Sofia Carvalho
Mythical Narratives in Stesichorus

Trends in Classics – Supplementary Volumes

Edited by
Franco Montanari and Antonios Rengakos

Associate Editors
Stavros Frangoulidis · Fausto Montana · Lara Pagani
Serena Perrone · Evina Sistakou · Christos Tsagalis

Scientific Committee
Alberto Bernabé · Margarethe Billerbeck
Claude Calame · Jonas Grethlein · Philip R. Hardie
Stephen J. Harrison · Stephen Hinds · Richard Hunter
Christina Kraus · Giuseppe Mastromarco
Gregory Nagy · Theodore D. Papanghelis
Giusto Picone · Alessandro Schiesaro
Tim Whitmarsh · Bernhard Zimmermann

Volume 115

Sofia Carvalho

Mythical Narratives in Stesichorus

Greek Heroes on the Move

DE GRUYTER

ISBN 978-3-11-126569-8
e-ISBN (PDF) 978-3-11-071573-6
e-ISBN (EPUB) 978-3-11-071588-0
ISSN 1868-4785

Library of Congress Control Number: 2021942026

Bibliographic information published by the Deutsche Nationalbibliothek
The Deutsche Nationalbibliothek lists this publication in the Deutsche Nationalbibliografie;
detailed bibliographic data are available on the Internet at http://dnb.dnb.de.

© 2023 Walter de Gruyter GmbH, Berlin/Boston
This volume is text- and page-identical with the hardback published in 2022.
Editorial Office: Alessia Ferreccio and Katerina Zianna
Logo: Christopher Schneider, Laufen
Printing and binding: CPI books GmbH, Leck

www.degruyter.com

To my daughter

Contents

Acknowledgements —— IX
Preliminary Note —— XI

Introduction —— XIII
Stesichorus' biography —— XIV
Stesichorus' professional context —— XXIII
Stesichorus' performance —— XXV
The myth in Stesichorus and travelling motifs —— XXXII

1   Adventure —— 1
1.1   The *Geryoneis* —— 2
1.1.1   Mapping the far west (frr. 8–10 F.) —— 8
1.1.2   Geryon's heroism (frr. 12–15 F.) —— 19
1.1.3   Callirhoe's plea (frr. 16 and 17 F.) —— 27
1.1.4   The gods' Assembly and a parallel with the Cycnus (frr. 18 and 166 F.) —— 32
1.1.5   Heracles' tactis and the example of the Boarhunters (frr. 19 and 183 F.) —— 35
1.1.6   Heracles in Thessaly (fr. 22a F.) —— 43

2   Escape and Returns —— 47
2.1   The *Sack of Troy* —— 47
2.1.1   Divine pity and Epeius (fr. 100 F.) —— 50
2.1.2   The Trojan Debate (frr. 103 and 104 F.) —— 59
2.1.3   Divine abandonment (fr. 114 F.) —— 68
2.1.4   The death of Astyanax (frr. 107 and 116 F.) —— 70
2.1.5   Polyxena's sacrifice (frr. 118 and 119 F.) —— 73
2.1.6   The recovery of Helen (frr. 106, 113, and 115 F.) —— 76
2.1.7   Hecuba's rescue (frr. 108 and 109 F.) —— 84
2.1.8   Aeneas' escape (fr. 105 F.) —— 87
2.2   The *Nostoi* —— 95
2.2.1   Aristomache (fr. 169 F.) —— 98
2.2.2   Telemachus in Sparta (fr. 170 F.) —— 99

3   Abduction —— 105
3.1   The *Europeia* —— 107
3.2   The *Helen* —— 115

3.2.1	Tyndareus' fault (fr. 85 F.) —— **116**
3.2.2	Helen in Athens (fr. 86 F.) —— **128**
3.2.3	Helen back to the Peloponnese (fr. 87 F.) —— **132**
3.2.4	Helen in Sparta (fr. 88 F.) —— **135**
3.3	The *Palinode* —— **138**
3.3.1	Helen in Egypt (frr. 90, 91a, and 91c F.) —— **138**
4	**Exile** —— **157**
4.1	The *Oresteia* —— **157**
4.1.1	The opening of Stesichorus' *Oresteia* (frr. 172–174 F.) —— **162**
4.1.2	Iphigenia's sacrifice (frr. 178 and 181.25–27 F.) —— **175**
4.1.3	Clytemnestra's dream (fr. 180 F.) —— **180**
4.1.4	The Nurse Laodamia (fr. 179 F.) —— **189**
4.1.5	Electra and the return of Orestes (fr. 181 F.) —— **192**
4.1.6	The bow of Apollo and the matricide (fr. 181.14–24 F.) —— **197**
4.2	The *Thebais*? —— **204**
4.2.1	Oedipus in (or out of) the *Thebais* —— **215**
4.2.2	Teiresias' Prophecy —— **218**
4.2.3	The identity of the Queen —— **223**
4.2.4	The Queen's speech (fr. 97.201–231 F.) —— **230**
4.2.5	Casting lots and Teiresias' advice (fr. 97.235–291 F.) —— **247**
4.2.6	Polynices' journey (fr. 97.291–303 F.) —— **250**
5	**Conclusion** —— **254**

Bibliography —— **259**
Index Nominum et Rerum —— **289**
Index of Sources —— **297**

Acknowledgements

This book is a result of my doctoral investigation awarded by the University of Coimbra and funded by the Foundation for Science and Technology (SFRH/BD/85173/2012) which allowed me to be dedicated in full to this enterprise and created the conditions for several visits to the University of Nottingham during the research. I am thankful for the guidance, knowledge, and generosity of Patrick Finglass who supervised and discussed the research outputs and the manuscript and to Frederico Lourenço who encouraged me to pursue higher goals and challenges. A word of thanks is also due to Carlos de Jesus who commented the manuscript and made relevant suggestions of improvements, and to João Baptista for his constant presence throughout the years that took this volume to be completed. This book could not have been successfully concluded without the help, the encouragement, and the marvellous work of the editors and staff of De Gruyter's *Trends in Classics*, especially Professors Franco Montanari and Antonios Rengakos for accepting the publication of this volume, and to Marco Michele Acquafredda, Katerina Zianna, and Anne Hiller.

Finally, I want to address my deepest gratitude and love to my family who stood by my side through the perils of this task, especially to Miguel whose love and support have guided me throughout all the aspects of this and other projects, and to our daughter to whom I dedicate this book.

Preliminary Note

In this book, I follow the edition and the numeration of M. Davies and P.J. Finglass 2014 *Stesichorus. The Poems*. Cambridge for the fragments of Stesichorus. The fragments are indicated by the number of this edition followed by the abbreviation F. For the testimonies (Ta, Tb), I follow the edition and numeration by Ercoles 2013 *Stesicoro: Le testimonianze antiche*, Bologna, cited with the reference to the work: Ercoles. The dates in this study refer mainly to the period before Christ, unless otherwise stated, except for the cases in which the date clearly refers to our era. Translations of the Greek text with no reference to the translator are mine.

Periodicals are referred according to *L'Année Philologique*. Ancient Greek authors are referred as in Liddell and Scott (LSJ) and Roman authors are referred as in *The Oxford Latin Dictionary*. Collections of Papyri, editions, are referred to by the abbreviations used in those works. The full list of abbreviations used in this study can be found in the bibliography. For dictionaries, encyclopaedias, and other collections the abbreviations I use are the following:

ABV	Beazley, J.D. (1959), *Attic Black-Figure Vase-Painters*. Oxford.
Add²	Carpenter, T.H. (1989), *Beazley Addenda: additional references to* ABV, ARV² *and Paralipomena*. 2nd edition. Oxford.
ARV²	Beazley, J.D. (1984), *Attic Red-Figure Vase-Painters*. 2nd edition. Oxford.
BAD	Beazley Archive Database [www.beazley.ox.ac.uk]
Chantraine	Chantraine, P. (2009), *Dictionaire Étymologique de la Langue Grecque. Histoire des Mots*. Paris.
LIMC	AA. (1981–1999), *Lexicon iconographicum mythologiae classicae*. Zurich/Munich.
Para.	Beazley, J.D. (1971), *Paralipomena: Additions to 'Attic Black-figure Vase-painters' and 'Attic Red-figure Vase-painters'*. 2nd edition. Oxford.
RE	Pauly, A.; Wissowa, G. and Kroll, W. (1893–1980), *Paulys Real-Encyclopaedia der classischen Altertumswissenschaft, Neue Bearbeitung*. Stuttgart.

Introduction

Stesichorus is perhaps the most enigmatic archaic lyric poet. Despite his exceptionally copious production when compared to the other names of the nine lyricists, and his pairing with Homer among the poetic authorities of the Ancient world, he is but a shade in our anthologies, a whisper of a once vivid, vibrant voice. From the 26 books that gathered his works in the Alexandrian edition, fewer than 600 lines survive, most of them severely damaged, which makes his poetry difficult to classify within the modern concept of archaic lyric. The gaps in our information regarding Stesichorus lead, inevitably, to some speculation, but they also open a window of possibilities to explore.

The uncertainties about this figure, however, do not undermine his importance in the wide panorama of Greek lyric as a key element in the development of Greek literature. The ancients regarded Stesichorus as one of the highest poetic authorities.[1] The earliest attestation for Stesichorus' place in Greek literature comes from no other than Simonides, who places the Himerian as a peer to Homer in poetic authority, which means that our poet's works took no more than two generations to become a reference for posterity. The greatness of Stesichorus' works is highlighted by later rhetoricians,[2] who emphasize his excelling poetic technique. This is why he should be revisited. Furthermore, his work, despite its scattered condition, bears witness to the relevance of the Greek west in the formation of an idea of panhellenism and Greek identity, which far from being confined to mainland Greece, extended from Asia Minor to Sicily and beyond.

In this book, I aim to discuss the uses and adaptations of myth in Stesichorus' work, with a particular emphasis on the mythic cycles dealing with the theme of travelling. In a context of great mobility as it was the Archaic Greek World,[3] it seems to me relevant to discuss the mythical maps Stesichorus' proposes and to evaluate its significance in the wider context of each poem and of the place of the Greeks in the Mediterranean during the archaic period.[4] I have, therefore, divided this work in four sections, each dealing with one travelling theme. Alas, in a corpus this mutilated it is difficult to assert patterns and

---

1 TTb37, 40–47, 50–52 Ercoles. See also Arrighetti 1994.
2 Tb9 and TTb49–52 (ii) Ercoles.
3 For a survey on the centrality of mobility and the idea of return (nostos) in all the aspects of Greek Culture see more recently Hornblower and Biffis 2018.
4 On the general topic see Hawes 2017 on the interaction between myth and space. The volume, however, ignores Stesichorus.

tendencies. Therefore, we can find in Stesichorus' oeuvre different degrees of relevance of the journey theme. The *Geryoneis* provides the more poignant example of our poet's treatment of mythical geography. In other poems, the traveling motif gives way to new versions of the myth, as happens, for example, in the *Sack of Troy* and in the *Palinode*. In the *Thebais*, the journey itself deserves little attention, but the relevance of Stesichorus' version lies in the way up to the moment of the travel, with the persona of the Theban Queen having the unprecedented spotlight. The aim of the assessment of the travelling motif in Stesichorus' poems in not so much focused on the journey itself, but rather on the implications of those journeys in the overall construction of the narrative and shaping of the myth and the characters. I will show how Stesichorus' reshaping of the myth in some minor and major aspects provides new routes, alternative paths, and different meanings for the narratives he composes. In order to appreciate the full significance of Stesichorus works and the versions presented by our poet in the wider context of archaic Greek lyric, we first need to address the controversial discussion on Stesichorus' chronology and the general context of poetic performance in his time.[5]

Stesichorus' biography

Stesichorus' biography has been problematic since antiquity. The fact that his poetry lacks any specific reference to the poet and to the occasion has left ancient commentators and biographers without their usual main source to reconstruct the biographies of the archaic poets: their poetry.[6] In what concerns his chronology, we find some inconsistencies. According to the *Suda*,[7] Stesichorus was born during the 37th Olympiad (= 632/628), forty years after Alcman,[8] and roughly contemporary of Sappho and Alcaeus.[9] This information seems consistent with other sources making Stesichorus younger than Terpander and

---

[5] For a detailed discussion of Stesichorus' chronology, see West 1971a: 305–312; Ercoles 2008; 2013: 116–127 (who presents his arguments against West's hypothesis of Stesichorus' activity to be placed in between 560–540, a considerably later date for that advocated by the vast majority of the sources), Finglass 2014: 1–6; Ornaghi 2014. Campbell 1991: 3–4, and Hutchinson 2001: 116 present brief considerations on the date of the poet.
[6] See Ornaghi 2010: 18–20.
[7] Ta10 Ercoles. The lexicon follows the chronological tradition of Apollodorus, see Ercoles 2008: 35; 2013: 116.
[8] s.v. Ἀλκμάν = Alcm. test. 1. Cf. Campbell 1991: 3.
[9] *Suda* Σ107 = Ta6 Ercoles.

Xanthus.¹⁰ This may thus have been compatible with Eusebius' information placing our poet's *floruit* in 610,¹¹ which, as we shall see, is a rather satisfactory date. However, despite the uncertainties regarding the exact date for Stesichorus' activity, its duration, and the occasions in which our poet performed, the overall idea provided by our sources is that Stesichorus lived a long life and that throughout his life he travelled around Magna Graecia and perhaps even to mainland Greece.

Two different cities claimed to be Stesichorus' birthplace. Most of the sources state that Stesichorus was a Himerian.¹² However, Stephanus of Byzantium clearly says that he was Metaurian by birth (Ta15 Ercoles). This evidence led some to consider that Stesichorus and his family moved to Himera shortly after his birth.¹³ An inscription found in Tivoli names Euclides as Stesichorus' father (Ta16 Ercoles). Burnett suggested that this man may be one of the colonists of Himera,¹⁴ since, according to Thucydides, one of the three οἰκίσται was called Euclides.¹⁵ However, Himera was founded in 648, sixteen years before the earliest date suggested in the traditional date for Stesichorus' birth.¹⁶ If our poet's father was indeed one of the founders of Himera, Stesichorus would have hardly been born in Metaurus around 630.

---

10 Ta4, Ta5(a–b), Tb20, and Tb22 Ercoles. Glaucus (Tb20) states that Stesichorus was older than Xenocritus, but we have no means to confirm or deny the validity of the observation, since we have no further evidence for Xenocritus' biography. [Plut.] *Mus.* 1134b says that the poet was involved in the reorganization of some festivals in the Peloponnese, with Sacadas (fr. 2 Campbell).
11 Ta5b(i) Ercoles.
12 Ta10 – Ta14(ii) Ercoles for Himera as his birthplace; Ta17, Ta42 and Tb20 Ercoles for his association with Himera.
13 Kleine 1828: 8–10; Ercoles 2013: 12 supports this view on which see Ercoles 2013: 260 n. 259 for further bibliography. Against this hypothesis, see Gigante 1987: 536. An information first attested in the sixteenth century by Maurolico 1568: 37 points Catania as Stesichorus' homeland, but there are no ancient sources which confirm this information.
14 Burnett 1988: 136 "First, the father of Stesichorus was living in this place [Metaurus] in 630 (...) this man later went to Himera among that city's founders, he must have originally been an inhabitant either of Zancle or Rhegium, the cities that sponsored the colony. Through his father, then, Stesichorus was a Chalcidian who knew in his earliest years the life of South Italy in its rougher and more temporary forms". The same opinion is suggested by Willi 2008: 51 n. 1.
15 Th. 6.5.1. Other names include: Euphemus (Ta15 and Ta17 Ercoles); Euphorbus (Ta10 Ercoles); for Euclides see Ta10 and Ta16 Ercoles.
16 Diodorus' account according to which the battle of 408 happened 240 years after the foundation of the city (D. S. 13.62.4) is consistent with the archaeological traces on site (thus Hansen and Nielsen 2004: 174; De Angelis 2016: 71–73).

Moreover, the evidence which names Euclides as Stesichorus' father does not mention his inclusion in any founding activity. The association of Stesichorus with one of the founders of Himera may well be a result of an attempt to link Stesichorus to the very origins of Himera, thus allowing the Himerians to claim the poet not only as their own but as a someone closely related to the existence of the city itself.[17] A more plausible solution is that Stesichorus' family moved to Himera after Stesichorus' was born.

The *testimonia* concerning his family suggest Italian origins, particularly in the names attributed to one of his brothers: Marmecus, Marmertius or Mamertinus, common in southern Italy and associated with the Oscan people known as the Mamertini.[18] However, the attribution of a name of Italian origin does not necessarily mean that Stesichorus' family had non-Greek ancestry; it may only indicate a common practice in the ancient world of naming the offspring after someone with whom the family had commercial or diplomatic ties, which would be expected both in Metaurus and in Himera.[19]

Himera was a strategically placed Greek settlement in the Mediterranean trading routes from east to west, hence, an important link to the Greek wider world.[20] The mobility of goods and people, as well as the ethnic diversity of multicultural Sicily, and particularly of Himera, would have been a key factor in Stesichorus' life,[21] perhaps beginning in his own family. Himera was indeed a

---

17 Finglass 2014: 17.
18 Clackson 2012: 139.
19 For this practice see the inscription in a gravestone of a Greek named Latinos *IGDS* II § 24 Λατίνο {η} ἐμί το Ῥεγίνο ἐμί; cf. Finglass 2014: 31 with n. 23. For a similar phenomenon in Egypt, Meiggs and Lewis 1989: § 7(4), *SEG* 12; *SEG* 43 1102. Archaeological findings show that Metaurus had a mixed population of Greeks with ties to Zancle, Rhegium, and Mylae, but also with indigenous people, which suggests a high level of cultural interaction between Greeks and non-Greeks (thus Finglass 2014: 13 n. 84, see also De Angelis 2016: 166 with n. 174 for Himera, mentioning this precise situation of Stesichorus' brother, and De Angelis 2016: 162 for evidence of mixed population in Metaurus). Cultural synergy among the various ethnic Greek groups and the indigenous peoples is a fundamental aspect of the cultural products (both from literary and material culture) from Magna Graecia. And this may well have influenced Stesichorus' poetic production.
20 Finglass 2014: 7, 10.
21 Thus Hornblower 2004: 195 "[Himera] was evidently, like Palermo in later centuries, a culturally, ethnically and linguistically heterogeneous place: on the city streets and harbourside of Himera you could no doubt jostle not only with these Dorian and Ionian Greeks, but with more exotic folk as well. The neighbours of Himera included not only Phoenicians and Carthaginians, who in peaceful times surely traded with the Greeks to the east of them, but also with Etruscans to the north and Elymians (who were neither Greeks nor Semites) from Egesta to the west or Entella to the south, and indigenous Sicilians of more than one variety."

multicultural and flourishing city. However, Stesichorus hardly limited his work to the public of his city. On the contrary, the ancient sources and the biographical tradition show a well-travelled Stesichorus, who is thought to have spent some time in other cities.

An example of this may be the tradition that makes Stesichorus Hesiod's son (Ta18–20 Ercoles). This information is probably best understood as a genealogical analogy emphasising the poetic affinity between the two poets. After all, Stesichorus knew the works of Hesiod to the point of referring to them. However, this association may have been an attempt from Locris to fabricate a genealogical link between our poet and the origins of the city.[22] Links between Stesichorus and Locris are found elsewhere, and the poet must have been well known there.[23] Pindar in his *Olympian* 10, composed for the Locrian Hagesidamus, winner in boys' boxing, refers to the episode of Heracles' encounter with Cycnus in similar terms to those presented in Stesichorus.[24]

It is precisely regarding the story of Cycnus that Stesichorus is said to have mentioned Hesiod. However, the fact that Stesichorus could have known Hesiod's works may be problematic if we follow West's assertions that the *Shield* was composed before c. 580–570,[25] a date which would make the poem hardly accessible to Stesichorus any time before 550. Such assumption would question the traditional date for Stesichorus' death in the 550's. However, the François Vase depicting a centaur labelled as *melanchaites* may suggest that a version of

---

22 Cf. Ta18; Ta19 (b). Kivilo 2010: 65–66. Kivilo follows Wilamowitz suggestion of the two distinct biographic traditions of Stesichorus; one deeply connected to Locris and other to Himera. The former presents various hints to a Pythagorean tradition which may have influenced the biographic tradition of our poet. On the literary affinity of Hesiod and Stesichorus and the possible relation of both poets see also West 1971a: 304; Ercoles 2008: 37; Finglass 2014: 5. For Hesiod's association with Locris, see Finglass 2013d: 162.
23 Cf. TTa28, 30, 32 Ercoles. As Sgobbi 2003: 36–38 pointed out this association may be motivated by the attempt to legitimize a political ideology to the authority of a famous poet, even if that association would turn out to be anachronistic. Ercoles 2008: 39 argues that the association of Stesichorus and the battle at Sagra show influence of Pythagorean background and with political intentions of Croton from the beginning if the fifth century which showed support to the Punics. However, the chronology of the battle between Crotonians and Locrians is disputed, with scholars defending the occurrence of the battle between 575–560 (Ercoles 2008: 39 n. 8) and others placing it c. 540 (Campbell 1991: 3), leaving us with little ground to make any relevant use of this testimony.
24 Pi. *O*. 10.14; Stes. fr. 168 F. See Ercoles 2013: 347.
25 The most recent date for the *Shield* is c. 590, but this assumption is based on the supposed references to the fall of Crisa, whose historicity is far from certain. On which see Robertson 1978; Davies 1994; Fowler 1998: 13 n. 30.

the *Shield* was already in circulation as early as 580–570, if both the poem and the vase were not following a common source. Since there are no means to establish the date of the *Shield* beyond reasonable doubt, the reference to the poem does not demand a revision of the chronological tradition for Stesichorus' career.

Another problematic piece of information derived from the works of Stesichorus and recurrently used to help in the chronology of our poet is a reference to a solar eclipse in fr. 300 F. I cite only Plutarch's passage:

> Θέων ἡμῖν οὗτος τὸν Μίμνερμον (fr. 20 *IEG*) ἐπάξει καὶ τὸν Κυδίαν (fr. 715 *PMG*) καὶ τὸν Ἀρχίλοχον (fr. 122 *IEG*), πρὸς δὲ τούτοις τὸν Στησίχορον καὶ τὸν Πίνδαρον (fr. 52k S–M) ἐν ταῖς ἐκλείψεσιν ὀλοφυρομένους ἄστρον φανερώτατον κλεπτόμενον καὶ μέσωι ἄματι νύκτα γινομένην καὶ τὴν ἀκτῖνα τοῦ ἡλίου σκότους ἀτραπὸν φάσκοντας.

> If you do not remember (*sc.* the recent eclipse of the sun) Theon here will quote us Mimnermus, and Cydias, and Archilochus, and in addition, Stesichorus and Pindar, who lament during the eclipses "the stealing of the most conspicuous star" and speak of "night falling at mid-day", or even of the sun's beam "racing along the path of darkness."

According to the calculations, eclipses happened in Sicily in 607, 585, 557. West argues that the eclipse to which Stesichorus would have referred is the one which occurred in 557, and which was in some regions of Italy a total eclipse.[26] However, assuming that poet was writing on the last eclipse implies that his death would have to be pushed to a later date, since 557 roughly coincides with the traditional date for his death. Perhaps it is safer to assume that the eclipse mentioned by Stesichorus need not be a total eclipse, and that the author was inspired by the phenomenon, which is a common literary *topos*, as Pliny's and Plutarch's oeuvres show,[27] even if it was a partial eclipse. Moreover, the observation of a total eclipse in 557 was only possible in the region of Locris. In Himera, this eclipse, as the previous ones, was partial. Wherever Stesichorus may have been, it is possible that even a partial eclipse would cause enough awe and apprehension as to motivate the poet to write about it.[28] Hence, the reference to the eclipse does not rule out the possibility that Stesichorus was born in the last

---

[26] West 1971a: 305; Campbell 1991: 3.
[27] Cf. Archil. fr. 122 *IEG*; Mimn. fr. 20 *IEG*; Hom. *Od.* 20.356–357; see Finglass 2014: 3, fr. 300 F.
[28] 'un occultamento di circa il novanta per cento della superficie solare à apprezzabile da un osservatore che si trovi nella zona interessata dalla congiunzione, anche se questi non è intent a guardare il cielo. Si tenga conto, poi, che un inconsapovole osservatore del periodo arcaico che assista per la prima volta ad un'eclisse sarà senz'altro fortemente colpito dal fenomeno anche se esso è soltanto parziale', Ercoles 2008: 44.

quarter of the seventh century, let alone confining his activity to the period from 560 to 540 as West argues.[29]

Another example of the problems when dealing with Stesichorus' biography concerns one testimony saying that Stesichorus was exiled to Pallantium in Arcadia (Ta10 Ercoles). Now, exile was a common fate for early Greek poets, especially those with complicated relationships with the city's tyrant.[30] Stesichorus was said to have publicly opposed the tyrant of Himera, Phalaris[31] and that would have put him at risk of exile. Moreover, Stesichorus elaborates on his works on themes of exile (the *Oresteia* and the *Thebais*).[32] However, the reference of Stesichorus' exile in Pallantium seems more an extrapolation of the poet's works than an historical fact.[33] Stesichorus refers to Pallantium in the *Geryoneis* (fr. 21 F.). Which Pallantium it is is a matter of discussion. It can be the Arcadian Pallantium, in which case the reference was part of the episode of Pholus attested in fr. 22 F.; or it could refer to a supposed encounter between Heracles and Evander in Italy, who fled the Arcadian Pallantium to found a colony in Italy. The Evander episode would have resonated considerably for a Western audience. Unfortunately, the presence of Evander in Stesichorus' poetry is not attested, unlike Pholus'. This passage may have led ancient biographers to take the episode of the poem and treat it as a sign that Stesichorus has experienced exile himself in the Arcadian Pallantium. Again, these ideas that Stesichorus was opposed to the tyrant, along with the presence in his poems of the motif of exile, may have contributed to the information from the *Suda* (Ta36(ii) Ercoles), which does not provide any details regarding the date of such event. Be that as it may, as Bowra noted, this account may have derived from a tradition based on an actual journey of Stesichorus to Greece, which is mentioned in two other testimonies.[34]

---

29 West 1971a: 305–307.
30 Sappho (Sicily) T251 V; Alcaeus fr. 307(d) V. On exile in Antiquity see Gaertner 2007, particularly, Bowie's (2007: 21–49) study on the motifs of displacement and exile in early Greek poetry; Bowie 2009: 118–122 explores the theme in Alcaeus.
31 Ta34 Ercoles. Cf. Kivilo 2010: 76–77. For other poet's civic intervention in their communities see also Kivilo 2010: 214. The story of rivalry of Stesichorus and Phalaris remained for posterity and originated a series of fictional letters from the imperial age, for which see Ercoles 2013: Ta43(xix) n.
32 On which see below Chapter 4. Exile.
33 This is the interpretation favoured by most scholars, among which Welcker 1844: 161, n. 7; Mancuso 1912: 167; Wilamowitz 1913: 236–240; Vürtheim 1919: 102–106; Maas 1929: 2460; Bowra 1934: 115; Podlecki 1971: 313; Lloyd-Jones 1980: 11; Ercoles 2013: 265, 376–377; Davies and Finglass 2014: 290.
34 Bowra 1934: 115.

Pseudo-Phalaris (Ta43(iv)) records a sojourn of Stesichorus and other two men, named Conon and Dropis, through the Peloponnese. Bowra had long advocated a visit by Stesichorus to Sparta. He sees in this anecdotal reference an allusion to what may have been Stesichorus' stay in Sparta. Journeys through the Peloponnese feature in Stesichorus' fr. 170 F. ascribed to the *Nostoi*,[35] in his *Helen*,[36] and in his *Thebais*.[37]

Another testimony concerning Stesichorus' presence in mainland Greece is provided by the *Marmor Parium* (inscribed c. 264/263), which reports that in 485/484 Stesichorus arrived in mainland Greece, the same year of Aeschylus' first victory and the birth of Euripides (Ta36 Ercoles).[38] The chronology is clearly wrong for an actual visit of our Stesichorus at that date, since Simonides mentions him in fr. 273 Poltera (= Stes. Tb37 Ercoles). The *Marmor* may be referring to another Stesichorus, whose work is unknown to us.[39] It may have been the case that a different poet paid homage to Stesichorus and took his name, or a family member who follow the same career.[40] However, the *Marmor* attests the existence of a second Stesichorus who is dated to the fourth century,[41] contradicting Wilamowitz's suggestion.

If, on the other hand, the *Marmor* refers to our Stesichorus, then it attests the poet's visit to Greece mainland, but the event, in the absence of a solid chronology, was synchronized with a crucial year for Athenian performance culture.[42] Alternatively, the *Marmor* may as well be referring to the posthumous

---

35 Cf. below Chapter 2.2 and fr. S166 if one considers this piece, commonly ascribed to Ibycus, to be part of Stesichorus' production, as is the case of West 2015: 70–76. But this is by no means a convincing case, as Finglass 2017b shows, since the poem is much closer to Ibycus' production than to any work by Stesichorus we know.
36 frr. 86, 87 F.; on which see below Chapter 3.2.
37 fr. 97.295–303 F.; on which see below Chapter 4.2.
38 For a discussion of Stesichorus' reception in Athens, see Bowie 2015: 111–124; and for an account focusing particularly in tragedy see Ercoles and Fiorentini 2011: 21–24.
39 Wilamowitz 1913: 233–242 suggested the possible existence of three poets named Stesichorus, the first of Locrian origin who lived in the archaic age, the other two from Himera who lived in the fifth and fourth centuries.
40 Thus Kleine 1828: 7, and Böckh *CIG* II 2374 (p. 319). D'Alessio 2015 suggested that 'Stesichorus' could have been a professional name to which a collection of poems by several mainly western poets is ascribed, since "Stesichorus' works (collected in 26 books, far more than any other lyric poet) look rather as a collection of narrative poems, mostly impersonal, and attributed to a 'professional' name apparently used by mainly western poets from the archaic period onward".
41 Fr. 841 *PMG*.
42 Ercoles 2008: 36.

re-performance of Stesichorus' works at Athens, as Bowie suggests,[43] which would have explained the Athenian dramatists' knowledge of Stesichorus.[44] The coincidence of the presence of Stesichorus in Greece when Aeschylus achieved his first victory may also indicate how much the latter poet owed to the former. We know of Stesichorus' influence on the tragedians by an anonymous commentator who, among other examples, demonstrates how innovative our poet was by giving the example of his version of Demophon in Egypt.[45] As the only attestation for such sojourn, this innovation suggests special interest in a figure and in Athenian mythology as a whole.[46] In the same fragment, the commentator elaborates on Demophon's and Acamas' genealogy in Stesichorus. Our poet has Demophon and Acamas sons of different mothers; the first is said to be Iope's son, thus grandson of Heracles' half-brother; the second was bore to Theseus by Phaedra. The fragment mentions even Hippolytus who is said to be the son of the Amazon. The reference to the Amazon denounces a considerably good knowledge of Theseus' story, to which we may add the episode of his abduction of Helen, although this was already told in the *Cypria* and in Alcman.[47] A further reference to Athenians in Stesichorus' oeuvre is found in his *Sack fo Troy* (fr. 105 F.) where, similarly to what happens in *Little Iliad*, fr. 17 *GEF* and *Iliou Persis*, arg. 4 and fr. 6 *GEF*, Demophon and Acamas rescue their grandmother. We see, therefore, that Athenian mythology which is residual in the Trojan saga, was integrated in many of Stesichorus' poems. This may suggest, as happens in the case for performance at Sparta, that our poet had contact with the tales of the city's heroes, which may imply a visit. Unfortunately, we have no means to prove that the references he makes to the Athenian mythology in his poems reflect performance there.[48] What this may illustrate is the growing influence of the city in the poetic circuits of the time.

Another reason to consider the extent that travelling marked Stesichorus' life and career is the fact that he is claimed to be buried in Catania, in the eastern coast of Sicily, founded soon after Leontini (729) by Chalcidians.[49] Claiming possession of the poet's bones demonstrates the lasting fame of Stesichorus in

---

43 Bowie 2015.
44 On the topic, see below Chapter 3.2, 3.3, and 4.
45 fr. 90 F. See too fr. 181 F. for the details in the Theban plays borrowed from Stesichorus.
46 Cf. Finglass 2013b; Morgan 2012: 43.
47 *Cypria* fr. 13 *GEF*; Alcm. fr. 21 *PMGF*.
48 Bowie 2015: 122–124 suggested that a possible visit of Stesichorus to Athens may have occurred by the time of the 566 reorganisation of the Panatheneia.
49 Th. 6.3.3. On which see De Angelis 2016: 69 n. 28.

the city, which may be the result of a few years of residence there.[50] The tradition that Stesichorus was buried in Catania prevailed in the literary fictional epitaph written by Antipater of Sidon.[51]

Cicero places Stesichorus' death in the 56th Olympiad (556/555),[52] the same year as Simonides was born.[53] This association between the two poets may be derived from the fact that Simonides provides the earliest reference to Stesichorus,[54] by citing him as an authority alongside with Homer in the treatment of Meleager's myth.[55] This implies that, by the time Simonides was writing, Stesichorus was already considered a poetic authority. Eusebius indicates the 55th Olympiad (560/559) for his death which slightly deviates from the other sources, but nevertheless suggests a long lifespan,[56] commonly attributed to distinguished figures, such as Simonides, Hellanicus, Anacreon, or Lycurgus.[57]

We do not know what took Stesichorus to Catania, nor if that happened much before his death. The close association of Stesichorus with Himera, suggests that the poet spent most of his life there. However, and in spite of being more directly connected to Himera, during his life (roughly from 630 to 550) Stesichorus is associated with six cities in the Greek world: Metaurus, Himera, Locris, Pallantium, Athens, and Catania, not to mention Sparta. One may wonder to what extent a poet confined to the vicinity of his homeland would have been attributed such a biography.

---

50 Ta39 Ercoles is the sole instance where Stesichorus is said to have been buried at Himera.
51 Antip. Sid. *AP*. 7.75 = Tb49 Ercoles. Ta10; Ta40 Ercoles. For the other *testimonia* concerning the funerary monuments to Stesichorus, including the one at Himera, see comm. TTa38–42 Ercoles.
52 Ta5(a) Ercoles. Cicero is probably relying on the information provided by Apollodorus of Athens.
53 Cf. *Suda* Σ 439, 1 A; Ta5(b)ii, Ta5(d). On Simonides' date, see Molyneux 1992 arguing for the first date provided by the *Suda*; Stella 1946, for the second. For the discussion of different sources on the subject, see Poltera 2008: 7–8; Ferreira 2013: 115–119.
54 Simon. fr. 273 Poltera = Stes. Tb37 Ercoles.
55 Cf. frr. 183, 184 and probably 189 F.
56 *Chron.* Ol. 42.2, 55.1 (Ta5(b) Ercoles). For Stesichorus as having lived a long life, see Cic. *Cato* 7.23 = Ta8(a) Ercoles; Ger. *Ep.* 52.3 = Ta8(b) Ercoles; Ps. Lucian *Macr.* 26 = Ta9 Ercoles. According to Ps. Lucian, Stesichorus died aged 85 years old which outdates the version provided by the *Suda* (76 to 80 years old). Cicero's account of a statue of the poet as an old man carrying a book (*Verr.* 2.2.87) confirms the tradition, which can also be inferred by the extension of Stesichorus' poetry. For a detailed discussion of the ancient sources, see Ercoles 2013: 127–130.
57 For Simonides' lifetime cf. TT 46–50 Poltera; for Hellanicus' cf. Ps. Lucian *Macr.* 22; for Anacreon's, Ps. Lucian *Macr.* 26; and for Lycurgus', Ps. Lucian *Macr.* 28. Cf. Jacoby 1902: 198 and Kivilo 2010: 216–217.

Stesichorus' professional context

Stesichorus' *floruit* can thus be placed in the last decade of the seventh century, in a context of well-established poetic culture going through "a fast-moving technical and musical development",[58] which depended in part on the mobility of its professionals.[59] Among Stesichorus' contemporaries we can find a sample of what would have been the poetic diversity of the late seventh and early sixth centuries.

On the one hand, we find poets whose activity seems confined to their homeland. Sappho is not exactly known for having been a travelling poet. The biographic tradition regards her as a very important piece in the cultural life of Lesbos, with little margin for wandering on duty.[60] Nevertheless, she is thought to have travelled to Sicily in exile, which may attest an interesting cultural environment in the island.[61] Alcaeus also seems to have been active only in Lesbos.

But there were cases where travelling was part of the job. Sparta is one of the most revealing examples. Although Alcman's biography is not clear as to the origins of the poet, his Sparta was a remarkable cultural centre attracting many foreign talents. Most of the more relevant names in the generation before Stesichorus are associated with Sparta. The evidence we possess on seventh century Sparta, shows its capacity to attract poets from different cities of the Greek world, including Magna Graecia,[62] who contributed to the institution or the renovations of several festivals in the city, and who are known to have made some musical innovations.[63] This indicates that these poets invested considera-

---

[58] Krummen 2009: 195; on poetic mobility in the Homeric epics, see Ferreira 2013: 15–26. For Hesiod's testimony on the poetic mobility of his own time, see Ferreira 2013: 27–31.
[59] See Bowie 2009; Kowalzig 2013; Ferreira 2013: 65–112.
[60] Note, however, the remarks on the idea of travelling in her more recently found poem published in 2014 where she elaborated on the distress of those who wait for someone to return safely from a sea journey, a poem which attests the trading activity of Lesbos in the seventh century.
[61] Sapph. test. 5 Campbell.
[62] Xenocritus of Locris was said to have been involved in the 668 *Gynmopaedia*. He is said to be from Eziphyrian Locris in Magna Graecia, but this is inconsistent with the traditional foundation date for the city in 673. Podlecki 1984: 154 suggested that he may have been among the first colonists. Xenocritus' poems may have been approximated to those of Stesichorus, since according to *De Musica* 9.1134c, 10.1134e, he composed heroic narratives, which some have understood to be dithyrambs. Ferreira 2013: 73 infers that his poems were performed by a chorus.
[63] Terpander (ca. 642–640) was originally from Lesbos. He is credited with important musical innovations (cf. frr. 1–2, 8, 13, 17–20 Campbell). See Gostoli 1990: 9–11; Ferreira 2013: 68–70.

ble time in this, which leads us to wonder to what extent could or would they have had another job.[64]

Another example of a professional travelling poet from roughly the same period as Stesichorus is Arion of Methymna.[65] Arion is credited with the invention of the dithyramb and for having been a famous citharode whose career took him to perform in Italy and Sicily,[66] although the poet is more directly associated with Corinth, an important city in the Mediterranean trading and colonial activity. The legend of Arion illustrates the increasing value of music and poetry which ultimately led to the establishment of the civic festivals and maps Sicily in the wider circuit for poetic performance.[67]

The case of Stesichorus is more complicated since we do not know if his poetry was confined to Himera, or if instead he was a travelling poet. As we have seen, the biographic tradition preserves an image of a travelled man, one who knew very well the frenzy of the Mediterranean routes. Moreover, his poems show a wide "geographical distribution of mythic content" which allowed the poet to "generate a narrative corpus which at least touches on all the major cycles across the whole Greece".[68] The Panhellenic scope of Stesichorus' poems with no mention or reference to a specific occasion for performance, have led scholars to consider the possibility of Stesichorus as a travelling poet.

Some scholars argue that "we have little ground for saying how far, if at all, his career took him beyond Himera or Sicily".[69] By the sixth century, Sicily, and Magna Graecia in general, was a flourishing region. As such, religious and civic festivals multiplied across the island and in Italy.[70] As pointed out by several scholars, Stesichorus' oeuvre seems a result of the cultural hybridity of the region, evident in the characteristics of his poetry, combining the Ionian flavour of epics with the Dorian lyric.[71] However, other aspects point to a wider scope,

---

[64] *Pace* Kurke 2000: 45 arguing that the phenomenon of the professionalization of the poets occurred only in the second half of the fifth century.
[65] Herodotus dates Periander's rule over Corinth around 625–585 (1.23–24) and the *Suda* (Arion fr. 1 Campbell) places Arion's *floruit* in the last quarter of the seventh century (cf. Eus. *Chron.* = fr. 2 Campbell).
[66] Hdt. 1.24.4–7.
[67] Thus Purcell 1990: 29–30; Kowalzig 2010: 32.
[68] Carey 2015: 55.
[69] Hutchinson 2001: 114.
[70] For a survey of the festivals in the west, see Burnett 1988: 141–145; Morgan 2012: 37–40.
[71] Willi 2008: 82–91 is his study on Stesichorus' language points out it hybridity resulting from the blending of Ionian epic and the morphology of Doric lyric, concluding that his style is a product of the cultural context of Sicily, which he dubs as a Sicilian *koine*. West 2015: 63–70

such as "the whole array of Greek myths, not on the themes specifically catering interests of the west Greek diaspora".⁷² Moreover, "there is a degree of productive cross-fertilization between local traditions and poets from elsewhere, who bring to those traditions an external and panhellenic perspective".⁷³ Although his poems would be consistent with the effort of the western communities to provide their cities with civic and religious festivals that would include the region in the circuit of poetic culture and help the consolidation of the institutions of the *poleis*, the panhellenic appeal of his works and their apparent detachment from any specific occasion leads us to wonder to what extent he would be confined to the western circuit. If Magna Graecia was becoming a recognized and highly prestigious cultural centre, the mainland cities may have been interested in welcoming a poet coming from such a promising place.⁷⁴

Now, the idea of Stesichorus as a travelling poet, either confined to Magna Graecia or including journeys across mainland Greece, may pose some questions regarding his performance. Would a poet whose works were considerably longer than the other known examples of choral lyric be able to either take with him a group of singers or train local, amateur choruses for each of his performances? Or is it preferable to think of Stesichorus as a solo-singer accompanied by a mute chorus?

Stesichorus' performance

The definition of Stesichorus as a choral lyric poet was widely accepted by modern scholars, but since the sixties, new possibilities have been discussed regarding Stesichorus' performance. The scepticism in accepting the traditional view of our poet's mode of execution brought up a fruitful discussion about the sharp and orthodox categories according to the modern dichotomy of choral vs monody.⁷⁵ Even though the debate provided interesting results and significantly enriched perspective on the nuances of archaic lyric poetry in general, the case of Stesichorus is far from being resolved.

---

speaks in an attempt to categorize the genre speaks of a lyric epic whose followers are particularly associated with western Greece.
72 Carey 2015: 51.
73 Carey 2015: 51.
74 See Stewart 2017: 34–42 on the motivation for poetic mobility; Hunter and Rutherford 2009: 1–15 for the festival networks and the idea of panhellenism, particularly Delphi, on which see also Malkin 2011: 55.
75 On which see Davies 1988 and Lourenço 2009: 22–24.

The *Suda* states that Stesichorus is a speaking name, meaning that he was the first to set up a chorus to the cithara. His name parallels others that point to the same concept of choral performance, such as Hagesichora, Alcman's *Parthenion* chorus-leader.[76] Until the publication of Stesichorus' poems, this claim was generally understood as proof for choral performance. However, after the poems came to light, scholars were compelled to approximate Stesichorus' performance to that of the citharodes, a hypothesis put forward by Kleine before the publication of the papyri,[77] and revived by Barrett and West,[78] to whom the length of the poems, revealed in the *Geryoneis*' papyrus,[79] would demand considerable perseverance from a chorus.[80] Moreover, with the publication of Stesichorus' works it was finally possible to evaluate the epic flavour of his poetry, which led scholars to extend the similarities between Stesichorus and epic to the performance, thus approximating our poet's performance to that of the citharodes, in particular Terpander.

According to Heraclides Ponticus,[81] Terpander, apart from performing the cithara to the verses of Homer, composed melodies for the lyre to accompany his own epic verses.[82] Pseudo-Plutarch claims that Stesichorus did the same, adapting his poems to the lyre.[83] Martin West considers these passages to be evidence for the similarity between Terpander and "the classical citharodes' practices", and Stesichorus' work.[84] However, the context of Heraclides' passage refers to compositional technique, not performance.[85]

---

76 Tb2 Ercoles: ἐκλήθη δὲ Στησίχορος ὅτι πρῶτος κιθαρῳδίαι χορὸν ἔστησεν. See Finglass 2007: 184.
77 Kleine 1828: 53.
78 Barrett 2007a (1968): 22; West 1971a: 309 and also 2015; Pavese 1972.
79 See, however, Ercoles 2013: 567 n. 1001, drawing attention to Page's colometry according to which each strophe would have 13 lines, and not the 26 presented in the papyrus, and thus a total of 750 lines.
80 Thus West 1971a: 309–313; Pavese 1972; Haslam 1974; Lloyd-Jones 1980: 22; Rossi 1983: 13; Russo 1999: 339; Schade 2003: 6–7; Lourenço 2009: 22–24. For the ancient sources pointing to citharodic performance, see TTb20–24 Ercoles.
81 *Ap.* [Plut] *De Mus.* 3.1132c = Terp. test 18 = Stes. Tb22 Ercoles.
82 Alexander Poliistor *ap*. [Plut.] *De Mus.* 3.1132f = Terp. test 21, refers to the poetic achievement of Terpander as a perfect balance between the words of Homer and the music of Orpheus: ἐζηλωκέναι δὲ τὸν Τέρπανδρον Ὁμήρου μὲν τὰ ἔπη, Ὀρφέως δὲ τὰ μέλη.
83 [Plut] *De Mus.* 3. 1132 b-c: τῶν ἀρχαίων μελοποιῶν, οἳ ποιοῦντες ἔπη τούτοις μέλη περιετίθεσαν. For a similar claim, see Tb42 Ercoles.
84 West 1971a: 307 = 2015: 123. [Plut] *De Mus.* 4 and 6.
85 Thus Burnett 1988: 130; D'Alfonso 1994: 64–71; Power 2010: 240; Ercoles 2013: 556.

Some scholars argue that Stesichorus' poems were performed by a solo singer who may have been accompanied by a silent chorus. The parallel these scholars draw in support of their view is Demodocus' second performance in the *Odyssey*. In the poem, the bard performs three times in two different manners.[86] The first and third songs are epic recitations, whereas the second – the one on Ares and Aphrodite – seems a different narrative genre, since it features a group of dancers at some point.[87] The argument of the supporters of this hypothesis is that the second song of Demodocus attests the existence of silent choruses dancing to his song. However, the text suggests that the bard starts singing only after the dancers began their dance.[88] So we might imagine a situation where the dancers would adapt their dance to Demodocus' song. Finglass believes that, if the dance continued, it was less exuberant than the previous one who marvelled Odysseus.[89] For Garvie, Demodocus' song starts only after the dance is over, but nothing in the text indicates that the dancers have stopped.[90] So the role of the chorus in this passage is not clear.

But even if we concede that a silent chorus accompanied Demodocus, the situation in the *Odyssey* is hardly comparable to what we would expect to be a performance by Stesichorus. Ercoles[91] remarks that they seem to be improvising their movements while hearing the music, since the situation itself seems to be improvised as a showcase of Phaeacians' skills presented to Odysseus.[92] In the

---

86 *Od.* 8.73–83, 266–366, 499–520.
87 Wilamowitz 1913: 238. Russo 1999: 341 draws attention to Gentili 1988: 15. Heraclides Ponticus, writing in the fourth century, traced a continuity of poetic tradition between this type of pre-Homeric composition and the post-Homeric lyric narratives of Stesichorus; and in the light of the Homeric evidence, his view should be accepted as historically valid, both as pertains to subject matter (heroic narrative) and to form (strophic song construction) and meter (dactyl-anapests and epitrites "in the enoplion manner [kat'enoplion]".
88 *Od.* 8.261–266: κῆρυξ δ' ἐγγύθεν ἦλθε φέρων φόρμιγγα λίγειαν | Δημοδόκωι· ὁ δ'ἔπειτα κί' ἐς μέσον· ἀμφὶ δὲ κοῦροι | πρωθῆβαι ἵστανο, δαήμονες ὀρχηθμοῖο | πέπληγον δὲ χορὸν θεῖον ποcίν. αὐτὰρ Ὀδυccεὺc | μαρμαρυγὰc θηεῖτο ποδῶν, θαύμαζε δὲ θυμῶι | αὐτὰρ ὁ φορμίζων ἀνεβάλλετο καλὸν ἀείδειν κτλ. "the herald arrived, bearing the clear-toned lyre for Demodocus, who then took place in the middle, and around him stood the boys in the first bloom of youth, experienced dancers, who hit the sacred floor with their feet. Odysseus saw the twinkling of their feet, marvelled in his heart. Then the bard playing the lyre began to beautiful song...".
89 Finglass 2017a: 75–80.
90 Garvie 1994: 291.
91 Ercoles 2012: 6–7.
92 Note Alcinous' words at 8.251–253, ὥc χ' ὁ ξεῖνοc ἐνίcπηι οἷcι φίλοιcιν | οἴκαδε νοcτήcαc, ὅccον περιγιγνόμεθ' ἄλλων | ναυτιλίηι καὶ ποccὶ καὶ ὀρχηcτυῖ καὶ ἀοιδῆι. "So that the stranger

case of Stesichorus, however, we would expect to find a rehearsed chorus, resulting in a symbiosis of music, words and dance, leaving it possible to assume that the dance would have been mimetic.[93] Moreover, if Stesichorus' performance was like that of Demodocus, why would he be known as the first to have set up a chorus to the cithara, as the *Suda* says?[94] If the existence of silent chorus dancing to the music played by the bard is attested already in the *Odyssey*, Stesichorus would not have been the first to do so. Hence, he should have added something new to the previous manner of performance.

In fact, if we look at the inventive part of Stesichorus' mythic details in the representation of his characters, such as the three-bodied Geryon, it is reasonable to think of a glamourous and eye-catching choreography that would awe the audience. Such a performance would hardly be improvised. Thus, the triadic structure would not be a mere musical feature, as suggested by West,[95] who consider that it may "be understood as a purely musical principle of composition, an alternation of melodies to alleviate the monotony of monostrophy",[96] but would find a choreographic parallel, which would make the changes not only heard but visible.[97] As Hutchinson puts it, "the form creates a narrative of a different kind from the flowing movement of Homeric hexameters: a distinct lyric mode of narrative".[98] The first two stanzas make it clear that the triad structure "imply motion. Both music and dance 'turned' and recommenced, the pairing of identical rhythmic units being emphasized by the intervening epode."[99] A singing chorus would bring further dynamics to the mere visual effect of a dancing chorus. Moreover, as Hutchinson stresses, "the poems of Stesichorus are plainly transforming the epic genre in some sense, and one does not see why the mode of performance should not be different as well as the metrical design".[100] Willi notes that if Stesichorus had the chorus dancing according to the rhythm of the triadic structure, it is likely that the chorus was the one singing

---

can tell his friends on returning home, how superior we are compared to the others in sailing, in swiftness of feet, in dance and in song."
93 Thus Willi 2008: 77–78.
94 Tb2 Ercoles.
95 For arguments against the implication of choral performance in the triadic compositions, see Lefkowitz 1991: 192; for the arguments in favour, Carey 1991: 192–200.
96 West 2015: 125.
97 Both fundamental features of Greek poetry and indeed culture as pointed out by Gentili 1988: 5–6.
98 Hutchinson 2001: 118.
99 Burnett 1988: 133.
100 Hutchinson 2001: 116.

too, particularly because of the only apparent self-referential occasion among Stesichorus' fragments (fr. 173 F.).

Another argument in favour of the choral performance concerns the recurrent use of μολπή and derivatives in Stesichorus' poems.[101] The term is associated with contexts of choral performance.[102] In the epic, it appears in different religious contexts where a chorus sings and dances for a specific deity.[103] However, the word μολπή occurs in the *Odyssey* in apparently two different contexts. It describes the dance of the acrobats accompanying the bard (*Od.* 4.17–19) and in a group dance in which Nausicaa is said to excelled in song (*Od.* 6.101) and is presumably assuming the function of *choregos*.[104] Cingano stresses that the emphasis on singing suggested by ἄρχετο μολπῆς in this episode seems similar to the meaning of the word in lyric,[105] particularly when compared to Stesichorus' *hapax* in which the Muse is ἀρχεcίμολποc (fr. 278 F.). In the *Palinode*, a deity, presumably the Muse, is given the epithet φιλόμολποc (fr. 90 F.), and in fr. 271 F. μολπή is associated with χορεύματα.[106] The opening of the *Oresteia* and its reference to the song for the people (δαμώματα) and the self-referential participle ἐξευρόντα<c> points to choral performance.[107]

The existence of a singing chorus seems, therefore, highly likely,[108] but does this mean that the chorus sang the whole poem? Martinéz and Adrados suggested that the *choregos* sang the proemia and the speeches, while the chorus would be confined to the performance of the narrative sections.[109] However, this hypothesis does not take into account that the triadic structure often does not coincide with the change of character.[110] Some speeches begin or end in mid-stanza which would result in an odd variation soloist/chorus.[111] A better hypoth-

---

101 Cf. Finglass 2017a: 70–72. Frr. 90.9, for which see below; and frr. 271.2; 278 F.
102 Chantraine 1968: s.v. μέλπω. See also Adrados 1978: 297.
103 *Il.* 1.474 (paean), 16.182 (dance of the chorus of Artemis), 18.572 (collective dance accompanied by the song of Linus); *h.Ap.* 197 (Artemis dances and sings before the other gods); *h.Pan.* 21–24 (choral song of the Nymphs); Hes. *Th.* 66, 69 and [Hes.] *Scut.* 206 (choral song of the Muse), Cingano 1993: 349. For further detail see Calame 1977: 85–86.
104 Thus Cingano 1993: 350 n. 15.
105 Cingano 1993: 350 provides examples where the word stresses the element of singing, such as hymns, paeans, dithyramb, and epinicians.
106 Finglass 2014: 31.
107 fr. 173 F. See below 4.1.1.
108 Webster 1970: 76–78; Calame 1977: 164; Burkert 1987: 51–54; Burnett 1988: 129–131; D'Alfonso 1994; Nagy 1990: 361–375; Ercoles 2013: 564–568; Finglass 2017a.
109 Martinéz 1974; Adrados 1978: 297.
110 Thus Haslam 1978: 29 n. 1; D'Alfonso 1994: 53 n. 59; Willi 2008: 72.
111 E.g. frr. 93.3, 97.290 F.

esis is that the chorus performs the entirety of the poem and the variations of characters and narrative would be operated by it.

As Burkert pointed out, the *Homeric Hymn to Apollo*, dating to the second half of the sixth century, seems to attest the choral capacity of impersonating different voices, and therefore different characters. This hymn refers to another performance, which is in fact a "heroic myth in the form of choral lyrics, in other words, a Stesichorean production," where the maidens are said to have mastered the art of "imitating the voices and chatter of all people".[112] The substantial amount of direct speech in Stesichorus' poems has been one of the most intriguing aspects for the defenders of choral performance. This *Hymn* seems to prove that such a performance would not have been as strange as it seems to a modern mind and audience. In this line, Ley suggested that the *rheseis* in the *Thebais* (fr. 97 F.) would suit choral performance, as happens, for example in Aeschylus' *Agamemnon*, where the chorus recreates the dialogue between Chalcas and Agamemnon.[113]

Ercoles draws attention to the existence in Stesichorus' own times of pre-dramatic choruses,[114] such as the tragic choruses in Sicyon,[115] the dithyrambs and other poems of Arion,[116] and the *Padded Dancers*.[117] In these performances, the narrative of lyric taste is accompanied by some dramatic form. The details are unknown to us, but the evidence suggests the dramatization of narrative elements, either through dance or by means of some dialogical structure. Stesichorus would have hardly ignored all these performance experiments, which he could have noticed in his own island, where choral performance was common.

---

112 Burkert 1987: 111.
113 Ley 1993: 115. The melody that accompanies the words on Agamemnon had the characteristics of the citharodic nomos, and that in the same tragedy (vv. 104–159) occurs a Stesichorean triadic structure. This may suggest the idea that Aeschylus was aware and an admirer of Stesichorus performative manner.
114 Ercoles 2012: 7–12. See also Csapo and Miller 2007 for a general overview of the pre-dramatic performances and Kowalzig and Wilson 2013 for a contextualization of the dithyramb.
115 Hdt 5.67.
116 Cf. Solon, fr. 30a W; Hdt. 1.23–27; *Suda* α 3886 A (Arion test. 1 Campbell); Schol. Ar. *Av.* 1406 (p. 254 White) = Arion test. 4 Campbell. See Lesky 1972: 52–68; Pickard-Cambridge 1962: 97–112; Ieranò 1997: 175–185; D'Angour 2013: 202.
117 Cf. Arist. *Po.* 1449a-15–25. The padded-dancers appear in Corinthians and Attic vases dated to the last quarter of the seventh, first half of the sixth century, cf. Seeberg 1995; Todisco 2002: 46–58; Green 2007: 96–107; Steinhart 2007. On the importance of these vases in the context of choral performance Sicily, see Wilson 2007: 357 n. 28.

Now, the status of the Delian maidens, as quasi-professional choruses, was possible because of their ties to the temple, to the site of performance.[118] The question is, if Stesichorus was a travelling poet, how would he have rehearsed his choruses? Did he have a professional chorus travelling with him? Or was he able to make an amateur chorus perform his long poems? If Stesichorus was working with a professional chorus, the preparation and rehearsal of text, music, and choreography are more likely to succeed than if he was dealing with an amateur group. Burkert and others hypothesised a semi-professionalised chorus accompanying Stesichorus in his tours.[119] He relies on the evidence of Pseudo-Xenophon according to which there was a time in Athens "when alien professionals showed their expertise".[120] However, Bierl points out that what persisted in Athens was the practiced of the amateur choruses, accompanied by an increasing professionalization of the *choregos*.[121] The choruses therefore, Bierl suggests, were composed by a non-professional "representative groups that on a cyclical basis formed a chorus",[122] instead of a "travelling group of *technitai* appearing wherever a public festival presented the occasion for a production".[123] Stesichorus' Sicily attracted famous choral poets in the sixth and fifth century and the training of chorus to the international festivals abroad was not rare practice. Pausanias tells us that there was a monument dated to the fifth century in memory of a chorus of boys and their *didaskalos* who drowned on their way from Messina to Rhegium.[124]

But other evidence suggests that a chorus need not be professional to be able to perform long compositions. Burnett mentions the example of tragic choruses dancing and singing up to 2000 lines throughout the three plays.[125] Moreover, in the case of the tragic choruses the variety of metres to memorize stands as a further difficulty which would not apply to Stesichorus.[126]

The hypothesis for the monodic performance of Stesichorus' poems seems therefore, too dependent on an idea of epic influence in his poetry, and fails to

---

118 Thus Power 2010: 102.
119 E.g. Cingano 1993: 361.
120 Ps. Xen. *Ath. Pol.* 1.13. Burkert 1987: 107.
121 Bierl 2009: Introduction n. 61.
122 Bierl 2009: Introduction n. 61.
123 Burkert 1987: 107, n. 54.
124 Pausanias 5.25.2–4.
125 Burnett 1988: 132–133.
126 Finglass 2017a: 85.

convince that this would be his primary mode of performance.[127] This does not exclude the possibility that Stesichorus could have performed some works as a solo singer to the cithara in particular contexts.[128] An archaic poet would hardly be confined to one mode of performance. But the idea that Stesichorus' poems were never performed by a chorus of singers is highly unlikely and therefore his place among the choral lyric should not be ignored.

The myth in Stesichorus and travelling motifs

"Travel and 'wandering' are persistent elements in both the reality and the *imaginaire* of Greek poetry, and intellectual and cultural life more generally, from the earliest days".[129] Thus begins the introduction of Hunter and Rutherford's volume on the wandering poets; a book that shows how recent scholarship has been drawing attention to the phenomenon of travelling, poetic mobility, and wandering as a central aspect of Greek and indeed Mediterranean culture. In the volume, Stesichorus' name is mentioned only seven times, all of which *en passant* or as a briefly cited example. However, his poems, although silent regarding the occasion, were likely to be performed in various locations throughout the Greek world. Travel, it seems, was part of Stesichorus' job as a poet. But it was also a common experience in his time and particularly in his city, and his poems carry the spirit of the new world emerging in the Mediterranean basin deeply marked by travelling.

As a poet dedicated to heroic narratives, Stesichorus' themes oscillate roughly between the Trojan Cycle, the Labours of archetypical heroes (Heracles, Meleager), and the Theban Cycle. All these mythical kernels focus on principals of displacement, exile, or adventures to the unknown or the savage; *topoi* closely associated with the idea of travelling and wandering, which may find in an

---

127 Finglass 2014: 31–32 does not exclude the possibility of citharodic reperformance, and concedes that Stesichorus would be able to sing is poems without a chorus in particular contexts. Arion, the legendary inventor of the dithyramb is said to have had citharodic performances.
128 Martinez 1974: 336 and Adrados 1978: 297 suggested independently a sort of mixed performance where the invocation was sung by the solo singer or the *choregos*, while the narrative was performed by the chorus, with the exception of the dialogues which would have been left to the *choregos* or the solo singer. Vetta 1999: 106–109, on the other hand, argues that the provision would be the part of the chorus and the narrative was left to the solo singer-poet. Cingano 2003: 21 believes that the chorus would dance and sing only the refrains while the rest was to be sung by the poet.
129 Hunter and Rutherford 2009: 1.

audience from the west an enhanced impact. Stesichorus' poetic production, and indeed his life, show a constant inclination for the highlighting of the idea of travelling as central to Greek perception of the world and of its own identity.

In the choices of the journeys of his heroes, Stesichorus maps Greek ambitions in the trading world, concerns regarding the institution of the polis; ideas characteristic to a world in rapid development, growth, and prosperity. I aim to show how these concerns and this spirit of the archaic Greece is expressed in one of its most recognized voices. I will discuss Stesichorus' works in four chapters, each dedicated to a particular motif involving travel. I have excluded from this study the spurious titles and I have focused on a selection of the more prominent fragments. Thus, in the first chapter, I discuss the narratives of adventure, traditionally associated with a conquer of nature by culture, in three poems: the *Geryoneis*, the *Cycnus*, and the *Boarhunters*. The chapter is focused primarily on the *Geryoneis* for two reasons. First, because it involves a far-off western journey where the hero reaches a known land, rather than an imprecise vague location. This has obvious implications in the understanding of Stesichorus' perception of the west, which may have differed from that of his predecessors. Second, because it is the poem of which more lines survived.

The second chapter is dedicated to the narratives of escape and return present in the *Sack of Troy* and in the *Nostoi*. The aftermath of the Trojan war tells a story of diffusion. I aim to show Stesichorus' treatment of this diffusion in the attribution of new routes to the Trojan fugitives, mainly Aeneas, who has here the earliest association with the west. As a fugitive, Aeneas will sail the same waters as the Greeks returning home. Our knowledge of the *Nostoi* is limited to one episode, which raises some questions regarding the possible wider scope of the narrative. It tells about Telemachus' visit to Sparta in the most significant fragment attesting Stesichorus' knowledge and intertext with Homer. Alas, details on the journeys in both accounts have not survived in enough extent for us to fully appreciate the literary treatment given to them by our poet. However, the surviving fragments of these poems illustrate to a relatively satisfying degree Stesichorus' adaptation of details of the myth from previous accounts, thus casting light on our poet's innovative and, at times, bold, changes to the narrative by focusing episodes in characters that are not as relevant in other accounts.

In the third chapter, we find a discussion on the abduction myths and the innovative aspects of these tales. I elaborate a short review of the later versions of the abduction of Europa discussing the possible contents of the homonymous poem, but the focus of the chapter falls on the abductions of Helen, and, again, on the alternative routes of Helen, proposed by the poet.

The last chapter concerns the motif of exile and *stasis* in the *Oresteia* and the *Thebais*. These two poems are perhaps the best examples of Stesichorus' place between epic and tragedy as they show a careful treatment of the characters, especially the female figures that we later find in the tragedy, suggesting Stesichorus' place as a source of the tragedians in the treatment of the myth. In this chapter the travelling theme is perhaps less central in the discussion, given that very little as survived from that part of the narratives, but they are crucial to our understanding of Stesichorus' poetic technique and innovative approach to these myths.

Through this I aim to contribute to the appreciation of Stesichorus' narrative technique, on his reworking of epic myths and his relevance to the wider context of Greek literature as a source to later poets, namely the tragedians. By idealizing the chapters opposing two different poems, in most of the cases, from two different narrative cycles, it is my purpose to show the different treatment given by Stesichorus to the same motif, the same situation, or the same character in several poems. For, enigmatic though he may be, Stesichorus is a central piece in the puzzle of Greek literature, and his name deserves to be heard much more.

1 Adventure

This chapter primarily focuses on one of the travelling heroes *par excellence*, the challenger of boundaries: Heracles, a hero to whom Stesichorus devoted no fewer than three poems: *Cycnus*, *Geryoneis*, and *Cerberus*.[1] These three titles alone suggest three levels of journey: one close to home, in Thessaly; another in far off western lands, in Cadiz; and, finally, one to the Underworld.

Unfortunately, from the *Cerberus* only one word is preserved: ἀρύβαλλος (fr. 165 F.), which is likely to refer to the recipient containing the meat to lure or poison the infernal dog Cerberus.[2] Not much can be said of Stesichorus' treatment of the subject apart from noting his interest in a journey to the Underworld, which, given the abundance of travelling themes in Stesichorus' oeuvre, is not surprising but nevertheless a lamentable loss. How would the poet have treated the journey itself? How did he describe the landscape of the Underworld?

The remaining fragments and quotations from Heracles' other journeys offer material for us to appreciate Stesichorus' treatment of the hero's encounters with monsters and the poet's approach to such episodes in comparison to other poems involving the encounter with monsters and beasts, namely the Calydonian Boar hunt, that displays a different set of motifs: the scene is set in the Greece mainland, the hero Meleager gathers an army to defeat the creature, whereas Heracles, even when facing monsters in Greek mainland, acts alone.

---

1 Some scholars have argued that the *Scylla* (fr. 182 F.) told of the encounter between Heracles and the monster when he was returning from Erytheia, and was thus part of, or a sequel to the *Geryoneis* (thus Bowra 1961: 94). Adrados 1978: 264–265 believes that the *Scylla* is part of the *Geryoneis* because he sees in the reference to Sarpedonia (fr. 6 F.) an allusion to Scylla's mother who is connected to the Gorgons. However, the reference to the island may well refer to Chrysaor, Geryon's father, born from the severed head of Medusa (Hes. *Th.* 276–281), thus Robertson 1969: 216; Antonelli 1996: 60. Waser 1894: 46; Bowra 1961: 94; Curtis 2011: x n. 4, 7, and 21, n. 88, who does not discuss problems with this argument. The encounter between the monster and Heracles is first attested only in Lycophron's *Alexandra* (44–49) and other sources of the Hellenistic period (Hedyle *ap.* Athenaeus 7.297b; Ov. *Met.* 13.728–14.74 and in the V scholium to *Od.* 12–85 which ascribes the story to a Dionysus whom Jacoby tentatively identified with Dionysus of Samos a third century author of *Kyklos Historikos*, on which see Hopman 2012: 196–199. The episode involving Scylla is better known from the *Odyssey* 12.85 (see too Pherecydes fr. 144 *EGM*) and, thus, it is best to think of Stesichorus' version as part of this tradition.
2 Cf. Verg. *Aen.* 6.417–425, thus West *ap.* Davies and Finglass 2014: 461.

2 — Adventure

A particularly relevant aspect of Stesichorus' versions of Heracles' encounters with Geryon and Cycnus is the emphasis on the monsters' *ethos*, as well as on the divine agency behind Heracles' success. I will focus on the better-preserved poem, the *Geryoneis*, since it contains a fundamental aspect of the journey motif, the journey westwards, into the streams of the Ocean. Throughout the chapter, I will establish and discuss parallels with the *Cycnus* and the *Boarhunters*. These two poems differ from the *Geryoneis* in the use of the travelling motif, since the *Geryoneis* is set in far-off western lands, whereas the other two poems imply a rather shorter terrestrial journey. However, the *Geryoneis* provides other very relevant aspects of Stesichorus' interaction with myth, namely in the focus that the poet casts on otherwise little explored characters, such as Callirhoe.

1.1 The *Geryoneis*

The publication of the *Geryoneis* papyrus in 1967 shed new light on several aspects of Stesichorus' poems. I have mentioned above the importance of the discovery for the understanding of their extension. In the present chapter, the focus is rather on Stesichorus' characterization of his poem's personae and on its apparent innovations, particularly in terms of mythical geography.[3]

Stesichorus' *Geryoneis* is the longest and more complete treatment of the Geryon's story known to us from antiquity. Before his detailed and expanded account, other versions provided the general outline of the story. The earliest record of Heracles' tenth Labour appears in Hesiod's *Theogony* (287–294):

> Χρυcάωρ δ' ἔτεκε τρικέφαλον Γηρυονῆα
> μιχθεὶc Καλλιρόηι κούρηι κλυτοῦ Ὠκεανοῖο·
> τὸν μὲν ἄρ' ἐξενάριξε βίη Ἡρακληείη
> βουcὶ παρ' εἰλιπόδεccι περιρρύτωι εἰν Ἐρυθείηι
> ἤματι τῶι, ὅτε περ βοῦc ἤλαcεν εὐρυμετώπουc
> Τίρυνθ' εἰc ἱερὴν, διαβὰc πόρον Ὠκεανοῖο,
> Ὄρθον τε κτείναc καὶ βουκόλον Εὐρυτίωνα
> cταθμῶι ἐν ἠερόεντι πέρην κλυτοῦ Ὠκεανοῖο.

---

[3] These aspects of the poem have drawn the attention of scholars resulting in copious bibliography. See e.g. the bibliography and state of the art in Lazzeri 2008; Curtis 2011; Davies and Finglass 2014: 230–298. Apart from the commentary by Davies and Finglass, other pieces have come to light on the *Geryoneis*, particularly, Noussia-Fantuzzi 2013; and others dealing with some particular aspects of the poem as for example Ercoles 2011; Bowie 2014: 99–106; Kelly 2015: 31–38, 41–42; Xanthou 2015: 38–45.

> Chrysaor then lay with Kallirhoe, daughter of glorious Okeanos,
> and sired the three-headed Geryones
> whom the might Herakles slew
> beside his shambling oxen at sea-girt Erytheia
> on the very day he crossed Ocean's stream
> and drove the broad-browed cattle to holy Tiryns.
> There he also slew Orthos and the oxherd Eurytion
> Out at the misty place, beyond glorious Ocean.[4]

According to the author of the *Theogony*, Geryon dwells in an island called Erytheia, located beyond the Ocean. No further detail related to its geographical location is given. The characterization of the island suggests a mysterious atmosphere, as the poet describes Erytheia as περιρρύτωι εἰν Ἐρυθείηι (290) and ἐν ἠερόεντι πέρην κλυτοῦ Ὠκεανοῖο (294), emphasising the isolation and remoteness of the island. This idea of isolation is recovered in another passage dedicated to Geryon (*Th.* 980–983) where the poet displays the same imagery: εἰλιπόδων ἀμφιρρύτωι εἰν Ἐρυθείηι (983).

However, here the characterization of Geryon is different from the previous one. In lines 287–294, Hesiod mentions Geryon in the context of Pontus' genealogy, a family of dreadful creatures that inhabit the furthest regions of the world. The approach to Geryon in lines 979–983 is rather different. Mentioned here among the list of the offspring resulting from unions of goddesses and mortal men, he is referred to as the most powerful of all mortals (βροτῶν κάρτιστον ἁπάντων, line 981). As noted by De Sanctis, the double perspective cast upon Geryon in the *Theogony* opens the way to the sympathetic and more humanized treatment of the character in later accounts.[5] In this sense, therefore, Stesichorus' treatment of Geryon is but an extension of the portrait hinted at by Hesiod, which will, nevertheless, surpass in many levels the version of his predecessor, as we shall see.

One of the aspects that Stesichorus maintains is the difficulty of the journey to Erytheia, something that requires divine collaboration; an aspect present in an earlier account of the myth offered by Pisander of Rhodes. The *Suda* places Pisander's activity in the 33th Olympiad (648–645), *i.e.* mid-seventh century, thus two generations before Stesichorus.[6] According to the same source, he is

---

4 Trans. Athanassakis 2004.
5 Thus De Sanctis 2011: 63. Cf. Clay 1993: 109–110 who argues that the generation of monsters in Hesiod matched the mixed breed of Greek heroes, such as Achilles, Aeneas, or Heracles himself.
6 West 2003: 23 disagrees with this chronology on the basis that the artistic evidence only shows Heracles with the lion skin, bow, and the club after 600 and postulates this date as a

considered the author of one epic *Heracleia* (fr. 5 *GEF*), of which little has survived. Only one fragment provides a reference to the Bowl of the Sun, the means by which Heracles manages to sail through the Ocean:

> Πείcανδρος ἐν δευτέρωι Ἡρακλείας τὸ δέπας ἐν ὧι διέπλευcεν ὁ Ἡρακλῆς τὸν Ὠκεανὸν εἶναι μέν φηcιν Ἡλίου, λαβεῖν δ' αὐτὸ παρ' Ὠκεαν<οῦ τ>ὸν Ἡρακλέα

> Pisander in Book II of his *Heracleia* says that the Bowl of the Sun in which Heracles sailed through the Ocean belonged to Helios, but Heracles obtained it from Oceanus.

This is the earliest attestation of the episode of Heracles' use of the Bowl of the Sun,[7] which will reappear in Stesichorus' account and in later depictions from 510 onwards.[8] It is not evident what episode of Heracles' Labours in far off locations this refers to, but the use Stesichorus makes of this means of transportation in his *Geryoneis* may indicate that Pisander did the same. No other literary evidence for the story of Geryon antedating Stesichorus survives. However, the artistic evidence shows that the theme was widely known and appreciated, at least from the last quarter of the seventh century, which may corroborate a generalised interest in the theme by different means of artistic representation in Stesichorus' times. In general, the surviving depictions of Heracles' tenth Labour focus on the battle between Heracles and a three-bodied Geryon, whose characterisation varies in the details.[9]

From the second half of the sixth century, Heracles and Geryon reappear in Ibycus, who refers briefly to the episode in fr. S 176.17–18 *PMGF*. The surviving

---

terminus post quem for Pisander's activity. Davies and Finglass 2014: 231 n. 6 point out that beside the appearance of the lion skin in a representation of Heracles dating to 625–600, the argument that the artistic evidence must stand as a precursor of literary and poetic creativity is unsatisfactory. See, however, Jesus 2017: 32–74, especially, 38–48 on the antecedents of art in poetry and vice-versa.

7 Mimnermus fr. 12 *IEG* may be the earliest reference to this means of transportation belonging to the Sun, if he predates Pisander, but he does not mention it in the context of Heracles' Labour, but rather in a description of the Sun's use of his chariot in a cosmological perspective.

8 For the representations of the Bowl of the Sun and Heracles, see Pinney and Ridgway 1981 and Brize 1990: §§ 2548, 2550–2552; for depictions where Heracles appears to be displaying a menacing posture, see §§ 2545–2546, 2549, which may echo the version first attested by Pherecydes (fr. 18a *EGM*) in which the hero obtains the bowl by threatening the god.

9 Other seventh century representations of Geryon focus solely on the characterization of the monster rather than on his encounter with Heracles (cf. Brize 1988: § 1–2, 5 and Davies and Finglass 2014: 232 n. 10 for a more recent and disputed depiction). Statues dating to the first quarter of the sixth century depict Geryon (Brize 1988: § 2a and §§ 3–4 from slightly later in the sixth century). For the representation of the episode in art, see further Robertson 1969.

lines focus on Heracles' athletic excellence in two episodes, the funeral games for Pelias and the tenth labour of Heracles; mythical episodes to which Stesichorus dedicated two poems: the *Geryoneis* and the *Funeral Games for Pelias*.[10] We cannot assess the exact use made by the poet of these episodes, but the context and encomiastic tone suggest that this was part of an epinician.[11] Hence, the episode with Geryon may have been intended to emphasise the supremacy of Heracles. The episode appears also in one fragment of Pindar, with a curious shift. In the fragment, Heracles' conquest is somehow criticised and the figure of Geryon appears as a victim of unjust deeds, a victim of fate (fr. 169 S-M). Here the focus is on the malice of Heracles' conquest, rather than on his heroic achievement, an aspect which may have derived from Stesichorus' treatment of the myth, as we shall see.

The fifth century shows a revived interest in the labours of Heracles. Panyassis' *Heracleia* preserves the Pholus episode (fr. 9 *GEF*), which featured in Stesichorus' *Geryoneis* (fr. 22 F.). West suggests that fr. 13 *GEF* is part of a dialogue between Geryon and Heracles.[12] Panyassis also makes use of the bowl of the sun in the context of Heracles' travel to Erytheia (fr. 12 *GEF*). The bowl appears again in Pherecydes, who tells us how Heracles gained possession of it by force and travelled in it to Erytheia (fr. 18a *EGM*). The theme recurs in mythographers and early historians, who provide rationalized versions of the earlier accounts of the myth particularly in geographical terms. Hecataeus' *Genealogies* denies the traditional setting of Geryon's dwelling-place in the west and places it in Ambracia, while in his *Periegesis* he maintains Heracles' traditional route westwards, with a stop in Sicily.[13] Italy and Sicily assume a growing importance in the route of Heracles' on his return from Erytheia.[14] Hellanicus treated the toils of Heracles during his return with the cattle, where a heifer escapes the

---

10 Thus Wilkinson 2013: 126, who notes, however, that the passing reference to these two poems may have been intended to recall the audience of Stesichorus' poems and appreciate the distinctiveness of Ibycus' poetry, as may have been the case in S151 *PMGF*.
11 Wilkinson 2013: 126 notes the encomiastic nature of several other poems by Ibycus, suggesting that fr. S 176 fits the epinician genre (thus Jenner 1986: 66–70; cf. Rawles 2012: 6–12) and hence using the myth as a paradigm rather than the core of the poem, as is the case in Stesichorus. In the fragment, Heracles is referred to six times and the focus seems to be drawn to his athletic excellence, a theme recurrent in encomiastic poetry.
12 West 2003: 201. See also McLeod 1966.
13 Hecat. fr. 26 *EGM*, *FGrHist* I FF 76–77.
14 Cf. fr. 21 F.

cattle and swims from Italy to Sicily.[15] Herodotus, on the other hand, has Heracles return to Greece via Scythia (4.8–10). Later historians such as Timaeus seem to have made use of the story to provide Sicily and Italy with cultic and political *aitia*.[16]

In tragedy, we have mere allusions to the episode,[17] although Pearson suggested that Sophocles treated the figure of Geryon in his lost play *Iberians*.[18] In comedy, the more substantial evidence on the treatment of the story is a play entitled *Geryon* attributed to Ephippus from the fourth century.[19]

More detailed versions of the myth after Stesichorus are only found in later accounts by Apollodorus and Diodorus. Apollodorus (*Bibl.* 2.5.10) identifies Erytheia with Gadeira, maintains Heracles' threatening attitude towards the Sun in the hopes of acquiring his cup to sail the Ocean, and features Menoetes, suggesting that he was familiar with Stesichorus' account.[20] Diodorus (4.17.1–25.1) pays close attention to this labour of Heracles, providing a detailed account of Heracles' travels to and from Erytheia, in a circular journey around all the significant shores of the Mediterranean.[21]

In art, the earliest attestation of the episode dates from the mid-seventh century, where Heracles attacks a three-bodied, four-legged Geryon armed with three shields, who is protecting his cattle, which is also depicted.[22] The battle scene, with further detail, appears in a relief dating to the last quarter of the seventh century, where Heracles appears with the lion-skin.[23] The scene portrays the battle not only in more detail, but also at a more advanced stage than

---

15 Hellanic. frr. 110–111 *EGM*; cf. Pearson 1975: 188–189 for the importance of Italy and Sicily in the fifth century and later tales of Heracles' return.
16 Timaeus *FGrHist* 566 F 90, cf. D. S. 4.22.6 and Pearson 1975: 171–196 and Baron 2012: 202–255 on Timaeus and his predecessors.
17 A. *Ag.* 870, fr. 74 *TrGF*; E. *Heracl.* 419–424.
18 *TrGF* 4 Radt. Note also the third century tragedian Nicomachus of Alexandria who wrote a play entitled *Geryon* (*TrGF* 127 F 3). For the use of the term Iberians, see further Aeschylus frr. 73a, 199 *TrGF*, and in comedy Cratinus fr. 108 *PCG* and Aristophanes fr. 564 *PCG*. The term Iberian is increasingly frequent in the fifth and fourth century because of the presence of mercenaries in the Carthaginian army (thus Celestino and López-Ruiz 2016: 45–46).
19 Diodorus (4.8.4) claims that the theme recurred in the genre, but the evidence available to us is very limited; on the use of monsters in comedy, see also Sommerstein 2013: 155–175.
20 Barrett 2007a (1968): 13 proposes that Apollodorus' ultimate source may have in fact been Stesichorus' *Geryoneis*.
21 For Tartessus in Greek Literature see Albuquerque 2010; Celestino and López-Ruiz 2016: 24–95, the latter a survey covering Greek, Roman and Phoenician sources.
22 Brize 1988: § 11; cf. fr. 19 F.
23 Brize 1988: § 8; Brize 1985 for a detailed survey.

the previous piece, since one of Geryon's heads is bended over, thanks, we may presume, to an arrow. The similarities of this depiction with Stesichorus' fr. 19 F. are striking, not least because the piece also depicts Eurytion who, despite figuring as one of the victims of Heracles along with his dog Orthos in Hesiod (*Th.* 293), seems to have received close attention from Stesichorus in frr. 9 and 10 F.

One vase from the first quarter of the sixth century depicts Geryon as a herdsman,[24] a version which will later appear in literary sources, although the most recurrent scene featuring Geryon is indeed the battle with Heracles. The other vase dating to the same period offers a similar battle scene as the one depicted in the relief mentioned above.[25] Depictions increase considerably after 550 BC, perhaps reflecting some aspects of Stesichorus' poem.[26] The most significant similarities between depictions and poem are found in two Chalcidian amphorae dating to the mid-sixth century representing a winged Geryon labelled in the Doric dialect.[27] As far as we know, the earliest literary representation of a winged Geryon is Stesichorean. Davies and Finglass point out the increasing presence from the mid-sixth century on of female figures in the battle scene between Heracles and Geryon: Athena, the protector of the son of Zeus, and Callirhoe, Geryon's mother.[28] Both figures have determinant roles in Stesichorus' battle scene; roles that, at least for Callirhoe as the *mater dolorosa*, as far as we can tell, were not developed by the earlier literary versions of the myth. Throughout the fifth century the story is still frequent in statuary, being present in the metopes of the treasury of Athens at Delphi, of the temple of Zeus in Olympia, and the temple of Hephaestus at Athens.[29] Its expression on vase-painting decreases by the end of the fifth century.

Stesichorus' *Geryoneis* seems to have remained as one of the sources of the story to poets and artists at least in some respects, such as the location of Erytheia, the inclusion of Callirhoe, and in the idea of a diversion during Heracles' return. However, the feeling that no other account in antiquity exactly matched Stesichorus' *Geryoneis* on the level of characterization and treatment of certain characters is inescapable. It still puzzles scholars today, making the *Geryoneis* one of, it not *the*, most commented poems by Stesichorus.

---

[24] Ivory pyxis from Chiusi (Brize 1988: § 7).
[25] Middle-Corinthian kylix from Perachora (cf. Robertson 1969: 208; Brize 1988: § 12).
[26] See Robertson 1969 on Stesichorus' influence on vase-painters.
[27] On which see Barrett 2007a (1968): 8; Robertson 1969: 208–209; Davies and Finglass 2014: 232–233.
[28] Davies and Finglass 2014: 232–233. On the roles of the female figures, see below frr. 17 and 18 F.
[29] Brize 1988: §§ 2506, 2507, 2475; also Robertson 1969: 207.

1.1.1 Mapping the far west (frr. 8–10 F.)

As we have seen above, the earliest account of the myth, by Hesiod, located Erytheia beyond the Ocean. To travel to Geryon's home, Heracles had to count with the collaboration of divine agents. One example of this is the acquisition of the bowl of the Sun, as we have seen, first attested in Pisander. The general idea and imagery of these two accounts is maintained by our poet, with slight, albeit significant, alterations. The crossing of the Ocean is a recurrent *topos* of the westwards heroic journeys. The Ocean establishes the limit of human realm in Greek cosmology since Homer.[30] In Homeric cosmology as depicted on the Shield of Achilles in the *Iliad* (18.478–608), Oceanus, although the origin of all the water streams,[31] is most commonly associated as the mass that circumscribes the world, enclosing it in a space beyond which nothing is nor can be known. Therefore, it is the boundary of the human realm, the limit beyond which no common mortal should ever adventure.[32] It is not surprising then that all the major heroic travelling narratives imply, at a certain point, the crossing of Oceanus.[33] Perseus travels westwards beyond the streams of Oceanus to defeat Medusa (Hes. *Th.* 274–280). Odysseus reaches the dusk region as he visits Aeolus' Island. In all these episodes, the victorious return of the hero implies the overcoming of the human condition.

Heracles' quest for Geryon's cattle is no exception, even though earlier accounts do not specify the region of Geryon' island. It is commonly accepted that the journey accompanies the movement of the Sun, and hence lies westwards. As a traditional example of the journey to the west, the crossing of the Ocean is present, since the western horizon and the Ocean share the same conceptualization.[34] These earlier accounts of Heracles' Labours in the west, Geryon's cattle,

---

[30] Espelosín 2009: 284 points out the fundamental role of the Homeric poems to early Greek cosmology and to the idea of *oikoumenê* (thus Strabo 1.1.2). Geographical references beyond the Greek space are vague and the sense of danger and uncertainty of what lays beyond the known land and seas is more marked as the journey moves westwards. For a recent survey on the aspects of the Sea in Greek imagination, see Beaulieu 2016: 21–89 and West 1997: 144–148, for parallels to the notions of the liminal stream of water in Near-Eastern cultures.
[31] *Il.* 21.195–197; Hes. *Th.* 337–370; Pi. fr. 326 S-M. West 1997: 144–148.
[32] Nesselrath 2005: 1. On the idea of the Pillars of Heracles as a barrier that should not be crossed see Pi. *O.* 3.44; *N.* 3.21. Cf. *I.* 4.13 for the metaphor of the grasping of the Pillars as a great deed. See Pavlou 2010 for a study on *Olympian* 3 and the elements of space and the conception of the periphery of earth. Cf. Alcaeus fr. 345V.
[33] For the crossing of the sea and its implications in Greek culture, see Beaulieu 2016: 46–57.
[34] See Celestino and López-Ruiz 2016: 96–124 for a survey on the conceptualization of the far west in Greek and Roman cultures.

the apples from the Garden of the Hesperides, and the taking of Cerberus, preserve the imagery of the far west as a mythical place of obscure contours commonly associated with the eschatological elements of the Underworld and afterlife.[35] The mythical landscape left its traces in the idea of the far west as the location of the most perilous adventures of the heroes.

The mysticism of the western shores and the themes associated with it prevail in the three fragments (8, 9, and 10 F.) that more clearly preserve the mythical ambience traditionally associated with tales set in the west. However, their interpretation is not unanimous. Let us begin with fr. 8 F., a quotation by Athenaeus, which deals with Heracles crossing the Ocean in the bowl of the Sun:

ὅτι δὲ καὶ ὁ Ἥλιος ἐπὶ ποτηρίου διεκομίζετο ἐπὶ τὴν δύcιν Cτηcίχοροc μὲν οὕτωc φηcίν·

†ἅλιος δ' Ὑπεριονίδας†   str./ant.
Δέπαc †ἐcκατέβαινε† χρύcεον ὄφ-
  Ρα δι' Ὠκεανοῖο περάcαc
ἀφίκοιθ' ἰαρᾶc ποτὶ βένθεα νυκ-
  τὸc ἐρεμνᾶc   5
ποτὶ ματέρα κουριδίαν τ' ἄλοχον
  παῖδαc τε φίλουc,
ὁ δ' ἐc ἄλcοc ἔβα δάφναιcι †καταc-
  κιον† ποcὶ παῖc Διὸc [–⏑⏑–

1 ἅλιοc], τᾶμοc Barrett | Ὑπεριονίδαc], Ὑπεριονίδα‹ἴ›c West ‖ **2** ἐcκατέβαινε], ἐcκατέβαιν' ἐc Pardini ‖ **4** ἀφίκοιθ' Blomfield: ἀφίκηθ' codd. | ἰαρᾶc Page: ἱερᾶc codd. ‖ **8–9** κατάcκιον], κατακcιόεν Barrett ‖ **9** ποcὶ Suchfort: ποcὶν codd. | [Ἡρακλέηc Page

and that the sun too is conveyed on a cup to the west is said by Stesichorus as follows:

The sun, son of Hyperion
stepped into the golden bowl
  so that, crossing the Ocean,
he might reach the depths of holy
  dark night
To his mother, his lawful wife,
  and his dear children;
But he, the son of Zeus, went into the grove
overshadowed with laurels by foot...

---

35 For Near Eastern parallels, see West 1997: 151–167. For the sea as a mediator between life and death, see Beaulieu 2016: 10, 28–32; Celestino and López-Ruiz 2016: 96–97.

As noted above, Heracles' use of the bowl of the Sun appears for the first time in Pisander who names Oceanus as a helper of Heracles in the acquisition of the bowl. The scene reappears with a clearer connection to the episode of Geryon in Panyassis and Pherecydes. In Panyassis, Heracles gains access to the bowl from Nereus, while in Pherecydes he obtains it by threatening Helios with his bow and arrow.[36] Although we lack the moment when Heracles obtains the bowl, scholars have suggested that in Stesichorus our hero may have also had an intermediary. One of the hypotheses suggested is Nereus, thus affording Panyassis' version a prestigious antecedent.[37] This suggestion is based on the mention of the sea-god in fr. 7 F. attributed to the *Geryoneis* by Rhode[38] and accepted by the majority of editors, including Davies and Finglass, who argue that the "hypothesis has the further advantage that Nereus (...) parallels Geryon in various respects", namely the association with the imagery of the far west.[39] Such encounter would thus anticipate the one with Geryon. Furthermore, Heracles' fighting Nereus is attested in art since the late seventh century.[40] Moreover, although there are significant pieces in which the Sun is absent,[41] the artistic evidence shows the presence of Sun on several occasions all dating to the fifth century. Some present a more hostile attitude, approximate to Pherecydes' contemporary account.[42] Other pieces imply a more amicable arrangement, as is the case of a scyphos dating to the second half of the sixth century or the beginning of the fifth century, found in Tarentum and attributed to the Theseus painter, which depicts Heracles with one hand extended as if greeting the Sun.[43]

The scene of fr. 8 F. seems more approximate to the idea that the Sun is approached by Heracles himself – not by an intermediary, as happens in Pherecydes (fr. 18a *EGM*) and Apollodorus (2.5.10). The Sun is present when Heracles leaves the bowl, which suggests that the use of the bowl was permitted by the Sun himself who agreed to concede the passage to the son of Zeus, whatever the means by which Heracles won the deity over.

---

36 Fr. 18a *EGM*.
37 Thus Davies 1988: 277–278.
38 Rhode 1872: 39.
39 Davies and Finglass 2014: 253. Brize 1980: 68–69, 77–78 rejects this hypothesis and prefers to ascribe the episode to a lost title of a poem dealing with the episode of Heracles' visit to the Garden of Hesperides on the grounds that Pherecydes' account of this labour described the fight of Heracles with a metamorphosing Nereus (fr. 16a *EGM*).
40 Glynn 1981; Westcoat 2012: 158–164.
41 Brize 1988: §§ 2550–2552.
42 Two lekythoi dating ca. 550–475 BC, which depict Athena; see Brize 1988: §§ 2548–2549.
43 Brize 1988: §§ 2545–2546; on which see also Pinney and Ridgway 1981: 141.

The fragment preserves the moment when Heracles arrives at his destination and the Sun embarks in his bowl to go and meet his family with whom he is to spend the night. Several aspects deserve attention in the passage. First, where does Heracles arrive? Page considers that the journey is eastwards, since that is the traditional direction of the Sun's travel in the bowl, whereas in the voyage westwards, the Sun uses his chariot.[44] This implies that the episode refers to Heracles' return from Erythia. However, Athenaeus explicitly tell us that the passage illustrates a westward voyage, thus meaning that the place to which Heracles' arrives is in the west. Moreover, the fact that no mention is made to the cattle, which would have accompanied Heracles if this was a return journey, strongly suggest that the land at which Heracles arrives in fr. 8 F. is Erythia.[45]

Despite Athenaeus' claims that the Sun is conveyed to the west on his cup, Stesichorus' version need not to have contradicted the traditional view according to which the travel eastwards is made in a cup while the one to its setting is performed in a chariot.[46] Barrett provides a satisfactory, albeit speculative, reconstruction of the preceding aspects of the narrative. Heracles travels by land until a point where he sees himself in the need to cross the Ocean. The Sun arrives in the west, dismounts his chariot and is about to embark on the cup to meet his family; Heracles appears and demands a passage to Erythia. The Sun, threatened or persuaded, agrees, suspends his return and concedes to give the passage to our hero, after which the Sun returns to his usual path to spend the night with his family.[47]

However, a problem arises: Heracles needs to go back across the Ocean, after getting the cattle. If fr. 8 F. describes the arrival at Erythia, how does Heracles travel back? Our fragment explicitly says that the Sun embarks in his bowl after leaving Heracles by the limits of a grove. This means that the hero does not keep the bowl (as in Apollodorus) and, by extension, that the hero either uses the vessel once more, or finds an alternative mean of transportation back to the continent.[48] This hypothetical scenario points to a further aspect of the scene

---

[44] Page 1967: 101.
[45] Thus Barrett 2007a (1968): 20–21.
[46] Thus Curtis 2011: 97; cf. Ath. 11.781; Apollod. 2.5.10; Eust. *Od.* 1632.23.
[47] Thus Barrett 2007a (1968): 20: "He will have gone out by foot to the hither shore of the Okeanos; but at that point he had the problem of crossing the Okeanos to Erytheia. Stesichoros solved the problem for him by having the Sun give him the loan of a golden cup."
[48] Apollod. 2.5.10 says that Heracles obtains the cup after his defiance of the Sun, whose heat was disturbing the son of Zeus. Heracles keeps the cup during his adventure in Erythia returning the cup to the Sun only after he gets the cattle and crosses over to the mainland.

provided by fr. 8 F.: Heracles' arrival at Erythia by dusk, an aspect which enriches the scene following his entrance in the grove.

Bowie has pointed out the peacefulness of the scene of fr. 8 F. which would contrast the violence of the following Heracles' encounter with Geryon.⁴⁹ The fact that Heracles arrives at Erythia and finds a grove which he would have to cross or wander into is significant. The imagery of the grove as, on the one hand, an idyllic and bucolic place, and on the other, a sacred wild space protected by the deities and home to beasts of all kinds, would anticipate the subsequent scene of the encounter between the hero and Geryon.⁵⁰

The imagery of Heracles' entrance in the grove parallels episodes of the *Odyssey* where the hero arrives to unknown locations. For instance, the landscape described in Odysseus' entrance in Persephone' grove (*Od.* 10.509) is similar to Heracles' arrival to Erytheia.⁵¹ On the other hand, the reference to the shade of the laurels may correspond to the episode of Odysseus' arrival to the land of the Cyclops (*Od.* 9.182–183), the monstrous creature with divine lineage that the hero will defeat.⁵² A further parallel is the episode of Odysseus in Phaeacia. Despite the variation in the word for woodland, reading ὕλη instead of ἄλcoc as in Stesichorus' passage, Homer presents Odysseus entering in a forest on his arrival to Scheria.⁵³ He is to spend the night in the forest sheltered by the vegetation from the winds and the cold of the night. He arrives alone, of course, and after a perilous sea journey. If indeed Stesichorus had this episode in mind and elaborated further on the parallels, the effect would have been significant, since Odysseus arrives in a friendly and civilized land in which he also behaves amicably, whereas Heracles arrives with an aggressive intent to a land inhabited by monsters, heroic though they may be.

The imagery of darkness, silence, and mystery created in the episode of Heracles' arrival and associated with unknown far-off lands reappears in the *Geryoneis* in a fragment which has drawn the attention of several scholars for its combination of mythical and historical geography. Unlike Hesiod, Stesichorus provides topographic details for Erythia, locating it in a specific land known to the Greeks (fr. 9 F.):

---

49 Thus Bowie 2014: 102.
50 Buxton 1994: 81–96; Horden and Purcell 2001: 182–183, 332–233, 414. On the relevance of woods, forests, and groves in Greek myth and religion, see Frazer 1890: 11–27; Burkert 1993: 73–74; Harrison 1992: 19–51.
51 Bowie 2014: 102–103.
52 Lazzeri 2008: *ad loc.*
53 Cf. the grove of Athena in the country of the Phaeacians, *Od.* 6.291–292.

ἐοίκασι δ' οἱ παλαιοὶ καλεῖν τὸν Βαῖτιν Ταρτησσόν, τὰ δὲ Γάδειρα καὶ
τὰς πρὸς αὐτὴν νήσους Ἐρύθειαν· διόπερ οὕτως εἰπεῖν ὑπολαμβάνουσι
Στησίχορον περὶ τοῦ Γηρυόνος βουκόλου διότι γεννηθείη

⌣⌣—⌣⌣—⌣⌣—cχεδὸν ἀν-   ep.
   Τιπέρας κλεινᾶς Ἐρυθείας
—⌣⌣—⌣⌣—⌣⌣
   —⌣⌣—⌣⌣—⌣⌣ Ταρτης-
cοῦ ποταμοῦ παρὰ παγὰς ἀπείρονας ἀρ-   5
γυρορίζους
ἐν κευθμῶνι πέτρας ⌣⌣—⌣⌣

2 Ἐρυθείας Xylander, Ἐρυθίας codd. || **3–4** lacunam statuit Page || **5–6** ἀργυρορίζους], ἀργυρορίζου Wilamowitz || **7** κευθμῶνι Hermann, κευθμώνων codd.

Ancient writers seem to call the Baetis Tartessos, and Gadeira and the nearby islands Erytheia. This, it is supposed, is why Stesichorus could say of Geryon's herdsman that he was born:
>   Right
> Opposite famous Erytheia
>   ...
> ... along the boundless
> Streams of Tartessos river
>   With roots of silver
> In the hollow of a rock.

We owe our knowledge of this passage to a citation by Strabo. However, it seems certain that the quotation omits some parts of the original, since, as we have them, these lines present some metrical difficulties. Even with emendations of Ἐρυθείας for -θίας and κευθμῶνι for -ώνων, the resultant schemes do not yield satisfying results, for either it does not give word-end after four dactyls and requires two successive contracted bicipitia, or it leaves the end of the stanzas (strophe and antistrophe) in mid-word.[54] Hence, Strabo seems to have quoted only the relevant lines for his argument omitting some parts of the original text, a tendency found elsewhere in his and others' works.[55]

---

[54] For discussion on this subject and possible reconstructions see Finglass and Davies 2014: 258–260 and Curtis 2011: 155–156.
[55] Cf. e.g. [Hes.] frr. 240, 70.21–23 M-W. For a study of the problems of quotation by ancient sources and the probability of omission see Most 1994 and related to Simonides of Ceos and his quotation by Stobaeus see Sider 2001.

The fragment concerns the birthplace of Eurytion, Geryon's herdsman, who is frequently associated with the latter in literature and art.[56] These lines from the *Geryoneis* maintain the mystery and fantastic ambiance of the landscape associated with mythical and distant places. In this passage, the narrative does not focus solely in the landscape *per se*, as it is mainly concerned with the episode of Eurytion' birth. Mythical births, particularly those of deities, are often concealed and occur in isolated areas, most frequently in caves[57] yet surrounded by a peaceful and idyllic scenario of abundance.[58]

However, this scenario hides a more concrete location. In our fragment, the idyllic environment is emphasised by the boundless stream (παγὰc ἀπείρονας) of the Tartessus river. Our poet's use of an adjective commonly applied to the sea, when referring to masses of water may acknowledge the vast extension of the Guadalquivir.[59] Moreover, the reference to the ἀργυρορίζους "roots of silver" of the river may allude to the mineral richness of the area, which was known in the eastern Mediterranean, primarily to the Phoenicians and later to the Greeks.[60]

---

56 Cf. Hes. *Th.* 293. For the artistic evidence, see Zervoudaki 1988: particularly § 2, dated to ca. 560. The depiction of Geryon's herdsman is popular in art during the last half of the sixth century (cf. Zervoudaki 1988: §§ 3, 5, 12, 18, 20, 25, 32, 34, 41, 44).
57 Cf. Zeus' birth in several locations all of them in the wilderness, in Hes. *Th.* 468–480; D. S. 5.70; Verg. *G.* 4.153; Call. *Jov.* 1.51; Ov. *Fast.* 4.207; Hermes' birth in *h. Merc.* 229; Pegasus' birth Hes. *Th.* 231–282. For the births of heroes in similar circumstances see e.g. Hom. *Il.* 4.475, 14.444–445; Pi. *P.* 4.46. Ustinova 2009: 3 for an association of caves with fertility, Hom. *Od.* 19.188. See also, Curtis 2011: 160. For other cultures, see e.g. the birth of Abraham (Binder 1964: 125, 127).
58 For ἀπείρων as a definition of the boundlessness of land and sea, see Hom. *Il.* 1.350, 7.446, 24.545 (here referring to the Hellespont); Hes. *Op.* 487, see further Romm 1992: 10–44. For a full account on the etymology and archaic usages of πεῖραρ see Bergren 1975: 22–23; 102–115. On the imagery of a "new territory" in the passage, see Jourdain-Annequin 1989 and Noussia-Fantuzzi 2015: 244.
59 The Guadalquivir is considerably longer than most rivers mentioned in Greek literature, with a length of 657 km today. Its mouth would have occupied a considerable wider area than verifiable today (for a survey on the geological and geographic changes in the landscape of the Guadalquivir basin, see Celestino and López-Ruiz 2016: 176–178); Himera, the river in Sicily (today Salso) extends for 144 km; Achelous in Greece Mainland runs for 220 km; another famous river in Greek mythical repertoire, Xanthus (today Eşen Çayı), extends for 120 km. In comparison to more familiar rivers to the Greeks, the river Guadalquivir may have been a cause for awe and justifiably perceived as "boundless".
60 The idea that Stesichorus intended to make an allusion to the region of Spain is generally accepted by scholars; thus Bowra 1961: 144 who, despite recognizing the epic echoes in the passage, argues that the *Geryoneis* was set in a real place known to sailors and merchants who

The more recent findings in excavations on the Tartessus area show that the western colony of Tyre in Cádiz was established at least by the end of ninth century, a less inhabited area when compared to Huelva or Málaga. But it is with Huelva that most of the trading activities seem to have taken place, both by Phoenician and Greeks, particularly Samians and Phocaeans.

The main interest in Tartessos for the Phoenicians and, later, the Greeks was its metal resources (gold, silver, and tin) and the Iberian expertise in the field, known to the Phoenicians presumably during the tenth century, before the first settlement attempts by Tyre.[61] Greek pottery dating to as early as the eighth century, but increasing in the seventh and the sixth is found in the region of Huelva, although the extent to which this is a result of Greek presence or Phoenician trading is not clear.[62] Tartessus' wealth was therefore known to the Greeks. Evidence of this can be found in other accounts of the region in early Greek historiography. Pherecydes identifies Erytheia with Gades.[63] In his *Periegesis*, Hecataeus refers to the mines of gold and silver in the region. Although the same author denies that Geryon's island was in Tartessus, he was aware of the region and its resources. So too Herodotus, in two different anecdotal passages, mentions Greeks travelling to Tartessus, some returning with great wealth.[64] But even in earlier times, Tartessus' wealth seems to have been known. For example, Anacreon (fr. 361 *PMG*) attests that a sixth century audience was expected to have heard of the region, which may well be derivative

---

brought back knowledge (first-handedly or otherwise) of the landscape and most importantly the precious metal wealth of the area; Lane Fox 2008: 206–207; Lazzeri 2008: 85; Curtis 2011: 152–155; Albuquerque 2013; Davies and Finglass 2014: 258–259.

61 Celestino and López-Ruiz 2016: 152.

62 Cf. Antonelli 1997: *passim*; Vanschoonwinkel 2006: 85; González de Canales *et al.* 2008: 633; Celestino and López-Ruiz 2016: 156–157. The existence of such evidence in Huelva led scholars to question the relation that the Greeks might have established with the local population of Iberia. Domínguez (2010: 33–36) argues that the situation in Iberia was considerably different from that of Sicily. The characteristics of Phocaean colonisation are marked by a mutually favourable relation between Greeks and natives. In places largely inhabited by native communities, the Phocaeans purposes of trading did not need political structures needed in Sicily. At the end of the sixth century the Greeks and natives developed an intense trading relation. Greek products attained the status of luxury goods to the native elite.

63 Fr. 18a *EGM*; and later, Apollod. *Bibl.* 2.5.10.

64 Hdt. 1.163.1–4 and 4.152.2–5. The primordial notion of the west thus suffered slight changes as Greek knowledge of the Mediterranean improved and expanded. The allocation of mythical episodes and imagery to geographical locations begin to emerge among the mythographers and the historians, creating a genre of 'ethnography-geography', Celestino and López-Ruiz 2016: 99.

from information provided by the Samian sailors. These examples show that Tartessus was generally known in Greek communities, especially those with a strong maritime trading engagement, such as Samos, or Himera, our poet's hometown. The transference of the mythical journeys to further western locations would then reflect an increasing geographical knowledge resulting from the broadening of trading networks across the Mediterranean which connected the sea from east to the west.[65] However, the progress of geographical knowledge need not imply that the features of a more traditional idea of west would no longer be found in mythical geography, a favourite theme in literature throughout the centuries.[66]

Stesichorus elaborates his landscape with characteristic elements of the Guadalquivir's mouth, in a subtle manner. The epithet describing the river (ἀργυρορίζoc) does not refer only to a quality strikingly coincident with the mineral resources of the area - the abundance of silver;[67] it also provides the Guadalquivir with an epithet that approximates it to the other rivers in Greek literature which are often described as ἀργυροδίνηc.[68]

Homer applies ἀργυροδίνηc to Peneus, and Scamander; Hesiod to Achelous; Bacchylides to Alpheus; and Euripides to the Simoeis.[69] Perhaps more relevantly, they are all perceived as river-gods, some of them intervening in the narrative. Guadalquivir had no such pedigree. One can suspect that the poet wanted to offer the western river the same treatment that other rivers enjoyed in Greek literature. However, in the majority of these occurrences, the river plays an important role as a topographic reference, as in Stesichorus' *Sack of Troy* (fr. 100 F.), where the river provides not only the location of the episode, but also the landscape and its idyllic, although temporary, ambiance, which eventually

---

[65] The bibliography on the network theory approach to the archaic Mediterranean is extensive and we indicate only a few examples, beginning with the ground-breaking study of the Mediterranean History by Horden and Purcell 2001: especially 7–50, 123–172, 342–400; Lane Fox 2008: 162–172; for the specific case of Tartessus, see Nienmeyer 2006; Celestino and López-Ruiz 2016: esp. 137–148; for the Greek networks, see Malkin 2011; Antonaccio 2013; Domínguez 2006.

[66] Allen 1976: 53 *ap.* Espelosín 2009: 283.

[67] Horden and Purcell 2001: 348–349 for the metallurgy in Greek and Roman Mediterranean: the more relevant silver mines in mainland Greece were in Thrace and Laurion, Attica.

[68] On the composition of epithets using compounds of epic diction and an innovative element, see Maingon 1979: 122–123.

[69] Hom. *Il.* 2.753, 21.8, 130; Hes. *Th.* 340; B. 8.26–27, 12.42; E. *IA* 752. Euripides uses ἀργυροειδήc applied to the Castalia in *Ion* 95. Alc. fr. 395 V. mentions the Xanthus. Note also the inscription of Douris (Lyr. Adesp. fr. 938(e) *PMG*).

contrasts with the mayhem that will unravel throughout the narrative.[70] In the *Geryoneis* the contrast would have been further emphasised if the fragment was part of a narrative diversion on the genealogy of Eurytion at the moment of his killing by Heracles.[71] Remembering Eurytion's birth in these idyllic landscape as a parenthesis in the story of his death[72] would have been particularly dramatic.

Fr. 10 F. may be a part of this digression, too. It mentions the Garden of the Hesperides, the idyllic garden beyond the Ocean, a divine place:

⏕] κ[ύ]μαθ' ἁλὸς βαθ[έ]ας ἀφίκον-　　　　　　　　str./ant.
  το θ]εῶν περικαλλέ[α ν]ᾶϲον
  τ[όθι Ἑcπερίδεc π[αγχρ]ύcεα δώ-
  μα]τ' ἔχοντι·
⏑⏑–⏑⏑] αcc̣[⏑⏑–⏑⏑]και　　　　　5
⏑⏑– κ]αλύκῳ[ν
........]λατ[

1 διὰ] Page, ἐπὶ] Barrett | κ[ύ] Lobel, [ἐ] Barrett || 2–4 Lobel || 6 Barrett

...
...the waves of the deep sea
They reached the fairest island of the gods
Where the Hesperides have
Their golden homes
...
...buds...
...

The reference to the Garden of the Hesperides, has led some scholars to suppose that the *Geryoneis* either included Heracles' quest for the apples, or an allusion to the episode.[73] Neither of these options is entirely satisfactory. In all the ac-

---

[70] See further, Chapter 2.1.1. Cf. Kelly 2015: 30 n. 45 for the importance of rivers in the epic topography.
[71] See further below.
[72] Davies and Finglass 2014: 263, comparing with similar digressions in *Il.* 4.475, 14.444–445; cf. Barrett 2007a (1968): 12.
[73] Bowie 2014: 103 assumes that the fragment refers to Heracles' visit to the Hesperides with no discussion on the issues of the fragments. Barrett 2007b (1978): 22 suggests that Stesichorus could have mentioned the Garden of Hesperides in the *Geryoneis* since the narrative was also set in the west. Curtis 2011: 60–61, 108–109 presents the hypothesis that the papyrus contained more than one poem by Stesichorus, and that this fragment should then be part of another poem on the Heraclean quest on the Garden of Hesperides, although he seems to be more inclined to believe that the fragment is an allusion to the episode, as Barrett suggested.

counts on the labours of Heracles, the quest for the cattle of Geryon and for the apples of the Hesperides are undertaken in separate times, not in one single journey as would have been the case according to this hypothesis.[74] The fragment can be a mere allusion to the island, which is also located in the far west. But in what context would such allusion be convenient in the poem? Barrett unconvincingly suggests that the episode is part of a detour in Heracles' journey.[75] Heracles would sail by the island and the poet took the chance to elaborate on the landscape. There is a problem with this hypothesis: the verb is in the plural (ἀφίκοντο), thus indicating that whoever arrives in the island is not alone. Barrett presents two solutions: either Heracles travels with a companion, such as Iolaus; or the plural refers not to people but to the cattle or to the bowl of the sun itself. However, in all the other remaining fragments of the *Geryoneis*, Heracles seems to be alone, since no reference is made to a companion. On the other hand, Heracles would hardly have been "put in the same footing as mere animals or his mean of conveyance".[76]

Perhaps the problem is in the assumption that Heracles undertakes the journey. What if the travellers are not Heracles and Iolaus or the cattle but someone else? And if so, who? Robertson suggested that fr. 10 F. may describe the journey of Eurytion and his mother Erytheia to the garden of Hesperides.[77] He presents a *exempli gratia* reconstruction of the episode. Erytheia gave birth to Eurytion in the cave by the Tartessus and afterwards would have taken him with her back home, to the garden of Hesperides. This suggestion received the approval of Page and later of Davies and Finglass.[78] There are several episodes of offspring of forbidden affairs or dangerous pregnancies in which the mothers wander the earth escaping,[79] or expelled,[80] from their homeland with their in-

---

[74] Thus Page 1973: 148; Davies and Finglass 2014: 264.
[75] Barrett 2007a (1968): 22.
[76] Davies and Finglass 2014: 264.
[77] Erytheia is considered Eurytion's mother in Hellanicus fr. 110 *EGM* and an Hesperid in Hes. fr. dub. 360 M-W; and later in Apollod. *Bibl.* 2.5.11, although later accounts present her as Geryon's daughter (cf. Paus. 10.17.5).
[78] Page 1973: 148; Davies and Finglass 2014: 264.
[79] E.g Leto (*h. Ap.* 14–18; Pi. *Pa.* 7, 12; E. *IT* 1235–1244; Call. *Del.* 55–196) and Io (Hdt. 1.1; A. *Supp.* 45, 313–315, 535, 1066; [A.] *Pr.* 645–657; Verg. *Aen.* 7.789–792). For examples of concealed births in caves, see above n. 58.
[80] E.g. Danae (Hom. *Il.* 14.379; Hes. fr. 135 M-W; Pherecyd. fr. 10 *EGM*; Simon. fr. 271 Poltera; S. *Acrisius* frr. 68–69 *TrGF* Danae's imprisonment, *Danae* fr. 165 *TrGF*.; E. *Danae, Dictys*; Verg. *Aen.* 7.409; A. R. *Arg.* 4.1091; Hyg. *Fab.* 63; see further Karamanou 2006: 1–17) and Auge (Hes. fr. 165 M-W; Hecat. fr. 110 *EGM*; A. *Mysians* 143–144 *TrGF*, *Telephus* 238–239 *TrGF*; E. *Auge* 265–

fant child. Although none of these cases present a direct parallel with Robertson's hypothesis for fr. 10 F., his suggestion is rather convenient.

Erytheia was not expelled from home, and she is not wandering, but returning home with her baby. A scene where Erytheia and Eurytion were the focus of the narrative would come in the context of fr. 9 F. in a digression on Eurytion's genealogy at the moment of his encounter with Heracles. Moreover, the fact that the episode is told only in Stesichorus is not a strong argument against Robertson's hypothesis. After all, Stesichorus is the only source known to us to have dealt with the herdsman's birth in detail. A scene of maternal love and dedication, of tenderness, as the one which would have resulted from fr. 10 F., associated with a minor character,[81] such as Eurytion would increase the dramatic tension of the episode and anticipate the central battle with Geryon, in the context of which aspects of maternal love and genealogy are present, as we shall see below. To provide the herdsman with a family and to bring the audience a reminiscence of Eurytion as an infant would then have the same effect as it does with Geryon: to emphasise Heracles' brutality.

1.1.2 Geryon's heroism (frr. 12–15 F.)

It is precisely Heracles' brutality, or at least his remarkable power, that is at stake in frr. 12–15 F. which in all likelihood belong to the same part of the poem. They form a series of speeches between Geryon and a messenger who came to inform the former of the attack on his cattle. Since its guardians, Eurytion and Orthos, must have been killed, as they are in the other accounts, Eurytion cannot be the messenger. It is generally accepted that Geryon' interlocutor is Menoetes, the herdsman of Hades.[82] The suggestion of this character is influenced by the account provided by Apollodorus, the fullest version of the episode known to us, and one which contains the detail of a dialogue between Geryon and a companion, found elsewhere only once, precisely in Stesichorus.

As we have seen above, frr. 9 and 10 F. are likely to have been placed in the narrative as a digression on the description of Eurytion's death, which suggests

---

281 *TrGF*, *Telephus* 696–727 *TrGF*; S. *Aleads* 74–96 *TrGF*, *Mysians* 375–391 *TrGF*; Apollod. *Bibl.* 2.103–104; Paus. 8.48.7; D. S. 4.33. 7–12; Str. 13.1.69).

81 The focus on a minor character is not the only example of our poet's attention to minor characters. The opening of the *Sack of Troy* focuses on Epeius describing his daily task in the Achaean camp and his inspiration by Athena to build the Trojan horse.

82 Barrett 2007a (1968): 13; followed by Page 1973: 145; Maingon 1979: 280; Lazzeri 2008: 350; Curtis 2011: 113–114; Davies and Finglass 2014: 267.

that his death was told not only in detail but also in a dramatic way, emphasising the herdsman's birth and childhood, presumably the dedication and love of his mother; a particularly emotional account. Menoetes would have witnessed Heracles' slaughter of Eurytion and Orthos.[83] Therefore the inclusion of a messenger such as Menoetes would, on the one hand, allow our poet to elaborate a dialogue describing Heracles' atrocities and his might, and, on the other, provide the occasion for development of the monster's psychology and dilemmas, aspects to which Stesichorus dedicated special attention in other works.

The fragments ascribed to the messenger speech are severely damaged, particularly fr. 12 F., from which only two, perhaps three words, survive intact: ἀνήρ (line 34), ἦτορ (line 35), and presumably ποκα (line 33), pointing to a speech. Nevertheless, the supplement provided by Lobel to line 31, κε]φαλάν and by Barrett to line 32, ὀϊστο]δόκα, may shed further light on the scene described here. ἀνήρ and ἦτορ may allude to Heracles' might, whereas the combination of ποκα and ὀϊστο]δόκα, a speech in which the "quiver" is in nominative concurs with the hypothesis of a "description of Heracles' appearance".[84] In fr. 13 F. the same Menoetes attempts to dissuade Geryon from facing the invader, by exhorting the creature to remember its parents:

[⏑⏑–⏑⏑–⏑⏑–⏑ ἀλ-] γινόεντος·] ἀλλ' ὦ φίλε ματ[έρα Καλλιρόαν καὶ ἀρηΐφιλο[ν Χρ[υσά]ορα ς.[–⏑⏑–⏑⏑– 5	str./ant.

1–2 Lobel ‖ 3–5 Barrett

...
  ...painful...
  But, my friend, ... your mother Callirhoe
  And warlike
  Chrysaor...

We may compare this fragment to another episode of a messenger delivering appalling news: fr. 191 F. which seems to describe the moment when Althaea

---

[83] The reason why Menoetes should be in the neighbourhood is not clear in Stesichorus or in Apollodorus; thus Barrett 2007a (1968): 13.
[84] Thus Barrett 2007a (1968): 14.

receives the news on her brothers' death and which would have anticipated her dilemma:[85]

>   ]. εὐπατέρει-   5
> α, τ]άχ' ἀγγελίας ἀμεγάρτου
> πε]ύσεαι ἐν μεγάροις· τεθνᾶσί τ[ο]ι
> ἄμα]τι τῶιδε παρ' αἶ-
>   cαν] ἀδελφ[εοί·] ἔκτανε δ' αὐτοὺς
>   ]φ[10

6–9 Haslam

>   ... lady with a noble father
>   Soon you will learn unenviable news
> In your palace: your brothers have died
>   today against
>   fate; their killer was
>   ...

Here too the news is brought to Althaea in her palace by a messenger, who delivers his message in asyndeton anticipating the urgent content of the message,[86] with the first word being the one which expressed death and pushing the subject of the verb to the end of the sentence. The name of the killer is also pushed to a later phase of the sentence. The following narrative would presumably deal with her decision-making on how to act, which would involve her dilemma whether to avenge her brothers by killing her own son or leave her brothers unavenged. The cases mentioned so far concern mainly domestic dilemmas associated with female characters. The *Geryoneis*, on the other hand,

---

85 Haslam 1990: 34 for the identification of the scene.
86 The use of asyndeton anticipating an urgent and important speech is recurrent in tragedy. Cf. the messenger bringing Clytemnestra the news of Iphigenia's sacrifice (E. *IA* [1607–1608]), and Antigone telling Oedipus that his sons are dead, as a result of his curses (E. *Ph.* 1555–1559; compare with Oedipus' curses in S. *OC* 1518–1521). Oedipus delivering the sentence for the assassin of Laius S. *OT* 236–240 (Finglass 2018: *ad loc.*), and the beginning of Teiresias' speech eventually revealing Oedipus as the killer (*OT* 412–415, 449). See also the guard announcing Antigona's return, and later Antigona defending her case (245–246, 908–912; cf. A. *Eu.* 657–659 Apollo introducing his speech on behalf of Orestes, and E. *Or.* 622–626 for Tyndareus' wish to see Orestes condemned). In S. *Tr.* 1130, Hilo announcing the death of Dejanira (cf. E. *HF.* 490–493 Megara addressing the dead Heracles to call him as a witness of his children's misfortunes). In S. *Ph.* 591–594, the merchant reveals to Neoptolemus the true reason for Philoctetes' rescue. In Euripides' *Ph.* [438–440], 503–506, 568–570 the reasons of each of the brothers present their reasons to fight each other.

while sharing the same narrative interest of exploring the psychology of the character, takes a different course. Geryon is presented with a dilemma on which he will elaborate in detail: should he follow Menoetes' advice and abstain from facing Heracles, or should he show his heroism, a motif of pride to all parents, and defy the hero?

The dilemma Stesichorus creates to Geryon allows the poet to focus on the psychology of Callirhoe's son, to explore his doubts about his own condition, to show his heroic *ethos* (fr. 15 F.):

χερςὶν δ[⏑⏑–⏓–⏓ τὸν   ant.
   δ' ἀπαμ[ειβόμενος
ποτέφα [⏑⏑– Χρυςάορος ἀ-
θανάτοιο [⏑–⏓–⏑⏑–.

"μή μοι θά[νατον ⏓–⏓–   5   ep.
   τα δεδίςκ[ε(ο) –⏑⏑– –
μηδέ μελ[–⏓–⏓–⏑⏑
   αἰ μὲν γὰ[ρ ⏑⏑ ἀθάνατος ⏓
μαι καὶ ἀγή[ραος –⏓–⏓–
   ἐν Ὀλύμπ[ωι   10
κρέςςον[(⏑) –⏓–⏓–⏑ ἐ-
   λέγχεα δ[–⏑⏑–

καὶ τ[–⏑⏑–⏑⏑– –   str.
   Κεραϊ[ζόμεν –⏓–⏓ ἀ-
μετέρω[ν ⏓–⏑⏑– –   15
   αἰ δ' ὦ φί[λε –⏓–⏓ γή-
ρας [ἱκ]έςθαι,
   ζώ[ει]ν τ' ἐν ἐ[παμερίοις ⏓–
θε θ[ε]ῶν μακάρω[ν,
   νῦν μοι πολὺ κά[λλιον –⏓–   20
ὅ τι μόρςιμ[ον –⏓–⏑⏑–

καὶ ὀνείδε[⏑–⏑⏑– –   ant.
   καὶ παντὶ γέ[νει ⏓–⏓ ἐξ-
οπίςω Χρυς[άο]ρο[ς υ]ἱόν.
   μ]ὴ τοῦτο φί[ί]λον μακά[ρε]ςςι θε[ο]ῖ-   25
ςι γ]ένοιτο
   ....].[.]..κε[..].[.] περὶ βουςὶν ἐμαῖς

1 χερςὶν Lobel: χηρςιν Π² | τὸν Barrett ‖ **2** Lobel ‖ **3** Χρυςάορος Barrett | ἀ- Lobel ‖ **5** Lobel, θροέων κρυόεν- Barrett ‖ **6** Lobel δεδίςκ[ε' ἀγάνορα θυμόν Barrett ‖ **8** Barrett ‖ **9** Page ‖ **10** Barrett ‖ **11** Lobel ‖ **12** Σ διο(ρθωτέον) ‖ **14** κεραϊζόμεν Barrett | ἀ- Lobel ‖ **16** [λε Lobel | γή- Barrett ‖ **17–19** Barrett **20** Lobel ‖ **21** Barrett ‖ **23** [νει West | ἐξ- Führer ‖ **24** Barrett ‖ **25** μ]ὴ Lobel, cett. Barrett ‖ **26** -ςι Barrett, γ] Lobel

With his hands ...
   In reply ...
   He addressed .... of Chrysaor
immortal....:

'Do not ... death...   5
   To frighten ...,
Nor ....
   For if I am .... [immortal]
   And ageless...
   On Olympus...   10
Better...
   shameful...

and...
carried off....
   far from my stalls.   15
But if, my friend ... reach ...
   old age,
And live among ephemeral ...
   ... of the blessed gods,
   For now it is much more noble for me 20
   What is fated...

And disgrace...
And for all my kind...
   ...future ... the son of Chrysaor.
   May this not be the wish of the blessed   25
   Gods...
...concerning my cattle'
   ...
   ...

The speech is focused on two conditional clauses expressing a dilemma. The fragment preserves the beginning of Geryon's speech (in lines 5–6)[87] where he

---

[87] That Geryon is the speaker seems unproblematic since there is a clear reference to the cattle as property of the speaker in line 27. Geryon's interlocutor is expected to be Menoetes, who had just informed Geryon of Heracles' presence and advised him not to fight the stranger, since fr. 15 F. seems to deal with Geryon's decision to do exactly that, *i.e.*, to contradict the counsels of Menoetes. Moreover, no other character seems to have been appropriate to feature in this episode. This character is male, hence Callirhoe is excluded. Eurytion must have been dead by now, and Chrysaor, Geryon's father, would have hardly been addressed by the vocative ὦ φί[λε; cf. Davies and Finglass 2014: 269.

seems to emphasise his courage towards the possibility of death,[88] thus demonstrating his heroic *ethos* by considering two possible scenarios, one involving his condition of mortality and the other involving the possibility of his immortality. The protasis is in the indicative, thus revealing that immortality is not excluded from the range of possibilities; it is a plausible consideration but presents some problems.

Page and Barrett have dealt with the issues at stake here. Page suggested that the general sense in these lines is that Geryon feels he should fight Heracles whether he is mortal, thus risking his life, or immortal, then not risking his life at all.[89] As Davies and Finglass note, this supposition offers a satisfactory sense, but Page does not provide any supplements which support his suggestion.[90] Moreover, this dilemma would imply that his decision is already taken: Geryon would fight Heracles whatever the outcome. While this suggestion makes the decision to fight inescapable and consequently easier to deal with, it renders it less interesting in terms of the character's psychology, since any of the outcomes would have been heroic: either Geryon defeats Heracles and saves his cattle and himself, or he dies as a hero, a rather expected end for a character that shares so many characteristics with epic heroes.

Barrett proposes a slightly different approach to Geryon's options.[91] According to the scholar, the sense of the first apodosis is not so much "fight, since he can't kill me", but rather "better not to fight" connected to a slightly altered protasis along the lines "if I am destined to be immortal, if not killed by Heracles, it is better for me not to fight and secure immortality". This suggestion presupposes a scenario in which someone told Geryon that he may be able to achieve immortality if he is to endure the shame of letting Heracles get away with his cattle. However, Geryon chooses to fight risking his own life, risking

---

88 Barrett's supplement θροέων is preferable to his own φράζων, to Page's προφέρων and to a sense of predication as προλέγων would convey (cf. Barrett 2007a (1968): 30; Davies and Finglass 2014: 270–271), since the sense here seems to be referring to an allusion, a reference made by Menoetes, rather than a prediction, an information, or a certain consequence of Geryon's intervention. For the adjective for θα[νάτον, Barrett suggested κρυόεν]τα, but Lazerri's cτονόεν]τα would also suit the context.

89 Page 1973: 149–150.

90 Davies and Finglass 2014: 273. Lazzeri follows the suggestion of Page but does not provide supplements. Rozokoki 2008: 68 doubts the general sense of Geryon's ignorance of his own condition and suggests a similar solution to that of Barrett presupposing a contingent immortality, but her supplement presents some problems, since if Geryon knew he was not immortal, he would not have expressed that possibility in the indicative, but rather, as happens in the episode of Sarpedon in the *Iliad*, in the optative.

91 Barrett 2007b (1978): 26–28.

any chance of attaining immortality. As pointed out by Barrett, this outcome does not eliminate Geryon's nobility or heroism.[92] On the contrary, it stresses it, since the character chooses to gamble his life. Davies and Finglass add another aspect to this scenario, questioning the extent to which Geryon was certain to be granted immortality should he avoid the battle.[93] If he doubted the claim, a further reason for engaging in the fight is put forward.

In fact, while Callirhoe's immortality seems to be unanimously agreed on, Chrysaor's is a matter of discussion. In the *Theogony* (979–983), the union of Callirhoe and Chrysaor appear in the context the relationships of goddesses and mortal men. If Stesichorus was following this tradition, Geryon was right in doubting his immortality. As a matter of fact, Chrysaor's condition is itself problematic, since he was born to Poseidon from the severed head of Medusa, the only mortal Gorgon. However, his brother Pegasus is reckoned as immortal by Hesiod (*Th.* 284–286). The reference to the island Sarpedonia in fr. 6 F. may have dealt with the genealogy of Chrysaor in detail or even his birth,[94] since Hesiod places the Gorgons in an island in the Ocean, near the garden of Hesperides (*Th.* 274–275). Such an episode as that of Eurytion may have appeared in the context of Geryon's ancestry, so emphasised in his speech in fr. 15 F.[95] Geryon thus replies to the herdsmen by weighing all the possible situations, as we as have seen, but he reaches the wise conclusion that, in the end, the outcome rests in the hands of the gods, who, Geryon hopes, will not allow the disgrace of dying and losing his cattle to fall upon him.

The final lines of the fragment resemble the sense of the Theban Queen's speech fr. 97.211–217 F. In the *Thebais*, the Queen expresses the wish that the gods may grant her death before she witnesses the dreadful events predicted by Teiresias. She too pleads with the gods to be benevolent to her and spare her the view of her sons killed or the city destroyed. But in the *Geryoneis* the context is more surprising; the wish that the gods may be on Geryon's side preventing him from dying in battle is particularly "striking in a context in which the speaker's

---

[92] Barrett 2007b (1978): 27. Curtis 2011: 119 says that the fragment does not preserve any reference to Geryon's noble heart, despite accepting the general sense of line 20 as Geryon's resolution to do what is noble.
[93] Davies and Finglass 2014: 273.
[94] Antonelli 1996: 60.
[95] Thus Robertson 1969: 216. The reference to Sarpedonia, may instead refer to a moment of Heracles' journey to or from Erytheia, but a reference to Chrysaor's birth and ancestry should not be excluded, particularly in a context where his condition of mortality or immortality is so germane.

status relative to mortals and immortals is probably at issue".⁹⁶ The passage informs us that Geryon decided to engage in fighting Heracles, whatever the circumstances and the possible consequences of this enterprise. Here Geryon wishes that the gods may prevent dishonour from falling on his lineage. It is with the wish that the gods may be on his side that Geryon decides to face Heracles, little knowing that the opposite is destined to happen. Despite having no guarantees of his immortality, the son of Callirhoe decides to act according to his heroic and noble ethics, to show himself worthy of his ancestry. However, his mother, Callirhoe, is not so much of a positivist as her son, as she attempts to persuade him not to engage into battle with the son of Zeus.

Instead of a roaring creature, we are presented with a heroic figure. The decision Geryon makes is based not upon passion, or pure unjustified violence, but on a matter of honour, for which Geryon is willing to risk is life. A Homeric reader recognises immediately the ethical principles of the epic heroes behind these words, in particular those in the episode of Sarpedon in the *Iliad* (12.322–328). However, in this Iliadic episode the protasis, in the case, the possibility of immortality is in the optative, thus indicating the impossibility of such outcome.⁹⁷ Curtis and Kelly have drawn attention to the risks of assuming the fragment as a specific interaction with Homer. Curtis stresses that most of the parallel elements between the two episodes result from supplements, which, in turn, may have been attempted to prove the interaction.⁹⁸ An example of this issue is provided by Kelly who argues that the best case for interaction is that of lines 8–9 (αἰ μὲν γὰ[ρ ⏑⏑ ἀθάνατος ⏓ μαι καὶ ἀγή[ραος) which results from restoration, and is, furthermore, a formulaic expression. However, as Kelly himself acknowledges, the similarity of the dilemma in both situations is remarkable, since the two characters ponder the best course of action.⁹⁹ The conditional in Sarpedon's speech is but a mere impossible solution, that will never become a reality, since Sarpedon is aware of his condition.

Other conditional clauses in the context of decision-making like those at lines 8–24, the first in αἰ μέν (line 8) and the second in αἰ δ' (line 16), can be found in Homer. Among them, Achilles' speech in Book 9 (lines 410–416) relates to Geryon's. Glory, honour, fate, and decision: these are present in Achilles' words in the same way that they are in Geryon's. Achilles can choose between

---

96 Spelman *ap.* Davies and Finglass 2014: 277.
97 Thus e.g. Davies and Finglass 2014: 272 for a parallel to the contingent immortality/mortality Davies and Finglass call attention to Pindar *N.* 10.83–88.
98 Curtis 2011: 118.
99 Kelly 2015: 42; n. 94 for examples where the formula appears in an epic context.

the glory, which will kill him, and the anonymity, which will allow him to survive Troy and return home to live a peaceful live until old age. In the same way, Geryon must choose between a heroic death and a life condemned to reach shameful old age, enduring the shame of being deprived from his cattle with no fighting back. This episode of the *Geryoneis* that is of major importance in the characterization of Geryon alludes semantically to Iliadic episodes played by both a Trojan and a Greek.

1.1.3 Callirhoe's plea (frr. 16 and 17 F.)

At this point, then, we have a warrior that, moved by his heroic urge, is willing to fight for his property. Here we get to the ultimate step in the humanization of the monster: when the poet reminds his audience that the monster has a mother. Again, the intervention of the Theban Queen comes to mind, but while in the *Thebais* the Queen elaborates a plan to avoid the terrible fate announced to his sons, in the *Geryoneis*, Callirhoe uses a highly emotional mean to persuade her son. Two fragments are understood to be Callirhoe's speeches: frr. 16 and 17 F. Fr. 16 F. presents us with a first plea for Geryon to avoid battle:

```
πεφ[⏑—⏓—                                          str.
ο.α.[..πε]φυλαγμε[ν⏑—⏓—
πεν ἰ[δοῖc]ά τε νιcόμ[ενον ⏑⏑—

"νίκα[⏑] κράτοc.[⏑⏑——                              ant.
cτυγε[ρ—⏓—⏓—⏓—         5
    χματε..γ λευκ[—⏑⏑——
π]είθεο τέκνον[—⏓—⏓—
    cα γ.[⏑——
κατα[—⏓—⏓—⏓ αἰ-
    γιοχρ[⏑⏑—           10
μεγα[—⏓—⏓—⏑⏑—
θήcε[ι ⏑⏑—⏓—⏑⏑—

οὐκε[⏑⏑—⏓—⏓—                                      ep.
    Θανατ[—⏓—⏓———
ἀλλ' ὑπ[⏑—⏓—⏓—⏓       15
    .αντ[⏓—⏓—⏓—⏓
αcαπ.[⏑—⏓—⏓—⏓—
χερὶ δ[— —
```

2 Lobel || **3** Barrett super νιc scr. ει et Σ οὔ(τωc) ἦν επι[|| **4** νίκα[c τι Barrett || **5** Barrett || **7** π]είθεο West, π]ειθου Π² Barrett || **9** Lobel || **12** Lobel

...
...caution...
...seeing him on his way...

"...victory...might...
    ...   5
Obey, my son
    ...
... ae-
gis-bearer...   10
    ...
    ...will place...

    ....no...
death...
But...   15
    ...
    ...
    ...

Castellaneta argues that this speech was uttered by Chrysaor, since the speech ascribed with certainty to Callirhoe (fr. 17 F.) occurred at least two columns later. The scholar suggests that Chrysaor would have urged his son to avoid battle and to hide in a safe place.[100] However, the presence of Chrysaor is doubtful, since he is absent from the episode in both literary and artistic accounts, in contrast to Callirhoe, whose presence is common. Moreover, we can perceive in this episode the same pattern as in the speech of the Theban Queen, as she pleads with her sons to obey her plan.[101] Callirhoe thus urges her son to obey her, presumably to return to safety and avoid battle. The presence of a mother pleading to her son not to rush into battle encourages the audience to sympathise further with Geryon. But it is with fr. 17 F. that the audience is led to appreciate Geryon's situation against the backdrop of the Homeric epic, to appreciate him as a hero whose home is invaded by a foreign force that threatens to destroy him:

---

100 Castellaneta 2005: 30–34, provides the following supplement for lines 2–3 –] πέ νι[ν ὦκ]ά τε νιcόμ[ενοc ⏑⏑–. On the problems of the sense for νίcομαι, see Lazzeri 2008: 130–131, n. 304. Barrett, on the other hand, supplements line 3 with the participle ἰ[δοῖ]cα, generally accepted by scholars who believe that the speaker in this fragment is Callirhoe not Chrysaor.
101 Cf. see below 4.2.4 and E. *Ph.* 1568 where Jocasta displays a similar attitude to the Theban Queen, but who is said to have made a reference to her maternal love by exposing her breasts.

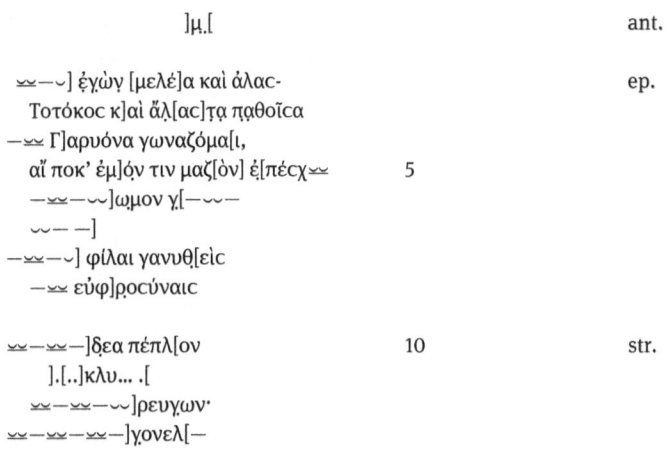

2 [μελέ]α Barrett || **3** -τοτόκος κ] Barrett | ἄλ[ας]τα Lobel || **4** Γ]αρυόνα γωναζόμα[ι Lobel || **5** αἴ ποκ' ἐμ] Barrett | μαζ[ὸν] Lobel | ἐ]πέςχεθον Page, ἀ]νέςχεθον Ucciardello || **8** γανυθ[εὶς Lobel || **9** εὐφ] Barrett || **10** πέπλ[ον Page

'...I, unhappy woman, miserable
  In the child I bore, miserable in my sufferings
  ... I beseech you, Geryon
If ever I offered you my breast   5
         ...
  At your dear...gladdened
  By [the meal]'

  ... robe   10

In this fragment two aspects of supplication ought to be considered: a lamentation and a supplication. Lines 2–3 express Callirhoe's grief. The supplement proposed by Barrett, ἀλαστοτόκος, results in a *hapax*, which imprints a deeper sense of disgrace experienced by the mother and foretell the future doom.[102] With these words of misery Callirhoe introduces her plea. Barrett's *hapax* is reminiscent of Thetis' lament to the Nereids where she refers to herself as δυσαριστοτόκεια, the "unhappy mother of a noble son" (*Il.* 18.54), reinforcing, at the moment of Achilles' imminent death, a feeling that she had already expressed in *Il.* 1.414. Callirhoe and Thetis share the same condition as nymphs, married to mortals, from which union is born a noble son fated to die young, heroically though it may be.

---

[102] Thus Xanthou 2015: 39.

We have seen how some parts of Geryon's dilemma may resemble Achilles' decision to stay at Troy and its implications. Hence it seems that Stesichorus had in mind Thetis and Achilles when composing his *Geryoneis*. After all, Thetis is the most interventive mother of the Homeric poems. Callirhoe, however, is not simply a variation of Thetis. Among the intricacy of references and allusions, Stesichorus finds yet another figure on which to model further aspects of his maternal figure.

In line 5, Callirhoe urges Geryon to consider his decision and to avoid battle by mentioning the tender image of her breast-feeding him. Scenes of breast exposure occur in highly tense moments and as a last resource for persuading or dissuading the interlocutor. They are common in tragedy,[103] but rare in lyric[104] and in epic. However, it is in epic that we find the most similar episode, in terms of context, to Callirhoe's situation: Hecuba's plea with Hector.[105] After failing to persuade her son to avoid battle with her rhetoric, Hecuba attempts a more emotional approach by exposing her breast. Likewise, and judging from the missing lines between fr. 16 and 17 F., Callirhoe's exposure occurs only after an extensive speech or dialogue where she tried to dissuade Geryon from fighting Heracles. The parallels with Hecuba's plea to Hector at *Il.* 22.82–83 are evident:

Ἕκτορ τέκνον ἐμὸν τάδε τ' αἴδεο καί μ' ἐλέηcον
αὐτήν, εἴ ποτέ τοι λαθικηδέα μαζὸν ἐπέcχον·

Hector, my child, respect these things and pity me
If I ever held you the breast that eases care;

Kelly argues that verbal interactions are not sufficient to establish a specific Homeric allusion.[106] Also, there may have been other instances before Stesicho-

---

103 E.g. A. *Cho.* 896–898; E. *El.* 1206–1207, *Or.* 527, 841, *Ph.* 1568, *Andr.* 629; also found in comedy Ar. *Lys.* 155–156 to inspire pity. For a survey of the theme, see Castellaneta 2013: especially 49–59 on Stesichorus' fragment; for maternal authority in Aeschylus, see Mc Clure 2006. The exposure of a breast occurs in several episodes, always to inspire pity or compassion. In the plays on the House of Atreus, Clytaemnestra mentions lactation to persuade Orestes to spare her life; in Euripides' *Andromache* the motif appears in a similar context, as a reminiscence of Helen's exposure of her breasts to avoid the Achaean host to kill her (627–631), which Hermione will repeat at 832. See further Chapter 2.1.6.
104 The use of the episode in the *Geryoneis*, at a highly dramatic moment and in an unexpected context may be a further aspect attesting Stesichorus' place as a link between the epic and tragedy, as pointed out by Arrighetti 1980: 135; Bremer 1980: 365–371; Curtis 2011: 117.
105 A similar use of the reference to the maternal breast in the context of an attempt to dissuade the children to engage in battle appears in E. *Ph.* 1568.
106 Kelly 2015: 38–39.

rus where the exposure of the breast functioned as a persuasion technique and from which he could have been inspired. For example, Helen in the epic *Iliou Persis* is said to have shown her breasts to dissuade the Achaean host to kill her (fr. 38 *GEF*).[107] However, in that episode the focus is not on maternal love and care, but rather on eroticism. To establish a parallel between Helen's scene and Callirhoe's would have been odd, to say the least. Conversely, the scene in the *Iliad* is remarkably appropriate. The language presents definite similarities, but it is the parallelism of the broader context, the coincidence of the moment when these episodes occur within the narrative, that strengthens the case for Homeric allusion. Moreover, there are other allusions to episodes of the *Iliad* in the poem; in these, Geryon assumes the place occupied in the *Iliad* by Trojan warriors or their allies. Hence the probability that Stesichorus had the scene of Hecuba in mind gains further weight. After all, the situation of Geryon is not very different from that of Hector.

Elsewhere in Stesichorus, we find another instance where a mother intervenes in the hopes to avoid their children's death. In the *Thebais* (fr. 97.201), the Queen's speech, which also displays vocabulary of suffering and sorrow (ἄλγεccι μὴ χαλεπὰc ποιεῖ μερίμναc) imprinting in it a distinct tone of maternal feeling, sets the mood for the subsequent utterance, where a pledge for obedience to avoid conflict takes place. Callirhoe also tries to make her son avoid conflict. However, although both interventions have the same purpose in the narrative, Callirhoe's plea is different from that of the Theban Queen. While the Queen pleads with Eteocles and Polynices for obedience in following her rational and practical plan, Callirhoe attempts to dissuade her son to engage in battle with Heracles and does so by a most moving means, alluding to Geryon's infancy. Stesichorus leads his audience to forget the monstrous condition of Geryon by focusing on the image of a tender and happy childhood that only maternal love can provide.[108] The effect on the narrative is the same as that of its Homeric parallel: the intensification of the nobility of the hero's decision emphasising its destructive power. The same audience led to imagine a baby Eurytion in fr. 9 and 10 F. is now urged to picture a tender baby Geryon. Here, as in the previous episode, the allusion to Geryon's childhood emphasises not only the suffering of Callirhoe as a mother, but also, and ultimately, Heracles' cruelty.

---

107 See also E. *Andr.* 629.
108 Cf. Xanthou 2015: 40–44.

1.1.4 The gods' Assembly and a parallel with the Cycnus (frr. 18 and 166 F.)

We have seen how Stesichorus treated in detail Geryon's decision-making as to whether he should face Heracles to retain his cattle, possibly avenge his herdsman, and eventually expel the stranger. I concluded that the most probable scenario for his dilemma was that he decided to risk his life trying to do so. We also know that he prayed for the gods to grant him success (fr. 15. 25–26 F.). Fr. 18 F. provides information about how the gods reacted to this prayer:

—⏑⏑—⏑⏑ μ]ίμνε παραὶ Δία	ep.
παμ[βαcιλῆα ⏑—.	
⏑⏑— γλαυκ]ῶπιc Ἀθάνα	str.
⏑⏑—⏑⏑—]c ποτὶ ὃν κρατερό-	
φρονα πάτρω' ἱ]πποκέλευθον· 5	
"⏑⏑—⏑⏑—]c μεμναμένοc α[	
⏑⏑— —]	
⏑⏑—⏑⏑ Γαρυ]όναν θ[αν]άτου	

1 μ]ίμνε Lobel || 2 Page || 3 Lobel || 5 -φρονα Lobel, πάτρω' Page, ἱ]πποκέλευθον· Lobel || 8 Lobel

...remained by the side of Zeus,
Who reigns of all things

...grey-eyed Athena...
... to her strong
-minded uncle, the driver of horses
"...remember...
...
...Geryon's death...

Athena's interlocutor is probably Poseidon,[109] although the epithets by which he is introduced are never applied to him elsewhere. However, while κρατερόφρων is associated with several figures,[110] Poseidon's association with horses is com-

---

[109] Thus Lobel 1967: 4; Page 1973: 150; Maingon 1979: 288–289; Barrett 2007a (1968): 17; Lazzeri 2008: 186; Curtis 2011: 131–134; Davies and Finglass 2014: 281–282.
[110] In the *Iliad*, it is applied to Heracles (14.324), and to wild beasts in the context of a simile (10.184); in the *Odyssey*, it refers to Odysseus (4.333) and to the Dioscuri (11.299). In lyric, it appears in Ibycus to characterise Athena (fr. 298.3 *PMGF*) as well as in Attic inscriptions from c. 510–480 (*CEG* I 206.2, 243.2, 295).

mon.¹¹¹ Moreover, Poseidon is Geryon's grandfather, and hence presumably interested in protecting his grandson.

In our fragment, Athena reminds Poseidon of something concerning Geryon. The relevant part is lost, but the supplements provided by Barrett give an overall satisfactory sense. Certainly, Athena is not urging Poseidon to save Geryon. Such words coming from Athena, the traditional and relentless protector of Heracles, would sound odd. Page's suggestion that Athena encouraged Poseidon to defend Geryon while she would support Heracles is not fully convincing either. Barrett's solution is preferable: ἄγ' ὑποσχέσιο]ς μεμναμένος ἄ[νπερ ὑπέστας | μὴ βούλεο Γαρυ]όναν θ[αν]άτου [ῥύσθαι στυγεροῦ, "Come, remember the promise you made, and do not wish to rescue Geryon from hateful death". Athena appears in several scenes demanding resolutions by the gods with regards to the mortals' affairs.

In the *Odyssey* (1.45–78), Athena complains about Poseidon's wrath against Odysseus which is preventing him from returning home. The wrath of the god was caused by Odysseus' killing of Polyphemus, Poseidon's son. But even Poseidon must accept the fate established for Odysseus and let go of his anger, as Zeus clearly states. A further Homeric parallel for the episode is found in book 22 of the *Iliad*. Barrett has compared the scene of fr. 18 F. to the Divine Assembly of *Iliad* 22.166–187, where Zeus pities Hector, who never failed to offer him sacrifices, and who is now in the verge of being killed by Achilles. Athena interprets Zeus' words as an attempt to intervene and change Fate, which she criticizes. Zeus replies to his daughter, saying that she is not to be worried, for he will not intervene; things will happen as fated. Athena leaves the Olympus to join Achilles in the battlefield.

In Stesichorus, Athena often intervenes on behalf of her protegés, either on the battlefield or in other circumstances. The *Sack of Troy* begins with her intervention on behalf of Epeius, whom she pitied for his menial service (fr. 100 F.). Athena appears again as Heracles' helper in the *Cycnus*, where we might have had a similar dispute or tension between the gods concerning their favourites. Stesichorus' version presents an important novelty: Heracles' flight. According

---

111 The epithet is applied to Patroclus (*Il.* 16.126, 584, 839), but Poseidon's connection to these animals is traditional. In Stesichorus the god appears as the tamer of horses in fr. 272 F. and, possibly, according to some, in fr. 187 F. (thus Haslam 1990: 32, although Schade 2003: 64 argues that the epithet refers to Artemis). For other instances of Poseidon as the master of horses see *h. Hom.* 22.5; Pi. *P.* 4.45, *I.* 1.54 and in Paus. 7.21.7. The same author mentions the custom of sacrificing horses to the god (8.7.2–3). See further Macedo 2016: 1–8.

to the fragments, Stesichorus' *Cycnus* presented the following story:[112] Cycnus lives in Thessaly, where he is a threat to travellers passing by, since he uses their skulls to build a temple to Apollo (fr. 166a F.). Heracles passes by Cycnus' home and fights with him. Cycnus' father, Ares, fights by his side, causing Heracles to flee (fr. 166 F.). He returns after a while, encouraged by Athena (fr. 167 F.), and defeats Cycnus, who this time was not in the company of his father.

The presence of Ares and Athena in the context of this story has a precedent in the *Aspis*. However, there Cycnus does not receive divine help, despite his attempts to summon Apollo to his side, who not only refuses to help him, but instead encourages Heracles to engage in the conflict (*Scut.* 57–74). Nevertheless, Cycnus counts on the presence of Ares (*Scut.* 59), who intervenes only after Cycnus' death at Heracles' hands (425–434, 450–461), despite Athena's efforts to keep the god away from the fight (443–450). Ares' intervention, however, proves unfruitful since Athena herself interferes on behalf of Heracles taking the force of the god's spear (455–457). Heracles responds to Ares attack by a strike that hits Ares on the thigh (458–462). The god falls wounded and is taken to Olympus by Phobos and Deimos (463–467), while Heracles takes the spoils and return victorious to Trachis (467–469).

In Stesichorus, Ares intervenes earlier, in what seems to have been the most distinct episode of our poet's account: the flight of Heracles. That Heracles flees the fight need not be understood as an effort to depict him as a coward.[113] It should perhaps be seen as an attempt to provide the narrative with further complexity and dramatic tension,[114] which, moreover, resembles in some ways the drama also latent in the *Geryoneis*. In the *Cycnus*, Ares intervenes on behalf of his son to avoid his defeat and eventual death at the hands of Heracles. In the *Geryoneis*, Athena ensures that Poseidon will follow whatever promise he made, and abstain from interfering in the battle to save his grandson. Stesichorus therefore was interested in playing with divine characters as parental figures who fight, or are ready to do so, on behalf of their offspring. In the *Cycnus*, Ares intervention is more effective, because it delays Cycnus' death, adding *pathos*. In the *Geryoneis*, Poseidon is prevented from intervening and forced to watch, impotently, his grandson dying at the hands of Heracles. Poseidon is thus an-

---

[112] The story of Cycnus was popular in archaic art, particularly in the sixth century; see Cambitoglou and Paspalas 1994; Zardini 2009. In literary evidence, a brief reference to the story appears in the epic *Thebaid* fr. 11 *GEF*, but the fullest surviving account is the Pseudo-Hesiodic *Aspis*. Pindar alludes to the myth in *O*. 10.13–19 as does Euripides in his *Heracles* (389–393).
[113] Thus Finglass 2015a: 86, with n. 12 for further examples.
[114] Thus Davies and Finglass 2014: 467.

other one of Geryon's legion of relatives that care for him and are incapable of intervening effectively to save him from death. The fact that Geryon is surrounded by loved ones who helplessly watch him heading to certain death encourages, once again, the audience's sympathy.

1.1.5 Heracles' tactis and the example of the Boarhunters (frr. 19 and 183 F.)

]ν.[		str.
⏑⏑–⏑⏑]ναντ[⏑⏑– –		
⏑⏑–⏑]αν δοιω. [⏑⏑–		
⏑⏑– –]		
⏑⏑–⏑⏑–]τα νόιω διελε[ν	5	
⏑⏑–⏑⏑–]ν·		
⏑⏑–⏑⏑–] πολὺ κέρδιον εἶν		
⏑⏑–⏑⏑]οντα λάθραι πολεμε[ῖν		
⏑⏑–⏑⏑–⏑] κραταιῶι·		ant.
⏑⏑– εὐρ]ὰξ κατεφράζετ[ό] οἱ	10	
⏑⏑–⏑⏑ πι]κρὸν ὄλεθρον·		
⏑⏑–⏑⏑– ἔ]χεν ἀcπίδα πρόc-		
θ' ⏑⏑– –		
⏑⏑–⏑⏑–]ετο· τοῦ δ' ἀπὸ κρα-		
τὸc (⏑) –⏑⏑–]	15	
⏑⏑–⏑⏑ ἱπ]πόκομοc τρυφάλει'·		
⏑⏑–⏑⏑–⏑] ἐπὶ ζαπέδωι·		
–]ν μεγ [⏑⏑–]. ρονεc ὠκυπετα[		ep.
⏑⏑–⏑⏑–⏑].ν ἐχοίcαι		
–⏑⏑–] ἐπ[ ]άξαν ἐπ[ὶ] χθόνα·	20	
–⏑⏑–]απε.η κεφαλὰ χαρ[⏑		
–⏑⏑–⏑⏑]ωcωcα.[.] ε...[		

desunt versus viii

⏑⏑–⏑⏑–⏑⏑]ων cτυγε[ρ]οῦ	31	str.
Θανάτοι]ο τέ[λοc		
κ]εφ[αλ]ᾶι πέρι [–⏑] ἔχων, πεφορυ-		
γ]μένοc αἵματ[ι –⏑⏑–]ι̣ τε χολ]ᾶι,		
ὀλεcάνοροc αἰολοδε[ίρ]ου	35	ant.
ὀδύναιcιν Ὕδραc· cιγᾶι δ' ὅ γ' ἐπι-		
κλοπάδαν ἐνέρειcε μετώπωι·		
διὰ δ' ἔcχιcε cάρκα [καὶ] ὀ[cτ]έα δαί-		
μονοc αἴcαι·		
διὰ δ' ἀντικρὺ cχέθεν οἰ[c]τὸc ἐπ' ἀ-	40	

       κροτάταν κορυφάν,
       ἐμίαινε δ' ἄρ' αἵματι πορφ[υρέωι
       θώρακά τε καὶ βροτόεντ[α μέλεα .

ἀπέκλινε δ' ἄρ' αὐχένα Γαρ[ύονας   ep.
    ἐπικάρσιον, ὡς ὅκα μ[ά]κω[ν   45
    ἅτε καταισχύνοις' ἁπαλὸν [δέμας
    αἶψ' ἀπὸ φύλλα βαλοίσᾳ γ[⏑—⏓

5-6 [ν Lobel || **8** Lobel || **10** εὐρ]ὰξ Barrett | κατεφράζετ[ό Lobel || **11** Lobel || **12-13** Page || **15** Lobel || **16** Lobel || **20** Lobel || **31** Lobel || **32** θανάτοι]ο Lobel | τέ[λος Barrett Σ cτυγεροιο το..[.]·[| cτυγεροῦ θανὰτ[, unde v.l. θανάτου cτυγεροῖο eruit Barrett || **33** Lobel || **34** Lobel || **35** Lobel || **38** Page || **40** Lobel || **42-44** Page || **45** Lobel || **46** Page

       ...
       ...
       ...two...
       ...in his mind he [decided   5
       ...
       ...it was much better...
       ...to fight by stealth...

       ...mighty...
       ...to one side he devised for him... 10
       ...bitter destruction...
       ...he held his shield in front of...
       ...
       ...from his head...
       ...   15
       ...helmet with its horse-hair plume...
       ...on the ground.

       ...swift-flying...
       ...hold...
       ...to the ground.   20
       ...head...
       ...ear...

       ...the e[nd of...   31
       ...hateful [death
       ...on his head...having... stained
       with blood and bile,

       With the agonies of the dapple-necked 35
       Hydra, destroyer of men. In silence, it stealthy
       Thrust into his forehead.
       It cut through the flesh and bones

according to the determination of a god.
And right through the crown of his head   40
the arrow went
and stained with gushing blood
his breastplate and gory limbs.

Geryon leaned his neck
to one side, like a poppy   45
which dishonouring its tender form,
at once, sheds its petals...

The first lines of the fragment appear to describe the approaching of Geryon from the perspective of Heracles. Lines 1–11 seem to deal with Heracles planning the attack. Spelman[115] supplements line 2 with ἐ]ναντ[ίον or ἐ]ναντ[ίβιον, which would give the sense of a face to face battle, an option that Heracles quickly sets aside (line 5) in favour of a more advantageous approach (line 7), an attack by stealth (line 8) by means of arrow and bow.[116] Heracles thus ponders the best options for making a successful approach to the opponent, thus anticipating a tough fight.

Stesichorus' interest in tactics is evident in other poems. We have seen how he presented a different version to the fight against Cycnus, from which Heracles flees only to return later with his valour revived by Athena, catching Cycnus by surprise and without Ares' protection. Another episode of the killing of a monster was told in Stesichorus' *Europeia* (fr. 96 F.). The only preserved part of the poem preserves the sowing of the dragon's teeth, implying that Cadmus faced the serpent. The context of the scholium to Euripides *Phoenician Women* tells that Athena sowed the teeth. The version of the myth is not unanimous in this aspect, although the most common account has Cadmus sowing the teeth.[117] Be that as it may, the relevant element here is that, in the *Europeia*, Cadmus defeats the dragon, presumably with the help of Athena. It would have been interesting to see how our poet dealt with the approach to the dragon in this account, which also involves a far-off journey by Cadmus.

In the *Boarhunters*, on the other hand, we have an example of a completely different scene, which nevertheless seems to have dealt in detail with the issue of how to approach and prepare for a battle in which the opponent is signifi-

---

115 *Ap.* Davies and Finglass 2014: 282.
116 Cf. Heracles using the same strategy against Diomedes in Pi. fr. 169a. 18–20 S-M.
117 Cadmus sowing the teeth, sometimes with the help of Athena: Hellanic. fr. 51 *EGM*; E. *Ph.* 666–669; Apollod. *Bibl.* 3.4.1; Hyg. *Fab.* 178.5. One source has Ares sowing the teeth: E. *HF.* 252–253, and another featuring both Ares and Athena (Pherecyd. fr. 22a *EGM*).

cantly stronger.[118] In fr. 183 F. we are presented with what seems to be the preparations to the hunt, with the arrival of hosts from different locations within Greece, many of which having in this fragment their earliest reference.[119] In lines 10–11 and 17–18, the poet "imagines the different contingents already in the field, ready to face the boar".[120] The contingents are placed in strategic places, apparently in two sides, to make the hunting more effective. Some hosts have defined roles. So, the Locrians, in line 11 are sitting as spearmen; they are joined by the Achaeans (lines 12–13) and the Boeotians (lines 14–16), and by the Aetolians and the Dryopes, on the other side, presumably, in a different contingent. This suggests careful planning of the attack, on the one hand, and, on the other, that the hunters would have been noticeable.

Heracles quietly observes Geryon approaching,[121] as he defines the wiser method to attack his opponent successfully. They are alone and about to engage in a duel, though Heracles may have been helped by Athena. The situation is unexpected since Heracles has quickly to decide which tactics he should follow

---

118 The poem tells the story of the Calydon Boar hunt, a popular theme in early literature and art. The boar hunting is, furthermore, a recurrent *topos* in Indo-European, Celtic folktale (cf. Davies 2001; West 2007: 430). The myth of the Calydon boar and the fate of Meleager appears for the first time in the *Iliad* 9.529–599; [Hes.] fr. 25.2-13, *Minyas* fr. 5 *GEF*; Ibyc. 290 *PMGF*; Pi. fr. 249a, 48 S-M; Phryn. Trag. *Pleuroniae TrGF* 3 F 6; B. 5.93–154; A. *Cho.* 602–612, *Atalanta*; S. *Meleager*; E. *Meleager* test. iiic, iiid, fr. 525 *TrGF*; Apollod. *Bibl.* 1.8.2.; two later mythographical papyri dated to the second century AD (P. Oxy. 4097 fr. 2 and P.Duk. inv. 752 = P.Robinson inv. 10). In Roman literature, we have Hyg. *Fab.* 173; Ov. *Met.* 8.298–328, 360. In art, the myth appears copiously in the sixth century, the 'François Vase' c. 570 (Woodford and Krauskopf 1992: § 7), and the Attic dinos c. 570–60 (§ 9) in fourteen Attic black-figure vases, in four non-Attic, and in the throne of Apollo in Amyclae, (cf. Woodford and Krauskopf 1992: §§ 6–23, 28); in the fourth century, there are a few depictions of Meleager and Atalanta (cf. Woodford and Krauskopf 1992: § 37–41). Pausanias 8.45.6–7 describes the front pediment of Scopas' temple of Athena at Tegea, where the myth was depicted.

119 E.g. Boeotia (lines 14–16) and the Dryopes (lines 17–18). See Finglass 2012 on the several cities represented and its implications. Davies and Finglass 2014: 525 note that the catalogue of the hunters is organized as to mentioning towards the end figures who will meet their fate in the hunt. Note, however, that the identity of the hunters is subject of variation in the several accounts of the myth referred above. See further Davies and Finglass 2014: 518–519.

120 Schade 2003: 30–34; Davies and Finglass 2014: 529. Lobel 1956: 13 argued that the scene presents two contending parties, but such a scene would have only been possible after the hunt, in a fight for the carcass of the boar which would hardly fit right after the catalogue of the hunters, expected to occur before the hunt and not afterwards. It seems that the scene here represents not two opposed parties but two sides of a host expecting the boar, which is presumably lured into some net (cf. X. *Cyn.* 10.19; Ov. *Met.* 8.331, for a parallel, see *Il.* 18.520–522).

121 In fr. 184 F. the description of the boar presumably searching for food may have been part of a scene on the approach of the hunters, who observe the behaviour of the beast.

to defeat Geryon. He opts for a furtive attack (line 8), which gives him the advantage of surprise and the safety of distance. The description of the attack shows a cunning Heracles whose strategy diminishes Geryon's heroic decision to die in battle, as he gets caught in an ambush with no opportunity to respond or to demonstrate his warrior excellency.

The recoverable words of lines 13–20 focus on the description of Geryon: ἀσπίδα, "shield" (line 12), κρατός "head" (lines 14–15), and τρυφάλει' "helmet" (line 16). All are singular. This may seem unexpected since in Stesichorus' poem Geryon's body was three-headed, six-handed, six-footed and winged (fr. 5 F.); hence our poet is not describing Geryon as a whole, but focusing on Heracles' first target, the one head from which the helmet falls. Barrett and Page agree that the helmet falls thanks to a stone or some other missile object thrown from afar by Heracles.[122]

Lines 18–20 seem to have explained how the helmet falls from Geryon's head. The reference to some swift-flying feminine entities preserved in the fragment led scholars to picture some sort of intervention by the goddesses of fate. The sense of the supplements presented to this passage pose four different scenarios. Either the Keres or the Moirai intervene in favour of Heracles and allow the helmet of Geryon to fall;[123] Keres/Moirai come to the battlefield and await near Geryon for his death;[124] or the reference to the Keres is a mere objectivation of Geryon's doom, a representation of a *kerostasia*.[125]

---

122 Thus Page 1973: 151 (with *exempli gratias*) and Barrett 2007a (1968): 20.
123 Thus Lerza 1978: 86–87, although the supplement provided presents some problems of misprints (cf. against some of Lerza suggestions Irvine 1997: 45; Lazzeri 2008: 216). Davies and Finglass 2014: 284 present *exempli gratia* the following lines: τὰ[ν (Lerza 1978: 86) μὲν [ῥ' ὀλοό]φρονες (Ercoles 2011: 358) ὠκυπέτα[ι (Lobel 1967: 3) Κῆρες κατὰ πότμ]ον (Ercoles 2011: 358) ἐχοίcαι [καρπαλίμωc] ἐπ[λ]άξαν ἐπ[ὶ] χθόνα, "Then the baleful, swift-flying Keres, who control the future, swiftly knocked it to the ground", which maintains the general sense of Lerza's interpretation but offers a less problematic solution.
124 This is the proposal of Lazzeri 1995: 43: τὸ]ν μὲν [δολιό]φρονες ὠκυπέτα[ι τόκα Μοῖραι (vel Κῆρες) πότμ]ον ἐχοίcαι [πίπτοντ' ἀμφ]επ[ι]άξαν ἐπ[ὶ] χθόνα "Now the insidious swift-flying Moirai, who hold the fate, went around the falling Geryon". Along the same lines, Ercoles 2011: 358: βὰ]ν μὲν [ῥ' ὀλοό]φρονες ὠκυπέτα[ι (Lobel 1967: 3) Κῆρες κατὰ πότμ]ον ἐχοίcαι [πὰρ δέ οἱ αἶψ'] ἐπ[τ]άξαν ἐπ[ὶ] χθόνα, "moved by the baleful swift-flying Keres, holding destiny of death, and near him suddenly cowered on the earth".
125 Irvine 1997: 41 n. 11, 45: τοῖ]ν μὲν [δαμαcί]φρονες ὠκυπέτα[ι ῥέπον αἶψα τάλαντ]ον ἐχοίcαι [Γαρυόνα καὶ] ἐπ[λ]άξαν ἐπ[ὶ] χθόνα, "and, in the case of the twain, straightaway did the swift-flying conquerors of the spirit who had control of the balance pertaining Geryon incline downwards, dashing it to the earth".

Let us begin by the last scenario. The idea of a *kerostasia* makes the scene rather enigmatic with no significant narrative gain. Moreover, it poses problems of authority concerning the balance itself, since usually, even in the examples cited by Irvine, Zeus controls the balance, not the Keres.[126]

More likely, the hypotheses of Lazzeri and Ercoles convey the notion that Geryon, from whom Poseidon is led to renounce protection, is abandoned at the hands of destiny which awaits its moment of completion by the side of the one they are to take. Such a scene would require the direct intervention of the Keres in battlefield. Although this is not very common, Lazzeri presents an important passage where the Keres intervene directly in the battlefield and are pictured not only as dragging corpses but also holding a wounded, but alive, warrior (*Il.* 18.535–540). Lazzeri argues that this may be a precedent for the intervention of the deities in the battle that are not necessarily the moment of the warrior's death.[127] However, the intervention of the Keres in this Iliadic scene shows their selection of those who die and those who live. Hence, the reference to the wounded warrior that the Keres hold and to the unharmed warrior: it is their fate to survive that battle. If this interpretation is correct, the scene in the *Iliad* is not exactly the same as the episode in this fragment of the *Geryoneis*. Ercoles, on the other hand, compares the scene of our fragment to the final line of Sarpedon's speech in *Il.* 12.326 – a speech that Stesichorus seems to have had in mind when composing the scene in fr. 15 F. – where the fates (κῆρες) are mentioned. However, they are not said to crouch by the warrior's side.

Finally, the first scenario presented above suggests that the Keres intervene to direct, or simply allow the projectile thrown by Heracles to travel to the helmet of Geryon, making it fall. Lerza's e.g. presents some undeniable problems,[128] but the suggestion by Davies and Finglass offers a plausible solution for the reference to Keres: they make Heracles' attempt successful. Given that they control the future, it is in their hands to conduct the events for the future to happen according to what is settled. This does not necessarily mean that they throw the object, nor even that they interfere in its trajectory, although it remains plausible that they did, since divine intervention in these cases is not rare. Our poet may have been reminded of the intervention of Athena to dimin-

---

126 Thus Ercoles 2011: 354–356. Cf. the role of Zeus in *Il.* 16.656–658 and the other examples presented by Irvine (*Il.* 8.66–74, 19.221–224, 22.208–213). Moreover, in the divine assembly that precedes the fight where Gorgythion is killed, a moment described by means of the poppy simile, it is Zeus who holds the balance (*Il.* 8.69). On *Kerostasia* and the dictates of Fate in the *Iliad*, see Morrison 1997.
127 Lazzeri 1995: 95.
128 Cf. Lazzeri 1995: 83–102; Ercoles 2011: 352 n. 9, 354.

ish the power of the spear Ares throws at Heracles in the battle against Cycnus.[129] In the *Iliad*, Apollo knocks Patroclus' helmet to the ground moments before the fatal injury.[130] Moreover, the fact that it is the Keres who intervene strengthens the sense of inexorable fate emphasised again in δαίμονοc αἴcαι ending the sentence, where the wound of the arrow is first described.[131] The lines do not justify in moral grounds the brutality of Heracles as some pretend;[132] it rather emphasises Geryon's vulnerability to it and adds further depth to his character, just as with any Homeric hero.[133]

With Geryon's helmet on the ground, Heracles has his opportunity to perform the first attack. The focus of the previous lines seems to have been in Geryon's helmet, in an almost zoomed-in perspective. In lines 33–34, the focus changes to another object: the arrow which Heracles shots, taking advantage of Geryon's exposed head.[134] According to this view, the κ]εφ[αλ]ᾶι of fr. 19.33 is not Geryon's, but that of the arrow which is stained with blood and gall from the Hydra. If this is correct, this is the earliest reference to the arrows poisoned with the Hydra's blood.[135] The diversion to refer to another labour of the hero is significant, because it acts as a reminder to the audience of Hydra's agonies (ὀδύναιcιν, line 36) inflicted by Heracles, thus anticipating Geryon's suffering. The focus on the arrow is maintained until line 43,[136] as the poet describes its trajectory and its effects in gory detail. Suspense is achieved by the way in which the poet drives our attention to the silence of the arrow movement; an undetectable threat (lines 36–37). The repetition of the διά sentences and its remarkable analytic precision and crudity, almost like a slow-motion sequence, a deceleration of time,[137] accentuates the gravity of the wound, further explored in the stains in Geryon's breastplate and limbs as it anticipates his death. The detailed and

---

129 [Hes.] *Scut.* 455–457. See Ercoles 2011: 355 on Lazzeri's supplement.
130 *Il.* 16.793–800. Thus Lerza 1978: 86–87; Davies and Finglass 2014: 284.
131 Barrett 2007a (1968): 19 remarks à propos of this line that the "success with the more chancy missile is what might more readily be ascribed to the working of the daimon". If this notion is applicable to the situation to line 39, it can equally be so to lines 18–20, if indeed the scene presented another object thrown at Geryon.
132 Segal 1985: 195; Cruz Andreotti 1991; Gentili 1976: 746; Curtis 2011: 143–144.
133 Noussia-Fantuzzi 2013: 242.
134 Thus Barrett 2007a (1968): 19.
135 The arrows reappear only in S. *Tr.* 572–577, 714–718 and E. *HF.* 1187–1188. See further Davies and Finglass 2014: 286–287.
136 Thus Page 1973: 152. Lobel 1967: 6 suggested that the subject is Heracles, but as pointed out by Davies and Finglass this would not only imply a sudden change of subject only to return to the previous subject in the next line, but it also results in an odd sense.
137 Cf. Noussia-Fantuzzi 2013: 251.

structurally repetitive description of the arrow penetrating Geryon's head and the excursus of the Hydra confers a heightened *pathos* to the scene. In the next lines the focus is back to Geryon's now wounded head. The simile with which our poet describes the scene detaches the audience from the reality and violence of it by evoking the delicate imagery of a poppy.

Much has been said about Stesichorus' remarkable simile and its parallels with the Iliadic episode of Gorgythion,[138] where the poppy bending itself on his own weight and the morning dew is applied to the moment of his death by an arrow. The other occurrence of the poppy appears in book 14.496–500. The context of this episode is also noteworthy, since the killer, Peneleus, rises the severed head of Ilioneus, which is compared to a poppy and shouts to the Trojans to go and tell the parents of the deceased to sing lamentations. Vegetation similes, particularly those containing flowers, evoke the inexorability of mortality; they illustrate the ephemerality of mortals and, by extension, the imminence of a hero's death.[139] The poppy simile in the *Iliad* is applied always to dying warriors, but the poppy in the similes is not necessarily dying, as happens in our fragment. The poppy of lines 44–47 deforms his beautiful shape as it casts away its leaves. This refers to the final moment of the flower, the loss of youth and beauty; the loss of life. In Stesichorus' simile, both Geryon's head and the poppy are depicted in their ultimate moments. Moreover, intertextuality *per se* is strikingly reduced, with the only shared word being μήκων, albeit a rare one, which appears again only in Aristophanes (*Av.* 160). But in terms of sense and occasion, the passages closely resemble each other. Apart from the poppy, the reference in both Iliadic episodes to deceased parents, namely their mothers, may further hint at the debt of our fragment to the Homeric episode. We have seen above how Stesichorus uses Homeric passages in contexts com-

---

[138] *Il.* 8.302–308. Barrett 2007a (1968): 20; Maingon 1980; Lazzeri 2008: 254–268; Franzen 2009: 70–75; Curtis 2011: 146–151; Davies and Finglass 2014: 288–289; Kelly 2015: 36–37, among others.

[139] Thus Kelly 2007b: 289–290 provides many examples which applied to several situations. The instances where the comparison of human ephemerality is compared to that of the flowers or leaves are *Il.* 6.146–148, 21.464–466. The similes of the warriors as trees appears in Anthemides' death (4.485–487), an episode which shares many aspects with the *Geryoneis*, e.g. the birth of the hero is reminded to the audience moments before his death, as happened with Eurytion; in Thetis lament to the Nereids and to Hephaestus in *Il.* 18.56, 437; and in the description of Euphorbus' death (17.9–109) where the warrior is compared to an olive tree, both situations evoking a premature death. For the metaphor for the multiplicity of warriors heading to the assembly or to the battlefield, see *Il.* 2.87–90, 2.468, 2.800. The case of *Il.* 21.257–263 and the simile of the gardener seems to fall into a distinct category.

pletely distinct from the original. By adapting the simile of the poppy, used in Homer in minor episodes involving marginal characters, in the most important and central scene of his *Geryoneis*, Stesichorus shows a refine knowledge of Homer, and a playful mind directed to surprise his audience. A three-headed monster is compared to one of the more fragile flowers. Ephemerality and vulnerability are combined in one perfect caption.

This scene corresponds, however, to the defeat of only one of Geryon's three heads. We expect that the following lines would describe how Heracles defeated the others, eventually killing Geryon. Fr. 20 F. refers to a second head stricken by the club, probably coming from the scene dealing with Heracles' second attack.[140] Geryon would have been weakened thank to the attack on the first head, which would allow Heracles to approach him more closely.

1.1.6 Heracles in Thessaly (fr. 22a F.)

Frr. 21 and 22 F. indicate that Stesichorus' *Geryoneis* did not end in Heracles' defeat of Geryon, but included his return home and took the opportunity to add another unamicable encounter. The episode refers to Heracles visit to the centaur Pholus and their consumption of some wine:

cκύφιον δὲ λαβὼν δέπαc ἔμμετρον ὡc
    τριλάγυνον
πί' ἐπιcχόμενοc, τό ῥά οἱ παρέθη-
    κε Φόλοc κεράcαc
	str./ant.

And taking his cup a vat of three flagons'
    measure
Which Pholus had mixed, and set before him,
    he put it to his lips and drank

The fullest archaic sources for the episode are provided by artistic evidence from the seventh and sixth centuries, suggesting a wide circulation. Most of the scenes depict Pholus holding a kantharos and Heracles pursuing the centaurs, although there are some Attic versions showing a peaceful resolution of the conflict.[141] Literary evidence is considerably poorer. The story may have featured

---

140 Curtis 2011: *ad loc.* suggests that the fragment may well refer to the fight against Orthos.
141 Drougou *et al.* 1997: §§ 365, 366, 368, 358. For the Attic depictions, see Drougou *et al.* 1997: §§ 349–350, 351–354, 355–357, 359, 360–363. Cf. Lucian 17.14 for an attestation of the popularity of the scene in art.

in the seventh century Pisander's epic (fr. 9 *GEF*) and in the fifth century account by Panyassis (fr. 9 *GEF*). It certainly featured in Epicharmus' play entitled *Heracles and Pholus* (fr. 66 *PCG*) and presumably in Aristophanes' *Dramata* or *Centaurs* (frr. 278–288 *PCG*). Theocritus mentions the episode in 7.149–150, but it is from Apollodorus' and Diodorus' accounts of this episode that we learn the general outline of the story which is associated within the context of Heracles' hunt for the Erymanthian boar:[142] Heracles was passing by Arcadia where he is entertained by Pholus, who, as a decent host, shares with the hero a special jar of wine, the gift of Dionysus. The wine attracts the other centaurs whom Heracles expels from the vicinity with his bow. The conflict results in the deaths of Chiron and Pholus, who are injured by poisoned arrows.

The only part of this story detectable in fr. 22 F. is Pholus serving the wine to Heracles in vast quantities. But this means that the story, usually associated with the Erymanthian boar is included by Stesichorus in Heracles' return from Erytheia, which, in turn, suggests that Heracles' journey back to Greece was made by foot, which would have allowed to poet to include further episodes with other characters along the way.

Fr. 21 F. states that Stesichorus mentioned the city of Pallantium, but the testimony does not specify which; if the one in Arcadia, which would have been easily accommodated in the context of Heracles' visit to Pholus, or the city of Italy, founded by Evander, which would have implied that at some point on his journey back to Greece, Heracles visited Italy. The *Suda* records information that associates Stesichorus with Pallantium, but this is generally taken to be a statement made about Evander and later taken as biographical.[143] A stop of Heracles in Italy would certainly be of interest to our poet, and Pallantium is indeed more directly connected to Evander than to Pholus. Heracles' stop in Italy, presumably in his return from Erytheia, would hint at the poet's interest to map the west in the major sagas of Greek mythology, and would demonstrate that Aeneas' escape to Italy or Sicily in the *Sack of Troy* was not a unique case for the inclusion of this region in the maps of the heroic journeys. Nevertheless, the inclusion of Heracles' encounter with Pholus in a poem primarily concerned with the quest for Geryon's cattle shows that the treatment given to Geryon went beyond his mere characterization as an uncivilized barbarian.

---

142 Apollod. *Bibl*. 2.5.4 and D. S. 4.12.
143 Ta10.3 Ercoles.

Curtis, following Andreotti,[144] argues that 'Herakles's triumph over Geryon symbolises the arrival of the new order and the dismissal of fear and unfamiliarity which the monster embodied', implying that the conflict between Heracles and Geryon is a dichotomy of civilization versus wildness.[145] However, his view seems too dependent on the assumption that the audience only appreciated Heracles' victory. The fragments of the *Geryoneis* show a tendency to highlight Heracles' malice. More importantly, the portrayal of Geryon tends to dissociate him from wild and chthonic characters, and instead to approximate him to heroic figures such as the Trojans. Moreover, Curtis' view excludes what may have been an important and perhaps even innovative addition to the quest: the visit to Pholus.

Similarly, Franzen implies that the poem is an analogy of the social situation at Himera.[146] The author argues that Geryon represents neither the Greeks nor the absolute other, but rather occupies a third space; here Geryon plays negotiator, linking the diverse cultures sharing territory in Sicily. This new ethnicity gives way to the creation of a new cultural discourse from which the *Geryoneis* emerges. Geryon represents the colonial interaction. Or in Burnett's words, the *Geryoneis* might provide the colonists with a reminder of their mainland/eastern heritage that make them part of the Greek world, by being part of the kinship of the Greeks.[147]

Van Dommelen, however, believes that a dualistic perspective in colonial situations reduces the colonial reality to a mere opposition between coloniser and colonised, which ignores social nuances among the various groups of the social and cultural milieu of the city emphasizing the dominant position of the coloniser.[148]

As Hall has noted,[149] in the archaic period, Greek perception of ethnicity was not oppositional, but aggregate. Instead of having a markedly dichotomy between Greek and Barbarian, we have a much more complex, mutually influen-

---

144 Andreotti 1991: 59 observes that "the clear humanization of the peninsular Geryon, which leads to heroic remaking in the Sicilian case, can be interpreted as enhancing the superiority of Heracles which is more comprehensive than aggressive against the barbarian", thereby illustrating a relation of contact and common acquaintance in terms of mythical conflict between Greek hero and his antagonist.
145 Curtis 2011: 22.
146 Franzen 2009. On the existence of cults of Heracles and Geryon in Himera, see Ercoles 2014.
147 Burnett 1988: 141; Lane Fox 2009: 180–181.
148 Van Dommelen 2005: 117.
149 Hall 1997: 47.

tial poetical images and perceptions. Stesichorus' Geryon is in perfect consonance with the parameters of Greek heroic excellence. Moreover, the inclusion of episodes in mainland Greece involving hybrid creatures such as the centaurs question the applicability of the notion of the "absolute other" to a figure like Geryon. What is more, the inclusion of the Pholus' episode shows that the action was not fixed in the west; it covered a substantial part of the Greek world. As such, the poem does not offer any reason to think of it as a Sicilian product targeted exclusively to the Sicilians, let alone Himerians.[150] Quite on the contrary, the *Geryoneis*, with its intensely dramatic scenes, Homeric references, geographical allusions, would have certainly be appreciated in every corner of the Greek world, as many, if not all, of Stesichorus' works.[151] Therefore, it is perhaps better to think of the *Geryoneis* and Geryon's characterisation as a product of a poet interested in exploring the literary potential of secondary, tendentially silenced, figures of Greek myth. This tendency is evident in the majority of his surviving poems. The extent to which this interest arises from his colonial background and from an urge to make a political statement regarding the colonial situation, however, is harder to determined. Be that as it may, the fact that his poetic interests may be biased by his colonial background does not imply that his poetry could only be appreciated by a colonial audience. Quite on the contrary, the circulation of his poetry in venues outside his hometown would only further the impact of his poetry and his message.

---

150 Burnett 1988: 147 suggested some occasions for the performance of the poem in Sicily; Curtis 2011: 37–40, with n. 150 for Geryon cults in Sicily (e.g. D.S. 5.4.2, although this cult took place in Syracuse). For the argument that the *Geryoneis* was designed to an Himerian audience see Franzen 2009: 59–61. Ercoles 2014: 73–74 calls attention to the fact that Athena was the patroness of Himera and explores the possibility of the *Geryoneis* to be included in a festival in honour of Athena or Heracles. Noussia-Fantuzzi 2013: 240–242 is sceptical regarding the applicability of these arguments to Stesichorus' *Geryoneis*.
151 Thus Finglass 2014a: 26; Carey 2015: 52.

2 Escape and Returns

In this chapter, I discuss the poems dealing more directly with the motifs of escape and return. The motif of return seems to have been recurrent in Stesichorus' poems, as may be expected in an oeuvre dealing with heroic narratives. However, here the motif gains depth because it is paralleled with the escape journeys, those taken by the more fortunate Trojans, namely Aeneas. To do so, I will discuss the *Sack of Troy*, which offers significant material for our purpose, not only providing Aeneas and Hecuba with alternative routes compared to those of earlier or contemporary accounts, but also by depicting the recovery of Helen in a different manner from that present in the vast majority of surviving material.

Having done so, I shall proceed to the commentary on the *Nostoi*, where I discuss the only piece of information certainly ascribed to the poem, the name of a certain Aristomache, showing that Stesichorus' *Nostoi* seems to have continued to give some emphasis to the Trojan royal family, even if to show their misfortune. I will also address fr. 170 F., which was tentatively ascribed to the poem but not without problems, since the content, similar to that of *Odyssey*'s book 15, indicates that it dealt in some detail with Telemachus in the context of the returns of the Greeks.

The episodes dealing with the travel of the heroes itself are unfortunately not preserved. However, the surviving evidence of their inclusion in Stesichorus' poems shed further light on how our poet dealt with myth and rearranged it creating new versions with new maps and protagonists.

2.1 The *Sack of Troy*

The contents of the *Sack of Troy* have come down to us in commentaries, paraphrases, in one quotation and two papyri: P. Oxy. 2803 (a first century AD papyrus published in 1971 by Lobel) and P. Oxy. 2619 (a late second or early third century AD papyrus published by Lobel in 1967). P. Oxy. 2803 preserves what seems to be a title for the content of the papyrus, but one of its scraps overlaps with one piece of P. Oxy. 2619, leading us to conclude that the *Sack of Troy* circulated in antiquity either with two alternative titles, or with titles for specific sections of the poem.[1] Apart from the literary evidence, Stesichorus' poem is

---

[1] Thus West 1971b: 264. Page 1973: 64 suggests the existence of two poems on the same subject but such option is unlikely. Given the importance of the horse in the opening of the poem (fr.

depicted in one iconographic piece of evidence, the *Tabula Iliaca Capitolina*, fr. 105 F., a calcite tablet from the first century AD, first published in the seventeenth century,[2] which among other things constitutes the only evidence for Stesichorus' version of Aeneas in the west. This means that despite the fragmentary state of the evidence, we have a relatively good idea of Stesichorus' version of the sack of Ilion.

The sack of Troy is first described in the *Odyssey*.[3] However, this account focuses on the key moments that precede the sack, such as the building of the Trojan horse. The sack *per se* is described towards the end of the *Little Iliad*, attributed to Lesches. Epeius builds the horse (arg. 4a–5a), and the Trojans debate what to do with it (arg. 5b) eventually taking it inside of the walls; the attack begins; Astyanax (fr. 18 *GEF*) and Priam are killed (fr. 25 *GEF*), Helen (fr. 28 *GEF*) and Aethra (fr. 17 *GEF*) are rescued, Aeneas is taken captive with Andromache by Neoptolemus (frr. 29–30 *GEF*), a different version from what happens in the *Iliou Persis* and in Stesichorus. It is likely that the poem contained the rape of Cassandra (fr. 3 *GEF*).[4]

A more detailed account was given in the epic *Iliou Persis*, attributed to Arctinus.[5] The *Iliou Persis* is likely to have begun with the building of the Trojan horse, followed by a debate on whether to take the horse inside the walls (fr. 1 *GEF*; arg 1a). Laocoon intervenes, attempting to dissuade his fellow citizens from taking the horse, and is attacked by serpents (arg. 1c). Aeneas takes this appalling attack as an omen of the destruction of Troy and escapes with his family to Ida (arg. 1d). During the night, the Greeks attack. Priam (arg. 2c) and Astyanax (arg. 3b, fr. 3 *GEF*) are killed, Cassandra is raped (arg. 3a), Polyxena sacrificed (arg. 4c). Helen (arg. 2d) and Aethra (fr. 4b) rescued.

In lyric poetry, some episodes of the sack survive. If his name is correctly emended in Athenaeus' passage, Sacadas mentioned the warriors inside the Trojan horse (Stes. fr. 102 F.). Alcaeus treated the episode of Cassandra's rape

---

100 F.) it seems more plausible to consider that the *Horse* was either an alternative title to the *Sack of Troy* or a title of a section of that poem. Davies and Finglass 2014: 406 nn. 49 and 50 present Hellenistic examples for other instances where the title *horse* is applied to poems dealing with the sack of Troy and other instances of lyric poems circulating under two titles. Adrados 1978: 270, who argues for the *Scylla* as a part of the *Geryoneis* (1978: 264–265) and the *Eriphyle* and *Thebais* being part of the same poem (1978: 274–275), agrees with West's suggestion that the *Horse* is likely to refer to a section of the *Sack of Troy*.

2 Fabretti 1683: 315–384.
3 *Od.* 4.266–289, 8.492–520, 11.523–537.
4 Thus West 2013: 122. For a discussion of the poem see Kelly 2015b: 318–341.
5 For the *Iliou Persis* in art and literature see Finglass 2015a.

(fr. 298 V). Ibycus is said to have treated the sacrifice of Polyxena (fr. 307 *PMGF*) but the context is lost. In his fr. S151 he mentions in his *recusatio* that it is not his intention to sing the destruction of Troy (lines 10–14).[6] Although tragedy dealt extensively with the events of the immediate aftermath of the Trojan War, the only surviving plays that elaborate on the events of the sack are Euripides' *Hecuba* and *Trojan Women*. The death of Priam is recalled by Hecuba in the *Trojan Women* (lines 481–485) and alluded to in *Hecuba* (line 21). The killing of Astyanax is dealt with in detail in the *Trojan Women* (709–799, 1133–1149; cf. *Andr.* 10). In *Hecuba*, Andromache alludes to the rape of Cassandra (*Hec.* 618–619), but it is the sacrifice of Polyxena that dominates the first half of the play (40–105, 140, 221, 919) although it is referred to in the *Trojan Women* (622–630, 641–650) and may have featured in a lost play by Sophocles (frr. 618–635 Radt). The rescue of Helen is an important episode of the *Trojan Women* (890–1059) where Menelaus says he intends to kill her by stoning (1037–1040), a version similar to that of Stesichorus. Among the historians, interest in the aftermath of the sack is evident in the many accounts of the Trojan escape to the west, which is found in Hecataeus (*FGrHist* 1 F 62), Thucydides (6.2.3), Hellanicus (fr. 84 *EGM* and fr. 31 *EGM*), Damastes (fr. 3 *EGM*), Timaeus (*FGrHist* 566 F 59) and Alcimus (*FGrHist* 560 F 4).

In art, the episodes of the sack of Troy are just as prominent. From the eighth to the mid-seventh century we find several depictions of the Trojan horse.[7] During the mid-sixth to the mid-fifth century, apart from occasional depictions of the horse similar to those found in the previous century,[8] we find a proliferation of individual episodes of the sack, in particular the more violent

---

[6] Wilkinson 2013: 15 notes that Polyxena may have featured in fr. S224 *PMGF* where Troilus appears. Robertson 1970: 11–15 suggests that she may have appeared in an earlier section of fr. S151. For the association between Polyxena and Troilus see Noussia-Fantuzzi 2015: 446–448.
[7] Fragmentary bronze Boeotian fibula dated to the late-eighth century; fragmentary relief pithos from Tenos dated to the mid-seventh century and the Mikonos relief pithos c. 675 (Sadurska 1986: §§ 22–24). The Mykonos relief is the more detailed depiction of the sack, since it includes other episodes, such as what seems to be either Helen's recovery or Cassandra's rape, the death of Astyanax, but the images are not labelled (cf. Ervin 1963: §§ 7, 17). See further Anderson 1997: 182–191; Carpenter 2015: 179–185.
[8] Sadurska 1986: §§ 1, 2, 17, 18. The first two vases (red-figure cup from Vulci c. 490 and from Chiusi c. 470–460, respectively) depict the building of the horse with Athena's supervision. § 1 has Epeius as the builder of the horse. The last two vases, a Corinthian aryballos from Caere ca. 560 and an Attic black-figure from Orbetello ca. 560–550 are similar to the representation of the horse from the Mykonos relief pithos. A further Corinthian kylos from Gela c. 580–570 depicts the horse with warriors inside, (cf. Ingoglia 2000).

scenes, such as the rape of Cassandra,[9] the deaths of Astyanax and of Priam,[10] the sacrifice of Polyxena,[11] but also the rescues of Helen and Aethra.[12] Artists focus on the more vulnerable characters (the elderly, women, and children). In paintings, the theme is treated in detail in the Stoa Poikile at Athens, the Cnidian Lesche at Delphi, and the northern metopes of the Parthenon, dated to the mid-fifth century.[13]

Stesichorus' poem follows the other versions of the sack, namely the *Odyssey* and the epic *Iliou Persis*. The poem began with Athena pitying Epeius for his inferior condition and inspiring him to build the wooden horse (fr. 100 F.), with enough room for a hundred warriors (fr. 102 F.). Such a massive piece of woodwork raises questions among the Trojans, who debate whether they should destroy it or take it into the city. They go for the second option probably because of a misinterpretation of an omen (fr. 103 F.), or, alternatively, the intervention of the deceiving Sinon (fr. 104 F.).[14] The Greeks assault the city; Helen is found (frr. 105, 106, 113, 115 F.), women are taken as slaves (fr. 110 F.), sacrificed (Polyxena, frr. 105, 118.5, 119.5 F.); children are murdered (Astyanax, fr. 107 F.). However, some Trojans escape: Hecuba is rescued and taken to Lycia (fr. 109 F.) and Aeneas escapes to the west with his companions (fr. 105 F.).

2.1.1 Divine pity and Epeius (fr. 100 F.)

For Stesichorus' *Sack of Troy* we can safely restore a substantial and revealing opening.[15] The restoration results from the connection of three scraps from P. Oxy. 2619 (frr. 15 (b), 30, 31 = S89 *SLG*) which were joined by Barrett[16] and a

---

9 See Touchefeu 1981: 336–351; Pipili 1997: § 7; Anderson 1997: 199–202; Hedreen 2001: 22–32; Carpenter 2015: 188–195. This is the more recurrent episode depicting of Cassandra in early art, particularly in the Argive shield-bands (cf. Carpenter 2015: 195).
10 The depictions of the deaths of Priam and Astyanax are often related, with Astyanax used as the weapon to kill Priam (see Touchefeu 1984: §§ 7–24, 27). There is no literary parallel for such an episode, which suggests that this scene was original to the artists (see Jesus 2017: 37–38, 426). The common literary account is that Priam is assassinated at the altar and that Astyanax is killed separately (e.g Stes. fr. 107 F.; E. *Tro.* 1175–1177).
11 Laurens 1988: § 57; Touchefeu-Meyneir 1994; Schwarz 2001.
12 For the rescue of Helen, see below 2.1.6. For Aethra's rescue by her grandsons, see Kron 1981; Finglass 2013b: 38 n. 4.
13 Paus. 1.15.2, 10.25–27. Cf. Stansbury-O'Donnell 1989; Ferrari 2000; Scott 2010: 325.
14 West 1969: 139.
15 Finglass 2013c.
16 Cf. West 1969: 140.

quotation by Athenaeus[17] which fits the meter and context except for one trace.[18] P. Oxy. 2619 fr. 15 (a) was added to S89 *SLG* by Pardini and confirmed by Schade.[19] Pardini's placement and reconstruction of the fragments was of high value to a correct understanding, leading to the conclusion that we have an invocation to the Muse and not a speech, as West suspected.[20] The first part of the first strophe is now lost,[21] but θεά in line 6 strongly suggest the invocation of the Muse, and thus that the fragment belongs to the beginning of the poem:[22]

]δρ		str. 1
θεά, τὺ [˘]δο[˘˘—×—˘—	6	
παρθέν[ε] χρυc[˘˘—×—˘˘—˘˘] ἱ-		
μείρει [δ'] ἀείδε[ιν.		
νῦν δ' ἄγε μοι λ<έγ>ε πῶc παρ[ὰ καλλιρόου(c)		ant. 1
δίνα[c] Cιμόεντοc ἀνὴρ	10	
θ]εᾶc ἱ[ό]τατι δαεὶc cεμν[ᾶc Ἀθάναc		
μέτ[ρα] τε καὶ cοφίαν τού[τοιc ἐπιπειθόμενοc		
ῥηξήνορ]οc ἀντὶ μάχα[c		
καὶ] φυ[λόπ]ιδοc κλέοc [×—˘		
εὐρυ]χόρ[ο]υ Τροΐαc ἁλώcι[μον ἆμαρ ˘—	15	
×—]ν ἔθηκεν		
(×)—˘˘].εccι πά .(.)ο [×—˘˘—˘˘—×		ep. 1
ὤικτιρε γὰ]ρ αὐτὸ[ν] ὕ[δωρ ἀεὶ φορέοντα Διὸc		
κούρα βαcιλ]ε[ύcι]ν α[˘—×		

---

17 10.456g.
18 Finglass 2013c: 1–7 discusses the results of the conjunction of Athenaeus' quotation with P. Oxy. 2619, advanced earlier by Kazansky 1976; 1997: 37, 90 and Führer 1977: 16 nn. 172–173 and showed that the resulting text should be considered the beginning of the poem (Finglass 2013c: 4–6), as Kazansky 1976 had suggested.
19 *Ap*. Schade 2003: 121–124.
20 West 1969: 141. For details see Davies and Finglass 2014: 414–415; for a syntactic overview of the problems related to the place of the fragment in the poem and to the supplements provided to line 9, see Tsitsibakou-Vasalos 2011.
21 Thus Finglass 2013c: 4–7. Bergk 1882: 223 ascribed fr. 277a F. (which presents many similarities to fr. 90 F.) to the *Sack of Troy*, following Tyschen's suggestion 1783: 31 that Eustathius' quotation was the first line of Stesichorus' poem. Bergk noted the metrical compatibility of the line with the *Sack of Troy* scheme. West 1969: 137 correctly pointed out that this 'might as well be attributed to almost any of Stesichorus' poems', since its dactylic metre could easily fit in other poems of Stesichorus. Finglass 2013c: 14–15, takes into account the possibility of fr. 277a F. as the opening line of the poem.
22 Finglass 2013c: 4–7 for the reconstruction of fr. 100 F. as the opening of the *Sack of Troy*.

7 παρθέν[ε] Kazansky | χρυς[οκόμα Finglass || 8 Führer || 9 ἄγε Kazansky post West | μοι Lobel | λ<έγ>ε Führer | πῶς Kazansky | παρ[ὰ West | καλλιρόου(ς) Barrett || 10 West || 11 Barrett || 12 μέτ[ρα] Barrett | τού[τοις ἐπιπειθόμενος Finglass || 13 ῥηξήνορ]ος (vel. φθιήνορ]ος) Führer | μαχα[ς Barrett || 14 Barrett || 15 εὐρυ]χόρ[ο]υ ... ἁλώςι[μον Barrett | Τροΐας Page post West: τρωας Π⁸ || 18 ὤικτιρε Page 19 ἀ[γαυοῖς Barrett, ἀ[τρείδαις Führer, ἀ[χαιῶν Kazansky

        ]...[
   Goddess, you ...   6
   Maiden ... gold ...
     Wishes to sing.

   Tell me now how by the fair-flowing
   eddies of the Simoeis, a man,   10
   By the will of the venerated goddess Athena, mastered the
   Measurements and the skill, and [trusting in these]
   Instead of in battle [breaker of men]
   And of strife...[won] glory [and]
   the ... capture of [spacious] Troy   15
   ...brought

     [Because of his toil]
   She pitied him as he was always carrying water for the kings,
   The daughter of Zeus...

The resulting invocation shows similarities between lines 6–7 of the strophe and fr. 90.8–10 F. θέα (...) χρυσόπτερε παρθένε, ascribed to the *Palinode(s)*.[23] The first line of the antistrophe reading νῦν δ' ἄγε μοι λ<έγ>ε πῶς suggests a progression in the song from the invocation to the beginning of the narrative. Despite the unsurprising structure of the invocation, this opening provides a strange beginning for a poem about the most important war in Greek mythology. It shows that the hero chosen by Stesichorus to open his poem is Epeius, water-carrier of the kings. However, his identity is not promptly revealed. Before it, the poem sets its spatial context providing the audience with subtle allusions to the Trojan war and to the importance of this man in its resolution.

Stesichorus initiates the narrative by providing the geographical location of the events he is about to narrate: παρ[ὰ καλλιρόου(ς)/ δίνα[ς Σιμόεντος (lines

---

[23] Cf. below 3.3. For other invocations to the Muses in Stesichorus' poems, see 4.1.1 and 278 F., and fr. 327 F. corresponding to the opening of *Rhadine*, a poem which recent editors tend to consider spurious, on which see Rutherford 2015.

9–10).²⁴ The reference to rivers gives a recognisable location where the events take place, in similar diction to that of Stesichorus' *Geryoneis* fr. 9 F., where παρά refers to the streams of a river, in that case to Tartessus.²⁵ In both poems, Stesichorus uses topography to provide the geographical location of the narrative and to enhance the dramatic effect of the violent events by first depicting the bucolic ambiance of the scene. Rivers, particularly those of Ilion, offer more than the location of the episode; they are associated with the landscape of certain events, and "trigger narrative development and eases mnemonic recall".²⁶

The ambivalent meaning of the allusion to rivers is evident in the *Iliad*, where the Simoeis and the Scamander are associated with the prosperity of Troy, recalling peaceful bucolic passages,²⁷ but they are also the background for the merciless slaughter during the war.²⁸ The reference to the rivers of Troy alludes to key moments of the war, a synecdoche for all the suffering a war causes. Such a parallel would remind the audience of the gruesomeness of battle, the maleficent effects of war. Stesichorus uses the allusion to intensify the dramatic effect of line 15 where the capture of Troy is mentioned in a relevant place, at the end of a stanza. The reference to the rivers in the opening of the stanza and the final revelation of the capture of Troy enclose and frame the rise of a hero, an unexpected one, whose activity in Troy is, moreover, closely related to the streams of these rivers.

---

24 Cf. also the fifth century hexameter inscription in Douris 'school cup' (Lyr. Adesp. fr. 938(e) PMG): Μοῖcά μοι ἀ<μ>φὶ Σκάμανδρον ἐύρ<ρ>οον ἄρχομ' ἀεί{ν}δε<ι>ν, once attributed to Stesichorus (Sider 2010: 544 n. 4).
25 See above 1.1.1. Also worthy of mention in this context is the supplements provided by Barrett to fr. 97.220 F. Barrett restores πα[ρὰ νάμαci Δίρκαc in what would be a reference to the kingdom of Thebes. This line occurs in the moment when the Theban Queen, after announcing her plan to divide Oedipus' inheritance between her two sons in two equal lots, specifies one of these lots. This lot is the one which concerns Thebes' throne. The other lot concerns the movable goods (gold, herd, etc). However, a reference to the rich and fertile lands of Thebes in this moment of the narrative would have been unexpected. For further discussion on this and other supplements see below 4.2.4 n. 269.
26 Tsagalis 2012.
27 For example, in *Il.* 22.145–156 the description of the fight between Hector and Achilles is paused to describe the landscape dominated by the Scamander and the springs where, the poet tells us, the women of Troy used to go to wash the clothes (note the reference to menial domestic tasks) before the Greeks' arrival.
28 The more significant examples of this ambivalence are the death scenes, particularly Hector's (*Il.* 22.145–156), where Scamander serves as a metonymic referent for the past prosperity and the present doom of Troy. In *Il.* 12.17–33 Simoeis' mud bears witness to the death of many heroes. *Il.* 4.473–487 recalls Anthemides' birth by the Simoeis immediately before his death.

However, our poet does not make this clear from the beginning. The final word of line 10 – ἀνήρ – draws attention to the figure of the man, just like the opening of the *Odyssey*. In the next line, we learn that this man enjoyed Athena's patronage: θ]εᾶς ἰ[ό]τατι δαεὶς σεμν[ᾶς Ἀθάνας. Up to this point, Odysseus would certainly be one of the options available, particularly because he is left unnamed in the *Odyssey* for over twenty lines.

Stesichorus quickly shifts to aspects not so identifiable with Odysseus or Neoptolemus, or in fact with any of the traditional Homeric heroes. The means by which this man achieves the destruction of Troy are quite surprising: through measurements and wisdom instead of battle (13 ἀντὶ μάχα[ς). The clear opposition between measurements and battle makes clear that the man cannot be Odysseus. In early epic, Odysseus is associated with diplomacy and cunning, but he is an excellent warrior. In the *Aethiopis* (fr. 3 *GEF*) he fights for the body of Achilles. In the *Iliad*, despite his recurring diplomatic interventions,[29] he is present in important battle scenes where his excellence is attested (e.g. 10.148–282). Even in the *Odyssey*, where his most outstanding quality is cunning, his warrior skills are not forgotten (e.g. 22.115). The idea of Odysseus as the coward and wicked-minded man, as for example in Sophocles' *Philoctetes*, is a later development. Moreover, μέτ[ρα] τε καὶ σοφίαν point to other skills, particularly those associated with craftsmanship, not with intellectual μῆτις.

The man who stands in the opening of a poem describing the end of the Trojan War is no warrior; he was the water-carrier for the kings. Exactly who these kings are is uncertain. The final word of line 19 beginning with α could be Ἀ[τρείδαις, as suggested by Führer, thus making Epeius a servant of Agamemnon and Menelaus, which is attested elsewhere, or Ἀ[χαιῶν, as proposed by Kazansky, which would imply a considerable harder task. However, other supplements are possible, such as ἀ[γαυοῖς, "the noble kings".[30] The identity of the water-carrier as Epeius reappears in an anecdote supposedly connected to Simonides' stance in Cartheia (Athen. 10.456e–f), where a donkey is called Epeius because of his function as a water-carrier.[31] The episode attests to the comic treatment of Epeius, perhaps also found elsewhere.[32] However, in Stesichorus,

---

[29] E.g. *Il*. 2.284–335, 9.179, 223–306.
[30] Führer 1977: 16 n. 171; Kazansky 1976; Barrett *ap*. Davies 1991. An example of the use of the adjective in a similar context can be found in *Il*. 3.268.
[31] See Bowra 1961: 309–310 for some brief considerations on the authority of Chamaeleon – the source of Athenaeus for this episode – and on the interactions between Simonides and Stesichorus.
[32] Finglass 2013c: 11–12, especially the satyr-play *Epeius* by Euripides (*TrGF* v/1 390), and in Plautus (fr. incert. 1 Leo) indicate a tendency to portray Epeius in a satirical manner. On the

Epeius' function is not comic, but shameful. The task of carrying water, as part of a wider range of domestic affairs, was traditionally a feminine function, well attested in art and in literature.³³ The scene appears often in art with no mythological context.³⁴ In mythological contexts, the Danaids appear regularly with this function in the Underworld, as a punishment for their crime, after the fourth century, but before that, some depictions of Sisyphus' toil were accompanied by the presence of winged creatures pouring water.³⁵ The association of the water-carrying with an eternal toil would emphasise Epeius' miserable condition. Representations of Achilles' ambush of Troilus featuring Polyxena fetching water are common.³⁶ There is, however, one relevant example of men carrying water. The north friezes of the Parthenon, show four male water-carriers.³⁷ This detail has puzzled the scholars, precisely because this was a task usually relegated to the maidens, especially daughters of metics.³⁸

---

domestic tasks attributed to Epeius see Davies 2014. On the other hand, Simias in his *Axe* presents a sympathetic portrait of Epeius as a water-carrier, on which see Finglass 2015b.

33 *Il.* 6.456–458; *Od.* 7.19–20, 10.105–106, 15.440–442, 20.153–154; Hes. *Th.* 784–787; A. *TrGF* III 131–133; Hdt. 5.12–13; E. *El.* 107–111; Ar. *Lys.* 327–334. See further Finglass 2013c: 12 with notes.

34 The earliest attestation of women fetching water is found in the seventeenth century Theran wall-painting. Attic black figure hydriae depicting women in fountains with hydriae dating to ca. 575–550 are found in 42176 *BAD* and Florence, Museo Archaeologico Etrusco 3792; (*BAD* 8054). For black-figure hydriae ca. 550–500, see e.g. the artefacts in Brussels, Musees Royaux R 346 (*BAD* 10964); Florence, Museo Archaeologico Etrusco 3793 (*BAD* 8098), and London, British Museum B338, 366.72 *ABV*, 97 *Add²* (*BAD* 302067). From ca. 525–475, see Paris, Musée du Louvre MNC18 (*BAD* 11267); Boston, Museum of Fine Arts 61.195, *Para.* 147.5BIS, *Add²* 91 (*BAD* 351087); Toledo, Museum of Art 1961.23, *Para.* 147.5TER, *Add²* 91 (*BAD* 351088); Rome, Mus. Naz. Etrusco di Villa Giulia 63610, *Para.* 148.5QUARTER, *Add²* 91 (*BAD* 351089); New York, Metropolitan Museum 06.1021.77, *Para.* 148 (*BAD* 351090). For the attic red figure hydriae with the same scene see London, British Museum E159, *ARV²* 24.9, 1620, *Add²* 155 (*BAD* 200130); and Detroit, Insitute of Arts 63.13, *ARV²* 565.40, *Para.* 389, *Add²* 260 (*BAD* 206470).

35 For the winged creatures pouring water, see Kossatz-Deissman 1981: § 2. For the Danaids in the Underworld as water-carriers, see Keuls 1974: 337–341 and Hansen 2002: 69–74.

36 The scene appears in several hydriae and amphorae of the sixth century depicting the two siblings approaching a fountain behind which Achilles is hiding. Polyxena brings a hydria most of the times. See further Robertson 1990.

37 Parthenon North Frieze, block (VI), scenes N 16–19. The general explanation for the oddity of having male water-carriers is the great demand for water that the sacrifices would require (cf. Dillon 2001: 311, n. 75). Traditionally the scene in the frieze is seen as the procession of the Panathenaea since Stuart and Revett 1787. See Boardman 1977 for the reading of the frieze as representing the last Panathenaea before Marathon, thus heroicising the warriors who are to depart; and Connelly 1996 for the theory that the frieze depicts the myth of the sacrifice of Erechtheus' daughters.

38 Cf. Demetrius of Phalerus *FGrHist* 288 F 5.

However, the association of Epeius with a lower status is present in the iconographic evidence since the third quarter of the sixth century in a marble relief found in Samothrace. This relief shows Epeius and Talthybius attending Agamemnon, all labelled.[39] The content of the marble relief is enigmatic. It has been suggested that it either alludes to Agamemnon's initiation in the cults of the Cabires in Samothrace,[40] or it is a representation of the moment when Epeius shows the wooden horse to the Atreid.[41] Epeius must therefore be presented simply as a servant of Agamemnon. In epic, on the other hand, the status of Epeius is not clear. He appears in Homer and in the Epic Cycle. In the *Iliad*, he is a boxer, in the *Odyssey* the builder of the horse. The idea that he is not quite skilled in battle is evident in the *Iliad* (23.669–670), and in his absence from the Catalogue of Ships (2.517–526). However, as shown in the Funeral Games for Patroclus (23.664–699), he masters boxing.

There has been a tendency to interpret the presentation of Epeius in the Funeral Games as a proof of his brutal nature; a man whose strength lacks any strategy. According to this view, he ignores the heroic standards and codes as he stands for mere force. However, some details of the Iliadic Epeius show that he was not ignorant of skill at all. In his speech, Epeius stresses the importance of being expert (δαήμονος) at something, whatever it may be. Even though boxing requires a particularly strong body structure, it depends mostly on skill. This is evident later in the episode (23.836–841) when Epeius participates in the iron-throwing. In this contest, he loses because he lacks skill, not strength.[42]

Epeius' participation in building the Trojan horse is a common feature of all the accounts concerning the episode. However, the importance of Epeius in the task varies, as does the focus on his character. He is mentioned twice in the *Odyssey*, where he is credited with giving physical form to Odysseus' brilliant

---

39 Wilamowitz 1899: 55, n. 18 suggested the association of Epeius with the condition of slave was not an innovation of Stesichorus, but an existing tradition perhaps from early epic. The evidence from the Samothracian throne and his characterization in the *Iliad* differentiate him from the other characters in terms of status. Therefore, the idea that Epeius was a servant, not necessarily a slave, seems to be present in the tradition. See Robertson 1986: § 7 and Touchefeu 1981: § 2; Hamiaux 2001: 84–85.
40 *Schol.* A. R. 1, 916–918, pp. 76–78 Wendel; D. S. 5.48–49. Hamiaux 2001: 84–85; Zachos 2013: 12 n. 51. For the initiation cults of the Cabires in Samothrace see Hdt. 2.51 and, for a general survey, see Burkert 1993: 539–544.
41 Picard 1935: 557 suggested that the marble relief depicts Epeius because, as the builder of the horse, he was a distinguished sculptor, a later tradition which perhaps owes something to Stesichorus' *Sack of Troy*. But, as Lehmann-Hartleben 1943: 130 n. 71 points out, Epeius' function in the marble is not clear.
42 Howland 1955: 15.

idea; that is, to build the Wooden horse, not to idealise it.[43] The Epic Cycle shows some variations of Epeius' ability. In the *Little Iliad*, it was according to Athena's command that Epeius built the horse.[44] Fr. 1 *GEF* of the *Iliou Persis* says that Epeius' horse had moving eyes, knees, and tail.[45] Here, Epeius is praised for his remarkable engineering technique. His work of art surpasses what would have been necessary to the occasion.

Stesichorus follows this tendency of giving him more relevance by focusing the opening of his poem on this character. Athena gives him the chance for glory (κλέος in line 14) by instructing Epeius on measurements and wisdom: θ]εᾶc ἰ[ό]τατι δαεὶc cεμν[ᾶc Ἀθάναc. | μέτ[ρα] τε καὶ coφίαν (lines 11–12). Despite having a menial – although necessary – function in the war, Epeius managed to be the one granting victory to the Achaeans. ῥηξήνορ]οc ἀντὶ μάχα[c (line 13) is quite surprising in the context of the sack of Troy. Amid all the terrible, merciless, and desperate action which took place in the several battles fought to win the war, it is by means other than battle that a man brought the capture of the city of Troy.

Finglass rightly emphasises the potential metaphorical power of the depiction of Epeius in the Cnidian Lesche at Delphi described by Pausanias (10.26.2–3).[46] Stansbury-O'Donnell reconstructed the painting which occupied three walls, each of them representing one episode of the sack according to Pausanias' description.[47] Epeius appears at the left part of the second scene. He is depicted naked, tearing down the wall of Troy, above which the Wooden horse could have been visible.[48] The other figures depicted naked are either corpses of the Trojans (10.27.1) or children (10.26.9). The fact that Epeius is not wearing any armour, unlike the other Achaeans in the scene, shows his detachment from the affairs of war: he does not own armour, nor did he require arms to bring an end to the war. Instead, he used his craft to render the wall ineffective. The consequences of his intervention were just as destructive. The same idea is present in our poet's opening of the *Sack of Troy*.

In Stesichorus, as we have seen, Epeius is unsuitable not only for battle, as he himself admits he is in the *Iliad* (23.670–671). Because of the shameful job he performs, he is, to some extent, also unsuitable for glory. The Epeius of the

---

43 *Od.* 8.492–493, 11.523–524.
44 Arg. 4a *GEF*: Καὶ Ἐπειὸc κατ' Ἀθηνᾶc προαίρεcιν τὸν δούρειον ἵππον καταcκευάζει.
45 Fr. 1 GEF: *Hunc tamen equum quidam longum centum uiginti <pedes>, latum triginta fuisse tradunt, cuius cauda genua oculi mouerentur.*
46 Finglass 2013c: 9.
47 Stansbury-O'Donnell 1989.
48 For details see Stansbury-O'Donnell 1989: 207.

menial job suffers a metamorphosis in the paths of craft inspired by divine will; an intervention that ultimately concedes to Epeius eternal fame and prestige in the tradition. Stesichorus draws attention to how the ability to build the horse – ability conceded not to a warrior but to a man with a menial occupation – grants victory over Troy, more than the ability to fight. The ability to build this cunning machine of war, which was so monumental as to carry one hundred Achaeans (fr. 102 F.),[49] granted Epeius the association with manual dexterity in the tradition. This is particularly evident in later authors. Plato compares his sculpture ability to Daedalus' (*Io.* 533a) and Theodorus of Samos (*R.* 620c). When Apollodorus refers to Epeius' role in the building of the horse, he calls him an architect.[50] In Callimachus he is said to have made a sculpture of Hermes.[51] Pausanias (2.19.6) credits him with the building of the sculpture of Apollo at Argos. Dictys (2.44) has Epeius repairing ships.

The building of the Trojan horse is told in two fragments from the Michingan Collection (fr. 1 ii. 5–11 and fr. 2 i. 1–5),[52] tentatively attributed to Timotheus but showing Euripidean flavour in diction and style.[53] The fragments use the Scamander and the Simoeis as a landmark of the Trojan landscape.[54] And they suggest some direct speech (beginning at fr. 1 ii.5 until fr. 2 i.5) or quotation. Someone commands others, the Danaans (fr. 1. i. 5), to head to the Mount Ida to cut wood to be floated down the streams of the Scamander (fr. 1 i. 4). The scene is described as a commander giving instruction to the Achaeans in an agitated manner. The fragmentary state of the poem presents many difficulties in interpreting the identities of the speaker and narrator.[55] The possibilities considered by Sampson point to Sinon as the narrator and Helenus as the speaker, and they may well be true. However, the argument Sampson gives to exclude Epeius as the speaker fails to consider the possible contribution of Stesichorus

---

[49] According to Eustathius (*Od.* 1698.2 = Stes. fr. 102 F.), Stesichorus referred to the capacity of the horse to contain one hundred Achaean warriors. However, he does not seem to have named them, at least according to Athenaeus' testimony. See further Davies and Finglass 2014: 420–421.

[50] *Epit.* 5.14: Ἐπειῶι, ὃς ἦν ἀρχιτέκτων.

[51] Call. *Iamb.* 7 = fr. 197 Pfeiffer.

[52] See Borges and Sampson 2015: 56–60. From the range of possibilities of lumber activity in the Trojan saga, Sampson considers that the building of the Wooden horse is the more likely, but it is also possible that the episode refers to the construction of a pyre, ships, or the Trojan Wall.

[53] On the attribution of fr. 1 P. Mich.inv. 3498+3250b verso and fr. 2 P.Mich.inv.3250c verso to Timotheus instead of Euripides, see Borges and Sampson 2015: 75–81.

[54] Φ]ρύγιος λιμήν fr. 1 i. 4 and Πριάμου πάτρας in fr. 2 i.5 corroborate the setting.

[55] See Borges and Sampson 2015: 62–75.

to this character. Sampson admits that we have enough evidence for the importance of Epeius in the process of the building of the horse, but 'in no point in the mythological tradition does he provide instructions for the horse's construction'.[56] This is in part true, but when we have the beginning of a poem drawing attention to Epeius and his importance in the building of the horse, we can no longer claim that he did never had some relevance to the point of being the instructor of the works.

Now, divine pity is a common primary trigger for the plot in epic context, evident not only in the *Odyssey*, but also in the *Iliad*. In the *Cypria*, Zeus' pity for Earth serves as the justification for the origin of the Trojan war.[57] The irony of an act of divine pity that brings destruction to the pitied opponent is no novelty. It is in fact a characteristic of divine nature in Greek myth and literature. But the irony in Stesichorus reaches another level because of the "disparity between the object of pity and the consequences of it".[58] Despite bringing victory to the Achaean community, the pity of Athena falls on a single man. The individuality of the choice of Athena implicates the devastation of Troy. Moreover, the exclusivity of Athena's pity and the emphasis on it in the opening of the poem will contrast deeply with the pitiless acts performed by the Greeks during the sack. Divine pity, as most divine emotions, is ambivalent.

2.1.2 The Trojan Debate (frr. 103 and 104 F.)

The ambivalence of divine pity and compassion in the context of the Trojan war is evident in many other occasions. It accompanies the dramatic tension and emphasises the problems of divine cunning (fr. 103 F.), or divine abandonment, as felt by the Trojans possibly referred to in fr. 114 F. and in the various merciless killing of innocent figures (frr. 116, 118, 119 F.).

One of the most effective ways to emphasise the Trojan *pathos* in the myth of the Sack of Troy is conveyed by the episode of the debate.[59] The Trojans gathered to decide what to do with the Wooden horse. The debate scene is mentioned in the *Odyssey* (8.500–510), the *Iliou Persis* (arg. 1a *GEF*), and probably in the *Little Iliad* (arg. 5b *GEF*).[60] However, Stesichorus' fragment shows interesting

---

56 See Borges and Sampson 2015: 71.
57 Thus Finglass 2013c: 6; *Od.* 1.19; *Il.* 1.56; *Cypria* fr. 1.3 *GEF*, on which see West 2013: 65–70.
58 Finglass 2013c: 13.
59 Cf. Carey 2015: 57 on Stesichorus' predilection for decision-making moments.
60 West 2013: 205–206.

variations from earlier or contemporary accounts. Fr. 103 F., containing the debate, is the result of the conjunction of three scraps of P. Oxy. 2619 by Lobel and Barrett.[61] It shows two speeches, and the two competing resolutions regarding the statue.

] ̣γα̣λα̣ϲα̣γα̣.[ ]		ant.
x—⏑⏑—⏑⏑—]		
x—⏑⏑—⏑⏑—x—]ακον		
—⏑⏑—⏑⏑—x—⏑⏑—]τε ̣ομωϲ		
x—⏑——]	5	
(x)—⏑⏑—⏑⏑—x—]ντι βίαι τε καὶ αἰχμᾶι		ep.
x—⏑⏑—⏑⏑—] πεποιθότεϲ· ἀλλ'ἄγε δή		
x—⏑⏑—⏑⏑—x]		
—⏑⏑—⏑⏑—x—]ο̣νεϲ ἀγκυλοτόξοι		
—⏖—⏑⏑—x]	10	
—⏑⏑—⏑⏑—x—]. ̣ϲ διάϲταν		
—⏑⏑—⏑⏑—]		
x—⏑—x—⏑—x—]ρ̣απαϲιν		
x—⏑⏑—⏑⏑—]ηϲων		
x—⏑⏑—⏑]Ἀχαιῶν	15	
—⏑⏑—⏑⏑—] τέλοϲ εὑρύο[πα		str.
x—⏑⏑—⏑]υναιϲ		
x—⏖—⏑⏑— π(τ)]ολέμου [τε]λευτά̣ [ ]		
—⏑⏑—⏑⏑—x—]ε̣ν πυκιν[άϲ] τε̣ φρ[έ]ν̣αϲ̣		
x—⏑⏑—⏑⏑—]	20	
x—⏑⏑—⏑⏑—] ῥηξάνορα̣		
—⏑⏑—⏑⏑— ὤτρ]υνε μέγαν φρ[α]ϲὶν ἐν		
x—⏑——]		
—⏑⏑—⏑ μετέ]πρεπε καὶ πιγ[υ]τᾶι		ant.
x—⏑⏑—⏑⏑—]	25	
x—⏖—⏑⏑—x—⏑]ε̣ργον		
—⏑⏑—⏑⏑—x—⏑⏑] ̣οπτολ[⏑—		
x—⏑⏑—⏑⏑—]		
x—⏑⏑—⏑⏑—x—⏑—]		
—⏑⏑—⏑⏑—x—⏑⏑—⏑⏑]νο	30	
x—⏑——].[		
τ̣ονδ[̣.] ̣δα̣ ̣υν λ.[ ] ̣μ̣.ε̣.[		ep.
πρὸϲ ναὸν ἐϲ ἀκρ[όπο]λ[ι]ν ϲπεύδοντεϲ [⏑—⏑⏑—		

---

61 Lobel 1967: 35; Barrett ap. West 1969: 135. For further information, see Davies and Finglass 2014: 421.

Τρῶες πολέες τ' ἐπίκ[ου]ροι
ἔλθετε μη[δ]ὲ λόγο[ις π]ειθώμεθ' ὅπως π[⏑⏑—×   35
τονδεκα.[...]ονι.[ ]..
ἁγνὸν ἄ[γαλ]μα [⏑—] ..αὐτεῖ καται-
    σχ]ύνωμε[ν ἀ]εικ[ελί]ως
×]νιν δὲ [—×—⏑] .ἀζώμεσθ' ἀγάς[ςας
×].ησογ[⏑—⏑⏑—⏓—]ρ   40
    .].[.].[   ].. α̣[].

ὣς[φά[τ]ο· τοὶ [δ(ὲ) ⏑—⏑⏑—⏑⏑—].[str.
φ[ρ]άζοντο .[⏑—⏑⏑—
ἵπ[π]ον με.[⏑—⏑⏑—×—⏑—×].[
ω .[.] ..φυλλοφ[ορ —×—⏑⏑—⏑⏑—   45
πυκινα[ῖ]ς πτερ[ύγεσσι ⏑—
κίρκον τανυσίπ[τερον —×—⏑—
—].ες ἀνεκράγον [—×—⏑⏑—
        ].τε.[

4 δ̱ Page || **16** εὐρύο̱[πα Page || **18** Lobel || **19** Lobel || **21** ῥηξάνορα̣ Lobel: ῥηξή– Π⁸ || **22** ὤτρ]υνε Page | φρ[α]cὶν Barrett post Lobel || **24** Lobel || **33** West || **34** Lobel || **35** West | ὅπως West: ο-πως Π⁸ || **37** Barrett || **38** cχ[West, [ύνωμε[ν Barrett | ἀ]εικ[ελί]ως Barrett || **39** West || **42–4** Barrett || **45–7** Lobel

...
...
...
...
...   5

...]in strength and spear
...]trusting. Come now
...
...] with curved bows
...   10
...] they were divided
...
...
...
...] of the Achaeans   15

...] the outcome...of the wide brows (Zeus?)
...
...] the end of the war
...] and his/their cunning minds
...   20
...] breaker of men
...] he exhorted on the great...in his/their heart(s)

...
...conspi]cuous also for wisdom
...   25
...]task
...
...
...
...   30
...

...
Dashing to the temple on the acropolis...
Trojans and their numerous allies
Come, do not obey the arguments...   35
...
...this sacred statue... destroy
Shamefully...
...let us respect...of the Lady
...   40
...

Thus he spoke; but they...
considered...
horse...
... leaf-bearing...   45
With impenetrable wings
A long-winged hawk...
They cried out...

The two concurring options over which the Trojans must decide are either the destruction of the statue, or its consecration to the goddess. In the *Odyssey*, the Trojans debate three options: break the horse open; roll it down the cliff; or take it inside the walls and offer it to Athena as a sacred object (*Od.* 8.506–507). The debate, however, takes place after the Trojan took the statue to the acropolis. In the *Iliou Persis* (arg. 1 *GEF*), some Trojans suggested setting it on fire, instead of cracking it open, thus maintaining the option of rolling it down the cliff.[62] The *Little Iliad* does not preserve any scene of the debate, although the *Tabula Iliaca Capitolina* depicts Cassandra's distress in front of the horse, which is being

---

62 See Finglass 2015c: 348, 352.

taken inside the walls, perhaps manifesting her opposition to the decision of the Trojans.[63]

In Stesichorus, the first option presented in the speech ongoing at line 7 and finishing before line 22 exhorts the Trojans not to lower their guard yet (lines 6–7). The identity of the speaker in Stesichorus is now lost, but he or she seems to be sceptical of an Achaean capitulation.[64] The reference to "his/their cunning minds" (line 19) emphasises the scepticism. Therefore, the strength and spear (βίαι τε καὶ αἰχμᾶι) in line 6, may indicate that the first speaker is proposing something close to the first option presented at the debate according to Demodocus' account (*Od.* 8.506): to use their weapons to break the wooden structure open and be ready to endure more battle.[65]

The final sense of the exhortation told of in line 22[66] may indicate that ὤτρ]υνε μέγαν φρ[α]cὶν̣ ἐν is not part of the first speaker's utterance, as Tsitsibakou-Vasalos[67] assumes, but rather a characterization made by the narrator about either the former or the next speaker. In the *Little Iliad*, Cassandra may have spoken against the decision, as we have seen, which makes her a suitable candidate as the first speaker of fr. 103 F. as Lloyd-Jones suggests.[68]

In the *Iliou Persis* (arg. 1c *GEF*), on the other hand, one of the opponents to the consecration of the statue seems to be Laocoon, who is killed along with one of his sons by two serpents.[69] In *Aeneid*, Laocoon intervenes trying to dissuade his audience to take the horse. After his desperate speech, he pierces the horse with a spear: "*validis ingentem viribus hastam | in latus inque feri curvam compagibus alvum contorsit*".[70] The reference to a spear finds a parallel in Stesichorus fr. 103.6 F. Virgil (*Aen.* 2.35) also names Capys as one of the proponents of

---

63 Cf. Verg. *Aen.* 2.246; Apollod. *Epit.* 5.17; cf. West 2013: 205.
64 Thus Page 1973: 50.
65 Similar phraseology appears in Homer to describe a battle scene in book 12 (12.135, 153) of the *Iliad*. The circumstance where we find the first parallel corresponds to a moment in the battle when the Trojans advance to the gates of the Achaean Wall in the hopes of making the Achaeans withdrawal to their ships. It was an illusory hope, since in the gates there were Polypoites and Leonteus who, trusting in their strength (12.135: χείρεccι πεποιθότες ἠδὲ βίηφιν), fought back. The ideas of misjudgement and of the inexorability of destiny underline the episode in the *Iliad* and the Stesichorean scene alike.
66 On which see Page 1973: 50 and Davies and Finglass 2014: 423.
67 Tsitsibakou-Vasalos 2011.
68 Lloyd-Jones 1980: 21.
69 Some accounts say that the serpents killed Laocoon's two sons (Verg. *Aen.* 2.199–227 and Apollod. *Epit.* 5.18). See West 2013: 231, n. 9 for other accounts where only one son his killed.
70 Verg. *Aen.* 2.50–52.

the dismissal of the Trojan horse, highlighting the wisdom and prudence of Capys and his supporters' view: "*at Capys, et quorum melior sententia menti*".

However, the main difficulty of the portent episode in the *Iliou Persis* is the location of the debate, since Arctinus' episode is likely to be taking place inside the walls of Troy.[71] The idea of movement conveyed in line 33 of the second speech (πρὸς ναὸν ἐς ἀκρ[όπο]λ[ι]ν cπεύδοντες) indicates that in Stesichorus the debate is taking place somewhere outside the walls, probably near the Achaean encampment, which means that the debate began in the moment when the Trojans found the horse and not after they took it inside.

The extent of the first speech is uncertain. It is not over until line 11 and not longer than 22. A reference to Zeus εὐρύο[πα (line 16) may imply the interference of the god to end the war (τέλος ... π(τ)]ολέμου [τε]λευτά̣ [ ], lines 16–17). τέλος so close to [τε]λευτά̣ emphasises an ambiguous sense of finality, since it draws attention to the power and final decision of Zeus: to end the war although not in the exact terms that the Trojans believe. Perhaps Zeus intervenes to change the direction of the debate, which apparently was favouring the option of destroying the horse. Zeus then would have taken action to bring the war to an end, by deceiving the Trojans and lead them to consecrate the statue to the goddess. Zeus thus seems to manipulate (πυκιν[άς] τε̣ φρ[έ]νας, line 19) the intervention of the next speaker who is introduced as someone who is known to excel in wisdom (]π̣ρεπε καὶ π̣ιν[υ]τᾶι, line 24). Of course, this quality attributed to the speaker would surely lead the Trojans to believe his words and take the horse inside the walls. The irony is more obvious when we see that the advice of the second speaker is based on the idea of piety.

The second speaker intervenes after a lacuna (lines 24–31). Schade suggests φι]λοπτόλ[εμ- in line 27, a common epithet used to refer to the Achaeans and Trojans in the *Iliad*.[72] Finglass supplements Ν]ε̣οπτόλ[εμ-, considering that a reference to the Greeks inside the horse at this point of the narrative, after the suggestion of destroying the horse somehow, would emphasise the critical moment experienced by the Greeks, where "Neoptolemus ... shows particular courage".[73] In favour of this option is also Davies and Finglass's assertion that the

---

[71] Proclus' summary does not explicitly state that the debate took place within the walls, as happens in the *Odyssey*. However, his text offers some hints regarding the location of the debate. Thus, κατακρημνίcαι indicates that there should have been some cliffs around where the debate takes places, and a setting in the plain or at the shore is unlikely to provide such topography. Furthermore, the feast that Proclus says to have followed the decision to consecrate the horse supports the setting within the walls. Thus Tsagalis *ap.* Finglass 2015c: 352.
[72] Schade 2003: 180.
[73] Davies and Finglass 2014: 423. *Od.* 11.523–532.

focus on the hidden warriors in the middle of the discussion of the Trojans would highlight the tension experienced by the Greeks.[74]

The second speaker addresses the Trojans and their allies (Τρῶες πολέες τ' ἐπίκ[ου]ροι, line 34) and dissuades them from believing in the previous arguments (ἔλθετε μη[δ]ὲ λόγο[ιc π]ειθώμεθ' ὅπως π[⌣⌣—×, line 35). The association of the word λόγο[ιc with the concept of deceptive arguments is also present in the *Theogony*,[75] and in Sophocles' *Philoctetes*,[76] where the repetition of λόγοιcιν and λέγων emphasises its victory over ψυχή.[77] The idea of stories as lies, or poets as tellers of lies, is an old Leitmotiv, evident since Hesiod or the *Odyssey* and latent in the debate over Stesichorus' *Palinode*.[78] Moreover, *Philoctetes'* central theme is "a complicated play of genuine pity and imposed deception".[79] The same variation between the idea of pity and deception is significant in Stesichorus' *Sack of Troy*.

The speaker advises instead the Trojans to accept the horse as a sacred statue (ἁγνὸν ἄ[γαλ]μα, line 37) and thus to offer it to the Lady or Queen, presumably Athena (ἀζώμεcθ' ἀνάc[cac, line 39). Destroying such a sacred object would be a shameful (ἀ]εικ[ελί]ως, line 38) treatment to the object and could provoke the god's anger.[80] The pious attitude of the speaker responds to his possible introduction as wise in line 24, if the poet is indeed referring to the second speaker[81] and not the first. The reverence of the goddess closes this speech marking the irony of the fact that the goddess to which the Trojans would demonstrate reverence is the same responsible for the building of the horse.

The Trojans must decide which option to accept (φ[ρ]άζοντο, line 42–43) when what seems to be an omen appears (lines 45–48). The content is uncertain. West suggests these lines describe a bird omen; Barrett is inclined to consider it as a simile illustrating the events.[82] Barrett supplements ὣ δ' [ἀ]πὸ in the beginning of line 18 and ψᾶ]ρες ἀνέκραγον [in line 48, citing Triphiodorus (247–279), a context which seems better applied to a moment of awe and fear

---

74 Davies and Finglass 2014: 423.
75 Thus West 1966 on *Th*. 26–28, 229.
76 S. *Ph*. 54–55 τὴν Φιλοκτήτου cε δεῖ | ψυχὴν ὅπως λόγοιcιν ἐκκλέψειc λέγων, "You must, in the course of your story as you tell it, allay suspicion in Philoctetes' mind" (trans. Ussher).
77 Thus Webster 1970: 72 *ad loc.*; Podlecki 1966: 244–245.
78 Cf. below 3.3; also, Sol. fr. 29 W.
79 Prauscello 2010: 209.
80 See Davies and Finglass 2014: 425 e.g. μᾶ]νιν δέ [τοι βαρειᾶ]ν expanding the suggestions of West 1969: 138. For such terms for divine anger, see Finglass on S. *Aj*. 654–656n.
81 Thus Page 1973: 50.
82 West 1969: 139.

when the Trojans find the horse, as Davies and Finglass note.[83] Page, considers it a simile, which completes the overall idea of these lines. The discussion among the Trojans did not obtain consensus. Hence, while some adorned the horse with garlands (φυλλοφ[ορ-, line 45),[84] others "flutter and shriek around the wooden horse like starlings finding a hawk in their company".[85] The scene would, therefore, describe the desperate reaction of the Trojans who believed in the first speaker. If Barrett and Page are right, the simile would emphasize discord among the Trojans, responding to line 11 and thus highlighting, somehow, the futility of the debate and Zeus' power of confusing wits, in lines 16–24. In the *Iliad*, the Trojans rarely obtain consensus in their assemblies; the choice of the king or the princes prevails in the vast majority of the scenes.[86] Even the wise counsel of Polydamas is frequently ignored.[87] The failure to listen to the good advice from the wisest of the Trojans (Antenor and Polydamas) has always appalling consequences for the Dardanids. The situation here is very similar.[88] Someone is advising a better course of action, that some of the Trojans, presumably those holding power, refuse to accept. The decision to take the horse inside seems, therefore, a resolution which did not hold consensus.

However, if we take this episode to be an omen, there is a further element to consider: the possible discord among the gods. If these lines describe a portent there is a chance that some god tried to dissuade the Trojans from taking the horse inside. West accepts Τρ]ῶες in line 48, and understood φυλλοφ[ορ-, line 45, not as a garland but as a bush. Hence the sense of the passage would be that the Trojans see a hawk coming out of a bush, which makes them burst in crying (ἀνέκραγον [, line 48). Davies and Finglass remark that a misinterpreted or ignored portent would fit the episode, since it would mirror the situation of the Trojans. Virgil includes the portent of the serpents in the same moment, when the Trojans have made their decision (*Aen.* 2.195–233).

The hypothesis that this passage is a portent that the Trojans ignored, and that the hawk, representing the hidden Achaeans, departs from the bush to attack another bird, symbolizing the Trojans caught by surprise, leads to the

---

[83] Davies and Finglass 2014: *ad loc.*
[84] Thus in Q.S. 12.434 and Triph. 316–317.
[85] Page 1973: 49.
[86] Elmer 2013: 132–145. Cf. e.g. *Il.* 7.357–364.
[87] E.g. *Il.* 12.231 and 18.285–313, with devastating consequences.
[88] Elmer 2013: 135 notes that when the Trojan "attempt to include the community in the decision-making process", the audience "has no part in actually deciding the outcome of the discussion" e.g. *Il.* 7.348, 368. Generally, he argues that the Trojan assemblies function more as a counsel for the king and princes rather than being an effective decisive body.

conclusion that there was some god trying to warn the Trojans of the menace the horse represents. This god is trying to act against what Zeus seems to have determined in lines 16–17, a desperate call to save the Trojans, perhaps.

However, gods are not sole agents in the development of the narrative. Fr. 104 F. seems to allude to the importance of the humans' role and decision during the events at Troy.

```
—⏑⏑—]. δ' ἐπώμοςε ϲεμ[ν ⏑⏑—×                    ep.
—⏖—⏑⏑—×]
—⏑⏑—×]εϲθ', ἐγὼν δ' αὐ
    —⏑⏑—⏑⏑—]
×—⏑—×—⏑—×—]γον εἴμειν            5
×—⏑⏑—⏑⏑—⏖—]..
    ×—⏑⏑—]...εϲαγυ

—⏑⏑—⏑⏑—]φαός ἀελίου [                            str.
×—⏑⏑—⏑⏑—]
×—⏖—⏑⏑—×]ᾳ . [κ]ατ' αἶϲαν [       10
    ] . [  ] ...εψ[
```

1 ϲεμν[ῶϲ West, Παλλ]άδ'... ϲεμν[ὰν Barrett || **10** ρ[Lobel, unde γ]άρ West | [κ]ατ' Lobel

... swore a false oath by ...

...

... you..., but I ...

...

... to be ...   5

...

...

... light of the sun ...

...

... fairly...   10

...

Comparing the general lines of Stesichorus' *Sack of Troy* with Virgil's *Aeneid*, West suggested that fr. 104 F. may be alluding to the decision over the horse,[89]

---

[89] West 1969: 139. Hornblower 2015: 351 suggests that this fragment is a reference to Epeius' father's perjury, which consisted in breaking an oath. Amphitryon gathers four allies among whom was Panopaeus. They all had to swear an oath according to which none of them should take possession of any sort of booty. Panopaeus broke this oath by retaining Lagaria. (Apollod. *Bibl.* 2.4.4–8 and also Hes. *Scut.* 15–27). Hornblower argues that "it is tempting to suppose that Stesichorus referred to this perjury in the opening of his *Sack of Troy* (...) If so, that would push

in which case the swearer of this false oath would be Sinon. In Virgil (*Aen.* 2.154–158), Sinon is left at Troy, as if abandoned by the Greeks, to persuade the Trojans of the votive purpose of the horse and encourage them to take the horse inside the wall. The earliest account including such a role for Sinon is present in the *Little Iliad*, where he intervenes in the debate of the Trojans and convinces them to take the horse as an offer to the goddess.[90] In the *Iliou Persis*, on the other hand, Sinon merely gives the sign to the Achaean army outside the horse, thus informing them that the horse is inside the walls of Troy.[91]

Fr. 104 F. may come from a speech where the Trojans realise that Sinon has been deceiving them and swearing false oaths.[92] Given the prominence of the debate scene, it seems likely that Stesichorus mentioned Sinon in terms closer to the *Little Iliad* then to the *Iliou Persis*. In any case, the reference in line 10 to 'destiny' or 'portion' may allude to the irreversible fate of the Trojans, to their miserable fortune, which would fit the moment when they disclose the Achaean stratagem and Sinon treachery. Tsitsibakou–Vasalos suggests that the second speech in fr. 103 F. would fit the character of Sinon, although the introduction of the second speaker as wise (fr. 103.24) seems rather ironic for a deceiver and a traitor.[93]

2.1.3 Divine abandonment (fr. 114 F.)

—⏑⏑—⏑⏑—]τ' ἐπικουρ[⏑⏑—   ant.
×—⏑⏑—⏑⏑—] ͜δαρ
×—⏓⏑—⏑⏑—×—]λιποῖϲα [

---

the motif of Epeius' cowardice – which goes hand-in-hand with his father's perjury – back to at least the sixth century" (Hornblower 2015: 351). However, we do not find in Stesichorus any allusion to the cowardice as punishment of Epeius, as is Callimachus (*Iamb.* 7 = fr. 197 Pfeiffer) or Lycophron (*Alex.* 932). On the contrary, as we have seen, Epeius is treated with sympathy, despite his menial job. If fr. 104.1 F. indeed refers to the swearing of a false oath as a justification for Epeius' punishment it is likely that it referred to the water-carrying and not to Epeius' supposed cowardice. The supplement by Barrett to line 1 – Παλλ]άδ'... ϲεμν[ὰν – presents similarities to fr. 100.10–12 F. This could suggest proximity between the two moments of the poem, supporting the possibility of having here a reference to Panopaeus' perjury and the consequent punishment of his son. However, there are other places in the *Sack of Troy* where the episode could fit.

90 Arg. 4c *GEF*.
91 Arg. 2a *GEF*.
92 Thus Davies and Finglass 2014: 427.
93 Thus Tsitsibakou-Vasalos 2011.

```
⏑–⏑–⏑–×–⏑–]ματακα[
×–⏑–⏑–]                                    5
×–⏑–⏑– γαι]αόχου
–⏑–⏑–]πίτνη πυ.[⏑–⏑–
    ×–⏑– –]

(×)–⏑– Δα]ναοὶ μεμ[αότ]ες ἔκθορον ἵ[π]π[ου        ep.
×–⏑ Ἐ]γνοσίδας γαιάοχος ἁγνὸς ε[–        10
×–⏑–]αρ Ἀπόλλων
–⏑–ἱ]αρὰν οὐδ' Ἄρταμις οὐδ' Ἀφροδίτα [
–⏓–⏑–×]
–⏑–⏑–] Τρώων π[ό]λιν Ζεὺς
  –⏑–⏑]ατων                               15
×–⏑–]ου Τρῶας .[×–⏑–]..μους
×–⏑–]ιν.μερ.[⏓–
  ×–⏑–]τοσα.[– –
```

6 West || **9** Δα]ναοὶ Lobel | μεμ[αότ]ες West et Führer | ἵ[π]π[ου West || **10** Lobel || **12** ἱ]αρὰν West || **14** π[ό]λιν West

    ...
    ...
... [she] leaving ...
    ...
    ...   5
... [of] the holder of the earth...
... falling ...
    ...

The Danaans eagerly leapt from the horse
the sacred, shaker of the earth, holder of the earth ...   10
... Apollo
... nor sacred Artemis, nor Aphrodite ...
...
Zeus ... the city of the Trojans ...
    ...   15
... Troy ...

Despite the reference to the Greeks leaping from the horse in line 9, fr. 114 F. must be part of a speech uttered by a Trojan recalling the moment. Such a short reference to the event by the narrator would be odd, since we expect more elaboration on the episode.[94] Furthermore, a discourse lamenting the misery that

---

[94] Thus Barrett *ap*. Page 1973: 65.

Troy is witnessing would fit the context. There would be several good opportunities for Stesichorus to display a lament over a city being burnt to ashes. One of these could be when the women of Troy are gathered, awaiting their fate (e.g. fr. 105 F.).

Line 3 refers to a female character. West suggested that this may be Cassandra, who leaves after failing to dissuade the Trojans from taking the statue to the city.[95] Davies and Finglass offer other options.[96] The character may be Helen, if Stesichorus had her trying to lure out the Greeks inside the horse, as she does in the *Odyssey* (4.274–289). Alternatively, the character may be a goddess abandoning the city, which would be appropriate given the context of the following lines (11–12) where the sense of divine abandonment is remarked on and which may be compared to Euripides' *Trojan Women*, when the chorus (857) and Hecuba (1281) say that it is of no use to pray for the gods.[97] This notion that the gods abandoned the Trojans to their inevitable fate, this sense of inexorability is emphasised by the many epithets attributed to Poseidon, perhaps reinforcing the sense that even him, of all gods, whose interest should be to defend the Trojans, departs and none of the other deities stayed behind to grant the city protection, nor Apollo, nor Artemis and not even Aphrodite. Spelman suggested that the emphasis on the catalogue of gods that deserted may have evoked sympathy towards the Trojans and Troy.[98] Moreover, the desertion of the gods stresses the brutality of the Achaean attack.

2.1.4 The death of Astyanax (frr. 107 and 116 F.)

In discussing the following fragments, I will use the *Tabula Iliaca Capitolina* to support my readings. However, this piece of evidence has met with some scepticism of some scholars who doubt that it presents a valid source for reconstructing Stesichorus' poem. I will address that issue in more detail when discussing one aspect of the *Iliou Persis* for which the *Tabula* is the sole surviving evidence: the escape of Aeneas to the west. For now, the *Tabula* will be used as a compar-

---

[95] West 1971: 263, citing Q. S. 12.580–585. Lloyd-Jones 1980: 21 suggests that she may have been the first speaker in fr. 103 F. In the *Little Iliad*, Cassandra may have attempted to persuade the Trojans to destroy the horse (cf. the depiction of the poem in *Tabula Iliaca Capitolina*, thus West 2013: 205). She has a similar role in Apollod. *epit.* 5.17; Verg. *Aen.* 2.246–250. Führer 1971: 253 supplements line 4]ματα Κα[c]cάνδρ–.
[96] Davies and Finglass 2014: 445.
[97] On the gods abandoning a fallen city cf. A. *Th.* 217–227.
[98] *Ap.* Davies and Finglass 2014: 446.

ative element to the information in the fragments. In the *Tabula Iliaca Capitolina*, Astyanax is first in the arms of Andromache (in the left part of Hector's tomb), but absent from the other depiction of Andromache at the right of Hector's tomb, which suggests that Talthybius was depicted in the former scene as he was coming to take Astyanax from Andromache.

We have seen above the recurrence of Astyanax and Priam's death in archaic art, presenting a version not attested in literary evidence: Astyanax used as a weapon to kill Priam. In fact, Astyanax's death, as appears in earlier accounts, does not take place at the same time as Priam's, although in many versions their killer is Neoptolemus. In most epic accounts, Astyanax dies by being thrown down the wall. This abhorrent scenario is present in the *Iliad* when Andromache imagines the possible end for her son, if his father dies in battle (*Il.* 24.732–738). The reference to the episode by Homer, however, suggests that the poet knew the story.

In the *Little Iliad*, Neoptolemus is the killer (fr. 29 *GEF*); in the *Iliou Persis* Odysseus performs this merciless act (fr. 3 *GEF* and Arg. 4). A scholium to *Andromache* (fr. 107 F.) remarks that Stesichorus referred to Astyanax's death but gives no further detail. However, a fragment within the scraps from the *Sack of Troy* could contain this episode:

```
x—⏑⏑—⏑ ἀϊcτ]ώcαc πόλ[ι]ν                            ant.
—⏑⏑—⏑⏑—x— τ]έκοc Αἰακιδᾶν
    x—⏑— —]

].[  ] περὶ ἄcτυ .. [⏑—x                             ep.
].αι. [.] c κατὰ φυ[                      5
x—⏑⏑—⏑⏑]εντα[]
—⏑⏑—⏑⏑— Cκ]αμάνδριον α[⏑⏑—x
—⏔—⏑⏑—x]
```

1 ἀϊcτ]ώcαc Führer | πόλ[ι]ν Lobel ‖ 2 τ]έκοc Lobel | vel – ίδαν Lobel ‖ 6 cιμό]εντα Diggle ‖ 7 cκ]αμάνδριον Lobel | ἀ[νθεμοέντα Führer, ἀ[κτάν Diggle, ἀ[cτυάνακτα Finglass

... [having destroyed] the city
... Aeacids' son
...

... around the city ...
...
...
... Scamandrios
...

This fragment (fr. 116 F.) describes events taking place presumably after the destruction of the city.⁹⁹ The son of the Aeacids is likely to be Neoptolemus. In line 7, Σκ]αμάνδριον led Diggle¹⁰⁰ to supplement line 6 with Σιμό]εντα suggesting, at this point, an allusion to the Iliadic reference to both rivers together.¹⁰¹ With the same imagery in mind, Führer suggested ἀ[νθεμοέντα in line 7, which would convey the idea of bloom and flowers, in deliberate contradiction to the scene of death which would have involved the sack of Troy.¹⁰² Tsitsibakou-Vasalos considers putting the epithet in line 6, hence ἀνθεμο]έντα.¹⁰³ This would emphasise the ambiguous potential of the epithet evident particularly in the *Odyssey* (12.159) where it 'qualifies the meadows of the Sirens', and, perhaps more significant to our present discussion, in the *Iliad* (2.459–468) where, "in a distinct metaphor, thousands of Greeks 'poured forward' in the meadow of flowery Scamander preparing for a long and deadly war".¹⁰⁴

However, given the presence of Neoptolemus in the previous line, line 7 might refer to Astyanax's alternative name: Scamandrios.¹⁰⁵ Davies and Finglass suggests the supplement Ἀ[cτυάνακτα after Scamandrios, thus providing Astyanax with an epithet. If these supplements are correct, this may be part of the episode of Astyanax's death, and his killer is the τ]έκος Αἰακίδαν: Neoptolemus, as in the *Little Iliad*. Davies and Finglass argue that the latter phrase enhances Neoptolemus' "status as the inheritor of Achilles' prowess".¹⁰⁶

The scholium to *Andromache* 10 (= fr. 107 F.) does not tell how Stesichorus imagined Astyanax's death, but implies that he did not portray the infant being thrown off the wall, as it ascribes that addition to *a* cyclic poet (Arctinus):

<οἳ δέ> φαcιν ὅτι <οὐκ ἔμελλεν> ὁ Εὐριπίδηc Ξάνθωι προcέχειν περὶ τῶν Τρωϊκῶν μύθων, τοῖc δὲ χρηcιμωτέροιc καὶ ἀξιοπιcτοτέροιc· Στηcίχορον μὲν γὰρ ἱcτορεῖν ὅτι τεθνήκοι καὶ τὸν τὴν Πέρcιδα cυντεταχότα κυκλικὸν ποιητὴν ὅτι καὶ ἀπὸ τοῦ τείχουc ῥιφθείη· ὧι ἠκολουθηκέναι Εὐριπίδην.

---

99 Führer 1977: 19 n. 192 suggested the supplement ἀϊcτ]ώcαc for fr. 116.1 and ἀϊcτ]ώcαντεc in fr. 120.14 F. Lobel 1971: 7 preferred the supplement ἀϊcτ]ώcαc to fr. 119.6 F.
100 Diggle 1990: 151.
101 Cf. e.g Hom. *Il*. 12.13–23.
102 Führer 1977: 19.
103 Tsitsibakou-Vasalos 2011.
104 Tsitsibakou-Vasalos 2011.
105 Thus Davies and Finglass 2014: 449 "Scamandrius is said to be Astyanax's real name in the *Iliad* (6.399–403). We might supply Ἀ]cτυάνακτα, which would make Σκ]αμάνδριον an epithet for him based on the Homeric passage".
106 Compare the use of Plesthenid to refer to Orestes in fr. 180 F., on which see 4.1.3.

<They say> that Euripides <is not likely to> have trusted in Xanthus, regarding the Trojan story, but rather in the more useful and trustworthy [poets]: for Stesichorus stated that he (sc. Astyanax) died, and the cyclic poet who composed the *Sack* added the that he was thrown from the wall; Euripides has followed him.

Perhaps Stesichorus wanted to spare the Trojan child this particularly horrific death for the sake of poetic variety. Or, as suggested by Davies and Finglass, Astyanax may have been thrown from the wall after being killed.[107] Be that as it may, what we do know is that in Stesichorus' version Astyanax dies, unlike what seems to have happened in Xanthus (*FGrHist* 765 F 21), and the author of this appalling killing is Neoptolemus, who is responsible for a number of other merciless acts of violence, such as Polyxena's sacrifice.

2.1.5 Polyxena's sacrifice (frr. 118 and 119 F.)

Among the papyri, two scraps may contain the episode of Polyxena's sacrifice. The story of the hateful end of the daughter of Priam and Hecuba is found in the epic *Iliou Persis* (arg. 4c *GEF*), although the author of the sacrifice is not specified. In the *Tabula Iliaca Capitolina*'s central panel Polyxena is portrayed twice. The first time she appears near Hecuba in the side facing towards the right of Hector's tomb. Odysseus is in the scene, perhaps to take Polyxena for the sacrifice. The second time she is depicted kneeling by the tomb of Achilles in the right of the panel, with her nude waist and arms bounded; Neoptolemus is about to perform the sacrifice: the same characters which appear in Euripides' accounts *Hecuba* and *Trojan Women*. Among Stesichorus' fragments, frr. 118 and 119 F. are likely to correspond to this episode.

```
×—⏑⏑—⏑⏑—×—⏑⏑]' Ἀκυ[⏑—                                    ep.
×—⏑⏑—⏑⏑—×]
—⏑⏑—⏑⏑—×—] θαλέας παρ[⏑—×
—⏖—⏑⏑—×]
—⏑⏑—⏑⏑—×]ραν Πολυξε[ν-              5
   —⏑⏑—⏑⏑—]
×—⏑—×—⏑—] τοτεχε[⏑—×
×—⏑⏑—⏑⏑—⏖]. νᾶρ
   ×—⏑⏑—⏑ δ]ρακοῖϲα

—⏑⏑—⏑⏑—⏑']χεν α[ἷ]ϲ ἀλόχ[οιϲ           10              str.
```

---

[107] Davies and Finglass 2014: 438–439.

desunt versus aliquot

```
        ]  [
        ]  [
        ]  [
        ]   .[
        ]  [
```
'15'

5 Πολυξέ[ν– Lobel, πολυξε[νώτατ– Finglass || **9** Lobel || **10** Lobel

...
...
... (cheering) ...
...
... Polyxena ...   5
...
...
...
... (she) seeing / leaving ...

... wives ...   10

In line 5 of fr. 118 F. the papyrus reads πολυξε[. Finglass's suggestion for πολυξε[νώτατος calls attention for the uncertainty of this fragment's theme. This supplement alludes to a context of feasting and hospitality, which could refer to some feasting scene of the Trojans before the Greeks' leap from the horse, or maybe recalling Paris' wrongdoing at Sparta. Lobel supplements Πολυξέ[να.[108] A reference to Polyxena would fit the context of sacrifice especially considering the reference to the tomb of Achilles in line 3 of fr. 119 F. as West suggested.[109] Lobel also supplemented line 9 δ]ρακοῖσα, which reinforces the female presence at the scene.

Furthermore, Lobel's supplement gives a highly dramatic scene of confrontation where victim and assailant could be facing each other. Polyxena's courage in Euripides' *Hecuba* (342–378 and 402–443) makes an extraordinary impression because she goes willingly to her death, whereas her mother stays

---

108 Lobel 1971: 6.
109 West 1971: 264.

behind watching her daughter being taken to the sacrifice.¹¹⁰ Polyxena chooses death over slavery, and this heroic deed motivates pity and admiration for the character on the part of both the audience and the Achaean characters. The shame of their actions could thus be what makes Odysseus stand in a pensive pose in the *Tabula* when Polyxena is sacrificed.¹¹¹

The scene in the *Tabula* shows that Polyxena is taken to the sacrifice from among the Trojan Women, which suggests that in Stesichorus too, the scene of the gathering of the prisoners may have had some significance. It may then be that the reference to the wives in line 10 does not refer to Priam's wives as Lobel suggests, but rather to the Trojan wives, now prisoners of war, about to be allocated as servants or concubines to a Greek master. In that sense, the reference to Medusa in fr. 110 F. may have appeared in a description or a scene of the Trojan women. Polygnotus includes Medusa in the Cnidian Lesche at Delphi, and Apollodorus in his catalogue of Priam's daughters says that Medusa is one of Priam's daughters from a wife other than Hecuba.¹¹²

We cannot determine whether Stesichorus dealt with the same dramatic features of the sacrifice of Polyxena and Astyanax as Euripides. However, the deaths of these two elements of Trojan offspring certainly conveyed an idea of Greek reckless deeds during the sack. Hecuba would have been particularly vulnerable to such suffering as a mother and a queen who witnesses the destruction of her city and the death of so many of her loved ones. It would have been interesting the see the parallels of Polyxena's sacrifice and Iphigenia's as described in the *Oresteia* (fr. 178 F.). Both maidens are sacrificed for the sake of the army, one at the beginning of the expedition, the other at the end of it. Both are innocent victims of the often capricious nature of heroes in their quest for glory. Polyxena is sacrificed for Achilles at his tomb, as it is suggested by West who associates fr. 118 with the reference to ἥ]ρως Ἀχιλλευ[in fr. 119.3 F., and as it happens in most of the accounts.¹¹³

Polyxena's sacrifice would have certainly be one of the most dramatic scenes in the sack. Her appearance twice in the *Tabula* may suggest that the episode of her being taken to the tomb and her sacrifice by Neoptolemus was treated with some detail. The episode of the sacrifice in Euripides' *Hecuba* 557–570 and the character of Polyxena herself deserved close attention, emphasising

---

110 Due 2006: 121.
111 Thus Davies and Finglass 2014: 432.
112 On the Cnidian Lesche see Paus. 10.27.1, Stansbury-O'Donnell 1989: 210; Apollod. *Bibl.* 3.12.5; see also Hyg. *Fab.* 90.6.
113 West 1971: 264.

her almost warlike courage despite her vulnerable condition. The disrobing of her bust is more an act of bravery, almost like a warrior who gives his breast to the spear, than an intended erotic appeal, so much so that her fallen body conceals her nudity.[114] Although no evidence survived of Stesichorus' treatment of the sacrifice of Polyxena, we do have some information regarding what may have been a similar episode of female vulnerability and exposure: Helen's near-stoning.

2.1.6 The recovery of Helen (frr. 106, 113, and 115 F.)

Stesichorus' account provides a unique version of the recovery of Helen.[115] In his *Sack of Troy*, Helen was about to be stoned by the army, but they drop the stones as soon as they see her (fr. 106 F.):

ἆρα εἰc τὸ τῆc Ἑλένηc κάλλοc βλέψαντεc οὐκ ἐχρήcαντο τοῖc ξίφεcιν; οἷόν το καὶ Cτηcίχοροc ὑπογράφει περὶ τῶν καταλεύειν αὐτὴν μελλόντων. φηcὶ γὰρ ἅμα τῶι τὴν ὄψιν αὐτῆc ἰδεῖν αὐτοὺc ἀφεῖναι τοὺc λίθουc ἐπὶ τὴν γῆν.

That is, after contemplating Helen's beauty they could not use their swords? Stesichorus indicates something similar about those who are assigned to stone her: he says that as soon as they saw her appearance, they dropped the stones on the ground.

The scene implies a public gathering involving the whole, or at least a significant part of the Greek army, in a quasi-judicial event of public lynching of the very reason why the war was fought over. In tragedy, we find arguable allusions to the episode in Euripides' *Trojan Women* 1039–1041 and more vaguely in *Orestes* 53–60.[116] However, in neither of these references is Helen about to be stoned to death. The more traditional version of Helen's recovery presents a more intimate encounter between husband and wife. The summary of the *Iliou Persis* says only that Menelaus took Helen to the ships (arg. 2 *GEF*). In the *Little Iliad* (fr. 28 *GEF*) and Ibycus (fr. 296 *PMGF*) Menelaus approaches Helen to kill her but drops his sword when he sees her. Ibycus' version provides more details, saying that Helen took refuge in the temple of Aphrodite and speaks from there to

---

114 Loraux 1987: 60; Finglass 2018a: 149.
115 In Lycophron's *Alexandra* 314–334 there is a prophecy of stoning in Thrace. In 1187 it seems Cassandra prophecises her stoning again, but this time it is Odysseus and the army that perform the attack. The inconsistency cannot be explained, cf. Hornblower 2015: *ad loc.*
116 Finglass 2018a: 147–149.

Menelaus. Euripides' *Andromache* 627–631 recalls the episode but adds the detail of Helen's exposed breast.

The same scene depicting the encounter between Helen and Menelaus recurs in Greek art from the seventh century.[117] It is progressively more detailed with some vases including other characters.[118] This tendency increases from the first half of the fifth century with Aphrodite and Eros featuring in some vases.[119] The vast majority of the depictions of Helen's rescue in art emphasises the couple, particularly, Menelaus' reaction.[120] The Hellenistic and Roman period tended to maintain the tradition.[121] Conversely, no iconographic evidence survives of Helen's near-stoning.

The effects of Helen's appearance on the community are noted since the *Iliad*, where the sight of her causes awe, amazement, and delight so overwhelming that it justifies the war to be fought over her. This verdict is uttered not by Paris, to whom such a remark would be of interest, but by those from whom one expects wise advice, the elders (3.154–160), and it allows the war to continue until the eventual sack of the city. Stesichorus' scene introduces a similar notion but with traces of irony: the Greek army (not the revengeful husband alone) are about to execute the person for whom they fought the war. The scholium which reports Helen's near-stoning is brief in its description, so we do not know exactly when the army dropped the stones. Was it at her approach? Highly unlikely

---

117 Buxton 1982: 46; Cf. Kahil 1988.

118 See, Krauskopf 1988: §§ 210–249). Krauskopf displays evidence attesting the different versions of the encounter of the couple. Hence, we find Menelaus threatening Helen but does not take her (§ 210–234) and Menelaus pursuing Helen with his sword in his hand both alone (only the couple represented § 235–242) and in the presence of other characters (§ 243–259).

119 E.g. an Attic red-figure crater (Louvre G424) from c. 450–440 presents Aphrodite at the moment of the encounter accompanied by a winged Eros. A red-figure oenochoe (Vatican H. 525) from c. 430–425 shows Menelaus chasing Helen who runs towards the temple of Athena. Aphrodite stands before him, and above her is, again, the winged Eros. Persuasion also figures on this pot. Although Persuasion is often associated with Aphrodite and erotic seduction, its presence in the pot may perhaps allude to Helen's attempt to softened Menelaus' anger with her rhetoric, as appears in Euripides' *Tro.* 896–1059.

120 §§ 210–372; Menelaus dropping his sword after seeing Helen (§§ 260–277); Uncertain gesture by Menelaus (§§ 278–283); Menelaus with a spear instead of a sword (§§ 284–289). Then the author presents the catalogue of the scenes allegedly deriving from the epic *Iliou Persis* by Arctinus. First, Menelaus taking Helen by the arm (§§ 291–314; Icard–Gianolio 2009: § add.6), a warrior grabbing a woman (§§ 294–305, 320–336), a warrior does not touch the woman (§§ 337–357); Helen seeks refuge in statues of the gods (§§ 358–372, the similarity of this scene to the pursuit of Cassandra by Ajax make the attribution of some evidence uncertain, § 372; see also Icard-Gianolio 2009: § add.7).

121 Krauskopf 1988: § 362a–b, 370–371. For the depiction of Eros in Roman reliefs see § 232–234.

since the tension of the scene would be missed by such a quick reaction. Did Helen tried to persuade the army with her rhetoric? One expects that she would present her arguments to the husband, as she does in in the *Trojan Women* (895–1032), not to the whole army. Or did she, in a desperate act, exposed her naked body in a last attempt to disarm the army, as happens in other accounts with Menelaus? Such a scene would emphasise the gravity of her situation which calls for desperate measures, shameful though they may be. However, the breast exposure in distressful moments recalls the pleas of Hecuba in the *Iliad* and Callirhoe in the *Geryoneis* (frr. 16–17 F.) to their sons. The allusion is striking, for in these cases, their desperate act is intended to save the lives of their children, not (at least directly) their own. The irony would be even more marked since it emphasises Helen's ego; an ego present even at the most inappropriate times, however persuasive her concern may be. Nevertheless, the reference to the child in the context of disrobing would not be out of place, so perhaps we should not promptly exclude the hypothesis that Helen addressed the army, while exposing her breasts, particularly when the subject is her longing for her daughter. This passage (fr. 113.13 F.) preserves an interesting adjective that may be connected to Helen and her presence at Troy:

```
—⏑—⏑] αἶψα [—⏑—⏑—×                              ep.
—⚌—⏑ ἐ]ναργές
—⏑—].ἐτύμως αιθ.[—⏑—×
    —⏑ ἀ]μιόνους
×—⏑]υραν πρωπε[—×—⏑—×                    5
×—⏑ κ]υπρογενὴς α[(⏑)—
×—] ἁλιπόρφυρον ἀγν[—

—⏑⏑]αιμεν ἐγὼν λέγω [—⏑⏑—                      str.
×—⏑].ι ἀθανάτοι-
   ϲιν εἴκε]λον Ἑρμιόναν τ.[—⏑—×           10
—⏑⏑]..ων ποθέω νύκτ[—⏑⏑—⏑⏑—
×—⏑—].λοπόδαν
×—⏑]ν ὑφαρπάγιμον [—×—⏑—
—⏑⏑—].ρομέναν κνακα[⏑⏑—⏑⏑—
    ×—⏑—]τα                                             15

—⏑⏑— κ]ορυφαῖϲι νάπαιϲ[(ί) τε                  ant.
×—⏑]ων ϲτυγερόν
×—⏑]δα παῖδα φίλον.[×—⏑—×
—⏑⏑—].ο λέγω μηδ[—⏑⏑—⏑⏑—
    ×—⏑]ῳ..ρο..πω[[ι]][                            20
×—⏑]οντο γένοιτ'.[×—⏑—
       ].[
```

2 Lobel || **4** West   post   Lobel || **6** Lobel || **9–10** ἀθανάτοι[cιν εἴκε]λον Page || **16** κ] Lobel | [(ἰ) τε Daly

...immediately...
... clear...
... truly...
... mules...
...   5
... born in Cyprus...
... holy sea-purple ...

... I say...
... (resembling of the?) immortals...
... for Hermione...   10
I long night...
... with her ... foot...
... snatched in secret...
... tawny...
...   15

... in the peaks and glens...
... abominable...
... dear child...
... I say, nor...
...   20
... might happen...

Lines 8–11 lead the reader to suppose that the speaker is Helen, but the next few lines suggest that this may not be the case. παίδα φίλον (line 18) refers to a male child, and no male child is ascribed to Helen. This led scholars to question the place of the fragment within the wider context of the *Sack of Troy*. Page suggests an alternative hypothesis for the fragment, relating it to the abduction of Persephone. 'Hermione' may signify the Argolid town from where Hades is said to have taken Persephone, or as Hesychius tells us, Hermione, may, in fact, denote an alternative name for either Demeter or Persephone at Himera.[122] Moreover, the reference to κνακα[in line 14 and the epithet αἰγ]λοπόδαν in line 12 would suit a reference to the abduction of Persephone. But where would an episode concerning Persephone fit in the context of the poem? In spite of the difficulties, Page's suggestion has some appeal particularly regarding the focus on the language of separation with ὑφαρπάγιμον in line 13, a compound of ἁρπάζω, common in the narratives of abduction and recurrent in the *Homeric Hymn to Deme-*

---

[122] Page 1973: 56. Hsch. ε 5957.

ter (3, 19, 82). The same hymn tells how Demeter reacts after fruitless attempts to recover her daughter, saying that she spent her days "consumed with longing for her daughter" (πόθωι μινύθουσα βαθυζώνοιο θυγατρός).

This idea of Demeter longing for her daughter is similar to Ἑρμιόναν... ποθέω of line 10 and 11 of fr. 113 F. Another parallel for a similar construction regarding Helen and Hermione is found is Triphiodorus. In his poem, Athena scolds Helen after she tries to deceive the Greek soldiers, hidden in the wooden horse, to reveal themselves and their trick, by imitating their wives' voices, as in *Odyssey* 4.280–289. Athena then asks Helen when her treason would ever end. The goddess not only remarks on Helen's deceiving action and very questionable repute; she wonders about Helen's maternal ability and asks if she does not long for her daughter (οὐδὲ θύγατρα | Ἑρμιόνην ποθέεις; Triph. 493–494). In the passage, Athena blames Helen for her extra-marital affair and for her abandonment of both her husband and her daughter. The goddess contests Helen' conduct in moral (πόθος) and even emotional terms (ποθέεις).

The accusation that Helen prefers a love affair over her own daughter has a strong emotional effect in the context of Athena's reprimand, especially given that it is Athena who confronts Helen with her failure as a mother in terms perhaps similar to lines 10 and 11 of Stesichorus' fr. 113 F. However, in Stesichorus it is Helen herself that speaks, saying that she longs for Hermione (the conjecture of 'day and night' in line 11 would make the passage still more emphatic and emotional). If this is indeed the case, line 13 ὑφαρπάγιμον may then refer to Helen's abduction by Paris, which if we consider Page's supplement for line 20 προλ[ίπω suggests active abandonment, an idea consistent with Tyndareus' curse upon his daughters "deserters of husbands" (λιπεσάνορας, fr. 85 F.). However, the closest parallel for the episode is in the *Odyssey*, when Helen remembers her joy when she realised that the Greeks were to capture Troy. She blames Aphrodite for having taken her from home, and for making her abandon her daughter (*Od.* 4.259–264).

But to whom would Helen address these words? Lines 1–3 suggest tension. The reference to the abduction/elopement of Helen is more appropriate in a scene of the encounter with Menelaus, but it would fit the context of the near-stoning if it accompanied the exposure of the breasts. She attempts to convince the army that she was taken to Troy against her will. On the other hand, if Menelaus is the addressee, the effect is even more poignant. The reference to their daughter would emphasise their marriage ties, recall their life as a couple, and suit a context where the couple finally meet.

Another fragment that suggests an encounter between Helen and Menelaus is fragment 115 F. Despite its mutilated condition, many scholars have provided enlightening supplements. If we accept Barrett's supplement for line 3 giving the interrogative adverb π]ῶϲ,[123] we may believe with West that the speaker is Helen and the addressee Menelaus:

ἱμερτὸν πρ[⌣⌣—×   ep.
ὧδε δέ νιν .[⌣⌣—×—⌣—×
  π]ῶϲ ἀγαπαζ[⌣⌣—
δ]υϲώνυμοϲ [×—⌣—×—⌣—×
×]ωδε τεκ[—⌣⌣—⌣⌣—   5
×].χοιϲ.[⌣⌣—⌣⌣— —

ὣϲ φά]το· τὰν]δ(ὲ)⌣—⌣⌣—⌣⌣—   str.
      ] ..[

3 Barrett || **4** Lobel || **7** Barrett

desirable...
Thus she addressed ...
"How ... love ...
... of ill repute
...   5
     ..."

Thus she spoke...

In the *Iliad* and the *Odyssey*, Helen is frequently self-loathing in similar terms to those in fr. 115 F., particularly when facing a Trojan audience.[124] She speaks relentlessly about herself and laments her fame. However, it is unlikely to imagine Helen addressing the Trojans at this stage. In Helen's words one can sense regret. A witness of the suffering the war brought to both Achaeans and Trojans, the Helen from the *Odyssey* continues to blame herself, as she does when she first addresses Telemachus.[125] In Stesichorus, she seems to have displayed a

---

123 *Ap.* West 1969: 141.
124 When speaking to Priam (*Il.* 3.172–176, 180), when speaking to or about Hector (4.344–356, 19.325, 24.775).
125 *Od.* 4.141–146. The word used by Helen to describe herself in this passage of the *Odyssey* is κυνῶπιϲ. This word is also used in the *Iliad* by Hephaestus (18.394–397) when the god recalls his mother's attempt to hide him embarrassed by his disability. In the *Odyssey*, the poet applies this adjective to another situation, much closer to the case of Helen: infidelity. In book 8, the same Hephaestus repeats the same word to insult his wife in the moment when he proves the love shared by Aphrodite and Ares (*Od.* 8.317–320). κυνῶπιϲ also characterizes Clytemnestra when Agamemnon narrates to Odysseus the events that took place in Mycenae when he re-

similar approach. The *exemplum* put forward by Slings provides a useful insight on what may have been Helen's rhetoric. For lines 3–4, he suggests *exempli gratia* the following reconstruction: πῶc ἀγαπάζ[εαι, ἃ | δ]υcώνυμοc [πάντεccιν ἀνθρώποιcίν εἰμι;, "How can you love me, I who am of ill repute among all people?".[126] According to this example, Helen seems humbled and incredulous at Menelaus' perseverant love.

In the Homeric poems, this sort of insult is used to refer to the infidelity of wives and to situations of negligence. These are the terms by which Helen defines herself in Stesichorus' *Sack of Troy*, as she recognizes the ill repute of her name: δ]υcώνυμοc.[127] Such a scene can take place either during or after the sack, which facilitates the identification of the addressee as Menelaus. This encounter would have followed the episode of Helen's near-stoning in fr. 106 F., since it implied that someone has shown affection towards Helen.

The existence of such encounter calls into question the scepticism of some scholars regarding the authenticity of the depiction of Stesichorus' poem in the *Tabula Iliaca Capitolina*, a calcite tablet found in a villa close to Bovillae and dated roughly to the last quarter of the first century.[128] According to these scholars, the *Tabula* should not be taken in consideration for the study of Stesichorus' *Sack of Troy*, because of the inconsistencies between the scenes depicted and the evidence from the fragments, and the absence of other sources attesting the Stesichorean origin of the story of Aeneas in the west as depicted in the *Tabula*. The latter subject will be discussed below. We shall now focus on the first objection presented by Horsfall: the inconsistency between image and text, especially in the scene of Helen and Menelaus.[129]

In the *Tabula Iliaca Capitolina*, the scene featuring Helen is nothing like a near-stoning. On the right of the central panel, we find a temple of Aphrodite (labelled), on the left of which stands a warrior holding a sword in his right hand and grabbing a woman's hair as if about to stab her in the neck. Neither of these characters is identified by name, but we can say with some degree of cer-

---

turned home and the circumstances of his humiliating death (*Od.* 11.423–426). For canine imagery characterizing Helen's mischievous behaviour see Franco 2014: 103–108.

126 Slings 1994: 105. Translation by Davies and Finglass 2014: 448.
127 Schade 2003: 210 indicates two occurrences of this adjective in the *Iliad*: first, when Priam refers to the "accursed sons of the Achaeans" (*Il.* 6.255 ἦ μάλα δὴ τείρουcι δυcώνυμοι υἷεc Ἀχαιῶν); secondly, in a narrative moment describing the "dark-named destiny" (12.116 πρόcθεν γάρ μιν μοῖρα δυcώνυμοc ἀμφεκάλυψεν/ἔγχεϊ Ἰδομενῆοc ἀγαυοῦ). In both circumstances the adjective emphasises the ill-repute of what they refer to.
128 For a discussion on the date of the *Tabula*, see Sadurska 1964: 32.
129 Horsfall 1979: 41.

tainty that the woman represented is Helen, since the scene resembles the episodes of Helen's rescue in other accounts, as seen above. This leads to the identification of the man: Menelaus. Instead of showing a host of warriors running after Helen as indicates fr. 106 F., there is a single man who carries a sword, not stones. Now, artistic depictions of Helen's recovery always represent her with Menelaus, sometimes accompanied by goddesses. In none is he carrying a stone. We have seen above that Stesichorus almost certainly included the encounter of Helen and Menelaus, although not exactly in the same manner as in other accounts or in the artistic evidence. The fact that Helen was about to be stoned to death by the army does not exclude the existence of an episode which concentrates on the encounter of the couple. Moreover, in the impossibility, for artistic and aesthetic reasons, to depict the scene as told in Stesichorus, the sculptor may well have chosen Menelaus to represent in a single, concise character, the army of the Achaeans and their vulnerability to the beauty of Helen.[130] It seems, therefore, safe to assume that the variation we have in the *Tabula* is justified by the artistic tradition and the dynamic of the panel itself. Given the popularity of the encounter between husband and wife in Greek and Roman art, and the absence of parallels for the depictions of Helen's near-stoning, the sculptor must have followed the iconographic tradition of the scene.

Moreover, this is not the only case where the scenes of the *Tabula* differ from the literary accounts. For example, in the first horizontal panel of the *Tabula*, which depicts the first books of the *Iliad*, the episode corresponding to the Achaean assembly in book one depicts a slightly different version from the one in the text.[131] In it, Agamemnon seems to be holding his sword, a detail that does not occur in the *Iliad*, but which is common in art.[132] This is one example of the need of the artists to deviate from literary accuracy to convey more effectively the emotions of particularly tense moments. Agamemnon holds his sword to convey what in the literary source is a verbal threat. The other 'inaccuracy' of the depiction of the *Iliad* occurs in the panel concerning book 18 of the *Iliad*, which depicts Hephaestus forging the armour for Achilles. In the *Tabula*, Hephaestus is accompanied by three figures, whereas in the *Iliad* he is alone. In Greek art, Hephaestus is usually depicted working alone.[133]

---

130 Thus Ercoles 2018: 8.
131 Valenzuela-Montenegro 2004: 393–395.
132 See Krauskopf and Touchefeu 1988: §§ 48–51, 69 for iconography and Davies and Finglass 2014: 429 for bibliography.
133 There is only one example in Greek art depicting Hephaestus with Satyrs, not Cyclopes as helpers (Hermary and Jacquemin 1988: § 15). On the depiction of the *Tabula* see Valenzuela-Montenegro 2004: 66–69, 386.

Therefore, the differences between the literary source and its artistic counterpart can be explained by the needs of art that demand a slight alteration of the episodes as presented in the poems and by the traditional depiction of certain scenes prolific in the plastic arts which would help the identification of a certain scene in its context.[134] It facilitates the identification of the scene to the viewer if the depiction is familiar. And it does not contradict the poem, since it featured the encounter between husband and wife.

Despite all the suffering Helen caused, she survives. The reason that saves Helen from the army is the same that brought her to Troy: the appalling effect of her looks. It is because of her appearance that she is taken to Troy, and thanks to it she returns to Sparta alive. Her beauty is both her doom and her salvation. Her looks can cause both violence and restraint. Her beauty can even buy Menelaus' love back.

2.1.7 Hecuba's rescue (frr. 108 and 109 F.)

Another character who survives the sack of Troy is, remarkably, Hecuba who is spared a more dishonourable fate thanks to the intervention of Apollo. Hecuba witnesses the sack of her city, the death of her husband, her children, and grandchildren, but contrary to what happens in the other versions of the myth, in Stesichorus her end is not one of captivity, nor death during the sack.

The fate of the Trojan Queen received little attention in the epic accounts. Homer does not mention it, and the fragments of the Epic Cycle preserve no information on the subject. Only in Euripides' *Trojan Women* and *Hecuba* do we find a treatment of Hecuba's destiny. In both plays, Hecuba is given to a Greek as a slave: in the *Trojan Women* to Odysseus, in *Hecuba* to Agamemnon. However, in neither of these plays does Hecuba lives on as a slave, since she dies before reaching Greece.

In *Hecuba*, Polymestor, already blind because of the Queen's revenge for Polydorus' death, announces Hecuba's metamorphosis into a dog and her death by drowning after leaping from the mast of the boat in which she embarked. Her

---

[134] Petrain 2014: 101 argues that the manner in which the poems are presented influences the extent to which the sculptor is free to manipulate the chronological order of the events in the poem. The *Iliad* which is presented in bands is less prone to modification than the Stesichorean depiction in a panel. This gives the sculptor more freedom to alter some details concerning some episode to maintain the purpose of his task, to produce a work of art (cf. Davies and Finglass 2014: 432). For an analysis of the central panel structural organization and its implication for the organization of the narrative see also Brilliant 1984: 15–20, 53–89.

grave, *cynosema*, "the tomb of the dog", will become a landmark for sailors (*Hec.* 1229–1243). Although this story appears for the first time in Euripides, Mossman is reluctant to believe that it is Euripides' innovation and prefers to see in it a hint at a local myth of the Chersonese to which the Athenians had access through their influence in the area.[135] We have no means to prove the precedence of the version. However, stories of metamorphosis as consequences for exacerbated grief are not rare in Greek myth. The metamorphosis of Hecuba into a dog in Euripides' play materialises the effects of the incommensurable pain experienced by the Queen which highest point surpasses the scale of human endurance.[136] This is particularly evident when a mother witnesses the suffering, or even the killing of her children,[137] as happens, for example, with Lamia, a character which Stesichorus mentions in his *Scylla* (fr. 182 F.), precisely the context of her offspring.[138]

In the *Trojan Women*, her fate is referred briefly by Cassandra, who says that Apollo had told Cassandra that Hecuba must die in the vicinity of Troy (427–431). The allusion to Apollo at this point connected to the fate of Hecuba is revealing and it may indicate that Euripides is alluding to some pre-existing story according to which Apollo is somehow involved in the matter of Hecuba's fate, as he is in Stesichorus' account. Euripides mentioned a possible role of Apollo in such context and chose not to have the god intervening to save Hecuba.[139] Perhaps the tragedian decided to explicitly deviate from another source, namely from Stesichorus.

Pausanias tells us that in Stesichorus Hecuba did not embark on the ships of the Greeks but was instead taken to Lycia (fr. 109 F.):

ἐc δὲ Ἑκάβην Cτηcίχοροc ἐν Ἰλίου Πέρcιδι ἐποίηcεν ἐc Λυκίαν ὑπὸ Ἀπόλλωνοc αὐτὴν κομιcθῆναι.

As to Hecuba, Stesichorus said in the *Sack of Troy* that she was carried to Lycia by Apollo.

The first problem with this piece of information is that it does not reveal if Hecuba is alive when Apollo takes her to Lycia.[140] The quotation comes from a part

---

135 Mossman 1995: 35 with n. 39.
136 Thus Fialho 2012: 177, 182; Silva 2005a: 95; Carson 2006: 90.
137 Johnston 1999: 161–199.
138 Lamia was too a Queen (Libyan) who was compelled by Hera to kill her own children; as a result, she was disfigured by grief. Cf. E. fr. 472m *TrGF*).
139 Thus Mossman 1995: 36.
140 Hecuba is found twice in the *Tabula*, one inside the walls, where she is taken away from Priam (about to be killed) and then outside the walls seated next to the other enslaved, where

of Pausanias' description of the Cnidian Lesches (10.27.2) where he is cataloguing the corpses of the Trojans. Moreover, Apollo rescuing someone from Troy and arranging their translation to Lycia is reminiscent of the episode of Sarpedon in the *Iliad* (16.666–683), where his corpse is taken from the battlefield, bathed and anointed by Apollo, and transported to Lycia for the burial by Sleep and Death.

If Hecuba is dead when Apollo takes her, the version of the *Trojan Women* has here a precedent. Although not saving the Queen of Troy, Apollo would, nevertheless, intervene, thus allowing her a respected burial, a restored dignity. However, as Stansbury-O'Donnell notes, Hecuba is mentioned nowhere else in Pausanias' account, so the reference to Stesichorus may be Pausanias' explanation for her absence,[141] which would therefore imply perhaps that she is taken by Apollo alive.

In many other occasions gods intervene on behalf of their protégées. Pausanias mentions a tradition according to which Creusa, Aeneas' wife, was rescued from Troy by Aphrodite to prevent her from a life of slavery.[142] Laodice, one of Priam's daughters, is miraculously swallowed by the earth at the moment of the sack.[143] In Euripides' *Orestes*, Helen mysteriously disappears from the chamber when she is about to be killed.

Among Stesichorus' fragments, we have further examples of divine intervention at critical moments. Iphigenia is rescued by Artemis in the last moment (fr. 178 F.) and Helen is taken to Egypt, tricking Paris into believing that he was bringing Helen to Troy (fr. 91b F.).[144] Moreover, in Stesichorus' *Sack of Troy* Apollo was said to be the father of Hector (fr. 108 F.).[145] In the *Iliad*, the bond between the god and Hector is evident: he acts on behalf of the Trojan prince eight times.[146] Hence, the extension of this bond into parentage would hardly

---

she is represented with Polyxena, about to be taken to the sacrifice which is depicted in the other side of the tablet, in the tomb of Achilles. In no instances does the tablet depict Apollo's rescue of Hecuba, but as Davies and Finglass 2014: 433–434 point out, Stesichorus may have made Hecuba witness her daughter's sacrifice before being taken by Apollo to Lycia. Anyway, the version does not contradict the idea that Apollo came for Hecuba.

141 Stansbury O' Donnell 1989: 211 with n. 30.
142 Paus. 10.26.1, cf. Heinze 1994: 62 n. 95.
143 Apollod. *Epit.* 5.25, Lyc. *Alex.* 314–318. See Hornblower 2015: 189.
144 On which see below 3.3 and 4.1.2.
145 The scholium to Lycophron which transmits this piece of information does not indicate the poem, but since it fits the context of the *Sack of Troy* and provides a possible explanation for the intervention of Apollo on behalf of Hecuba, it is likely to be part of the poem.
146 7.271–272, 15.236–262, 21.599–22.20, 22.202–204, 23.188–191, 24.18–54.

sound odd and is in fact adopted in later accounts by Euphorion, Alexander Aetolus and Lycophron.[147] The fact that Apollo fathers Hector in the Stesichorean account supports the hypothesis of Apollo's intervention to rescue Hecuba rather than simply providing her a decent burial. Moreover, such an episode would provide a response to the idea expressed in fr. 114 F. that the gods have abandoned Troy. Unable to defend their protégés in a more useful manner, the gods had to find other ways to comfort the Trojans after the sack of the city. Therefore, the likeliest moment for Apollo's intervention is in a highly emotional tense moment for Hecuba, perhaps right before the sacrifice of Polyxena, thus sparing Hecuba yet another sight of utter violence by taking her to a safe location.

As Troy's closest ally in the *Iliad* and a place of wealth, peace and prosperity, Lycia is an expected place to take the Queen of Troy.[148] Moreover, Apollo is strongly associated with Lycia and may have wished to provide Hecuba, his past consort, with a welcoming place to spend her life after Troy. Stesichorus' account, therefore, presents a completely distinct version form the Euripidean. In Stesichorus, not only does Hecuba seems to survive Troy, she is taken to an allied prosperous city. Hecuba may enjoy a more dignified end in a land that will provide her refuge. But this journey not only allows a more pleasant end for Hecuba; it allows the memory of Troy to live on in the figure of its Queen. But if Hecuba takes with her the memory of Troy to the east, there are others who take it to the west.

2.1.8 Aeneas' escape (fr. 105 F.)

To discuss Stesichorus' account of Aeneas' fate we need to discuss the *Tabula Iliaca Capitolina* in more detail. This piece depicts the *Aethiopis* ascribed to Arctinus, the *Little Iliad* by Lesches, the *Iliad*, and the *Sack of Troy* by Stesichorus, as indicated by a statement Ἰλίου Πέρcιc κατὰ Cτηcίχορον. However, some scholars have expressed their scepticism regarding the authenticity of the claim, based on three aspects. First, could Theodorus, the sculptor of the piece, have known our poet's *Sack of Troy*? Second, is it conceivable that the story of

---

[147] Fr. 80 Lightfoot, fr. 12 Magnelli, *Alex.* 265., respectively. Porphyry adds Ibycus (fr. 295 *PMGF*) to the list of authors who followed the version of Apollo as Hector's son, but he fails to mention Stesichorus, probably, as Cingano 1990: 199–200 suggests, as a result of some confusion between the two western poets.
[148] E.g. *Il.* 5.478–481.

Aeneas' escape to the west goes back to Stesichorus? Third, can we trust a version which seems to contradict at times the existing evidence on the content of the poem?

The last question was addressed above where I argued that the *Tabula* does not necessarily contradict Stesichorus' version regarding Helen's recovery, since an encounter between Helen and Menelaus featured in the poem. Moreover, the sculptor's choice to depict the encounter of husband and wife rather than the near-stoning of Helen is consistent with the artistic tradition of the episode and with the aesthetic concerns of the piece, not to mention the fact that this is not a sole example, inasmuch as the *Iliad* depiction also presents variations.

The other two arguments, however, deserve our attention. Let us begin by addressing the first one. Horsfall doubts that Stesichorus could be the source for an artistic piece of Roman Imperial times and believes that the story depicted by Theodorus would have cited Stesichorus only to show the alleged refined literary taste of his clientele or patrons, rather than provide an accurate depiction of the poem. His scepticism is based on the idea that Stesichorus would sound more exotic and unexpected than the epic version of the sack: Arctinus' *Iliou Persis*.[149] However, Stesichorus was by no means an obscure and forgotten poet in this period. Quite on the contrary, as Petrain shows, the use of Stesichorus' name would function "as part of Theodorus' strategy to convince the viewer that the tablets bear the wisdom of the most famous poets in Greek tradition",[150] not because it is a bizarre and farfetched reference, but because Stesichorus would have been a famous name. He was one of the nine great lyric poets according to the Alexandrian canon (TTb3 Ercoles), and a well-established peer to Homer (Tb37–52 Ercoles). Furthermore, his *Sack of Troy* was not unworthy of Homer to an audience from the reign of Alexander the Great, as the testimony by Dio Chrysostom attests.[151] Following the testimony of the ancient sources on the lasting fame of Stesichorus, Petrain asserts that the sculptor uses Stesichorus' version precisely because "[h]e [Theodorus] could hardly aim higher than Stesichorus and Homer, both given pride of place at the head of their respective sections in the tablet's list of its poetic sources".[152] When speaking of the sack of

---

149 Horsfall 1979: 43.
150 Petrain 2014: 100.
151 fr. 98 F.: Στησιχόρου δὲ καὶ Πινδάρου ἐπεμνήσθη, τοῦ μὲν ὅτι μιμητὴς Ὁμήρου γενέσθαι δοκεῖ καὶ τὴν ἅλωσιν οὐκ ἀναξίως ἐποίησε τῆς Τροίας. "He mentioned Stesichorus and Pindar, because the former seems to have been an imitator of Homer and composed the capture of Troy in a manner not unworthy of him".
152 Petrain 2014: 100.

Troy, Stesichorus would have been anything but a surprising reference. Moreover, there is other aspect that suggests that the sculptor knew Stesichorus' text quite well. The sculptor' *sphragis* found on the bottom of the central panel presents a compelling similarity to fr. 100 F. It reads:

τέχνην τὴν Θεοδ]ώρηον μάθε Ὁμήρου
ὄφρα δαεὶς πάσης μέτρον ἔχηις σοφίας

Learn the technique of Theodorus, so that from Homer
you may know the measurements of all wisdom

The similarity between the *sphragis*, although supplemented by Mancuso[153] and the opening of Stesichorus' poem (fr. 100.11–13 F.) is remarkable and leaves little space for doubting the allusion to the sculptor's source. Petrain is overly cautious when he asserts that the couplet "points to a nexus of concepts and terms that is amply attested in the poetic tradition".[154] The opening lines of the poem, lines which are the easier to remember, reproduce, recognise, and celebrate Epeius' craftsmanship, just as the couplet does in exalting Theodorus' work of art. It seems too much of a coincidence that an allusion to Stesichorus was not intended.

The doubts whether the *Tabula* is to be trusted as a valid source to reconstruct the poem are more problematic when the presence of certain characters is only attested in it. This is the case of Aeneas who is depicted three times. First, in the lower left part of the depiction of Troy inside the walls a figure labelled as Aeneas seems to be taking something from another Trojan, presumably the sacred objects.[155] At the main gate Aeneas' family is depicted. Aeneas, in the centre, carries his father on his shoulder, Ascanius is holding his father's hand, and there is a female figure, not labelled (presumably Aeneas' wife). Hermes accompanies them. Finally, the last scene corresponds to the moment when Aeneas is preparing to depart from Troy.

Now, Aeneas is not mentioned in the papyri, but nor is Odysseus, Agamemnon or Menelaus; and Aeneas is a fairly common presence in the accounts of the

---

153 Mancuso 1911: 730.
154 Petrain 2014: 101. See e.g. the *Homeric Hymn to Hermes* (4.483, 509–511), in a context where the vocabulary associated with song, skill, and learning is abundant, which is in part also what is at stake in Stesichorus' text; cf. Davies and Finglass 2014: 417–418. For further philological aspects of the *Tabula*, see also Carlini 1982: 632–633.
155 Compare Hellanicus' account in his *Troika* (fr. 31 *EGM* = D.H. 1.45.4–47.1–5), described below.

sack. Therefore, more puzzling than the presence of Aeneas is the inscription of his destiny in the bottom right corner of the central panel of the stone:

Αἰνείας cὺν τοῖc ἰδίοιc ἀπαίρων εἰc τὴν Ἑcπερίαν

Aeneas with his companions departing to Hesperia

To Horsfall, "the presence of Aeneas at the very centre of the panel will have been an emphasis given by the Augustan artist, not the Himerian poet".[156] This may well be true – Aeneas could have been a less central character in the poem than the *Tabula* may lead us to perceive – but it does not imply that the *Sack of Troy* did not tell of Aeneas' escape and his journey westwards. In fact, as Mancuso suggested, it was perhaps because Stesichorus' version put Aeneas in the west that Theodorus chose his account for the *Tabula*.[157]

The idea that Aeneas survives Troy is central to the myth and unanimous. It is already present in the *Iliad* when Poseidon prophesises that Aeneas will survive and rule over the Trojans (*Il.* 20.293–308), but this account gives no precise location for Aeneas' future home. In the *Homeric Hymn to Aphrodite* (196–199) the goddess predicts the same fate for Aeneas to his father Anchises.[158] These are the most disputed lines of the poem because, like in the *Iliad*, they give no further detail on where Aeneas is supposed to go after Troy is destroyed.[159] Reinhardt argues that this poem was a eulogy in honour of the Aeneads of Scepsis, because Scepsis lies near Mount Ida and said to have been called Aeneas' seat.[160]

The Epic Cycle maintains the tradition but gives further details. The escape of Aeneas to Ida is specifically told only in the *Iliou Persis*,[161] and appears again in Sophocles' *Laocoon* (fr. 373.3–5 *TrGF*). West connects both accounts to the tradition present in the *Iliad* and the *Homeric Hymn to Aphrodite*, and suggests that the escape to Ida implies the establishment of the Aenead dynasty there.[162]

---

156 Horsfall 1979: 38.
157 Mancuso 1912: 185–186.
158 The dating of the *Hymn* was far from unanimous among scholars, but recently, it is commonly accepted that the *Hymn* antedates the sixth century: see Faulkner 2008: 47–49.
159 For a recent discussion of the bibliography related to the prominence of the Aenead dynasty see Faulkner 2008: 3–18; for older literature see van Eck 1978: 69–72.
160 Reinhardt *ap.* van Eck 1978: 69, see also Strabo 13.1.53.
161 West 2013: 232–233. Proclus, Arg. 1d *GEF*. On the relation of the flight of Aeneas to Mt Ida and earlier episodes of Aeneas' story see Anderson 1997: 72–74. For a discussion of the subject and its relevance to the name Hesperia see Mele 2014: 41–44.
162 West 2013: 226.

Anderson points out the prominence of Aeneas' withdrawal to Mt Ida, since Ida is a recurrent element in the Trojan saga.[163] Stansbury-O'Donnell observed the parallels of the beginning and the end of Polygnotus' painting of the *Iliou Persis*.[164] The painting begins with the ship of Menelaus and the dismantling of his tent at the left part of the first composition. The last scene of the third composition represents the survivors of Troy departing from their devastated city.[165] However, whereas the Greeks are preparing the ships to undergo a sea travel, the Trojans only have the help of a donkey, which suggest a journey by land, probably to Mount Ida, as in the *Iliou Persis*. All these accounts, relying on the same tradition, leave Aeneas in Anatolia; no movement further west is implied.

However, another tradition from at least the sixth century associates Aeneas with other routes. The *Little Iliad*,[166] also represented in the *Tabula Iliaca Capitolina*, gives an unusual account of Aeneas' fate. He and Andromache were captured and taken in Neoptolemus' ships as captives. Such a shameful fate for the son of Aphrodite, who was granted dominion over the Trojans according to the prophecies referred above, may seem quite inappropriate. Nevertheless, his association with Neoptolemus integrates Aeneas into the returns of the Greek warriors to their land.

The epic poem dedicated to the homecoming of the warriors, the *Nostoi*, had Neoptolemus travelling by land through Thrace, Maronea, and finally to the land of the Molossians. Despite the absence of any mention of Aeneas in the remains of this poem,[167] this version of the Neoptolemus' *nostos* and his stop in the Molossians seems to have had an impact on historical sources as early as the fifth century. Hellanicus' account of the fate of Aeneas seems to incorporate both accounts of the *Nostoi* and the *Little Iliad* in the detail of associating Aeneas and Neoptolemus in Troy's aftermath. According to Hellanicus' version, Aeneas somehow reaches the Molossians, the same people that Neoptolemus met on his way home. In Hellanicus' *Priestesses of Hera at Argos*, after meeting Odysseus in the land of the Molossians, both Aeneas and the king of Ithaca depart to a city in Italy, presumably Rome.[168] Hellanicus presents yet another account in his *Troika*[169] where he presents Aeneas sailing through the Helles-

---

[163] Anderson 1997: 72–74.
[164] Stansbury-O'Donnell 1989: 213.
[165] Stansbury-O'Donnell 1989: 211–212.
[166] F 30 *GEF*.
[167] See Erskine 2001: 122–124.
[168] Fr. 84 *EGM*. See also D.H. 1.72.1 for Aeneas in Rome. For his account of the sack, see 1.45–48.1.
[169] Fr. 31 *EGM* = D.H. 1.45.4–47.1–5.

pont and reached Chalcis accompanied by his father and the sacred images of the gods.[170]

Sending Aeneas out of the Troad to locations further west indicates an interest in widening his route and approximating it to the routes taken by the Greek heroes. Moreover, it could mean that the son of Anchises was already being associated with Italy by previous authors, especially if we consider the detail in Hellanicus' fr. 31 *EGM* according to which Aeneas reaches Chalcis, a prominent town in the Greek presence in the west, particularly in Sicily.[171] The Euboeans' early (eighth century) presence across Italian shores is attested by archaeology in the finding of Euboean pottery in Pontecagnano, Capua, Campania, and Naples.[172] Aeneas association with Chalcis, may therefore denounce the existence of a version which somehow connected him to the west. Furthermore, the Trojan presence in Italy is first attested from the early fifth century by Hecataeus, who says that the Trojan refugee Capys founded Capua.[173] Thucydides (6.2.3–4), in a more historical approach, ascribes the foundation of Segesta to the Trojan fugitives, among other groups.[174]

We see that from at least the fifth century onwards stories of Trojans in the west circulated, namely in Italy and Sicily. This indicates that an association of Aeneas with this location in the sixth century may not be far-fetched. However,

---

170 See Canciani 1981: 388 § 92, a coin from Aeneia, Chalcis from c. 490–480, depicting Aeneas carrying his father in his back.

171 This version would also serve the development of a contemporary colonial movement, that of the Chalcidians who were beginning to have particular presence in Tyrrhenus and in Campania which would legitimate an encounter between the wandering Odysseus and the newly arrived Aeneas (cf. Mele 2014: 43). For the Euboeans in the west, see Domínguez 2006: 256–258; Greco 2006: 171–173; Tsetskhladze 2006: l–li.

172 Lane Fox 2009: 133.

173 *FGrHist* 1 F 62 (cf. Fowler 2013: 566). For more details on the legend of Aeneas in historiography, see Fowler 2013: 561–568.

174 Ἰλίου δὲ ἁλισκομένου τῶν Τρώων τινὲς διαφυγόντες Ἀχαιοὺς πλοίοις ἀφικνοῦνται πρὸς τὴν Σικελίαν, καὶ ὅμοροι τοῖς Σικανοῖς οἰκήσαντες ξύμπαντες μὲν Ἔλυμοι ἐκλήθησαν, πόλεις δ' αὐτῶν Ἔρυξ τε καὶ Ἔγεστα, "As Troy fell some of the Trojans, escaping from the Achaeans in small vessels, arrived in Sicily. They settled near the Sicanians and were generically called Elymoi (cf. D.H. 1.47.2) but their two cities were Eryx and Egesta". On the passage and its implications of a synoikismos between Trojans and Phocians, see Ridgeway 1888: 180 who claims scribal error and emends φωκέων to φρυγῶν (thus also Rigby 1987: 334–335). Hornblower 2008: 270 notes that such an emendation would result in redundancy since Trojans and Phrygians were generally understood as the same ethnic group, and suggests the emendation of φωκέων to φωκαῆς, while Kahrstedt 1947: 17 proposes φωκαιῶν. However, the editors (Gomme, Andrewes, Dover 1970: 212) prefer to maintain the manuscript's reading, which seems the more likely option.

such association does not necessarily mean that a clear link was established between Aeneas and Rome. After all, we are told only that Stesichorus has Aeneas travelling to "Hesperia". 'Hesperia' referring to the land of the west, existed long before its more precise connotation with Italy, which is first attested in Ennius (*Ann.* 20). The earlier occurrence of the use of Hesperia in such terms appears in [Hes.] fr. 150.6 M-W Ἑσπε[ρί]ην, which provides evidence for the association of the term with a geographical location. Apart from this hint, we commonly find the adjective ἕσπερος and other words built on the stem ἑσπερ-, referring to either the mystical and primordial ideas associating the west with ideas of night (fr. 360 M-W),[175] darkness, death, and the dwelling place of some deities,[176] or as a specific reference to the compass point.[177] The word is therefore ambivalent since it can refer to far distant mythical places or the more palpable location, presumably with a more concrete sense of either Sicily, Italy or even Rome, as Finglass suggests.[178]

The main argument against such an association is that Rome in Stesichorus' time was not yet important enough to be integrated in the Trojan saga as the city where the Trojan fugitives fled. Moreover, Dionysus does not mention Stesichorus on his account on the antecedents of the foundation of Rome (1.48–64). However, contacts between Latins and western Greeks are attested in the sixth century.[179] Art also attests the knowledge of Aeneas in the west, particularly on objects found in Italy. This may lead us to conclude that the story was known not only to Greeks but also to the native populations in the west.

In fact, Aeneas' escape from Troy is a common episode in art, particularly in black-figure pottery, which proves at least that the idea of Aeneas fleeing Troy travelled itself as far as Etruria. Canciani's survey illustrates this by presenting examples of the representation of the family similar to the one depicted in the *Tabula*.[180] Particularly relevant to our argument are the vases and other iconographic sources up until the beginning of the fifth century.[181]

---

175 See West 1966: 215n., 275n., 517n.
176 E.g. Hes. *Th.* 27; Pi. *P.* 4.40, 11.10, *I.* 8.47; A. *Pr.* 348; S. *OT* 177; Pl. *Phdr.* 59e, *Smp.* 223d.
177 E.g. S. *Aj.* 805; E. *Or.* 1260; Hdt. 1.28.2; Th. 6.2.
178 Finglass 2014b: 31–33. For the significance of the term Hesperia in the context of the *Tabula*, see Sadurska 1964: 34–35. For a more comprehensive discussion of the term Hesperia and its ambivalence, see Malkin 1998: 191–194 and Debiasi 2004: 170, 172–173.
179 Thus Finglass 2014b: 31 citing a gravestone found in Sicily which informs us that the deceased was a Greek called Latinos (*IGSD* II § 24). Note also Hesiod *Th.* 1008–1016, who mentions the birth son of Anchises before the birth of Latinos.
180 Canciani 1981: §§ 386–390.
181 Canciani 1981: §§ 59–87, 92–95.

Most of the vases representing Aeneas' escape from Troy as depicted in the *Tabula* were found in Italy, particularly Etruria.[182] From Etruria there is also a scarab dating to the late sixth or early fifth century[183] depicting the same episode with Anchises bringing the *sacra* from Troy. Furthermore, in the last quarter of the sixth century Etruria imported considerable quantities of Attic black-figure vases depicting Aeneas.[184] Also of importance to these considerations are the terracotta votive statuettes found in Veii, particularly the one depicting a bearded young man carrying an old man in his shoulders, considered a representation of Aeneas and Anchises.[185] The date of the statuettes is controversial as well as their purpose, since they seem analogous to other statuettes associated with founder-cults.[186]

As in the case of Helen and Menelaus discussed above, the similarity of these depictions to the relief in the tablet is striking. They belong and respond to the same mythological tradition, which in turn may indicate that the sculptor of the *Tabula* was gathering elements from earlier pictorial tradition associated with the departure of Aeneas from Troy in the minds of a western audience familiar with Stesichorus' poems.[187]

For all these reasons, it is safe to conclude that the version in the *Tabula* illustrates Stesichorus' poem. This means that Stesichorus provides the earliest account where Aeneas embarks with his companions in a far-off journey westward. Given the interest of Stesichorus in western mythology, or at least mythology located in the west, and since Aeneas and other Trojans were integrated

---

182 Canciani 1981: §§ 94, 395.
183 Late–sixth century: Furtwängler 1900; Texier 1939: 15; Alföldi 1971: 286; and Galinsky 1971: 60 n. 115. Early fifth century: Pallotino 1958 and Canciani 1981.
184 Momigliano 1989: 59 argues that such evidence does not imply knowledge of the myth of Aeneas among the Etruscans and could result from coincidence. On the same subject Osborne 2009: 87 argues that the figured pottery among non-Greeks, particularly Etruscans implies the knowledge of the imagery and the stories associated with them, supporting the view that the Etruscans were familiar with Greek mythology and with Aeneas' story in particular to which they had access through both iconography and story-telling.
185 Terracotta statuary group from Veii, Museo Nazionale di Villa Giulia Museum 40272, Rome; see Canciani 1981: § 96. For the relevance of the geographical position of Veii to the discussion see Lane Fox 2009: 133 "The Etruscans' big southern outposts at Veii or Capua stood out among the villages of the Latins and Campanians among whom they were established".
186 For a detailed analysis see Giglioli 1941: 8–15; Bendinelli 1948: 88–97; Alföldi 1957: 16–17; Gagé 1950: 73 n. 5 for the argument in favour of dating the statuettes to the early fourth century. Of the same opinion is Torelli 1973: 404. On the sanctuaries and the possible votive character of the statuettes see Galinsky 1971: 133–135 and Nagy 2011: 113–125.
187 Thus Valenzuela-Montenegro 2004: 383.

in foundation narratives by the fifth century, Stesichorus might have taken this opportunity to include his homeland in this major topic of Greek mythology, with which his audience, at home and in other places of the Greek world, would have been indubitably familiar.

Our poet takes a myth traditionally set in Eastern Mediterranean – a location emphasised in the opening of the poem with the reference to the streams of the Simoeis – and ends it in the west. Aeneas' journey, unlike that of Heracles, Helen, or Demophon, is a journey with no return. The place where he is heading must grant him the suitable conditions for a permanent stay, for a stable future, for a new beginning. It was precisely in Italy and Sicily that many Greeks and other peoples found that shelter. One wonders to what extent is the journey of Aeneas mimicking the movement of migrants, traders, settlers, that a Greek living in Sicily or Italy in the sixth century, would witness every day.

Our evidence from the *Sack of Troy* indicates a rather sympathetic treatment of the Trojan side, emphasising the pathos of a destroyed city of which the only surviving members are women enslaved after seeing their offspring mercilessly killed by the enemy. The motif of travelling or escaping appears as an alternative to this fate. Apollo's rescue of Hecuba saves her from being enslave and Aeneas' escape not only saves him but allows the survival of the Trojan *ethnos*.

On the other hand, the brutality of the Achaean enterprise must therefore have been latent in Stesichorus' *Sack of Troy* with a pejorative sense, as in the epics dealing with the subject. The Greeks won the war and achieved their difficult goal at Troy, as fr. 118 F. could allude to. However, the violence of their deeds goes beyond what it was acceptable to the gods, and hence their return is troublesome and uncertain. Fr. 121 F., whose context is lost to us, seems to refer to a sea-journey. Lines 5–6 of the fragment refer to κῦμα and in line 2, Lobel supplemented πον]τοπόρου[. This may be part of either Aeneas' or the Greeks' departure from Troy, the beginning of new and perilous adventures, which were dealt in detail in Stesichorus' *Nostoi*.

2.2 The *Nostoi*

The fact that Stesichorus composed a poem entirely dedicated to the return journey of the Greek heroes from Troy is not surprising. It was a theme widely known since Homer's *Odyssey*. The epic *Nostoi* also dealt in detail with the subject, describing the journeys of a variety of heroes, in particular Agamemnon's return and the revenge of Orestes.¹⁸⁸ Telemachus' journey to Sparta, however, is not recorded in the evidence on the poem.¹⁸⁹ Pindar's *Nemean* 7.35-50 and *Paean* 6 refer to the journey of Neoptolemus. The mythographers were interested in the theme and provide precious information on the role of the Trojan captives in the *nostos* narratives, particularly, as we have seen, Aeneas.¹⁹⁰ Tragedy was more concerned with the dramatic potential of the νόστος from the perspective of those who await the return of the hero and the subsequent events caused by it, rather than exploring the journey per se.¹⁹¹ Euripides' *Helen* is perhaps the most relevant account of the returns as such, since it occurs during Menelaus' journey. Aeschylus' *Agamemnon* and Euripides' *Andromache* contain a residual reference to the Trojan captives. Telemachus visit to Sparta is again missing. In later authors, we find an extensive record of the returns in Apollodorus (*Epit.* 5.20–6.15), and in Lycophron's *Alexandra* (417–1089).

Stesichorus dealt with the returns of the Achaeans in three poems: the *Palinode*, the *Oresteia* and the *Nostoi*.¹⁹² From the last poem, little survives. We have one testimony, one tentatively ascribed fragment and two other references, one epistle from Pseudo-Phalaris¹⁹³ and the other from Tzetzes.¹⁹⁴ While these testi-

---

188 For a general account of the story, see Danek 2015. The epic treated in some detail the journeys of Menelaus (fr. 1c *GEF*), Agamemnon (arg. 3a, 5 *GEF*), Neoptolemus (arg. 4a *GEF*), Diomedes and Nestor (arg. 1b *GEF*), and Calchas (arg. 2 *GEF*) among others. Odysseus is referred in passing in arg 4b. The poem covers the returns until Orestes' revenge, thus allowing the poem to cover other wanderings, such as Odysseus' and Menelaus (West 2013: 272).
189 Eustathius in his commentary to the *Odyssey* (*Telegony* fr. 6 *GEF*) wrongly ascribes to the *Nostoi* the story of Telemachus' marriage to Circe and Penelope's to Telegonus; this story is rather part of the epic *Telegony*. On the *Telegony* as a spin-off of the *Odyssey*, see West 2013: 289 and Fowler 2013: 557 on Hellanic. fr. 156 *EGM*.
190 On the subject see Fowler 2013: 545–568. Pherecydes treated the death of Calchas (fr. 142 *EGM*), and the wanderings of Odysseus (fr. 144 *EGM*, so too Acus. fr. 4 and Herodor. fr. 65 *EGM*); Hellanicus provides an account of Menelaus in Egypt (fr. 153 *EGM*), on Odysseus' (fr. 77 *EGM*) and Ajax's (fr. 152a *EGM*, so too Acus. fr. 450 *EGM*) returns and on Aeneas' escape (frr. 31, 84 *EGM*, see also Acus. fr. 39, Damocr. fr. 3 and Menecr. Xanth. fr. 3 *EGM*).
191 From the considerable amount of plays on the Trojan cycle only a few may have dealt with the journeys, e.g. A. *Proteus*?; Sophocles' *Teucer* TrGF FF 576, 579; Euripides' *Helen*. On the subject, see Sommerstein 2015 and Alexopoulou 2009: 37–83.
192 The scope of the *Helen* is unlikely to have covered the events up until the return from Troy.
193 Ta43(iii) Ercoles καὶ τοὺς μὲν τῶν Ἀχαιῶν νόστους πυνθάνομαί σε συγγράφειν καὶ τισι τῶν ἡρώων ἐκείνων ἀβουλίαν ἐπιτιμᾶν ἱκανῶς· ὅπως δ' αὐτὸς ἀπονοστέσεις ἀπαθὴς ἐξ Ἀλαίσης εἰς Ἱμέραν οὐδὲν φροντίζεις. ἀλλ' εὖ ἴσθι ὅτι μένουσί σε καὶ Καφηρίδες πέτραι καὶ Πλαγκταὶ καὶ ὁ ναύπλιος στόλος [δόλος West], καὶ οὐκ ἂν ἐκφύγοις ὅλως τὰς ἐμὰς χεῖρας, οὐδ' ἂν εἰ θεῶν σέ τις καθ' ὑμᾶς ποιητὰς ἀϊστώσειεν ("I understand you are writing about the returns of the Achaeans and that you censure some of the heroes for their folly; not considering how can you

monies attest the fame of Stesichorus in a later period, they lack specific references to the *Nostoi*. Tzetzes' lines may apply to the *Nostoi* but could also be referring to the *Oresteia* or the *Palinode*. Nothing in them suggests that Tzetzes was better informed about the poem than we are.[195] The epistle, on the other hand, has been regarded as a potential source for information on the poem. Bruno attempted to show how the references to the mythical topography associated with the returns of the Greeks from Troy may have been part of Stesichorus' *Nostoi*.[196] Ercoles recognizes that the argument fails to convince, but nevertheless believes that these references should be considered as a fragment *sine auctoris ipsissima verbis* and thus integrated in Stesichorean editions, not necessarily under the *Nostoi*.[197] However, it is uncertain whether these allusions to the works of Stesichorus are derivate of direct knowledge of some details now lost, or if the details present in the epistle are but an extension added by the author who knew, as we do thanks to Pausanias, that Stesichorus wrote a poem on the returns of the Achaeans.[198] Moreover, the episodes alluded to in the epistle need not come from the *Nostoi*. The reference to Nauplius may well have been part of the *Oresteia* (175 F.),[199] and the reference to Charybdis could be part of the *Scylla*. So, these two elements do not add to our knowledge of the poem.

Only fr. 169 F., a testimony by Pausanias, is certainly part of the *Nostoi*. Fr. 170 F. is tentatively ascribed to the poem based on its content, but it may well be part of a poem whose title is now lost. Let us begin with the testimony.

---

return unharmed from Alaesa to Himera yourself. For you should know that the Rock of Capharaeus, the Wandering Rocks, Charybdis and the stratagem [*vel* journey] of Nauplius await you and from my hands you shall not escape, not even if a God – as in the tales of your poets – renders you invisible.")

194 *Posth*. 750.2 Στηςίχορος δ' ἐρέηςιν ἐοῖς ἐπέεςςιν νόςτον | ἠμὲν ὅςοι πελάγει φθάρεν ἠδ' ὅςοι ἤλυθον ἄλληι, | ἠδ' ὅςοι εἰςαφίκοντο φίλην παρὰ πατρίδα γαῖαν ("Stesichorus treated in his poems their return journey | Many died at sea, others when they arrived | and many others returned to their beloved homeland.")
195 Thus Davies and Finglass 2014: 471.
196 Bruno 1967.
197 Ercoles 2013: 465; Pardini 1997: 98.
198 Thus Davies and Finglass 2014: 471.
199 For a discussion of the inclusion of fr. 175 F. in the *Oresteia*, see below 4.1.5.

2.2.1 Aristomache (fr. 169 F.)

The allusion to Aristomache in the context of a *nostos* poem implies that the Trojans, and particularly the royal family, played a part in the poem, as they do in the epic. The fates of the Trojan captives appear in the *Little Iliad* where Andromache and Aeneas were made captives of Neoptolemus (frr. 29–30 *GEF*). In tragedy, Andromache appears again as a captive of Neoptolemus (Euripides' *Andromache*); Cassandra is taken by Agamemnon in Aeschylus' *Agamemnon* and in Euripides' *Trojan Women*, Hecuba is given to Odysseus, and to Agamemnon in *Hecuba*, although she does not reach Greece in any of the accounts. The information provided by Pausanias contains more names for Priam's daughters (fr. 110 F.):

> τῶν δὲ γυναικῶν τῶν μεταξὺ τῆς τε Αἴθρας καὶ Νέστορός εἰσιν ἄνωθεν τούτων αἰχμάλωτοι καὶ αὗται Κλυμένη τε καὶ Κρέουσα καὶ Ἀριστομάχη καὶ Ξενοδίκη. Κλυμένην μὲν οὖν Στησίχορος ἐν Ἰλίου Πέρcιδι κατηρίθμηκεν ἐν ταῖc αἰχμαλώτοιc· ὡcαύτωc δὲ καὶ Ἀριστομάχην ἐποίηcεν ἐν Νόcτοιc θυγατέρα μὲν Πριάμου, Κριτολάου δὲ γυναῖκα εἶναι τοῦ Ἰκετάονος.

> Above the women between Aethra and Nestor are other captives: Clymene, Creousa, Aristomache, and Xenodice. Stesichorus includes Clymene among the captives in the *Sack of Troy*; and similarly, in the *Nostoi* he makes Aristomache Priam's daughter and wife of Critolaus, son of Hicetaon.

This testimony includes two poems of Stesichorus. The first concerns the *Sack of Troy* and mentions that Clymene was among the captives (fr. 110 F.). Clymene appears in the *Iliad* as a handmaid of Helen, but in a problematic passage, which many believe to be an Attic interpolation.[200] So it is not certain if she was indeed a daughter of Priam, or even Trojan. Later accounts say that she was Aethra's daughter by Hippalces and that both women are rescued by Demophon and Acamas.[201] She may have been mentioned in the *Sack of Troy* alongside Aethra as in the *Iliad*, but in Stesichorus she had a slightly different treatment: listed among the captives and thus perhaps Trojan. Later in Pausanias, Stesichorus is said to have named Medusa as one of Priam's daughters in the *Sack of Troy* (fr. 111 F.). The context of her appearance is unknown, but she may well have been named among the captives. Medusa is found nowhere else in earlier poetry. As seen, it seems that the *Sack of Troy* provided a detailed account of the suffering of the Trojans. In this context, it is not surprising to sup-

---

200 Hom. *Il.* 3.143–144. For the interpolation, see West 1999: 186–187 and Finglass 2006. For the contrary argument, see Kelly 2008.
201 Dictys 5.13, 6.2 and Σ Hom. *Il.* 3.144.

pose that Stesichorus catalogued Priam's daughters to emphasise the scale of the Achaean victory and its massive impact on the surviving Trojans.

The reference to Priam's daughters in the context of Pausanias' description suggests that Aristomache is a war prisoner. Her name and Critolaus' appear only here in the context of the Trojan war. Hicetaon, on the other hand, appears four times in the *Iliad*. He is among the elders who, despite recognizing Helen's marvellous beauty, advise that she should be taken to the ships of the Greeks (3.147). He is said to be one of Priam's brothers (20.238) and the father of Melanippus who dies in battle (15.546–547, 576). The fact that Stesichorus names Aristomache and Critolaus may indicate that he had had an intention, in the *Nostoi* too to give relevance to characters that were forgotten in other accounts of the myth.

2.2.2 Telemachus in Sparta (fr. 170 F.)

The other fragment we have refers to Telemachus' visit to Sparta. Scholars have suggested that the episode could have featured in other compositions. Lloyd-Jones argued that the fragment could be part of the *Oresteia*,[202] but that is highly unlikely. First, the content of the *Oresteia* does not suggest room for a shift from the House of Agamemnon to the concerns of Ithaca. True, the fate of Agamemnon plays an important role in the *Odyssey* as a constant vision of what may await Odysseus at home and provides, in the figure of Orestes, a *paradeigma* to Telemachus. Furthermore, the return of Agamemnon and the revenge of Orestes frame the five books of the epic *Nostoi*. Yet what we have of the *Oresteia* suggests a very detailed narrative, focused on the events that concern the House of Agamemnon.[203] Moreover, for the episode of fr. 170 F. to be part of the *Oresteia* all the fragments we possess of the poem would have to be parts of the epode unless the two books had different metres, which is unconvincing.[204]

The *Helen*, a poem which dealt with a number of events covering a considerable amount of time (since Helen's youth to her departure to Troy),[205] would hardly accommodate a visit of a 20-year-old Telemachus. Moreover, the metre also presents some problems. Little is preserved from the *Helen* to allow a con-

---

[202] Lloyd-Jones 1958: 17.
[203] West 2015: 75.
[204] Thus Haslam 1974: 45 n. 86. For the unconvincing argument for different metres within the same poem, see 4.2.
[205] See below 3.2.

clusive comparison, but the lines we have suggest that the verses would integrate epitrites and dactyls, whereas in the *Nostoi* the lines we have suggest that there was no integration of both units in the same verse.[206] The *Palinode* presents the same metrical issues (epitrites and dactyls integrated in the same verse, fr. 91a.2 F.), but it seems to have dealt with a more confined timeframe, from Paris' visit to Sparta and his attempted seduction or abduction of Helen to Menelaus' and Demophon's diversion in Egypt on their return.[207] Carey suggests that fr. 170 F. belonged to a story focalised on Menelaus' return, in a kind of reversion of the *Odyssey*.[208] In such a scenario a visit of Telemachus to Sparta may not be completely unthinkable. Moreover, Helen in fr. 170 F. enjoys remarkable authority and shows signs of compassion towards the maternal sufferings of Penelope, which would be consistent with a poem where she is not seen as responsible for the Trojan war.[209]

Another option, put forward by West and Carey independently, is that the fragment may come from a sort of lyric *Telemachy* where the stories of the heroes' returns would be framed by the context of Telemachus' visit to Sparta. But a *Telemachy* deprived of the wider context of the *Odyssey* is hard to imagine; and an *Odyssey* by Stesichorus would not have passed unnoticed.[210] On the other hand, could a poem in which an omen announced Odysseus' return end without treating it? If not, can we imagine a context in which Odysseus appears only towards the end? If yes, then we may have here a reason for Telemachus' appearance: he could have been introduced as a bridge in the narrative that ends a part of the poem focused on Menelaus and introduces that of Odysseus' return. Therefore, Stesichorus would have obtain a more linear narrative that included a detailed account of the journeys of Menelaus and others, which ended with the last man to return home: Odysseus, while including yet another journey in the poem. In this scenario, rather than a mere allusion of what was known from the myth, leaving it as an unresolved issue, the omen interpreted

---

206 Thus Haslam 1974: 45.
207 Doria 1963: 84 n. 12 suggests that Demophon's diversion through Egypt was not part of the *Palinode*, but of the *Nostoi*. However, the absence of any remarks on the title or the origin of such account lead me to believe that the tale come from the same poem as that which was being discussed in the previous lines. See further Finglass 2013b: 43.
208 Carey 2015: 57.
209 Maingon 1979: 139 n. 36 "Do we attribute this representation [a dutiful wife and hostess] of Helen as the poet's development of what is inherent in the *Odyssey*, or as being composed after his formal recantation?"
210 Thus West 2015: 75, so too Maingon 1979: 139.

by Helen would have had a more relevant function in the poem as a prediction of what will happen later.

Θε[ῖ]ον ἐ[ξ]αίφνας τέρας ἰδοῖςα νύμφα,
ὧδε δ' ἔ[ει]φ᾽ Ἑλένα φωναῖ ποτ[ὶ] παῖδ᾽ Ὀδύςειο[ν·
"Τηλέμαχ᾽, [ἦ] τις ὅδ᾽ ἀμὶν ἄγγελ[ο]ς ὠρανόθεν
δι᾽ αἰθέρο[ς ἀτ]ρυγέτας κατέπτατο, βᾶ δ[
          ]., φοινᾷ κεκλαγώ[ς   5
     ]…ς ὑμετέρους δόμους προφα. [……]υς
            ]….. αν, υς ἀνήρ
     βο]υλαῖς Ἀθάνας
               ].ηις αυτα λακέρυζα κορώνα
—◡—×—◡]].μ᾽ οὐδ᾽ ἐγώ ς᾽ ἐρύ[ξ]ω   10
—◡◡ Παν]ελόπα ς᾽ ἰδοῖςα φίλου πατ[ρ]ὸς υἱὸν
          ]ςο.[.]τ…ς ἐςθλ[
            ] [.] θειον μ[
   ]   [
       ] [15
        ].γ...[
  ].α...[
        ] [
        ]αμο[
        ].οιω[20
        ].ντ[
desunt versus aliquot
     ἀργυρέαν τε.[◡—
     χρυςῶι ὕπερθε[
     ἐκ Δαρδανιδ..[—◡◡—
     Πλεισθενίδας.[◡◡—
     καὶ τὰ μὲν ευ.[◡◡—
     ςυνθ.[..].[.].[
     χρυς[

1–2 Lobel ‖ **3** [ἦ] Lloyd–Jones | ἄγγελ[ο]ς Lobel ‖ **4** Lobel ‖ **5** κεκλαγώ[ς Lobel, –γγ– Π³ ‖ **6** ἐς Lobel, προφαν[εὶς Lobel (vel προφαν[εῖτ᾽) Ὀδυς[εύς Lobel ‖ **8 –11** Lobel

the woman, suddenly seeing the divine portent,
and thus aloud Helen spoke to the son of Odysseus:
"Telemachus, indeed this is a messenger which flown
from the sky through the air for us, and went…
          … screeching … blood(y) …   5
     … your home (appears Odysseus)…
     … man …
     …by the counsels of Athena…
     …chattering crow…
     …nor will I detain you…   10

                ...Penelope, seeing you, the son of a dear father
                ...
                ...
                ...
                ...   15
                ...
                ...
                ...
                ...
                ...   20
silver...
from Dardanian...
Pleisthenid...
and these (things)
(gold)...

The similarities between this fragment and book 15 of the *Odyssey* have long been noted. We have seen above how Stesichorus makes use of Homeric episodes in unexpected contexts and characters. Here the situation is different. The episode and the characters are the same as in Homer. On the other hand, it is also a relatively minor episode of the *Odyssey*, like the death of Gorgythion, or the dilemma of Sarpedon in the *Iliad*. This attests once more Stesichorus' thorough familiarity with the Homeric poems, providing a valuable testimony for the circulation of the *Odyssey*, in the late seventh and the early sixth centuries.

The fragment begins by presenting Helen, referred to as νύμφα perhaps stressing her condition as a returned and renewed bride. She sees a bird omen and interprets it as a prediction of Odysseus' return. Helen thus encourages Telemachus to return home and mentions the joy Penelope will feel in seeing him. Then Helen and presumably Menelaus offer Telemachus some artwork in silver and gold. The fragment breaks off here. Although sharing many aspects with the scene in *Od.* 15.170–184, there are aspects distinguishing both accounts.

First, in Stesichorus Helen spots the omen, describes and interprets it (lines 1–8), whereas in the *Odyssey*, the narrator says that they all see the eagle approaching and react to it. Peisistratus asks Menelaus' opinion, but it is Helen who provides an interpretation (*Od.* 15.160–165). Second, while in the *Odyssey* Menelaus and Helen give the presents to Telemachus before the omen (15.67–130), in Stesichorus this occurs afterwards. True, in both cases the presents are given when Telemachus expresses the wish to return home (15.43–66), which in the *Odyssey* occurs through Athena's inspiration and to which Menelaus responds (15.1–42). In Stesichorus Telemachus' wish seems motivated by the meaning of the omen and it is Helen who delivers the customary reassurance that it is not the host's job to keep a guest from leaving.[211]

Menelaus remains silent throughout, being mentioned only once in line 25, if indeed the patronymic refers to him. In fact, the line in the *Odyssey* 15.68 where he expresses sympathy for Telemachus' decision (Τηλέμαχ' οὔ τί c' ἐγώ γε πολὺν χρόνον ἐνθάδ' ἐρύξω) is alluded to in Helen's speech in Stesichorus (Τηλέμαχ'...] μ'οὐδ' ἐγώ c' ἐρύ[ξ]ω). This variation allows the poet to elaborate more on the maternal side of Helen. She expresses understanding for Telemachus' wish, as we have seen, but adds an aspect not present in the *Odyssey*: a reference to Penelope's joy in seeing her son back home safe. In the *Odyssey*, she may be moved by maternal sentiment when she offers the dress for the future wife of Telemachus to wear,[212] but in Stesichorus she shows compassion for the distress of a mother whose son is abroad (line 11), vulnerable to every peril which a journey of this sort may imply.[213]

The omen may have also differed in both accounts depending on the interpretation of line 9. In the *Odyssey*, the bird in question is an eagle, usually perceived as a good portent.[214] The eagle snatching a goose anticipates Penelope's premonitory dream at 19.536–545 which announces the return of Odysseus. The type of bird of Stesichorus' episode is not certain. Davies and Finglass, following Peek's supplement, accept that the crow refers to Helen's pejorative remarks on herself,[215] thus assuming that the bird in the omen is not a crow but an eagle.[216] Furthermore, the reference to the cry of the bird in the omen would be odd in a context where Helen is not describing what she sees, but interpreting it, and the next line presents a negative clause that stresses in the first person something that she shall excuse herself to do. Other scholars take line 9 as a reference to the bird in the omen, which therefore means the omen involved the

---

211 Cf. *Od.* 7.315, where Alcinous affirms that no Phaeacian shall detain Odysseus if it is his will to leave. Cf. Kelly 2015b: 40.
212 Thus Lourenço 2007: 52.
213 Cf. Noussia-Fantuzzi 2015: 436.
214 E.g. *Il.* 24.315–321, where lines 320–321 repeat those at *Od.* 15.164–165 with a slight alteration: δεξιὸc ἀΐξαc διὰ ἄcτεοc: οἳ δὲ ἰδόντεc | γήθηcαν, καὶ πᾶcιν ἐνὶ φρεcὶ θυμὸc ἰάνθη and in the *Odyssey* δεξιὸc ἤϊξε πρόcθ' ἵππων: οἱ δὲ ἰδόντεc | γήθηcαν, καὶ πᾶcιν ἐνὶ φρεcὶ θυμὸc ἰάνθη. For further examples of eagles as good omens see *Il.* 24.292; *Od.* 15.526; B. 5.19–20; E. *Ion* 158–159; and see Dillon 2017: 145–146; Kelly 2015a: 40 n. 91.
215 Something which is not rare from Helen, as we have seen above apropos fr. 115 F.
216 Peek 1958: 170; Grossardt 2012: 41–42; Davies and Finglass 2014: 480; Noussia-Fantuzzi 2015: 436.

appearance of a crow.[217] The chattering would be consistent with the reference in line 5 to the cry of the bird, applied to crows in a context of a favourable omen in *Il.* 10.276. Either an eagle or a crow, Helen interpreted the omen as a sign of Odysseus' return according to Athena's plans (lines 6–8).

Line 12 suggests some reference to Zeus or to the gods pleading for the prophecy of Helen to become true, perhaps a line uttered by Telemachus replying to and thanking Helen, as happens at *Odyssey* 15.180. There is a lacuna in the papyrus on the sequence of which appears to be a list of the presents of Menelaus and Helen to Telemachus, which involve a silver item, something that came from or belonged to Priam (line 24). This suggests that one of the gifts offered to Telemachus comes from Troy, presumably part of the war exploits. In the *Odyssey*, Helen offers him a refulgent dress for his bride to wear (15.125–129), while Menelaus gives Telemachus a silver crater with a golden rim, obtained from the king of the Sidonians (15.115). In Stesichorus the list may have continued, as the reference to gold in line 27 seems to suggest, but we cannot prove that. Telemachus should have left soon afterwards, judging by the rapid departure depicted in the *Odyssey*, although it is plausible that they enjoyed a meal before heading to Ithaca, as indeed happens in the *Odyssey*. Whether the poem extended until Odysseus' return, we cannot tell with certainty, but it seems likely.

By including Telemachus' journey to Sparta and back home, Stesichorus not only has the chance to display once more his creativity in dealing with Homer, he also seizes the opportunity to include another journey, one confined to a familiar space, to the comfort zone of the Greek mainland. Stesichorus' Helen in fr. 170 F. is more dedicated and more active than her epic counterpart. She dominates the scene as she assumes the roles of prophet, host, mother-nurse. In the next chapter, we will discuss the poems where Helen is not so much of an independent and self-determined woman.

---

217 Thus, Kelly 2015b: 41.

3 Abduction

In the earlier chapters, I have shown how myth provided a "representational geography" which helps in shaping the world geographically and ethnographically in Stesichorus' poems.[1] So far, the conceptualization of real space in fictional terms was mainly connected to the imaginary journeys of men. However, the myths of abduction and escape provide a different pattern for mobility: the mobility of women in myth. This influences the response to the ethnographic or genealogical reality and can explain the presence of both Greeks[2] and other peoples in a certain place, as the example of the genealogical poems show.[3] But as narratives of abduction, these episodes often present conflicting moral issues which oscillate between the themes of seduction and violence.

This chapter discusses how Stesichorus treats the two examples of abduction in his corpus, Europa and Helen, and the patterns and impact of the movement of female characters. I will first discuss the original fault which provokes the abduction (whether divine anger or lust) and, by extension, the agency of women in the process; secondly, I will examine the imagery and circumstantial elements of the moment of the abduction and its parallels with the ritualistic representations of marriage; and finally, I will look at the motif of the failed and/or illusory abduction.

The motif of abduction of young girls and women, perhaps because of its recurrence as a historical fact, is frequent in world literature and myth.[4] Abduction may happen "through tyrannical brute force, [or] through the use of trick-

---

[1] Thus Mitchell 2007: 169.
[2] Mitchell 2007: 172–174; Rutherford 2000: 81–83.
[3] Thus D'Alessio 2005: 224, 224 n. 32 on the motif of the displacement of women by gods. Stesichorus seem to have had a profound interest in genealogy considering the alternative versions he presents for filiation, for example, Hector being Apollo's son (fr. 108b F.) and Iphigenia being Helen's daughter (fr. 86 F.) or other fragments attesting this interest, as shown in frr. 15, 286, 287, 288 F.
[4] For abduction as a folktale motif see Frenzel 1999: 160–170, for a discussion of the myth of Helen in the scope of folktale, see Edmunds 2016: 20–65, and for a comparative study of the motif of the abduction of women, see Avsenik Nabergoj 2009: 122–139. In the realm of Greek literature the interconnection of the mythical abductions and the historical facts is clear for example in Herodotus (1.1–5) who begins his *Histories* "with a series of abductions and counter-abductions of women" (Hornblower 2015: 452, n. 1283–1450) and explains the historical facts behind the myth in an approach that withdraws from a mythical perspective in favour of a more historical one; and in Lycophron, as noted by Hornblower 2015: 452 n. 1238–1450, who in his *Alexandra*, which deals extensively with the motif of abducted women, uses the historical facts as the main thread for his narrative.

ery and temptation",[5] i.e. seduction, to quote Avsenik Nabergoj, in her study on the motifs of longing and temptation and its relation to myths of abduction. Whether motivated by demonstrations of force from an invader, or by a military or political agenda; or more directed, as a form of reprisal against a certain family, or indeed a certain man; or even as the result of seduction, abduction involves displacement of women. It is therefore no wonder that it is in the mythical narratives treating the theme of abduction that we find the most insidious representation of travelling women within Greek literature.

In other works, Stesichorus shows interest in female characters.[6] In what concerns their travels, we have seen his alternative version for the destiny of Hecuba in the *Sack of Troy*, which implies a journey undertaken by Hecuba, which does not result from abduction. This journey is nevertheless commanded by Apollo, who escorts Hecuba to Lycia. We cannot tell, therefore, to what extent Hecuba had a say in her rescue, although the aura of seduction common in the abduction myths seems to be absent from the episode. It is worth noting, however, that, according to Stesichorus, Hecuba had had previous encounters with Apollo, to whom Hector was born. One may wonder to what extent was Hecuba vulnerable to Apollo's seduction or violence in the past.

Some have found it hard to distinguish between abduction and seduction[7] in Greek myth as the versions vary regarding the role of the abductee. However, the vulnerable place of women is a common denominator of these stories,[8] even when the escape is consensual. This accentuates the problem in defining the agency of women in context of female displacement in Stesichorus since in both cases we are dealing with the abduction can arguably be an elopement, hence a consequence of seduction. We do not know how Stesichorus treated the abduction of Europa. In the traditional version, the princess is attracted to Zeus disguised as a bull, but she is not asked in any moment if she wants to depart with him. The case of agency is more of an issue regarding Helen, and particularly Stesichorus' Helen, since her agency in her disappearance from Sparta is precisely the point in her characterization, especially in the *Palinode*. In any case, Helen seems to have had no word regarding her abduction by Theseus, an epi-

---

[5] Avsenik Nabergoj 2009: 124.
[6] On maternal figures in the works of Stesichorus, see Xanthou 2015.
[7] Thus Morales 2016: 61 n. 2. However, see Zeitlin 1986 on the nuances of the rape myths.
[8] On the problematic of consent vs sexual violence, see Sommerstein 2006 championing the distinction in Greek Tragedy of consensual and non-consensual intercourse. Rabinowitz 2011 draws attention to the recurrence of sexual violence upon women in Greek Tragedy.

sode which is told by Stesichorus (fr. 86 F.), making her a victim of abduction by force at least once.

3.1 The *Europeia*

Europa's abduction by Zeus was known to early epic, lyric, and drama. However, in contrast with the case of Helen, whose myth appears in many surviving works from early and classical Greek literature and art,[9] no detailed version of the myth of Europa survives from those periods. Her abduction is referred in Homer in the catalogue of Zeus' affairs.[10] To find detailed versions of the abduction of Europa in an epic context we have to turn to Eumelus' *Europeia*[11] and the *Catalogue of Women*,[12] although the date of these works is a matter of debate. In lyric, apart from Stesichorus, the myth of Europa was explored in lost poems by Simonides[13] and Bacchylides.[14] In tragedy, Aeschylus treats the episode as a background for the present event, where Europa shows concern regarding the

---

9 Robertson 1988; Barringer 1991; López Monteagudo and San Nicolas Pedraz 1991; Robertson 1992; Wintle 2006: 81–152; Marconi 2007: 90–96; Westcoat 2012: 176–179.
10 E.g. Hom. *Il.* 14.321–323. Rocha Pereira 2005: 7 notes that in the *Catalogue*, a scholium to *Il.* 12.292 (fr. 140 M-W), where the myth of Europa is mentioned, Europa is Phoenix's daughter, whereas other versions make Europa daughter of Agenor and sister of both Phoenix and Cadmus. However, the *Iliad* recognizes Cadmus as the founder of Thebes. Stesichorus told about Cadmus in his *Europeia* (fr. 96 F.) so we should therefore consider that he adopted the version according to which Europa was his sister, thus either she is daughter of Agenor, or Cadmus son of Phoenix. See further Apollod. *Bibl.* 3.1.1., and West 2005b: 83.
11 See West 2002: 129–132.
12 [Hes] fr. 140–141 M-W. Not to be confused with the Europa from Hes. *Th.* 361. The *Catalogue* is the first instance where Sarpedon is son of Europa. For discussion on the date of the *Catalogue*, see West 2005b: 130–137.
13 This information is provided by Aristophanes of Byzantium (fr. 124 Slater), who says that the composition, likely a dithyramb (on the discussion see Ferreira 2013: 134), was entitled *Europa*. However, the sole information provided refers to the bull in three different ways, suggesting that the episode of the abduction was quite long.
14 Europa is mentioned as Minos' mother at B. 1.124. Fr. 10 M informs us that Bacchylides composed another poem on the abduction of Europa. It is uncertain whether the scholium was referring to an independent poem entitled *Europa* (lost dithyramb or hymn: Jebb 1905: 429; Robert 1917: 308–313), or to the content of *Dith.* 17.28–32, 52–54 (thus e.g., Schwartz 1904: 642) which mentions Europa's love affair with Zeus.

fate of her son, Sarpedon, commander of the Lycians at Troy.[15] Euripides mentions the episode in passing.[16]

The most extensive and moving account of the abduction itself is found only in the Hellenistic poetry with Moschus' *Europa*,[17] which emphasises the eroticism of a scene easily compared to many other myths of seduction and marriage.[18] Achilles Tatius opens his novel *Leucippe and Clitophon* (1.1.1–13) with an ecphrasis of an image depicting the abduction of Europa by Zeus metamorphosed into a bull. In similar terms, the *Anacreontea* preserves another ecphrasis (fr. 54) of a representation of the abduction of Europa ("the Sidonian woman") by Zeus and their journey crossing the sea.[19]

In general terms, the episode of the abduction should not have differed much from what the information provided by a scholium to the *Iliad* 12.292:

Εὐρώπην τὴν Φοίνικος Ζεὺς θεασάμενος ἔν τινι λειμῶνι μετὰ νυμφῶν ἄνθη ἀναλέγουσαν ἠράσθη, καὶ κατελθὼν ἤλλαξεν ἑαυτὸν εἰς ταῦρον καὶ ἀπὸ τοῦ στόματος κρόκον ἔπνει· οὕτως τε τὴν Εὐρώπην ἀπατήσας ἐβάστασε, καὶ διαπορθμεύσας εἰς Κρήτην ἐμίγη αὐτῆι. εἶθ' οὕτως συνώικισεν αὐτὴν Ἀστερίωνι τῶι Κρητῶν βασιλεῖ. Γενομένη δὲ ἔγκυος ἐκείνη τρεῖς παῖδας ἐγέννησε Μίνωα Σαρπηδόνα Ῥαδάμανθυν. ἡ ἱστορία παρ' Ἡσιόδωι καὶ Βακχυλίδηι.

Zeus saw Phoenix's daughter Europa plucking flowers together with maidens in a meadow, and he was seized by desire for her. He came down and changed himself into a bull whose breath was saffron-scented. Deceiving Europa in this way he let her mount him, and carrying her across the sea to Crete he mingled with her. Then he gave her as wife to Asterion, the king of the Cretans. She became pregnant and bore three children: Minos, Sarpedon, and Rhadamanthys. The story is in Hesiod and Bacchylides.[20]

The part of the *Catalogue* which preserves the episode confirms the version in the scholia regarding what follows Zeus' success in deceiving Europa. The fragment thus begins when Zeus and Europa having already "crossed the salty

---

15 Fr. 99 *TrGF*. The connection between Troy, Lycia and desperate mothers is emphasised by Stesichorus in the *Sack of Troy*, where Hecuba is rescued from Troy by Apollo and taken to Lycia (fr. 109 F.), as discussed above in 2.1.7.
16 Frr. 472.1–2, 752g.18–23, 820 *TrGF*.
17 On Moschus' *Europa*, see Bühler 1960.
18 Hunter 2005: 254–256.
19 The chronology of fr. 54 is hard to define. However, most scholars agree that fr. 54 is among the latest poems of the group, hence composed roughly between the second and the fourth centuries AD. See Baumann 2014: 122–124. For chronology of the *Anacreontea*, see Brioso Sanchéz 1970; West 1984; Campbell 1988: 10–18; Müller 2010: 121–124.
20 Schol. A+B Hom. *Il.* 12.292 Dindorf = fr. 140 M-W = Bacchyl. fr. 10 M. Transl. Most 2007: 159–161.

sea" after Europa had been Διὸς δμηθεῖϲα δόλοιϲι "overpowered by the tricks of Zeus", and "carried across" (διαπορθμεύϲαϲ)[21] the sea to Crete (fr. 141.1–2 M-W), and develops from the moment of the union of Europa and Zeus once in Crete. The imagery, suggested by fr. 140 M-W, of the group of young girls gathering flowers, repeated by Moschus (*Europa* 44–71), is a central motif in the narratives of abduction and is also present in episodes of erotic flavour such as Nausicaa's in the *Odyssey*, or of abduction, as in the *Homeric Hymn to Demeter*, and in some accounts of Helen's abduction by Theseus. It would have been interesting to see how the author of the *Catalogue* dealt with it. The romantic scenes in Hesiod are present only in the aftermath of the intercourse in fr. 141.14, where Zeus gives Europa a necklace made by Hephaestus, suggesting not only a romantic but also a marital scene. The fragment proceeds in describing the achievements of the sons of Europa and Zeus (frr. 141.13–31; 144 M-W.).

The accuracy of the scholiast regarding Bacchylides is harder to verify, since from Bacchylides' works even less survives. Some scholars have pointed out that Bacchylides had composed a poem fully dedicated to Europa;[22] others consider that the information of the scholium refers to *Dithyramb* 17.29–32, where, upon the arrival of Theseus to Crete, Minos challenges his divine origin, to which the first responds reminding the latter that he is not the only one with divine ancestry, despite being the son of Zeus and Europa.[23] The references to Europa merely allude to her union with Zeus in Ida and Crete, and her Phoenician origin, which implies knowledge of the abduction, but not necessarily a detailed treatment.

Only with Moschus do we have a more detailed account of the abduction, which is in dialogue with the *Catalogue*.[24] Moschus seems to follow the blueprint of the narrative of the *Catalogue*, according to fr. 140 M-W, but displays variations, the most significant of which is the treatment given to Europa and Zeus' offspring. Moschus ends the narrative when the three children's names are revealed, whereas that is Hesiod's main interest,[25] and indeed that of most accounts of the abduction. Another different aspect of the treatment of Moschus is the vocabulary used to refer to the abduction. While Hesiod treats the abduction in descriptive terms, referring only to the movement of the girl carried

---

21 Cf. Acusilaus fr. 29 *EGM*: ἀγαγεῖν ταῦρον. τοῦτον Ἀκουϲίλαοϲ μὲν εἶναί φηϲι τὸν διαπορθμεύϲαντα Εὐρώπην Διί.
22 Thus Jebb 1905: 429.
23 Schwartz 1904: 642. On the debate, see Jesus 2014: 134–135, 216–217.
24 Hunter 2005: 254–256. Hunter focuses on the deviations or reworkings of Moschus in, for example, the active role of Europa in the narrative as opposed to the silent character of Hesiod.
25 Campbell 1991: 1.

across the sea (διαπορθμεύϲαϲ), Moschus' classifies the action through the term ἁρπάξαϲ (line 110), common in situations of abduction, in particular, in the account of the abduction of Persephone in the *Homeric Hymn to Demeter* (lines 3, 55, 80, 414), where the idea of unwillingness of the victim is clear.

We do not know how Stesichorus dealt with the abduction in his *Europeia*, but one may suspect that it was a crucial moment in the narrative, a trigger to the plot. It is because Europa is abducted that Cadmus had to leave Phoenicia and eventually founded Thebes, the only episode certainly ascribed to Stesichorus (fr. 96 F.). If not the abduction itself, at least its consequences were certainly explored by Stesichorus, which makes him the earliest surviving source of the connection between Europa and Cadmus, otherwise known from Herodotus.[26]

Eumelus' *Europeia* shares affinities with the recoverable part of Stesichorus' account, since he connects Europa' abduction, the foundation of Thebes and the treatment of Theban genealogy; but the extent to which it was treated by Eumelus cannot be told with certainty.[27] The existent pieces attributed to Eumelus' *Europeia* are almost all related to the genealogy of Cadmus.[28] However, Philodemus makes an interesting point regarding the abduction of Europa that differs from what we have in the other sources (fr. 26 *GEF*):

ὁ δὲ [τὴν Εὐ]ρώπειαν γράψα[ϲ] καὶ αὑτῆϲ τὸν α[ὑ]τὸν ἐραϲθῆνα[ί] φηϲιν, καὶ διὰ τ[ὸ] μὴ ὑπομεῖνα[ι μι]χθῆναι Διὶ αὐτ[ὸν] αὐτὴν [τὸν] Δ[ία [πα]ρῃρῆϲ[θαι

The author of the *Europeia* says that the same god fell in love with her too, and that because she would not submit to intercourse with Zeus, Zeus himself abducted her.

Unlike other accounts, here Philodemus suggests that Eumelus had Europa abducted by force and against her will, in which case the narrative loses its romantic potential, and approximates the myth of Europa to Persephone's, for example. However, the sense of παραιρέω is not clear, since it can mean both

---

26 Hdt. 4.147.4. However, Herodotus, in his rationalizing manner, has Europa being abducted by Cretan men, not Zeus (Hdt. 1.2.1, for a similar version see Lycophron 1296–1311, Hornblower 2015: 456–458). However, the only element that connects Cadmus and Europa in the oeuvre of Euripides is, in fact, a scholium to E. *Ph*. 670, which relates the episode where the chorus remember the sowing of the dragon's teeth by Cadmus to Stesichorus' *Europeia* (fr. 96 F.).

27 It is likely that in Eumelus' *Europeia*, the abduction of Europa and the foundation of Thebes have been connected. The testimonies also point to a very interesting detail of Eumelus' version concerning Menelaus' visit to Crete in whose absence Helen was taken by Paris (Apollod. *Bibl*. 3.11.1 = fr. 33 *GEF*), on which see West 2002: 127).

28 Eumelus' *Europeia* fr. 27 *GEF*.

"seize" and "persuade".²⁹ Lefkowitz has argued that, in Greek myth, women are not raped but rather seduced or abducted and their consent in the intercourse is emphasised. The romantic and harmonious set of these scenes enhances the amorous, thus non-coercive environment.³⁰ However, the fragment of Philodemus stresses the lack of consent by Europa, which makes this abduction more of a rape.

The violence of the abduction is also stressed, but in different terms, in Aeschylus' *Cares* or *Europa* (fr. 99 *TrGF*):

ταύρωι τε λειμών ξένια πάμβοτος παρῆν.
τοιόνδ' ἐμὲ Ζεὺς κλέμμα πρεσβύτου πατρὸς
αὐτοῦ μένων ἄμοχθον ἤνυσεν λαβεῖν.
τί οὖν τὰ πολλὰ κεῖνα; διὰ παύρων λέγω·
γυνὴ θεῶι μειχθεῖσα παρθένου σέβας
ἤμειψα, παίδων δ' ἐζύγην ξυνωνίαι.

A lush meadow welcomed the bull.
In his exaltation, Zeus succeeded in his
Untroubled theft of me from my aged father.
Why all this? I tell you in few words.
I, a mortal women united to a god, lost the holiness
of maidenhood, and am now subdued to him by these children.

Aeschylus' Europa emphasises the trickery of Zeus, who sent an actual bull as his agent to Sidon, by stressing how her theft was untroubled to the god, who remain wherever he was, probably in Crete. The fact that it was a bull to take Europa implies that there was no seduction, and therefore, that Europa was taken unwillingly, kidnapped from her parental home, while alone and defenceless in the meadow, and lost her status as a *parthenos* to become subdued to the god.³¹

This context for abduction is closer to what we see in later historians. The tendency to elide the metamorphosis of the god from the myth is present already by the sixth century mythographer Acusilaus³² according to whom it was a real bull, sent by the god, which abducted Europa and brought her to Crete. Herodotus³³ ignores the version of the abduction by Zeus and frames it exclusively within the realm of human affairs. He relates that the abduction of Euro-

---

29 Thus Chantraine 1968 s.v. αἱρέω.
30 Lefkowitz 1993: 19–20.
31 Deacy 1997: 45.
32 Fr. 29 *EGM*, see Fowler 2013: 286.
33 Hdt. 1.1.2.

pa was undertaken by the Cretans, in a revenge action for the previous abduction of Io by the Tyrians.[34] Malalas,[35] in the fourth century AD, recalls how in the absence of Agenor and his sons, Tauros, the king of Crete, came from the sea and sacked Tyre making its inhabitants, among whom Europa was found, prisoners of war in Crete. Some poetic accounts are based in this less fictional version. Euripides[36] seems to have oscillated between the two, but Lycophron draws his version from Herodotus', emphasising that the girl was dragged off (ἤμπρευcαν) by the Cretans.[37]

Whether as a consenting victim of the enchantment of Zeus, or an innocent abducted girl, Europa is taken from her home by a foreigner or an alien element of the *oikos* without her consent or her father's authorisation. From the multiplicity of meanings that the myth may have in its different accounts, the idea that Europa is taken as a girl, not as a woman, is significant since the myths of rape and abduction "can be regarded as the mythical embodiment of marriage".[38]

As pointed out by Barringer,[39] the myth of Europa, as the marriage rites, consists in a literal voyage from the maiden homeland to her future marital home. This literal voyage parallels the symbolic path from maidenhood to womanhood. However, unlike marriage, this union results from seduction and abduction or elopement; hence, parental authority is challenged inasmuch as there is no consent from the father of the maiden. This is what triggers the departure of Cadmus in search for his sister, an element presented for the first time, as far as we know, in Stesichorus.[40] Therefore, in the case of Europa,

---

34 Hdt. 1.2.1: μετὰ δὲ ταῦτα Ἑλλήνων τινάc (οὐ γὰρ ἔχουcι τοὔνομα ἀπεγήcαcθαι) φαcὶ τῆc Φοινίκηc ἐc Τύρον προccχόνταc ἁρπάcαι τοῦ βαcιλέοc τὴν θυγατέρα Εὐρώπην. εἴηcαν δ' ἂν οὗτοι Κρῆτεc. "According to the story, some Greeks (they cannot say who) arrived in Tyre in Phoenicia and abducted Europa, the king's daughter. I suppose they must have been Cretans."
35 *Chron.* 2.34.
36 E. fr. 820a–b. *TrGF*.
37 Lyc. *Alex.* 1296, see Hornblower 2015 *ad loc.*
38 Thus Robson 1997: 79, on the parallels of rape and marriage and rape see esp. pp. 78–82; Lefkowitz 1986: 30, 31, 43 and 48; Perlman 1983: 126 n. 61.
39 Barringer 1991: 659, 662.
40 The Phoenician origin of Cadmus is not certain to antedate the sixth or fifth centuries (cf. Gomme 1913; Vermeule 1971; Hall 1996; Gruen 2011: 223–236; Skinner 2012: 87, n. 127). In Homer, and indeed in some Pindaric works (*P.* 3.88, 8.47, *O.* 2.78, *I.* 6.76.), Cadmus' origins are left unclear. However, scholars such as Edwards 1979; Vermeule 1971; and West 1997 have argued for a genuine Phoenician origin of Cadmus. West 1997: 607 points the Semitic etymology of Cadmeians, meaning either 'easterners' or 'men of old'. Furthermore, as the scholars suggests, the Phoenician ancestry of Cadmus may be explained by the attribution of the ruins

whose accounts generally depict a seduced, and not abducted, maiden, the problem is perhaps not so much the free will of the maiden or bride, since her say in the matter was indubitably reduced, if any at all, but the significance it has to the father or *kurios* of the maiden. Whether the maiden is taken willing or unwillingly, the power and authority of the *kurios* is harmed, and this is all the more relevant, as the myth of Helen so clearly shows and to which we shall return.

In Stesichorus' *Europeia*, the harmed authority of the king has its repercussions in the figure of Cadmus, Europa's brother, who is sent by their father to recover his sister Europa. This chain of events is similar to Stesichorus' account of the abduction of Helen by Theseus and the subsequent search and recover of her by her brothers, the Dioscuri, as we shall see. However, whereas in the account of Helen, the Dioscuri are successful, in the myth of Europa Cadmus is not.

But the story of Europa and the failure of Cadmus to accomplish his task allow Stesichorus to elaborate other themes. While the symbolic meaning of marriage would hardly have been the main concern of the poet, it seems that he nevertheless dealt with marriage, or union, to elaborate on other issues, which are derivatives of marriage, such as aetiology and genealogy. Adrados suggested that the poem concerned the whole genealogy of Cadmus, beginning in Agenor's own genealogy (fr. 286 F.), and moving to the origins of Thebes and its earlier history.[41] According to him, the poem elaborated on the theme of marriage, perhaps mentioning Cadmus and Harmonia's wedding and indeed the conflict between Zeus and Acteon over Semele (fr. 285 F.),[42] Agave and Penthe-

---

of the Mycenaean citadel to the 'men of old' by the Phoenician migrants' settled in Boeotia in the ninth and eighth centuries. Despite the absence of material evidence attesting Phoenician presence in Thebes, there are some connections between the eastern elements of Dionysus and the house of Cadmus as early as the *Homeric Hymn to Dionysus* (1.5–9), on which see Mitchell 2007: 183.

41 Adrados 1978: 289. Ἡcίοδος δ' ἐν Καταλόγωι φηcί· "καὶ κούρην Ἀράβοιο, τὸν Ἑρμάων ἀκάκητα γείνατο καὶ Θρονίη, κούρη Βήλοιο ἄνακτος" οὕτω δὲ καὶ Στηcίχορος λέγει. εἰκάζειν οὖν ἔcτιν ὅτι ἀπὸ τούτου καὶ ἡ χώρα Ἀραβία ἤδη τότε ὠνομάζετο, κατὰ δὲ τοὺς ἥρωας τυχὸν ἴcως οὔπω. "Hesiod says in the *Catalogue* 'and the daughter of Arabus, son of gracious Hermaon and Thronia, daughter of lord Belus'. Stesichorus says the same. So, one can infer that by their time the country was already called Arabia, although it presumably did not have the same name in the age of the heroes". On Hermes as the father of the Arabs, see Finglass 2014d.

42 Rose 1932a; Adrados 1978: 289; Davies and Finglass 2014: 571–574. Fr. 285 F.: τοῖc δὲ ἐκ Μεγάρων ἰοῦcι πηγή τέ ἐcτιν ἐν δεξιᾶι καὶ προελθοῦcιν ὀλίγον πέτρα· καλοῦcι δὲ τὴν μὲν Ἀκταίωνοc κοίτην, ἐπὶ ταύτηι καθεύδειν φάμενοι τῆι πέτραι τὸν Ἀκταίωνα ὁπότε κάμοι θηρεύων, ἐc δὲ τὴν πηγὴν ἐνιδεῖν λέγουcιν αὐτὸν λουομένης Ἀρτέμιδοc {ἐν τῆι πηγῆι}. Στηcίχοροc δὲ

us. Monteagudo and Nicolás Pedraz⁴³ note that the archaic and classical literary sources for the myth of Europa demonstrate a concern for its historical, geographical, and aetiological consequences, from which several sources draw the justifications for eastern presence and expansion across the western Mediterranean.

The travels implied in the myth of Europa are significant inasmuch as they concern the movement not of Greeks, but of easterners within the Greek genealogical realm, which creates an idea of a shared and common space and the movement across it. The shared space thus become a common origin, which is materialized in genealogy.⁴⁴ The movement of Europa to Crete, Cadmus from Crete to Delphi, and from there to Thebes motivate the mixed genealogy of the Thebans, therefore, tied to the ruling family of Crete, which implies the connection with the ruling family of Lycia (if Stesichorus indeed made Sarpedon the son of Europa and Zeus, as happens in most accounts).

We have then a map of Phoenician presence across the eastern Mediterranean. The voyage of Europa to Crete triggers a whole series of other travels, but more significantly creates a temporal dimension of the phenomenon of Phoenician presence within the realm of Greek influence. As the genealogical poems which "provided an interconnected genealogy of the whole world",⁴⁵ the story of Europa, Cadmus, and their travels has the potential to create a more comprehensive, inclusive account of affairs throughout the Mediterranean. It is then significant that the first poets, as far as we know, to have connected Cadmus to Europa are Stesichorus – a poet from Sicily, where the Phoenician presence was quite intense,⁴⁶ and who composed a poem whose action was settled in a territory under Phoenician influence, Cadiz (the *Geryoneis*) – and probably Eumelus, from Corinth, a city with early relations with the Near East.⁴⁷

ὁ Ἱμεραῖος ἔγραψεν ἐλάφου περιβαλεῖν δέρμα Ἀκταίωνι τὴν θεόν, παρασκευάζουσάν οἱ τὸν ἐκ τῶν κυνῶν θάνατον, ἵνα δὴ μὴ γυναῖκα Σεμέλην λάβοι. "On the road from Megara have there is a spring on the right and a rock further on. The rock is called 'Actaeon's bed', for they say that Actaeon used to sleep on it when weary with hunting, and from there he looked into the spring when Artemis was bathing in it. Stesichorus of Himera wrote that the goddess wrapped a deerskin round Actaeon to make sure his hounds would kill him, and thus prevent his marriage with Semele".
43 Nicolás Pedraz 1995: 2–3.
44 On which see Mitchell 2007: 177–183.
45 Mitchell 2007: 177–183.
46 Domínguez 2008: 149–159; De Angelis 2016: 36–41, 46–53, 161–162, 167.
47 Ziskowski 2016: 91–110; Morris and Papadopoulos 1998: 251–264.

Using the traditional motifs of the tales of abduction such as the abduction of the maiden from the meadow, and the departure of the brother is her search, Stesichorus includes foreigners as a determinant element of the genealogy of the Greek myth, particularly the Theban. Moreover, he establishes an interesting parallel for the other instance where he elaborates on abduction: the story of Helen. In both accounts the element of displacement is crucial.

3.2 The *Helen*

Despite being one of the most famous mythical personae, the story of Helen is never told from beginning to end,[48] but is rather divided in relatively independent episodes in various works of both literature and art. Stesichorus composed at least four poems on which Helen played a part: *Helen* (frr. 84–89 F.), *Sack of Troy* (frr. 105, 106, 112, and 115 F.), *Nostoi?* (fr. 170 F.), and the *Palinode* (frr. 90–91j F., if one considers the *Palinode* to be a different poem from *Helen*).[49] The *Helen*, overshadowed in scholarly discussion by the *Palinode*, occupied two books in the Alexandrian edition of Stesichorus. Unfortunately, it only survives from quotations and it is difficult to prove the original order of events. But, to put them in a chronological order, we have the following reasonable sequence.

Tyndareus forgets to honour Aphrodite in a sacrifice to the gods (fr. 85 F.). This enrages the goddess, who curses each of Tyndareus' daughters with a plurality of marriages. The first event motivated by the punishment of Tyndareus through his daughters is the abduction of Helen by Theseus, followed by her rescue and the birth of Iphigenia at Argos, where the baby is left under the custody of Clytemnestra (fr. 86 F.). After returning home, Helen's suitors gather in Lacedaemon and woo her (fr. 87 F.), Menelaus wins and, after the oath exacted by Tyndareus, he marries her (fr. 88 F.). Finglass suggests that the procession in fr. 88 F and the epithalamium song referred in fr. 84 F. "would make a suitable point for a Hellenistic editor to insert a book division".[50] If this was the case, then the second book of *Helen* would have dealt with events subsequent to the troubled marriage, among which were Helen's elopement with Paris and her arrival at Troy. Furthermore, the reference to the oath on the occasion of Helen's wooing (fr. 87 F.) makes it likely that the poem explored the resulting marriage

---

48 Thus Edmunds 2016: 103.
49 For a discussion in favour of the *Palinode* as the same poem as *Helen*, see Kelly 2008.
50 Finglass 2015a: 93.

described later in the narrative. If so, the gathering of the troops may well have been treated in the *Helen*.

Abduction myths in Greek mythology are often motivated by an erotic appeal of a god towards a woman (whether a young unmarried girl, as in the case of Europa shown above, and Persephone, or a married woman, such as Pasiphae or Danae). There is no other reason behind the abduction except the erotic impetus of the deity. The case of Helen, however, cannot be included in this pattern, because the gods, in most versions, do not intervene directly; they make humans their agents in the plot.

Although responsible and the ultimate coordinators of the events leading to the Trojan War, the gods are no direct agents of the abduction of Helen. In fact, in the case of Stesichorus' *Helen*, the anger of the gods is not even caused by any of the characters traditionally involved in the event at Troy. And this has a reason: Stesichorus' *Helen* is not concerned only with the justification of the Trojan War, but compelled to explain the questionable conduct of the house of Tyndareus and to bring together in the story of Helen another tradition otherwise strange to the epic, concerning the ancestral hero of Athens, Theseus, thus including his house in the wider and "foundational" heroic cycle of Troy. The curse of Tyndareus encompasses both stories of abductions and marriage, providing them with the same single cause, and thus deserves closer attention.

3.2.1 Tyndareus' fault (fr. 85 F.)

The curse of Tyndareus resultant from his disregard towards Aphrodite is known to us from a scholium to Euripides' *Orestes* 249:

> Στησίχορός φηcιν ὡc θύων τοῖc θεοῖc Τυνδάρεωc Ἀφροδίτηc ἐπελάθετο· διὸ ὀργιcθεῖcαν τὴν θεὸν διγάμουc τε καὶ τριγάμουc καὶ λειψάνδρουc αὐτοῦ τὰc θυγατέραc ποιῆcαι. ἔχει δὲ ἡ χρῆcιc οὕτωc·
>
> οὕνεκα Τυνδάρεοc
> ῥέζων ποκὰ πᾶcι θεοῖc μόναc λάθετ' ἠπιοδώρου
> Κύπριδοc· κείνα δὲ Τυνδαρέου κόραc
> χολωcαμένα διγάμουc τε καὶ τριγάμουc ἐτίθει
> καὶ λιπεcάνοραc.   5
>
> Stesichorus says that Tyndareus forgot Aphrodite when he was sacrificing to the gods; the goddess was angry and made his daughters twice-wed, and thrice-wed, and deserters of husbands. The passage runs as follows:

> Because Tyndareus
> when he was sacrificing to all the gods, forgot only bountiful
> Aphrodite. So in her anger, she made the daughters of Tyndareus
> Twice-wedded and even thrice-wedded and
> Deserters of husbands.   5

This fragment is ascribed to *Helen* in Davies and Finglass's edition, reviving the suggestions of Blomfield and Bergk.[51] However, this has not been unanimous among scholars, who have been debating the subject since the nineteenth century. This discussion eventually led to the cautious decision of Page followed by Davies[52] to assign it to the *incerti loci* deviating from earlier editions, thus leaving the ascription of the poem a matter open to debate, which led to tentative ascriptions to other Stesichorean poems, namely the *Sack of Troy* and the *Oresteia*.[53]

In his edition, Schneidewin ascribes fr. 85 F. (= fr. 9 Schneidewin) to the *Sack of Troy* following the suggestion of Welcker, who relates the information provided in the *Tabula Iliaca Capitolina* regarding the sons of Theseus and Aethra to frr. 85 and 86 F., which mention the original fault of Tyndareus and the abduction of Helen by Theseus.[54] Perhaps due to this attribution, Detienne categorically assumes that this fragment belongs to the poem on the sack of Troy without further discussion.[55] These suggestions were made, lest we forget, before the discovery of the papyri of the *Sack of Troy*, published by Lobel in 1967 (P. Oxy. 2619) and 1971 (P. Oxy. 2803); hence before a more solid knowledge of the metre, which shows incompatibility with fr. 85 F.,[56] thus invalidating this possibility.

The consideration of fr. 85 F. as part of the *Oresteia* is also problematic. Geel and Wilamowitz considered the fragment fitted for the context of the *Oresteia*, since it provides the context for the events of the poem. It is ultimately the bigamy or trigamy of Clytaemnestra what leads to the death of Agamemnon and

---

51 Blomfield 1816: 261; Bergk 1882: 214 (fr. 26); Grossardt 2012: 27.
52 fr. 223 *PMG*.
53 For a general overview of the debate see Geel 1839: 7; Campbell 1998: 260; Gerber 1970: 152; Aloni 1994: 99; Ragusa 2010: 252 nn. 109 and 110; Grossardt 2012: 26–28. *Oresteia*: Colonna 1963: 211. *Sack of Troy*: Schneidewin 1838 fr. 9 and Detienne 1959: 139.
54 Schneidewin 1838: fr. 9; Welcker 1829: 260.
55 Detienne 1957: 139.
56 The remains in the papyri of the *Sack of Troy* allow us to have an idea the metre of both strophe/antistrophe and epode, and neither of them allow an inclusion of a sequence such as the presented in fr. 85 F. Compare the metre of e.g. frr. 100 F. and 103 F. (see Davies and Finglass 2014: 406–414) and fr. 85 F. (Davies and Finglass 2014: 317).

Orestes' revenge.⁵⁷ Defradas (followed by Bowie) argues that Stesichorus "almost certainly depicted the shameful conduct of Helen in the *Helen* and in the *Oresteia*".⁵⁸ He mentions fr. 85 F. as part of the *Oresteia* without acknowledging the controversy of that assumption. As Grossardt⁵⁹ notes, some supporters of this view point out that fr. 85 F. comes from a scholium to the *Orestes* of Euripides, which may indicate that the fragment was part of Stesichorus' *Oresteia* because the scholiast would have had a tendency to consult the homonymous poem when commenting on Euripides' version. However, the *Oresteia* fragment are in dactyl-anapaests, which rules out the hypothesis.

Moreover, in his discussion against the attribution of fr. 85 F. to the *Oresteia*, Grossardt asserts that the fragment makes no sense in the context of that poem because it would emphasise a character not central to the poem. Helen, he assumes, is central to fr. 85, but I fail to see why is Helen more central in this fragment than the other daughters. The central character here is not Helen, nor Clytemnestra, but Tyndareus.

Would Tyndareus occupy such an important role in the *Oresteia* as to be responsible for the mayhem in the poem? We have no evidence for Tyndareus presence in the *Oresteia*. But we do have a fragment ascribed convincingly by modern editors to the *Helen* where he is a central figure. Fr. 87 F., a scholium to the *Iliad*, does not mention where the story was told, but is generally accepted as belonging to *Helen* since it concerns her wooing, and such episode would fit a poem where the wedding of Helen and Menelaus would be told (fr. 88 F.). It seems too hypercritical to exclude fr. 87 F. from the *Helen*.

If the assumption is correct, Tyndareus appears to be a prominent character in the course of the *Helen*.⁶⁰ What is more, he is a central character in an episode (fr. 87 F.) where he shows awareness of his fault against Aphrodite; he knows or suspects how Aphrodite will seek her revenge and anticipates the consequences of a possible future desertion of Helen by means of an oath which ties the suitors to act, should anything happen to his daughter. Both frr. 85 F. and 87 F. reflect moral judgments on Tyndareus and his daughters that denigrate their

---

57 Geel 1839: 7; Wilamowitz 1896: 248.
58 Defradas 1954: 174; Bowie 1993: 23.
59 Grossardt 2012: 26.
60 The attention paid to Tyndareus in this fragment may provide a context for fr. 287 F., which is not ascribed to any poem in Davies and Finglass' edition. Fr. 287 F. says that, in Stesichorus, Tyndareus was son of Perieres and Gorgophone, daughter of Perseus. The genealogical background of Tyndareus would suit a context where the man in question received some prominence, as it is the case with Geryon as seen above in 1.1.2.

reputation in a different way than Homer.[61] It seems therefore that the *Helen* is the likeliest poem to contain this characterization of both father and daughters.[62] The arguments presented by Finglass for attribution of fr. 85 to *Helen* are convincing, since it is the only known title to present the ideal metre and content to accommodate it.[63]

Fr. 85 F. casts light on a particularly significant part of the poem where the poet presents the motives and the justification for the subsequent narrative. The recuperation of older (mostly forgotten) solutions for the arrangement of Stesichorus' fragments carried out in Davies and Finglass's edition of Stesichorus have been proven fruitful regarding the *Sack of Troy*,[64] where the opening stanza has been partly recovered. Taking this into account and the importance of the information preserved in the fragment, it may have occupied a place in the opening of the poem. If so, this represents a valuable addition when considering the structure of the poem and indeed Stesichorus' narrative technique. In these lines, Stesichorus is explaining the bad repute of Tyndareus' daughters. Tyndareus failed to honour Aphrodite with a sacrifice and the goddess, in her anger, inflicts the penalty for such a fault in the culprit's daughters.

The series of abductions, elopement, and failed marriages, among which is the abduction of Helen by Paris and the Trojan War, will unfold by means of erotic and marital misbehaviour because of their father's impiety towards Aphrodite. The daughters of Tyndareus are, therefore, not the cause for Aphrodite's anger, unlike in Hesiod, but her instruments for fulfilling her revenge against Tyndareus. He is thus the central figure in the fragment, and his name figures as the sole responsible for his daughters' ill repute. This stresses not only the capricious nature of the deity but, more importantly, casts light on a character otherwise secondary in other versions of the myth.

The emphasis on unexpected characters as the origin and cause of the subsequent events is found in another Stesichorean fragment. The opening of the *Iliou Persis* (fr. 100 F.) encompasses the reaction of Athena towards Epeius. As we have seen above in the previous chapter, the goddess pities him for his toil as a water-carrier and therefore decides to inspire him in building the horse, thus giving him the opportunity to win glory. This kind gesture of the goddess,

---

[61] Thus Bowra 1961: 111; Cingano 1982: 32 n. 47; for a discussion on this matter, see also Ragusa 2010: 251.
[62] Rozokoki 2014: 205 is perhaps hypercritical regarding the attribution of the fragment to the *Helen* rather than to the *Oresteia* or the *Sack of Troy*.
[63] Davies and Finglass 2014: 319–320.
[64] The hypothesis of fr. 100 F. to be the opening of the *Sack of Troy* was first put forward by Kazansky, as seen above in 2.1.1.

however, has appalling consequences for an entire city and its people. Her pity for one man results in the death of hundreds, a fact that clearly illustrates the capricious *modus operandi* of deities. The structure of both fragments would thus result similar, although they present some contrasting elements.

First, the man in question is mentioned (fr. 85.1 F. and fr. 100.10 F. ἀνήρ). In the *Iliou Persis* the identity of the man is not revealed for another eight lines, whereas in fr. 85 F. Tyndareus is referred to by name. In the next line, both of the fragments have the goddesses mentioned by name and an epithet (fr. 85.3 F. and fr. 100.11: cεμν[ᾶc Ἀθάναc), followed by the indication of how they intend to favour or punish these men. Epeius is favoured by Athena who grants him the wisdom and skill to build the horse (fr. 100.11–12: θ]εᾶc ἰ[ό]τατι δαεὶc .../ μέτ[ρα] τε καὶ coφίαν), whereas Aphrodite's punishment of Tyndareus will have direct repercussions not on himself but on his daughters. While Athena grants Epeius the wisdom for which she herself is renowned, Aphrodite inflicts the daughters of Tyndareus with erotic misconduct, the appanage of the goddess. Although both interventions are motivated by contrasting and even opposed emotions towards the mortal in question, their actions have roughly the same dire repercussions. The gravity of the consequences of Aphrodite's wrath is by no means proportional to the offence of Tyndareus, just as the pity (fr. 100.18: ὤικτιρε) of Athena towards Epeius contrasts deeply with the massacre that results from her intervention.

The similarities of both accounts in terms of structure and function suggest that the fragments may have occupied the same position within the poems, *i.e.*, in the beginning, after an invocation to the Muse, which in the case of fr. 85 F. is lost. The same arguments presented by Finglass regarding the opening of the *Sack of Troy* apply to fr. 85 F. The argument that the openings of the poems are the most cited and therefore most known parts of the poem may also be true in the case of the scholiast who transmitted our fragment. The scholiast is commenting on Euripides *Orestes* 249, where there is merely a reference to the fact that Tyndareus begot a race of daughters notorious by blame, no mention is made regarding his fault towards Aphrodite.

If this information was in fact in the beginning of the poem, it would have been easier for the scholiast to remember (or to find) it, and hence to provide the quotation. This may be the passage to which Isocrates is referring to in his *Encomium of Helen* when he says that Stesichorus had pronounced blasphemies regarding Helen in the beginning of his poem (ἀρχόμενος τῆς ὠιδῆς, 64). Moreover, the content of the fragment presents the "divinity's motives [which] suits the start of a poem",⁶⁵ as indeed the opening of the *Iliad*, the *Odyssey*, and the *Aeneid* show, in a very similar way to fr. 85 F.

Divine anger motivated by human fault is common a *topos* in the epic poems from Homer to Virgil, particularly in their openings, as they provide a justification for the subsequent events. In the opening of the *Odyssey*, we learn that the delay of Odysseus' return is owed to Poseidon.

> θεοὶ δ' ἐλέαιρον ἅπαντες
> νόσφι Ποσειδάωνος: ὁ δ' ἀσπερχὲς μενέαινεν   20
> ἀντιθέωι Ὀδυσῆι πάρος ἧν γαῖαν ἱκέσθαι.

> All the gods now pity him
> Except Poseidon: he is unceasingly enraged
> At godlike Odysseus and would not let him go home.

Despite being pitied by the gods (line 19) and appreciated for honouring all of them (lines 66–67), Odysseus is nevertheless affected by the wrath of Poseidon. The juxtaposition of the emphatic θεοὶ ... ἅπαντες in line 19 and νόσφι Ποσειδάωνος in line 20 is similar to the juxtaposition in fr., 85 F. of πᾶσι θεοῖς μόνας in line 2 and Κύπριδος in the opening of line 3, which stresses the failure of Tyndareus. Here as in the *Odyssey* the events are owed to the will of a single deity. Later in book 1, the episode of the Assembly of gods elaborates on the causes for Poseidon's wrath (*Od.* 1.65–69):

> πῶς ἂν ἔπειτ' Ὀδυσῆος ἐγὼ θείοιο λαθοίμην,   65
> ὃς περὶ μὲν νόον ἐστὶ βροτῶν, περὶ δ' ἱρὰ θεοῖσιν
> ἀθανάτοισιν ἔδωκε, τοὶ οὐρανὸν εὐρὺν ἔχουσιν;
> ἀλλὰ Ποσειδάων γαιήοχος ἀσκελὲς αἰεὶ
> Κύκλωπος κεχόλωται

> How should I then forget divine Odysseus,
> Who is beyond all mortals in wisdom, and above all
> Has given sacrifices to the gods, who hold broad heaven?
> But the earth-holder Poseidon is ever filled
> With stubborn wrath because of the Cyclops

Here Athena accuses Zeus of forgetting about Odysseus, to which he responds that he did not forget (λαθοίμην) Odysseus who had always offered sacrifices to the gods, but it is the wrath of Poseidon (κεχόλωται) for what he did to Polyphemus that motivates his suffering. This passage highlights the value of the

---

65 Finglass 2013c: 6.

sacrifices to the gods, as a guarantee of divine favour. In the case of Odysseus, the injustice of his situation is emphasised by the fact that he sacrifices to the gods. However, he incurred in another very serious fault against Poseidon: harming his child. Furthemore, κεχόλωται resembles fr. 85.4 F. χολωσαμένα.

A similar reason for divine anger is presented in the *Iliad* 1.8–11, where the poet asks the Muse to tell him who were the gods behind the strife between Achilles and Agamemnon:

> τίc τ' ἄρ cφωε θεῶν ἔριδι ξυνέηκε μάχεcθαι;   8
> Λητοῦc καὶ Διὸc υἱόc: ὃ γὰρ βαcιλῆϊ χολωθεὶc
> νοῦcον ἀνὰ cτρατὸν ὄρcε κακήν, ὀλέκοντο δὲ λαοί,
> οὕνεκα τὸν Χρύcην ἠτίμαcεν ἀρητῆρα
> Ἀτρεΐδηc:

> Which of the gods was it who set them to quarrel and fight?
> The son of Leto and Zeus; for he was angry with the king
> And roused an evil plague through the camp, and people went on dying because the son of Atreus had dishonoured his priest Chryses

Apollo is angry at Agamemnon because he offended Chryses, his priest. Many elements in this passage are also present in fr. 85 F., although the structure is slightly inverted. First, instead of the name of the culprit of causing the deity's intervention, we have the identification of the god (Λητοῦc καὶ Διὸc υἱόc, line 9), followed, in the same line, by the cause for his action, the wrath (χολωθεὶc) the same term applied to Aphrodite in fr. 85 F. In the next line (line 10) we have the materialization of divine anger, and only after this are we presented with the identity of the culprit and his crime (οὕνεκα τὸν Χρύcην ἠτίμαcεν ἀρητῆρα | Ἀτρεΐδηc, lines 11–12), introduced by the clause in οὕνεκα, the same displayed in our fragment (οὕνεκα Τυνδάρεοc, fr. 85.1 F.), which explains the motives for the divine intervention.[66]

The passage explains the quarrel between Achilles and Agamemnon, primordial *aitia* for the theme of the poem: Achilles' anger, which ultimately results from Agamemnon's offence of Chryses. To make Agamemnon pay for his misdeed, Apollo uses a whole army as an instrument of his revenge, just as in fr. 85 F. Aphrodite uses Tyndareus' daughters as instruments to get to the culprit, by inflicting in them bad repute, which will eventually cause the suffering of a considerable number of people.

---

[66] Thus, Finglass 2013c: 6, where he presents this precise example for the suitability of such themes in the opening of the poems.

It is thus likely that fr. 85 F. would suit the beginning of Stesichorus' *Helen*, on the basis of both structure and content. In the cases where the opening of a poem by Stesichorus is preserved, we have a pattern of emphasis on surprise, whether by means of presenting an unexpected character, or by an unexpected, and perhaps even misleading start, as in the case of *Oresteia*, fr. 172 F.[67] The focus on a menial character as Epeius capable of incurring Athena's compassion in the *Sack of Troy* (fr. 100 F.) demonstrates Stesichorus' ability to surprise his audience in the beginning of his works by casting light on a character who does not deserve such attention in other accounts. If fr. 85 F. featured the beginning of *Helen* it would have the same effect when the audience learns that all that Helen and her sister(s) were blamed for was in fact a fault of their father; the daughters were but instruments, and also victims, of Aphrodite's anger.

The responsibility of Aphrodite for the events leading to the sack of Troy is a common feature of the myth.[68] In Sappho's fr. 16 V. Helen is ultimately a victim of the power of Aphrodite.[69] Although not exactly exempt of some extent of agency she acts according to the expected reaction before Beauty and Eros. In other words, she is ultimately the agent of abandonment of her family as she elopes with Paris, something clear from fr. 16.9 V (καλλίποιϲ' ἔβα). In the same way, λιπεϲάνοραϲ in fr. 85 F. suggests an active part from the daughters of Tyndareus. The focus is on the effects of the divine principles of κάλλοϲ and ἔρωϲ but in a perspective of divine force, rather than divine agency, which is what is at stake in most of the versions blaming the gods. In Sappho's 16 V., it is ultimately Paris' beauty that arouses Helen's desire to elope, forgetting and leaving behind her child, her parents and her husband, whom Helen, apparently, did not love. In Stesichorus, the tendency to embark on promiscuous behaviour is prompted by Aphrodite herself.

Alcaeus stressed the inescapability of Eros and considered Helen to suffer from *mania* of love. Helen does nothing more than obeying the designs of Eros,[70]

---

67 Finglass 2013c: 8, also draws attention to the unexpected opening of the *Oresteia* as a parallel to the surprising beginning of the *Sack of Troy*. Again, the same can be apply as an argument in favour of the hypothesis of fr. 85 F. to be the opening of the *Helen*, occupying perhaps the first antistrophe or the first epode.
68 In Homer the tendency is to blame Paris for his disregard for the norms of hospitality (*Il.* 3.99–100, 24.27–28). However, he is also accused of unjust judgement of beauty of the goddesses, which is directly related to Aphrodite. For archaic lyric, see Sapph. fr. 16 V.; Ibyc. fr. S151.9; Theog. 1232. In tragedy, see e.g. E. *Hec.* 629–657.
69 See Bierl 2003; Torre 2007: 60–62 nn. *ad loc.*; Carvalho 2012: 79–91.
70 Fr. 283 V. However, in fr. 42 V. he draws upon the reasons provided by the epic traditions for the war and Helen is the one and only responsible for it.

which is not far from the concept presented by Stesichorus in fr. 85 F. In *Paean* 6.95–98 Pindar evokes the destruction of Troy as a consequence of Helen's promiscuous nature,[71] also sharing the same principle that fr. 85 F. Helen's ill repute is also a central aspect of the account provided by the *Catalogue of Women*. In fr. 176 M-W, as in Stesichorus, the bad fame of Tyndareus daughters is a result of Aphrodite's rage:

τῆιϲιν δὲ φιλομμειδὴϲ Ἀφροδίτη
ἠγάϲθη προϲιδοῦϲα, κακῆι δέ ϲφ' ἔμβαλε φήμηι.
Τιμάνδρη μὲν ἔπειτ' Ἔχεμον προλιποῦϲ' ἐβεβήκει,
ἵκετο δ' ἐϲ Φυλῆα φίλον μακάρεϲϲι θεοῖϲιν·
ὣϲ δὲ Κλυταιμνήϲτρη <προ>λιποῦϲ' Ἀγαμέμνονα δῖον
Αἰγίϲθωι παρέλεκτο καὶ εἵλετο χείρον' ἀκοίτην·
ὣϲ δ' Ἑλένη ἤιϲχυνε λέχοϲ ξανθοῦ Μενελάου

Smile-loving Aphrodite
Enraged as she saw them, threw bad fame upon them
Timandra left Echemus and ran away,
And came to Phyleus, dear to the blessed gods;
thus Clytemnestra leaving godly Agamemnon
Chose a worse husband and lay beside Aegisthus;
thus Helen shamed the marriage-bed of blond Menelaus

Hesiod does not state a clear reason for Aphrodite's anger towards the daughters of Tyndareus, although one may infer that it was related to their beauty.[72] Therefore, the culprits for Aphrodite's anger are to some extent the daughters themselves. Despite of their innocence, the wrath of the goddess will manifest directly on them. The frivolous nature of Aphrodite is clear in the Hesiodic account, since she is willing to bring utter misfortune to a considerable number of people because of her jealousy for some mortals' beauty. In Stesichorus' account, the motive of the goddess is somehow less frivolous. The failure in offering sacrifices to the gods is a serious offence. But the surprising element in this account is that it differentiates the culprit from the subjects of divine punishment. If in Hesiod the goddess punished who causes her anger, the daughters of Tyndareus, in Stesichorus, the culprit and the victim are different entities. In

---

[71] *P.* 11.51, Pindar blames Helen for the death of Agamemnon and Cassandra. However, in other instances he leaves the figure of Helen without judgement (*O.* 3.1, *O.* 13.58–60, *P.* 5.83).
[72] With Davies and Finglass 2014: 321.

other words, the anger of Aphrodite will not be directed towards the culprit of the fault against her, but on others.[73]

There are many other examples of this divine *modus operandi*. In the *Iliad*[74] we are told that Oeneus forgot to sacrifice to Artemis alone and the goddess retaliates on the offender's children, provides presents a similar account on the gravity of forgetting a to sacrifice to the gods. In *Hippolytus*, we have the reverse, where the punishment of Aphrodite will fall on the stepmother for Hippolytus' disregard for the goddess, contrasting with the offerings and reverence he gives to Artemis. The revenge of Aphrodite will, similarly to fr. 85 F., materialize in the erotic misconduct of Phaedra, the victim chosen by Aphrodite to serve as her vehicle in the consummation of her revenge.[75]

The gravity of these faults towards the gods is evident, as explained by Burkert,[76] only when the mortals fail to honour one of them. On the other hand, as Dover[77] pointed out, the Greeks were not unaware of the merciless nature of their gods. In fact, they were very aware that everything that might affect the gods' honour was a good reason to trigger the anger of the divinity. Forgiveness was not to be expected from the gods.[78] In the case of Tyndareus, the fault towards the goddess is particularly emphasised.

The fault of Tyndareus has consequences for his daughters, but it is not clear whether the formulation of his curse (διγάμουc τε καὶ τριγάμουc ἐτίθει/ καὶ λιπεcάνορας, lines 4–5) is a rhetorical means to express the persistence his daughter's promiscuity, or an accurate description of their faults, where each of the faults refers to one daughter. If so, who is the third daughter?

In the Hesiodic account quoted above, the daughters of Tyndareus are Timandra, Clytemnestra and Helen. There is no record of Timandra in Stesichorus' fragments. The only other daughter of Tyndareus mentioned in Stesichorus is, of course, Clytemnestra, who is likely to have figured in *Helen,* and receives close attention in the *Oresteia*. The most famous version of the myth concerning Clytemnestra attributes her with only two husbands, Agamemnon and Aegisthus. We can assume that διγάμουc in line 4 refers to the wedding of Clytemnestra first to Agamemnon and then to Aegisthus. However, Euripides reminds us in his *Iphigenia at Aulis* that Clytemnestra was once married to another man,

---

[73] Thus Davies 2010, on the episodes in Greek Literature and folk-tale of episodes where the punishment of the faults of the fathers fall upon the children.
[74] Cf. *Il.* 9.533–539, on which see Davies 2010.
[75] Thus Ragusa 2010: 242–245.
[76] Burkert 1993: 422.
[77] Dover 1994: 156.
[78] Thus Bowra 1967: 83.

Tantalus,[79] and that they had a child together, whom Agamemnon brutally killed, along with the child's father. It is Clytemnestra herself who recalls the event, as a justification for her utmost disgust towards Agamemnon:

> τὸν πρόcθεν ἄνδρα Τάνταλον κατακτανών: 1150
> βρέφοc τε τοὐμὸν cῶι προcούδιcαc πάλωι,
> μαcτῶν βιαίωc τῶν ἐμῶν ἀποcπάcαc

> You have killed my former husband Tantalus,
> You dashed my new-born baby to the ground
> violently ripping him from my breast.

If Tantalus is to be considered the son of Thyestes, as Pausanias assumes, he would be Agamemnon's cousin and Aegisthus' uncle and brother, given that Tantalus was brother of Pelopia (both children of Thyestes).[80] However, it seems unlikely that Stesichorus would have elaborated on this subject in his *Helen*, since it illustrates better the fault of the house of Pelops than that of the house of Tyndareus, which, as we have seen, is central to Stesichorus' poem.

The affairs of Helen in the context of the homonymous poem, on the other hand, seem to fit her characterization as "twice-married, thrice-married and deserter of husbands", since in the poem she is taken, presumably, by three men: Theseus, Menelaus, and Paris. Some scholars suggested that, instead of Theseus, the poet could be referring to Deiphobus as one of the husbands,[81] partially because the episode of Helen and Theseus was not a marriage, rather an abduction, while Deiphobus' union to Helen was official.

---

79 According to Pausanias, Tantalus was son of Thyestes: Paus. 2.18.2: ὕcτερον δὲ οὐκ ἔχω cαφῶc εἰπεῖν πότερον ἀδικίαc ἦρξεν Αἴγιcθοc ἢ προϋπῆρξεν Ἀγαμέμνονι φόνοc Ταντάλου τοῦ Θυέcτου· cυνοικεῖν δέ φαcιν αὐτὸν Κλυταιμνήcτραι παρθένωι παρὰ Τυνδάρεω λαβόντα. "I cannot say with certainty whether Aegisthus committed the injustice first or whether Agamemnon started it by murdering Tantalus, son of Thyestes. It is said that Tantalus received the maiden Clytaemnestra in marriage from Tyndareus."
80 After the killing of Thyestes' children with Aeropa by Atreus in the consequence of the finding of adultery of Aeropa (who was married to Atreus and mother of Agamemnon and Menelaus), Thyestes consults an oracle which says that Pelopia, his daughter, could bore him a son who would avenge the previous killing of the children, by killing Agamemnon. This makes even more sense if we think that Agamemnon himself was about to kill Pelopia's brother Tantalus.
81 Grossardt 2012: 35; Woodbury 1967: 167 suggested Deiphobus as one candidate for the list of Helen's husbands, whereas Smyth 1900: fr. 5; Colonna 1963: 212; Bowra 1963: 251–252; Degani and Burzacchini 1977: 302 defend that Helen's three husbands are Theseus, Menelaus, and Deiphobus.

According to Grossardt, the wrath of Aphrodite is inflicted on Helen only after her marriage to Menelaus; hence Theseus was not included among her husbands referred to in fr. 85 F., but only Paris, Deiphobus, and perhaps even Achilles. However, as Noussia-Fantuzzi points out, the meaning of the compounds of γαμεῖν in the fragment can mean both marriage and merely sexual intercourse.[82] The ambiguity of the term is particularly relevant here and can in fact be an argument in favour of Theseus rather than Deiphobus, since intercourse was quite clearly present.

Pausanias tells us that in the sequence of her abduction by Theseus, Helen bore Iphigenia to him. This means that Helen had a baby before she got married, hence her decision to leave Iphigenia with Clytemnestra before returning home (fr. 84 F.). This episode cannot be part of the *Oresteia*, since, in it, Iphigenia is daughter of Agamemnon (fr. 178 F.). The only other known poem by Stesichorus where the reference to Iphigenia as Helen and Theseus' daughter would fit is the *Helen*. Therefore, the story of Helen and Theseus should have been part of this poem.[83] Furthermore, as argued above, fr. 85 F. is likely to have occupied a place in the opening of the poem as a cause for the following events. Hence, Theseus' episode should be the first consequence of Aphrodite's wrath which would then not be solely related to the Trojan War, but to the general biography of these women, Helen in particular.

An episode such as this would emphasise Helen's bad reputation on a much larger scale than her marriage to Deiphobus, in the sequence of Paris' death. Furthermore, it seems more likely that the *Helen* elaborated on the life of the heroine before the beginning of the Trojan War. Therefore, the inclusion of the episode of Theseus, alongside Menelaus and Paris, would provide a pre-marital stain in Helen's reputation, which suits the context of the poem. Menelaus plays the role of the legitimate husband, who is abandoned (fr. 85.5 F. λιπεcάνορας) for a post-marital relation with Paris. The cadence of lines 85.4–5 F. highlights the continuous pattern of Helen love-life – never finished, never settled – which is also what lies behind the motive for the oath of the suitors demanded by Tyndareus. He is aware that at least Helen among his daughters is destined to be continuously changing her marital partner. Furthermore, as we shall see, the abduction by Theseus provides an outcome in many ways similar to that of Paris, since the consequence of both abductions is the departure of men to rescue Helen and the sack of a city.

---

[82] Noussia-Fantuzzi 2015: 434 n. 20.
[83] Thus Grossardt 2012: 10.

These two abductions – one prior to the wedding to Menelaus and the other after it – complement one another. The poem would start with an innocent Helen dragged away from her home unwillingly and whom her brothers rescue after sacking the city where she is kept, and would end with another, slightly different abduction, but with the same consequences, the sack of the city, this time Troy. In between lies a rapid illusion of a happy marriage to Menelaus framed by the two abductions, forming a thematic ring-composition subordinated to the theme of abduction.

3.2.2 Helen in Athens (fr. 86 F.)

The abduction of Helen by Theseus, himself the abductor *par excellence*, is a well-known episode attested in literature and art as early as the seventh century.[84] Although ignored in Homer, a scholium to the *Iliad* 3.242 informs that the story of Theseus' abduction of Helen was told in the *Cypria* (fr. 12 *GEF*) and in Alcman (fr. 21 *PMG*), before Stesichorus. After him, the episode survived in the versions of Herodotus (9.73), Hellanicus (fr. 168a *EGM*), and later in Diodorus (4.63) and Plutarch (*Thes.* 31–34).

These accounts tell how Theseus and Peirithous abducted Helen. The Dioscuri depart to recover their sister and to gain revenge.[85] In the *Cypria* they sack

---

[84] See Davies and Finglass 2014: fr. 86n. On the other victims of Theseus' "conquests", see Athenaeus 13.557a–b and, for a different catalogue Plut. *Thes.* 36.1–2. Edmunds 2016: 74.

[85] Cavallini 1999 argued that the military enterprise of Ibyc. S166 refers precisely to the expedition of the Dioscuri to Attica where they went to rescue their sister. This is a poem which was attributed to Stesichorus by Lobel 1968: 9, who argues that "manuscripts of [Stesichorus'] poems have turned up in Oxyrhynchus many times more often than those of Ibycus". Furthermore, the content of fr. 11 may have had some connexion to the *Funeral Games for Pelias*, and mentions some aspects we know Stesichorus have dealt with. It is West 1969: 142–149, however, who argues for Stesichorean authorship on grounds of metre, and, more recently, in 2015: 70–74, where he displays more arguments, such as the fact that we have evidence on Stesichorus' interest on Sparta, but not on Ibycus (e.g. fr. 177, 170 F.), and Stesichorus' copious treatment of Helen, namely in what concerns her abduction by Theseus and the subsequent departure of the Dioscuri to recover her, something which is not documented, he says, for Ibycus. On the other hand, Page 1969: 71 defended the authorship of Ibycus, arguing that the theme and scope of the poem would be more suited to the poet of Rhegium, who we know had had patrons (see Finglass 2014: 215 n. 47) and composed laudatory songs for them (see Rawles 2012). Page 1971: 93 adds that if the fragment corresponds to one roll, which Lobel disagrees, a poem by Stesichorus would have occupied at least the entire roll. Moreover, and according to the same scholar, the allusions of fr. 11 to themes worked by Stesichorus seem unlikely to have figured in a poem of the author, particularly because of the brevity in which they are presented.

Aphidnae, where Helen was hidden and taken care of by Aethra, whom the Dioscuri take in reprisal. In Alcman, the action takes place in a different location. The Dioscuri bring their sister and Aethra from Athens after sacking the city, which was deprived from Theseus' defence, since he was absent.[86] In the *Cypria* and in Alcman, therefore, the first abduction of Helen results in the sacking of a city by the Dioscuri.[87]

Stesichorus (fr. 86 F.) adds an important detail: when rescued by her brothers, Helen is pregnant with Theseus' child, Iphigenia. On the way back they stop at Argos, where Helen delivers Iphigenia. However, she does not keep the child but instead gives it to her sister Clytemnestra, perhaps motivated by the fact that the baby was illegitimate and should hence be hidden:

Πληcίον δὲ τῶν Ἀνάκτων Εἰληθυίαc ἐcτὶν ἱερὸν ἀνάθημα Ἑλένηc, ὅτε cὺν Πειρίθωι Θηcέωc ἀπελθόντοc ἐc Θεcπρωτοὺc Ἄφιδνά τε ὑπὸ Διοcκούρων ἑάλω καὶ ἤγετο ἐc Λακεδαίμονα Ἑλένη. ἔχειν μὲν γὰρ αὐτὴν λέγουcιν ἐν γαcτρί, τεκοῦcαν δὲ ἐν Ἄργει καὶ τῆc Εἰληθυίαc ἱδρυcαμένην τὸ ἱερὸν τὴν μὲν παῖδα ἣν ἔτεκε Κλυταιμνήcτραι δοῦναι – cυνοικεῖν γὰρ ἤδη Κλυταιμνήcτραν Ἀγαμέμνονι –, αὐτὴν δὲ ὕcτερον τούτων Μενελάωι γήμαcθαι. καὶ ἐπὶ τῶιδε Εὐφορίων Χαλκιδεὺc καὶ Πλευρώνιοc Ἀλέξανδροc ἔπη ποιήcαντεc, πρότερον δὲ ἔτι Cτηcίχοροc ὁ Ἱμεραῖοc κατὰ ταὐτά φαcιν Ἀργείοιc Θηcέωc εἶναι θυγατέρα Ἰφιγένειαν.

Near to the Lords is a shrine of Eilethyia dedicated by Helen when, in the absence of Theseus among the Thesprotians with Peirithous, Aphidna was captured by the Dioscuri, and she was being brought to Lacedaemon; they say that she was pregnant and was delivered in Argos ...and they gave the daughter who she had bore to Clytaemnestra, who was already married to Agamemnon; after that Helen married Menelaus. Consequently, both Euphorion of Chalcis and Alexander of Pleuron, both epic poets, and before them Stesichorus of Himera agree with the Argives that Iphigenia was Theseus' daughter.

The same is argued by Wilkinson 2013: 88–93, who also calls attention for the discussion of Fogelmark entertaining possible authors other than Stesichorus and Ibycus. Stesichorus is credited with the composition of erotic songs and παιδικά, as the testimonies inform us (Tb7 Ercoles), and should, therefore, be open to the possibility of finding such poems attributed to Stesichorus. S166 offers no solid element for such an ascription, as more recently argued by Finglass 2017b.

86 Hes. *Lex.* = Alcm. fr. 22 *PMG* explains that Alcman's version according to which Helen was in Athens, Ἀcαναίων πόλιν, should be emended to τὰc Ἀφίδναc, as according to the versions presented by both Plutarch (*The.* 32–33) and Pausanias (2.22.6–7).

87 The celebration of the victory of the Dioscuri was the prior concern of Alcman's account and is also a recurrent aspect on the Peloponnesian art, as noted by Neils 1987: 20–21.

This child-bearing Helen conflicts with Plutarch's account,[88] according to which, when Theseus abducted Helen, she was still a child (*Thes.* 31.2–3):

> ἦλθον [Theseus and Peirithoo] μὲν εἰς Σπάρτην ἀμφότεροι, καὶ τὴν κόρην ἐν ἱερῶι Ἀρτέμιδος Ὀρθίας χορεύουσαν ἁρπάσαντες ἔφυγον. τῶν δὲ πεμφθέντων ἐπὶ τὴν δίωξιν οὐ πορρωτέρω Τεγέας ἐπακολουθησάντων, ἐν ἀδείαι γενόμενοι καὶ διελθόντες τὴν Πελοπόννησον ἐποιήσαντο συνθήκας, τὸν μὲν λαχόντα κλήρωι τὴν Ἑλένην ἔχειν γυναῖκα, συμπράττειν δὲ θατέρωι γάμον ἄλλον. ἐπὶ ταύταις δὲ κληρουμένων ταῖς ὁμολογίαις, ἔλαχε Θησεύς, καὶ παραλαβὼν τὴν παρθένον οὔπω γάμων ὥραν ἔχουσαν εἰς Ἀφίδνας ἐκόμισε, καὶ τὴν μητέρα καταστήσας μετ' αὐτῆς Ἀφίδνωι παρέδωκεν ὄντι φίλωι, διακελευσάμενος φυλάττειν καὶ λανθάνειν τοὺς ἄλλους.

> Theseus and Peirithoo were heading to Sparta when they abducted the little girl as she was dancing in the temple of Artemis Orthia, and fled. The men sent to capture them did not go farther than Tegea. So, when the abductors crossed the Peloponnese and were out of danger, they made a pact according to which whomever the lot fell should have Helen to wife, providing that he would assist the other in getting a wife for him. They cast lots and it was Theseus who won the prize. He took the girl, who was not yet in the age for marriage, and escorted her to Aphidnae, where he made her mother a companion of the girl and entrusted both to his friend Aphidno with orders to guard and hide them from strangers.

The fact that Helen was dancing on the precinct of Artemis Orthia implies that Helen was a child around seven to twelve years old.[89] This is even more significant when, in Hellanicus' account, Theseus is not exactly an ephebe, but a fifty-year-old man (fr. 168b *EGM*). Such an age gap between abductor and abducted is not present in the artistic representations of the episode. Cohen attributes the absence of such depiction not to the difficulty in depicting a young girl, or a female child, but rather as a sign of the artists' "discomfort about the inappropriately wide age inequalities between sexual partners",[90] also implicit in Plutarch's οὐ καθ' ὥραν. The decorum shown by the artists in hiding this version may be in part motivated by a revision of Theseus as the national hero of Athens, which included the exclusion of some of his less laudatory deeds.[91]

However, most of the depictions of the episode, even those representing Theseus as a young man, include the imagery of forced abduction, which would

---

[88] Gumpert 2016: 70 believes that this version can be considered to be also attributed to Hellanicus, but it is hard to tell with certainty.
[89] Tzetz. Ad. Lyc. 513 says that Helen was seven when abducted; whereas Apollod. *Epit.* 1.23 says she was twelve. See further, Calame 1977: 160, 196; Fowler 2013: 488–489; Edmunds 2016: 70 n. 27.
[90] Cohen 2007: 273; also Shapiro 2000: 275.
[91] Thus Sourvinou-Inwood 1988: 53–54; 93–94; Mills 1997: 8.

easily fit in a context of child abduction – a kidnap really – by a relatively old man. Cohen observes that "in the images Theseus usually abducts Helen with the aid of a horse-drawn chariot, and she expresses her vehement objection through eloquent poses of distress, while her female companions watch the gesture helplessly".[92] This forced abduction imagery, together with the accounts that make Helen a child when abducted, exculpates Helen for this primal abduction, and make it distinct from the episode of Paris.

When the abduction by Theseus took place, Helen was not married, and therefore could not have been charged with leaving her husband (λιπεϲάνορας, fr. 85.5 F.), but such accusation could well apply to the idea that Helen had many sexual partners, implicit, as we have seen, in the διγάμουϲ καὶ τριγάμουϲ of fr. 85 F. In fact, the version of a young woman, *i.e.* nubile but unmarried, taken by a stranger and eventually rescued by her brother(s), is very similar to other accounts of abduction, particularly that of Europa.

The abductions of Helen by Theseus and Europa by Zeus share many similarities. Both are young unmarried girls accompanied by other girls, and hence defenceless. Both abductions result in offspring, although in the case of Europa the children are accepted by her future husband, whereas Helen entrusts Iphigenia to Clytemnestra. And these abductions eventually lead to the departure of the brothers of the girls in search for them. However, while the Dioscuri are successful in bringing Helen home, Europa's brother Cadmus fails to recover her. Another contrasting aspect is that the demand of the brothers of Helen results in a sack of a city, whereas Cadmus is known to have founded one. Moreover, as Cingano notes,[93] the Dioscuri depart in search for their sister without any demand from Tyndareus, as far as we know, whereas Cadmus is in many accounts urged by his father to do so and threatened not to come back home should he fail in his mission, much like the brother of Medea, Apsyrtos.[94]

If in the *Helen* we have her brothers departing to Athens or Aphidnae to recover her, in the *Palinode* this idea of recovery is also at play regarding the recovery not of a sister, but of a grandmother. In the *Palinode* Demophon recovered his grandmother who had accompanied Helen in her refuge in Egypt. The *Palinode*, a song composed to exculpate Helen, maintains the connection between her and Athens, here personified in Aethra. The connection between the two poems, therefore, suggests that Helen is not much to blame for the abduction by Theseus as she may be in the episode involving Paris. Although Helen may be innocent in

---

92 Cohen 2007: 263.
93 Cingano 2005: 134, n. 59; cf. Apollod. *Bibl.* 3.11.
94 A. R. 4.224–225, 303–481 for Medea.

this episode, the fact that the series of events which will materialize the anger of Aphrodite starts with Theseus, the abductor *par excellence* and a well-travelled hero, is significant and a constant feature of Helen's entourage in the *Sack of Troy* (fr. 105 F.) but also in the *Palinode*, almost as a constant reminder of Helen's first fault, her first abduction, her first imposed journey.

The map that comes out of this episode is restricted to Greek mainland, from Lacedaemonia to Athens and back again, with a stop at Argos, but it implies the movement of many characters. Theseus and Peirithoo come from Athens or (Aphidnae?) to Lacedaemonia, and then return to Attica with Helen. The Dioscuri depart on her track. They recover Helen and bring her back: Helen's first *nostos*. But the return is always more perilous than the first trip, and as such they stop at Argos where Iphigenia is born, and only then return to their parents' home. This is a small-scale anticipation of the events of the Trojan War. It does not involve the whole of Greece, since it is reduced to the family unit. And it does not demand a sea journey – the rescuing trip is made by land. The return has a stop in Argos, where Iphigenia is born. They eventually return home and Helen is then ready to be wooed. This episode envisages not any journey trodden by Helen, but instead the travels of the prospective husbands to her wooing, which is the topic of the next section.

3.2.3 Helen back to the Peloponnese (fr. 87 F.)

The episode of the wooing of Helen, despite of its importance in the events concerning the Trojan war, is absent from the remains of all the major epic poems and art. The earlier literary versions of the episode appear in a fragment of the *Catalogue of Women* (fr. 204. 75–85 M-W) and in Stesichorus' fr. 87 F. Later it is found in Euripides (*IA.* 51–71), Isocrates (*Helen* 39–41), Pausanias (3.20.9), Apollodorus (*Bibl.* 3.10.8–9), and Hyginus (*Fab.* 81).

The information about how Stesichorus dealt with the wooing is not so much concerned with the process of wooing itself, but rather with the details of an oath that Tyndareus made the suitors swear before he revealed the man he chose to marry his daughter Helen. This was transmitted to us by a scholium to *Iliad* 2.339 that relates this passage of Nestor[95] to the oath mentioned in Stesichorus (fr. 87 F.):

---

[95] Apart from Nestor's reference to the oaths sworn by the Greek army, there are two more occasion where promises are mentioned in the *Iliad*: 2.236–239 and 4.266–267, but Davies and Finglass 2014: 326 note that neither of these speak of the path sworn by the suitors of Helen.

Τῶν ἐκ τῆς Ἑλλάδος ἀρίστων ἐπὶ μνηστείαν τῆς Ἑλένης παρόντων διὰ γένος καὶ κάλλος, Τυνδάρεως ὁ πατὴρ αὐτῆς, ὥς τινές φασι φυλασσόμενος μήποτε ἕνα αὐτῶν προκρίνας τοὺς ἄλλους ἐχθροὺς ποιήσηται, κοινὸν αὐτῶν ὅρκον ἔλαβεν ἦ μὴν τῶι ληψομένωι τὴν παῖδα ἀδικουμένωι περὶ αὐτὴν σφόδρα πάντας ἐπαμύνειν· διόπερ Μενελάωι αὐτὴν ἐκδίδωσιν καὶ μετ' οὐ πολὺν χρόνον ἁρπαχθείσης ὑπὸ Ἀλεξάνδρου ἐκοινώνησαντο τῆι στρατείαι διὰ τοὺς γενομένους ὅρκους. ἡ ἱστορία παρὰ Στησιχόρωι.

When the best men among the Greeks came to woo Helen on the account of her lineage and beauty, her father Tyndareus, as some say, to protect himself from making enemies in the others by choosing one of them, made them all swear an oath according to which the others should come energetically to help the man who received the girl, should he ever be wronged in respect of her. That is why he gave her to Menelaus. Not long after that, when she was carried off by Alexander, they took part in the expedition because of the oath they sworn. The story is in Stesichorus.

The information focuses on the motif of the oath, but there is good reason to believe that Stesichorus' poem contemplated a broader account of the wooing, because it is on the occasion of this gathering that the core of the Greek army that will defeat Troy is defined. It is likely that Stesichorus listed the heroes who fought and will "fight" for Helen. However, we know that Hesiod did so. The version of Helen's wooing in the *Catalogue of Women* deserves particular attention from the poet (frr. 196–204 M-W), who elaborates on the event and provides a considerably long catalogue of the suitors (fr. 204 M-W), anticipating the unprecedented scale of the Trojan enterprise. By displaying a catalogue of the suitors and their origins, the poet makes this event a major panhellenic gathering.

The episodes of wooing of a bride proliferate in the *Catalogue*; they all involve the same idea of combined movement of heroes to a single place, to engage in some sort of challenge or contest.[96] The wooing contest of Helen has the same agonistic component found in the wooing of other well sought women, such as the daughters of Proitos (fr. 130 M-W), or Mestra (fr. 43a M-W). The fact that these women are wooed by many Greek heroes implies that their wooings will result in a considerable number of suitors, from a myriad of locations within the Greek world. The competitive element among the suitors found in wooing scenes as Atalanta's (fr. 74–6 M-W),[97] Hippodameia's (fr. 259 M-W),[98] or Penelo-

---

96 The theme of winning brides is, as a matter of fact, a common *topos* in Indo-European folktale as shown by West 2007: 432–436, or Edmunds 2016: 53–54. Cingano 2005: 124–127 discusses the wooing contests present in the *Catalogue*.
97 The case of Atalanta's wooing differs from these deadly contests only in the figure of the adversary of the suitors. Instead of being defied by the father of the future bride, the suitors of Atalanta have to race and win over the bride herself.

pe's (to draw on other sources: *Od.* 21.1–4; 67–79), on the one hand; and the challenge or quest that the suitor has to surpass to win the bride, a motif shared in many European mythologies, as in the case of Melampus winning Pero for his brother Bias (fr. 37 M-W),[99] on the other, allow these episodes to sit neatly among the other mythological instances where massive gatherings of Greek heroes take place.

Commenting on the catalogue of Helen's suitors in the *Catalogue* we have been referring to, West notes that "mythology knew of certain other great occasions for which the heroes gathered from far and wide".[100] He then names some of the examples of such encounters: the Argo expedition, the Calydonian boar hunt, and the funeral games for Pelias. Coincidently, Stesichorus composed poems on two of these three events: the *Funeral Games for Pelias* (frr. 1–4 F.), and the Calydonian *Boarhunters* (frr. 183–184 F.).

The surviving material from these poems is scarce, but it allows us to understand our poet's concern in stressing the element of the gathering of the Greek heroes in a common event. The surviving material from the Calydonian Boar hunt by Stesichorus is more enlightening when it comes to the origin of those gathered to fight the beast sent by Artemis as a punishment for Oeneus failure in offering her sacrifice – interestingly another event ultimately caused by the same fault that triggered the event in the *Helen*. Fr. 183 F. tells of the arrival of all the Greeks who responded to Oeneus' appeal for help; the list includes the Locrians, the Boeotians, the Dryopes, and the Achaeans, among others. The *Funeral Games* elaborated on the sporting events championed by several Greek heroes from different locations, such as Sparta (the Dioscuri), Argos (Amphiaraus), and Calydon (Meleager), to name the ones that certainly featured in the poem. Fr. 3 F. preserves the most intriguing scene where different sorts of cakes, associated with wedding gastronomy, are brought to a young woman, presumably Atalanta.[101] If this was the case, there was a clear connection between the sporting event of the funeral games and a wooing or court scene.

Another wooing scene in the context of a considerable gathering of heroes appears in the fragment of *Eriphyle* (fr. 93 F.). The context of the scene is uncer-

---

98 Pelops is the victor after thirteen listed suitors lost their lives. Cf. Pi. *O*.1.75–81; Apollod. *Epit.* 2.3–5. See also the myth of Marpessa in B. *Dith.* 20, fr. 20a M.
99 Melampus succeeds in bringing the cattle of Iphiclus to Neleus, thus winning Pero for his brother Bias.
100 West 1985: 114–115.
101 See Davies and Finglass 2014: 227–228.

tain. After a banquet scene, where a bard is reciting, we are told that there is a mother, rather than the father or the brother, who departs in search for a bride for her son, who is identified in our fragment as Anaxander's son. The name is unprecedented in mythology and it is not certain how the episode fits in the context of the scene. In any case, the departure of this mother deserves to be described with some details, particularly in what concerns the mode of transportation chosen to the journey. Fr. 93. '13' describes the yoking of a wagon (ὁπῶς ἀπήναν ζευ[⏓–⏑⏑–) and how after this the mother departed to woo a wife (lines '14–15' -ναδ' ἔβα παράκοιτι[ν ⏑–⏑⏑–– | μναστεύсοιса μάτη[ρ). The ἀπήνη is a mule drawn wagon which in Homer is used to transport a considerable heavy cargo.[102] This usage of the wagon implies that the mother was transporting some gifts to offer to the bride upon her arrival. She travels by land, but this would have been a quite perilous journey to undertake alone, especially for a woman. This fact highlights the utter importance of a marriageable young hero to be present or at least represented in such events, even if (or perhaps precisely because) it implies a long perilous trip.

The case of the wooing of Helen in Stesichorus must have had the same aura of grand scale panhellenic gathering as it does in the Hesiodic *Catalogue of Women*. We do not know the extent of Stesichorus' catalogue, if there was one. But we do know that it involved the vast majority of the heroes who went to Troy, because of the reference to the oath of Tyndareus. We should have had in this episode a mass movement of heroes from all over Greece, the same ones that later will join to sail to Troy to recover Helen.

3.2.4 Helen in Sparta (fr. 88 F.)

The agonistic and indeed heroic valour of this wooing, taken as a difficult, well fought and thus deserved task, is made evident in the scene describing the arrival of Menelaus and his bride Helen at Sparta (fr. 88 F.):

κυδωνίων δὲ μήλων μνημονεύει Στηсίχοροс ἐν Ἑλένηι οὕτως·

πολλὰ μὲν κυδώνια μᾶλα ποτερρίπτουν ποτὶ δίφρον ἄνακτι,
πολλὰ δὲ μύρсινα φύλλα
καὶ ῥοδίνους стεφάνους ἴων τε κορωνίδας οὔλας

---

[102] In the *Iliad* it is used to carry the ransom for Hector's body and his corpse: 24.266, 324, 502, 556, 576–579, 590; in the *Odyssey* Nausicaa and her slaves use it to carry the laundry down to the river, 6.57, 69, 72–73.

> Stesichorus mentions Cydonian apples in his *Helen*:
>
> Many Cydonian apples they throw at the chariot of their lord,
> Many myrtle leaves,
> And garlands of roses, and crowns of violets.

This scene has usually been interpreted as the wedding procession of Helen and Menelaus. Rozokoki challenged this traditional view and suggested that the scene describes "Menelaus' triumphant entry into Sparta as a bridegroom after the difficult contest in which he brushed aside many fine candidates".[103] The basis for this view lies in the fact that the attention is focused on the man (line 1, ἄνακτι), at whom fruits, leaves and garlands are thrown, a common practice in the celebration of athletic and military victories. However, evidence attests the throwing of fruit, flowers, or other sorts of plants in ancient Greek wedding ceremonies.[104] As Hague shows, wedding processions are similar to the panhellenic victory processions.[105] In both there were praise songs and φυλλοβολία.[106] The hypothesis that this fragment describes the consecration of Menelaus as a victor in the wooing contest is problematic, since in the other account of the wooing of Helen, that of the *Catalogue of Women*, Menelaus is absent and Agamemnon woos for him.[107] Stesichorus may or may not have followed this version; if he did, the victor's procession of fr. 88 F. makes little sense. However, Stesichorus altered some aspects in his account, namely the figures who presided over the wooing: in the *Catalogue* the Dioscuri are in charge of the competition, whereas in Stesichorus it seems that it was the father of the bride who made the final choice.

But the reason to believe that fr. 88 F. describes a wedding procession rather than a victor's celebration lies in the irony of the episode. If we consider that the scene described is the wedding procession, the episode has a remarkable symbolism within the wider context of the narrative. If fr. 88 F. is a victor's celebration the impact it has in the narrative is considerably reduced. Menelaus'

---

[103] Rozokoki 2013; the quotation is from Rozokoki 2014: 205.
[104] Cf. Theopompus fr. 15.1–2 *PCG*.
[105] Hague 1984, *apud* Robinson 2010: 13.
[106] φυλλοβολία is the common praise of the athletic victor, a sort of applause. See Anagianou 1990: 16 and Carson 1982: 123–125 on Pindar's use of the motif combined with a wedding ritual scene in *P*. 9.123–125.
[107] Fr. 197.1–5 M-W. On the role of Agamemnon in the wooing, see Cingano 2005: 135–139. For other instances where the suitor is replaced by a member of the family among Stesichorus' works, see fr. 93 F. For other examples on this solution in other wooing scenes, see e.g. fr. 37.5 M-W.

excellence is emphasised, since he accomplished a remarkable victory among many suitors, and Helen is seen as a mere prize. On the other hand, if this episode depicts the wedding procession, the implications for the whole narrative are far more significant.

The ritualistic procession of the bride to her new home is attested as early as the *Iliad* (18.491–497), in the pseudo-Hesiodic ecphrastic *Aspis* (273–274)[108] and in Sappho fr. 44.13–17 V. Two of these accounts refer to the chariot. In fr. 88 F. the man at whom the fruits, leaves and flowers are thrown is generally understood to be Menelaus. He also travels in a chariot (δίφρον, line 1), which is often associated with marriage in art.[109]

The wedding procession, particularly the moment when the bridegroom takes his bride from her father's house, the central action in wedding ceremonies,[110] marks an important point in the life of women in ancient Greece: they change *kurios*. The procession thus marks the "metaphorical and physical passage of the bride from her old to her new home".[111] This travel, that also mark the transition from maiden to adulthood, "was regarded as the female's ultimate and definite destination".[112]

Fr. 88 F. depicts this desirable last travel of Helen, who, lest we forget, had already been involved in a similar occasion, as seen in the last chapter. Helen is here once again taken from her home, this time, of course, with the legitimacy of the marriage agreement – although not necessarily with her consent. The emphasis on the wooing and on the wedding procession thus highlights the significance of the marriage of Helen and Menelaus in the wider narrative. It is intended to wash away Helen's past with Theseus and restore her social "maiden to adulthood" process. The fact that Helen has had already a child makes the wedding procession, as a symbol of the passage from maiden to adulthood, a farce. So too the oath, as a manifestation of Tyndareus' awareness of the possible (if not certain) future elopement of Helen, anticipates that this marriage is

---

[108] Note ἀπήνη in line 273, the same word used by Stesichorus in fr. 93.13 F.
[109] Chariots in the context of weddings are represented in art as early as the eighth century (Diez de Velascos 1992: § 36), in the sixth century we have some examples (London B 174), in the fifth century (see, Lorimer 1902: 132; London B 1920.12–21.1, on which see also Blundell 1998: 50; B London 298). See also Kahil 1988: § 61 for a representation of Helen and Menelaus in the chariot. Also, the portrayal of the man taking a young woman in a chariot away from her home is also common artistic motif to depict abduction, as shown above. See, on the subject of abduction in art, Cohen 1996, and, for Helen in particular, Shapiro 2000.
[110] Carson 1982: 122.
[111] Clark 1998: 13.
[112] Blundell 1998: 44.

bound to fail with appalling consequences not only for Menelaus, but for the entirety of Greece.

3.3 The *Palinode*

3.3.1 Helen in Egypt (frr. 90, 91a, and 91c F.)

So far, I have been discussing the nuances of the presentation of Helen in the homonymous poem. The information we have about the contents of this work includes the original fault of Tyndareus, the abduction of Helen by Theseus, her wooing, and finally her marriage to Menelaus, in what is probably a wedding scene and song, as discussed above. It is rather unfortunate that we do not have elements of the treatment of the aftermath of this fateful matrimony.

We can but speculate on what would have been Stesichorus' treatment of the episode with Paris at Sparta in a song where Helen is represented as a victim of Aphrodite's anger. Given that Aphrodite's wrath involves the infliction of a deviant behaviour for the daughters of Tyndareus, namely their propensity to leave their husbands, it seems likely that the following narrative would tell of how Helen succumbed to Paris' seduction and departed to Troy. Moreover, the reference in fr. 87 F. to the oath that required the suitors to act in case of an elopement of Helen is likely to have had repercussions later in the poem.[113] However, we do not know in what terms it took shape.

Conversely, the information we have on the *Palinode(s)* offers some hints about Stesichorus' treatment of this exact point of the narrative – the moment of eminent departure – and the subsequent events. There are more doubts than certainties regarding this composition. The content is generally accepted among scholars: the *Palinode(s)* told how Helen did not go to Troy (fr. 91a F.), but instead remained in Egypt under the guard of Proteus (fr. 90 F.). To Troy went an *eidolon* for which both Greeks and Trojans fought (fr. 91b F.). The *Palinode* also described how Demophon arrived in Egypt and rescued his grandmother Aethra (fr. 90 F.).

What survived from this poem came down to us in quotations; few suggest first-hand knowledge of the work of Stesichorus.[114] The earliest information we have regarding the "so called Palinode" is provided by Plato in his *Phaedrus* (fr.

---

[113] Thus Davies and Finglass 2014: 308.
[114] For a study of the derivative testimonia on the *Palinode*, see Davies 1982; Davies and Finglass 2014: 341–343.

91a F.) and Isocrates (fr. 91c F.). In the *Phaedrus*, Plato quotes Stesichorus' poem in the context of Socrates' urge to sing a song to Eros, whom he might have offended by a previous utterance. He explains that he is about to proceed to the recantation in the hopes of avoiding a punishment from the deity, just as Stesichorus did when he learnt that the cause for his blindness was the anger of Helen for his defamatory portrait of her:

ἔcτι δὲ τοῖc ἁμαρτάνουcι περὶ μυθολογίαν καθαρμὸc ἀρχαῖοc, ὃν Ὅμηροc μὲν οὐκ ἤιcθετο, Cτηcίχοροc δὲ· τῶν γὰρ ὀμμάτων cτερηθεὶc διὰ τὴν Ἑλένηc κακηγορίαν οὐκ ἠγνόηcεν ὥcπερ Ὅμηροc, ἀλλ' ἅτε μουcικὸc ὢν ἔγνω τὴν αἰτίαν καὶ ποιεῖ εὐθύc·

> οὐκ ἔcτ' ἔτυμοc λόγοc οὗτοc,
> οὐδ' ἔβαc ἐν νηυcὶν ἐϋccέλμοιc
> οὐδ' ἵκεο πέργαμα Τροίαc

καὶ ποιήcαc δὴ πᾶcαν τὴν καλουμένην Παλινωιδίαν παραχρῆμα ἀνέβλεψεν.

There is an ancient purification for those who have sinned in matters of mythology, known not to Homer but to Stesichorus. When he lost his sight because of his slander of Helen he was not ignorant of the cause, like Homer, but devoted to the muses as he was, he recognised the origin and immediately wrote:

> That story is not true
> You did not go on the well-benched ships
> And you did not arrive at the citadel of Troy

And having composed the so-called Palinode he instantly recovered his sight.

Plato informs us that the so-called *Palinode* intended to correct a previous slander of Helen. In this recantation, Helen never betrayed her husband, since she never accompanied Paris; she never eloped. The version of her elopement with Paris may be what Isocrates vaguely refers to as a blasphemy (fr. 91c F.):

ἐνεδείξατο δὲ καὶ Cτηcιχόρωι τῶι ποιητῆι τὴν αὑτῆc δύναμιν· ὅτε μὲν γὰρ ἀρχόμενοc τῆc ὠιδῆc ἐβλαcφήμηcέ τι περὶ αὐτῆc, ἀνέcτη τῶν ὀφθαλμῶν ἐcτερημένοc, ἐπειδὴ δὲ γνοὺc τὴν αἰτίαν τῆc cυμφορᾶc τὴν καλουμένην Παλινωιδίαν ἐποίηcε, πάλιν αὐτὸν εἰc τὴν αὐτὴν φύcιν κατέcτηcεν.

She manifested her power also to the poet Stesichorus: for when in the beginning of his song he uttered a blasphemy about her, he stood up deprived of his sight; but after he realised the reason for his misfortune and composed the so-called Palinode, she restored his condition.

Both testimonies speak of a composition in uncertain terms; they merely mention a "so-called Palinode", which indicates that the poem was known by this name but need not have had this title. The account of Isocrates is particularly relevant in this matter, since it seems to indicate that the recantation was preceded by a more defamatory content,[115] but the opposition ὅτε μὲν ... ἐπειδὴ δὲ suggests different occasions.[116] Hence the defamatory song and the recantation are two separate compositions: the *Helen* and the *Palinode*.

This was the general belief until 1963, when P. Oxy. 2506 (= fr. 90 F.) came to light and shook the general view about the *Palinode*. Fr. 90 F. consists in the testimony of an anonymous commentator on the mythological innovations of Stesichorus. The fragment tells us the following:

    [μέμ-
φεται τὸν Ὅμηρο[ν ὅτι Ἑ-
λέ]νην ἐποίηcεν ἐν Τ[ροίαι
καὶ οὐ τὸ εἴδωλον αὐτῆ[c, ἔν
τε τ[ῆι] ἑτέραι τὸν Ἡcίοδ[ον   5
μέμ[φετ]αι· διτταὶ γάρ εἰcι πα-
λινω<ι>δ[ίαι <δια>]λλάττουcαι, καὶ ἔ-
cτιν <τ>ῆ<c> μὲν ἀρχή· δεῦρ' αὖτε θεὰ φιλόμολπε, τῆc δὲ·
χρυcόπτερε παρθέγε, [[ερ]] ὡc   10
ἀνέγραψε Χαμαιλέων· αὐ-
τὸ[c δ]έ φηc[ιν ὁ] Στηcίχορο[c
τὸ μὲν ε[ἴδωλο]ν ἐλθεῖ[ν εἰc
Τροίαν, τὴν δ' Ἑλένην π[αρὰ
τῶι Πρωτεῖ καταμεῖν[αι· οὕ-   15
τωc δὴ ἐκ[α]ινοποίηcε τ[ὰc]
ἱcτορ[ί]αc [ὥ]cτε Δημοφῶντ[α
μὲν τ[ὸ]ν Θηcέωc ἐν τ[ῶ]ι νό-
cτωι με[τὰ] τῶν Θε.[..]δων [
ἀπενεχ[θῆναι λέγ[ειν ε[ἰ]c [Αἴ-   20
γυπτον, [γενέcθα]ι δὲ Θηc[εῖ
Δημοφῶ[ντα μ]ὲν ἐξ Ἰό[πηc
τῆc Ἰφικ[λέουc, Ἀ]κάμαν[τα δὲ
ἐκ] Φα[ίδραc,] ἐκ δὲ τῆc Ἀμ[α-
ζόνοc Ἱππο]λύτη[c].ελη.[25
  ] περὶ τ[ο]ύτων [
  ]τηc [Ἑ]λένηc [

---

[115] Thus, for example, Kelly 2007 who suggests that the *Helen* and the *Palinode* are the same poem.
[116] Thus Davies and Finglass 2014: 338.

```
]ε Ἀγαμέμ[ν–
].ον τον.[
Ἀ]μφίλοχον [                    30
]ωνουδε[
[τ]
```

1–5 Lobel || **6** μέμ[φετ]αι Lobel | διτταί... εἰcι Π²ᵖᶜ, διττά... εἰcι Π²ᵃᶜ || **7** Lobel, –ωδ[⁸]λλ– Π² || **8** <τ>ῆ<c> Fraenkel et West || **10** –ρθεγε[[ερ]]ωc Π² || **12–18** Lobel || **19** Θεc[τορι]δῶγ Lloyd Jones || **20–23** Lobel || **24** ἐκ] Φα[ίδραc Page | Ἀμ[α– Lobel || **25** Lobel || **26–30** Page

```
...
censures Homer for
putting Helen in Troy
and not her image, and
in the other it is Hesiod           5
That he blames. For there are
two distinct palinodes, and this
is their beginning: "Hither again
goddess lover of song", and:
"Maiden of the golden wings", [as]  10
Chamaeleon wrote. Stesichorus
himself says that the image went to
Troy, and Helen stayed
with Proteus.                       15
He innovates his stories
so as to say that Demophon,
son of Theseus, in his return
with the The[...]ids, was carried away
to Egypt, and that Demophon         20
[was son] of Theseus by Io[pe
daughter of Iphicles, Acamas
by Phaedra, and by the Amazon,
Hippo]lytus ...                     25
    ...
...Helen...
...Agamem[non...
    ...
A]mphilochus                        30
    ...
```

This piece enlightens us about the content of the *Palinode(s)*. It says that Stesichorus puts the Helen's image in Troy and not Helen herself, and that the *Palinode* included a detour of Demophon to Egypt. But the part which had caught more attention is that there was not one *Palinode*, as the earliest testimonies suggested, but two, for which the commentator provides two invocations to the Muses. These two invocations correspond to two different poems or sections of poems where Stesichorus criticised Homer (in the first) and Hesiod (in the second). The general interpretation of this papyrus maintains that both invocations, and thus both "palinodes", refer to the myth of Helen. Page accepted the validity of this source since the commentator[117] cites Chamaeleon, a Peripatetic philosopher who must have had direct access to the works of Stesichorus, as he is the author of a book on him. The authority of Chamaeleon was often contested,[118] but Bowra, who had previously argued that the *Palinode* and the *Helen* were the same poem, elaborates on the validity of Chamaeleon's words on the basis that, despite his sensationalistic tendencies, the commentator usually supports his views on reliable and accurate sources.[119]

Another aspect that led scholars to read in fr. 90 F. the existence of two palinodes for Helen is the fact that the Church Fathers (frr. 91i and 91j F.) also attest the tradition of more than one palinode. These later accounts, presumably derived from secondary tradition, did not make much of a case before the publication of fr. 90 F., but have since received a revitalized attention from the supporters of this view. Cingano points out that not only these pieces should be regarded with more consideration,[120] but also that the idea of the existence of only one poem is the result of a misinterpretation of the earlier sources (sc. Plato and Isocrates), which very likely are quoting the most famous *Palinode*.[121]

Bowra,[122] followed by Doria, suggested that the quotation of Plato (fr. 91a F.) was part of the first *Palinode*, and that the second, less well known than the first,[123] was focused on the criticism of Hesiod's version according to which Helen was abducted by Theseus, which is what Stesichorus presented in his *Helen*, as we have seen. This suggestion is not fully convincing for the following reasons. First, fr. 90 F. refers to the *nostos* of Demophon via Egypt. True, the papy-

---

[117] Page 1963: 36. The supposition that fr. 90 F. refers to two *Palinodes*, that is, two independent poems written by Stesichorus with the purpose of retracting from a yet another, previous and defamatory account on the conduct of Helen is followed, among others, by Bowra 1963; Doria 1963; Devereux 1973; Pulquério 1974; Podlecki 1971: 321–327; Cataudella 1972: 91; Rossi 1983: 25; Gentili 1985: 126; Massimilla 1990a: 370; Cingano 1982; Segal 1990: 191; Davies 1991; Brilliante 2002: 134; Ragusa 2010: 249; Edmunds 2016: 136–139.

[118] Woodbury 1967: 160–161 highlights the possible bias in Chamaeleon's account, from which the commentator of fr. 90 F. is citing, because he often shows elsewhere a concern with poetic disputes, of which Woodbury provides a list.

[119] Bowra 1961: 112; 1963; 1970: 81.

[120] For a discussion on the validity of the information provided by the Church Fathers, see Cingano 1982: 25–29.

[121] Hesiod fr. 358 M-W; Cingano 1982: 30–31.

[122] Bowra 1963: 245.

[123] Thus Campbell 1967: 260; Cingano 1982: 30–31.

rus says only that the son of Theseus "was brought to Egypt". But, if there was such a *Palinode* recalling the abduction of Helen by Theseus, it is remarkable that the poet decided to maintain a connection between Helen and the family of the Athenian hero. Second, if one considers the first *Palinode* to include the full exculpation of Helen, as it is implied by the quotation of Plato, a second *Palinode* would have been pointless.

More convincingly, Pulquério argued, against the previous hypothesis, that the *Palinode* quoted by Plato refers to the second poem,[124] precisely because the poet was deviating from this version where Helen departs with Paris. Hence the first line quoted by Plato does not refer to a general story but to a previous version told in the first *Palinode*, he argues. Thus, the first *Palinode* would have included the version attributed to Hesiod where Helen departs with Paris but is detained in Egypt, and the second would have revised this version and said that she would not have left Sparta. Hence, according to this view, both Plato and Isocrates (fr. 91a–c) are referring to the second, and the effective, *Palinode*. This means that a first *Palinode* was not as exculpatory as one may have expected.

However, the content of the "first *Palinode*", as suggested by Pulquério among others, is far from certain, since there are good reasons to believe that the testimony which attributes to Hesiod the first version of Helen's sojourn in Egypt, and her *eidolon* in Troy is not accurate. Pulquério, and later Cingano, considered the scholium to Lycophron's *Alexandra* which names Hesiod as the predecessor of the *eidolon* of Helen and conclude that he maintained the elopement of Helen with Paris, but altered their route.[125] Instead of sailing directly from the Peloponnese to Troy, they diverted and stopped in Egypt where they encountered Proteus who intervenes and keeps the real Helen, giving to Paris her *eidolon* (fr. 91h F.). Although less serious, since the betrayal of the marriage is not entirely fulfilled, Helen is not entirely exculpated from adultery.[126] Stesichorus would have adopted this version in the first *Palinode*, maintaining the agency of Helen in the elopement, which is interrupted only by the intervention of Proteus.

However, as Davies and Finglass point out, this testimony presents some problems. The *Catalogue of Women*, which is probably the poem the scholiast is referring to, does not intend to exculpate Helen, and the *eidolon* would fit oddly in the narrative. More relevant is the fact that fr. 90 F. cites the *eidolon* as an

---

[124] Thus Pulquério 1974.
[125] Pulquério 1974: 268; Cingano 1982: 32. The problems with this fragment have been pointed out by Dale 1967: 23, but it is generally accepted, cf. Doria 1968: 88.
[126] Edmunds 2016: 138.

innovation of Stesichorus, which is intended to differ poignantly from the traditional versions presented both by Homer and Hesiod. Moreover, the idea that Helen is maintained as a deserter of her husband, as Solmsen points out,[127] would not fit in the context of a palinode, whose goal is to revise the unflattering content of a previous song. The information we have about the recantation suggests that it was effective and that Stesichorus recovered his (metaphorical or physical) sight, which was the price he paid for denigrating Helen. Both Plato and Isocrates agree that he regained his sight only after composing the *Palinode*. If we consider the hypothesis of two *Palinodes* on the theme of Helen in which only the second is effective, as advocated by Pulquério, we need to reckon that the *Palinode* quoted by Plato and Isocrates is a recantation of a recantation, since the first attempt would have failed to fulfil its purpose. If the first song maintained the slander of Helen by making her elope with Paris, then it would hardly be called a palinode.

If the song referred to in fr. 90 F. is not a palinode on the theme of Helen, then what is it? The reference to criticism of Hesiod in fr. 90 F. is rather vague. It is true that we do not know of any other poem by Stesichorus where he would have told a myth and then proposed an alternative version apart from the myth of Helen, but we know of another poem where Stesichorus diverted in many aspects from Hesiod.[128] It is possible, then, that the reference to the criticism of Hesiod had nothing to do with Helen. Davies and Finglass suggest this hypothesis on the basis that the idea of a poem focusing solely on the criticism of Hesiod's version of Helen is redundant, speculative and possibly a misinterpretation of Chamaeleon's words who provide only the theme for the poem criticising Homer, while the other only says the Stesichorus censured Hesiod.[129] According to this view, there was only one, effective, *Palinode*, as our earliest sources suggest, that revised the traditional version thoroughly, and that had Paris taking a phantom with him in the ships, and over which the war of Troy was fought.

Woodbury considers the possibility that the two poems mentioned by the commentator may in fact be the *Helen* and the *Palinode*.[130] The first would be a

---

[127] Solmsen 1932: 119 n. 4.
[128] Davies and Finglass 2014: 316–317, the *Cycnus* by Stesichorus presented a different version from the Hesiodic account presented in the *Aspis*, which he mentions in fr. 168 F. This involved criticism of Hesiod, but it would hardly classify as a recantation, since the version of Stesichorus would not have included a previous one closer to the Hesiodic version.
[129] Davies and Finglass 2014: 316–317.
[130] Woodbury 1967 is generally held as the reference study for this issue, but see, before him, Sisti 1965: 301. This hypothesis has been accepted, followed, and complemented by Farina

defamatory song that nevertheless deviated from Homer is some aspects, and the second would be the recantation. Although Woodbury fails to convince that Chamaeleon's authority should be discredited, he may be right in considering that the two "palinodes" are in fact *Helen* and "*the*" *Palinode*. The *Palinode* would therefore describe how Helen never left Sparta with Paris, thus exculpating her. The emphasis on line 2 of fr. 91a F.: οὐδ' ἵκεο πέργαμα Τροίας implies a former account where Helen did arrive at Troy. This may be a reference to the traditional version of the myth, an allusion to another work of Stesichorus (for example, the *Sack of Troy*), or a reminiscence of what was told in the *Helen*.

In the hopes of reconciling the three different outcomes for Helen (leaving Sparta with Paris and reaching Troy; eloping with Paris but being stopped in Egypt by Proteus; never leaving Sparta but being taken to Egypt by some deity), some scholars argued that the *Palinode* included both versions of the journeys of Tyndareus' daughter. Bowie put forward the hypothesis that the poem known as the *Palinode* could have had two beginnings, or two *prooemia*.[131] This can explain the existence of two invocations to the Muses, one taking place in the beginning which would censure Homer, and the other later on retracting from Hesiod's account.[132] This hypothesis is compatible with the testimony of Isocrates, according to which the defamatory song and the palinode took place in two different occasions, as seen above, and also with fr. 90 F., if we consider the palinodes as sections and not as independent compositions. However, the hypothesis of the first opening as part of the *Helen* and the second as part of the *Palinode*, remains possible, if not likely.

The idea of the two *prooemia* allowed some scholars to revisit Blomfield's suggestion that that the *Helen* and the *Palinode* were the same poem, even after the publication of fr. 90 F.[133] The most satisfying argument for such a reading is

---

1968; Gerber 1970: 149–151; Adrados 1978: 283–287; Austin 1994; Bowie 1993; Ercoles 2013: 309–326; Davies and Finglass 2014: 314–316.

131 Bowie 1993: 24; Willi 2008: 112 favours this hypothesis.

132 See also Ercoles 2013: 309, which relates this hypothesis with the testimony of Conon in Ta30(a) Ercoles, which mentions the ὕμνοι composed by Stesichorus at the request of Helen. The hypothesis of the two beginnings is partially influenced by Aristides' words (see Baudy 2001), according to which it was a known practice of Stesichorus to compose more than one preface in his works: fr. 296 F.: μέτειμι δ' ἐφ' ἕτερον προοίμιον κατὰ Στησίχορον. "I shall now move over to the next preface like Stesichorus". In the sequence of this reference to this Stesichorean mannerism, Aristides criticises his opponents. The multiple prefaces introducing some sort of criticism of distinct views would thus replicate the structure of Stesichorus' *Palinode*. These two *prooemia* would first blamed Homer and then Hesiod, but not necessarily naming them.

133 Kannicht 1969; Bertini 1970; Sider 1989.

the one provided by Kelly, who argues that fr. 90 F. does not imply the existence of two poems, but of two invocations opening two hymnodic sections that belonged to the same poem. The first section, generally ascribed to the *Helen*, was more defamatory, while the second part, in an apologetic tone, would deny the previous account and propose an alternative version, known as the *Palinode*.[134] The scholars in favour of this hypothesis suggest that the first part of the poem would begin with the first invocation to the Muses provided by fr. 90 F. and would include the story of Tyndareus' oath, the wooing of Helen, and the betrayal of Menelaus; and the second would focus on the recantation of the elopement, saying that Helen was not seduced by Paris. This is similar in terms of content to what suggested the supporters of the hypothesis of only one *Palinode*. The problem with this view is that it assumes that the *Helen* and the *Palinode* were not independent compositions, which is problematic as seen above, not to mention fr. 90 F.

Be that as it may, supporters of this view have argued that the change in the course of the poem where Helen, instead of being taken by Paris, remains in Sparta, would be operated by means of a *persona* narrative[135] in which the story of the poet's blindness and its recovery (frr. 91a–g F.) would have been be told to justify the alternative version and to postulate its poetic authority,[136] derived

---

134 The existence of two titles for the same composition is a phenomenon observed elsewhere in the works of Stesichorus, and thus should not be dismissed on those grounds. Stesichorus' poem on the sack of Troy was more widely known by the title *Sack of Troy*, but fr. 99 F. presents the alternative title *Horse* (perhaps *Trojan* or *Wooden*), thus West 1971b: 264. Page 1973: 64 argues for the existence of two poems on the sack of Troy, a suggestion rejected by Davies and Finglass 2014: 406 n. 48 on the grounds that such a "hypothesis thus requires us to suppose two poems by Stesichorus on exactly the same subject". See also the last page of Haslam 1974.

135 Sider, with Blomfield, argued that the blindness of Stesichorus should be understood "as an act of theatre in which Stesichorus himself performed as if unable to see" (Sider 1989: 430). Carreusco 2017: 180–183, also argues that the encounter of Stesichorus and Helen must have been told in the poem as a factor of attesting poetic authority, in the same way as Hesiod and the Muses in or Sappho's Aphrodite (fr. 1 Voigt). Helen comes to Stesichorus with a version which contradicts the Homeric epic. On the other hand, Finglass 2018a: 145–146 correctly points out the risk in assuming such personal references in a surviving work of Stesichorus, whose style was closer to the epic, and thus had the tendency to hide the persona of the narrator. However, the address to Helen, in the quotation of Plato, seems to allow a more personal kind of narrative, on which see Kelly 2007: 2–11. For the use of 'I' in epic see Griffith 1983: 37–65. For a general account of the poetic 'I' in lyric, see Slings 1990: 1–30.

136 On the issue of poetic authority in the context of the *Palinode*, see besides Sider 1989: 430; Bowie 1993: 24–25; Kelly 2007: 11–12; Torre 2007: 66–67; Boedeker 2012: 67; Davies and Finglass 2014: 306–307. Morrison 2007: 80–81 draws attention to the Muses as a means to authenticate the new version.

from the intervention of Helen herself demanding a revision of the events (frr. 91c–g F.). This suggestion seems more appropriate to the context than the view put forward by Bowra, according to whom the poet needed to alter his version to please a Spartan audience.[137] While there is a good chance that Stesichorus performed in Sparta, it seems rather unlikely that he offended Helen, a goddess for Spartans, when there were other poems, certainly familiar to this audience, that provided a similar defamatory account of Helen.[138] It seems, therefore, preferable to consider that this new version of the myth of Helen was motivated only by Stesichorus' will to provide a different account of this widely known myth. However, a Spartan (or Doric) audience would be perhaps more open to accept a godlike intervention of Helen, *qua* goddess, in her ability to struck someone blind and cure them.[139]

The agency of Helen as a goddess is therefore a mere prop used by the poet to justify his alternative versions of the events. This scene would be required by the fact that a radical change in the canonical version could lead to the discrediting of the poet, particularly when he defies the truth of the epic version.[140] After the presentation of the reasons that led him to alter the traditional narrative, Stesichorus would have proceeded to tell how Helen never embarked in the ships of Paris but was instead taken to Egypt where she spent the ten years of war, and how she was recovered by Menelaus, presumably after the visit of Demophon in search of his grandmother Aethra.

If a *persona* narrative should be considered, *i.e.* a narrative where the poet speaks in the first person and about events occurred to him – and the address to Helen implied in fr. 91a F. seems to suggest so –,[141] it should have included,

---

[137] Bowra 1934: 116–118.
[138] Thus Bowie 1993: 25.
[139] The worship of Helen as a goddess (on which see Edmunds 2016: 162–186) was not restricted to Sparta, but it was indeed a general practice in the Doric communities across the Greek world. See Rozokoki 2014: 202 for a criticism of Grossardt's interpretation of Stesichorus' *Palinode* as a dichotomy between Panhellenic versus epichoric traditions. See also Beecroft 2006 for a study of the tension between Panhellenic and epichoric traditions in Stesichorus.
[140] Bowie 1993: 25–27; Torre 2007: 66–67.
[141] Calame 2015: 264–269, on poetic authority and truth. Cf. e.g. Pi. *O*. 1.25–55, where the poet first points out in general terms the countless lies perpetrated in the stories as an introduction to the alternative version he is about to present regarding the story of Pelops, whom he addresses in the first person. This alternative version has Pelops being taken by Poseidon to the Olympus, thus surviving and avoiding the horrifying cannibalistic episode in the traditional narrative. Pindar does so, he says, because he does wish to offend the gods by calling them cannibals, and adds, for the slanderous there are seldom profit. The fact that this story speaks of poetic truths and lies, slanderous versions told by the poets, and even divine intervention

probably after the invocation to the Muses, the poet's explanation for his blindness, and its solution. At this point he would start the recantation.[142] If so, it is perhaps better to assume that the *Palinode*, containing an address to the Muses and a direct appeal to Helen, was an independent poem, retracting from the previous more defamatory account, rather than a part of a longer one.[143]

Every suggestion offers its own problems; none is entirely satisfactory. Our knowledge of the contents of the poem is limited and the sources are not always helpful or fully reliable. Nevertheless, we can safely say that the *Palinode* elaborated on an alternative journey for Helen, and this is what is significant for our purposes.[144] This alternative journey of Helen does not implicate her alone. In fact, Stesichorus seems to have taken this opportunity to add new characters in a detour to Egypt who are not traditionally associated with this region: Demophon and Calchas. In what follows, I will address the possible meanings for such innovations.

We cannot move forward in this discussion of an alternative journey of Helen without addressing the motif of the *eidolon* and its implications to the narrative as a false and deceptive element.[145] Despite the considerable fame of the Stesichorean *eidolon* of Helen in modern scholarship, it must be said that very

---

that materializes in a god taking the relevant character for a safe place, is remarkably close to what we know of outline of the *Palinode*.

142 See, e.g. the invocation to the Muses ascribed to the *Oresteia* (fr. 172 F.). The retraction can refer to a previous composition (e.g. Hes. *Op.* 11–12), or to a change in the course of the present poem, see Kelly 2007: 9–10.

143 See, however, Pi. *O.* 1.25–50.

144 Wright 2005: 101: "There is still no good reason, then, to think that the Palinode described a phantom-Helen or Helen's sojourn to Egypt. If we discount the plot-summary of fragment 193 [fr. 90 F.], certain facts remain there which have seemed to shed some light on the content of the Palinode. However, these facts are too highly suspect". Apart from discounting, quite lightly, the testimony of fr. 90 F. (Wright 2005: 104–110) casts doubt on the validity of *Phaedrus*' quotation of the *Palinode*, arguing that Plato is often caught misquoting the works of the poets for argumentative purposes and thus may have adulterated the quotation of Stesichorus, something Lefkowitz 1981: 32 had highlighted Wright 2005: 108–109 argues that the testimony of Isocrates is the true one, and that it shows that Stesichorus' blasphemy was to make Helen a mortal and not a goddess, on the basis of what follows Isocrates' discourse. The implication of such assumption is that we are left with no content for Stesichorus' *Palinode* whatsoever. It is important to keep in mind the nature and reliability of our sources of the *Palinode*, but Wright's intention to dismiss all of them is unconvincing, particularly in what concerns fr. 90 F. For a study of the structure of the *Phaedrus* and the importance of the *Palinode* in the context of this dialogue see Demos 1997; Halliwell 2000; Rozokoki 2010; Campos 2016.

145 For a general survey on the uses of the *eidolon*, in particular when applied to the images of the dead, see Vernant 1993: 29–35.

few sources attest it. The earliest account for Stesichorus' version of the *eidolon* is provided by Plato in his *Republic* 9.586c (= fr. 91b F.):

> τὸ τῆς Ἑλένης εἴδωλον ὑπὸ τῶν ἐν Τροίαι Στηςίχορός φηςι γενέςθαι περιμάχητον ἀγνοίαι τοῦ ἀληθοῦς
>
> Just as, according to Stesichorus, the *eidolon* of Helen was fought over in Troy, in ignorance of the truth.

The same content is also found in Aristides (*Or.* 2.234 and 1.128)[146] even if it adds nothing to Plato's testimony. There are later testimonies where the details of the sojourn of Helen in Egypt with Proteus survive.[147] Fr. 90.13–15 F., as seen above, confirms the version of Helen's *eidolon* and her sojourn with Proteus:

> τὸ[c δ]έ φης[ιν ὁ] Στηςίχορο[c
> τὸ μὲν ε[ἴδωλο]ν ἐλθεῖ[ν εἰc
> Τροίαν, τὴν δ' Ἑλένην π[αρὰ
> τῶι Πρωτεῖ καταμεῖν[αι·   15
>
> Stesichorus
> himself says that the image went to
> Troy, and Helen stayed
> with Proteus.   15

Fr. 90 F. provides two important details: it mentions the *eidolon* and enlightens us on the whereabouts of Helen during the war. Let us first focus on the *eidolon*. The *eidolon* motif, as an episode where the real person is replaced by an image when he or she is safely elsewhere, is not hard to find in Greek literature, but is applied in the story of Helen only by Stesichorus and Euripides.[148] There are many episodes paralleled by this particular story of Helen, such as Heracles' *eidolon* in the Underworld, while the real hero sits joyfully in Olympus (*Od.* 11.601–604). But perhaps it is more useful to look for parallels in episodes where a god rescues one of his or her protégés, thus saving them from death.

---

[146] 1.128: ὥςπερ τῶν ποιητῶν φαςὶ τινες τὸν Ἀλέξανδρον τῆς Ἑλένης τὸ εἴδωλον λαβεῖν, αὐτὴν δὲ οὐ δυνηθῆναι: "some poets say Alexander took Helen's *eidolon* but could not take her"; 2.234: ὥςπερ οἱ Στηςιχόρου Τρῶες οἱ τὸ τῆς Ἑλένης εἴδωλον ἔχοντες ὡς αὐτήν: "as the Trojans in Stesichorus, who have the *eidolon* of Helen, convinced that it is Helen herself".
[147] Fr. 90 F. dates between 150 BC and 100 AD Page 1963; Davies and Finglass 2014: 81, suggests an earlier rather than later date. Fr. 91h F. postdates Aristides, since it is a scholium to his works, hence from after the second century AD.
[148] On the typology of the eidolon motif see Kannicht 1969: 33–38.

In book 5 of the *Iliad*, Aeneas is in the imminence of dying in battle, but Apollo rescues him, leaving in the battlefield an *eidolon* over which the Trojans and Greeks fight. This image of the Greeks and Trojans fighting over an image – ἀμφὶ δ' ἄρ' εἰδώλωι Τρῶες καὶ δῖοι Ἀχαιοί / δήιουν ἀλλήλων (5.449–453) – is paralleled with the idea expressed in fr. 91b. F. concerning Helen's *eidolon*. However, the *eidolon* of Aeneas has a shorter duration. The same can be said of Iphimede/Iphigenia in the *Catalogue of Women*, where Artemis replaces Iphimede by an *eidolon*, thus saving her from sacrifice (fr. [Hes.] fr. 23a.17–26 M-W), a version adopted by Euripides in his *Iphigenia at Tauris*.[149]

The *eidola* in these episodes, as in the *Palinode*, allow the narrative to proceed on two distinct but parallel paths. The narrative is left unaltered, while another path is created. This allows the poet to explore new meanings and new settings. We do not know how Stesichorus arranged the motif of the *eidolon* within his narrative. It is likely, as seen above, that the image was produced by the gods, since it is unlikely that Helen had travelled to Egypt with Paris. Therefore, the image appeared in Sparta, so that it could be taken by Paris, ignorant of the fact that he was taking a hologram with him and not the real Helen. If this is true, how could Helen have reached Egypt? Stesichorus may have applied the same principle as Euripides in his *Helen*, where the *eidolon* is created by Hera, while the real Helen is taken by Hermes through the air to Egypt.[150] This is similar to the episode of Iphigenia being rescued by Artemis in the moment of the sacrifice. If Stesichorus used the motif of the *eidolon*, which seems to be true, it is likely that the transportation of the real Helen to Egypt was performed by a god. Such an intervention is validated when seen in parallel with another, otherwise unknown, episode of the destination of an important female character of the Trojan War in Stesichorus (and indeed Euripides): Hecuba.

Although not involving an *eidolon*, Hecuba's rescue by Apollo in the *Sack of Troy* shares some aspects with these scenes of divine intervention to save a protégé. As seen in the previous chapter, Hecuba is rescued by Apollo and taken to Lycia (fr. 109 F.) in the sequence of the sack of her city. I have argued that her rescue, in contrast to the alternative versions in which she metamorphoses into a she-dog, maintains her dignity and nobility as Queen of Troy. Moreover, Lycia is commonly known to be an ally of Troy and a land of incredible wealth, an

---

149 For the antecedents of the rescue of Iphigenia, see Kyriadou 2006: 16–30; Parker 2016: xix–xxx; further below 4.1.2.
150 E. *Hel.* 31–55. Hermes also accompanies Europa in her sea journey (see e.g. Attic black-figure amphora 500–490, in Boston; Robertson 1988: § 31 and further § 57 and § 74.

image similar to that of Egypt, the place where Helen was taken to spend the ten years of war.

That Helen spent the time of the war with Proteus in Egypt is the unanimous account of the versions that do not have Helen eloping or being taken to Troy. Unfortunately, we know little of how Stesichorus treated this sojourn of hers. Fr. 91h F., a scholium to Aristides *Or.* 1.131.1, is the only other source to mention Proteus in association with Helen in Egypt, thus corroborating the story present in fr. 90 F., but adds further details:

> Στησίχορος ἐν τῆι ποιήσει λέγει ὡς ἡρπακὼς τὴν Ἑλένην Ἀλέξανδρος, καὶ διὰ τῆς Φάρου ἐρχόμενος, ἀφηιρέθη μὲν ταύτην παρὰ Πρωτέως, ἔλαβε δὲ παρ' αὐτοῦ ἐν πίνακι τὸ εἴδωλον αὐτῆς γεγραμμένον.

> Stesichorus in his poetry says that when Alexander had taken Helen and was sailing past Pharos, Proteus robbed her from him, and Alexander took with him a *pinax* with her image painted on it.

The scholium, unlike fr. 90 F., attributes to Stesichorus the version according to which Helen leaves Sparta but, when passing by Pharos, is taken from Paris by Proteus, who gives Paris a picture instead. As argued above, such a version is unlikely to be part of a *Palinode*, since it maintains Helen elopement, and substitutes the *eidolon*, for an image, perhaps in a rationalization of the earlier version,[151] since the passage on which the scholiast is commenting refers to the *eidolon* of Helen.[152] The version told by the scholiast, however, is similar to the story presented by Herodotus (2.112–120), the earliest source, besides Stesichorus, to have Helen staying in Egypt during the Trojan war. Herodotus eliminates the episode of the *eidolon* and instead has the Trojan prince to come back to Troy empty-handed. The Greeks fail to believe this story and pursue the war that ultimately led to the sack, which eventually proved that Helen was not in Troy after all, but safely in Egypt.

In fact, Helen's presence in Egypt had a long tradition. Egypt is associated with the *nostoi* of the Greeks in the aftermath of the Trojan War since the *Odyssey*. In this poem, we are told of the stop of Helen and Menelaus in the land of the Nile, from where they bring luxurious gifts (4.125–127; 131–132), and analgesic drugs to ease pain, wrath, and similar conditions (4.220–234). Homer made

---

[151] I owe the suggestion to Carlos de Jesus.
[152] Arist. *Or.* 1.128. Aristides mentions the *eidolon* again in 2.234. Note the similarity between Aristides' words and Plato's in the *Republic* (fr. 91b F.). This led scholars to believe that the passage of Aristides derives from Plato rather than from direct knowledge of Stesichorus (thus Davies and Finglass 2014: 341).

Menelaus and Helen spend twenty days in Egypt, waiting for more favourable winds to bring them back home (4.351–362). Homer's Egypt is a land of mystery, magic, wisdom; but it is also a wealthy and splendid place. It is a distant land which nevertheless attracts Greek attention for his marvels. Menelaus' sojourn in the Nile for twenty days suggests that Egypt was no longer a distant unknown land for the Greeks. Quite on the contrary, his stay there with Helen, and the hospitality they found, implies a closer Egypt; a place which was not only a mystery, but also a refuge, a "necessary stop in the journeys from Greece to Troy and vice-versa".[153]

This image of Egypt as a stop for sailors and travellers crossing the sea from Troy to Greece in their return is maintained in Stesichorus' *Palinode*. Most scholarship on fr. 90 F. focuses on its first 10 lines. However, important details in the following lines elucidate other aspects regarding the centrality of Egypt in the poem, and indeed in the *nostoi* narratives.

In lines 20–25 of fr. 90 F. Stesichorus includes Demophon among the warriors who are driven off to far-off lands, in the case, Egypt. The commentator introduces this information to illustrate one of the many innovative aspects of Stesichorus' poetry. Demophon and Acamas are among the Achaeans in the Epic Cycle, although their greatest achievement there is the rescue of their grandmother Aethra.[154] Stesichorus' *Sack of Troy* is thought to have depicted this episode (fr. 105 F.), thus attesting that throughout the sixth century Theseus and his sons make their way into episodes of the Trojan Cycle, and suggesting an Attic effort to "enhance its mythological prestige" by including their most famous hero among the Trojan warriors.[155] However, it is also possible that the presence of Theseus and his family in Stesichorus' poems reflect either a poetic effort to please his audience, thus suggesting his presence in Athens, or that the Attic myths were less epichoric than we may have thought, having rather a panhellenic appeal which made elements associated with this region to pene-

---

[153] Rodrigues 2004: 482.
[154] Cf. Stesichorus' *Sack of Troy* (fr. 105 F.), but also in the epics *Iliou Persis* (fr. 6, arg. 4 *GEF*) and *Little Iliad* (fr. 17 *GEF*). West 2013: 241 points out that "the recovery of Aithra was the only point of Akamas' and Demophon's presence at Troy. There is nothing to suggest that they did anything else." For the rescue of Aethra in Stesichorus' *Sack of Troy* see above 2.1.8. However, West notes that the presence within the Trojan cycle is "unlikely to go back to the 7th century BC", since the references to Aethra and Theseus in the *Iliad* (3.114 and 1.265, respectively) are likely to be interpolations.
[155] Thus Finglass 2013b: 38.

trate in the tradition at an earlier stage.[156] The presence of these Athenian family members also brings into question the traditional view of the *Palinode* as a pro-Spartan composition. As a matter of fact, the information provided by fr. 90 F., shows a mixture of provenances and genealogical elements, that enhance the ethnic and genealogical diversity of the Achaean heroes.

Stesichorus' *Palinode* extends the presence of Theseus' sons and their importance in the overall expedition to Troy. If the Epic Cycle and Stesichorus' *Sack of Troy* offered a circumscribed role to the grandsons of Aethra, in the *Palinode* the poet presents a different treatment, inasmuch as it includes one of them, Demophon, in the tales of the *nostoi* and in a stop-off: Egypt. Apart from this, in the *Palinode* Demophon does not travel with his usual companion and brother Acamas, but with someone else.

Acamas, however, is mentioned in the fragment, but in a rather different circumstance. After mentioning Demophon, the anonymous commentator elaborates on the lineage of Theseus' sons. We are told that Demophon is son of Iope, niece of Heracles, and Acamas had Phaedra as his mother. Theseus has another son by Antiope, probably Hippolytus. Finglass suggests that this catalogue is intended to place Theseus' copious love conquests in direct contrast to Helen's virtue implied in the *Palinode*, which, in turn, is the opposite of the woman of many husbands depicted in the *Helen*.[157] Such opposition would enhance Helen's chastity particularly since in the poem which the *Palinode* is intended to recant, Helen would have been part of such a catalogue of Theseus' lovers, indeed bearing him a child. We may then ask if this reference to the lovers of Theseus and the resulting offspring was supposed to stress Helen's absence, thus subtly recanting the Athenian abduction of Helen.[158] The "Catalogue of Theseus' Wives", in lines 21–25 of fr. 90 F., is also relevant in the context of the *Palinode* as it encapsulates the travels of Theseus, which most often result in a scene of abduction: a discrete way of mimicking the purpose of Menelaus' (and indeed the Greeks') travel that is the main topic. A reference to Theseus'

---

156 Finglass 2013b: 47. n. 108; Bowie 2015. [Xen.] *Ath. Pol.* 1.13 is taken by Burkert 1987: 52 as a testimony that professional poets performed in Athens in the sixth century.
157 Finglass 2013b: 47: "Helen's virtue would thus become more prominent when set alongside Theseus' laxer morality. The *Helen* united the pair in shameful sexual conduct; the *Palinode(s)* distinguished chaste woman from promiscuous man." In the same piece, Finglass elaborates on the problems of the text.
158 Bowra 1963: 245, who argues for the existence of two *Palinodes* on the theme of Helen, suggests that the hypothetical censure of Hesiod may have been related to his version of Helen's abduction by Theseus.

expertise in far-off journeys and encounters with "barbarians" may have legitimized the same ability in one of his sons.

Such a recognition would be required since Demophon's travelling record was rather confined to Troy before Stesichorus. Later sources tell of his passage to Thrace on his return from Troy, and the subsequent stop in Cyprus (Aeschines 2.31). However, this may be connected to the Athenian colonial presence in Thrace,[159] as it is the case for several Athenian foundations in the Troad credited to Acamas.[160] We may therefore see in Demophon's presence in Egypt a sign of the Athenian interest in the region.

The fact that Demophon travels without Acamas presents serious problems. The identity of Demophon's companions is seriously damaged. There are three hypothesis θες[τορι]δῶν, the sons of Thestor, θες[πια]δῶν Thespiadae, the children of Heracles by the daughters of Thespius, and θες[τια]δῶν the sons of Thestius. Of these the first seems best, since it involves Calchas, a well-travelled hero in the *Nostoi*.[161] However, this implies that Demophon is accompanied by more than one Thestorid, which is odd. The most famous Thestorid, Calchas, is in fact a well-travelled hero in the context of the *Nostoi*, with whom many foundations are associated,[162] but who nevertheless is not otherwise known to have visited Egypt. Calchas' divinatory powers could have played a part in their encounter with Helen in Egypt, facilitating the recognition, predicting Menelaus' soon arrival.[163] But a problem remains: the fragment refers to more than one Thestorid. A dubious source does say that Calchas had Theoclymenus as a brother,[164] but this is probably a result of corruption. With no brothers to be found for Calchas, there are two options: either Stesichorus mentioned an otherwise unknown brother for Calchas, or he is referring to one or both of his sisters, as D'Alessio suggests.[165] Calchas' sisters Theonoe and Leucippe are known from their wanderings in the sequence of the former's abduction by pirates. In the sequence of this, her father and sister depart in search for her, much like

---

159 Parker 1996: 86.
160 Thus Finglass 2013b: 39.
161 Thus Finglass 2013b: 43; D'Alessio 2013: 36.
162 In the *Nostoi* (arg. 2) Calchas returns from Troy in the company of Leonteus and Polypoetes. He is *oikistes* of Colophon in Lycophron *Alex*. 424–438 (see also Σ Hom. *Od*. 13.259 = II 570.16–19 Dindorf). His devination competition with Mopsus is said to have occurred in a myriad of places in Asia Minor ([Hes.] fr. 278 M-W; Pherecyd. fr. 142 *EGM*; S. fr. 180 *TrGF*; Apollod. *Ep*. 2.6; Conon *FGrHist* 26 F 1.VI).
163 Thus Finglass 2013b: 43.
164 Hyg. *Fab*. 128; see also Johnston 2008: 110.
165 D'Alessio 2013: 36–37.

Cadmus did when Europa disappeared. They succeed and bring her back home. The story of Theonoe, therefore, would be similar to that of the innocent and chaste Helen in the *Palinode*. She too was taken from her home against her will. She too will be rescued by her family and brought back home. The coincidence of the names of Calchas' sister and the daughter of Proteus and prophetess in Euripides' *Helen* should also be stressed. In a poem which rewrites the map of Helen's journeys it would have been interesting to have a female counterpart with a similar story.

In the story of Demophon and the Thestorids we have the representation of Egypt as a short-term sojourn, a place of passage. This idea of Egypt may parallel the above-mentioned Athenian interest in the Nile. Their passage via Egypt in the *Palinode* opens the region to other Greek communities, and by doing that renders it a more familiar place. Archaeological finds at Naucratis provide evidence for a Greek presence at the Nile delta at least from 620,[166] and attest the popularity of this *emporion*[167] in several other Greek cities or regions which by the seventh century were expanding.[168] Naucratis was, then, a quasi-panhellenic trading city where the Greeks had established good diplomatic

---

[166] Thus Boardman 1999: 121. Von Bissing argues for a later foundation, in the reign of Psammetichos II that reigned from 595–589, since he finds no references to an earlier king. However, the presence of Greek mercenaries, traders and settlers in Egypt can be pushed further back to the seventh century. An inscription at Abu Simbel Meiggs and Lewis 1989: § 7(4); *SEG* 12; *SEG* 43 1102 shows a host of Greek mercenaries whose commander was probably a second-generation Greek mercenary bearing an Egyptian name, Psammetichos, son of Theokles (see Lloyd 1975: 14–38). The inscription predates the foundation of the Hellenion at Naukratis by twenty years. Their self-representation as *alloglossoi* implies the assimilation of the Egyptian perspective towards the Greeks, this mutual awareness of the other was determinant to Amasis' treatment of the Greek settlement at Naucratis. Furthermore, Greek pottery findings attest with a certain degree of certainty a Greek presence in Naucratis before the sixth century (see Malkin 2011: 82–84). For the archaeological findings in Naucratis see Boardman 1999: 121–128; Jenkins 2001.

[167] For the organization of *emporia* see Horden and Purcell 2000: 395–400; Reed 2004: 34–42.

[168] The importance of Naucratis in the Greek trading network is evident from the existence of several temples dedicated to Greek gods and by the pottery findings from several Greek cities. Furthermore, the relevance of prophecies in exile narratives in the context of a world in movement is also noteworthy. The importance of a settlement such as Naucratis was noted above, particularly in what concerns its place within the convergence between Greeks and their relations with non-Greeks and the extension of this model to other places in the Mediterranean. Finally, it is worth mentioning the attention given by Malkin to the meaning of myth to the understanding of Greek network, especially a myth as central to Greek culture as the Trojan Cycle.

relations.[169] By making Helen stay in Egypt during the ten years of war, Stesichorus makes Egypt a place of permanence (for the Greeks) rather than a place of mere passage. This is significant when seen in parallel with the construction of the Hellenion in Naucratis in the sixth century, or perhaps even the seventh.

The *Palinode* is thus about much more than Helen's exculpation. In this poem, Stesichorus includes new characters on familiar routes. He widens the map of the *nostoi* of the Greeks, as he explores Egypt's potential as a friendly, wealthy, and welcoming place. More than just restoring the virtue of Helen, Stesichorus renovates the image of Egypt, which is no more a mysterious, distant place, but rather a part of the Greek world network.

---

[169] For the Greek presence in Naucratis, see Braun 1982 and Boardman 2006.

4 Exile

In this chapter, I focus on the two poems dealing with the motif of exile, the *Oresteia* and the *Thebais*, although this motif is not equally present in the remains. Both poems seem to have had considerable impact in later versions of the myths in what concerns the shaping of the characters and some details of the stories. The strong-mindedness of the tragic Jocasta may trace back to Stesichorus' Theban Queen. Some aspects of the tragic accounts of Orestes' revenge are said to have a Stesichorean precedence, such as the use of the bow of Apollo, and the recognition of the siblings by the lock of hair. Overall, these are the poems from which we can perceive more clearly Stesichorus' proto-tragic elements: his attention to the psychology of the female characters, their relevance to the narrative, and tense moments of suspense.

4.1 The *Oresteia*

The *Oresteia* is perhaps the best surviving example of the place of Stesichorus' poetry as a link between epic and tragedy. The innovations attributed to his version of the myth of Orestes (fr. 181 F.) illustrate his contribution to the shape of the story later found in the tragedians. The myth of Orestes and the abhorrent fate of the House of Atreus is one of the most prolific themes of surviving Greek tragedy, presented sometimes in more than one play by the three major tragedians. Although these versions of the myth deserved copious scholarly attention, their epic and lyric precedents are considerably less discussed. This may be because the most prestigious antecedent of the myth – Homer's *Odyssey* – is silent regarding the matricide performed by Orestes, which is the focus of the plays on the theme by the three tragedians. However, the antecedents of the story of Orestes in epic and lyric deserve a closer look since they provide the essential background for the story; the episodes that led to the matricide by Orestes and his subsequent persecution by the Erinyes. Therefore, before studying in detail the contributions of Stesichorus to the myth of Orestes, we should take a brief look at the versions presented by previous authors.

As said above, the earliest appearance of the myth of Orestes is found in Homer's *Odyssey*, since in the *Iliad* there is no mention of *stasis* within the family of Agamemnon, nor even to what is sometimes regarded as the reason for

Clytemnestra's revenge against her husband: the sacrifice of Iphigenia.[1] The events concerning the death of Agamemnon and the revenge of Orestes are told on several occasions in the *Odyssey*, although never from beginning to end and emphasising each time different aspects of the story depending on its relevance to the economy of the narrative.

The general outline of the story, however, can be summarized as follows: Agamemnon departs to Troy leaving his wife entrusted to the bard of the house at Mycenae (3.254–275; 9.452–461). Aegisthus, seeing in Agamemnon's absence an opportunity to seize power, tries to seduce Clytemnestra, who at first rejects him, but eventually capitulates (3.254–275). Anticipating the imminent return of the victorious Agamemnon, Aegisthus places a guard by the shore of the Argolid, where the fleet of Agamemnon is driven by the winds (4.512–528). Once Agamemnon returns, Aegisthus receives him with a sumptuous feast at which the king of Mycenae is to meet his fate together with his companions (4.529–539; 9.409–430; 11.405–434; 14.96–97). In the sequence of the slaughter of Agamemnon, Clytemnestra kills Cassandra and refuses to provide a proper funeral for her deceased husband or for his concubine (4.422–425). Aegisthus assumes the rule over Agamemnon's kingdom and remains in power until the return of Orestes from exile, eight years after the murder of Agamemnon (3.303–310). Orestes kills Aegisthus and offers a proper funeral to him and Clytemnestra (3.258), although we are never told how Clytemnestra died, since in the *Odyssey* there is no reference to the matricide.

As noted long ago, the version of the myth of Orestes in the *Odyssey* is used on two different occasions and serves as a parallel and an antithesis to the story of both Odysseus and Telemachus.[2] Orestes functions as an *exemplum* to Telemachus of a dedicated son who avenges his father.[3] In turn, when told by Agamemnon in book 11, the myth is modelled to highlight the differences between

---

[1] In Hom. *Il.* 2.299–332 Odysseus narrates the gathering of the Greeks in Aulis. Although he refers to sacrifices dedicated to the gods and to a portent in which a serpent devoured the *innocent* chicks of a sparrow before the eyes of their helpless mother, no direct reference to the sacrifice of Agamemnon's daughter is made. In fact, Iphigenia is absent from the Homeric accounts: she is not listed among Agamemnon's daughters at *Il.* 9.145 and 287. Her attempted sacrifice, however, was described in the *Cypria* and in the Hesiodic *Catalogue of Women* (see below).

[2] On the myth of the Atreids in the *Odyssey*, see D'Arms and Hulley 1946; Hölscher 1967; Lesky 1967; West 1988: 60; Marks 2008.

[3] Thus, e.g., Maingon 1978: 245 "In the *Odyssey* the theme of Orestes as the avenger of his father's murder is introduced into the complex design of the narrative as a foil to the dominant plot of the Telemacheia in books I–IV".

Clytemnestra and Penelope, and the analogy between Aegisthus and the suitors.[4]

For the most part, the story of the death of Agamemnon and the revenge of Orestes is told in the first four books of the *Odyssey*. Precisely because the story of Orestes stands as a model for Telemachus' task of protecting and possibly avenging the house of his father, no mention to the matricide nor to Orestes' subsequent sufferings is made. The story of Orestes is focused on his role as the glorious avenger of his father (e.g. 1.298; 3.254–306). Furthermore, as the Assembly of the gods with which the poem starts shows, the responsible party for the murder of Agamemnon, within the *Telemachy*, is Aegisthus.

Only in the speech of Agamemnon do we learn that Clytemnestra had a more active role in the killing (11.405–434). But here the story serves another purpose. If in the first four books of the *Odyssey* the story served to encourage Telemachus to act, in book 11, the tale of Agamemnon is directed to Odysseus as a warning of what he may find upon his return home, which ultimately serves to delineate the oppositions between Clytemnestra and Penelope.

While Homer is silent regarding the main faults among the house of Agamemnon, two poems of the Epic Cycle dealt with some of these episodes. The *Cypria* (arg. 8 *GEF*) stands as one of the earliest sources for the sacrifice of Iphigenia. When the Greeks were gathered at Aulis, Agamemnon killed a deer. Artemis, angry, prevents them from sailing to Troy. Calchas advises Agamemnon to sacrifice Iphigenia to Artemis in the hopes of appeasing the goddess and obtain her favour. They then elaborate the plan to lure Iphigenia to Aulis under the pretext of a supposed marriage to Achilles. The girl is then brought to Aulis only to find herself not as a bride, but as a victim of a sacrifice to be performed by her own father. The goddess intervenes at the last moment and rescues the girl, translating her to the Taurians (arg. 8 *GEF*) and making her immortal.[5] Iphigenia, it turns out, was not sacrificed, as seems to have been the case in most of the accounts of the episode in tragedy.

The *Nostoi* offers some details on the myth of Orestes. This poem is particularly interested in telling the stories of the Atreids' returns, although it includes,

---

[4] Also, Neschke 1986: 289 "C'est celui d'utiliser le récit des Atrides comme contrast du récit principal pour mettre en relief les parallèles et les oppositions entre le sort des personages de chaque récit et en particulier du protagonist Ulysses avec Agamemnon".

[5] For more details on the episode within the context of the *Cypria*, see Currie 2015: 241 who draws attention to the parallels of this episode and *Iliad* 1. Currie argues that the episode of the sacrifice of Iphigenia in the *Cypria* may be the model for Euripides' *Iphigenia among the Taurians*, but this is far from certain since we find a similar version in the Hesiodic *Catalogue of Women* and in Stesichorus, as we shall see.

as expected, other *nostoi*,⁶ such as Calchas' and Neoptolemus'. The plot of the *Nostoi* would extend from the departure from Troy to Menelaus' arrival.⁷ This means that it covered at least eight years, enough time to include Agamemnon's murder and the return of Orestes to avenge his father. The remains of the *Nostoi* concerning these episodes are minimal, but chances are that the account was rather similar to what we knew from the *Odyssey*, in particular, the story as told by Menelaus to Telemachus at 4.530–537 (recalling the information provided by Proteus) and by Agamemnon to Odysseus at 11.409–434.

It is likely that in the *Nostoi* Agamemnon was killed by Aegisthus during a feast, as in the *Odyssey*.⁸ Aegisthus takes over the throne in Mycenae. Orestes, absent from Mycenae in exile during the seven years that separate the death of his father and his return, appears towards the end of the poem. No information reveals how the *Nostoi* treated the return of Orestes. How was his appearance in Mycenae described? Did he use some disguise? We do know, however, that, unlike what is told in the *Odyssey*, Orestes is accompanied by Pylades (arg. 5 GEF). Fr. 11 GEF suggests a fight presumably between Orestes and Aegisthus.⁹

The presence of Pylades as a companion of Orestes raises some problems since in the *Odyssey* (3.306), Orestes takes refuge in Athens after his father's murder and not in Phocis, the homeland of Pylades, as in later accounts. Either the *Nostoi* is following a different version from that of the *Odyssey*, or the presence of Pylades is an error by Proclus. Since fr. 11 *GEF* may be seen as further proof for Pylades' role as an ally of Orestes, perhaps the likeliest option is that the poet of the *Nostoi* placed Orestes' exile in Phocis, rather than Attica, as it is the case in the *Catalogue of Women*.

In fact, many of the elements presented in the *Catalogue of Women* are similar to the events attested in the two poems of the Epic Cycle we have been discussing. From the remaining fragments of the *Catalogue*, we know that the poet dealt with the sacrifice of Iphigenia who is rescued by Artemis (fr. 23a. 13–27 M-W) and with the revenge of Orestes (fr. 23a. 28–30 M-W). In the *Catalogue*, the daughter of Agamemnon sent to be sacrificed at Aulis is not called Iphigenia but

---

6 Cf. Bethe 1929: 263–283; West 2013: 244–250. Athenaeus refers to at least three parts of this poem as ἡ τῶν Ἀτρειδῶν κάθοδος (F 3 and 12 West), which may mean that part of the poem was known as the *Return of the Atreids*, as suggested by Bernabé, *PEG* 93. See further, West 2013: 244, n. 1.
7 On the contents of the *Nostoi* in general, see the commentary of West 2013: 245–287, for the myth of Orestes in particular, see West 2013: 282–284 and Danek 2015.
8 Cf. frr. 10 and 12 *GEF*.
9 Thus West 2013: 283. Cf. the painting described by Pausanias (1.22.6) where, as Orestes murders Aegisthus, Pylades was depicted killing the sons of Nauplius, Aegisthus' allies.

Iphimede. The name and indeed existence of Iphigenia as the daughter of Agamemnon is problematic in the *Iliad*. Homer does not refer to the sacrifice of Iphigenia at all. Agamemnon is said to have three daughters: Chrysothemis, Laodike, and Iphianassa. No mention is made of Iphigenia, nor Electra. However, there are elements that may hint at a connection between Iphianassa and Iphigenia.

Iphianassa appears in the list of Agamemnon's daughters, Iphigenia does not. If Homer had in mind the sacrifice of the girl at Aulis, this absence is of course understandable. However, the context of the appearance of Iphianassa as a possible wife for Achilles alludes to the circumstances in which Iphigenia is taken to Aulis.[10] As we have seen above, the excuse used to take Iphigenia to Aulis is a stratagem that leads the girl to believe that she will marry Achilles. It seems, therefore, that the absence of the sacrifice of Iphigenia from the *Iliad* (and the *Odyssey*) reflects a poetic choice.[11] It is also possible that the fake wedding to Achilles is inspired in this episode of the *Iliad*. Therefore, it seems likely that Iphianassa and Iphigenia refer to the same character.[12] The case of Electra, on the other hand, is more problematic. She appears in the *Catalogue* and in Xanthus, but apart from that, does not seem to have had great relevance in the epic versions of the myth.

As to the revenge of Orestes, the *Catalogue*, contradicting the *Odyssey*, places Orestes' exile in Phocis under Strophius' protection, instead of Athens. Another relevant detail presented by the *Catalogue* strengthens the association of Strophius and by extension Pylades with Orestes. As noted by Sommerstein, fr. 194 M-W mentions an otherwise unknown "sister of Agamemnon and Menelaus, named Anaxibia, who looks very much as though she had been invented for the purpose of becoming the wife of Strophius", [13] thus making the exile of Orestes among the Phocians a more natural and justified solution, as opposed to the somewhat obscure circumstance of Orestes' refuge in Athens.

---

10 For parallels in the episodes of the *Iliad* and the episode of the sacrifice of Iphigenia in the *Cypria*, see Bremmer 2002: 29; Parker 2016: xxi–xxii.
11 See further, Dowden 1989: 11–12. Note, however, Σ A *Il.* 9.145 Erbse: <Χρυcόθεμιc καὶ Λαοδίκη καὶ Ἰφιάναccα> ὅτι οὐκ οἶδε τὴν παρὰ τοῖc νεωτέροιc cφαγὴν Ἰφιγενείαc, which seems to imply that the poet did not know the story.
12 *Il.* 9.145; 247. On the possible etymological associations of Iphigenia and Iphianassa, see Nagy 1990: 143–201; Palaima 2006: 58–62. Lucr. 1.85 names the sacrificed daughter of Agamemnon Iphianassa; Currie 2015: 291–292, esp. 292 n. 90.
13 Sommerstein 2013: 141. In E. *Or.* 1233, Agamemnon is considered a relative of Pylades. Paus. 2.29.3 says that the mother of Pylades was indeed called Anaxibia but does not mention any familiar bond between her and the Atreids.

Among the lyric poets, the only reference we have for the treatment of the myth of Orestes before Stesichorus is Xanthus, who is said to have treated this theme. In fact, one of the few details we know about Xanthus is related to his *Oresteia*. Athenaeus tells us that, according to Megaclides, Stesichorus adapted (παραπεποίηκεν) many of Xanthus' poems (fr. 699 Campbell = Stes. fr. 171 F.) including his *Oresteia*. Of this poem, we only know that in Xanthus (fr. 700) Electra was not the original name of the daughter of Agamemnon and Clytemnestra. She was born Laodice, but because she remained unmarried, she was later called Electra (ἄλεκτρος).[14] This may be an attempt to maintain the names of Agamemnon's daughters as they appear in Homer. Note, however, that in Hesiod fr. 23a.15 Electra is mentioned together with Iphimede/Iphigenia. Aelian puts this information in a way which leads us to believe that Xanthus may have told of Electra's misfortune in the aftermath of Agamemnon's death. This, in turn, may indicate, together with the title of the poem itself, that Xanthus dealt with the revenge of Orestes in further depth than Homer.

The earlier versions of the myth do not provide any details about the aftermath of Orestes' revenge, the central aspect of the myth later explored by the tragedians. Stesichorus' *Oresteia* seems to have focused on details otherwise ignored in earlier versions known to us. Elements of the myth common to the later plays such as the dream of Clytemnestra, the recognition of Orestes by Electra and the persecution by the Erinyes, are found for the first time in Stesichorus, and are likely to be his innovations (fr. 181 F.).

Stesichorus' *Oresteia* is said to have occupied at least two books in the Alexandrian edition, like the *Helen*. As in that poem, the diegesis of the *Oresteia* seem to have extended for a considerable time frame, possibly covering the events at Aulis (fr. 178 F.) to the Orestes' pursuit by the Erinyes (fr. 181.14–24 F.). It is likely that the central episode of the poem was, contrarily to what seems to have been the case in the versions we have seen above, the revenge of Orestes.

4.1.1 The opening of Stesichorus' *Oresteia* (frr. 172–174 F.)

It has long been suggested that the quotations provided in the scholia to Aristophanes' *Peace* should all belong to the same poem of Stesichorus. Since fr. 173 F. specifically mentions the *Oresteia*, editors have generally printed the three

---

[14] Cf. Finglass 2007a: 401–402 and Campbell 1991: 26–27.

fragments under this title.[15] These fragments offer a glimpse at the tone with which the poem began, something which has puzzled the modern readers of Stesichorus. The lines of the three fragments have elements that allow us to speculate on the type of song and occasion for Stesichorus' *Oresteia*. Here are the fragments (fr. 172–174 F.):

> Μοῦσα, cὺ μὲν πολέμουc ἀπωcαμένη μετ' ἐμοῦ τοῦ φίλου χόρευcον, κλείουcα θεῶν τε γάμουc ἀνδρῶν τε δαῖταc καὶ θαλίαc μακάρων. ad haec Σ^VΓ 775f αὕτη <παρα>πλοκή ἐcτι καὶ †ἔλαθεν†. cφόδρα δὲ γλαφυρὸν εἴρηται· καὶ ἔcτι Στηcιχόρειοc.

ita forte Stesichorus:

⊗   Μοῖcα cὺ μὲν πολέμουc ἀπωcαμένα πεδ' ἐμοῦ
     κλείοιcα θεῶν τε γάμουc ἀνδρῶν τε δαῖταc
     καὶ θαλίαc μακάρων

"Muse set the war aside and come to preside over the dances with me, your friend, and to celebrate the weddings of the gods, the banquets of the mortals and the feasts of the blessed". This is interwoven and has remained unnoticed. It is more elegantly expressed and it is Stesichorean:

> Muse, set the wars aside and, celebrating
> with me the weddings of gods, the banquets of men,
> And the feasts of the blessed ...

Since fr. 173 F. is metrically equivalent to fr. 172 F., Davies and Finglass suggested that it may have been the initial part of the antistrophe of the first triad of the poem:[16]

> τοιάδε χρὴ Χαρίτων δαμώματα καλλικόμων τὸν cοφὸν ποιητὴν ὑμνεῖν ὅταν ἠρινὰ μὲν κτλ. ad haec Σ^VΓLh (p. 125 Holwerda) ἔcτι δὲ παρὰ Στηcιχόρωι ἐκ τῆc Ὀρεcτείαc·

> τοιάδε χρὴ Χαρίτων δαμώματα καλλικόμων
> ὑμνεῖν Φρύγιον μέλοc ἐξευρόντα<c> ἁβρῶc
> ἦροc ἐπερχομένου.

δαμώματα δὲ τὰ δημοιcίαι ἀιδόμενα.

"Such public songs of the Graces of beautiful hair must the wise poet sing when the spring..." This is from the Stesichorus' *Oresteia*:

---

[15] Bergk 1843: 643. Finglass's edition agree with the hypothesis and prints fr. 172 F. as the opening strophe.
[16] Thus Davies and Finglass 2014: 493.

> Such public songs of beautiful haired Graces
> We must sing, discovering the Phrygian melody delicately
> As spring approaches.

'Public songs' are songs sung in public.

The scholia to Aristophanes' *Peace* give us yet another couple of lines (fr. 174 F.) which seems to fit the context of the previous ones, and so are thought to belong to the same part of the poem:

> ὅταν ἠρινὰ μὲν φωνῆι χελιδὼν ἑζομένη κελαδῆι. ad haec Σ⁵ (p. 125 Holwerda) καὶ αὕτη <παρα>πλοκή Στησιχόρειοc· φηcὶ γὰρ οὕτωc·
>
> <—⌣⌣—> ὅκα ἦροc
> ὥραι κελαδῆι χελιδών.

"when in spring the swallow tweets with joyful voice". This is also an interweaving of Stesichorus, who says:

> ... when in spring-time
> the swallow babbles.

There are good reasons to consider the three fragments as part of the opening of the *Oresteia*.[17] First, they present the invocation to the Muse, which is expected to happen at the beginning of the song,[18] as in the *Sack of Troy*, in the *Palinode*, and elsewhere,[19] where the poet calls the Muse the beginner of the song (ἀρχεcίμολπον, fr. 278 F.). As argued when discussing fr. 85 F. in the previous chapter, the beginnings are more likely to be quoted and remembered, hence, to be used in contexts such as Aristophanes' *Peace* speech. Since the lines commented by

---

17 See Davies and Finglass 2014: 172–174 comm.; contra Bornmann 1978: 149, who argued against the attribution of fr. 172 and 174 F. to Stesichorus' *Oresteia*, since he considers that the story of Orestes was impossible to be associated with the celebratory tone of fr. 172 F.
18 For invocation to the Muses before Stesichorus in epic and lyric context, see Finglass 2013c: 4–5. As noted by Davies and Finglass 2014: 331, we seldom find invocations to the Muses in the several openings preserved from Pindar and Bacchylides. See West 2015: 68–69 for discussion on the form of Stesichorus' poems between epic and lyric and for the remarks on how the opening of the *Oresteia* attest that Stesichorus' works were far from being a mere adaptation of epic themes to a lyric form.
19 Cf. *Sack of Troy* fr. 100 F. for the most complete opening preserved; note also the indication that Stesichorus began the *Palinode* with an invocation to the Muses in fr. 90 F. Other invocations are preserved but they are not ascribed to any title (frr. 277–279 F.), and in fr. 327 F. in the spurious *Rhadine* (on which see D'Alfonso 1994: 92–95, 102; Rutherford 2015).

the scholia all come from the same speech in the play, which is, moreover, the opening of a lyric section, it is likely that they refer to the same poem, and roughly to the same part of it.[20] Furthermore, from what we can tell of the first strophe of fr. 100 F. of the *Sack of Troy*, our poet dedicated quite a few lines to the invocation, so it should not surprise us to find a long invocation in other poems. The reference to the spring and the swallow also fit the opening of the poem which mentions springtime early on.

We learn from frr. 172–174 F. what would be the tone of the beginning of the narrative, but what caught most of the scholarly attention were the apparent allusions to the occasion and even perhaps the genre of the performance. The poem opens with the invocation to the Muse and elaborates on the theme which the poet is willing to sing (festivities instead of wars). Later, we learn what he wants to sing (the public songs of the Χαρίτες);[21] how he will sing it (by means of a Phrygian melody);[22] and when (at the approach of the spring).

It is agreed that the "public songs" (δαμώματα) mentioned in fr. 173.1 F. presuppose some sort of public ceremony, as opposed to a private occasion.[23] These allusions to a public setting for the performance have encouraged scholars to investigate possible scenarios where the poem could have been presented and the genre in which it was performed. The reference to the spring in frr. 173 and 174 F. supports the hypothesis that the performance took place during a celebration, perhaps a festival, upon the arrival of the season. The relevance of Apollo in the *Oresteia*, moreover, may suggest a ceremony in honour of the god associated with the return of spring.[24]

---

20 Ar. *Pax.* 775–780, 796–800. Thus Davies and Finglass 2014: 493.
21 Demetrius argues that the graceful songs are connected to the themes of weddings, gardens, spring (132, 133). On the ancient appreciation of Stesichorus' song as "sweet" γλαφυρός and the contribution of frr. 172 and 173 F. to the sweetness of Stesichorus' style, see Hunter 2015: 147–150. For the theme of the *Charites* in Greek poetry, see Rosado Fernandes 1962.
22 The Phrygian mode could be "appropriate for a range of moods, from cheerful bonhomie or piety to wild excitement or religious frenzy", West 1992: 180. Ieranò 1997: 196 argued for a dithyrambic composition on the account of the reference to the Phrygian mode of the song; see Prauscello 2012: 70–77 for other examples.
23 Morgan 2012: 42; Cingano 1993: 354; D'Alfonso 1994: 105–119; Davies and Finglass 2014: 29; Carey 2015: 52–53; West 2015: 68–70. Less unanimous is the assumption that the term implies choral performance. Thus Rossi 1983: 12; Willi 2008: 81 n. 124; Pucci 2015: 28–29 who argues that Demodocus' song in *Od.* 8.260–384 was also sung to the public; Finglass 2017a: 71–73.
24 Cf. [Theogn.] 776–779; Alcaeus fr. 307(a) Voigt for Apollo's return in a chariot pulled by swans, while nightingales and swallows celebrate with songs his arrival, on which see Bowie 2009: 119–121.

The combination of elements, i.e., the theme of spring, the Phrygian melody and Apollo, led Delatte to hypothesise that the *Oresteia* was a paean performed at the spring festivals with a cathartic function.²⁵ The classification of some of Stesichorus' works as paeans was already claimed in antiquity, and Delatte's suggestion provides a socio-religious context for Stesichorus' poems in Magna Graecia and Sicily, something which found favour among other scholars.²⁶ D'Alfonso, for example, following and refining the argument put forward by Delatte, argues that the structure of fr. 173 F. presents similarities with examples of other poets and concludes that in such poems, the relevance of the δῆμος as an active part of the poem is paralleled to the place occupied by the hapax δαμώματα in Stesichorus.²⁷ This hypothesis, however, presupposes that the chorus, as part of the δῆμος, was essentially amateur and local.²⁸

But would a non-professional and local chorus be able to perform Stesichorus' *Oresteia*, which in the Alexandrian edition comprised two books? Against the view of the *Oresteia* as a paean to be performed by a non-professional chorus, Cingano²⁹ argued that the passages on which Delatte based his argument reveal that the paeans aimed at purification rites were relatively short compositions, sang by an amateur chorus, and were, in terms of content, primarily focused on the occasion rather than on mythical narratives, which would hardly have been the case in Stesichorus' *Oresteia*.³⁰ Moreover, the length of the poem would represent a problem if represented by a non-professional chorus, as proposed by Delatte and D'Alfonso. Cingano thus suggests that the *Oresteia* was a composition to be performed at a religious festival in honour of Apollo by a professional chorus on a formalised occasion.³¹

---

25 Delatte 1938; cf. Rutherford 2001: 54.
26 Tb5 and Tb5(a) Ercoles. For a survey on the problematic classification of some of Stesichorus' works as paeans or hymns, see Ercoles 2013: 516–526.
27 D'Alfonso 1994: 108–119, especially 114–116 for the similarity of structure between fr. 173 F. and other poems, particularly Pi. *P*. 2, 3 M. For such parallels see also Cingano 1993: 354–356.
28 D'Alfonso 1994: 117 "È noto che nelle grandi feste a carattere religioso della Grecia arcaica (πανηγύρεις) il λαός non è solo spettatore ma ativo protagonista delle attività musicali e atletiche in esse previste. Ciò si verificava in modo tanto più evidente ne, caso dell'esecuzione di carmi religiosi tradizionalmente legati alle festività e ala divinità locale (inni, peani, iporchemi, etc.), in cui, come abbiamo visto, era recorrente il riferimento al δῆμος in quanto esecutore (non professionista) e al contempo destinatario del canto."
29 Cingano 1993: 356–357.
30 Thus also Gostoli 1998: 151 who considers Stesichorus' poems to have been performed in a citharode mode, given the similarity in content and themes to the epic. See above XXV–XXIX.
31 Cingano 1993: 357–358; so also, Carey 2015: 52.

Other scholars are sceptical of the ability of a chorus to perform long poems such as Stesichorus' all together. Carey stressing the length of Stesichorus' poems as a difficulty in contextualizing their performance,[32] asserts that while δαμώματα refers to a civic festival, perhaps "commissioned for performance on their own in public festivals",[33] the poem is considerably longer than the surviving evidence for compositions by other choral poets created for such ritualistic and cultic context, such as Alcman's partheneia or Pindar's epinicians. Carey prefers to consider the possibility of competitive performance, along with the lines of rhapsodic and dithyrambic competitions.[34]

So too in terms of the competitive performance scholars have argued for a monodic performance of the citharodic type. Against the view of the *Oresteia* as poem to be performed by a chorus, Rossi pointed out three aspects that may tell against the idea of choral performance and favour instead a citharodic execution.[35] The narrative element of the *Oresteia* makes it possible to imagine a context of a public gathering involving citharodic *agones* or festivals where song and symposium were connected. Rossi notes that the attribution of titles to the compositions has affinities to the practice of epic poems executed by the rhapsodes of archaic times. On the other hand, Vox argued that the themes of fr. 172 F. allude to epic-lyric subjects, which the scholar associates with monodic performance. Other aspects in the *Oresteia* may allow such interpretation. The partisans of this hypothesis argue that δαμώματα need not imply choral performance alone.[36] Moreover, the uncertainty regarding the plural of the participle ἐξευρόντα<ς> in fr. 173 F. is frequently used in the argument against for the choral performance, since the plural ἐξευρόντα<ς> is owed to Kleine who corrects the transmitted ἐξευρόντα to avoid an odd hiatus,[37] and thus giving a bet-

---

[32] The difficulty in classifying poems such as Stesichorus' is a problem which affected even ancient scholars. Stesichorus' Alexandrian edition was presumably collected in separate volumes, each containing one poem, or part of a poem, organized by title. This is rather distinct for other choral poets, e.g. Bacchylides, whose works were separated by sub-genres, epinicians, dithyrambs, paeans, hymns, etc. See further Lowe 2006: 169–171.
[33] Carey 2015: 53.
[34] Ieranò 1997: 196 suggested that the *Oresteia* might have been a dithyrambic composition. Ibycus is also credited with the composition of dithyrambs in fr. 296 *PMGF* (cf. Wilkinson 2013: 19–20, 266–268; Fearn 2007: 167 n. 13). For poetic competitions in the archaic period, see Herington 1985: 6–12; Rhodes 2003: 108; Carey 2015: 47–48. For Stesichorus' performance as proto-tragic, see Ercoles 2012.
[35] Rossi 1983: 12.
[36] Thus Rossi 1983: 12; Willi 2008: 81 n. 124; Ercoles 2013: 565; Pucci 2015: 29.
[37] Kleine 1828: 84. Schneidewin 1839: 332 rejects the proposition. Davies 1979: 893 warns for the problem of drawing conclusions on the mode of performance from the participle.

ter sense to the sentence as a whole. The resulting participle conveys the notion of a plural subject, thus presumably the chorus.

This brief survey on the opinions on the performance mode leads us to the next enigma: where was Stesichorus' *Oresteia* designed to be performed? The most famous hypothesis is the one most commonly attributed to Bowra,[38] but originally put forward by Wilamowitz,[39] that Stesichorus' *Oresteia*, like the *Helen* and *Palinode*, was aimed at a Spartan audience, since in our poem the palace of Agamemnon in located in Lacedaemon (fr. 177 F.):

φανερὸν ὅτι ἐν Ἄργει ἡ cκηνὴ τοῦ δράματοc ὑπόκειται. Ὅμηροc δὲ ἐν Μυκήναιc φηcὶ τὰ βαcίλεια Ἀγαμέμνονοc, Στηcίχοροc δὲ καὶ Σιμωνίδηc ἐν Λακεδαίμονι.

It is evident that the drama is set in Argos. Homer says that Agamemnon's kingdom was in Mycenae,[40] Stesichorus, and Simonides[41] in Lacedaemon.

However, as the variation in Homer tells us, the exact location of Agamemnon's palace was a matter of debate in antiquity and our poet may have deliberately distanced his version from Homer's and thus presented a different kingdom for Agamemnon. Pindar is hardly influenced by epichoric details of the myth when he composes his *Pythian* 11. Addressed to a Theban audience, the ode sets Agamemnon's palace in Amyclae. Bowra also argued that the name chosen for the nurse of Orestes, Laodamia (fr. 179 F.), reflects a Spartan oriented narrative, which is a weak argument given that it is not necessarily a Spartan name.[42] Another element that Bowra sees as an indication of a Spartan audience is the distinct lineage of Agamemnon (or Orestes) in our poem. Stesichorus says the being emerging from the head of the serpent in Clytemnestra's dream is a Pleisthenid king, which would mean that our poet tried to find a more blameless parentage for the king. However, this alternative parentage of Agamemnon was already found in the *Catalogue of Women* (fr. 194 M-W) which hardly had any political associations with Sparta. Moreover, the fact that Atreus is not the father of Agamemnon does not imply that the family was any less exposed to the faults of its antecedents. Pucci also argues in favour of a Spartan audience, suggesting that the role of Apollo in the *Oresteia* in his defence of Orestes, an

---

[38] Bowra 1934: 117–118.
[39] Wilamowitz 1932: 113.
[40] E.g. *Il.* 2.569.
[41] Fr. 276 Poltera.
[42] Thus Davies and Finglass 2014: 28, who note that the different parentage of Agamemnon need not have excluded Atreus from the genealogy.

ephebe and the rightful heir to the throne, would be appropriate to be performed at the Hyakinthia.[43]

If these aspects support a pro-Spartan audience, they would also apply to other regions in the Greek west, particularly those claiming Doric ancestry or under its influence. Neschke argues for performance at Tarentum, where, she maintains, the cults from the motherland were also celebrated. While the relationship between Sparta and Tarentum is attested to the late sixth century, there is no firm ground to claim that, by the time of Stesichorus, the "colony" was dependent on the metropolis to such a degree as to import and replicate the hero cults of the mainland,[44] which, of course, need not implicate that the city itself did not have its own festivals at which such a poem could have been performed. But such assumption is by no means beyond reasonable doubt.

Burnett,[45] on the other hand, saw in the festivals in honour of Artemis at Rhegium a possible occasion for Stesichorus' *Oresteia*, since the city held a cult of Apollo and Artemis which seems to have been an important venue for choral performance in the west mobilizing people (and choruses) from several other cities.[46] As stressed by Burnett, Rhegium and Matauros were associated with the legend of Orestes' purification. Orestes came to Rhegium with Pylades and was there cleansed in a river which he found on instructions of Artemis.[47] Indeed, Artemis played a role in Stesichorus' *Oresteia* by rescuing Iphigenia from the sacrifice and making her immortal (fr. 178 F.), but we do not know her role in the poem after that. Apollo, on the other hand, seems to have been more prominent, and so, if we are to connect the *Oresteia* to a festival in honour of any particular god, Apollo is perhaps preferable. In any case, both Apollo and Artemis intervene on behalf of Agamemnon's offspring. Unfortunately, this is not sufficient to prove a link between the poem and the festival at Rhegium.

Attempts to suggest occasions for Stesichorus' *Oresteia* remain conjectural. I am, however, inclined to agree with the hypothesis of choral performance in civic festivals whether or not competition was involved.[48] Based on what we

---

43 Pucci 2015: 27, 32, 34.
44 Hall 2012: 29–30 (see, however, Morgan 2012: 44 who claims the contrary).
45 Burnett 1988: 146–148.
46 Morgan 2012: 38.
47 Hyg. *Fab.* 261. From an earlier period, we have a crater depicting Orestes, Pylades, and Iphigenia attributed to the Ilioupersis painter, thus dating form the second quarter of the fourth century, but little can be made of this piece of evidence regarding the association of Orestes with Rhegium.
48 Cf. Morgan 2012: 37–39; for competitions, see Ercoles 2013: 594; Davies and Finglass 2014: 29; Carey 2015: 53.

have from Stesichorus' poems, the occasion itself seems to have merited little attention in the composition; the primary concern of the poet was the myth and the plot, although, as noted by West, the initial fragments of the *Oresteia* do present significant detail that "goes rather beyond what could be found in an epic prooimion".[49] This is particularly relevant in fr. 173.2 F. φρύγιον μέλος ἐξευρόντα<c>, implying that it is the poet/the chorus who discovers the melody, rather than the Muse singing it to him/to the chorus; the chorus or the poet is its creator, thus distinguishing the poetic craft of our poet from the epic bard.[50] This may be seen in comparison to fr. 172.1 F. if the Doric form πεδ' ἐμοῦ is correctly restored, where the poet asks the Muse to join him in setting aside wars.

However, in other openings of Stesichorus' poems, the Muse has a more decisive role is aiding the poet in his task. The most illustrating parallel is fr. 100.9 F. where the poet asks the Muse to come and tell how Epeius was inspired by Athena in the construction of the Trojan Horse (νῦν δ' ἄγε μοι λ<έγ>ε πῶς κτλ.).[51] The request to the Muse to come to the poet, ἄγε, is used in lyric songs.[52] The use of the verb λ<έγ>ε is a single occurrence applied to the Muse, but other verbs with the same sense appear again in both epic and lyric.[53] Note, however, that the invocation to the Muse in Stesichorus' *Oresteia* is more elaborate and coloured than the invocations from epic and lyric.[54] Even among Stesichorus' works, the other surviving invocation seems to have been rather distinct.

If we compare the *Oresteia* to the beginning of the *Sack of Troy* we see that in the latter the poem moves quickly from the invocation to the theme of the poem, narrowing down already in the antistrophe to the main topic of the po-

---

49 West 2015: 70.
50 Thus Davies and Finglass 2014: 469; West 1999: 365. For the implications of μέλος in the context of choral performance, see above XXIX.
51 Thus Davies and Finglass 2014: 416.
52 Elsewhere in Stesichorus: frr. 277a F. δεῦρ' ἄγε Καλλιόπεια λίγεια and the spurious 327 F. ἄγε Μοῦcα λίγει' ἄρξον ἀοιδᾶc κτλ. In other lyric poets, Alcm. fr. 14 *PMGF* Μῶc' ἄγε Μῶcα λίγηα πολυμμελέc | αἰὲν ἀοιδὲ μέλος | νεοχμὸν ἄρχε παρcένοιc ἀείδην, and 27 *PMGF* Μῶc' ἄγε Καλλιόπα, θύγατερ Διὸc | ἀρχ' ἐρατῶν ϝεπέων, ἐπὶ δ' ἵμερον ὕμνωι καὶ χαρίεντα τίθη χορόν; Pi. *P.* 1.60: Μοῖcα, καὶ πὰρ Δεινομένει κελαδῆcαι | πιθέο μοι ποινὰν τεθρίππων. Χάρμα δ'οὐκ | ἀλλότριον νικαφορία πατέροc. | ἄγ' ἔπειτ' Αἴτναc βαcιλεῖ φίλιον ἐξεύρωμεν ὕμνον; *N.* 6.28: εὔθυν' ἐπὶ τοῦτον, ἄγε, Μοῖcα οὖρον ἐπέων εὐκλέα.
53 Hom. *Od.* 1.10: τῶν ἁμόθεν γε, θεά, θύγατερ Διός, εἰπὲ καὶ ἡμῖν; Hes. *Th.* 24–25: τόνδε δὲ με πρώτιcτα θεαὶ πρὸc μῦθον ἔειπον, Μοῦcαι Ὀλυμπιάδεc, κοῦραι Διὸc αἰγιόχοιο; Pi. fr. 520.32–34 S-M.
54 The impersonal narrator and absence of direct reference to the occasion, help in differentiating Stesichorus from the parochial compositions of Alcman. Cf. e.g. Arighetti 1994: 22; Hutchinson 2001: 117.

em.⁵⁵ In the *Oresteia*, our poet spent a little more time in the prooimion as if he was prolonging the happy and joyful elements of spring, swallows, and feasts only to prepare for a sudden break in the ambiance.

The happy festivities are set in the second line of the fragment (fr. 172.2 F.). We will hear not of wars, but of festivities, like those of the gods and the blessed. However, the *Oresteia* is rather limited when it comes to joyful events. We might not hear about wars, but we will certainly hear about strife; strife among the family of Agamemnon. How, then, could the poet have moved from the scenario in the first lines of the poem to the mythical narrative?

First, let us consider, that frr. 173 F. and 174 F. make direct references to spring and to elements traditionally associated with it (the swallow, the Phrygian song). The return of spring is emphasised in fr. 174 F. by the birdsong of the swallows in the subtle alliteration κελαδῆι χελιδών and by the repetition of the contracted ἦρος in fr. 173.3 and fr. 174.1 F. The motif of return of the spring is expressed in fr. 173.3 F. ἦρος ἐπερχομένου and in fr. 174 F. by the song of the swallow, the bird of spring.⁵⁶ Now, the return of spring is associated with Apollo and his return from the country of the Hyperboreans, where he had spent the winter. Hence, swallows, spring, and Apollo himself express a general notion of return; a return which ought to be celebrated. The *Oresteia* is a story of returns. In fact, it is the celebration of Agamemnon's return that sets the narrative in motion in the other versions of the myth.

The episode of the return and death of Agamemnon, as told in the majority of versions, takes place, contrarily to Aeschylus' *Agamemnon*, during a feast. This is no ordinary feast: it is designed to appear to be a celebration of the victory of the Achaeans over Troy, and the successful return of king Agamemnon, which will lead to his tragic death. The circumstances of Agamemnon' death, perpetrated by Aegisthus, are first described in book 11 of the *Odyssey*, to Odysseus (11.409–416):

ἀλλά μοι Αἴγισθος τεύξας θάνατόν τε μόρον τε
ἔκτα σὺν οὐλομένηι ἀλόχωι, οἶκόνδε καλέσσας,   410
δειπνίσσας, ὥς τίς τε κατέκτανε βοῦν ἐπὶ φάτνηι.
ὣς θάνον οἰκτίστωι θανάτωι· περὶ δ' ἄλλοι ἑταῖροι

---

55 See above 2.1.1; Finglass 2013c: 14–15; West 2015: 69.
56 The first literary attestation for the swallow as a token of springtime appears in Hes. *Op.* 568–569, and then in Simon. fr. 307 Poltera. For more sources see Arnott 2007: § Chelidōn. On swallows as migratory birds announcing the spring and therefore the sailing season, see Morton 2001: 296–308; note however that some believed the swallows hibernate during winter (Arist. *HA*.600a10–16).

νωλεμέως κτείνοντο σύες ὣς ἀργιόδοντες,
οἵ ῥά τ' ἐν ἀφνειοῦ ἀνδρὸς μέγα δυναμένοιο
ἢ γάμωι ἢ ἐράνωι ἢ εἰλαπίνηι τεθαλυίηι.   415

But for me, Aegisthus wrought death and fate
and killed me with the aid of my accursed wife, after he invited me
to his home for a feast, as one slays the ox at the stall.
So I died a pitiful death: around me my companions
Were slain one after the other, as if they were white-toothed swines
Whose slaughter, in the house of a rich and powerful man,
Takes place during a wedding, a banquet, or a cheerful feast.

Of importance to our discussion are the last three lines where Agamemnon compares himself and his companions to sacrificial victims slaughtered in the context of weddings, banquets, and feasts: ἢ γάμωι ἢ ἐράνωι ἢ εἰλαπίνηι τεθαλυίηι. The sentence is similar in its conveyed sense to Stesichorus' fr. 172.2–3 F.: θεῶν τε γάμους ἀνδρῶν τε δαῖτας /καὶ θαλίας μακάρων, the themes that the Muse is asked to celebrate with the poet. Stesichorus' use of the same imagery of the speech of Agamemnon in his invocation to the Muse could then be a hint of what would follow.

Davies and Finglass note that a divine wedding is difficult to imagine as a narrative episode in the *Oresteia*.[57] However, they suggest that the "wedding of the gods" could refer to the marriage of Peleus and Thetis, as the trigger of the Trojan War, although they do note the difficulties of such hypothesis. Perhaps we should consider instead that the poet is here alluding to Agamemnon's family, whose misfortune is marked by the chain of homicides, the majority of which happens to take place in contexts of banquets and feasts.

That said, let us turn to the episodes of the House of Agamemnon which might fit this invocation. First, the wedding of the gods. Tantalus was the son of Zeus with the nymph Plouto. This union is referred to in Euripides' *Orestes* as θεογόνων γάμων (line 346), thus making it a plausible candidate to the θεῶν τε γάμους of Stesichorus' fr. 173 F. After all, the "curse" of Agamemnon's family begins with Tantalus. Thus, the reference to the wedding of Zeus and Plouto and the subsequent episodes of misdeed within the family of Agamemnon may perhaps be seen as the ἀρχή κακῶν.

The curse of the family seems an overall present element of the myth of Orestes. In the case of Aeschylus' *Oresteia*, for example, the motif of inherited guilt is central. The chorus of the *Agamemnon* refers the *daimon* that inhabits in

---

57 Davies and Finglass 2014: 494.

the house of Atreus. Euripides' *Orestes* opens with Electra listing her genealogy, naming Tantalus, Atreus, and Thyestes (lines 1–27), thus contextualizing the events about to happen in the vicious chain of family bloodshed.[58] The motif is alluded to in Sophocles' *Electra* (10, 1498), where these past sufferings of the house of Atreus are introduced by the chorus in an epode that follows a rather "optimistic" attitude, thus marking a sudden change of tone from joyful to grim.

Tantalus is known for his afterlife of punishment associated in most cases with the context of banqueting. He is never mentioned in the *Iliad* and his appearance in the *Odyssey* (11.582–592) among the transgressors provides no explanation for his eternal punishment of being unable to drink or eat. His penalty is different in the *Nostoi* and melic poets.[59] In these instances, he is condemned to stay under a rock which hangs above his head so he would live in constant anxiety unable to enjoy anything. Again, no reference to the cause of the punishment is given.

Only with Pindar do we learn why Tantalus was punished, in a poem where the issues of truth and falsehood delineate the narrative section in a similar way to what we find in Stesichorus' *Palinode*. *Olympian* 1 refers to Pelops' ivory shoulder in an allusion to the feast where he is given as the meal offered by his father Tantalus to the gods, who afterwards resurrect him; thus also the reference to the cauldron.[60] In lines 35–55, the poet presents his version, which provides an alternative justification for Pelops' disappearance: Poseidon seizes him. Unable to explain the absence of the boy, someone spreads the false rumour that he had been dismembered, cooked, and eaten by the guests of his father. This implies that the story of the cannibalistic feast of Tantalus was already known to the audience.[61] But Pindar promised his audience an alternative story, which is what caused Tantalus' punishment.[62] He stole the nectar and ambrosia from the gods, so he could enjoy divine delicacies with his mortal companions (lines 56–63). Both the versions presented by Pindar, however, associate Tantalus' fortune with events taking place at feasts.

The quarrel between the brothers Atreus and Thyestes is another episode of the internal strife of Agamemnon's lineage, which is referred or alluded to in most of the plays on the myth of Orestes. Apart from the *Iliad*, where the transi-

---

[58] On the motif of inherited guilt or family curse in Euripides' *Orestes*, see Willink on 807–843. The story of the family is also told in Euripides' *Electra* 699–750 and *IT* 191–202.
[59] *Nostoi* fr. 3 GEF. Alcm. fr. 79 PMGF; Alc. fr. 365 V.; in Archil. fr. 91.14 IEG and Pi. *I.* 8.9–10 the "rock of Tantalus" is applied as a proverbial expression.
[60] Pi. *O.* 1.24–27; cf. also B. fr. 42 S-M.
[61] See Gantz 1993: 531–536.
[62] See above 3.3 for a discussion on truth and falsehood in poetics.

tion of power has always been peaceful in the House of Atreus (2.100–108), the story of the two brothers is one of conflict. However, we have no detailed account of the quarrel between the brothers before Aeschylus' *Agamemnon*. Cassandra alludes to the episode in the play at *Ag.* 1191–1193 and 1219–1222 and Aegisthus provides a more elaborate account.[63] In Sophocles' *Electra* these past episodes are less central, but Sophocles dealt with them elsewhere.[64] Euripides used the story of Atreus and Thyestes more frequently in his plays, particularly in his *Orestes* (especially lines 982–1012) where the "famous feasts" of Thyestes are mentioned in a context of the fortune of the house of Agamemnon.

These episodes of the curse of Agamemnon's family are recurrent in the plays dealing with the story of Orestes' revenge. In that sense, lines of fr. 172 F. are not a mere catalog of festivities, but rather have a specific, subtle function of preparing the audience for the upcoming narrative. The joyful tone of these lines and frr. 173 and 174 F., speaking of returns, need not be seen as a misleading trick by the poet, but a true contextualization of the narrative, especially if the poem began likewise: in an occasion of joy upon the victorious return of someone long gone.[65]

However, the *Oresteia* mentioned events that happened before the return of Agamemnon, namely Iphigenia's sacrifice at Aulis. This means that the poem dealt with events covering at least eighteen years: from the moment when the Greek army gathers in Aulis to Orestes' revenge and probably even his wanderings. Could this have been told in a linear manner respecting the order of the events over the years, or were some of these episodes described in speeches in a more chronologically restricted narrative?

Among the surviving works of Stesichorus, we find examples of narratives that covered relatively short periods of time, as the *Sack of Troy*, and poems which dealt with a considerably long duration, as the *Helen*. Given that the *Oresteia* dealt at least with the death of Agamemnon and the revenge of Orestes, covering a timespan of roughly eight years, it is more likely that the narrative

---

[63] *Ag.* 1583–1611; Gantz 1993: 545–550.
[64] On which see S. *El.* Finglass comm. lines 472–575. Sophocles composed two or three other tragedies (P. London. Inv. 2110) on the antecedents of the house of Agamemnon: *Atreus* and *Thyestes (in Sicyon?)*. For the problems concerning the titles of these plays and their content see Jebb, Headlam, and Pearson 1917: 91–93; and Lloyd-Jones 2003: 106; who argue that the first of these plays (of which only frr. 140–141 survive) probably dealt with the Thyestean feast and the golden lamb (fr. 738), and that the latter told about the story of Thyestes in Sicyon, which presupposed the incestuous relationship with his daughter Pelopia (to which are ascribed frr. 247–269).
[65] Maingon 1978: 248.

was more approximate to the *Helen* in its management of considerable periods of time. Both poems occupied two books in the Alexandrian edition, indicating that both works had relatively similar lengths. As Finglass points out,[66] Stesichorus' 'Thebais' shows that our poet can manage to present some episodes in impressive detail, while merely mentioning in passing important turning points in the narrative, as for example the journey of Polynices (fr. 97.288–303 F.) throughout Greece which one expects to have lasted for some days is told with impressive concision, thus allowing the narrative to extend to relatively long periods of time, as we shall see.

Hence, some important episodes of the *Oresteia* were perhaps merely mentioned. Davies and Finglass suggest that the events happening before the Trojan War were "described by means of a speech".[67] If this hypothesis is correct, the episode of Iphigenia would have been one of these cases and hence told in retrospect either in a speech or by the narrator.[68] This hypothesis is preferable to the alternative scenario, which is to consider that the narrative of the *Oresteia* extended from the gathering at Aulis to the persecution of Orestes by the Erinyes in chronological order. We know of no other episode from the period corresponding to the time between the sacrifice and the arrival of Agamemnon.[69] If then, the episode of the sacrifice was told by means of a speech, it is likely that the speaker was Clytemnestra, and, therefore, it may enlighten us regarding her role, motivations, and responsibility in Stesichorus' poem.

4.1.2 Iphigenia's sacrifice (frr. 178 and 181.25–27 F.)

The sacrifice of Iphigenia is ascribed to the *Oresteia* by Philodemus and is the only surviving episode of the events occurred before Agamemnon's return to Lacedaemon. The elements of the episode are approximate to those found in the

---

66 Finglass 2015a: 91.
67 Davies and Finglass 2014: 489.
68 For *analepses* inside speeches in the Epic Cycle, see Torres-Guerra 2015: 232, suggesting that the curse of Oedipus in the *Thebaid* may have been told in a speech and too the *Cypria* when Nestor tells Menelaus the stories about Epopeus (Proclus' summary lines 114–117 Severyns).
69 The presence of the nurse Laodamia (fr. 179 F.) may have happened before Agamemnon's arrival. As argued below, a preferable option is to consider the intervention of the nurse after Agamemnon's death, as happens in Pindar (*P.* 11) and Pherecydes (fr. 134 *EGM*).

earlier accounts of the sacrifice: the epic poem *Cypria* and Hesiod.⁷⁰ Stesichorus fr. 181a 25–27 F. further informs us that the stratagem used by Agamemnon to get Iphigenia to Aulis is the fictitious marriage to Achilles, that Euripides uses too:

> Εὑριπίδ[ης δὲ καὶ τὴν Ἰφιγέ–   25
> νειαν ἐ]ποί(ησε γαμουμέ[νην
> Ἀχιλλεῖ] ...cατ[.]ρ.[

25–7 Lobel

> And Euripides makes
> Iphigenia (believe she was?) marrying Achilles...
> ...

These lines are part of a fragment where a commentator enumerates some of the tragedians' borrowings from Stesichorus. However, from the little evidence we have on Stesichorus' treatment of the episode, his version was very similar to that of his predecessors. The luring of Iphigenia to Aulis under the pretext of marrying Achilles is a motive that is found in the *Cypria*.⁷¹ Agamemnon incurred in the wrath of Artemis after having killed a deer. The goddess punishes the Greeks preventing them to set sail by casting unfavourable winds. Calchas then advises Agamemnon to sacrifice his own daughter, who was, of course, at home. The Greeks then elaborate the plan to take the maiden to Aulis, so that the sacrifice may be performed: they tell the girl she is to marry Achilles. Iphigenia is then taken to Aulis only to find herself as a victim of a sacrifice. The

---

70 For more details on the episode within the context of the *Cypria*, see Currie 2015: 241 who draws attention to the parallels of this episode and *Iliad* 1. Currie also argues that the *Cypria* episode of the sacrifice of Iphigenia may be the model for Euripides' *Iphigenia in Tauris*. Some scholars have been sceptical in attributing to the *Cypria* the translation of Iphigenia to Tauris (thus Burnett 1971: 73; Hall 1989: 111; for a more detailed discussion, see Wright 2005: 113–116). However, we know that the association of Iphigenia with Tauris is not an Euripidean innovation since it appears in Herodotus (4.103).

71 *Cypria* arg. 8 *GEF*. The marriage to Achilles as a pretext for Iphigenia's journey to Aulis is also found in E. *El.* 1020–1022; *IA* 98–100, 358–365, 433–434, 457–459, 609–612, 884–885, 1108, *IT* 214–217, 372, 537–538, 798–799, 818, 856–861; Hyg. *Fab.* 98; Nonn. *Dion.* 13, 110–112, and it is part of the primary Aulidian legend (cf. Dowden 1989: 12–13). See Foley 1982; Seaford 1987: 108; Bonnechere 1994: 42 n. 106 on the motif of the marriage. Bonnechere suggests that the choice for Achilles may be an analogy, so to speak, to the *Iliad* 9.144–147; 286–289, where Agamemnon offers the hand of one of his daughters to Achilles, Iphigenia is not listed among them as we have seen.

sacrifice is conducted, but, at the last moment, Artemis intervenes and rescues the girl, translating her to Tauris and making her immortal. This version shares many aspects with the Euripidean account, Stesichorus' account was probably approximate. Moreover, another fragment confirms that Stesichorus (and Hesiod) had Artemis rescue Iphigenia from the sacrifice (fr. 178 F.):

    Στη-
cίχορο]c δ' ἐν Ὀρεcτεί-
αι κατ]ακολουθήcαc
Ἡcιό]δωι τὴν Ἀγαμέ-
μνονοc Ἰ]φιγένειαν εἶ-
ναι τὴ]ν Ἑκάτην νῦν
ὀνομαζ]ομένην [....] ερι
.....]αιανρητ[.]νε
...] κατὰ δὲ τιναc [....]. α καὶ ἀνθρω-
π,...] τάφον εἰδ
.....].τηιπο[..] με[

1–7. Bücheler

Ste-
sichorus in his Oresteia
follows
Hesiod: Agamemnon's
Iphigenia is in fact   5
identified with
Hecate...
...
... mortal(s)
...grave (funerary rites?)   10

'Hesiod' is likely to refer to the *Catalogue of Women* (fr. 23a M-W) where Iphimede is rescued from the sacrificial sword by Artemis. Iphimede is immortalised as Artemis of the Road,[72] who presents some similarities to Hecate, with whom Iphigenia is identified in Stesichorus. Fr. 23b M-W of the *Catalogue* has Artemis turning Iphimede into Hecate, an account even closer to Stesichorus, which may indicate a confusion by Pausanias between the *Catalogue* and our poem.[73]

---

[72] The identification of Iphigenia, Einodia and Hecate is known since the fifth century in Thessaly and Arcadia (Paus. 1.43.1). Cf. Mili 2015: 147–158 for the cults of Einodia and Hecate in the region, Bremmer 2002: 31 n. 47; Davies and Finglass 2014: 502–503.
[73] On the identification of Iphigenia to Hecate, see Johnston 1999: 241–242. The author argues for the sake of her argument that Iphigenia is killed and then identified with Hecate, the venge-

In the *Catalogue*, Artemis substitutes Iphigenia with an *eidolon*, whereas in the *Cypria* the real victim is a deer.

We have no evidence for these details in Stesichorus' account, but since Philodemus indicates Hesiod as the source for Stesichorus' episode, in the *Oresteia* too Artemis may have substituted Iphigenia by either an animal or an *eidolon*. Episodes of divine intervention at such high points of the characters' fates are not uncommon in Stesichorus as we have seen above. Hecuba is rescued by Apollo in the *Sack of Troy* (fr. 109 F.) and in the *Palinode*, when Helen is rescued she is not experiencing any sort of life-threatening situation, but is substituted by an *eidolon* intended to maintain the illusion of her presence while she is taken safely and chastely to Egypt. The rescue of Iphigenia gathers elements from both episodes: the dramatic moment of the rescue and a possible stratagem by the gods to perpetuate the illusion of a sacrifice that was never fulfilled. But what impact does the rescue of Iphigenia have in the narrative?

The poet of the *Catalogue* proceeds to give an account of the birth of Orestes and the avenging of his father. No association is made between the sacrifice of Iphimede/Iphigenia and subsequent events upon the arrival of Agamemnon. The *Catalogue* considers Aegisthus the killer, πατροφο[ν]ῆα, of Agamemnon (fr. 23a 29 M-W), using the exact term found in the *Odyssey* (1.299 and 3.197) to describe Aegisthus, not Clytemnestra, as the murderer of Agamemnon.[74] There are good reasons, however, to believe that in Stesichorus the perpetrator of Agamemnon's assassination was not Aegisthus, but Clytemnestra. Several elements sustain the idea that in Stesichorus Clytemnestra had a more relevant role than in earlier accounts.[75]

In later versions, where Clytemnestra is held responsible for the murder of Agamemnon, the sacrifice of Iphigenia is commonly presented as a justification. Such association is clear for the first time in Pindar (*P.* 11.23–24) and is later a common element in tragedy.[76] Although suggesting that the sacrifice of Iphige-

---

ful ghost of the prematurely dead and their "quintessential leader" (Johnston 1999: 242). However, in the *Catalogue* Iphigenia is not killed but replaced by an *eidolon*, and in Stesichorus it is likely that she is also rescued.

74 Sommerstein 2010: 138 notes that in the Hesiodic *Catalogue* the emphasis on the guilt of sacrifice is not so thoroughly connected to Agamemnon as in Aeschylus, but rather in the Achaean army in general.

75 In the *Odyssey*, Clytemnestra seems to have had a secondary role in the murder, being Aegisthus the perpetrator of the deed, as demonstrated above.

76 Pi. *P.* 11.23–24. For tragedy: A. *Ag.* 154, 185–246, 1412–1436, 1525–1527; S. *El.* 530–533; E. *El.* 1018–1029, *Or.* 658. For the discussion on the validity of the sacrifice as a justification for Clytemnestra's deed in Aeschylus' *Agamemnon*, see Pulquério 1970; Neitzel 1979. Note, however,

nia may have been a justification for the mariticide, Pindar seems more inclined to believe that Clytemnestra was moved by rather different motivations. In his commentary to Pindar's *Pythian* 11, Finglass cautiously suggested that the sacrifice of Iphigenia as the motive for Clytemnestra's killing of Agamemnon may go back to Stesichorus.[77] Later, in his joint edition with Davies, he seems more convinced that there must be something to it.[78]

There is no plausible reason for the episode of the sacrifice to feature in the context of the *Oresteia* if not to add to the plot a deeper sense of conflict and to raise some questions regarding Clytemnestra's decision to kill her husband.[79] It is possible that it was used by Clytemnestra to justify her position, to highlight the justice of her deed.[80] However, as we know, the sacrifice of Iphigenia in Stesichorus is not fulfilled. And it is here that Stesichorus may have made things more interesting.

If Clytemnestra used the sacrifice of Iphigenia in these terms, she is basing her revenge on something that never happened. Such arrangement of the plot shares with the *Palinode* the sense that all the events that were allegedly legitimised by this episode are deprived of justification. The expedition of Troy in the *Palinode* is motivated by the assumption that Helen was taken by Paris and is now at Troy. So too Clytemnestra takes revenge on Agamemnon because she thought he perpetrated the dreadful act of sacrificing Iphigenia. It happens, however, that Iphigenia is not dead. The motives for the Trojan expedition and for the revenge of Clytemnestra were hence based on false premises, wrong assumptions. The survival of Iphigenia not only exposes the futility of Agamemnon's death and the subsequent chain of revenge, it adds to the *Oresteia* the debate over the consequences of human ignorance and misdirected emotion.[81] While exonerating Agamemnon from the dreadful deed of killing his own

---

that the sacrifice is rather absent from the other plays of the trilogy (thus Parker 2016: xxiv–xxv). For Sophocles' *Electra*, see Finglass 2007a: comm. 516–633.

77 Finglass 2008: 16.

78 Davies and Finglass 2014: 489. Kurke 2013: 124–125, on the other hand, favours the debt of Pindar to Aeschylus, rejecting categorically Stesichorus' very likely influence (cf. fr. 181 F.) on both accounts.

79 Unless we consider the hypothesis that Stesichorus' *Oresteia* featured the encounter of Orestes and Iphigenia in exile, for which we have no evidence. Thus O'Brien 1988: 98 n. 1: the encounter of Iphigenia and Orestes "cannot be traced back with probability to any work of art or literature earlier than Euripides' play". See also Kyriakou 2006: 19–21.

80 Cf. Maingon 1978: 248; Davies and Finglass 2014: 489.

81 Kyriakou 2006: 23. Kyriakou uses a similar formulation but in negative terms, since the author is commenting on Euripides' *Iphigenia in Tauris*. She argues that the *IT* is not concerned with the aspects of justice and revenge, given that it largely ignores the motivation of Clytem-

daughter, the rescue of Iphigenia emphasises Clytemnestra's sense of guilt and imprints on her deed against her husband a deeper sense of injustice, which will haunt her in the form of a dream, even if she was unaware of what truly happened at Aulis.[82] However, regardless of what may have happened, for Clytemnestra Iphigenia is, for all matters, dead by the hands of her father who would have indeed sacrificed his daughter if the goddess had not intervened by rescuing the girl.

4.1.3 Clytemnestra's dream (fr. 180 F.)

Stesichorus is our earliest source for Clytemnestra's premonitory dream, a motif of considerable importance to the plot of Aeschylus' *Choephori* and Sophocles' *Electra*. Its presence in Stesichorus' composition is fundamental for our understanding of Clytemnestra's role in the poem as the murderer of Agamemnon and as the principal victim of Orestes' revenge. But it is also an interesting aspect of Stesichorus' narrative technique and its relation to the Homeric epics.

The dream often appears in Greek literature as a narrative trigger.[83] It may represent a way for the gods to communicate with mortals (a vision which presents the events in a clearer way), or it may be a symbolic portent message for the dreamer or someone else to interpret. In both cases, it points to future events and it has the mission to lead the dreamer to act in a certain way.[84] In Homer, for the majority of the cases, more than being a premonitory vision, the dream operates as a device used by the gods or by the ghost of the deceased in order to persuade the mortals into action. Therefore, they provide clear instructions on how the dreamer should proceed.

---

nestra. However, she notes that in Euripides' *Helen* the case is rather different: "the play cannot be thought to share the theme of futile bloodshed with *Helen*, in which it receives considerable emphasis in the laments of the Greek characters for the suffering and slaughter of a war fought for the sake of an illusion". In Stesichorus, however, it seems that the *Oresteia* and the *Palinode* share the theme of a course of events based on wrong information, unfair assumptions, or simply human ignorance of the divine designs.

82 Neschke 1986: 296 emphasises rather the use of the sacrifice as a false pretext of Clytemnestra to justify her deeds. This is of course plausible that she makes a rhetoric use of the sacrifice, but we should nevertheless, allow the presumption that Clytemnestra thought her daughter to be dead, even if Iphigenia's supposed death is a mere rhetoric instrument.

83 Lattimore 1964: 72; Silva 2005b: 139–143.

84 For the debate on dreams in Antiquity, see Dodds 1951: 102–134; Kessels 1978; Del Corno 1982; Lev Kenaan 2016. For the different types of dreams, see Dodds 1951: 106–107; Dodson 2009: 42–51.

There is one exception to this pattern of dreams in Homer. In the *Odyssey*, Penelope tells the disguised Odysseus about a dream she had. Unlike the other instances of dreams in Homer, this vision of Penelope is more similar to a portent and the only instance where a dream has a symbolic meaning and interpretation:[85]

ἀλλ' ἄγε μοι τὸν ὄνειρον ὑπόκριναι καὶ ἄκουσον.
χῆνές μοι κατὰ οἶκον ἐείκοσι πυρὸν ἔδουσιν
ἐξ ὕδατος, καί τέ σφιν ἰαίνομαι εἰσορόωσα·
ἐλθὼν δ' ἐξ ὄρεος μέγας αἰετὸς ἀγκυλοχείλης
πᾶσι κατ' αὐχένας ἦξε καὶ ἔκτανεν· οἱ δ' ἐκέχυντο
ἀθρόοι ἐν μεγάροις, ὁ δ' ἐς αἰθέρα δῖαν ἀέρθη.
αὐτὰρ ἐγὼ κλαῖον καὶ ἐκώκυον ἔν περ ὀνείρωι,
ἀμφὶ δ' ἔμ' ἠγερέθοντο ἐϋπλοκαμῖδες Ἀχαιαί,
οἴκτρ' ὀλοφυρομένην ὅ μοι αἰετὸς ἔκτανε χῆνας.
ἂψ δ' ἐλθὼν κατ' ἄρ' ἕζετ' ἐπὶ προὔχοντι μελάθρωι,
φωνῆι δὲ βροτέηι κατερήτυε φώνησέν τε·
θάρσει, Ἰκαρίου κούρη τηλεκλειτοῖο·
οὐκ ὄναρ, ἀλλ' ὕπαρ ἐσθλόν, ὅ τοι τετελεσμένον ἔσται.
χῆνες μὲν μνηστῆρες, ἐγὼ δέ τοι αἰετὸς ὄρνις
ἦα πάρος, νῦν αὖτε τεὸς πόσις εἰλήλουθα,
ὃς πᾶσι μνηστῆρσιν ἀεικέα πότμον ἐφήσω.

Interpret this dream to me and listen.
I keep twenty geese in the house, from the water trough
They come and peck their wheat – I love to watch them all.
But down from a mountain swooped this great hook-beaked eagle,
And he snapped their necks and killed them one and all
And they lay in heaps throughout the halls while he,
Back to the clear blue sky, he soared at once.
But I wept and wailed, although I was dreaming
And the well-groomed wives of the Achaeans came and clustered round me,
Sobbing, stricken: the eagle killed my geese. But down
He swooped again and settling onto a jutting rafter
Called out in a human voice that dried my tears:
"Courage!, daughter of famous Icarius.
This is no dream but a happy waking vision,
Real as day, that will come true for you.
These geese were your suitors, I was once the eagle
But now I am your husband, back again at last
About to launch a terrible fate against them all".

---

[85] *Od.* 19.535–550. Thus Dodds 1951: 106; Del Corno 1982: 56; Russo 1992: 102.

Penelope's dream is a "wish-fulfilment symbolic dream",[86] whose meaning, although apparently evident is nevertheless doubted by Penelope herself. The fact that in the dream the eagle addresses Penelope and tells her what will happen, shares many aspects with other dreams in Homer, where a vision of a certain person (an *eidolon*, a ghost) appears to the dreamer to tell him/her what is about to happen.[87] In many cases, these dreams are deceptive and orchestrated by the gods in order to persuade humans into a course of action.[88] This is perhaps why Penelope is so reluctant to believe in the words of Odysseus in her dream.[89] To Odysseus in disguise, the dream is unequivocal: the eagle representing him is telling the truth and the hero will return and kill the suitors. Yet, Penelope is sceptical of the meaning of what she is told in the dream because they are too optimistic for a woman whose defence mechanism in the final books of the *Odyssey* is to doubt and re-evaluate all the potential false hopes.[90]

Penelope's mourning of the geese fits oddly in the dream if they represent the suitors. Against the attempts of some scholars to see in this dream a Freudian sign that Penelope subconsciously enjoyed the wooing, Pratt has suggested that, in Penelope's interpretation, the geese do not represent the suitors but rather the twenty years of her waiting and longing for Odysseus. There are not twenty suitors, but Odysseus' absence did last twenty years. If Penelope interprets the killing of the geese as the end of this period of waiting and hopes for Odysseus' return,[91] the mourning, and weeping of Penelope and the Achaean women are legitimate. Penelope must decide to give up her hopes for the return of her husband.

Penelope's worries are responded to in the dream, although she refuses to accept its optimistic message, emphasised by the beggar Odysseus. The dream is the opposite of what she understands from it. It is an announcement of the return of the hero, which will bring justice to the palace and restore peace and prosperity. The only example of a symbolic prophetic dream in the Homeric

---

[86] Dodds 1951: 106.
[87] In *Il.* 2.79–83 Zeus sends a deceitful dream to Agamemnon encouraging him to attack the Trojans which will turn out to be a disaster. In *Od.* 6.15–36 Athena disguised as one of Nausicaa's friends instructs the daughter of Alcinous to go to the riverbanks to wash the clothes, which will allow her to meet with Odysseus. Patroclus' ghost appears to Achilles in *Il.* 23.62–90 stressing his need to have a proper funeral and tomb.
[88] Marques 2014: 30.
[89] Penelope later in her dialogue with the beggar Odysseus elaborates on the twofold nature of dreams, thus partly explaining her scepticism (*Od.* 19.560–581).
[90] Russo 1992: 10; Pratt 1994: 152.
[91] Calchas' interpretation and the number of birds representing a period of time.

poems is dreamt by Penelope and appears in the book where her psychological state, her concerns, her position, are central. Kessels is sceptical in accepting that Homer could have established any direct "relationship between dreams and the psyche",[92] but this claim seems to ignore the dream of Penelope and the *kairos* of its appearance, *i.e.* the eminent return of the hero.

The fact that the first example of a symbolic dream in Greek literature appears in this context helps us understanding why the motif was so common in *nostos* narratives later in tragedy.[93] These dreams announcing the return of the hero appear recurrently to women. However, not all the hero's returns are good news for the dreamer. By associating a motif that was first connected to Penelope to Clytemnestra, Stesichorus establishes a striking contrast between the two queens, a contrast which Homer so recurrently exposed. Here, the dreamer is the one upon whom revenge is falling. The dream is also a mirror of the character's inner concerns. In Clytemnestra's dream, as Plutarch indicates, the psychological state of the dreamer is marked by a sentiment of remorse, of distress (fr. 180 F.):

ἡ γὰρ ἰταμότης ἐκείνη καὶ τὸ θρασὺ τῆς κακίας ἄχρι τῶν ἀδικημάτων ἰσχυρόν ἐστι καὶ πρόχειρον, εἶτα τοῦ πάθους ὥσπερ πνεύματος ὑπολείποντος ἀσθενὲς καὶ ταπεινὸν ὑποπίπτει τοῖς φόβοις καὶ ταῖς δεισιδαιμονίαις· ὥστε πρὸς τὰ γιγνόμενα καὶ πρὸς τὴν ἀλήθειαν ἀποπλάττεσθαι τὸ τῆς Κλυταιμήστρας ἐνύπνιον τὸν Στησίχορον, οὑτωσί πως λέγοντα·

τᾶι δὲ δράκων ἐδόκησε μολεῖν κάρα βεβροτωμένος ἄκρον,
ἐκ δ' ἄρα τοῦ βασιλεὺς Πλεισθενίδας ἐφάνη.

καὶ γὰρ ὄψεις ἐνυπνίων καὶ φάσματα μεθημερινὰ καὶ χρησμοὶ καὶ καταιβασίαι, καὶ ὅ το δόξαν ἔσχον αἰτίαι θεοῦ περαίνεσθαι, χειμῶνας ἐπάγει καὶ φόβους τοῖς οὕτω διακειμένοις.

For the vigour and boldness of damage is violent and ready to hand until the evil deed is perpetrated; but thereafter the passion, like a blast, falls short and weak, and surrenders itself to superstition and terrors. So Stesichorus modelled the dream of Clytemnestra on real events and truth of things when he tells this:

Towards her a snake seemed to come, the top of its head stained with gore,
and from it appeared the Pleisthenid king.

---

[92] Kessels 1978: 13.
[93] The dreams have particular relevance in the plays involving a returning hero, cf. A. *Pers.* 176–230; A. *Cho.* 32–46, 523–550, 928–929; S. *El.* 410–427; Cf. Silva 2005b: 139–143 for a comparison of Atossa and Clytemnestra's dream in Aeschylus and McClure 2006 who emphasises the role of the waiting mother in A. *Persae.*

> For visions in dreams, epiphanies by day, oracles, thunderbolts, and the like that is accomplished by and from the gods bring troubles and fear to those in this state.

In the dream, Clytemnestra sees a snake approaching. The imagery of the snake is commonly found in the tragedies on the myth of Orestes.[94] In Aeschylus' *Choephori* (514–552) the snake to which Clytemnestra gives birth in her dream clearly represents Orestes. In Euripides' *Orestes* (479–480) Tyndareus refers to his grandson as a matricide serpent. In other instances, it is Clytemnestra who is associated with serpentine creatures.[95] It has been noted that in Aeschylus the snake symbolizes either an ill-omen, Orestes, or/and the agent of divine retribution.[96] Although, in Sophocles, Agamemnon appears to Clytemnestra in dreams,[97] there is no allusion to any chthonic creature as a metaphorical representation of the king as in Stesichorus' *Oresteia*.

In our poet's version, the serpent represents Agamemnon,[98] and the blood on the serpent's crest is likely to represent his fatal wound,[99] inflicted by a blow of a sharp object in the head. This is the first interesting detail provided by the fragment: how Agamemnon was killed.

In the *Odyssey*, Aegisthus kills Agamemnon with a sword (*Od.* 11.425). In this passage, we learn more details told in the first person of the event that occurred in the fateful banquet. It is also here where the role of Clytemnestra in the episode is emphasised; she not only kills Cassandra; she witnessed the last breath of Agamemnon with striking distance and detachment as she goes away (*Od.* 11.405–434). The sword appears again in Aeschylus' *Agamemnon* 1380–1405. Here Clytemnestra's hand performs the deed. The episode takes place not in a banquet but rather in the private ambiance of the bath.[100]

---

[94] For bibliography on the subject, particularly in the *Oresteia*, see Catenaccio 2011: 215 n. 30. For the association of snakes with the dead, see Plut. *Ag. et Cleom.* 60; Küster 1913: 62–85; Burkert 1993: 380; Bremmer 1983: 80 nn. 21–22.
[95] E.g. A. *Ag.* 48–59, 1233; *Cho.* 994, 1047.
[96] Cf. Catenaccio 2011: 221.
[97] E.g. S. *El.* 406–425, 459–460, 478–481.
[98] Cf. Maingon 1978: 248; Davies and Finglass 2014: 503. Neschke 1986: 297 considers that the serpent represents Agamemnon's Erinyes. For the association of serpents and the Furies, see Finglass 2005: 41 n. 16.
[99] See Davies and Finglass 2014: 503 for the common assumption that the ghosts of the dead maintained their fatal wounds with examples, esp. A. *Eu.* 103 where Clytemnestra's ghost shows the wounds inflicted to her by Orestes.
[100] Since Fraenkel appendix B of his commentary on the *Agamemnon* it has been generally agreed that the weapon used by Clytemnestra in the play was a sword. Davies 1987 argued against this view and proposed that Aeschylus envisaged an axe as the weapon rather than a

Iconography shows the use of a sword or dagger by Clytemnestra to stab Agamemnon since the seventh century. A terracotta plaque found in Gortyn – the earliest certain depiction of the king's death – shows Agamemnon sitting on a throne, Aegisthus holds him, while Clytemnestra stabs the king in the back.[101] The first iconographic association of Clytemnestra and the axe may be seen in the sixth century metopes from the temple of Hera at Foce del Sele.[102] In one metope a woman holds an axe while another female, probably the nurse, attempts to stop her. The woman's movement is likely to be connected to the other metope depicting a man, probably Orestes who, in turn, is stabbing a man, most likely Aegisthus. Only in the Boston Crater, dating to the early fifth century,[103] is Clytemnestra holding an axe at the moment of Agamemnon's murder. Clytemnestra appears behind Aegisthus, carrying an axe, while he performs the attack on Agamemnon who is involved in some sort of cloth or fabric, a similar immobilization strategy to that used by Clytemnestra in Aeschylus' *Agamemnon*. From these, it becomes clear that the use of the sword would hardly have caused a wound in the head. Such injury is more likely to have been caused by the alternative weapon associated with the death of Agamemnon: the axe, used in Sophocles' *Electra* and Euripides' *Orestes*.

In Sophocles, it is not clear who was holding the axe, but such ambiguity emphasises the deed as a joint action of Clytemnestra and Aegisthus, stressing the advantage of the attackers in number who cowardly attack an unarmed and off-guard Agamemnon, as he feasts celebrating his return. The fatal injury of Agamemnon, Electra tells us, is inflicted in his neck, decapitating him (*El.* 132). The chorus also alludes to a blow to the head (*El.* 263). In Euripides' *Electra*, Clytemnestra kills Agamemnon with the axe (160, 279, 1160), while Aegisthus holds a sword. The use of the sword in these descriptions and depictions, suggests that Agamemnon was stabbed.

---

sword, since the axe is the preferable weapon in other accounts. Sommerstein 1989 and Prag 1991 have responded to the article convincingly emphasising the perilous ground on which Davies' argument stands. Sommerstein stresses the evidence on the text for the use of the sword, particularly *Ag.* 1528 and *Cho.* 1010–1011; Prag compares the iconographic evidence reiterating many of his arguments on Prag 1985: 1–10.

101 Touchefeu and Krauskopf 1981: § 91; Prag 1985: 1–2. Davies 1969: 224–240 draws a comparison between the iconography of the Gortyn's pinax and a steatite disk also from Crete but earlier (ca. late eighth-early seventh centuries) to conclude that the latter is likely to depict the same scene, and therefore to have had Clytemnestra killing Agamemnon.
102 Van Buren 1942: 438 for the myth represented; Prag 1985: 11–13, 44; Morizot 1992: § 20 on the identification of Clytemnestra; Davies and Finglass 2014: 487.
103 Vermeule 1966; Clairmont 1966; Toucheferd and Krauskopf 1981: § 89; Prag 1985: 3–4.

Since in Stesichorus' dream the serpent is wounded in the crest, it is more plausible that in our poet's account the fatal blow was inflicted by an axe, in perhaps similar terms to Sophocles' version. Hence, there seems to be little room for doubting that the serpent, associated as it might be to the Erinyes, represents the dead Agamemnon, who still preserves his fatal wound. Conversely, the identity of the ambiguous "Pleisthenid king" rising from the top of the serpent's head is not so obvious, since there are good reasons to advocate for either Agamemnon or Orestes.

Pleisthenes' place in the genealogy is obscure and variable. He appears in the *Catalogue of Women* as the son of Atreus and Aerope. Cleolla, daughter of Dias, bores him Agamemnon, Menelaus, and Anaxibia.[104] Pleisthenes may have appeared as the father of Agamemnon and Menelaus in Euripides' *Cressae*.[105] Another variant combines both traditions: Agamemnon and Menelaus were Pleisthenes' sons, but were brought up by their uncle Atreus after the death of their father.[106]

Stesichorus may have followed the Hesiodic *Catalogue* and made Pleisthenes father of Agamemnon and Menelaus. Hence, the expression "Pleisthenid king" would be the patronymic referring to Agamemnon. Therefore, it would be Agamemnon's ghost that appears to Clytemnestra. Supporting this view, some scholars have pointed out the inadequacy of βαϲιλεύϲ applied to someone Orestes' circumstances, exiled and not yet ruling, and the rarity of the use of papponymic in such contexts.[107]

However, there are complying arguments to champion the latter hypothesis. First, the papponymic is applied to Achilles and Eurycleia in the Homeric poems, on occasions where the noble lineage of the person is to be emphasised.[108] As someone about to avenge one of the noble descendants of Pleisthe-

---

[104] [Hes.] fr. 194 M-W. His heroic *ethos* is questioned by another testimony who says that he was described as a hermaphrodite and a transvestite in the Hesiodic account (fr. 137c Most).
[105] E. *Cres.* test. iiia, iiic *TrGF*.
[106] Grimal 1986: 377.
[107] Several scholars support the view that the man who emerges from the snake is Agamemnon: Hartung 1856: 170–171; Robert 1881: 171; Bowra 1934: 118; Davies 1969: 246; Neschke 1986: 247; Garvie 1986: xx.
[108] West 1988: 80 argues that the use of the papponymic is abnormal in Homer except for Achilles. However, the use of the papponymic applies to Eurycleia in the *Odyssey* (1.429, 2.347, 20.148); thus Higbie 1995: 8. Higbie 1995: 6 argues that Orestes, in his first appearance in the *Odyssey* is referred to by the papponymic "Atreid", but it is unclear if the Atreid refers to Orestes or to Agamemnon. There are other instances where the use of the ancestors in more general terms is common, for example in Priam's epithet Dardanid, and in, among others single occurences (*Il.* 23.514, for Nestor; *Il.* 2.763 for Eumelus; *Il.* 2.621, 11.709, 13.185).

nids, being himself part of that lineage, it is not odd to find Orestes' place in the genealogy being highlighted here. He is the legitimate heir to the throne, and he should recover it from the usurpers.[109]

Moreover, the reference to the noble lineage need not apply only to the father or grandfather of the person in question. The patronymic can refer to a broader concept of ancestry, in which case there would be no problem in accepting that the figure that emerges is Orestes. In Ibycus fr. S151.21–22, a passage marked by the prolific use of epithets, Agamemnon is described as follows:

> ... Πλεισθ[ενί]δας βασιλ[εὺ]c ἀγὸc ἀνδρῶν
> Ἀτρέοc ἐc[θλὸc π]άιc ἔκγ[ο]νοc
>
> ...Pleisthenid king, leader of men
> noble son born to Atreus.

The use of the Πλεισθενίδας βασιλεύc in Ibycus, as a mere reinforcement of the noble ancestry of Agamemnon,[110] allows us to suppose that Stesichorus was implying the same in his fr. 180 F. Maingon suggests that we should understand Stesichorus' Πλεισθενίδας βασιλεύc as a reference to Pleisthenes' dynasty, rather than a direct reference to Agamemnon's parentage.[111] The same can be said regarding the other occurrence of the patronymic in Stesichorus. The context of fr. 170.'25' F. is irrecoverable but Πλεισθενίδας, close as it is to 'Dardanid' in the previous line, may indicate a similar general reference to the lineage. If we approach the line considering that it refers in more general terms to the dynasty and the lineage of Agamemnon, similarly to what happens in Ibycus, the reference to Orestes as the "Pleisthenid" figure who appears to Clytemnestra is less problematic. Orestes is the legitimate heir to the throne, born into the line of Pleisthenes, the future βασιλεύc.[112] The sense of the dream, therefore, is symbolically similar to the dream in Sophocles' *Electra*, where the idea of the transmis-

---

109 Mueller-Goldingen 2000: 10.
110 Wilkinson 2013: 70–71.
111 Maingon 1978: 256.
112 We need not exclude the possibility that Pleisthenes was indeed Agamemnon and Menelaus' father in Stesichorus to believe that the figure rising from the serpent crest is Orestes. Thus Reiske 1755: 90; Devereux 1976: 171–176 makes relevant points against the idea of a metamorphosis on the snake into Agamemnon (Devereux 1976: 172); Maingon 1978: 256; Mueller-Goldingen 2000: 9–13; Davies and Finglass 2014: 506–507, among others.

sion of power from father to son is clearly emphasised. The dynasty of Pleisthenes will continue in its legitimate heirs.[113]

The dream is structured in a "movement from enigma to clarity"[114] in the gradual pace of the serpent approaching, showing its wound from where Orestes emerges. It is likely that in the sequence of the episode preserved by Plutarch the figure of Orestes addressed somehow Clytemnestra, perhaps anticipating her death, or even attacking her, as in the Aeschylean dream. The quotation of Plutarch allows us to glimpse at the context and the implications of the episode. The dream, Plutarch tells us, illustrates the criminal mind of Clytemnestra assailed by her deeds.

However, by having Orestes emerge from the serpents' crest, Stesichorus does not limit the dream to a reflection of Clytemnestra's psychology. The poet uses the dream in the more traditional way of an epiphany that informs the dreamer of future events. Therefore, the dream is not a mere result of Clytemnestra's anxiety or remorse over the murder of her husband, it also the announcement of the imminent return of Orestes. Through the epiphany of the father from whose head the son appears, Stesichorus establishes a more intimate connection between Agamemnon and Orestes. The emergence of Orestes from the serpent's crest emphasises the complete exclusion of Clytemnestra from the maternal role, thus stressing Orestes' connection to his father and his lineage, thus denying Clytemnestra the role of a mother.[115]

The deviant behaviour of Clytemnestra as a wife and, more importantly, a mother is a determining aspect of her characterization. Xanthou noted that the maternal figures deserved Stesichorus' close attention, since he acknowledges their dramatic potential. As seen throughout this study, the maternal figures proliferate in his oeuvre usually as agents on behalf of their children. There are exceptions. Xanthou treats in detail one of them: Althaea, who Stesichorus may have "presented as hovering between her maternal feeling and affection towards her brother" ultimately deciding to privilege the latter over the former".[116]

---

113 Hom. *Il.* 2.100–108 offers an unexpected account of the traditional harmonious transition of power in the house of Atreus. This idealistic scenario contrast deeply with the myth of Orestes. But the dream and its announcement of the return of Orestes anticipated the hoped restoration of power to the rightful heir.

114 Lebeck 1971: 31. Although these words refer to the intricate structure of Aeschylus' *Oresteia*, they apply to the sequence in which Clytemnestra's dream unfolds.

115 Thus Davies and Finglass 2014: 506.

116 Xanthou 2015: 33–38, quotation p. 37. Althaea's treatment is hard to define. She appears in frr. 189 F. and 191 F., which, despite the thematic correspondence to the *Boarhunters*, is ruled out as part of that poem since they are metrically incompatible. We know that she learns

Three other deviating mothers are left out; Eriphyle, Helen, and Clytemnestra; all problematic maternal figures. Helen's case was already discussed in the previous chapter, so we shall leave her aside, and focus on the two other problematic wives and mothers: Eriphyle and Clytemnestra, who share a story similar in many ways. The characterization of Stesichorus' Eriphyle does not survive, although the fact that the poem bears her name as a title suggests that she was if not the main, at least one of the major characters. Since Homer, Eriphyle is condemned as a hateful woman for having accepted a bribe which she knows would lead to her husband's death. Clytemnestra either kills or helps to kill Agamemnon. Eriphyle and Clytemnestra would eventually be killed by their sons who spent a considerable period away from home and return to perpetrate the matricide, thus avenging their fathers. As matricides, they both face the punishment of being persecuted by the Erinyes of their mothers. It would be interesting to see how Stesichorus treated the character of Eriphyle as she decided to accept the bribe thus condemning her husband to die, and the subsequent vengeance of Alcmeon (fr. 93 F.) and to compare the two poems of matricide.

These mothers, particularly Clytemnestra, represent a challenge to Stesichorus' characterization of the maternal figures. Clytemnestra's children are by no means her priority, at least not Orestes and Electra. Their relationship is one of distance and detachment in many of the accounts of the myth of Orestes. In Stesichorus' *Oresteia* the mother does not intervene on behalf of her children, as, for example, in the *Thebais* or in the *Geryoneis*. But Stesichorus felt the need to include a proper maternal figure in his account: the nurse Laodamia.

4.1.4 The Nurse Laodamia (fr. 179 F.)

Stesichorus' *Oresteia* is the first account to include the figure of the nurse. Nurses, and tutors (*Paedagogus*), for that matter, occur in Greek literature as early as the *Odyssey*,[117] although having a subordinate status in the household, servants as they are, they enjoy some authority, which derives from their roles as super-

---

the news of the killing of her brother from a messenger (fr. 189 F. and 191 F.) and we should expect that this moment triggered the subsequent plot. Our poet would have explored her reaction to the news and her decision to avenge her brother, which would require her involvement in the death of Meleager.

[117] Thalmann 1998: 27–29 discusses the figure of Eurycleia in the context of female slaves in the poem.

visors and, many times, as maternal figures to children. They are frequently addressed as authority figures who offer advice.[118] But perhaps the most defining aspect of the nurse is her role as a maternal figure whose affection to the nursling is often recalled.[119] It seems likely that Stesichorus includes Laodamia in the *Oresteia* with this in mind. The content of the information provided by the scholium to Aeschylus' *Choephori* is minimum. However, it may suggest some similarity between the treatment of the figure in the three accounts (fr. 179 F.):

> Κίλισσαν δὲ φησι τὴν Ὀρέστου τροφόν, Πίνδαρος δὲ Ἀρσινόην, Στησίχορος Λαοδάμειαν.

> [Aeschylus] says that Orestes' nurse is Cilissa, Pindar Arsinoe, Stesichorus Laodamia.

In the versions of Aeschylus and Pindar, the nurse plays distinct roles. In Pindar's *Pythian* 11.17–18 Arsinoe is responsible for Orestes' rescue. She snatches him away as Clytemnestra kills Agamemnon, and sends him to the house of Strophius, a guest-friend, in the foot of Mount Parnassus (line 36). A similar account is presented by Pherecydes. In his account, the rescue of Orestes implicates the sacrifice of the nurse's own child (fr. 134 *EGM*). Aegisthus kills the nurse's child believing that he was Orestes. The fragment does not preserve what happens next, nor to what extent the nurse is involved in Orestes' escape from his home (here unknown), but it is probable that she had a central role in it.[120]

Aeschylus, the only tragedian who includes the figure of the nurse in the myth of Orestes, gives her a less active role, since it is Clytemnestra herself who sends Orestes away to Strophius (*Ag.* 877–886). This is, therefore, the sole account in which Orestes faces exile imposed to him by his mother, something that he recalls in their encounter at the *Choephori* (913–915). In the Aeschylean account, the nurse features expressing her unconditional love for Orestes, and her grief for thinking him dead (*Cho.* 734–782). Her intervention in Aeschylus' account occurs after Orestes' return whereas her primary role in Pindar and Pherecydes seems to have been in the rescue of Orestes. Although her late ap-

---

118 E.g. Phoenix, Achilles' tutor, tries to persuade him to return to battle in *Il.* 9.
119 Fletcher 1999 in her review of Karydas' study of the figure of the nurse stresses the lack of discussion of the historical role of nurses in the Greek quotidian. To illustrate the potential of such discussion, Fletcher mentions a fourth century epitaph (*IG* II² 7873. G) dedicated to a nurse by her former nursling (named Hippostrate) reveals the long-lasting affection of nursling to the nurse; Wrenhaven 2012 study fills in part this gap.
120 Gantz 1993: 675 suspects the nurse intentionally substituted Orestes for her child.

pearance in the trilogy, her maternal affection for Orestes is strongly emphasised.

It is conceivable that Stesichorus made her central to the rescue, perhaps in a similar manner as Pindar.[121] Nevertheless, her participation in the revenge plot, as happens in Aeschylus, remains a possibility. An aspect of Stesichorus' nurse that drawn the attention of scholars is her name, Laodamia. One of Bowra's argument for the Spartan audience of Stesichorus' *Oresteia* is precisely the nurse's name which recalls the king of Lacedaemon, Amyclas' daughter (Paus. 10.9.5).[122] However, and despite the coincidence, Laodamia is the name given to other mythical women with no connection to Sparta, as for instance the daughter of Bellerophon and the mother of Sarpedon in *Il.* 6.196–205, or the daughter of Acastus and wife of Protesilaus.[123] The name Laodamia, however, does suggest an aristocratic lineage, an aspect shared with the epic nurses in the *Odyssey*: Eurycleia and Eurymedusa.

In the versions where the nurse appears, her affection for Orestes is emphasised, either by rescuing him sacrificing her own son in Pherecydes or by lamenting over the supposed death of Orestes and recalling the time when he was a baby in Aeschylus. She assumes in these accounts a truly maternal role, which is particularly relevant in the case of Orestes given his relationship with his mother. Since in Stesichorus it seems that Clytemnestra assumed a more active role in the death of Agamemnon, it seems appropriate to have the nurse as the rescuer of Orestes, cast as a maternal and nurturing figure, similarly to what happens with the character of Cilissa in Aeschylus' *Choephori*. As said above regarding the maternal figures, it is interesting that in the tale of a matricide the figure of maternal love is replaced by a nurse and the dramatic potential of such figure is remarkable, as the *Odyssey* and *Choephori* so poignantly show.

Sophocles and Euripides exclude the nurse but maintained a servant in the episode.[124] In these accounts, the Paedagogus ensures Orestes' safety in exile,

---

121 Thus Finglass 2007b: 97; Davies and Finglass 2014: 503.
122 Bowra 1934: 117–118.
123 Thus Davies and Finglass 2014: 28.
124 Karydas 1999: 56 noted that the authority of the nurses in Greek literature derives from their role as supervisors of the children and in many cases in their role as teachers (cf. Pl. *Prt.* 325cd). In this sense, in terms of authority over the children, the figure of the nurse and the tutor are quite similar, which could explain the substitution in tragedy of the Nurse by the Paedagogus. The figure of the tutor as an authority figure capable of advising and even persuade his pupil is event in the relationship of Phoenix and Achilles in *Il.* 9.476–486. Eurycleia

although his role varies. In Sophocles' *Electra*, the protagonist rescues Orestes from the palace fearing the murderous hands of Aegisthus and Clytemnestra[125] and gives him to the Paedagogus so that he can take the child to a safe location.[126] The Paedagogus in Sophocles' *Electra* takes Orestes from his sister and raises him during his time in exile, assuming a parental role to young Orestes. Electra's involvement in the rescue is a Sophoclean innovation, appearing later in Hyginus (*Fab.* 117.2) and Seneca (*Ag.* 918–946). Euripides excludes Electra from the rescuing. In his *Electra*, the Paedagogus alone rescues Orestes and gives him to Strophius.[127] In these accounts, Electra assumes particular relevance, namely in Sophocles' *Electra*, whereas the accounts of Pindar and Pherecydes give prominence to the nurse in the rescue and exclude Electra.

4.1.5 Electra and the return of Orestes (fr. 181 F.)

Along with the figure of the nurse as a maternal character, another female character seems to have gained relevance in Stesichorus' account: Electra. Her character is similar to that of the female waiting-figures of the *nostos*-plots.[128] Electra, however, is not a passive character in the plays on the myth of Orestes, "but also as her complement, and eventually (at least, in Sophocles and Euripides), as an active co-conspirator in the actual conduct of the revenge".[129] We know that she featured in the poem of Xanthus (fr. 700) and that the death of Agamemnon had serious consequences on her adult life, casting her aside from the social status where she belonged and leaving her unmarried. No information survives regarding the status of Electra in the aftermath Agamemnon' death in Stesichorus' *Oresteia*, but the recognition by means of the lock of hair make it likely that she played a role in the revenge plot (fr. 181.7–13 F.):

    ... Αἰϲχύλο[ϲ μὲν γὰρ
'Ορέϲτ[εια]ν ποιήϲα[ϲ τριλο–

---

tries to persuade Telemachus to stay home *Od.* 2.349–379, and the nurse of *Hyppolytus* functions as Phaedra's adviser.
125 S. *El.* 296–297, 601, 1132–1133.
126 S. *El.* 11–14, 296–297, 321, 1132–1133, 1348–1352.
127 *El.* 16–18, 416.
128 For the importance of women in the *nostos* stories, see Alexopoulou 2009: 68–70; Sultan 1999: 4: "the woman ... is responsible for managing his [the man's] return from exile"; see further Sultan 1999: 53–99 and Sultan 1999: 3 for bibliography on the subject.
129 Zeitlin 2012: 362.

γίαν [Ἀ]γαμέμνον[α .....
Χ]οηφ[όρ]ους Εὐμεν[ίδας ...   10
...]..[.] τὸν ἀναγ[νωρισμὸν
τὸ]ν διὰ τοῦ βοστρύχο[υ ....
Στ]ηςίχορωι γὰρ ἐςτιν [....

7 Lobel ‖ **8–9** Ὀρέςτ[εια]ν ποιήςα[ς Lobel | τριλο]γίαν Radt post Page | [Ἀ]γαμέμνον[α Lobel ‖ **10–11** Χ]οηφ[όρ]ους Εὐμεν[ίδας Lobel | παρ|έλα]βε[ν Haslam | ἀναγ[νωριςμὸν Haslam ‖ **12** τὸ]ν Haslam | [υ Lobel ‖ **13** Lobel

    Aeschylus
When composing his trilogy *Oresteia* –
Agamemnon,
    Choephori, Eumenides – (treated?)   10
the recognition
by means of a lock of hair:
this is in Stesichorus...

As seen above, the episode of Clytemnestra's dream, as a *nostos* motif of the prophetic dream, announces Orestes' return. The shared elements of Clytemnestra's dream and Penelope's should have prepared the audience for a typical *nostos* scene, in which the hero arrives in disguise and goes through a process of recognition.[130] The dream of Clytemnestra, moreover, motivates the offerings at the tomb of Agamemnon, the place where Orestes leaves his lock of hair in the tragic accounts. In Aeschylus, Clytemnestra sends Electra with libations to the tomb, whereas in Euripides and Sophocles the task is attributed to other characters. It seems likely that Stesichorus set the recognition in the same place as the other accounts: at the tomb of Agamemnon and that Electra herself was sent there, since, according to Davies and Finglass, the versions of Sophocles and Euripides casting a third person to bring the lock to Electra seem like a secondary innovation. In the same line of thought, it is more probable that Electra recognized the lock than any other character. First, because the token of recognition, the lock of hair, would be easier to recognize by a family member. Secondly, because the majority of recognition scenes happen between close relatives.[131] Furthermore, the fragment highlights the similarities of the scenes. Hence, we would expect to hear some remarks, in case there were any significant alterations.

---

130 Perrin 1909: 371–376 evaluates the recognitions scenes in the *Odyssey* according to Aristotle's categorization of such scenes in this *Poetics* 1454b19–1455a. For the pattern of the *nostos*-story and the recognition scenes in epic and tragedy, see Alexopoulou 2009: 31–41; 68–70; 104.
131 Davies and Finglass 2014: 508–509.

The siblings are about to reunite after almost a decade apart. In Aeschylus, Electra finds the lock of hair while Orestes is hidden from her view. The recognition scenes have the potential of serving as a highly dramatic scene for the audience, but they play an important part in the structure of the narrative as they serve as a barometer for the character who returns to test the loyalty of a certain figure before revealing themselves. The character can thus evaluate the risks of disclosure and ponder the course of action. This is the use of Odysseus' disguise and the main difference between his caution (leading to success) and Agamemnon's triumphal return (which ended in gore). By displaying the lock of hair in Agamemnon's tomb, Orestes learns how Electra feels about him, allowing for a safer revelation and recognition. Another important aspect of the recognition scene by means of the lock of hair is that it implies a long separation. In the *Odyssey*, one can infer that Orestes was still at the palace when Agamemnon returned (11.452) and in 3.303–312 it is said that Orestes returns in the eighth year of Aegisthus' rule. Therefore, Orestes was absent for eight years. In Aeschylus, however, Orestes was sent into exile before Agamemnon's return, which makes his absence more prolonged.[132] We cannot determine how long Orestes was exiled in Stesichorus' account since we do not know when Orestes left. The earlier accounts agree on the presence of Orestes in the moment of Agamemnon' death, as happens in the accounts where the nurse rescues him. Perhaps Stesichorus followed this chronology.

The long absence of Orestes explains the need for multiple proofs of identity in the tragic accounts.[133] Like Penelope, Electra seems reluctant to give up scepticism and believe that her brother returned, which is more clearly represented in Sophocles' *Electra*, where the effective recognition is a result of Orestes' self-revelation.[134] Aeschylus opts for a more immediate recognition to allow the play to evolve; hence, the proliferation of recognition tokens. Apart from the lock of hair which leaves Electra reluctant to accept it as a sign of Orestes' return (*Cho.* 168–204), Aeschylus adds the sign of footprints (*Cho.* 205–211), Orestes' self-revelation (*Cho.* 219), and the piece of cloth (*Cho.* 231–232). Euripides, whose account has the Pedagogue recognizing Orestes immediate and instinctively, adds the scar as a proof of Orestes' identity to Electra (*El.* 573–579).

---

[132] Herodorus (fr. 11 *EGM*) says that Orestes was sent to exile with three years old, thus long before Agamemnon's return. This implies that Clytemnestra's affair with Aegisthus happen shortly after the beginning of the Trojan War.

[133] For a comparison of the recognition scene of Orestes and Electra in the three tragedians, see Solmsen 1967.

[134] Electra's recognition of Orestes in Sophocles happens only in 1221–1222, after a series of hints about Orestes' presence (thus Finglass 2007a: 5–6).

In Stesichorus, we only have evidence for the token of the lock in the recognition episode. It is, however, significant since it shows that Stesichorus, unlike his predecessors, dealt in detail with the episode of the return of Orestes. The return, as we seen, was anticipated in Clytemnestra's dream, but some have argued that Electra and Orestes may have kept contact during the times of the former's exile. This suggestion derives from an often-ignored fragment attributed to the second book of the *Oresteia* concerning Palamedes, who is credited with the invention of the alphabet. I cite here only fr. 175a F., for the contents of fr. 175b are identical:

Δοσιάδης δὲ ἐν Κρήτηι φησὶν εὑρεθῆναι αὐτά· Αἰσχύλος δὲ Προμηθέα φησὶν εὑρηκέναι ἐν τῶι ὁμωνύμωι δράματι, Στησίχορος δὲ ἐν δευτέρωι Ὀρεστείας καὶ Εὐριπίδης τὸν Παλαμήδην φησὶν εὑρηκέναι, Μνασέας δὲ Ἑρμῆν, ἄλλοι δὲ ἄλλον. πιθανὸν δὲ κατὰ πάντα τόπον εὑρετὰς γεγενῆσθαι.

Dosiadas says that it was invented in Crete (sc. the alphabet). Aeschylus says it was invented by Prometheus in the homonymous play; Stesichorus in his second *Oresteia* and Euripides say that it was Palamedes who invented it, Mnaseas [says it was] Hermes, and others credit another figure. It is possible that every region had its own inventor.

There are some possible contexts for the appearance of Palamedes in Stesichorus' *Oresteia*. The story of Palamedes is one of treason and revenge, thus providing an interesting parallel for the *Oresteia*.[135] The reference to him occurred in the second book, which probably rules out the hypothesis that he was associated with Nauplius' attempt to persuade Greek wives to leave their husbands,

---

135 For the story of Palamedes throughout Greek Literature, see Scodel 1980: 43–61; Gantz 1993: 603–607; Sommerstein 2000: 123 n.10; Davies and Finglass 2014: 498–500. Palamedes appears in the *Cypria* with the purpose of convincing Odysseus to go to war. Odysseus first refuses and upon the threat made by Palamedes to Telemachus, Odysseus stops pretending that he is mad. Eventually, though, Odysseus takes revenge on Palamedes, drowning him (arg. 5 and 12 *GEF*). Tragedy was prolific in plays on the story of Palamedes with the three tragedians dedicating their plot to the trial of Palamedes, who was framed for theft and treachery. Euripides includes a reference to Oeax ability to write (fr. 588 *TrGF*) as he sends a message to his father warning him about Palamedes' fortune. Aeschylus deals with Nauplius' arrival at Troy seeking revenge (fr. 181 *TrGF*.; thus Sommerstein 2000) Although Sophocles' *Palamedes* is lost, we have fragments for other plays featuring the story of Palamedes: *Nauplius sails in* and *Nauplius the Fire-Kindler*. The first described Nauplius arrival at Troy upon hearing the news of his son; the second probably concerned Nauplius stratagem of the beacon.

unless Clytemnestra uses this argument later as a justification for her adultery and as an attempt to dissuade Orestes from his matricidal plans.[136]

The same reason could apply to the ruling out of the inclusion of the episode of Palamedes' trial and execution at Aulis, preserved in the scholium to Euripides' *Orestes* 432 unless the episode was recalled as a justification for Oeax's present behaviour as a companion of Aegisthus who claims revenge for the deceased Palamedes. This is the hypothesis presented by Robert.[137]

Another possibility is that Palamedes is mentioned merely as the inventor of the alphabet. If so it would be probable that the siblings exchanged letters during Orestes' exile, as Stephanopoulos and Neschke suggests.[138] Sophocles and Euripides mention in passing that Electra sent messages to Orestes in exile.[139] The reference to Palamedes as the inventor of writing encourages us to expect that the context of his reference was somehow related to the skill. Moreover, the messages shared between siblings would illustrate their complicity and provide an emotional link between the two that overcomes their absence and solitude.

We have no means of determining the context in which Palamedes appeared in the *Oresteia*. It seems, however, that the idea that the two siblings kept in contact during Orestes' exile would diminish the dramatic potential of their encounter and recognition which would have had more impact if his return was clandestine. In turn, the possible revenge of Oeax would provide a parallel instance of fraternal affection, something that would perhaps highlight

---

136 Apollodorus (*Ep.* 6.9–10). The father of Palamedes, after the failed plan to go to Troy and make justice over his son's death, decides to try and persuade the Greeks' wives to leave their absent husbands and find themselves a lover. He pays a visit to Clytemnestra and succeeds in convincing her to commit adultery.

137 Robert 1881: 184. The scholium says that Palamedes was responsible for a plan for distribution of food at Aulis which involved him teaching the Greeks the Phoenician alphabet. Agamemnon, Odysseus, and Diomedes were unhappy with the scheme and plot against Palamedes by forging a letter which denounced a supposed plan between Priam and Palamedes. The Greek chiefs accuse Palamedes of treachery and condemn him to death by stoning. The idea that Oeax attempts to take revenge on Orestes is preserved in Pausanias 1.22.6 (cf. West 2013: 283). This suggestion may be seen in parallel with the reference to stones in fr. 176 F. The penalty of stoning to death in not alien to Stesichorus (cf. fr. 106 F.) and it was Palamedes' penalty for his crime, orchestrated by Agamemnon Odysseus and Diomedes. Unfortunately, the reference to stones could refer to a series of other relevant episodes in the *Oresteia*, for example, the tomb of Agamemnon (see Burkert 1983: 55, 133 for symbolic stoning in funerary rites), or to the penalty of Tantalus as in E. *Or.* (see O'Brien 1988). Another possibility is the threat of public stoning of Orestes, as told in Euripides' *Orestes*, but this seems even more unlikely. On stoning as a penalty in general, see Pease 1907 and Finglass S. *Aj.* 254n for further bibliography.

138 Stephanopoulos 1980: 137; Neschke 1986: 296.

139 S. *El.* 168–170, on which see Finglass *ad loc.*; E. *Or.* 615–621.

the role of Electra herself as the loyal and determined sister who did not succumb to hopelessness but waited patiently for her brother to lead the revenge in which she would perhaps have taken some part.

4.1.6 The bow of Apollo and the matricide (fr. 181.14–24 F.)

We have no clear evidence on how Stesichorus treated Orestes' exile. The only episode providing some details on Orestes' decision to return and avenge his father while still in exile is preserved, again, in fr. 181 F. These lines may offer clues about the role of Apollo in the *Oresteia* and Stesichorus' treatment of the character of Orestes. The commentator in fr. 181a F. and a scholium to Euripides' *Orestes* 268 (fr. 181b F.)[140] ascribes to Stesichorus the precedence of the motif of the bow of Apollo in Euripides' *Orestes*:

...]. Ε[ὐ]ριπίδης δὲ τὸ τ[όξον
τὸ Ὀρέστου ὅτι ἐςτὶν δε[δο-   15
μέ]νον αὐτῶι δῶρον πα[ρὰ
τ]οῦ Ἀπόλλωνος· παρ' ὧ[ι [μὲν
γ]ὰρ λέγεται· δὸς τόξα μ[οι
κ]ερουλκά, δῶρα Λοξίου, οἷς εἶ-
π'] Ἀπόλλων μ' ἐξαμύ[νας]θαι   20
θε]άς· παρὰ δὲ Στηςιχ[όρω]ι·
                                    τό-
ξα .....] τάδε δώςω παλά-
μα]ιςιν ἐμαῖςι κεκαςμένα
...].. [ἐ]πικρατέως βάλλειν·

14–21 Lobel || **16** δῶ–, δο– Π^r || **21–2** τό|[ξα δέ τιν Haslam (δὲ coί iam Page), τό|[ξα δ' ἐγὼ Page || **23–4** Lobel

    ... Euripides (says?) that the bow
        Of Orestes was given   15
   To him as a gift from
   Apollo, for in this work
he says: "Give me the horned
bow, the gift of Loxias, with which
      Apollo said I would ward off from   20
the goddesses." And in Stesichorus:
"I will give you the bow

---

[140] Στηςιχόρωι ἑπόμενος τόξα φηςὶν αὐτὸν εἰληφέναι παρὰ Ἀπόλλωνος: [Euripides] follows Stesichorus in saying that the bow was given to Orestes by Apollo.

which excelled in the palms of my hands
...to shoot with mastery."

The context of the quotation suggests that the bow would have had a similar purpose in both accounts. It follows that Orestes was tormented by the Erinyes in our poet's work as well. Therefore, Stesichorus' poem is our earliest source implying their appearance in the context of the myth of Orestes, which is significant since it suggests that Stesichorus explored the problem of guilt and the moral dilemma of the matricide in greater depth than his predecessors.[141] The threat of the intervention of the Erinyes on behalf of Clytemnestra indicate that Stesichorus' poem did not end with her death,[142] but rather went on to explore the subsequent torment of Orestes. What is more, it puts it beyond reasonable doubt that Clytemnestra was Orestes' main target, which in turn confirms that the murderer of Agamemnon was indeed Clytemnestra. On the other hand, the fact that Apollo loans his weapon to Orestes suggests that the god is providing protection to Agamemnon's son,[143] and acting as his guardian.[144] This implies that Apollo is somehow involved in Orestes' decision to avenge his father, an aspect of the myth shared with tragic accounts.

In Aeschylus, the god demanded Orestes' revenge on his father or else he should be condemned with some gruesome penalties. If Orestes decides not to proceed with the revenge, he will suffer Apollo' wrath. Orestes eventually opts to face the Erinyes and obeys Apollo. In the *Choephori*, the oracle of Apollo is revealed only gradually. We first learn of the command of Apollo and of the risks of disobedience (*Cho.* 269–296). Only after the vengeance is completed are we told that the oracle also promised protection (*Cho.* 1026–1034).[145] The protective role of Apollo is not evident until his appearance in the *Eumenides* where he expels the Furies. Only when Apollo appears in person does Orestes have the protection promised to him (*Eu.* 64–66).[146] Apollo presents himself as Orestes'

---

[141] Thus Ferrari 1938: 24; Davies and Finglass 2014: 491.
[142] Dyer 1967: 175 ignores Stesichorus' contribution and argues that it was Aeschylus who first questioned the glory of Orestes' deed. M.I. Davies 1969: 250 considers that Stesichorus' *Oresteia* ended with Orestes' revenge, thus excluding the highly likely episode of Orestes' persecution by the Erinyes which would have been a fundamental part of the poem, as pointed out by Davies and Finglass 2014: 491.
[143] Apollo loans his bow to Heracles in [Hes.] fr. 33(a). 29 M-W.
[144] Thus Swift 2015: 130.
[145] The bibliography on the subject is extensive. See Garvie 1986: xxxi, xxxvii–xxxix, 269–305n., 901–902n., 948–951n., 1030–1039n. On the oracle and Apollo's role in the trilogy, see Winnington-Ingram 1933; Roberts 1984; Sommerstein 2010: 189–194.
[146] Taplin 1977: 363–365, 403–407.

guardian to the end. Significantly, it is also in this scene that Apollo uses his bow to threaten the Erinyes.

Swift has drawn a comparison between the Apollo of the *Eumenides* in this scene and that of Stesichorus' fr. 181 F.: while in Aeschylus the protection provided by the god against the Erinyes is "merely rhetorical" and "diverted into the realm of metaphor",[147] in Stesichorus, it materializes into the weapon itself. In Aeschylus, Apollo can only instruct Orestes in the course of action; in Stesichorus, the god provides Orestes with the means to secure his safety.

Despite pointing out the precedence of the Euripidean episode of the bow, the testimony of the commentator of fr. 181 F. allows us to detect here, too, the differences between the Euripidean version and Stesichorus'. First, the bow is, in Euripides, a mere hallucination of an Orestes tormented and maddened by his mother's Erinyes (*Or.* 269–276). When Orestes regains lucidity, he blames Apollo for having persuaded him to commit the murder granting him protection, but now failing to fulfil it (*Or.* 285–293). The bow as a product of Orestes' visions emphasises the vainness of Apollo's promises,[148] which contrasts with the Stesichorean version where the bow is a palpable "talisman of protection".[149] In Euripides, Orestes, in his delusional state, says that the bow was given to him by Apollo. However, only in the theophany is the protection of Apollo assured which occurs in line 1665, *i.e.* thirty lines from the end of the play. Apollo reveals by his appearance that he owes Orestes protection because he ordered the matricide, something recalled throughout the play.[150]

Here too Orestes is faced with a difficult choice between committing the matricide or face Apollo's wrath. He opts for the former option but is on the verge of regretting it thanks to the torment caused by the Erinyes. Euripides thus distorts the symbolism of the bow as a token of protection, leaving Orestes deprived of any defence. In Stesichorus, on the contrary, Apollo addresses Orestes directly. This suggests that in our poet's *Oresteia*, Orestes encountered Apollo in person and received the weapon. He equips Orestes with his own defence mechanism. By having Apollo lending him the bow, Stesichorus makes Orestes capable of escaping the Erinyes.

Now, in Aeschylus as in Euripides, the bow appears, in distinct circumstances as we have seen, but in approximately the same moment, which is when

---

147 Swift 2015: 131.
148 Papadimitropoulos 2011: 505 correctly points out that Apollo's delay in showing his support and protection to Orestes may be perceived as a test of the hero's endurance.
149 Swift 2015: 131.
150 E. *Or.* 29–30, 269, 416.

Orestes is being assaulted by the Erinyes. We are not told when Orestes is visited by Apollo in Stesichorus, but the hallucination of Orestes in the Euripidean account may provide a clue. The conditional clause of line 270 – εἴ μ' ἐκφοβοῖεν μανιάσιν λυσσήμασιν –indicates that, in his *mania*, Orestes imagines a scene where Apollo gives him the bow before the appearance of the Erinyes.

The epiphany of Apollo to Orestes in Stesichorus may have also occurred when the threat of the Erinyes was still imminent. Therefore, the speech of the god preserved in the fragment may have taken placed before Orestes returned home; when he searched for guidance and advice on how to proceed. In tragic accounts of the myth, Orestes visits the oracle of Apollo before returning to avenge his father, so such a scene is not excluded *a priori*. Furthermore, as in all the accounts, the role of Apollo in the determination of Orestes' action is crucial and often recalled.[151] However, communication between Orestes and Apollo is operated by means of oracles, not by epiphanies.

Apollo's direct speech in Stesichorus suggests a different scene where the contact between god and mortal is direct, as is the form in which Apollo decides to show his commitment to the protection of Orestes: by loaning him the bow. Apollo and Orestes appear to have a closer relation in Stesichorus, one that would hardly be effected by means of the oracle alone. The possession of the bow would have contributed to Orestes' decisiveness in proceeding with the matricide. Whether it was demanded by Apollo, as in Aeschylus and Euripides, or only supported by him we cannot tell with certainty. However, the predisposition of Apollo to offer a defence weapon suggests that the god's involvement surpassed mere guidance and logistical support. Whether the episode was placed in its chronological order or told in analepsis is not possible to determine, although I am inclined to the former hypothesis because of the use of direct speech, indicating that the god appeared to Orestes. If so, this would imply Stesichorus' *Oresteia* included Orestes' return to Laconia. The other poem among our poet's works that deal with a matricide may too have dealt in detail with the return of the avenger of the father.

---

151 The Sophoclean Apollo has a slightly different role. As pointed out by Fialho among others, the gods are strikingly absent from the play. Orestes seemed determined to go and avenge his father before consulting Apollo, although Electra and the Chorus see in his deed the manifestation of divine will (Fialho 2007: 49). He consults the oracle for advice on how he should do it, which in fact is more in accordance to the practice (cf. Fialho 2007: 36). Electra is somehow excluded from Orestes' revenge plot.

The episode preserved in the surviving lines from the *Eriphyle* (fr. 93 F.) allows only speculation. However, in it, Alcmeon is about to depart from a feast. His uncle tries to hold him back to enjoy the symposium:

>   ]‥μελα‥[ ]
>   ] ὧδε ποτήνεπε κ[ ]
>   Ἄδρας[τος ἥρως· "Ἀλκμαον, πόσε[[ι]] δαι-
>   τυμόν[ας τε λιπὼν καὶ ἄριστον ἀοιδὸν
>   - - -⏑]. ἀνέστας;"   5
>
>   ὡς ἔφα· τ]ὸν δ' ὧδ' ἀμειβόμενος ποτέει-
>   πεν Ἄρηι] φ[ίλ]ος Ἀμφιαρητεΐδας·
>   "cὺ μὲν φ]ίλε πῖνέ τε καὶ θαλίαις
>   εὔφραιν]ε θυμόν· αὐτὰρ ἐγὼν ἐπὶ πρά-

desunt versus aliquot

>   ]κτοσθεπ['10'
>   ]νεcαμον[
>   εκα‥ [.].ιονα.ονιμ[
>   θ' ὅπῶς ἀπῆναν ζευ[⏒—⏑—
>   ναδ' ἔβα παράκοιτι[ν ⏑—⏑— —
>   μναcτεύcοιcα μάτη[ρ   '15'
>
>   παῖδ' Ἀναξάνδροιο .[—⏑—⏑ ὑπερ-
>   φιάλου γαμὲν ἔκγο[νον —⏑—

3 Lobel | ποcε[[ι]] Π⁴ || **4** Page || **6–7** ὡς Barrett | ἔφα· τ] ὸν Page || **8** Barrett post Lobel || **9** Lobel || **14–7** Lobel || **17** γάμεν Lobel, γα μέν Barrett

> ...
> The hero Adrastus addressed
> him in this way: "Alcmeon, to where do you
> get up to go, leaving the men in the feast and our
> noblest bard....?"   5
>
> So he spoke and answering him
> the son of Amphiaraus, dear to Ares said:
> "My friend, you drink and with the feast
>   Rejoice your heart. I ... thing   10
>   ..."
>
>   ...
>   ...
>   ...
> How, (yoking?) a mule-wagon

>   the mother went to woo   '15'
> a wife...
> the son of Anaxander
> to marry the offspring of the arrogant

Davies and Finglass pointed out that these lines may refer to Alcmeon's departure back home to avenge his father.[152] Alcmeon's words denounce a certain urgency to leave. The opposition cὺ μὲν ... αὐτὰρ ἐγών emphasise the contrast between the two characters and their conflictions, but it would also create an interesting opposition between the happy and celebratory ambiance of the scene from where Alcmeon departs and the deeds he is about to commit against his mother.

The following lines refer to journeys, but we have no way to determine to what extent is the journey of fr. 93 F. related to Alcmeon's departure. Fr. 95 F. is severely fragmented and the only surviving word is ἐcθλά ('good things', line 4). Lobel supplemented κακ[οῖc, which may lead to the meaning present in Hesiod *Op.* 197 of 'good things mixed with bad'.[153] Führer suggested that the fragment may describe the preparations for a departure.[154] The supplement he provides for line 14 καρπαλ[ίμωc makes the scene approximate to that of fr. 93 F. describing the yoking of the mule wagon. We have no certainty regarding the place or context of these lines within the text, which makes any further assumption entirely speculative. Nevertheless, in a poem dedicated to the story of Eriphyle, a tale which deals with a wife of questionable conduct, who is behind the events leading to her husband's death, and eventually killed by her son in revenge for his father, in the sequence of which he experiences the persecution of the Erinyes, in a story such as this it is not surprising to find several episodes involving travels. A more extensive knowledge of Stesichorus' *Eriphyle* would allow an interesting comparison of the treatment of treacherous wives and revengeful offspring in the works of Stesichorus. The example from the *Oresteia* and the scraps from the *Eriphyle* show that the dramatic potential of these characters was a major interest of our poet.

The persecutions by the Erinyes involve the purification of the assaulted. Therefore, Stesichorus would have dealt with Orestes' wanderings after the matricide. Burnett points out the relevance of Stesichorus' *Oresteia* to the western legend of Orestes, according to which he is purified by Artemis in the river

---

[152] Davies and Finglass 2014: 346.
[153] Lobel 1967: 33.
[154] Führer 1977: 24.

Matauros.[155] However, this hypothesis is impossible to prove, since in the remains of the poem the only role ascribed to Artemis is the rescue of Iphigenia. Moreover, several cities claimed to be the purification site of Orestes. In Aeschylus, Orestes is purified in Delphi. In Euripides, *Iphigenia in Tauris*, he needs to go to Tauris and snatch away the image of Artemis. Arcadia was often associated with the wanderings of Orestes since Pherecydes (fr. 135 *EGM*), Herodotus (1.67–68), and Asclepiades (*FGrHist* 13 F 25).[156] Euripides maintains Arcadia as central to the process of wandering and purification. In *Orestes*, Euripides places Orestes' exile after the matricide in the Parrhasion and before the trial (*Or.* 1644–1660). Conversely, in *Electra*, Orestes should return to Arcadia after the trial. Later developments of the myths associated Orestes with colonial foundations.[157]

A hero with such a remarkable history of travels and wandering is likely to be top choice for a founding ancestor. His status of the purified protégé of the most respected advisor in the colonial enterprises makes Orestes a good omen for the colonial adventure. Stesichorus may have contributed significantly to the idea of Orestes as a wanderer in the archaic period since earlier versions of the myth known to us do not refer the aftermath of the killing of Clytemnestra. The extent to which this contribution influenced Orestes' associations with colonial enterprises or foundations of rites and cults is, unfortunately, impossible to secure. However, the impact of Stesichorus' version may have influenced the development of later western legends of Orestes in the same way as it did regarding the various versions of the myth in Attic Drama.

---

155 Burnett 1988: 146–147. The story according to which Orestes accompanied by Pylades goes to Rhegium to be purified by Artemis is preserved in Hyg. *Fab.* 261. See also, Cato *Orig.* fr. 71 Peter, and Pliny *NH* 3.73.
156 On the Spartan claims over Tegea and Arcadian territory in the sixth century and the use of the myth, see Boedeker 1993 and Malkin 1994: 26–33.
157 On Orestes and the Aeolian migration, see Fowler 2013: 597–602. On the appropriation of myths involving murder and purification as colonial foundation stories, see Dougherty 1998: 192. She argues that "the myths and legends of the archaic colonial movement reveal a strong ideological link between purification and colonization". Particularly relevant for her argument is the differences of the story of Tlepolemus in Homer (*Il.* 2.661–669) and in Pindar *O.* 7 (Dougherty 1998: 189–193). An important aspect of Dougherty's argument is the centrality of Apollo in both the purification episodes and the colonial enterprise.

4.2 The *Thebais*?

The evidence for Stesichorus' works shows his interest in Theban myth, to which he dedicated part of at least three poems: *Europa*, *Eriphyle*, and the untitled poem preserved in the Lille papyrus (fr. 97 F.), commonly known to modern scholarship as the *Thebais*.[158] Despite preserving only one episode of the Theban Saga, fr. 97 F. adds important aspects to our knowledge of the Theban myth in the archaic times and presents innovative aspects. For reasons of conciseness, I concentrate merely on versions useful to our discussion of fr. 97 F.

The earliest reference to the Theban Saga appears in the *Iliad* which reports the events at Thebes, that is, after the episode preserved in our fragment.[159] Despite the reference to Polynices and Eteocles, no mention is made to their familiar ties in Homer. This is not surprising given that the *Iliad* tends to avoid family strife and thus omits such episodes.[160] Furthermore, in the *Iliad*, Oedipus was understood to have kept ruling over Thebes until his death and before the attack on the city, since *Il.* 23.679 refers to the Funeral Games of the Labdacid king. So too in the *Odyssey*, Oedipus remains king after becoming aware of his crimes.

---

158 Some scholars have suggested that the fragments preserved in the Lille papyrus are part of the *Eriphyle*, despite the metrical problems. The epode of fr. 93 F., which content provides a stronger claim for belonging to the *Eriphyle*, has an extra dactyl than the epodes of the Lille papyrus, making the two fragments incompatible in metrical terms. Adrados 1978: 274–275 argues, however, that the *Eriphyle* was divided, like the *Helen* and the *Oresteia*, in two books each with a different metre. However, it is unlikely that compositions under the same title would have had different metres, even if divided in two parts. Moreover, the affinity in the theme and the mythical sequence covered by the theme of fr. 97 F. and fr. 93 F. are insufficient to prove that they belong to the same poem. March 1987: 131–133 argues that the contents of the Lille Papyrus would fit better in the *Eriphyle* than fr. 93 F., but this is highly unlikely, since we would have an unplaced fragment that fits perfectly in a poem dedicated to the strife in the house of Amphiaraus. Second, it would imply that the *Eriphyle* would begin by focusing quite extensively on the problems of the house of Oedipus. Therefore, it is better to assume that there are some titles of Stesichorus' poems unknown to us, and that the *Thebais* and the *Eriphyle* were two separate compositions.
159 *Il.* 4.370–410, 5.800–813, 6.222–223, 14.113–125.
160 Cf. above on the *Iliad* omission of the strife in Agamemnon's house. For Oedipus' story in Homer see Mastronade 1994: 21.

The episode of the *Odyssey* (11.271–280) describes the major aspects of the myth: the killing of Laius, the marriage to Epicaste, and the discovery of the crime. Homer tells us that Epicaste, after learning the truth, hangs herself "overpowered by her sufferings (ἄλγεα)" (11.280). The account implies that Oedipus is still to suffer punishment for his crime. Despite the reference to future doom no mention is made to Oedipus' exile nor to the strife between his sons. This is because the children did not exist when Epicaste committed suicide, in accordance with the earlier versions of the myth where Epicaste/Jocasta does not bear incestuous children to Oedipus, a point to which we shall return.

The *Oedipodeia* concerns the events prior to the quarrel, but little survives of it.[161] We are told that the son of Creon is killed by the Sphinx, and Pausanias informs us that in the poem Oedipus had the four children with Euryganeia (fr. 1 *GEF*).[162] Pausanias' argument illustrates that the identity of mother of Oedipus' children was a matter of debate among ancient commentators. He argues that, if according to the *Odyssey* Epicaste hangs herself ἄφαρ, that is "right away", she could not have been the mother of Oedipus' four children and in supporting his view he mentions the *Oedipodeia*. We have no direct evidence for the identity of this Euryganeia, but from Pausanias' testimony it seems clear that Euryganeia and Epicaste/Jocasta are not the same character.[163]

---

161 The Peisander scholium (Σ E. *Ph.* 1760) should be treated with caution in the reconstruction of the *Oedipodeia*. The majority of scholars are inclined to doubt that the entire content of the scholium may date back as far as the *Oedipodeia*, among them Schneidewin 1852: 159–160; Jacoby 1923: 493–494 and 1957: 544–545; Wilamowitz 1925: 280–281; Keydell 1935: 301–302; Deubner 1942; Fraenkel 1963: 6–7; Mastronade 1994: 31–38; Kock 1962: 5, 7–8, doubts its fidelity to the *Oedipodeia*; Bernabé 1996: 17 n. 7 argues that the scholium contains elements from other sources; West 1999: 41 is sceptical in accepting that the story of Chryssipus was part of the *Oedipodeia*; Finglass 2014: 361 n. 20 is sceptical of considering the scholium a reliable source to reconstruct the epic and Cingano 2015: 112 agrees that the scholium is a multi-layered account of the myth); Bethe 1891: 22; Gruppe 1906: 24, n. 3; Pearson 1909: xviii; Alves 1975: 31–32; Lloyd-Jones 2002: 5–10 are inclined to accept that the source of the scholium is mainly the *Oedipodeia*. Given the state of our knowledge of the earlier versions of the myth this issue should remain open. Be that as it may, for the purpose of this study, the more relevant information from the *Oedipodeia* is the identity of the mother of Eteocles and Polynices, information not only present in the Peisander scholium but also attested by Pausanias (cf. *Oedipodeia* fr. 2 *GEF*).
162 Robert 1915: 110 implies that Euryganeia is yet another name for Jocasta, since it would be difficult to imagine Oedipus remarrying again after the first marriage to his mother (on which see further Cingano 2015: 221–222). If this was the case, then the version of Pherecydes (fr. 95 *EGM*) is the first to clearly differentiate Jocasta and Euryganeia and to go as far as to give Oedipus yet a third wife, Asteymedusa (D schol. *Il.* 4.376; on which see Fowler 2013: 406).
163 Cf. *contra* Davies 1989: 21.

The earliest detailed version of the fratricidal quarrel occurs in the Epic Cycle's *Thebaid*.¹⁶⁴ This is also the first instance where Polynices and Eteocles are explicitly said to be Oedipus' sons, although we lack information regarding the identity of their mother. The poem focused on the brothers' dispute and told about the attack of the Seven with considerable detail (dispute between Adrastus and Amphiaraus and the arbitration of Eriphyle fr. 7 *GEF*; descriptions of battle, fr. 9; the dead and funerals of the Seven, fr. 6). According to this account, the enmity between Polynices and Eteocles and ultimately the attack of the Seven results from a curse uttered by Oedipus. In Homer and Pindar, the future misfortune of the house of Oedipus is caused by the Erinyes of Jocasta and Laius, respectively. In Stesichorus, the curse is replaced by a prophecy from Teiresias. However, the motif of the curse is recurrent in the surviving accounts of the myth by the tragedians. Two reasons are presented for Oedipus to curse his sons, both related to the failure of the brothers to care for their father. Oedipus complains about being treated disrespectfully on at least two occasions.¹⁶⁵

First, Polynices serves his father in a silver table and the golden cup, items which cause a clear discomfort to Oedipus, leading him to curse his sons praying that they ought to enjoy the inheritance amidst war (fr. 2 *GEF*). Scholars agree that these objects are a reminder of Oedipus' parricide, or even a token of royal luxury recalling a glorious past that is so sharply contrasted to the present misery.¹⁶⁶ This episode informs us about Oedipus' situation in Thebes. In the *Thebaid*, as in the *Odyssey*, he stays in Thebes after learning the truth. However, unlike in the *Odyssey* where Oedipus remains in power, in the *Thebaid* he seems deprived of access to his possessions and does not participate in the sacrifices, as is implied from the occasion where he curses his sons. At a sacrifice, Oedipus is served the haunch instead of the shoulder, a less honourable part of the meat. This attitude by his sons angers him, leading to the utterance of a curse which anticipates future events: may they kill each other.¹⁶⁷ The curse in such context highlights Oedipus' helplessness and vulnerability.¹⁶⁸ Cingano, on the other hand, suggests that Oedipus is still king of Thebes in the epic *Thebaid*, and that

---

164 Howald 1939: 7 argues that the Oedipus story and the Seven against Thebes were originally independent stories, which were later connected by means of the curse of Oedipus on his sons. See also, Davies 2015.
165 Fowler 2013: 408 argues that one of the curses may have belonged to another poem, such as the *Oedipodea*, since they imply the same outcome.
166 Welcker 1865: 334; Robert 1915: 175; Davies 2015.
167 Fr. 3 *GEF*. Cf. Torres-Guerra 2015: 230–231.
168 Thus Davies 2015; on the curse as a last resource, see Watson 1991: 38, 95.

his sons want to undermine his ruling power, which is plausible.[169] Be that as it may, the humiliation caused by the disrespectful behaviour of Polynices and Eteocles explains the anger of Oedipus towards his sons.

The three tragedians use the motif of the curse found in the *Thebaid* with slight alterations. Aeschylus' *Septem* 782–784 seems to indicate (the text is partially corrupt), that the curse was uttered shortly after Oedipus' learning of the truth about his deeds.[170] In Euripides' *Phoenissae*, the curse comes after Oedipus' detention by his sons. Here, Oedipus remains in Thebes, imprisoned by his sons (lines 63–65). Their improper behaviour towards their father, which appears in the *Thebaid*, seems here too the cause of Oedipus' curse, praying that they shall divide the wealth and the throne by military means (lines 67–68). In Sophocles' *Oedipus at Colonus*, the curse is recurrent, but not only directed at his sons. He curses Creon for his opportunism in lines 893–906 and again at 988–993. The curses upon Polynices and Eteocles are motivated by the passivity of his sons before his condemnation to exile and their disregard for his situation (431–460, 788–789, 1370–1379), which contrast sharply with the dedication of Antigone and Ismene (lines 365–375), whose fate and situation Oedipus laments. In the final curse (lines 1370–1379), he predicts the end for the brothers. This curse, Oedipus tells us, repeats another uttered long ago, presumably while he was still in Thebes, which implies that the curse is of the same content and motivated by the same issues.

The *Thebais* fragment (fr. 97 F.) preserves the episode concerning the prediction of future *stasis* among Oedipus' sons, Polynices and Eteocles. Teiresias reveals a prophecy to the Theban Queen that her sons will die at each other's hands. In an attempt to negotiate with the Fate and the Gods and to prevent the prophecy from being fulfilled while she is alive, the Queen elaborates a plan of dividing the inheritance of Oedipus to placate a possible dispute between her sons. They are to divide throne and possessions by casting lots. Eteocles takes the throne, while Polynices is to leave Thebes with the movable goods. From this point onwards, the text is severely damaged, and we are left with some incomplete lines. However, there are a few conjectures that are worth considering. As we shall see, it is likely that, upon the result of the lottery, Teiresias advices Eteocles to accept the result and avoid conflict, and prophesizes a successful arrival and a welcoming exile at Argos for Polynices. The poem describes Polynices' journey until Cleonae and breaks off at this point. Since the poem

---

[169] Cingano 2004: 274–277.
[170] Cf. West 1990: 116–118; Hutchinson 1985: xxv, argues that the curse is likely to have been uttered in the *Oedipus*.

dealt profusely with the episode of the reaction of the Queen to the prophecy and her attempts to assure that it goes unfulfilled, it is likely that the poem included the episode of the conflict itself, otherwise the poem would end without the necessary sense of closure.[171]

In Stesichorus there is no reference to any curse. The focus seems to be directed to Teiresias' prophecy.[172] And that seems to be what triggers the plot, rather than a curse, as in the majority of the accounts. Even if there was a curse, it does not have the same impact to the narrative as the prophecy revealed by Teiresias, which is what causes the reaction of the Theban Queen and all the subsequent events, since the prophecy seem to have been revealed shortly after the beginning of the poem:

```
—⏑⏑—⏑⏑—×—⥕—] Κρονίδας            176        ant.
—⏑⏑—⏑⏑—⥕—⏑—  —]
—⏑⏑—⏑⏑—⥕—⏑⏑—⏑] ͅος υἱος
—⏑⏑—⏑⏑—]
⥕—⏑⏑—⏑⏑—×—] ͅας ἐνθεῖν            180
—⏑⏑—⏑⏑—]
⥕—⏑—⏑—⏑—  —].

—⏑⏑—⏑⏑—]                                     ep.
⏑—⏑⏑—⏑⏑—⏑—⏑] ͅυτας
—⏑—⏑—⏑—  —]                         185
—⏑⏑—⏑⏑—×—⥕—⏑⏑] ͅ… πρίν
```

---

171 Thus Finglass 2015a: 89, *contra* Burnett 1988: 111 who argues that the poem ends with Polynices' arrival to Argos, which would mean that the poem would finish not far from where the papyrus breaks. To support this view, Burnett suggests that a prayer for divine favour and the final remarks addressing the audience and the occasion would follow and end the song. However, if we exclude, with Finglass 2017b, the problematic attribution of Ibycus' fr. S166 to Stesichorus suggested by West 2015: 70–76, no end of a poem by Stesichorus is preserved, and to claim that his poems would end likewise is far too speculative. Moreover, as Finglass 2015a: 89 n. 24 points out, if the poem was to end with the arrival of Polynices to Argos, we would have a poem where no significant action had happened, the prophecy would be left with no major relevance to the narrative, the characters would have presented little development, let alone the fact that if the poem was to end shortly after line 303, this poem would have been unusually short for Stesichorus.
172 Thus Parsons 1977: 20; Burnett 1988: 111; Finglass 2014: 367. Hutchinson 2001: 121 argues that the prophecy has nothing to do with Laius' oracle, since Stesichorus seems to focus the attention on the divinatory powers of Teiresias. However, in Pindar *O*. 2 Laius is held responsible for the future doom of Eteocles and Polynices. There may have been some hint at hereditary guilt in Stesichorus too. As we have seen, the motif of inherited guilt appears in the works of our poet in the *Helen* and was considered in the discussion of the *Oresteia* above.

⏓–⏑–⏑]
–⏖–⏑⏑–×–⏑⏑– μ]έγα νεῖκοc
––⏑– –]
–⏑⏑–⏑⏑–×–⏖–⏑] ἐν εἴcω   190   str.
–⏑⏑–⏑⏑–⏖–⏑–]...ρ
–⏑⏑–⏑⏑–⏖–⏑⏑–⏑⏑] παίδαc
–⏑⏑–⏑⏑–   ]
 ⏓–⏑⏑–⏑⏑–×–⏑– –]
–⏑⏑–⏑⏑–]   195
 ⏓–⏑–⏑–⏑–] .[].

–⏑⏑–⏑⏑–×–⏖–] ος ἔγειρεν   ant.
–⏑⏑–⏑⏑–⏖–⏑– –]
–⏑⏑–⏑⏑–⏖–⏑⏑–⏑] .....
–⏑⏑–⏑⏑–]   200
    ἐπ' ἄλγεc<c>ι μὴ χαλεπὰc ποίει μερίμναc,
  μηδέ μοι ἐξοπίcω
    πρόφαινε ἐλπίδαc βαρείαc

οὔτε γὰρ αἰὲν ὁμῶc   ep.
    θεοὶ θέcαν ἀθανάτοι κατ' αἶαν ἰράν   205
νεῖκοc ἔμπεδον βροτοῖcιν
οὐδέ γα μὰν φιλότατ', ἐπὶ δ'ἀμε.α. νόον ἀνδρῶν
θεοὶ τιθεῖcι.
μαντοcύναc δὲ τεὰc ἄναξ ἑκάεργοc Ἀπόλλων
μὴ πάcαc τελέccαι.   210

αἰ δέ με παῖδαc ἰδέcθαι ὑπ' ἀλλάλοιcι δαμέντac   str.
μόρcιμόν ἐcτιν, ἐπεκλώcαν δὲ Μοίρα[ι,
αὐτίκα μοι θανάτου τέλοc cτυγερο[ῖο] γέν[οιτο,
πρίν ποκα ταῦτ' ἐcιδεῖν
    †ἄλγεcι† πολύcτονα δακρυόεντα[– –, 215
  παίδαc ἐνὶ μεγάροιc
    θανόνταc ἢ πόλιν ἁλοῖcαν.

ἀλλ' ἄγε παῖδεc ἐμοῖc μύθοιc, φίλα [–⏑–·   ant.
ταῖδε γὰρ ὑμὶν ἐγὼν τέλοc προφα[ίνω·
    τὸν μὲν ἔχοντα δόμουc ναίειν πα[⏑–⏑⏑– –, 220
  τὸν δ' ἀπίμεν κτεάνη
    καὶ χρυcὸν ἔχοντα φίλου cύμπαντα [πατρόc,
κλαροπαληδὸν ὅc ἂν
    πρᾶτοc λάχηι ἕκατι Μοιρᾶν.

τοῦτο γὰρ ἄν, δοκέω,   225   ep.
    λυτήριον ὔμμι κακοῦ γένοιτο πότμο[υ,
μάντιοc φραδαῖcι θείου,
αἴτε νέον Κρονίδαc γένοc τε καὶ ἄcτυ [⏑– –

Κάδμου ἄνακτος
ἀμβάλλων κακότατα πολὺν χρόνον [—⏑— —]ς   230
πέπρωται γεν.[.]. αι."
ὣς φάτ[ο] δῖα γυνὰ μύθοις ἀγ[α]γοῖς ἐνέποιςα,   str.
νείκεος ἐν μεγάροις. [...]ιςα παίδας,
cὺν δ' ἄμα Τειρ[ε]cίας τ[εραςπό]λος· οἱ δ' [ἐ]πίθο[ντο
    α .[⏑⏑—⏑⏑—   235
    το .[—⏑⏑—⏑⏑—×—⏑] Θηβαν
γαια[⏑—⏑⏑—
    κατ .[—⏑⏑—⏑⏑—]α

τον..[⏑⏑—⏑⏑— χρ]υςόν τ' ἐρίτιμον ἔχοντα   ant.
παμ[⏑⏑—⏑⏑—⤫—]..cθενηcαν   240
ηδρς.[⏑—⏑⏑—⤫— κ]λυτὰ μῆλα νέμοντο
...[⏑⏑—⏑⏑—].
    [] .μ[⏑⏑—⏑⏑—×] .ιραc ἵππους
.[.]. [⏑—⏑⏑—
    . [—⏑—⏑⏑— —   245

[⏑⏑—⏑⏑—   ep.
    . [—⏑⏑—⏑⏑— χρη]cμοὺς ἀcάμους
—⏑—⏑—⏑— —]
—⏑⏑—⏑⏑— ἐ]γὶ cτήθεccι φίλοιcι
⤫—⏑—⏑]   250
—⤫—⏑⏑—×—]ρος, ἂν δ' ἔθορ' αὐτὸς
— —⏑— —]

—⏑⏑—⏑⏑—×—⤫ μ]ῦθον ἔειπε   str.
—⏑⏑—⏑⏑—⤫—⏑—] λως
—⏑⏑—⏑⏑—⤫—⏑⏑—] .ατε βουλὰν   255
—⏑⏑—⏑⏑—]
    ⤫—⏑⏑—⏑⏑—×—]ιc πιθήcαc
—⏑⏑—⏑⏑—]
    ⤫—⏑—⏑⏑—⏑— —]

—⏑⏑—⏑⏑—×—⏑]ε. πολλὰ γὰρ ὑμὶν   ant.
—⏑⏑—⏑⏑—⤫—⏑—] .α   260
—⏑⏑—⏑⏑—⤫—⏑⏑—⏑⏑— —]
—⏑⏑—⏑⏑—]
    ⤫—⏑⏑—⏑⏑—×—⏑—]cαc
πολλα[⏑—⏑⏑—   265
    θεοὶ δόμεγ[⏑—⏑— —

τῶν ταμ[⏑—⏑⏑—   ep.
    αγεν ταδ[⏑—⏑⏑—⏑—⏑—].αιc
πολλὰ δ[—⏑—⏑— —
    .[—⏑⏑—⏑]υςιν θέντες μεγάλαις ε .[⏑— —   270

.[⏑−⏑−]γος
.[−⏓−⏑⏑].εν ἕλικας βόας ἠδὲ καὶ ἵπ[πους
.[− − −⏑−].αιϲαν

..[⏑⏑−⏑⏑].οι τὸ μὀρϲιμόν ἐϲτι γεγ[− — str.
...[⏑⏑−⏑]μον Ἀδράϲτοι' ἄνακτος   275
.[−⏑⏑−⏑⏑]γος δώϲει περικαλλέα κο[ύραν
.[−⏑⏑−⏑⏑]α
   .[⏑−⏑⏑−⏑⏑]τον δώϲοντι δᾶμος
..[−⏑⏑−⏑⏑]ο̣υ
   ⏑−⏑⏑−⏑]οι' ἄνακτος   280

—⏑⏑−⏑⏑]ω διαμπερέως Ἐτεο[κλ⏑   ant.
—⏑⏑−⏑⏑].εν ϲτήθεϲϲιν αἰνω[
θ.[−⏑⏑− ⏑⏑−].ν ἔχεν Πολυνείκεος [− —
ω.[⏑⏑−⏑⏑−].
   τευξ[−⏑⏑−⏑⏑]ταν πόλει τε πάϲαι   285
μα.[⏑⏑−⏑⏑]αν
   ἀεὶ π.[⏑−⏑−]ε πένθος

του[⏑⏑−⏑⏑]ο̣υ   ep.
   θεω[⏑⏑−⏑⏑].ϲη̣ι μάλιϲτα παντῶν
..[−⏑−⏑−]τοιϲιν.   290
ὣς φάτ[ο Τειρεϲίας ὁ]νυμάκλυτος, αἶψα δ' α[− —
δόμω.[⏑−⏑
ᾤχετ[⏑−⏑⏑−].το φίλωι Πολυνείκεϊ .[− —
Θηβαι.[−⏑− —

...ομ.[−⏑⏑].ν ϲτεῖχεν μέγα τεῖχ[ος ⏑−⏑   295   str.
..... [⏑−⏑⏑−⏑]....α̣ὐτῶι
.....[⏑−⏑⏑−] . ππ̣οις τ' ἴϲα̣ν ἄκρο[ν ⏑− —
ἄνδρε.[⏑−⏑⏑−
   πο̣μπ.[−⏑⏑−⏑⏑−]. δ' ἵκοντο Ἰϲθμὸν
ποντιο. [−⏑⏑—   300
   κραι .. [⏑−⏑−⏑] . υχαιϲ

αὐτὰ̣[ρ ⏑⏑−⏑⏑−×] ἄϲτεα καλὰ Κορίνθου   ant.
ῥίμφα δ' [ἐϋκτιμέναϲ] Κλεωνὰς ἤνθον

frustula ante versum 176 || **188** Parsons || **199** versus fortasse aliena manu scriptus || **212** multi || **213** ϲτυγερο[ῖο multi | γέγ[οιτο Meiller, Pavese || **214** ποκα West, τόκα Π¹ || **215** ἄλγεϲ<ϲ>ι Meillier || **219** προφα[ίνω multi || **222** πατρόϲ multi || **228 αἴτε** Parsons, **ἆι τε** Neri || **232** φάτ[ο Parsons | ἀγ[α]νοῖϲ Barrett || **234** Τειρ[ε]ϲίαϲ Meiller | τ[εραϲπό]λος· οἱ δ' [ἐ]π[θο[ντο Barrett || **236** Θηβᾶν Haslam || **239** Barrett || **241** Barrett, μῆλα West, μᾶλα Π¹ || **247** Meillier || **249** ἐ]νὶ Meillier || **253** μ]ῦ̣θον Carlini, Parsons || **273** κα]τ' αἶϲαν multi **275** δό]μον Haslam, Parsons **276** ὅ̣[ς δὲ ϲε δεξάμε]νος West κο[ύραν multi **278** δώϲοντι Cassio: δωϲουντι Π¹ **281** Barrigazzi **282** αἰνῶ[ϲ Barrett, Schwartz **285** τεύξ[ηι Page **286** ματ[ρί τ' Page ἀμαχανί]α̣ν

Parsons **290** βρο]τοῖϲιν Haslam, West **291** Parsons ἀ[ναϲτὰϲ Parsons: ἄ[ποικοϲ Page: ἀ[πῆνθε Hutchinson **293** ἔπο[υτο Page **295** ερχομεν Parsons **296**]..ἄμ' vel]..ἐπ' Parsons **297** Meillier **298** ϲ[Parsons **300** πόντιον [ἀμφίαλον Parsons: πόντιον ['Εννοϲίδα West **302** West **303** Barrett, West

    ... Cronid   176
    ...
    ... son
    ...
    ... to go   180
    ...
    ...

    ...
      ...
    ...   185
    ... before
    ...
    ... great quarrel
    ...

    ... into   190
    ...
    ... sons
    ...   ]
           ]
    ...   195
    ...

    ... stiring
    ...
    ...
    ...   200
Do not add to my sufferings appalling worries,
nor for my future
reveal heavy hopes.

Not for all times alike
do the immortal gods set among mortals perpetual   205
strife across the holy earth,
nor friendship either; rather ...the mind of men...
the gods set.
Your prophecies, may Lord Apollo, who works from afar,
not accomplish them all.   210

If I should see my sons killed by each other
As it is fated and as what the Fates have spun

May the hateful end of death be mine at once.
Before I ever see these things,
grievous, tearful...   215
My sons killed in the palace and the city captured.

But come children, ... my words, dear
This is how *I* reveal the resolution for you.
One of you should have the palace and dwell...
The other should depart   220
taking the cattle
and all the gold of his dear father,
he who in the shaking of the lots
is the first to obtain his allotment by the will of the Fates.

This, it seems to me,   225
may be your release from evil fate
(given?) the advice of the divine seer,
... the Cronid ... the latest offspring and the city
of Lord Cadmus,
delaying the evils...   230
...is fated..."

Thus said the noble woman, speaking with gentle words,
...her children from their strife in the palace,
Teiresias [the seer] promptly reiterated, and they obeyed.
    ...   235
...] Thebes
...
...

...should take the precious gold
...   240
...splendid sheep were at pasture
...
... horses
...
...   245

...
...] unclear oracles
...
... in his breast...
...   250
... and he himself jumped...
...

... uttered a speech...

...
... counsel   255
...obeying...
...
...
...

...many things...you   260
   ...
   ...
   ...
...many things...   265
The gods...

...
...
many things...
...setting ... great...   270
...(Argos?)
... twisted–horned cattle and the horses...
...(according to what is destined to happen)

...what is fated....
...Lord Adrastus   275
...give his beautiful daughter
...
...the people will give you
...
...lord   280

...straight ... Eteocles...
...in heart...
...have...Polynices'...
...
...to the whole city...   285
...
...always ... grief...

...
... most of all...
...   290
...Thus spoke the famous named Teiresias, and immediately home...
he left...for dear Polynices...
Thebes...

```
...walked through great wall...                    295
...with him...
...(many)...(horses)...they came to the extremity...
(men)...
...arrived at Isthmus...
...(sea)...                                         300
...

...beautiful cities of Corinth,
and swiftly reached well-built Cleonae.
```

According to Parsons' edition, the papyrus begins at line 176, as a result of the arrangement of the fragments and the stichometric gamma indicating line 300 in P. Lille 111c. The remaining lines preserve one triad with minor lacunae, from which we can infer that each triad had twenty-one lines. This implies that our fragment was preceded by eight triads and the strophe of the ninth. One, or at least part of one of these triads was occupied by the opening of the poem. The other instances where we have the openings of Stesichorus' poems, the *Sack of Troy* (fr. 100 F.), and the *Oresteia* (frr. 172–174 F.) both occupy at least part of one triad of the composition. The same is likely to have happened in the opening of the *Thebais*. The remaining seven triads would have introduced the theme delineated the version which the poet would follow. These lines should have included some important information regarding the situation in the house of Oedipus, namely the whereabouts of Oedipus.

4.2.1 Oedipus in (or out of) the *Thebais*

Oedipus is strikingly absent from the remaining lines of Stesichorus' *Thebais*. No reference is made to his name, crimes, punishment, or incest. What can this absence tell us? Is Oedipus exiled? Locked away? Dead?

Of these three options, the first is the least likely. The versions according to which Oedipus experienced exile appear for the first time in the fifth century in Sophocles' *Oedipus at Colonus* (although anticipated in *Oedipus Rex*) and in Euripides' *Phoenissae*. In Sophocles, Oedipus is sent to exile after learning the truth of his deeds. In Euripides, on the other hand, Oedipus is sent into exile only after the death of Polynices and Eteocles (lines 1584–1594). This is the earliest account where Oedipus outlives his sons.

The majority of the versions of the myth suggest that Oedipus remained in Thebes after discovering the parricide and the incestuous marriage to Epicaste/Jocasta.[173] However, these versions present some important divergences. While in the Homeric poems, Oedipus remains in power (*Od.* 11.275–276) presumably until his death, which is celebrated in a sumptuous burial (*Il.* 23.678–680), in the Epic Cycle his condition is different. In the *Oedipodeia* fr. 2 *GEF*, Oedipus remains king after the death of Jocasta/Epicaste and remarries, indicating that he had some years of apparently peaceful government after the revelation of his crimes. This scenario changes in the *Thebaid* (fr. 2 *GEF*), where he is depicted as a defenceless outcast, a neglected elder, with an apparent diminished power, deprived of dignity, as seen above.[174] In Euripides' *Phoenissae*, Oedipus remains in Thebes, but his sons locked him away (line 64), an act that Teiresias condemns (lines 834). Since the king is imprisoned, Euripides needed to feature Creon as the regent, as appears in the Sophoclean *King Oedipus*, *Oedipus at Colonus*, and *Antigone*. In Stesichorus, it is the Queen that seems to hold the regency of the throne. This would require that the throne be recently vacated, as a Queen would not be expected to remain the regent for long. Therefore, either Oedipus died, or he was locked away soon before the scene preserved in fr. 97 F.

Now, if Stesichorus drawn his version from the epic counterparts, we would expect that Oedipus remained somehow in power until his death, which would have happened soon before the scene in fr. 97 F. With the death of the king, the inheritance is to be taken care of and the rightful successor to assume power. If, on the other hand, Stesichorus anticipated what we would find later in Euripides, Oedipus' sons would have locked him away. It is true that in Euripides' version the imprisonment of Oedipus leads his sons to immediately make an arrangement concerning the inheritance. But they do it between themselves in reaction to Oedipus' curses and their mother has no intervention in the arrangement (*Ph.* 64–75). This is a different context from what we seem to have in Stesichorus. Moreover, if this was the case not only would we expect a reference to the curse, but the prophecy would be expendable, and the Queen would have reacted differently to it. It is therefore better to think of a beginning in slightly

---

[173] *Od.* 11.275–276; *Il.* 23.678–680; Σ *Il.* 23.679; Hes. fr. 192 M-W; *Oedipodeia* fr. 2 *GEF*; *Thebaid* frr. 2–3 *GEF*; E. *Ph.* until lines 1584. Cf. Gantz 1993: 505 "In all, our evidence suggests that for Archaic period, Oedipus' old age at Thebes and ill-treatment by his sons was an important part of his story, perhaps even as important as the catastrophe of the earlier days".
[174] Cf. Cingano 2004 who argues that the sons' attitude towards Oedipus reflect an urge to hold the throne, implying that in the *Thebaid* Oedipus was still officially ruling Thebes.

different terms, one that begins with a scene where the presence of Teiresias would be required, and which could be related to the following scene.

Some scholars have suggested that Teiresias is summoned to the palace to interpret a dream by the Queen.[175] Peron supports his suggestion by drawing some parallels with the dream in Aeschylus' *Septem* (710–711), which present some problems, but his suggestion regarding the tentative reconstruction of the dream convinced Massimilla who points that the reference to Zeus, the use of δοκέω in line 225, and the reluctance of the Queen in accepting the words of Teiresias resemble other episodes of prophetic dreams, dreamt by mothers and Queens.[176] Burnett and Aluja agree that the dream would solve some problems of the text, namely the "unusually closed to the colloquial expression" (Hutchinson 2001: 131) δοκέω and would explain the agreement of Teiresias to the Queen's resolution.[177]

However, Finglass remarks, this scenario presents some problems since "[s]uch a dream would have allowed [the Queen] to counter Teiresias' prophecy with greater confidence".[178] Moreover, one would expect more references to the dream in her speech. In the absence of more evidence and given the emphasis that the Queen puts in the deities more directly associated with ideas of Fate and prophecy, it is perhaps preferable to consider that Teiresias is summoned to the palace in the sequence of an important event either to interpret an omen, to provide advice or to reveal a prophecy. The problems derived from a recently vacant throne, either caused by the ruler's withdrawal from power, or by his death, which seems more likely,[179] would "provide impetus for the plot, immediately presenting the characters with an insoluble dilemma":[180] how would the succession of Oedipus be resolved between his sons.

---

175 Peron 1979: 81–83 followed by Burnett 1988: 112 and Massimilla 1990.
176 Massimila 1990: 192–193. As pointed out by Peron and Massimilla, the dream is a recurrent motif in epic and tragedy e.g. Penelope in *Od.* 19.535–569 and Clytemnestra's in Stesichorus fr. 180 F., in Aeschylus *Cho.* 523–539, Sophocles' *El.* 409–427 and Euripides *Or.* 618; the dream of Hecuba in Pindar fr. 52i (A) S-M and in Euripides *Hec.* 68–97; and the dream of Atossa in A. *Pers.* 176–204.
177 Burnett 1988: 112; Aluja 2014: 20.
178 Finglass 2015a: 91 n. 29.
179 Thus Meillier 1978: 13; Bremer 1987: 137; Wick 2003: 168–169; Finglass 2015a: 88, *contra* Bollack, La Combe, Wissman 1977: 37 and 39, who considers that the death of Oedipus did not feature Stesichorus' poem. Wick 2003: 168 argues that the poem, as an isolated *Thebais* is likelier to have begun in a scene who would not depend entirely on previous events.
180 Finglass 2015a: 88.

4.2.2 Teiresias' Prophecy

The exact content of Teiresias' prophecy is lost and thus can only be reconstructed from the Queen's reply (201–231). Lines 176–200 are severely damaged but some of the remains can be ascribed either to the prophecy of Teiresias or to the narrator's reaction to it. For example, the references to Zeus (line 176) and to a great strife (line 188) indicate that the prophecy of the seer dealt with the future doom of Eteocles or Polynices and can thus be part of Teiresias' speech. On the other hand, the first preserved epode (lines 190–196) may be the beginning of the speech of the Queen if we consider, with Hutchinson,[181] that the εἴcω refers to the "mother summoning her sons inside", the sons who are referred to in line 192.

Given the preserved lines of her speech in 201, it is likely that her speech had begun shortly before, since they show a negative "statement concerning an adverse situation", a common beginning to epic speeches where the speaker opposes the resolution or the advice of the interlocutor.[182] A similar pattern of a negative reaction, an opposition to the course of events suggested to the speaker, is found in the speech of Geryon in fr. 15.5 F.[183] Geryon's speech is introduced by the previous four lines, probably identifying his lineage (line 3). He begins his speech (in the epode) with negative imperatives suggesting that he is rejecting the advice of his interlocutor. The fact that these negative imperatives open the speech may indicate, as the epic examples cited by Maingon, that the Queen's speech began shortly before line 201, perhaps in line 198.[184] From what we can reconstruct from the speech of the Queen, the prophecy predicted the mutual fratricide of Eteocles and Polynices (lines 188, 211–212, 214, 227–228), but also implied the future of the *polis* (lines 217, 228). The question is in what terms.

The debate concerns precisely the relation between the fate of the sons and the future of the city, which derives from, among other things, the meaning of ἤ in line 217. The particle led scholars to question whether the prophecy was con-

---

181 Hutchinson 2001: 123.
182 Cf. Maingon 1989: 49–51 for the epic speeches where the same structural pattern of the Lille Queen's.
183 Thus Hutchinson 2001: 124.
184 Thus Hutchinson 2001: 124. Unlike Pindar and Bacchylides, whose speeches openings and conclusion coincide with the start and end of the stanzas (on which see Führer 1967: 66–76), Stesichorus triadic structure is less severe in this matter. For speeches beginning in mid-stanza, see frr. 18.6, 92.8, 170.3, 93.3 (beginning not only in the mid-stanza but also in mid-line), and in our fragment 97.254 F.

ditional and posed a dilemma *genos* vs *polis* to the Queen, or whether the prophet predicted both the mutual fratricide *and* the destruction of the city. Given the other accounts of the myth, it seems preferable to consider that Teiresias' prophecy did not impose a dilemma, but rather predicted both events. The disjunctive expression in lines 216–217 does not refer to the form of the prophecy per se, but to her wish of not seeing either of the events, since either one or the other would cause her deep sorrow (line 216). Furthermore, none of the arguments for the conditional prophecy in form of a dilemma is entirely satisfactory.

Bollack, La Combe, and Wissman, inspired by the earliest appearance of Teiresias in Greek literature, drew a parallel between Stesichorus' poem and *Odyssey* 11.100–137, where Teiresias reveals to Odysseus the perils he will face before he returns to Ithaca.[185] Everything will go well *if* he proceeds in a certain manner; *if* not, disgrace shall descend upon the companions and possibly even upon Odysseus (*Od.* 11.105–115). In the same way, according to Bollack, La Combe, and Wissman's view, in Stesichorus, Teiresias would have alerted the Queen that *if* both of sons stay in Thebes and insist on the quarrel, they will suffer the abhorrent fate of mutual fratricide *or* the city will be destroyed.[186]

Along these lines, Bremer explored the hypothesis of the prophecy to present a clearer dilemma to the Queen: the choice between her sons and the safety of the city.[187] Bremer argument implies that Stesichorus would be the first to focus on the dilemma *genos* vs *polis*. The dichotomy, however, is not clearly expressed in the speech of the Queen, nor in the subsequent action, which weakens the hypothesis. Moreover, his suggestion is contradictory on his own terms. If the prophecy was alternative, the Queen would be presented with two possible outcomes. She chooses to avoid the mutual fratricide. This would require that the city would be caught by enemies. However, this is not what happens in the myth, where both the mutual fratricide and the capture of the city occur.[188] One may argue, that in the likely scope of the poem, the attack on

---

[185] Bollack, La Combe, Wissman 1977: 49.
[186] So too Bremer 1989: 149: "If [your sons] insist on [reigning over Thebes], the result is bound to be disastrous, for *either* their present quarrel about the succession will become worse and end in fratricide, *or* if that is avoided, enemies will come and take the city". His suggestion implies that the prophecy imposed a dilemma.
[187] Bremer 1987: 144.
[188] MacInnes 2007: 97 draws attention to the poor sense of the second part of the prophecy as suggested by Bremer. She argues that the city being taken by enemies makes no sense in the context of the myth, arguing, quite rightly that "Thebes would be more likely to be sacked with both heirs dead than with both alive to defend it".

Thebes by the Seven was ultimately unsuccessful and the city was saved. Hence, the Queen managed to save the city. However, this would not be what she chose, since her attempts in the poem are focused on avoiding the prophecies (plural) from being accomplished.

Ercoles and Fiorentini elaborate a similar case to Bremer's, pointing out the recurrent use of such prophecies in the episodes of the Theban saga in tragedy particularly in the prophecy that Teiresias reveals to Creon in Euripides' *Phoenissae*.[189] Opposing Hutchinson's argument, according to which the dilemma in the prophecy would fit oddly in the *rhesis* since the Queen refers to it only later in her speech, Ercoles and Fiorentini suggest that the delay of reference to Thebes (lines 217, 228) may result from the Queen's priorities. She first emphasises her concern towards her sons and only later remembers that she is the regent; hence, it is her duty to grant the safety of the city.[190]

It would have been interesting to have a Queen deciding whether to let her sons die at each other's hands or to save the city; the pathos of such scene would have emphasised the inner conflict of a mother and a Queen presented with a choice between family and city, a scene recurrent in Greek literature, and which perhaps has its most striking examples in the dilemma of Agamemnon at Aulis, and Creon in Euripides. Unfortunately, there is no clear evidence that this is the case in Stesichorus' *Thebais*. Quite the contrary, the emphasis seems on the misfortune of having to witness both events. The structure of the Queen's *rhesis* points to a determinism that the Queen tries to avoid, rather than to struggle to choose one of the options, as in Creon's dilemma. As Hutchinson points out "the prophecy made the future certain and fixed" and "the bold wish that Apollo would not fulfil a prophecy or a part of one would hardly be called for or make plausible sense if the prophecy were merely conditional".[191]

---

189 A. *Th.* 745–749; E. *Ph.* 898–969, esp. 952.

190 Ercoles and Fiorentini 2011: 27: "Per quel che concerne poi l'incongruenza tra l'esclusiva preoccupazione della regina per i propri fi gli ai vv. 204–212 e la dicotomia tra il destino dei fi gli e quello della città ai vv. 216s., si può rilevare come l'accento cada piuttosto sul ruolo materno che su quello politico, tale da lasciare in secondo piano il destino di Tebe fi no ai vv. 216s., quando ella torna ad essere donna di Stato".

191 Hutchinson 2001: 128 draws attention to how the Queen's reaction to the prophecy indicates that she is left with no options, since her reaction, if the prophecy was conditional "would itself seem rather overblown if the killing is merely a possible event which can be avoided. The abstract arguments addressed to Teiresias in 204–08 would also seem somewhat out of place if the queen were merely contending that the condition he has spoken of will not in fact be realized. And if she intended simply to act on his advice, why does she tell him not to reveal grim expectations about the future? Certainly 209–10, and probably the whole preceding passage, do not fit a mere conditional warning which can be readily heeded."

The wish that Apollo does not fulfil all of what is predicted implies that the prophecy included a series of dreadful events, rather than two alternative outcomes. Moreover, the stanza 211–217 opens with a sense that the prophecy stated that she will witness the mutual fratricide. The emphasis that the Queen puts on this outcome implies that the mutual fratricide is bound to happen, rather than one of the options available. Therefore, the disjunctive sense of lines 214–217 was not a paraphrasis of the prophecy itself, but instead a reflection of the wish that the gods may spare her from seeing at least one of these most mournful, tearful, and painful events: the sons killed, or the city captured.[192]

If the prophecy imposed a dilemma it would stress her decision-making and focused on the ethical implication of her final decision. By having the Queen reacting to a prophecy revealing both events, the emphasis is drawn instead to her negotiation with Fate and the gods in an attempt to save both offspring and city, an attempt made clear in the last lines of her speech (228–231). Her desire not to witness one of the events highlight the cumulative set of disasters that will unfold,[193] should her attempts to prevent the abhorrent prediction fail.[194]

In the final stanza of her speech, the Queen hopes that the fulfilment of the prophecies would be delayed until the next generation (lines 228–231), thus again emphasising the unconditionality and assertiveness of the words uttered by Teiresias. However, some scholars have seen problems in aligning this hypothesis with the references to Teiresias' advices in line 227 and with his intervention in lines 275–290. Bremer remarks that if the prophecy of Teiresias was indeed ineluctable, it would be odd for the Queen to hope to revert the fate by moving to a completely different path, and even more surprising to have Teiresias obey her designs.[195]

---

[192] So rightly MacInnes 2007: 98, and Finglass 2015a: 89 n. 23.
[193] MacInnes 2007: 109. Vagnone 1982 compares the Homeric scenes of *desiderium mortis* with the scene of Stesichorus, with particular attention to *Od.* 20.315–319
[194] This wish may have been granted. Carlini 1977: 66 saw a parallel in these lines of the Queen and Euripides' Jocasta (1282), who, he argues, threatens to commit suicide. Bremer 1987: 146–147 is reluctant to see any threat in either instance, since in Euripides her speech at lines 435–637 does not mention the option and in 1282 it would be too late to impact the action. The same applies to Stesichorus, since there is no hint that the Queen needs to blackmail her sons with suicide to make them accept her solution. However, as Segal 1985: 199 points out, this plea to the gods in sparing her the sight of both her sons killed and the city captured "may be a foreshadowing of her suicide", if indeed the mother of the sons does indeed die after seeing her sons killed, as in Euripides' *Phoenissae*.
[195] Bremer 1987: 157.

These remarks are valid if we insist on approaching the prophecy either as an alternative conditional or as certain one that would only announce that the sons are to kill each other, and the city is to be destroyed. However, if we assume that the inheritance plays a central role in the prophecy as the cause for the future doom, things get slightly clearer. Say, the prophecy ran along these lines: "The inheritance of Oedipus will cause great strife between your sons, who are fated to fight and kill each other for it, bringing destruction to Thebes".

This hypothesis is, moreover, conveniently approximate to the terms in which Oedipus utters his curse in the epic *Thebaid* (fr. 3 *GEF*), and thus more likely to have been used as a replacement for it in Stesichorus' poem. Furthermore, the idea that there is an element that is causing trouble and that would eventually lead to a more serious problem would not be a single case, not to Teiresias. The idea is present in Sophocles' *Antigone*, where Teiresias' prophecy reveals that the unburied corpse of Polynices is causing the trouble and advises Creon to bury him (lines 1025–1032). Creon refuses to accept the prophet's advice to which Teiresias responds with the revelation of the future doom (1064–1090). It seems that the fate of Creon's family could have been adverted if he had wished to do so. There is an element, that, if treated with the due caution, could have prevented the events. Now, if the inheritance caused the strife among the brothers, as in other versions of the myth, the Queen's solution would be clever. It does not contradict the prophecy, it does not question Teiresias' authority, and it explains why the prophet shows support for it in line 234 and later in his intervention at lines 274–290, advising the brothers. Unlike Creon, the Queen shows that she is learning from Teiresias' prophecy, rather than dismissing it, unlike what will happen with her sons. Faced with the threat that the inheritance poses, the Queen decides to divide it and cast the lots to attribute the two equal parts to each of the sons. Providing her sons comply to the plan, the cause for the fight and the subsequent trouble would be avoidable. Alas, Polynices and Eteocles will not be content for long.

When we see the prophecy in these terms, with the inheritance as the cause of the strife, one more question arises. Is Teiresias convinced that the plan can work or is he simply complying with it to spare the Queen the trouble of seeing her efforts rendered futile? In tragedy, Teiresias shows reluctance in revealing the entirety of his predictions.[196] It may be that Teiresias is here showing the same decorum, perhaps out of pity for the Queen. Or it may be that Teiresias is materializing the conflict "between foreknowledge and human action",[197] revis-

---

[196] E.g. S. *Ant.* 1060; *OT* 320–332, 344, 360; E. *Ph.* 865–929.
[197] Hutchinson 2001: 132.

ing his previous prediction and adapting it to the new conditions that the Queen's plan would have established.

The element of the inheritance and its division among the brothers is central to our fragment, as to the myth in general. It would be only natural if it were the central element of the prophecy of Teiresias and the point which allows some modification, that allows some inventive human intervention, without contradicting the other elements in our poem, as we shall see in further detail.

4.2.3 The identity of the Queen

We have so far seen how the Queen reacts to the prophecies of Teiresias. It has been suggested that this figure is clearly Jocasta. However, this matter is far from established and the discussion deserves a closer look. Although consisting mainly of a speech by the Queen, fr. 97 F. does not preserve her name. Most scholars assume that the Queen and mother of Eteocles and Polynices is Jocasta.[198] But such assumption is problematic for two main reasons. First, the earlier accounts of the myth do not consider Jocasta to be the mother of Polynices and Eteocles. Second, the main argument for Jocasta as the Lille Queen derives from some loose similarities between the Lille Queen and Sophocles and Euripides' Jocasta.[199]

In the earlier versions of the Theban saga, Jocasta meets her death after discovering the incest. In the *Odyssey* (11.271–280), Epicaste, kills herself after learning the identity of Oedipus. Because no children are referred in the poem and her suicide seem to have occurred soon after the marriage, it is generally considered that no offspring resulted from the incestuous union. This idea is

---

198 Ancher, Boyaval, Meillier 1976: 327–328; Bollack, La Combe, Wissman 1977: 39–41; Carlini 1977: 63; Adrados 1978: 274; Carmignani 1981; Vagnone 1982; Burnett 1988: 120–125; Tsitsibakou-Vasalos 1989; Ugolini 1990: 61–64; Martin 2007; MacInnes 2007: 95 (assuming that the mother is Jocasta based on the assumption that the *Thebaid* presented a similar account, which is far from certain); Ercoles and Fiorentini 2011: 25–27; Noussia-Fantuzzi 2015: 438 (similar case to that of MacInnes, assuming that Jocasta is the Queen based on the supposed parallel with the *Thebaid*).
199 The scholars questioning this assumption divide in two groups: those who discuss both options, but present some scepticism towards the identification of the Queen with Jocasta (Parsons 1977: 20; Gostoli 1978: 23–25; Haslam 1978; Lloyd-Jones 1980: 16; Bremer 1987: 166; Maingon 1989: 53; Mastronade 1994: 20–22; Cingano 2015: 223; Xanthou 2015: 45), and those who argue that the Lille Queen is more likely to be Euryganeia (Christyakova 1980: 45; Ryzhkina 1984: 115; March 1987: 128–130; Morenilla and Bañuls 1991: 66 n. 9; Aluja 2014: 27–37; Finglass 2014: 366, 2015: 88, 2018b: 29–31.

further supported by the Epic Cycle.²⁰⁰ In the *Oedipodea*, the mother of Antigone, Ismene, Eteocles and Polynices is Euryganea (fr. 1 *GEF*), who is not Oedipus' mother but his second wife. The same account is preserved in Pherecydes (fr. 95 *EGM*), although the mythographer speaks of two children born to Oedipus, the obscure Phrastor and Laolytus, by his mother. Pherecydes speaks of a third wife, Astymedusa, who is the reason for Oedipus to utter the curses on his sons, since they are accused by their stepmother to have attempted to rape her.²⁰¹ Another mythographer, Epimenides, names Oedipus' mother Eurycleia (fr. 16 *EGM*).²⁰² In the same fragment an anonymous source ascribes two wives to Laius, Eurycleia and Epicaste. Epicaste is Oedipus' mother and subsequently his wife, but Oedipus remarried a woman called Eurygane.

Despite the clear conflict between the various sources regarding the names of Oedipus' mother and wives, one thing is clear: nowhere in the remaining sources prior to tragedy does the mother of Oedipus, whatever her name might be, gives birth to Polynices, Eteocles, Antigone and Ismene. It seems that until the fifth century the incestuous origin of the children of Oedipus was not explored by the poets.²⁰³ Tragedy, in particular Sophocles and Euripides, emphasised precisely that aspect of the myth: the condemned nature of the children.²⁰⁴ What is more, nowhere does Jocasta outlive Oedipus.²⁰⁵

Burnett argues that Stesichorus' version is not compatible with Homer's nor the *Oedipodeia* because of the detail presented in Hesiod fr. 192 M-W according to which the marriage of Polynices to Argeia occurred before the death of the king.²⁰⁶ This is a dangerous assumption. Burnett uses a Hesiodic fragment to argue that Stesichorus did not follow Homer, and that Oedipus did not rule over Thebes until his death, but was cast away from power, as in the epic *Thebaid*. However, if we turn to the fragments of the epic *Thebaid*, the situation of Oedipus is by no means clear, with some scholars arguing against his withdrawal

---

200 The date of the Theban Epics is uncertain, on which see Cingano 2015: 227–230.
201 Σ^D Hom. *Il.* 4.376.
202 Finglass 2014: 361 n. 24 suggests that Eurycleia may be a variant for Euryganeia.
203 Mastronade 1994: 21 argues that the omission of the offspring resultant from the incest in these accounts may be due to the fact that many families claimed descent from Thersandros (e.g. Pi. *O.* 2).
204 In Aeschylus (*Th.* 926–932), Oedipus' mother is given no name, but she seems to have been the mother of Polynices and Eteocles.
205 The *Thebaid* does not provide any reliable information on the mother of the children, whoever she may have been.
206 Burnett 1988: 1988: 120–125. For the Funeral Games of Oedipus before the attack of the Seven, see Davies 2015.

from power. He may well have continued to be king.²⁰⁷ Moreover, there is no secure evidence for the role of Oedipus' wife in the *Thebaid*; we do not even know her name. It follows that the justification for the identity of the queen cannot be safely assumed from apparent parallels with the *Thebaid*.²⁰⁸

Tsitsibakou-Vasalos, on the other hand, proposed a reading of *Od.* 11.270–276 attempting to prove that the Homeric account does not imply that Jocasta became aware of the incest right after it was consummated, and thus the revelation may have been delayed long enough to produce offspring, in similar terms to the Sophoclean version.²⁰⁹ Moreover, she argues that the figure of Euryganeia seems to have had significance only in the *Oedipodeia*, which Tsitsibakou-Vasalos considers to have had little panhellenic influence and thus less likely to have reached Stesichorus than the Homeric poems, which mention only Jocasta and no other wives.²¹⁰ She does not explore how in the *Odyssey*, the latent idea is that Oedipus was to endure "endless ἄλγεα", while holding the throne of Thebes (lines 275–276, 280–281), and one would have expected that a king is not to remain a widower for long. Moreover, Tsitsibakou-Vasalos's argument requires us to accept that both the Homeric and the Lille poems presented Eteocles and Polynices as the offspring of an incestuous union. Yet, Tsitsibakou gives little attention to this, as if it was a minor detail and would not present a serious problem for her argument, particularly because she credits Stesichorus with making Jocasta live after the revelation of the incest.²¹¹ An argument of this sort, that implies that the Lille Queen lives on after learning the truth, requires some explanation regarding the fate of Oedipus, for it would be unlikely that both the incestuous parties would live on peacefully and happily after such revelation.

It seems, therefore, that the identification of the Lille Queen with Jocasta on the grounds of epic evidence seems unstable. This does not prove that Stesichorus did not present Jocasta in his poem. But if he did, he was the first to make her the mother of Eteocles and Polynices, and to enjoy some authority even after

---

207 Cingano 2004: 274–277.
208 For example, Noussia-Fantuzzi 2015: 438, following Burnett, argues that "in making the Queen survive the discovery of the incest and continue the reign at Thebes, Stesichorus is following the tradition of the *Thebaid*", as opposed to that of the Homer epics, where Epicaste commits suicide after knowing she had married her son. However, we cannot prove that in the *Thebaid* Jocasta was alive, or even that the sons are a result of incest.
209 Tsitsibakou-Vasalos 1989: 60–76.
210 Tsitsibakou-Vasalos 1989: 86, argues that the figure of Euryganeia was "not firmly embedded in an epic poem so influential as to resist effacement and oblivion".
211 Tsitsibakou-Vasalos 1989: 88.

knowing that these children were the offspring of an incestuous marriage. Since there are no previous versions of Jocasta surviving long after the revelation of her crimes, scholars have searched for the parallels between Stesichorus' versions and those of tragedy, which, as we have discussed in chapter three and in the previous section of this chapter, owes much to Stesichorus' mythical innovations.

It has been recognised, that in Sophocles and Euripides, Jocasta is a respected member of the state and pillar of the family with considerable moral authority, aspects that to some degree match the characterization of the Lille Queen and may suggest an equivalence between the Lille Queen and Jocasta.

Sophocles maintains the anonymity of the mother of Oedipus and his offspring in the *Antigone* and in the *Oedipus at Coloneus* (*Ant.* 49–57; *OC, passim*). However, in the *Oedipus Rex* Oedipus' mother given the name of Jocasta and some scholars have drawn attention to the similarities of both Queens. Ugolini compares the psychology of the Lille Queen and Sophocles' Jocasta in their scepticism towards the arts of divination, which he takes as further argument for the consideration of the Lille Queen to be Jocasta.[212] Along the same lines, Martin argues that the significance of Jocasta in the *Oedipus King* depends on the audience's previous knowledge of Stesichorus' Queen.[213] By questioning the fidelity of the prophecies and mediating between the quarrelling Creon and Oedipus, Sophocles' Jocasta allows the audience to anticipate the doom of the house of Oedipus, and to prepare for the failure of her attempts and fragility of her beliefs. However, the scepticism of Jocasta in Sophocles does not match the attitude of Stesichorus' Theban Queen. As pointed out by Xanthou, the Lille Queen "exhibits extreme politeness towards Teiresias" showing that she is "learning from, and not defying, him".[214]

Moreover, one decisive aspect differentiates between the two characters. The Sophoclean version does not contradict the tradition according to which Jocasta commits suicide after learning the identity of Oedipus and realises that the oracles she so vehemently doubted were in fact fulfilled. Moreover, Sophocles' Jocasta kills herself immediately after she realises the incest, and thus she has a distinct function from the Lille Queen, who makes no references to the stain of incest.[215]

---

212 Ugolini 1990: 67–71.
213 Martin 2007: 322–327.
214 Xanthou 2015: 48.
215 Ugolini 1990: 63 defends that the importance that references to *genos* assumes in the poem are indicative of of the fact that the sons are a product of incest. However, the emphasis

A Jocasta alive during the attack of the Seven on Thebes presents further difficulties, since it would mean that she is aware of the incest but remains in Thebes as Queen and maintains the incestuous marriage. This version appears from the first time in Euripides' *Phoenissae* and is likely to be an Euripidean innovation.[216] There have been attempts to draw parallels between the Lille papyrus and Euripides' *Phoenissae*, in order to justify the identification of the Lille Queen to Jocasta.[217] The argument of Ercoles and Fiorentini relies on the apparent similarity between Jocasta's and the Lille Queen pleas. Euripides' Jocasta pleas to Zeus for peace among her sons, since, she argues, it is unfair for a mortal to be permanently affected by misfortune (lines 86–87).[218] The scholars argue that these lines correspond to lines 204–208 of fr. 97 F., where the Theban Queen presents the same theological principle. However, this fails to convince that Euripides is indeed taking the character of Jocasta, *qua* Jocasta from Stesichorus. Finglass shows that the parallels pointed by Ercoles and Fiorentini offer no solid evidence for intertextuality, for they lack verbal equivalence.[219] Furthermore, the Euripidean account presents considerable differences. In Stesichorus, as we have seen, Oedipus is likely to be dead, while in Euripides he is alive; in Stesichorus, the Queen intervenes to settle the division of the inheritance, whereas in Euripides the brothers themselves make an agreement in the hope of avoiding the fulfilment of Oedipus' curses; these curses are absent from Stesichorus' account which instead focuses on the prophecy of Teiresias as the trigger of the subsequent actions.[220]

Although the Euripidean Jocasta tries to prevent the fratricidal quarrel through mediation, an apparent similar function to that of the Lille Queen, this episode is different in timing, scope, and impact from the one preserved in our fragment, since the mediation of Jocasta in Euripides happens when the fight is imminent (Polynices is already at the Gates of Thebes with the Seven's army)

---

of *genos* within the context of the fragment seems to point rather to the dreadful fact that the Queen will witness the end of her *genos* and with it the end of the royal family of Thebes (cf. Aluja 2014: 33).

216 There are aspects of the Euripidean play that influenced the later accounts of the myth. In the play, her role is confined to a presentation of the past misfortunes of the lineage of Oedipus (lines 12–63); her more prominent action is to mediates between her sons (cf. also Sen. *Phoen*. 407–651 and Stat. *Theb*. 7.470) and she witnessed the battle between them (cf. also Accio, *Phoen*.).

217 Among them Tosi 1978; Ercoles e Fiorentini 2011: 25–27.
218 χρὴ δ', εἰ cοφὸc πέφυκαc, οὐκ ἐᾶν βροτὸν | τὸν αὐτὸν αἰεὶ δυcτυχῆ καθεcτάναι.
219 Finglass 2018b: 23–25.
220 Cf. Lamari 2010: 126; Aluja 2014: 31–33; Finglass 2018b: 30.

and it does not achieve its goal of preventing the mutual killing, which is imminent in the play, unlike in Stesichorus, where the quarrel is delayed for some time.[221] Moreover, Euripides' Jocasta does not have the same role in the Lille papyrus. In fr. 97 F. her role ultimately resumes with the elaboration of a plan to share the inheritance, thus hoping to avoid the quarrel. In Euripides, she plays no part in this whatsoever, since the brothers define the terms (lines 69–76).

Such differences allow us to wonder to what extent the Euripidean Queen was the same that Stesichorus sang.[222] Moreover, the use made of the Theban myth by Euripides should be taken into account when drawing these apparent parallels. Lamari notes that "[b]eing all aware of the previous literary treatments of the Theban myth, Euripides is both repetitive and innovative, endorsing or rejecting preceding variations. In this way, he manages to create a narrative that informs those who are not familiar with all the details of the story of the Theban royal family, while he can still keep the suspense for those who are mythical experts".[223]

With this in mind, we may assume that Euripides makes use of some of the features of the Stesichorean Queen to characterize his Jocasta, but this does not imply that the character is the same. The use of elements that might have led some of the audience to recognize Stesichorus' work would function a lot better in terms of poetic innovation and artistry if drawn from a blameless, honourable, and immaculate Queen, such as the Lille mother. The comparison between the two characters would perhaps be more effective if the audience were asked to compare the attitude and the outcome of the episode precisely by emphasising the different impact of a Jocasta, who is *still* married to her son, albeit knowing the truth, and a blameless Euryganeia. While Euryganeia has the authority and respect to demand the obedience of her sons on the one hand, Jocasta simply has not. Hence, her intervention does not bear the moral authority required to impose anything to her quarrelling sons. The contrast would be tremendous for those who knew their Stesichorus, perhaps recognisable also in the reference to the Spartoi (lines 5–6, 931–941), a tale in Stesichorus' *Europeia* (fr. 96 F.).

To sum up, the identification of the Lille Queen with Jocasta raises more problems than does the alternative, Euryganeia. Euryganeia is credited as the

---

221 Mueller-Goldingen 1985: 34–36; Ugolini 1990 and Ercoles and Fiorentini 2011: 25–26 argue that the similarities between the two texts suggests Stesichorean precedence. However, many scholars have pointed out the differences. Bremer 1987: 169–170; Maingon 1989: 51–53; Mastronade 1994: 20–22.
222 Aluja 2014: 31–33.
223 Lamari 2010: 17.

mother of Eteocles and Polynices in every version where she is mentioned.²²⁴ But this in itself is not sufficient reason to question Euryganeia's identification with the Queen. What is significant is that the presence of a Jocasta in fr. 97 F. would imply that both she and Oedipus maintain their wedding even after knowing their family ties. That is, they would have lived as husband and wife knowing that they were mother and son without suffering any punishment or public disapproval; they would have held royal power despite their moral miasma; the Queen would doubt divine power and the truth of Teiresias' oracles even after having experienced the most dreadful revelation. Would it not be more consistent with Stesichorus' interest in exploring the inexorability of human existence to make a blameless Euryganeia see her sons killing each other?²²⁵ We have no means to provide a conclusive answer to this problem. If on the one hand, we should not simply assume that she is Jocasta, this remains a possibility. What we should not do is merely assume her identity without a careful consideration of the consequences of such assumption. Hence, we shall refer to the mother of the Eteocles and Polynices as the "Queen", although I believe that the Queen of fr. 97 F. is a figure equivalent to Euryganeia (whether or not she actually had that name).

However, the fact that tragedians chose Jocasta and not Euryganeia as the Theban Queen in their accounts, does not mean that they have not known or have not been inspired by some other aspects of Stesichorus' version of the Theban myth. On the contrary, there are many elements in the three tragedians may trace back to Stesichorus, which would therefore have been influential in his shaping of the myth. This is particularly relevant in the use made by the tragedians of three motives: the scepticism of the Queen regarding the inexora-

---

224 Pausanias (9.5.10) mentions a painting by Onasias where Euryganeia is depicted in grief from witnessing the quarrel between her sons. The reference appears in a context where Pausanias is discussing precisely the issue of the identity of the mother of the children, in support for the view that the mother of Eteocles and Polynices in the *Oedipodeia* is Euryganeia and not Jocasta.

225 Thus March 1987: 130 points out the unlikeliness of Stesichorus having portrayed the incestuous Jocasta exercising moral authority; also, Aluja 2014: 36 who argues that the incest is punished in every account of the myth, either by the suicide of Jocasta or by the imprisonment/exile of Oedipus. In Stesichorus, if we accept that he continues to reign over Thebes, the incest goes unpunished for a long time (i.e. until the death of the brothers witnessed by their mother); so too Finglass 2015a: 88: "It is improbable that an archaic poet could have portrayed a woman who had committed incest (albeit unknowingly) exercising moral and/or political authority within the state. This is Stesichorus, not Euripides".

bility of prophecies, her role as a mediator, and the imagery of the sortition by lots.

4.2.4 The Queen's speech (fr. 97.201–231 F.)

The Queen's reaction to Teiresias' prophecy is surprisingly rational. She is no hopeless *mater dolorosa*, like Callirhoe in the *Geryoneis*. Rather, her speech shows an articulate discourse that goes further beyond mere lamentation. She is determined to act and avoid the predictions of the seer. It has been argued that her words express scepticism at the prophet's ability to interpret the will of the gods correctly. This may be true when applied to the first lines of the epode (204–208) but would hardly be applicable to the rest.

Her speech shows "the mental dynamism of a woman engaged in making a crucial decision while under pressure of strongest emotion".[226] Naturally, we detect some interference of her emotion as a mother trying to elaborate a plan that would avoid the mutual killing of her sons. So much so, that her final words, which contain the plan of the shared inheritance, do not exclude the gods, but rather put the final decision in their hands, particularly those of the Moirai. The Queen's speech moves from immediate denial to a very well pondered, pious, and reasonable solution that attempts to prevent or at least delay the prophet's predictions. As in any negotiation, the Queen concedes some of her initial demands.

The first three lines draw attention to the Queen's present situation, showing a mother in denial when confronted with the prediction of her children's mutual slaughter. In a sequence of negative imperatives, she urges the prophet not to add further worries to her already existing ἄλγεα (lines 201–203). What ἄλγεα may have been haunting the Queen before the revelation of Teiresias? To this question scholars have provided several hypotheses.

Some read in it an allusion to the discovery of the incest, and the subsequent shame that the Queen and the King would have gone through in later years.[227] However, there is no indication that the sorrows she refers to go long back in time. Moreover, as we have seen, the Queen is probably not Oedipus' mother. Hence, she should be referring to some other cause for sorrow. Parsons also suggested that these sorrows were caused by the death of Oedipus, a rea-

---

[226] Burnett 1988: 113.
[227] Parsons 1977: 21; Bremer 1987: 137; Burnett 1988: 113.

sonable explanation for grief from his wife.²²⁸ However, her speech seems to emphasise that the cause of her sorrows go beyond mourning for Oedipus. Hutchinson suggests that the Queen refers to the sorrow of witnessing her sons' dispute over the throne, something that she must resolve.²²⁹ Teiresias would have predicted that the dispute would not be easily resolved, and that Eteocles and Polynices were to kill each other as a consequence of it. Thus, the "appalling worries" (χαλεπάς μερίμνας) may be seen not only as further concerns regarding her sons, but also a reference to the matters of state, which, too, was part of Teiresias' prophecy (lines 217, 228). The Queen distinguishes between the present ἄλγεα, in the opening of the line, and the future μερίμνας, at the end, which, unlike the present suffering, she hopes she can avert.²³⁰

On the other hand, the "heavy hopes" (ἐλπίδας βαρείας), emphatically occupying the end of the stanza, may instead stress the anticipation of a grim future of Eteocles and Polynices, which contrasts with a mother's hopes for the future of her sons.²³¹ The sense is rather uncommon in archaic poetry, for hope is almost always a positive element, and the combination of ἐλπίς and the epithet βαρείας is unique in archaic literature up until the fifth century.²³² The sense of these heavy hopes is all the more emphatic as it refers to the future of the Queen and her sons. However, it is remarkable that she treats Teiresias' prophecy as predicting expectations or possibilities as if they would not necessarily come true. This principal shapes her speech and her place in the negotiation with the gods. This is different from being absolutely sceptical. Nevertheless, in the following stanza she defies the content of the prophecy, as she argues that these expectations (i.e. the fatal quarrel between Eteocles and Polynices) sit on thin ice because they imply a certain stability in human affairs, an assertion that, to the Queen's eyes, is simply not accurate.

In the epode (lines 204–210), the Queen presents a metaphysical argument to support her belief that the prophecies of Teiresias contradict observable

---

228 Parsons 1977: 21.
229 Thus Hutchinson 2001: 124 suggesting that the ἄλγεσι refers to the present quarrel.
230 Thus Finglass 2014a: 372.
231 Thus Burnett 1988: 113.
232 For the significance of the combination, not found anywhere else in literature between the eighth and fifth centuries, see Hutchinson 2001: 124; Maingon 1989: 43–44 argues that the resultant combination conveys an unprecedented negative sense of ἐλπίς which will only reappear in tragedy. Bremer 1987: 137 points some instances in the *Iliad* where the verbal form ἔλπω has a negative sense of anticipating with fear, the more convincing is *Il.* 16.281 but it does not correspond exactly to the Stesichorean expression. On Hope in archaic and classical literature see Cairns 2016.

laws.²³³ It seems likely that Teiresias predicted permanent strife between Eteocles and Polynices leading ultimately to the fratricide. The Queen opposes the idea that strife may be permanent since human life is intrinsically changeable. The structure of these lines merits further examination since it provides a glimpse at Stesichorus' poetic technique.

Lines 205–208 begin and end with two similar expressions: θεοὶ θέcαν and θεοὶ τιθεῖcι, which stress the dominance of the gods in the process, implying that the prophecy is contrary to the practices of the gods regarding the affairs of the mortals. Tsitsibakou-Vasalos draws attention to the meaning of the formula θεοὶ θέcαν in Homeric contexts. She argues that it is used mainly in contexts adverse to mortals. One example is found significantly in *Od.* 11.274, in the context of the story of Oedipus, where the gods are said to have revealed the truth. This revelation caused a sequence of dreadful events that caused many sufferings to Oedipus. The formula is recurrent in other episodes "accompanied by a description of the evils provoked" by the intervention of the gods.²³⁴ The use of the formula by Stesichorus plays with this notion of the will of the deities and renders their intervention ambiguous, because the notion associated with the formula – that the gods' intervention is a source of evil to the humans – is denied and the gods suddenly appear not only as the agents of discord, but also as grantors of amicability among the mortals.

The chiasm of θεοὶ θέcαν ... βροτοῖcι and ...ἀνδρῶν | θεοὶ τιθεῖcι is, thus, elegantly achieved. The chiasm may extend to the relation between ἔμπεδον and the general sense of the supplements provided by Parsons (owing to West) and Pavese to line 207.²³⁵ Parsons suggests ἀμέρα<ι ἐ>γ, thus imprinting in the line

---

233 Universal law established by the gods can be seen in Hes. *Op.* 289, and Archil. fr. 13.5–7 W. The cosmogonic view of the conflict and opposition of *neikos* and *philotes* is frequent in Empedocles (fr. 31 B 17, 26, 35 D-K); the maxim uttered by Ajax in the Sophocles (lines 678–682), on the oscillation between friendship and enmity is attributed to Bias of Priene one of the Seven Sages (cf. Hipponax fr. 123 *IEG* and Hdt. 1.170). Overall, this traditional principle was widely accepted and can hardly be used to demonstrate intertextuality.

234 Tsitsibakou-Vasalos 1986: 171; the examples provided by the scholar are *Od.* 11.555, 23.11; *Il.* 9.637.

235 Parsons 1977: 22; Pavese 1997: 263. The gap in line 207 after ἐπιδα- has been subject to thorough payrological analysis. Meiller 1977: 65 and 1978: 14 argues for the reading ἐπιδαλλ- or ἐπιδαμ-, excluding, however, the possibility of ἁμερα. So too Bremer 1987: 14, who gives as two equally likely readings επιδαλλοιαννοον and επιδαμεραννοον. Pavese 1997: 263 and Hutchinson 2001: 126 have argued that by the traces in the papyrus it is more likely that the letter following α was a μ, hence επιδαμερα- For a detailed discussion of the supplements provided for this line, see Bremer 1987: 141; Neri 2008: 16–17.

the sense that the gods set men's mind for a day.[236] However, as pointed out by Finglass, the supplement is not without some problems since it requires us to accept scribal error, for the absence of the epsilon, and to leave the ἐν without the suitable dative.[237] On a similar sense, Pavese suggests ἀμερίαν which results in the notion that the gods placed in the humans mind the notion of the day in its constant mutability. As observed by Neri,[238] this supplement, which is compatible with the traces in the papyrus and is less problematic for it does not imply scribal error, complements the concept of the mutability of human mind, in an immediate sense, and, in a broader sense, the fragility of their condition. These two supplements seem to be those which present less papyrological problems and that concur with the general meaning of the line, when seen in the context of the chiasm which is likely have alluded to the ephemeral condition of human dispositions.

This structure is particularly revealing of the change operated by the Queen's speech and her convenient reading of the gods' *modus operandi*. Neri draws attention to the significant variation of the verbal tenses.[239] The aorist θέcαν conveys a sense of an action that is finished and, thus, immutable, whereas the present τιθεῖcι stresses the continuous and possibly changeable decrees of the gods concerning human disposition. The first lines respond and deny the meaning of the formula in the Homeric context, which we may assume was the notion conveyed by the prophecy of Teiresias, whereas the latter lines emphasise the ambiguity of their action. The ambiguity of the gods' action is ultimately what allows her intervention, the window of opportunity to the Queen's hopes for a brighter future.

This notion of changeability and ambiguity is precisely the opposite of that expressed in the epic *Thebaid* (ὡc οὔ οἱ πατρώϊ' ἐνηέϊ ἐν φιλότητι δάccαιντ',

---

[236] Similar expressions are found in Hom. *Od*. 18.136–137; S. *Aj*. 208; Archil. fr. 131.2 W.; Semon. fr. 1.3 W. νόον θεῖναι in a similar context of the gods establishing in the mind of men a certain disposition is found in Hom. *Il*. 13.732–735. In [Aesch]. *Pr*. 164 the expression is used for the expression of the gods' setting of their mind.

[237] Finglass 2014a: 374.

[238] Neri 2008: 20 for details on the implications of the supplement on metre. Hutchinson 2001: 126 notes that Pavese does not provide convincing evidence for the suitability of the supplement with the verb ἐπιτίθημι. However, Neri provides some examples of similar uses, namely Hom. *Il*. 13.732–734, which context is the most approximate to the general meaning of the Stesichorean line.

[239] Neri 2008: 20, "[l]a struttura chiastica sottolinea il concetto che come gli dèi «posero» (aor.: una volta per sempre) la legge della mutevolezza dei sentimenti umani, così essi «pongono» (pres.: azione che si ripete ogni giorno) di giorno in giorno negli uomini le loro instabili inclinazioni."

ἀμφοτέροισι δ' ἀεὶ πόλεμοί τε μάχαι τε, fr. 2 *GEF*). In the curse of Oedipus, the idea is that his sons shall be in permanent strife, expressed by ἀεὶ πόλεμοί τε μάχαι opposed to ἐν φιλότητι.[240] In Stesichorus, the Queen is left with some hope, as she challenges the idea of the fixity of the human affairs. However, it is precisely because human emotion is volatile that her efforts are pointless in the long term, since the truce that the Queen achieves is also subject to such variation, vulnerable to same principle. οὐδέ γα μὰν φιλότατ' coordinates with οὔτε of line 204, drawing attention to the second limb,[241] where the irony of the Queen's intervention lies.

The irony of the Queen's argument, absent from the epic *Thebaid*, was not ignored by the tragedians. In Euripides' *Phoenissae*, Jocasta pleads with Zeus to save Eteocles and Polynices, since it is not fair, she says, that Zeus allows the same person to remain permanently wretched (lines 84–87).[242] The use of such notion implies that Euripides' Jocasta too is hopeful that the strife may come to an end. Unlike Euripides' Jocasta, however, the Lille Queen succeeds in putting a (temporary) end to the strife. Another use of the Lille Queen's argument that human affairs are not permanent is found in Sophocles' *Oedipus at Colonus* where Oedipus reverses the Theban Queen's approach.[243] Oedipus elaborates on the constant mutability of human emotions emphasising the fragility not of strife, but of friendship (lines 612–615):

καὶ πνεῦμα ταὐτὸν οὔποτ' οὔτ' ἐν ἀνδράσιν
φίλοις βέβηκεν οὔτε πρὸς πόλιν πόλει.
τοῖς μὲν γὰρ ἤδη, τοῖς δ' ἐν ὑστέρωι χρόνωι
τὰ τερπνὰ πικρὰ γίγνεται καὖθις φίλα.

---

[240] Maingon 1989: 54–55, draws attention to certain similarities between the Lille papyrus and Hesiod, in a significant passage that deals with strife within the *oikos* that eventually leads to strife within the *polis* (*Op*. 179, 188, 191). But Hesiod is pessimistic, whereas the Queen reveals obstinate in trying to achieve success in her negotiation. It is true that the scholar compares the Queen's speech to Hesiod in order to highlight the innovative lines in which the former's speech in conceived. However, Maingon stresses the positive approach of the Queen opposed to Hesiod' pessimism, but it seems that the point of the changeability is missing in Maingon's analysis.
[241] Denniston 1954: 193.
[242] The parallel is drawn by Mueller-Goldingen 1985: 34; see too Ercoles and Fiorentini 2011: 26 and Swift 2015: 140. For the problems of the argument that the parallel shows Euripides' debt to Stesichorus in the shaping of his Jocasta, see Mastronade 1994: 26 n. 1 and Finglass 2018b: 29–32.
[243] Bremer 1987: 143.

> And the same spirit never holds steady
> Among friends nor between one city and the other.
> For some of us sooner, for others later,
> Joyful things turn bitter, and then back again to being dear.

Theseus expresses scepticism towards Oedipus' announcement that some war may oppose Athens and Thebes. He cannot see how the two cities can ever engage in conflict. Oedipus points out to Theseus the rapid changeability of the human affairs, which matches their mutable and ephemeral condition. Nothing about human life is timeless, not even friendship.

It is on the Lille Queen's interest to argue that strife is not perpetual, but as the response of Oedipus in Sophocles shows, this applies equally to friendship. This principle renders the Lille Queen's attempts ineffective.

Although the Queen questions the applicability of Teiresias' prophecy to the real world, we can hardly argue that the Queen is not aware of the problem that her case creates, since in lines 209–210 she addresses Apollo and pleads for the god not to fulfil all the prophecies revealed by Teiresias. This could not have come from someone entirely sceptical of the truth that the prophet's words may bear.[244] The Queen is, thus, aware that the universal law of oscillating dispositions among men need the gods' approval. Hence, she turns to Apollo seeking his support.

Given the grimness of the revelation, the Queen could have asked the gods to prevent these events from happening, as does Sophocles' Jocasta, who begs for the god to provide an escape from the events predicted by his oracle. However, she does not do so. She merely pleas for Apollo not to fulfil *all* of them. It is not the same attitude as that presented by Jocasta in Sophocles. On the contrary, given that a plea for the god to avert all the prophecies may have been rather bold, the Queen merely asks that at least some can be avoided. Some have argued that this plea is a desperate solution, and to some extent it is.[245] However, it emphasises her reverence of the gods' will; her belief (and fear) is that the prophecies may be accomplished. This is in accordance, not in opposition as some have argued, with the following stanza where the Queen pleas not to see the mutual killing or the city captured. Burnett argued that the triad break in line 210 brings a change in the psychology of the Queen, "for [her] regal assertiveness is now replaced by a histrionic attitude of submission". However, such

---

244 Cf. Finglass 2015a: 91.
245 Thus MacInnes 2007: 100; comparing with the scene in E. *Ph.* 69–70.

significant change can only be sustained if we consider, with Burnett, that the Queen did "not humble herself before this god [sc. Apollo]".²⁴⁶

However, there is no arrogance towards Apollo in the words of the Queen. She may have cast doubts on the accuracy of the seer but she does not question the power of Apollo. The reverence of the Queen for the god is evident if we accept that the ἄναξ in line 209 is part of the formula ἄναξ ἑκαέργος Ἀπόλλων, rather than a vocative addressed to Teiresias.²⁴⁷ Tsitsibakou-Vasalos makes a suggestive point regarding the use of ἑκαέργος, arguing that in Homer the epithet is not a mere alternative for the more common Διὸς υἱός,²⁴⁸ but a meaningful variation.²⁴⁹ In the Homeric poems, ἑκαέργος is used when Apollo acts on his own will, as opposed to episodes where he intervenes on behalf of Zeus. By referring to the god in these terms, the Queen stresses his independence, summoning him as protector,²⁵⁰ and acknowledging his power of acting on his own will.

Therefore, far from incurring in a hybristic discourse, as some claim,²⁵¹ the Queen acknowledges the power of the god. This is clearly expressed not only in the chiasm of lines 204–208 that forms an elegant ring-composition, but by the emphatic μὴ πάσας τελέσσαι ending the triad in line 210 which emphasises "the force of the Queen's wish".²⁵² Such line could hardly have come from someone who defies the power of the gods in determining the fate of mortals. The unmistakable sense of finality of the clausula marks the end of her denial, which has been at the centre of her speech so far. From now on she will propose solutions.

---

246 Burnett 1988: 114.
247 Thus Tsitsibakou-Vasalos 1986; Finglass 2014a: 374–375. Parsons 1977: 22 rejects this alternative, as he prefers to see ἄναξ as a vocative, and, thus an address to Teiresias; Bremer 1987: 144; Burnett 1988: 109 n. 10; follow this suggestion on the grounds that the Queen addresses Teiresias in the previous lines (Bremer), (Burnett). The use of this would emphasise the prophet's high status (cf. Calchas *Il.* 11.107–108), so too MacInnes 2007: 100, who nevertheless recognizes that both options are valid. However, this hypothesis seems to ignore that for the Queen's purposes, it would be of more use to please Apollo than Teiresias.
248 Parry 1987: 277–278.
249 Tsitsibakou-Vasalos 1986: 173–184. For the controversy in the use of Homeric formulae and the contestation of Parry's approach see Tsitsibakou-Vasalos 1986: 173–175 nn. 1–5; more recent studies on the subject can be found in Friedrich 2007: 87–90; Finkelberg 2012; Yamagata 2012.
250 Cf. the role of Apollo as a protector of the Trojans against Zeus' commands in *Il.* 17.545–596.
251 Thus e.g. Maingon 1989: 52.
252 Haslam 1978: 37–38.

The following stanza elaborates more profoundly on the Queen's emotions. If in lines 204–210 she presents a more general and universal law, she now focuses on her own suffering. The resulting speech is, thus, highly emotional, at times illogical (lines 213–215). Once more, the Queen is far from defying the gods. She is aware that although the mechanics of the world, to use an expression from Mueller-Goldingen,[253] show that a quarrel cannot be permanent, it rests with the gods to intervene and change the dispositions of humans. She knows that, for her plan to succeed, she needs more than a clever observation or mere lamentation: she needs to gain the gods' favour and as soon as possible to establish the conditions for the quarrel to stop.

The next stanza begins with a conditional.[254] The content of these lines (211–217) is studied in detail in the section above, in an attempt to reconstruct the prophecy of Teiresias. The references to the multiplicity of prophecies in line 210 suggest that Teiresias' revelation did not present alternative outcomes, but rather a myriad of grim events. Overall, the Queen's wish to die before witnessing these events is a further element contradicting the view of her as sceptical towards the prophecies.[255] In line 212, her attention is focused no longer on Apollo, but on the Moirai and on what they may have assigned to her and to her sons.[256] The notion of the fixity of the fate contrasts with the idea of changeability developed in the earlier stanza. The idea of inflexibility is stressed in line 212, μόρcιμον ἐcτιν, ἐπεκλώcαν δὲ Μοῖρα[ι. The opening of the line is reinforced in the last word, which personifies the determinism of destiny conveyed by μόρcιμον.[257]

---

253 Mueller-Goldingen 1985: 34.
254 Cf. Hom. *Il.* 12.232 where Hector expresses some reluctance in accepting the utterance of Polydamas.
255 Vagnone 1982 provides Homeric parallels of the formulaic wish of death, concluding, however, that Stesichorus expands the *topos* and makes it more dynamic and dramatic.
256 Hutchinson 2001: 127 prefers the reading according to which the Moirai are acting with reference to the sons and not to the Queen. If so, it is interesting to see how the Queen includes herself and her suffering in the equation beginning the first (211) and third line (213) with emphasis on her position.
257 The plural Μοῖραι appears in Homer only once (24.49) where the endurance of mourning of the heart that the Μοῖραι gave to mortals is praised. It is more common to find references to the singular Μοῖρα (cf. *Il.* 24.209 and in A. *Eum.* 335). On Μοῖρα(ι) as personal deity(ies), see Dietrich 1965: 194–231 and for a different opinion, Chantraine 1952: 71. Overall, in Homer the action of spinning fates is generally attributed to the gods (*Il.* 24.525; *Od.* 1.17, 3.208, 8.579, 11.139, 16.64); thus, the gods, and more precisely, Zeus determines fate. However, the episode of Sarpedon (*Il.* 16.431–461) shows that Zeus is somehow constrained to go against what is destined, since it would create a precedent for the other gods to act according to their own will

Again, line 212 shows that the Queen manifests, not her scepticism, but her fear that some aspects of the prophecy are already established and cannot be averted. Her wish that she may be a subject of divine pity and die before witnessing the events occupies line 213, creating a clearer opposition between her wish and the inexorability of Fate. Her desperation is made evident by the illogical terms in which her wish is expressed. The repetition of verbs of sight in lines 211 and 213 makes the request of the Queen impossible to fulfil, since if it is destined that she will see her sons die at each other's hands, she cannot ask to die before seeing it. The emphasis of the verbs of sight (lines 211, 214) requires us to read these lines either as a manifestation of the intense maternal *pathos* leading to a diminished attention to matters of logic and consistency, or as a subtle plea for the event not to happen at all. If it is destined that she sees the death of her sons, and she asks that she may be spared from that sight, she is either begging the Fates to concede her the wish and thus alter what they have determined, to eliminate her presence when that moment arrives. Another possibility is that her wish refers to all the events that the prophecy included, reiterating her plea to Apollo not to accomplish all of what was revealed. If it is indeed her fate to see her sons killed, may she be spared the other grim event predicted, the destruction of the city. Seen in these terms, the wish of the Queen is less problematic, but no less emotional.[258]

(*Il.* 16.433); but it seems that should Zeus want to, he could have altered what was fated. A similar situation can be found in *Il.* 22.179–181, a scene to which Barrett 2007a (1968): 17 compared fr. 18 F. where Athena intervenes apparently to prevent Geryon from being rescued. See further Sewel-Rutter 2007: 141–143. Hesiod (*Th.* 211–217) makes the Μοῖραι daughters of Night, but in *Th.* 901–906 they are daughters of Zeus and Themis, thus suggesting that they are his subordinates (thus West 1966: comm. 37, cf. comm. 217, 904; Solmsen 1949: 36; Sewel-Rutter 2007: 143). This conflicting origin and authority of the Moirai may be seen as a reflection of the human perception of Fate, at times arbitrary and harsh, other times as part of a just world order of the Olympians (thus Solmsen 1949: 37). In the Lille poem, both notions are implied, since when the Queen refers to the Μοῖραι, she seems to imply that they act on their own terms (thus MacInnes 2007: 101); but the pleas to the gods, Apollo and Zeus, in the hopes that they may intervene in her favour, show that the gods can alter what the Μοῖραι establish.

258 The lacuna in line 215 presents difficulties. No supplement (for which see Bremer 1987: 148–149; Neri 2008: 23) is entirely satisfactory. Problems begin with the dative ἄλγες‹c›ι, which scarcely fits in the sense whether the lacuna is supplemented by a noun (Meillier 1977: 65; Tosi 1979: 134–135; Massimilla 1988: 26–28) or with a dative adjective as suggested by Barrett (*ap.* Meillier 1976: 298). Hutchinson approaches the question from another perspective and posits corruption on ἄλγες‹c›ι, suggesting ἄλγιcτα, but does supplement the lacuna. Barrett's supplement ἀ[λαcτοιc is preferred by Morenilla and Bañuls 199: 67 since it alters an Homeric formula and creates a chiasmic structure which is quite abundant in the poem (apart from the chiasmus in lines 204–208, and the idea of repetition in line 212, Xanthou 2015: 48 n. 1

This stanza shows a mother who, like Hecuba in *Il.* 22.82–89, expresses deep despair towards the prospect of seeing her sons killed, but who does not limit her action to laments and persuasion. ἀλλ' ἄγε in line 218, marking a "change on the direction away from adverse situation to a new proposal or solution",[259] shows that the Theban Queen is determined to take action.

Maingon provides several Iliadic parallels for speeches where ἀλλ' ἄγε is used in contexts of a shift in the attitude, when a speaker urges the interlocutor to leave behind present concerns and adopt another posture.[260] The speech of Diomedes to Capanaeus in *Il.* 4.412–418 presents a different structure from that of the Lille Queen, but they share some significant aspects. Diomedes begins by asking Capanaeus to obey his words (τέττα, cιωπῆι ἧcο, ἐμῶι δ' ἐπιπείθεο μύθωι) and leave behind the worries to focus on battle (ἀλλ' ἄγε δὴ καὶ νῶι μεδώμεθα θούριδος ἀλκῆc). Line 218 does not preserve the verb, but West supplements πιθέcθε after Maltomini's suggestion of τέκνα, thus giving ἀλλ' ἄγε παῖδεc ἐμοῖc μύθοιc, φίλα [τέκνα, πιθέcθε.[261] Both scenes show concern for demonstrating respect and affection to the addressee. The repetition of παῖδεc and φίλα [τέκνα (if we accept the supplement), emphasises the Queen's affection for her children and the maternal bond and thus is effective in persuading them to act according to her designs. The same strategy is found in tragedy, where the mothers (or maternal figures) address their children in critical moments to prevent them from doing something (A. *Cho.* 896), to advise them to listen to them and act accordingly.[262] After presenting her pleas to Apollo and after wishing to die before witnessing the dreadful events predicted, she turns to her sons – the only addressees whom the Queen can urge to obey – to fulfil

---

notes in lines 216–217 the "reversely chiastic metrical responsion of the two participial (παῖδαc — ⏑ ... θανόνταc — — ⏑ πόλιν — ⏑ ἀλοίcαν ⏑ — —), probably implying the disjunctive inevitability of fated evils."). Also, Neri 2008: 24 accepts the supplement of Barrett and that of Slings 1978: 432 n. 2, ἀ[γεῖcαν, although he does not rule out the possibility of [πολλοῖc, given the common association of ἄλγεα and πολλά (13 times in Homer cf. Neri 2008: 24 n. 35). Be that as it may, the central idea to all the supplements is that in this line the Queen elaborates on themes of suffering and mourning, emotions that either of the events (mutual fratricide or the city's destruction) would cause to the Queen.

259 Maingon 1989: 50.
260 Maingon 1989: 51–53, e.g. *Il.* 2.433, 3.441, 5.249, 12.195, 18.249.
261 West *ap* Meillier 1976: 298; Maltomini *ap* Meillier 1976: 347, 1977: 71. The hypothesis of the two supplements combined is preferable to the suggestion νῦν φρονέοιτε by Barigazzi *ap.* Meillier 1976: 298, since although the sense is acceptable, but it would require a dative of the person to whom the attitude is directed; thus Finglass 2014a: 377.
262 A. *Cho.* 264–265; E. *Hec.* 172; S. *Trach.* 61, although here it is not the mother but the servants who address Orestes and Electra in the affectionate term.

her plan. This plan, she believes, will allow a different outcome from the one presented by Teiresias.

Line 219 is particularly telling for the hopes of the Queen regarding her plan. Scholars see in the Queen's choice of words a bold and perhaps even hybristic attitude. ταῖδε γὰρ ὑμὶν ἐγὼν τέλος προφα[ίνω implies that the Queen is attempting to take the place of Teiresias in the utterances of prophecies to her children. προφα[ίνω recalls the earlier use of this word, in line 203, where it was accompanied by the reference to "heavy hopes" for the future. [263] Burnett suggests that these hopes contrast with the expectations of a mother to the future of her sons.[264] In line 219, by using the vocabulary associated with the prophet, the Queen affirms her authority. Moreover, τέλος has a strong meaning in the previous stanzas, in line 203, in her appeal to Apollo to forestall the events prophesised by Teiresias, and in line 213 as the concretization of her wish to die before these events take place.

τέλος combined with προφα[ίνω anticipates the failure of her plan, conveying a stronger sense of inexorability of fate to the episode and the poem in a whole.[265] It is therefore surprising that, instead of rejecting the Queen's attempt, Teiresias shows support. He does not feel attacked by her stand against his prophecies.[266] Nor should he, since, as the Queen puts it in line 227, her intervention and the plan are motivated by his prophecy. She is thus acting according to, not against, the advice of the seer.[267] Now, the question is whether Teiresias is also convinced that this may indeed avert the destiny he predicted, or if he is acting as he believes so in order to spare the Queen from suffering in anticipation.

The Queen's plan, revealed in lines 220–224, shows a well pondered course of action, which establishes an opposition with lines 211–217.[268] While in line 211 ἀλλάλοισι stresses the reciprocity implied in the brothers' fate, τὸν μέν ... τὸν δέ of lines 220–221 dissolves the reciprocity by establishing the separation of the brothers. The presentation of the portions in these lines introduced by the coordinate clauses τὸν μέν ... τὸν δέ, shows again a chiastic structure ἔχοντα ... ναίειν ...ἀπίμεν ... ἔχοντα, which produces a rhetorically satisfactory emphasis on

---

[263] Bremer 1987: 153; Hutchinson 2001: 130 "However, it would be unlikely that the queen, who will be supported by Teiresias, is here emphatically overruling his pronouncement".
[264] Burnett 1988: 113.
[265] Thus Hutchinson 2001: 130.
[266] Thus Hutchinson 2001: 130 contra Meillier 1978: 36, 39; Bremer 1987: 156; for the notion that the Queen defies the prophecies of Teiresias.
[267] Xanthou 2015: 48.
[268] Thus Morenilla-Bañuls 1991: 75.

the justice of the terms according to which the inheritance is to be divided: one lot being the throne of Thebes; the other the movable goods.[269] Her plan is entirely focused on the separation of the brothers to avoid the quarrel. Since that quarrel is likely to result from the conflict over the inheritance, the Queen, instead of choosing one heir for the whole inheritance of Oedipus, search for a compromise solution, which involves the division of the inheritance in two equal parts. Rather than having a "winner takes all" solution, the Queen, aware of the possibility that such a solution can cause the other brother to retaliate, establishes the principle that both brothers should have access to part of the inheritance.

However, the attribution of the portions to each of the brothers is not made by the Queen,[270] but through the casting of lots, which again puts the decision in the hands of the Moirai. The hapax κλαροπαληδόν, an adverb combining

---

[269] The line where the first lot is described is incomplete. Being such a relevant piece of information in the fragment, scholars have provided a considerable number of supplements for this line-end. It is unanimous that the Queen would somehow refer to the kingdom or the city of Thebes. Davies and Finglass 2014: 378 point out that the dotted letter is an alpha and not an epsilon or an omicron, as Bremer 1987: 153 suggested. Therefore, supplements as Neri's 2008: 28 πε[ρὶ νάματα Δίρκας, and Sisti's 1976: 54 πό[λιν εὐρυάγυιαν can be ruled out. πα[. Among the variety of supplements derived from πα[, Diggle's 1979 πα[τρίαις ἐνὶ Θήβαις is perhaps the one that would better fit the context which requires a neutral and accurate content. Barrett's suggestion πα[ρὰ νάμασι Δίρκας remains a possibility. However, it presents some problems on its own. It is in fact true that Stesichorus seems to enjoy the topographic references when setting his episodes and this may indeed corroborate Barrett's supplement, being the spring of Dirce a common metonymy for the kingdom of Thebes (see, for example, Pi. O. 8.29, I. 1.29, 6.74, and especially 8.20). Moreover, Statius' Thebaid – which has considerable parallels with Stesichorus' account (see Finglass 2016) – also alludes to the fields of Dirce referring to the kingdom of Thebes, precisely when referring to the cast of the lots. That is the same point of the narrative as the passage of Stesichorus here in discussion. Therefore, it seems that the reference to Dirce is not entirely unexpected. However, when considering Barrett's supplement, we should ask ourselves if it would make sense rhetorically. The Queen's speech is carefully designed to show her impartial position. She makes a considerable effort to try and show how the lots are equivalent in value. A reference to the kingdom as a whole alluding to its value as a land and not only the city itself, would have unbalanced the lots, making one seem more valuable than other. That is exactly what the Queen should avoid at this point. In this sense, so too Maltomini's attempt πα[ρὰ ματέρι κεδνᾶι seems to "associate the mother too closely to one of the brothers at the very moment when she needs to show herself a neutral arbiter" (Davies and Finglass 2014: 378).

[270] On the content of each portion, see Pindar P. 4.145–155, where Jason returns to recover the throne of his father and suggests Pelias a fair division of property: Jason is to keep the throne and Pelias the herds and some land. Jason stresses the generosity of his offer, which is aimed at solving their issues peacefully.

κλῆρος and πάλλω attested in epic and tragedy in such contexts,[271] is thus central to the overall sense of the stanza, since it implies that the Queen's sphere of action is limited, ultimately leaving the decision to the Fates. She merely establishes the terms.[272]

The closest approximation to this method is presented by Hellanicus with a slight but significant variation.[273] In his account, the division of the inheritance was settled by Eteocles and Polynices themselves. Instead of using sortition, the brothers choose between throne and wealth. Thalmann argues that in practical terms both methods were used in fourth century Athens, and thus the variation of both accounts is a mere detail.[274] However, while the solutions may be practically equivalent, in dramatic and poetic terms they are distinct since in Stesichorus the sortition constitutes not only an unprecedented role for the Queen, but also increases the irony of her attempt, anticipating as it does the failure of the settlement, and providing further insight on the "broader theological and ethical questions"[275] presented throughout her speech. The dramatic potential of the arrangement in Stesichorus is appropriated by Aeschylus, who uses the imagery to describe the fatal quarrel, the outcome that the allotment attempts to avert.

---

271 For further parallels, see Scarpanti 2003: 301–302; Neri 2008: 25 n. 41.
272 The casting of lots is a common method to divide inheritances. In the *Iliad*, it is once applied to the division of the world between Zeus, Hades, and Poseidon. They have divided the earth in three equal portions (so Poseidon insists) and casted the lots. In the *Odyssey* (14.208), Odysseus in disguise tells how the sons of the king of Crete shared the inheritance between them by casting lots. In both examples the sharing is proposed and conducted by the heirs themselves. It appears in other contexts of decision-making, e.g *Il.* 3.314–325, 23.861, 7.161–199; *Od.* 10.205–207. See further Thalmann 1978 for a survey on the motif of the allotment and for its use in sharing inheritances in fifth and fourth century Athens.
273 fr. 98 *EGM*. The details on the growing tension between Eteocles and Polynices are not preserved in the *Thebais*. Distinct accounts of the sharing of the inheritance are found in Euripides *Phoenissae* where the inheritance is not divided. Rather, each brother is to rule in alternate years, and enjoy the wealth of the palace (E. *Ph.* 69–76). The brothers solve the problem on their own, as in Hellanicus (fr. 98 *EGM*). The youngest Polynices is to go to exile in the first year, while Eteocles, the oldest, is to rule over Thebes. Statius presents the same solution of the ruling in alternate years. However, the decision as to who is to rule first is based not on seniority, but on the casting of lots (*Theb.* 1.164). Gostoli 1978: 26–27 draws attention to Euripides' *Suppl.* 14 where παγκληρία may refer to the χρήματα to which Polynices would be entitled to reclaim, should a division of the wealth take place. Pherecydes (fr. 96 *EGM*) and Sophocles (*OC* 1295–1298, 1330) present a more contentious version, where Eteocles expels Polynices. In these versions, there was no attempt to reach an agreement of any sort.
274 Thalmann 1882: 387.
275 Swift 2015: 136.

Aeschylus makes a particularly violent use of the imagery of inheritance division by casting lots, using it as a metaphor for Eteocles and Polynices' fate to kill each other. It occurs in the beginning of the play when the Argive army is allotting the warriors to specific gates (*Sept.* 375–376, 423, 458–459). The process is described by the messenger/ scout in a particularly vivid manner that emphasises that the outcome is the product not of free choice, but of fate (*Sept.* 816–818), thus preparing the audience for the inevitable mutual fratricide (*Sept.* 727–733, 906–991, 941–946), which is described using precisely the motif of allotment as a metaphor.[276] The mutual fratricide is presented as the one true heritage that Oedipus left his sons: violence, and death, which they will both receive in equal portions.[277] Ares, the arbiter figure, guarantees that both brothers will obtain their allotted portion, *i.e.* that they both meet death in battle. The paradox of the metaphor lies in general terms in the fact that the procedure is usually implemented to find a peaceful and amicable solution for the division of the inheritance.

Although the case for any intertext between Aeschylus and Stesichorus lacks strong evidence, Aeschylus reverses the use of the allotment in the Lille poem.[278] In Aeschylus and in Stesichorus the imagery of the lot "symbolises the power of fate and the gods",[279] but in Stesichorus' use of the lot comes as a glimpse of hope for the Queen, a desperate attempt to condition the gods' sphere of action, whose designs are, of course, irreversible, as it is made clear by the emphatic position of ἕκατι Μοιρᾶν.

Lines 223–224 repeat the emphatic and severe sense of lines 209–210, where the Queen implores Apollo not to fulfil all the prophecies revealed by Teiresias; and recall the central role of the Moirai in defining human fate as presented in lines 212. The Queen summons the same entities who designated the mutual killing of her sons to play a determining role in a plan that attempts to avert their decision. She is seeking their support in turning her hopes into destiny. Moreover, the Moirai in line 212 are again summoned in the antistrophe as the agents of the sortition in line 224. The ring structure configured by both stanzas emphasises the opposition between the fated prophesised by Teiresias and the Queen attempted reversion of it.[280]

---

[276] Cf. Wick 2003: 171–172; Swift 2015: 137–138.
[277] Cf. A. *Th.* 727–733, see also Wick 2003: 172.
[278] Wick 2003: 174; Swift 2015: 13.
[279] Swift 2015: 13.
[280] Morenilla-Bañuls 1991: 75.

Hutchinson argues that the Queen is confident, since the first person δοκέω in line 225 conveys an idea of modest authority, rather than hesitancy.[281] However, the Queen is aware of the fragility of her plan. Parenthetic δοκέω and optative γένοιτο stress not confidence, but caution. This subtle, shy, but resilient hope lies beneath her words; a hope that runs against, opposes, and ultimately eliminates the ἐλπίδας βαρείας announced by Teiresias in line 203. The three preserved stanzas all manifest this hope that motivates the Queen to keep going, to find possible solutions. In the final stanza, the Queen mentions again the prophecies of Teiresias directly, as she had in line 209. However, while there the word referring to the prophecies is μαντοσύνας, here φραδή has the more immediate sense "advice", "counsel" (A. *Cho.* 941; E. *Ph.* 667), "recommendation" (A. *Eu.* 245). The sense of μάντιος φραδαῖσι θείου is not clear, but most scholars take it as a dative of cause,[282] conveying the idea that the Queen's solution derives from the warnings or advices of the prophet, and that she is not dismissing them, but rather building upon them what she envisages as a possible path away from a grim future. The fact that the solution presented by the Queen is caused by the advice of Teiresias, does not mean that he predicted this exact procedure. Rather, the previous stanza seems to make clear that the casting of lots was the Queen's idea.

As argued above, Teiresias' prophecy was more probably a prophecy of certain doom, but the possible reference in it to Oedipus' succession as the cause of the quarrel between the brothers, opens the way to the Queen' plan, without implying her disregard for the prophet's intervention. By proposing the division of the inheritance, she eliminates the cause of the quarrel and establish a new scenario. With the inheritance divided in equal shares, her sons have no reason to fight. This reading does not oppose the hypothesis of a definite prophecy, as argued above, and allows a better understanding of the role of Teiresias in the following lines.

In tragedy, Teiresias shows reluctance to reveal the grim future that awaits his masters. In Sophocles' *Oedipus Ring* and in Euripides' *Phoenissae*, the prophet begs not to be asked to speak. In the *Antigone*, Teiresias' words to Creon in lines 1023–1032, seem to imply that something can still be done to avoid future doom, but he later reveals that disaster will occur (1060), showing that he had the knowledge all along, but nevertheless tried a different approach. This behaviour is found with other prophets. In the *Septem* 377–383, 568–591, Amphiaraus attempts to detain the Argives, but according to the tradition was fully

---

281 Hutchinson 2001: 131.
282 Parson 1977; Bremer 1987: 157; Finglass 2014a: 379.

aware of the future that awaited him. Thus, the figures of seers are in a middle ground between foreknowledge, that they usually try to veil, and human action. Therefore, a Teiresias hopeful that something may be achieved from this solution would not be completely strange. However, Teiresias may be aware of the future failure of the agreement, but chooses not to reveal it.[283] Moreover, his words to Polynices predicting a happy and wealthy life in exile, and his advice to Eteocles (lines 281–285) not to be too ambitious and to comply with the agreement, shows that Teiresias is not entirely convinced that the plan would work. On the contrary, he is aware of the risk which it entails.

The Queen too is aware that she cannot guarantee the success of her plan without the favour of the gods. In the previous epode (lines 204–210) she pleads with Apollo not to fulfil all his prophecies. She now turns to Zeus, implying that he has the power to intervene in order to save, or, at least, spare the Queen' suffering in witnessing the mutual killing of her sons and the city's ruin by delaying the doomed future (lines 228–231). The lacunae present problems, and scholars have paid close attention to them.[284] Parsons's preferred solution, αἰ γ' ἐτέον (owed to Lloyd-Jones and Barrett),[285] contradicts the traces on the papyrus which read τ rather than γ. Moreover, such a sentence would imply that the Queen assumes that Zeus will save the city, which would be odd.[286] Assuming an even wider corruption, Hutchinson suggested αἴ γε νοεῖ with infinitive, which would better account for the unusual position of νέον.[287] There are problems in maintaining the transmitted τ, but there are two hypotheses that seem reasonable: αἴτε or ἄι τε. Bremer doubts the sense of the construction with αἴτε, because, he argues, a "whether...or" clause in the ending of the Queen's speech would undermine the optimism that inspires it.[288] However, if we accept the supplement provided by Gallavotti to the lacuna in line 230 αἴτε καὶ ἄλλω]ς, providing the correspondent αἴτε for that in line 228, and the conjecture of Barigazzi and Ancher γενέ[c]θαι for line 231, the sense seems rather appropriate, and accounts for the probable final sigma at 230. In another approach to the

---

283 Thus Maingon 1989: 55: "the fact that Teiresias is singled out in line 232 suggests that for the moment he chose not to contradict the proposal".
284 For a survey on the supplements, see Neri 2008: 35–41.
285 Parsons 1977: 24; Tsitsibakou-Vasalos 1988: 141–142 suggests αἴ γε + relative clause + γενέ[c]θαι, acknowledging, nevertheless, the problems it causes in making the fated grim expected, which would contradict not only the Queen's words in the previous line, but the sense of the speech.
286 Thus Hutchinson 2001: 133; Neri 2008: 35–38; Finglass 2014a: 382.
287 Hutchinson 2001: 133; Finglass 2014a: 382.
288 Bremer 1987: 159.

lacunae, Neri argues that the supplement causes problems in an otherwise rhetorically consistent speech for it implies that the Queen, at the end of her utterance, casts some doubts on the way in which her plan may be successful.[289] For that reason, Neri suggests the supplement line 228 with ἅι τε which, he argues, would reinforce the Queen's confident τᾶιδε of line 219. The relative would exclude the need for a corresponding αἴτε in line 230. To this lacuna Neri suggests [ἃ κατὰ Μοίρα[c, a hypothesis that includes the final sigma in line 230 and which would result in an interesting repetition of the power and centrality of the Moirai referred to in the course of the Queen's speech in lines 211 and 223.[290]

In both readings the Queen would, therefore, recognize that, at the end, the decision to save Oedipus' kin and city would only be possible if the gods and Fates allow it. This final pious note in the speech would imprint to it a less hopeless note than the supplement by Gallavotti and would reinforce the Queen's reverence to the gods.

The Queen declares that she hopes that her plan will release them from grim destiny. Note the correspondence of λυτήριον ...κακοῦ πότμου (226) in the opening of the line and ἀμβάλλων κακότατα ... πέπρωται... (line 228–229), the latter being a more extended and detailed repetition of the former, thus establishing a cohesive structure of the stanza.

The speech concludes in the end of the triad – the same metre as line 210 – "highlighting for the listener the grimness of the real position"[291] and closing the emotional crescendo obtained throughout the stanza with a tonality of hopeful expectations that will later be crushed. This sense would be better achieved if the lacuna is to be supplemented with γενέ[c]θαι, thus recalling the μὴ πάcαc τελέccαι of line 210, although in terms of sense, metre, and syntax, the other suggestions are equally valid.

The narrator's words suggest that by the end of her speech, the Queen succeeded in persuading her sons and the prophet to comply with her plan and act accordingly.[292] From now on, however, the Queen disappears. No trace of her is detectable from the casting of lots or during Polynices' departure. A puzzling absence, indeed, given her dedication to elaborate a plan that might avert or delay the fated doom. Not a word of comfort to the exiled son, no advice to the

---

[289] Neri 2008: 37–38.
[290] Neri 2008: 40–41.
[291] Hutchinson 2001: 134.
[292] The narrator stresses the rhetorical effectiveness of the Queen's speech. Note the parallel, pointed out by Tosi (ap. Bremer 1987: 162), with Pi. *I.* 8.30–50, esp. 49, and Hutchinson 2001: 134–135, drawing attention to the parallel with *Od.* 15.53.

ruling Eteocles. Such absence emphasises her impotence in intervening from this moment on. This role is delegated to the prophet, who assists to the casting of the lots and provides advice to each of the brothers after the allotment.

4.2.5 Casting lots and Teiresias' advice (fr. 97.235–291 F.)

The Queen's plan is put to practice in the next lines (239–252) where the components of each portion are repeated (lines 221–223) and presented in more detail, emphasising the fairness of the solution. Lines 234–237 seem to refer to the lot that includes the throne of Thebes and the power over the territory, lines 239–241, which are slightly better preserved, to the movable goods, the gold and herd. The addition of adjectives, perhaps also added to the portion of the throne and territory in lines 234–237, stress value, thus making this portion equal to the perhaps more disputed lot of the throne. While the Queen refers only to gold and cattle, in these lines the gold is ἐρίτιμος,[293] the sheep are κλυτά, here to be understood in the sense of "splendid", or "noble", rather than "bleating",[294] and the horses in line 243 are probably introduced by an epithet such as εὐέθ]ειρας or ἀγλαέθειρας.[295] These adjectives are not mere formulae included to add an epicizing flavour to the passage; they inflate the value of a portion that may have been perceived as the less attractive. Parsons considers that, similarly to other scenes of casting of lots, the first lot to jump is usually the worse.[296] In the passage, there is a clear effort to eliminate the difference. Thus, both portions were intended to be equal shares. However, the fact that the portions are equal does not necessarily mean that the brothers would have been happy with any the result; they may be equal in value but are certainly not equal in prestige.

The decisive moment occurs in lines 246–252. It occupies the epode, which we have seen to have a metre particularly appropriate to emphasise tension. This moment may have conveyed an important emotional reaction from one of

---

293 Cf. Hom. Il. 9.126, where "precious gold" appears as one of many elements in the list of gift Agamemnon offers Achilles to persuade him to return to battle.
294 Finglass 2014a: 385 prefers bleating, but in the context of the scene it seems that the adjective would highlight the value of the portion.
295 Conjectures by West ap. Meillier 1976: 303 and Finglass 2014a: 385, respectively.
296 Parsons 1977: 24; Finglass 2013a: 10. For scenes of sortition where the first portion may be perceived as the worse, see Il. 3.314–325; Od. 10.205–207. In Pindar, although there is no casting of lots, Jason's offers Pelias the portion of the movable goods, while he is to keep the sceptre. Pelias does not accept it, but his rejection does not necessarily make the proposal unequal; it merely stresses Pelias' immoderate ambition.

the brothers, precisely when the lot leaps from the helmet. The sense of the passage is not unanimous among scholars. Some consider that the ἂν δ' ἔθορ' αὐτός refers to the leaping of the lot *itself*,[297] but idea that the lot jumps up is not entirely convincing. So, the likeliest option is that αὐτός refers not to the lot but to the person to whom it was ascribed. The order of the lots was probably defined in advance, as it is in the other episodes of allotment: the less favourable portion is attributed to the one whose lot jumps first;[298] αὐτός should, therefore, refer to Polynices.[299] Parsons suggested that the line implies either that Polynices jumped to his horse, or that Teiresias jumped up in emotion. This is motivated by a supposed speech by Polynices or Teiresias before line 251, perhaps a dispute over the authority of Teiresias' oracles.[300]

It seems, however, preferable to reconstruct these lines and the episode in a different manner. Finglass argues that lines 232–253 "belong to the narrator, perhaps focalised through (one of) the characters", describing the scene of the allotment.[301] These lines reveal a particularly tense moment of the poem, as the brothers are about to know which part of the inheritance is to be attributed to each of them.[302] The agitation implied in line 249 ἐ]νὶ στήθεσσι shows that, despite obeying their mother, the brothers are by no means indifferent to the result of the allotment as they demonstrate anxiety towards the result. Such a sense would stress the fragility of the agreement supposedly achieved by the mother.[303] This reading allows a different interpretation for line 251. It is not Teiresias who jumps up in anger towards Polynices, as suggested by Parsons, nor is it Polynices that jumps to his horse. Let us not forget line 190, which suggests that the action inside the palace, an odd place to have a horse. Moreover, Teiresias will speak to Polynices later on. It would seem awkward to have Polynices hearing the predictions of Teiresias while mounted. Therefore, ἂν δ' ἔθορ' αὐτός is likely to refer to Polynices' reaction to the jumping of his lot. He jumps in a sudden movement expressing disappointment at the result, since as Finglass suggests, the "αὐτός transfers the idea from token to man".[304] Moreo-

---

[297] Bakker 2012: 6.
[298] Thus Parsons 1977: 24 with examples.
[299] The supplements provided by West (*ap.* Finglass 2014a: 386) and Parsons (1977: 29)– ἐκ δ' ἔθορεν κλᾶρος Πολυνεί[κ]εος, ἂν δ' ἔθορ' αὐτός – convey a satisfactory sense to the line.
[300] Parsons 1977: 28.
[301] Finglass 2014a: 386.
[302] Thus Hutchinson 2001: 135.
[303] Thus Hutchinson 2001: 135; Finglass 2013a: 10, n. 9.
[304] Finglass 2013a, 2014a: 386.

ver, such a reaction from Polynices justifies the thirty-seven line intervention of Teiresias.[305]

The prophet addresses each of the brothers with predictions of the future and advices them to abide by the plan and by the outcome of the sortition. Before revealing his prophecies, he seems to have reinforced the justice of the plan and its power to avoid doom, perhaps referent to line 270[306] and in line 273 if we supplement κα]τ' αἶcαν,[307] a probable solution not only for its similar use elsewhere in Stesichorus (fr. 104.10 F.), but because it would again recall the final line of two other epodes (lines 210, 231). Repetition of πολλάc in lines 260, 266, 269 may again stress the value in each of the portions, in particular Polynices', whose share is mentioned once more in line 272–273,[308] always highlighting its advantages, which are complemented in the following lines, where Teiresias predicts the wealth and prestige that awaits Polynices in Argos (lines 274–280). He is to be exiled, but will be no miserable wanderer, as he seems to have been in Euripides' *Phoenissae* (lines 389–407). μόρcιμόν ἐcτι introducing the revelation of the future awaiting Polynices in Argos in line 274 conveys a sense of certain and fixed future, and emphasises the authority of the prophet.[309] Polynices will receive Adrastus' daughter in marriage (lines 275–276), which would make him a son-in-law of the king of Argos: a promising position which would allow him to gather an army and attack Thebes.[310]

In the next stanza, Teiresias may be addressing Eteocles, if we accept the supplement Ἐτεο[κλ.[311] Parsons further suggests that Teiresias is either emphasising his address to Eteocles, or urging him to be cautious.[312] In either case, the next line can refer to the distress of Teiresias, as he witnesses the discontent of Polynices and the probable failure of the agreement, or it may refer to the Eteocles' state of mind. In any case, the sense conveyed is one of deep negative emo-

---

305 Burnett 1988: 110 argues that the speech is delivered by one of the brothers. However, as shown by Hutchinson 2001: 136 and Finglass 2014a: 387, the use ὑμίν in line 260, the identification of the speaker in line 274–280, and the references to the gods in line 266, the naming of Adrastus (line 275), to Eteocles (line 281) and to Polynices (line 283), together with the absence of any signs that the speaker have changed, favour the consideration that these lines are part of a speech by Teiresias.
306 Parsons 1977: 30 suggests ἄν]υcιν θέντεc μεγάλαιc ἐπ[ὶ λύπαιc.
307 Thus, Haslam, Parsons, and West *ap*. Meillier 1976: 301.
308 Thus Hutchinson 2001: 136; Finglass 2014a: 388.
309 Hutchinson 2001: 137.
310 Cf. S. *OC* 410–416.
311 Barigazzi *ap*. Meillier 1976: 301.
312 ἐνέπ]ω διαμπερέωc Ἐτεο[κλεῖ or μελέτ]ω διαμπερέωc Ἐτεο[κλεῖ, respectively (Parsons 1977: 31).

tion, probably connected to line 283, where Polynices is mentioned. Parsons suggests and rejects ἐθέλ]ων ἔχεν Πολυνείκεος [αἶϲαν, which would add a further concern to Teiresias, since it would mean that the risk to break the agreement would not come exclusively from Polynices. According to Parsons, the fault is to be expected from Polynices, not Eteocles.[313] However, many accounts of the myth blame Eteocles for misconduct, for either acting by force and expelling his brother,[314] or for not having abide by the plan (E. *Ph.* 69–76). The responsibility for the breaking of the agreement in Stesichorus is thus better left open.

Teiresias' next lines (285–287) read "whole city" (πόλει τε πάϲαι), "pain" (πένθοϲ), "ever"/ "always" (ἀεί). If Eteocles is being urged to comply to his share of the inheritance, the sense may be that Teiresias is explaining what will happen if he fails to do so: disaster (will affect?) the whole city, and (cause?) pain (to their mother?). The closing lines are more difficult. Parsons offers an *exempli gratia* reconstruction: τοῦ[το ῥύοιτο κακ]όν, θεῶ[ν ὅτιϲ εὔνο]οϲ ἧι μάλιϲτα πάντων | το[ῖϲ ὀϊζυροῖϲ βρο]τοῖϲι.[315] This replicates, or paraphrases, the final lines of the Queen's speech. Such a reading, although far from certain, would stress Teiresias' sympathy for the Queen. But it would also indicate that Teiresias is aware of the futility of the plan. In this context, it would be more likely that Teiresias provides advice in roughly the same manner as he does in the *Odyssey*, aware though he may be of the outcome.

4.2.6 Polynices' journey (fr. 97.291–303 F.)

Line 291 marks the end of Teiresias' speech with the formular ὣϲ φάτο likely followed by the name and certainly by the epithet of the seer. The lacunae in the lines prevent us from knowing exactly to whom they refer. The subject of αἶψα δ' ... δόμω ... may also be Teiresias, who after revealing his prophecies leaves the palace, in which case line 293 ὤιχετ[ο would refer to Polynices. Parsons draws the parallel with *Il.* 1.387 where the subject of αἶψα is the person referred to in the previous clause. Moreover, such an attitude from Teiresias would anticipate his behaviour in the tragic accounts where he leaves the scene immediately after revealing his prophecies.[316]

---

[313] Parsons 1977: 32.
[314] Pherecyd. fr. 96 *EGM*; S. *OC* 404–409, 1295–1298, 1330.
[315] Parsons 1977: 33, βρο]τοῖϲι is owed to Haslam and West *ap.* Meillier 1976: 301.
[316] Cf. S. *OT.* 444, *Ant.* 1085–1090; E. *Ph.* 953–959.

However, the suggestion put forward by Page and supported by Parsons is perhaps more satisfactory given the following lines. Page argued that the subject of αἶψα δ' ... δόμω ... is Polynices and the subject of ὤιχετ[ο are his companions, thus conveying the sense that he departs accompanied by some men immediately after the speech of Teiresias.[317] As pointed out by Hutchinson, such a scene would emphasise the annoyance of Polynices with the allotment, as he departs abruptly. Finglass suggests that the "swift acquiescence of the brother in their mother's proposal (...) may contrast with later recriminations and insults during their conflict over the city".[318] Stesichorus' choice to depict a certain passivity on the part of the brothers would allow a more surprising development of the narrative upon the return of Polynices with the Argive army. Moreover, as noted by Parsons, it makes sense that the emphasis on departure is focused on Polynices and his entourage, rather than Teiresias. The suggestion is further supported by the plural in lines 298 and 303, which indicate that Polynices does not travel alone. It would make sense to make some reference to his companions at this point of the narrative where Polynices departs.

We have seen that Polynices is not entirely satisfied with the result of the allotment. Yet he departs without manifesting his emotions at the result of the allotment. Conversely, the mapping of his journey to Argos, which follows his rapid departure, occupies more than a stanza, beginning in line 295 with Polynices and his partisans leaving Thebes as they cross over the wall. Since the previous line is likely to refer to the departure of Polynices and his companions from the palace, the wall in line 295 must refer to the Theban one, rather than to any other city's fortifications.[319] The line refers to Polynices crossing the wall alone; the reference to his companions appears only in next line. Finglass points out the ironic flavour of the passage: the wall which Polynices now crosses easily will be heavily blocked upon his return; it will be the scene of his battle against Eteocles, the landmark of the fate he agreed to escape from. It is then significant that the poet isolates Polynices' crossing from that of his companions. Moreover, the pattern of a reference primarily focused on Polynices and only afterwards depicting the companions is applied to lines 293–294.

The journey from Boeotia to the Argolid occupies the last seven lines of the fragment, but the first preserved city name occurs in line 298, Isthmus, with a reference to the sea (line 300). Corinth and Cleonae are the other legible names

---

317 Page's supplement *ap.* Parsons 1977: 33: ἄ[οικος | δόμων̣ [ὅ γ' ἥρως] | ὤικετ[ο· cὺν δ' ἄρ' ἕπο]ντο φίλων Πολυνείκεϊ τ[αγοί] | Θηβαίω[ν ἄριστοι.
318 Finglass 2015a: 92.
319 Parsons 1977: 34–35; see also Finglass 2014a: 393.

of cities through which Polynices passes. The journey from Corinth to Cleonae is emphatically rapid, as denoted by ῥίμφα at the opening of line 303.

Despite the detailed description of the journey, providing information about the cities that Polynices and his entourage pass by, the general sense of these lines is one of a straightforward, direct, and rapid journey, with no delays, no unexpected sojourns; a rather unheroic journey, which opposes to the more elaborated and colourful account we have for Polynices' journey in Statius' *Thebaid* (1.328–335).[320] Moreover, in Statius, Polynices travels alone. In Stesichorus he is followed by his partisans, which may be significant to the meaning of the poem and to the overall status of Polynices as a political exile.

Burnett pointed that the whole scene of the division of the inheritance by allotment and the departure of Polynices is similar to some accounts of foundational tales involving precisely the division of the paternal wealth and power, leading to the exile of one brother who eventually founds a new city.[321] She argues that the dispute over the inheritance "between Eteocles and Polynices was a subject that reflected both the facts and the fictions of colonial life", as it "proposes a mythic doublet for the colonists' departure", "a story of a foundation tale gone wrong" due to Polynices incapability to let go of the throne of his homeland.[322] She concludes that this would have an impact on a colonial audience as a reversed or negative example of colonial enterprises and would have alerted the community to the dangers of civil strife.[323]

While the observation regarding the concerns of civil strife seems central to the poem, the function of it as a distorted colonial narrative is perhaps farfetched. The fact that Polynices departs from Thebes with a defined destination that involves no attempt at founding a city seem to contradict Burnett's claims. More than a negative example of what a colonist should do, the poem is a warning about civil strife. The focus is on the disregard of a resolution that

---

[320] Thus Parsons 1977: 32–33; Finglass 2016.
[321] Burnett 1988: 148–150. For some examples of the Brother's Quarrel motif in foundational narratives, see Strab. 8.7.1, Deucalion's grandsons divide the inheritance between them and the throne is ascribed to only one of them; Hdt. 1.173, Sarpedon and Minos fight over the throne of Crete, Minos takes the throne and expels Sarpedon, who in turn founds Lycia; Paus. 7.2.1 Neilus and Medon solve their dispute with the help of the oracle of Delphi which ascribed the throne of Athens to Medon and predicts that Neilus shall depart and found new cities in Asia Minor; Hdt. 5.42 on Dorieus' attempt to found a city in Motya as a result of a dispute with his elder brother.
[322] Burnett 1988: 150, 151.
[323] Burnett 1988: 148, n. 149, for some problems in the sharing of inheritances in newly founded colonies.

attempted to prevent family/civil/political strife that endanger a given city. This would be valid in mainland Greece and colonies alike. The tradition credits Stesichorus with a concern to intervene in situations of imminent civil strife to restore peace (Ta30 Ercoles). The account of Eteocles and Polynices, as well as Orestes' claim for revenge, would alert the community to the dangers of civil strife, of fraternal disputes, of violence among peers with dire consequences; a reality which, alas, was common throughout the Greek world.

5 Conclusion

My purpose with this study was to analyse Stesichorus' narrative technique and his innovative treatment of myths, particularly in the characterization of his hero(in)es. I have done so against the backdrop of four motifs connected with travel: the journeys which imply an encounter with monstrous creatures; narratives of return and escape, which allow reflections on the implications of war; abduction tales and their variations in three poems; and exile. These journeys provide unity for this volume and allow it to explore the different treatments of one theme in various poems and in different degrees of influence in the narrative itself. I also mapped the journeys of Stesichorus' heroes in order to understand the significance of mobility in our poet's shaping of the narrative and the extent to which, if at all, these travels may have reflected the reality of sixth century Greece and Mediterranean.

Stesichorus had an interest in bringing some of his heroes to further western locations. In the *Sack of Troy*, Aeneas escapes the city and embarks towards Hesperia (fr. 105 F.), presumably Italy or Sicily. In placing Aeneas in the west, Stesichorus includes his own region in the most relevant cycle of Greek myth. In other cases, we see a different concern in the mapping of the heroes' routes across other important regions of the seventh and sixth century Mediterranean. Helen's stay in Egypt and Demophon's sojourn there (fr. 90 F.) allude to more approximate ties with the region. No longer a place of passage, Egypt becomes a place of permanence. Phoenicia's influence in the Mediterranean, and in the Greek sphere in particular, is alluded to in the *Europeia*, where Europa is abducted by Zeus and taken to Crete, whereas Cadmus leaves the same place in search for his sister and ends up founding Thebes. Even the far west is mapped in Stesichorus' poetry, where the reference to the Tartessus in the *Geryoneis* (fr. 9 F.) shows knowledge of the topographic attributes of the region.

Stesichorus' mythical journeys were by no means confined to far off western locations. In fact, the majority takes place in mainland Greece. The fragment ascribed to the *Nostoi*, which told of the returns of the heroes presumably involving longer travels, includes Telemachus' journey to Sparta (fr. 170 F.). The *Geryoneis* told of Heracles' encounter with Pholus (fr. 21 F.) in Thessaly, thus suggesting that the poem covered the journey to Erytheia and back again. In the *Boarhunters*, although travelling is not specified, we find a catalogue of different *ethnê*, some mentioned there for the first time, which suggests the encounter of several Greek people in Calydon. In the *Funeral Games for Pelias* (frr. 3–4 F.) and in the episode of Helen's wooing (fr. 87 F.) too we see a gathering of heroes from several places in the Greek world in athletic competitions. These stories, together with the Labours of Heracles, provide mythical parallels for the sports culture of archaic Greece.

The poems dealing with the themes of exile or abduction also shows some geographical variations. In the *Oresteia*, Agamemnon's palace is in Lacedaemon, not Mycenae nor Argos (fr. 177 F.). In the *Helen*, the heroine is taken to Athens by Theseus, and on her way back to Sparta after being rescued by her brothers, Helen makes a stop in Argos (here Agamemnon's palace) to give birth to Iphigenia whom she leaves with Clytemnestra (fr. 86 F.). In the *Thebais*, we accompany Polynices on his journey from Thebes to Argos (fr. 97.295–303 F.). Polynices' exile is particularly illustrative of Stesichorus' elaboration on the motif's dramatic potential, by featuring his mother as the deviser of the plan that would eventually lead to his exile and consequently his offensive against Thebes. Surprisingly, the journey itself is treated with very little detail. Despite of not having survived, the episode of the return of Orestes, on the other hand, and the recognition scene also allowed our poet to present an emotional encounter of the siblings. It is in the tales of exile, therefore, that we can better observe the pre-dramatic features of Stesichorus' poetry and the effects of these journeys, even though the episodes of the exile itself are not preserved or deserve little attention from our poet. But these tales also allow a glimpse of what may have been a genuine concern about the affairs of the polis which deserves to be addressed and reflected upon by the community. Hence, although confined to mainland Greece, the narratives involving exile will be applicable to the newly founded cities in the west, as a warning of the potentially devastating consequences of political stasis.

However, and despite the recurrence of the theme in the poems, Stesichorus' use of travelling motifs is of little help in providing specific evidence for his target audience. Although we can understand the relevance of these themes to the new cities in Magna Graecia, the translation of concerns into mythical *paradeigmata* would have been appreciated throughout the whole Greek world. On the other hand, the references to Sparta, Athens, and Thebes do not imply that these poems were composed with the audiences of these cities in mind. His inclusion of Theseus' abduction of Helen (fr. 86 F.), Demophon and Acamas in the *Sack of Troy*, the sojourn of the first in Egypt in the *Palinode* may suggest an Athenian audience, although the focus of the poem is not on these characters. The reference to Athenian mythology, as happens with Egypt, for example, may merely suggest the increasing influence of Athens in the Greek world. Moreover, some of the poems which show interest in Athenian characters (*Helen* and the *Oresteia*) have long been used as evidence for performance in Sparta. We see therefore that the attempt to find in Stesichorus' shaping of the myth references which tie his performance to a particular place are problematic. Nevertheless, the silence regarding the specificities of the audience, on the one hand, and the broader panhellenic scope of his works, on the other, encourages us to conclude that more than providing heroic narratives exclusively to a western audience, Stesichorus created heroic narratives for his time which mapped the routes of the heroes across the Mediterranean, from east to west.

Stesichorus' poetry and his innovations, however, do not concern merely geography and travelling. On the contrary, his narrative technique provides significant clues which help us map his contribution to the sixth century Greek literature. Stesichorus' interaction with Homer is particularly telling, since it points to a level of Homeric intertextuality that goes beyond the mere use of Homeric diction and formulae, or the repetition of attributes of the major characters. This is best observed in the *Nostoi* and in the *Geryoneis*. In the *Nostoi* (fr. 170 F.), we are presented with a scene very similar to the *Odyssey* 15.170–185. The characters are the same, and even some parts of the preserved speech resemble what we find in Homer. However, in Stesichorus Helen has a more prominent role than her epic counterpart, since she assumes the role of prophet, host, and demonstrates sympathy towards Penelope. Menelaus is silent throughout the scene. This suggests that Stesichorus and his audiences had knowledge of the *Odyssey* to the point of remembering speeches from less central episodes. In the *Geryoneis*, on the other hand, our poet applies Homeric episodes to a different context, involving characters from a completely different myth. The case here, as we have seen, shows that our poet not only knew secondary episodes of the *Iliad* in detail, but also expected his audience to react to the irony caused by the adaptation of scenes to the story of Geryon (e.g. fr. 19 F.) and his mother (fr. 17 F.). The reminiscence of Hecuba pleading with Hector not to go into battle here applied to Callirhoe imploring to Geryon not to face Heracles emphasises the *pathos* of his death and the heroism of his deed, while encouraging sympathy for him.

Stesichorus poses dilemmas and creates tense situations for his characters, which allows him to elaborate on their psychology and on the drama of their situations. The incidence of these episodes goes well beyond what we find in Homer. We have seen how our poet dealt in detail with Geryon's dilemma on whether to fight Heracles (fr. 15 F.). But there are other instances throughout his poems where he invests a considerable number of lines in describing such dilemmas and decision-making scenes. The Trojans' debate over the Horse seems to have been an important and tense moment of the *Sack of Troy* (fr. 103 F.). Orestes' decision to avenge his father may have involved something of a dilemma (fr. 181 F.). Althaea seems to have been confronted with the need of killing her son; the Theban Queen, after learning the terrifying future that awaits her sons, attempted to design a plan that would change or delay fate (fr. 97 F.).

In elaborating on the psyche of his characters, the inclusion of Clytemnestra's dream (fr. 180 F.) also deserves mention, since it provides a unique example of Stesichorus' attention to the heroines' psychology that anticipates the character of tragedy. In fact, throughout the four chapters, female characters have a central role. The characterization of Callirhoe as a *mater dolorosa* who witnesses the death of her son adds dramatic depth to the poem and to the myth. The scenes in the *Sack of Troy*, featuring Hecuba, Andromache, or Polyxena should have enriched the drama of the story, as they do later in Euripides. Helen's concern with Penelope's anxiety regarding the absence of her son implies that in the *Nostoi* Helen is more considerate with the suffering of the Greek wives and mothers. In the *Oresteia*, the female characters also play a central role. Clytemnestra represents the deviant mother and wife. However, Stesichorus feels the need to adds to the story a maternal figure, the Nurse, who by invocating Orestes' childhood and her love for him would have created an interesting contrast with the careless Clytemnestra. So too, the recognition by means of the lock of hair, later adapted by the tragedians, again with all the reminiscences from the childhood of the Electra and Orestes must have been a moving passage. And finally, one of the most striking and enigmatic female characters of Stesichorus, the Theban Queen, who plays the twin roles of mother and ruler, a pragmatic and yet emotional character. Although the interest in maternal figures may indicate a genealogical interest of Stesichorus' works, he is not interested in them as an accessory in the lineage of his heroes. Our poet saw the dramatic potential of these figures, of the impact of their emotive words, of their authority towards their offspring, of their profound suffering for their children and the value of these characters to the narrative and to the myth. He saw too the force of a negligent mother in the figures of Clytemnestra in the *Oresteia* and perhaps Helen (fr. 115 F.). Stesichorus' female characters are a central aspect of his poetry and encourage us to consider the pre-dramatic aspects of his oeuvre as important sources of inspiration to the tragedians and even the comedians.

We have seen how our poet reworks epic material and creates something new from it. Stesichorus' aestheticisation of maternal suffering, of human vulnerability to the actions and caprices of the gods, owes much to epic material, but somehow transcends it. His poetry is a symbiosis of the best of epic poetry and the first steps towards what would become one of the major contributions of ancient Greece to world literature: Greek tragedy. The works of this Himerian are perhaps the best example attesting the cultural maturity of sixth century Magna Graecia so often ignored, denied, or diminished as an amalgam of several different influences from mainland Greece with no significant artistic value *per se*. Stesichorus' works prove these assumptions wrong. And although Stesichorus' revival from the second half of the twentieth century onwards brought further knowledge of our poet, we still possess a very small fraction of the monumental poems he composed. And yet, we can perceive in these tiny examples, in these shy details, the colossal value of his works and his fundamental contribution. The ancients recognized his value as a peer to Homer and an innovator; it is time for the moderns to acknowledge this too, to overcome the obstacles, as his heroes, and embark themselves on a Stesichorean journey.

Bibliography

Abbreviations

EGM	Fowler, R. (2000–2013), *Early Greek Mythography*, 2 vols. Oxford.
FGE	Page, D.L. (1981), *Further Greek Epigrams. Epigrams before A.D. 50 from the Greek Anthology and other sources, not included in 'Hellenistic Epigrams' or 'The Garland of Philip'*. Revised and prepared for publication by R.D. Dawe and J. Diggle. Cambridge.
FGrHist	Jacoby, F. et al. (1923 –), *Die Fragmente Der Griechischen Historiker*. Leiden/Brill.
GEF	West, M.L. (2003), *Greek Epic Fragments from the Seventh to the Fifth Centuries BC*. Loeb Classical Library. Cambridge/London.
CIG	Böckh, A. *et al.* (1828–1877), *Corpus Inscriptionum Graecarum*. 4 vols. Berlin
IEG	West, M.L. (1971–1972), *Iambi et Elegi Graeci ante Alexandrum cantati*, 2 vols, Oxford.
IGDS	Dubois, L. (1989–2008), *Inscriptions Grécques dialectales de Sicilie*. II vols. Rome/Genéve.
MW	Merkelbach, R./West, M.L. (1967), *Fragmenta Hesiodea*. Oxford.
PCG	Kassel, R./Austin, C.F.L. (1983–2001), *Poetae Comici Graeci*. 8 vols. Berlin/New York.
PLF	Lobel, E./Page, D. (1955), *Poetarum Lesbiorum Fragmenta*. Oxford.
PLG	Bergk, T. (1882), *Poetae Lyrici Graeci*. 4th edition. Lipsiae.
PMG	Page, D.L. (1967), *Poetae Melici Graeci*. Oxford.
PMGF	Davies, M. (1991), *Poetarum Melicorum Graecorum Fragmenta*. Oxford.
SEG	Chaniotis, A. et al. (1923–), *Supplementum Epigraphicum Graecum*. Leiden/Boston/Köln.
SLG	Page, D.L (1974), *Supplementum lyricis Graecis. Poetarum lyricorum Graecorum fragmenta quae recens innotuerunt*. Oxford.
TrGF	Snell, B./Kannicht, R./Radt, S. (1977), *Tragicorum Graecourm Fragmenta*. Göttingen.

Editions, Translations, and Commentaries

Accius
D'Antò, V. (1980), *Accio. I frammenti delle tragedie*. Lecce.

Aeschylus
Collard, C. (2002), *Aeschylus*. Oresteia. Oxford.
Fraenkel, E.D.M. (1950), *Aeschylus*. Agamemnon. Oxford.
Garvie, A.F. (1986), *Aeschylus*. Choephori. Oxford.
Griffith, M. (1983), *Aeschylus*. Prometheus Bound (Cambridge Greek and Latin Classics). Cambridge.
Hecht, A./Bacon, H. (1973), *Aeschylus*. Seven Against Thebes (trans.). New York/London.
Hutchinson, G.O. (1985), *Aeschylus*. Septem Contra Thebas. Oxford.
Pulquério, M.O. (2008), *Ésquilo*. Oresteia. Agamémnon, Coéforas, Euménides. Lisboa.

Smyth, H.W. (1926), *Aeschylus.* Agamemnon, Libation-Bearers, Eumenides, *Fragments.* vol. II. (Loeb Classical Library). London/New York.
Sommerstein, A. (1989), *Aeschylus.* Eumenides, Cambridge.
Sommerstein, A. (2008), *Aeschylus.* Fragments. vol III. (Loeb Classical Library). London/New York.
Wilamowitz-Moellendorf, E.F.W.U. (1896), *Aischylos Orestie. Griechische und Deutsch. Zweites Stück. Das Opfer am Grabe.* Berlin.

Anacreon (and *Anacreontea*)
Jesus, C.A.M. (2009), *Anacreontea. Poemas à maneira de Anacreonte.* Coimbra.
West, M.L. (1984), *Carmina Anacreontea.* Leipzig.

Apollonius
Wendel, C.T.E. (1935), *Scholia in Apollonium Rhodium vetera.* Berlin.

Aristophanes
Olson, S.D. (1998), *Aristophanes. Peace.* Oxford.
Silva, M.F./Magueijo, C. (2006), *Aristófanes. Comédias I.* Lisboa
Silva, M.F./Jesus, C.A.M. (2006), *Aristófanes. Comédias II.* Lisboa.
White, J.W. (1915), *The Scholia on the Aves Of Aristophanes. With an introduction on the Origin, Development, Transmission, and the Extant Sources of the Old Greek Comedy.* Michigan.

Aristotle
Valente, A.M. (2008^3), *Aristóteles. Poética.* Lisboa.

Athenaeus
Olson, S.D. (2006), *Athenaeus. The Learned Banqueters.* 8 vols. Cambridge, MA/London.

Bacchylides
Jebb, R.C. (1905), *Bacchylides: the Poems and Fragments.* Cambridge.
Jesus, C.A.M. (2013), *Baquílides. Odes e Fragmentos.* Coimbra.

Callimachus
Pfeiffer, R. (1949–1953), *Callimachus.* 2 vols. Oxford.

Dionysus
Fromentin, V. (1998), *Dionysus of Halicarnassus.* Antiquités Romaines. Tome I. Belles Lettres. Paris.

Epic Cycle
West, M.L. (2013), *The Epic Cycle. A Commentary on the Lost Troy Epics.* Oxford.

Euripides
Alves, M.C. (1975), *Eurípides. As Fenícias.* (trad.). Coimbra.
Carson, A. (2006), *Euripides. Grief Lessons.* New York.
Cropp, M.J. (2000), *Euripides.* Iphigenia in Tauris. Warminster.
Dale, A.M. (1967), *Euripides.* Helena. Oxford.

Kannicht, R. (1969), *Euripides*. Helena. 2 vol. Heidelberg.
Karamanou, I. (2006), *Euripides* Danae *and* Dictys: *Introduction, Text, and Commentary*. Munich.
Kyriakou, P. (2006), *A commentary on Euripides'* Iphigenia in Tauris. Berlin/New York.
Mastronade, D.J. (1994), *Euripides*. Phoenissae. Cambridge.
Mastronade, D.J. (2010), Euripidean scholia available at http://euripidesscholia.org [Last access 22/05/21].
Parker, L.P.E. (2016), *Euripides*. Iphigenia in Tauris. Oxford.
Pearson, A.C. (1909), *Euripides*. Phoenissae. Cambridge.
Silva, A.F.O. (1982), Orestes. *Eurípides*. Coimbra.
Willink, C.W. (1986), *Euripides*. Orestes. Oxford.

Herodotus
Lloyd, A. (1975), *Herodotus. Book II. Introduction*. Leiden/Brill.
Waterfield, R. (2008²), *Herodotus*. Histories. Oxford.

Hesiod
Athanassaki, A. (2004²), *Hesiod: Theogony, Works and Days, Shield*. Baltimore.
Merkelbach, R. and West, M.L. (1970), *Hesiodi Fragmenta Selecta*. Oxford.
Most, G. (2007), *Hesiod*. The Shield. Catalogue of Women. *Other fragments*. London/Cambridge, MA.
West, M.L. (1966), *Hesiod*. Theogony. Oxford.

Homer
Dindorf, W. (1855), *Scholia Graeca in Homeri* Odysseam. 2 vols. Oxford.
Dindorf, W. (1875–1877), *Scholia Graeca in Homeri* Iliadem. 3 vols. Oxford.
Edwards, M.W. (1991), *The Iliad: A Commentary*. Vol. V. Cambridge.
Erbse, H. (1969–1999), *Scholia Graeca in Homeri* Iliadem. 7 vols. Berlin.
Hainsworth, B. (1993), *The Iliad: A Commentary*. Vol. III. Cambridge.
Heubeck, A./Hoekstra, A. (1989), *A Commentary on Homer's* Odyssey. Vol. II. Oxford.
Heubeck, A./West, S./Hainsworth, J.B. (1988), *Commentary on Homer's* Odyssey, vol. I. Introduction and Books I–VIII, Oxford.
Janko, R. (1992), *The Iliad: A Commentary*. Vol. IV. Cambridge.
Kirk, G.S. (1985), *The Iliad: A Commentary*. Vol. I. Cambridge.
Kirk, G.S. (1990), *The Iliad: A Commentary*. Vol. II. Cambridge.
Lattimore, R. (2011²), *The Iliad of Homer*. Chicago.
Lourenço, F. (2003), *Homero*. Odisseia. Lisboa.
Lourenço, F. (2005), *Homero*. Ilíada. Lisboa.
Richardson, N.J. (1993), *The Iliad: A Commentary*. Vol. VI. Cambridge.
Russo, J./Fernandéz-Galiano, M./Heubeck, A. (1992), *A Commentary on Homer's* Odyssey. Vol. III. Oxford.
Van Thiel, H. (1991), *Homeri Odyssea*. Hildesheim/Zürich/New York.
Van Thiel, H. (1996), *Homeri Ilias*. Hildesheim/Zürick/New York.
West, M.L. (1998), *Homerus Ilias* (I–XII). Stutgardie et Lipsae.
West, M.L. (2000), *Homerus Iliad* (XIII–XXIV). Stutgardie et Lispae.

Homeric Hymns
Faulkner, A. (2008), *Homeric Hymn to Aphrodite: introduction, text, and commentary*. Oxford.
West, M.L. (2003), *Homeric Hymns. Homeric Apocrypha. Lives of Homer*. Cambridge, MA.

Ibycus
Wilkinson, C.-L. (2013), *The Lyric of Ibycus*. Berlin/Boston.

Inscriptions
Meiggs, R./Lewis, D. (1969), *A Selection of Greek Historical Inscriptions*. Oxford.

Lycophron
Hornblower, S. (2015), *Lykophron Alexandra: Greek Text, Translation, Commentary and Introduction*. Oxford.

Melic, iambic, and elegiac Poets
Aloni, A. (1994), *Lirici Graeci. Alcmane e Stesicoro. in appendice Simonides*. Milano.
Bergk, T. (1843), *Poetae Lyrici Graeci*. Vol I. Leipzig.
Bergk, T. (1853), *Poetae Lyrici Graeci*. Vol. 2. Leipzig/London.
Bergk, T. (1867), *Poetae Lyrici Graeci*. Vol. 3. Leipzig.
Bergk, T. (1882), *Poetae Lyrici Graeci*. Vol. 4. Leipzig.
Campbell, D.A. (1990–1993), *Greek Lyric*. 5 vols. London/Cambridge, MA.
Campbell, D.A. (1988), *Vol. II: Anacreon, Anacreontea, Choral Lyric from Olympus to Alcman*. London/Cambridge, MA.
Campbell, D.A. (1991), *Vol. III: Stesichorus, Ibycus, Simonides, and Others*. London/Cambridge, MA.
Hartung, J.A. (1856), *Die griechischen Lyriker V*. Leipzig.
Hutchinson, G.O. (2001), *Greek Lyric Poetry. A Commentary on Selected Larger Pieces*. Oxford.
Lourenço, F. (2006), *Poesia Grega de Álcman a Teócrito*. Lisboa.
Schneidewin, F.W. (1839), *Delectus poesis Graecorum elegiacae, iambicae, melicae. II et III. Poetae iambici et melici*. Göttingen.
Vetta, M.V. (1999), *ΣΥΜΠΟΣΙΟΝ. Antologia della lirica greca*. Napoli.
Voigt, E.-M. (1971), *Sappho et Alcaeus. Fragmenta*. Amsterdam.

Moschus
Bühler, W. (1960), *Die Europa des Mochos. Text, Übersetzung und Kommentar*. München.
Campbell, M. (1991), *Moschus: Europa*. Hildesheim/Zurich/New York.
Hopkinson, N. (2015), *Theocritus, Moschus, Bion*. London/Cambridge, MA.

Ovid
Alberto, P.F. (2007), *Ovídio. Metamorfoses*. (trans.). Lisboa.

Pausanias
Rocha Pereira, M.H. (1989–1990), *Pausaniae Graeciae Descriptio*. 3 vols. Lipsiae.

Pindar
Finglass, P.J. (2007b), *Pindar. Pythian Eleven*, Cambridge.
Snell, B./Maehler, H. (1987), *Pindarus. Pars I: Epinicia*. Leipzig.

Maehler, H. (1989), *Pindarus. Pars II: Fragmenta, Indices*. Leipzig.
Verity, A. (2007), *Pindar. The Complete Odes*. Oxford.

Quintus Smyrnaeus
Tyschen, T.C. (1783), *Commentatio de Quinti Smyrnaei Paralipomenis Homeri*. Göttingen.

Seneca
Frank, M. (1994), *Seneca's Phoenissae*, Leiden.

Simonides
Molyneux, J.H.M. (1992), *Simonides. A Historical Study*. Wauconda.
Poltera, O. (2008), *Simonides Lyricus. Testimonia und Fragmente*. Basel.

Sophocles
Dawe, R.D. (20062), *Sophocles*. Oedipus Rex (Cambridge Greek and Latin Classics). Cambridge.
Fialho, M.C. (2004), *Sófocles*. Electra. (trad.). Coimbra.
Fialho, M.C. (2006), *Sófocles*. Rei Édipo. (trad.). Coimbra
Finglass, P.J. (2007a), *Sophocles*. Electra, Cambridge.
Finglass, P.J. (2011), *Sophocles*. Ajax, Cambridge.
Finglass, P.J. (2018), *Sophocles*. Oedipus Rex, Cambridge.
Jebb, R.C. (1883–1894), *Sophocles. The Plays and Fragments*. 6 vols. Cambridge.
Jebb, R.C./Headlam, W.G./Pearson, A.C. (1917), *The Fragments of Sophocles*. 3 vols. Cambridge.
Lloyd-Jones, P.H.J. (1994–1996), *Sophocles*. 3 vols. London/Cambridge, MA.
Lloyd-Jones, P.H.J. (2003²), *Sophocles*. Fragments. London/Cambridge, MA.
Rocha Pereira, M.H. (2007), *Sófocles*. Antigona (trans.). Lisboa.
Ussher, R.G. (1990–2001), *Sophocles*. Philoctetes. Warminster.

Statius
Mulder, H.M. (1954), *Publii Papinii Statii Thebaidos liber secundus*. Groningen.

Stesichorus
Blomsfield, C.J. (1816), "Stesichori fragmenta", *Museum Criticum* 6: 256–272.
Curtis, P. (2011), *Stesichoros' Geryoneis*. Leiden/Boston.
Davies, M./Finglass, P.J. (2014), *Stesichorus. The Poems*. Cambridge.
Ercoles, M. (2013), *Stesicoro: Le testimonianze antiche*. Bologna.
Kleine, O.F. (1828), *Stesichori Himerensis fragmenta*. Berlin.
Schade, G. (2003), *Stesichoros. Papyrus Oxyrhynchus 2359, 3876, 2619, 2803*. Leiden/Boston/Köln.
Vürtheim, J. (1919), *Stesichoros' Fragmente und Biographie*. Leiden.

Terpander
Gostoli, A. (1990), *Terpander. Veterum testimonia collegit fragmenta edidit*. Roma.

Thucydides
Classen, J. (1963), *Thukydides*. Berlin.

Gomme, A.W./Andrewes, A./Dover, K.J. (1970), *A Historical Commentary on Thucydides*. Oxford.
Hornblower, S. (1991–2008), *A Commentary to Thucydides*. Oxford.

Virgil
Fagles, R. (2006), *Virgil. Aeneid*. London.
Fairclough, H.R./Goold, G.P. (1999¹⁵), *Virgil. Eclogues, Georgics, Aeneid Books 1–6*. London/Cambridge, MA.
Fairclough, H.R./Goold, G.P. (1999¹⁵), *Virgil. Aeneid Books 7–12*. London/Cambridge, MA.
Horsfall, N.M. (2008), *Virgil, Aeneid 2. A Commentary*. Leiden/Boston.

Studies

Achilli, A./Olivieri, A./Pala, M. et al., (2007), "Mitochondrial DNA variation of modern Tuscans supports the Near Eastern origin of Etruscans", *The American Journal of Human Genetics* 80: 759–768.
Adrados, F.R. (1978), "Propuestas para una nueva edición e interpretación de Estesícoro", *Emerita* 46: 251–299.
Agócs, P./Carey, C./Rawles, R. (eds.) (2012), *Receiving the Komos. Ancient and Modern Receptions of Victory Odes*. London.
Albuquerque, P. (2010), *Tartessos: entre mitos e representações*. Lisboa
Albuquerque, P. (2013), "Alguns pontos de interrogação sobre identidade(s) e território(s) em Tartessos", *SPAL* 22: 47–60.
Alexopoulou, M. (2009), *The Theme of Returning Home in Ancient Greek Literature. The Nostos of the epic heroes*. New York/Ontario.
Alföldi, A. (1971), *Early Rome and the Latins*. Ann Arbor.
Aluja, R. (2014), "Reexamining the Lille Stesichorus: about the Theban version of Stesich. *PMGF* 222b", in M. Reig and X. Rin (eds.), *Drama, Philosophy, Politics in Ancient Greece. Contexts and Receptions*. Barcelona, 15–38.
Anderson, M. (1997), *The Fall of Troy in Early Greek Poetry and Art*. Oxford.
Andreotti, G.C. (1991), "Estesícoro y Tartessos", *Habis* 22: 49–62.
Antonaccio, C. (1999), "Colonization and the Origins of the Hero-Cult" in Hägg (ed.), *Ancient Greek Hero-Cult*. Stockholm, 109–121.
Antonaccio, C. (2009), "The Western Mediterranean", in K. Raaflaub and H. van Wees (eds.), *A Companion to Archaic Greece*. Blackwell: 314–329.
Antonaccio, C. (2013), "Networking the Middle Ground? Greek Diaspora, tenth to fifth century BC", *Archaeological Review from Cambridge* 28: 237–251.
Antonelli, L. (1996), "Stesicoro e l'isola Sarpedonia", *Hesperìa* 7: 57–61.
Araújo, L./Rodrigues, N.S. (2006), *As comunicações na Antiguidade*. Lisboa.
Arnott, W.G. (2007), *Birds in the Ancient World from A to Z*. New York.
Arrighetti, G. (1980), "Civiltà letteraria della Sicilia antica da II séc. a.C. al IV sécolo d.C.", in E. Gabba and G. Vallet (eds.), *La Sicilia antica*. 2 vols. Napoli, 129–153.
Arrighetti, G. (1994), "Stesicoro e il suo pubblico", *MD* 32: 9–30.
Arrighetti, G. (1995), "L'arte di Stesicoro nel giudizio degli antichi", in L. Dubois (ed.), *Poésie et lyrique antiques. Actes du coloque organisé par Claude Meillier à l'Université Charles-de-Gaulle Lille III du 2 au 4 juin 1993*. Villeneuve, 55–72.

Arsenik Nabergoj, I. (2009), *Longing, Weakness, and Temptation. From Myth to Artistic Creations*. Cambridge.
Austin, N. (1994), *Helen and her Shameless Phantom*. New York/London.
Avagianou, A. (1990), *Sacred Marriage in the Rituals of Greek Religion*. New York.
Bakker, E.J. (ed.) (2017), *Authorship and Greek Song: Authority, Authenticity, and Performance*. vol. 3. Leiden/Boston.
Bakker, N. (2012), "A New Solution for the Lille Stesichorus' vv. 235–52", *ZPE* 181: 4–7.
Baron, C. (2012), *Timaeus of Tauromenium and Hellenistic Historiography*. Cambridge/New York.
Barringer, J. (1991), "Europa and the Nereids: Wedding or Funeral?", *AJA* 95: 657–667.
Barrett, W.S. (2007a) [1968], "Stesichoros and the Story of Geryon" in *Greek Lyric, Tragedy, and Textual Criticism. Collected Papers*. Oxford, 1–24.
Barrett, W.S. (2007b) [1978] "Stesichoros, *Geryoneis* SLG 11" in *Greek Lyric, Tragedy, and Textual Criticism. Collected Papers*. Oxford, 25–37.
Bassi, K. (1993), "Helen and the discourse of denial in Stesichorus' Palinode", *Arethusa* 26: 51–75.
Baudy, G. (2001), "Blindheit und Wahnsinn. Das Kultibild in poetplogischen Diskurs der Antike: Stesichoros und die homerische Helena", in G. v. Graevenitz, S. Rieger, and F. Thürlemann (eds.), *Die Unvermeidlichkeit der Bilder*. Tübingen, 31–57.
Baumann, M. (2014), "'Come now, best of painters, paint my lover' The Poetics of Ecphrasis in the *Anacreontea*", in M. Baumbach and N. Dümmler (eds.), *Imitate Anacreon! Mimesis. Poiesis and the Poetic Inspiration in the* Carmina Anacreontea. Berlin/Boston, 113–130.
Beaulieu, M.-C. (2016), *The Sea in the Greek imagination*. Pennsylvania.
Beecroft, A.J. (2006), "Stesichorus' Palinode and the revenge of the epichoric", *TAPhA* 136: 47–69.
Bergren, A. (1975), *The Etymology and Usage of Peirar in Early Greek Poetry*. Pennsylvania.
Bertini, F. (1970), "L'εἴδωλον di Elena", in AA. VV. *Myhtos. Scripta in Honorem Marii Untersteiner*. Genove, 81–96.
Bethe, J.A.E. (1891), *Thebanische Heldenleider. Untersuchungen über die Epen des tebanisch-argivischen Sagenkreises*. Leipzig.
Bethe, J.A.E. (1929²), *Homer. Dichtung und Sage. Zweiter Band. Odyssee, Kyklos, Zeitbestimmung*. Leipzig/Berlin.
Bhabha, H. (1994), *The Location of Culture*. London/New York.
Bierl, A. (2003), "'Ich aber (sage) das Schönste ist, was einer leibt!' Eine pragmatische Deutung von Sappho fr. 16 LP/V", *QUCC* 103: 91–124.
Bierl, A. (2009), *Ritual and Performativity: The chorus in Old Comedy*. Washington DC: https://chs.harvard.edu/book/bierl-anton-ritual-and-performativity-the-chorus-in-old-comedy/ [Last access 22/05/21]
Binder, G. (1964), *Die Aussetzung des Königskinde Kyros und Romulus*. Meisenheim.
Bissing, F.W. von (1951), "Naukratis", *Bulletin de la société royale d'Archéologie d' Alexandrie* 39: 32–82.
Blázquez Martínez, J.M. (1984), "Gerión y otros mitos griegos en Occidente", *Gerión* 1, 21–38.
Blondell, R. et al. (eds.) (1999), *Women on the edge. Four plays of Euripides. Alcestis, Medea, Helen, Iphigenia at Aulis*. New York/London.
Blondell, R. et al. (2010), "Refractions of Homer's Helen in Archaic Lyric", *AJPh* 131: 349–391.
Blundell, S./Williamson, M. (eds.) (1998), *The Sacred and the Feminine in Ancient Greece*. London/New York.

Boardman, J. (1977), "The Parthenon Frieze – Another Look", in U. Höckmann and A. Krug (eds.), *Festschrift für F. Brommer*. Mainz, 39–49.
Boardman, J. (1998), "Heracles' monsters: indigenous or Oriental?", in C. Bonnet, C. Jourdain-Annequin, and V. Pirenne-Delforge (eds.), *Le Bestiaire d'Héraclès. III*ème *Rencontre héracléenne. Actes du Colloque organicé à l'Université de Liège et aux Facultés Universitaires Notre-Dame de la Paix de Namur, du 14 au 16 novembre 1996*. Liège, 27–35.
Boardman, J. (1999[4]), *The Greeks Overseas: their early colonies and trade*. London.
Boardman, J. (2002), *Nostalgia. How Greeks re-created their Mythical Past*. London.
Boardman, J. (2006), "Greeks in the East Mediterranean (South Anatolia, Syria, Egypt)" in G. Tsetskhladze (ed.), *Greek Colonisation and Other Settlements Overseas*, vol I. Leiden, 507–534.
Boardman, J. (2009), Europe I, *LIMC suppl.*: 214.
Boardman, J./Hammond, N.G.L. (eds.) (2006[7]), *The Cambridge Ancient History. Vol. III, Part 3. The Expansion of the Greek World, Eighth to Sixth Centuries BC*. Cambridge.
Boedekker, D. (1993), "Hero Cult and Politics in Herodotus. The bones of Orestes", in C. Dougherty and L. Kurke (eds.), *Cultural Poetics in Archaic Greece*. Cambridge, 164–177.
Boedekker, D. (2012), "Helen and the 'I' in Greek lyric", in J. Marincola, L. Llewellyn-Jones, and C. Maciver (eds.), *Greek Notions of the Past in the Archaic and Classical Eras. History without Historians*. Edinburgh.
Bollack, J./La Combe, P.J. de/Wissman, H. (1977), *La Répilque de Jocasta. Sur les fragments d'un poème lyrique découverts à Lille*. Lille.
Bonnechere, P. (1994), *Le sacrifice humain dans la Grèce ancienne*. Liège.
Borges, C./Sampson, M.C. (2015[4]), *New Literary Papyri from the Michigan Collection*. Ann Arbour.
Bornmann, F. (1978), "Zur *Geryoneis* des Stesichoros und Pindars Herakles–Dithyrambos", *ZPE* 31: 33–35.
Bosher, K. (ed.) (2012), *Theatre Outside Athens. Drama in Sicily and South Italy*. Cambridge.
Bowie, E. (1993), "Lies, fiction, and slander in early Greek poetry", in C. Gill and T.P. Wiseman (eds.), *Lies and Fiction in the Ancient World*. Exeter, 1–37.
Bowie, E. (2007), "Early Expatriates: displacement and exile in archaic poetry", in J.F. Gaertner (ed.), *Writing Exile: The discourse of displacement in Graeco-Roman Antiquity and Beyond*. Leiden, 21–49.
Bowie, E. (2009), "Wandering poets, archaic style", in R. Hunter and I. Rutherford (eds.), *Wandering Poets in Ancient Greek Culture*. Cambridge, 105–136.
Bowie, E. (2010), "Performing and re-performing Helen: Stesichorus' 'Palinode'", in A.M. González de Tobia (ed.), *Mito y Performance, de Grecia a la Modernidad*. La Plata, 385–407.
Bowie, E. (2014), "Stesichorus' *Geryoneis*", in L. Breglia and A. Moleti (eds.), *Hespería. Tradizioni, Rotte, Paesaggi*. Paestum, 99–106.
Bowie, E. (2015), "Stesichorus at Athens", in A. Kelly and P.J. Finglass (eds.), *Stesichorus in Context*. Cambridge, 111–124.
Bowra, C.M. (1934), "Stesichorus in the Peloponnese", *CQ* 28: 115–119.
Bowra, C.M. (1961[2]), *Greek Lyric Poetry*. Oxford.
Bowra, C.M. (1963), "The two palinodes of Stesichorus", *CR* 13: 245–252.
Bowra, C.M. (1967), *A Experiência Grega*. Trans. Maria Isabel Belchior. Lisboa
Brasete, M.F. (2014), "Agamemnon na lírica arcaica grega", *Ágora* 16: 11–28.

Braun, T. (2004), "Hecateus' knowledge of the Western Mediterranean" in K. Lomas (ed.), *Greek Identity in the Western Mediterranean*. Leiden/Boston, 288–347.
Braun, T. (2006⁷), "The Greeks in Egypt" in J. Boardman and N.G.L. Hammond (eds.), *The Cambridge Ancient History. Vol. III, Part 3. The Expansion of the Greek World, Eighth to Sixth Centuries BC*. Cambridge, 32–57.
Bremer, J.N. (1980), "Stesichorus", *Lampas* 13: 355–371.
Bremer, J.N. (1987), "Stesichorus. The Lille Papyrus", in J.N. Bremer, A.M. van Erp Taalman Kip, and S.R. Slings, *Some Recently Found Greek Poems*. Leiden/New York/Copenhagen/Cologne, 128–174.
Bremmer, J. (2002), "Sacrificing a child in ancient Greece: the case of Iphigeneia", in E. Noort and E. Tigchelaar (eds.), *The Sacrifice of Isaac. The Aqedah (Genesis 22) and its Interpretations*. Leiden/Boston/Cologne, 21–43.
Brilliant, R. (1984), *Visual Narratives. Storytelling in Etruscan and Roman Art*. New York.
Brilliante, C. (2002), "L'Elena di Troia", in M. Bettini and C. Brilliante, *Il mito di Elena. Immagini e racconti dalla Grecia a oggi*. Turin, 37–186.
Brioso Sanchéz, M. (1970), *Anacreontea: Un ensayo para su datación*. Salamanca.
Brize, P. (1985), "Stesichoros und Samos. Zu einem fruharchaischen bronzeblech", *MDAI(I)* 100: 53–96.
Brize, P. (1988), "Geryoneus", *LIMC* IV/I: 186–190.
Brize, P. (1990), "L. Heracles and Geryon (Labour X)", *LIMC* V/I: 73–85.
Bruno, O. (1967), "L'epistola 92 dello Pseudo–Falaride e i *Nostoi* di Stesicoro", *Helikon* 7: 323–356.
Bücheler, F. (1865), "Philodemus Περὶ Εὐcεβίαc", *Neue Jahrbücher für Philologie und Paedagogik* 81: 334–372.
Buchner, G. (1966), "Pithekoussai. Oldest Greek Colony in the West", *Expedition* 8: 5–12.
Buren, A. W. van (1942), "News items from Rome", *AJA* 46: 428–440.
Burgess, J. (2001), *The Tradition of the Trojan War in Homer and the Epic Cycle*. Baltimore/London.
Burkert, W. (1983²), *Homo Necans. The Anthropology of ancient Greek Sacrifical Ritual and Myth*. Berkeley/Los Angeles/London.
Burkert, W. (1987), "The Making of Homer in the Sixth Century BC: Rhapsodes versus Stesichorus", in True (ed.), *Papers on Amasis Painter and his World. Colloquium sponsored by the Getty Center for the History of Art and the Humanities and Symposium sponsored by the J. Paul Getty Museum*. Malibu, 43–62.
Burkert, W. (1992), *The Orientalizing revolution*. Massachusetts/London.
Burkert, W. (1993) [1977³], *Religião grega na época clássica*. Trans. M.J. Simões Loureiro. Lisboa.
Burkert, W. (2001) [1987], "The Making of Homer in the Sixth Century BC: Rhapsodes versus Stesichorus", in *Kleine Schriften I: Homerica*. Göttingen, 189–197.
Burnett, A.P. (1979), *Catastrophe Survived: Euripides' plays of mixed reversal*. Oxford.
Burnett, A.P. (1988), "Jocasta in the West: the Lille Stesichorus", *ClAnt* 7: 107–154.
Buxton, R.G.A. (1982), *Persuasion in Greek Tragedy: a study of peitho*. Cambridge.
Buxton, R.G.A. (1994), *Imaginary Greece. The contexts of mythology*. Cambridge,
Buxton, R.G.A. (2009), *Forms of Astonishment. Greek myths of metamorphosis*. Oxford.
Cairns, D. (2016), "Metaphors for Hope in Archaic and Classical Greek Poetry", in R.R. Caston, and R.A. Kaster (eds.), *Hope, Joy, and Affection in the Classical World Emotions of the Past*. Oxford, 1–22.

Calame, C. (1977), *Les choeurs de jeunes filles en Grèce archaïque. Morphologie, fonction religieuse et sociale*. Roma.
Calame, C. (2015), *Qu'est-ce que la mythologie grecque?* Gallimard.
Cambitoglou, A./Psapalas, S. (1994), "Kyknos I", *LIMC* VII/I: 970–991.
Campbell, D. (1967), *Greek Lyric Poetry: a selection of early Greek lyric, elegiac, and iambic poetry*. London.
Campos, R. (2016), "Estesícoro e as tópicas da poesia arcaica no *Fedro*: do ídolo (eídolon) de Helena à Carta III", *Nuntius Antiquus* 12: 47–68.
Canciani, F. (1981), "Aineias" s.v. *LIMC* I.1, 381–396.
Carey, C. (1991), "The Victory ode in Performance: the case for the Chorus", *CPh* 85: 192–200.
Carey, C. (2015), "Stesichorus and the Epic Cycle" in Finglass and Kelly (eds.), *Stesichorus in Context*. Cambridge, 74–100.
Carlini, A. (1977), "Osservazioni critische al Papiro di Lille attribuito a Stesicoro", *QUCC* 25: 61–68.
Carlini, A. (1982), "Omero, Stesicoro e la «firma» di Teodoro", in AAVV, *ΑΠΑΡΧΑΙ. Nuove ricerche e studi sulla Magna Grecia e la Sicilia antica in onore di Paolo Enrico Arias*. Pisa, 631–633.
Carmignani, L. (1981), "Stile e técnica narrative in Stesicoro", in M. Fusillo (ed.), *Richerche di folologia clássica I. Studi di letteratura greca*. Pisa, 25–60.
Carpenter, T.H. (2015), "The Trojan War in early Greek art", in M. Fantuzzi and C. Tsagalis (eds.), *The Greek Epic Cycle and its Ancient Reception*. Cambridge, 178–195.
Carruesco, J. (2017), "The invention of Stesichorus: Hesiod, Helen, and the Muse", in E.J. Bakker (ed.), *Authorship and Greek Song: Authority, Authenticity, and Performance*. vol. 3, Leiden/Boston, 178–196.
Carson, A. (1982), "Wedding at Noon in Pindar's *Ninth Pythian*", *GRBS* 23: 121–128.
Carvalho, S.D.G. (2013), "O episódio das ΛΙΤΑΙ e o destino de Aquiles", *Boletim de Estudos Clássicos* 58: 75–90.
Castellaneta, S. (2005), "Note alla *Gerioneide* di Stesicoro", *ZPE* 153: 21–42.
Cataudella, Q. (1972), *Intorno ai Lirici Greci. Contributi alla critica del testo e all'interpretazione*. Roma.
Catenaccio, C. (2011), "Dream as Image and Action in Aeschylus' *Oresteia*", *GRBS* 51: 202–231.
Cavallini, E. (1999), "Ibico, fr. S166, 15–21 Dav.: la presa di Afidna?", *GIF* 51: 213–218.
Celestino, S./López-Ruíz, C. (2016), *Tartessos and the Phoenicians in Iberia*. Oxford.
Chantraine, P. (1954), "Le divin et les dieux chez Homère", in *La notion du divin depuis Homère jusqu'à Platon*. Genéve, 45–94.
Chistyakova, N.A. (1980), "Early Poetry of the Greek West", *Vetnik drevnej istorii* 154: 36–52.
Cingano, E. (1982), "Quante testimonanze sulle Palinodie di Stesicoro", *QUCC* 12: 21–33.
Cingano, E. (1990), "L'opera di Ibico e di stesicoro nella classificazione degli antichi e dei moderni", *Annnali dell'Instituto Universitario Orientale di Napoli Sezione Filologico-Letteraria* 12: 189–224.
Cingano, E. (1992), "The Death of Oedipus in the Epic tradition", *Phoenix* 46: 1–11.
Cingano, E. (1993), "Indizi di esecuzione corale in Stesicoro", in R. Pretagostini (ed.), *Tradizione e Innovazione nella cultura Greca da Omero all'Età Ellenistica. Studi In onore di B. Gentili*. Roma, 347–361.
Cingano, E. (2003), "Entre skolion et enkomion: refléxions sur le genre et la performance de la lyrique chorale grècque", in J. Jouanna and J. Leclant (eds.), *La poésie grecque antique*.

Actes du 13éme colloque de la Ville Kérylos à Beaulieu-sur-Mer, 18–19 octobre 2002. Paris, 17–45.

Cingano, E. (2004), "The Sacrificial Cut and the Sense of Honour Wronged in the Greek Epic Poetry: Thebais fr. 2–3 D.", in C. Grotanelli and L. Milano (eds.), *Food and Identity in the Ancient World*. Padua, 269–279.

Cingano, E. (2005), "A catalogue within a catalogue: Helen's suitors in the Hesiodic *Catalogue of Women* (frr. 196–204)", in R. Hunter (ed.), *The Hesiodic* Catalogue of Women. *Constructions and Reconstructions*. Cambridge, 118–152.

Cingano, E. (2015), "Oedipodea", in M. Fantuzzi and C. Tsagalis (eds.), *The Epic Cycle and its Ancient Reception: A Companion*. Cambridge, 213–225.

Clackson, J. (2012), "Oscan in Sicily", in O. Tribulato (ed.), *Language and Linguistic Contact in Ancient Sicily*. Cambridge, 132–148.

Clairmont, C. (1966), "Zum Oresteia-Krater in Boston", *Antike Kunst* 9: 125–127.

Clark, I. (1998), "The gamos of Hera. Myth and Ritual", in S. Blundell and M. Williamson (eds.), *The Sacred and the Feminine in Ancient Greece*. London/New York, 12–23.

Clay, J.S. (1993), "The Generation of Monsters in Hesiod", *CPh* 88: 105–116.

Cohen, A. (2007), "Gendering the Age Gap: Boys, Girls and Abduction in Ancient Greek Art", in A. Cohen and J. Rutter (eds.), *Constructions of Childhood in Ancient Greece and Italy*. Hesperia Supplement 41. Athens, 257–278.

Collar, A. (2009), "Network Theory and the Religious Innovation", in I. Malkin, C. Constantakopoulou, and K. Panagopoulou, K. (eds.) (2009), *Greek and Roman Networks in the Mediterranean*. London/New York, 144–157.

Colonna, A. (1963⁶), *L'antica lirica greca*. Torino.

Connelly, J.B. (1996), "Parthenon and Parthenoi: A Mythological Interpretation of the Parthenon Frieze", *AJA* 100: 53–80.

Csapo, E./Miller, M.C. (eds.) (2007), *The Origins of Theatre in Ancient Greece and Beyond*. Oxford.

Currie, B. (2015), "*Cypria*", in M. Fantuzzi and C. Tsagalis (eds.), *The Epic Cycle and its Ancient Reception: A Companion*. Cambridge, 281–305.

D'Agostino, B. (2006), "The first Greeks in Italy", in Tsetskhladze (ed.) *Greek Colonisation. An account of Greek Colonies and Other Settlements Overseas*. Leiden/Boston, 201–238.

D'Alessio, G. (2005), "The *Megalai Ehoiai*: A survey of the fragments", in R. Hunter (ed.), *The Hesiodic* Catalogue of Women. *Constructions and Reconstructions*. Cambridge, 176–216.

D'Alessio, G. (2013), "The Wanderings of the Thestorids (Stesichorus fr. 193.16–22 *PMGF*)", *ZPE* 186: 36–37.

D'Alessio, G. (2015), Review of M. Davies and P.J. Finglass (2014). *BMCR* 2015.10.40.

D'Alfonso, F. (1994), *Stesicoro e la performance. Studio sulle modalità esecutive dei carmi stesicorei*. Rome.

D'Alfonso, F. (1995), "Sacada, Xanto e Stesicoro", *QUCC* 51: 49–61.

D'Angour, A. (2013), "Music and movement in the dithyramb", in B. Kowalzig and P. Wilson (eds.), *Dithyramb in Context*. Oxford, 198–210.

D'Arms, F./Hulley, K.K. (1946), "The Oresteia-story in the *Odyssey*", *TAPhA* 77: 207–213.

Danek, G. (2015), "*Nostoi*", in M. Fantuzzi and C. Tsagalis (eds.), *The Epic Cycle and its Ancient Reception: A Companion*. Cambridge, 355–379.

D'Arms, E./Hulley, K.K. (1946), "The Oresteia story in the *Odyssey*", *TAPhA* 77: 207–13.

Davies, J.K. (1994), "The tradition of the First Sacred War", in S. Hornblower (ed.), *Greek Historiography*. Oxford, 193–212.

Davies, M.I. (1969), "Thoughts on the Oresteia before Aeschylus", *BCH* 93: 214–260.
Davies, M. (1979), *A Commentary to Stesichorus*. 2 vols. PhD Diss. Oxford.
Davies, M. (1982), "Derivative and Proverbial Testimonia concerning Stesichorus' 'Palinode'", *QUCC* 12: 7–16.
Davies, M. (1987), "Aeschylus' Clytemnestra: Sword or Axe?", *CQ* 37: 65–75.
Davies, M. (1988), "Stesichorus' Geryoneis and its Folk-Tale Origins", *CQ* 38: 277–290.
Davies, M. (1989), *The Epic Cycle*. Bristol.
Davies, M. (2010), "'sins of the fathers': omitted sacrifices and offended deities in Greek literature and Folk-tale", *Eikasmos* 21: 331–355.
Davies, M. (2014), "Epeius in the Kitchen", *Greece & Rome* 61: 91–101.
Davies, M. (2015), *The Theban Epics*. Washington DC. https://chs.harvard.edu/book/davies-malcolm-the-theban-epics/ [Last access 22/05/21]
Davison, J.A. (1968), "Stesichorus and Helen", in *From Archilochus to Pindar*. London, 196–225.
Deacy, S./Pierce, K. (eds.) (1997), *Rape in Antiquity*. Swansea/London.
Deacy, S. (1997), "The vulnerability of Athena: *parthenoi* and rape in Greek Myth", in S. Deacy and K. Pierce (eds.), *Rape in antiquity*. Swansea/London, 43–63.
De Angelis, F. (2016), *Archaic and Classical Greek Sicily: A social and Economic History*. Oxford.
Debiasi, A. (2004), *L'epica perduta. Eumelo, il Ciclo, l'occidente*. Roma.
Defradas, J. (1954), *Les thèmes de la propagande delphique*. Paris.
Degani, E./Burzacchini, G. (1977), *Lirici Greci*. Firenze.
De Kock, E.L. (1962), "The Peisandros Scholium. Its Sources, Unity, and Relationships to Euripides' *Chryssipus*", *ActaClass* 5: 15–37.
Delatte, L. (1938), "Note sur un fragment de Stésicore", *AC* 7: 23–29.
Del Corno, D. (1982), "Dreams and their interpretation in Ancient Greece", *BCIS* 29: 55–62.
Demos, M. (1997), "Stesichorus' palinode in the *Phaedrus*", *CW* 90: 235–249.
Dench, E. (1995), *From Barbarian to New Man: Greek, Roman, and modern perceptions of the central Apennines*. Oxford.
Denniston, J.D. (1954²), *The Greek Particles*. Revised by K.J. Dover. Oxford.
De Sanctis, D. (2012), "«Quando Eracle giunse ad Erytheia...» Gerione in Esiodo, Stesicoro ed Ecateo", *SCO* 57: 57–72.
Detienne, M. (1956), "La legend pythagoricienne d'Hélène", *RHR* 152: 129–152.
Deubner, L. (1942), *Oedipusprobleme*. Berlin.
Devereux, G. (1973), "Stesichorus' palinodes: two further testimonia and come comments", *RhM* 116: 206–209.
Devereux, G. (1976), *Dreams in Greek Tragedy. An ethno-psycho-analytical study*. Oxford.
Dewan, R. (2014), "A Mediterranean Mosaic: The Archaeological Evidence for Ethnic Diversity at Pithekoussai", *LUJA*: 1–28.
Dietler, M./López-Ruiz, C. (eds.) (2009), *Colonial Encounters in Ancient Iberia*, Chicago/London.
Dietrich, B.C. (1965), *Death, Fate, and the Gods*. London.
Diéz de Velasco, F. (1992), "Nessos", *LIMC* VI/I: 838–847.
Diggle, J. (1979), "Stesichorus, P.Lille 76.220", *ZPE* 35: 32.
Diggle, J. (1990), "Notes on Supplementum Lyricis Graecis", in M. Capasso et al. (eds.), *Miscellanea Papyrologica in Occasione del Bicentenario dell'Edizione della Charta Borgiana* I. Florence, 151.
Dillon, M. (2001), *Girls and Women in Classical Greek Religion*. Oxford.

Dillon, M. (2017), *Omens and Oracles: Divination in Ancient Greece*. London.
Dipla, A. (1997), "Helen, the seductress?", in O. Palagria (ed.), *Greek Offerings. Essays on Greek Art in Honour of John Boardman*. Oxford, 119–130.
Dodds, E.R. (1951), *The Greeks and the Irrational*. Berkeley.
Dodson, D.S. (2009), *Reading Dreams: an audience critical approach to the dream in the Gospel of Matthew*. London.
Dodson-Robinson, E. (2010), "Helen's 'Judgement of Paris' and Greek Marriage Ritual in Sappho 16", *Arethusa* 43: 1–20.
Dommelen, P. van (2005), "Colonial Interactions and Hybrid Practices", in G.J. Stein (ed.), *The Archaeology of Colonial Encounters: Comparative Perspectives*. New Mexico, 109–141.
Dominguéz, A.J. (2004), "Greek Identity in the Phocaean Colonies", in K. Lomas (ed.), *Greek Identity in the Western Mediterranean*. Leiden/Boston, 429–456.
Dominguéz, A.J. (2006a), "Greeks in Sicily", in G.R. Tsetskhladze (ed.), *Greek Colonisation. An Account of Greek Colonies and Other Settlements Overseas*, Leiden/Boston, 233–357.
Dominguéz, A.J. (2006b), "Greeks in the Iberian Peninsula", in G.R. Tsetskhladze (ed.), *Greek Colonisation. An Account of Greek Colonies and Other Settlements Overseas*, Leiden/Boston, 429–505.
Dominguéz, A.J. (2008), "Los contactos 'precoloniales' de griegos y fenicios en Sicilia", in S. Celestino, N. Rafel, and X.L. Armada (eds.), *Contacto cultural entre el Mediterráneo y el Atlántico (siglos XII–VIII ane). La precolonización a debate*. Madrid, 149–159.
Dominguéz, A.J. (2010), "Greeks and the Local Population in the Mediterranean: Sicily and the Iberian Peninsula", in S. Solovyov (ed.), *Archaic Greek Culture: History, Archaeology, Art & Museology*. St Petersburg, 25–36.
Doria, M. (1963), "La due Palinodie do Stesicoro", *PP* 89: 81–93.
Dougherty, C. (1993), *The Poetics of Colonization*. Oxford.
Dougherty, C. (1998), "It's murder to found a colony", in C. Dougherty and L. Kurke (eds.), *Cultural Poetics in Archaic Greece*. Oxford, 178–198.
Dougherty, C. (2001), *The Raft of Odysseus*. Oxford.
Dougherty, C./Kurke, L. (2003), *The Cultures within Ancient Greek Culture. Contact, Conflict and Collaboration*. Cambridge.
Dover, K. (1994²), *Greek Popular Morality in the Time of Plato and Aristotle*. Indianapolis.
Dowden, K. (1989), *The Death and the Maiden. Girls' Initiation Rites in Greek Mythology*. London.
Drougou, S. et al. (1997), "Kentauroi et Kentaurides", *LIMC* VIII/I: 671–721.
Due, C. (2006), *The Captive Woman's Lament in Greek Tragedy*. Austin.
Dueck, D. (2012), *Geography in Classical Antiquity*. Cambridge.
Dyer, R.R. (1967), "The iconography of the Oresteia after Aeschylus", *AJA* 71: 175–176.
Edmunds, L. (2016), *Stealing Helen: The Myth of the Abducted Wife in Comparative Perspectives*. Princeton/Oxford.
Edwards, R.B. (1979), *Kadmos the Phoenician. A study in Greek legend and the Mycenaean Age*. Amsterdam.
Elícuegi, E.G. (1998), "'*Gerioneidas*'. Desarrollo Literario Griego en contacto con el Proximo Oriente", *EM* 66: 231–256.
Elmer, D.R. (2013), *Poetics of Consent. Collective Decision-Making and the Iliad*. Baltimore.
Ercoles, M. (2008), "La cronologia di Stesicoro e l'eclisse. Testimonianze letterarie e dati scientifici", *Prometheus* 34, 35–47.

Ercoles, M. (2012), "Tra monodia e coralità: aspetti drammatici della performance di Stescioro", *Dionysus ex machina* III: 1–22.
Ercoles, M. (2014), "Stesicoro e i culti di Imera", in A. Bellia (ed.), *Musica, Culti e Riti nell' Occidente Greco*. Pisa/Roma, 67–78.
Ercoles, M. (2018), review of *Stesichorus. The Poems*. Edited with Introduction, Translation and Commentary by M. Davies and P.J. Finglass. Cambridge. Cambridge University Press, *Gnomon* 90: 1–9.
Ercoles, M./Fiorentini, L. (2011), "Giocasta tra Stesicoro (*PMGF* 222b) ed Euripide (Fenicie)", *ZPE* 179: 21–34.
Erskine, A. (2001), *Troy between Greece and Rome. Local Tradition and Imperial Power*. Oxford.
Ervin, M. (1963), "A relief pithis from Mykonos", Ἀρχαιολογικὸν Δέλτιον 18: 37–75.
Espelosín, J.L. (2009), "Iberia in the Greek Geographical Imagination", in M. Dietler and C. López-Ruiz (eds.), *Colonial Encounters in Ancient Iberia*, Chicago/London, 281–298.
Fabretti, R. (1683), *De columna Traiani syntagma. Accesserunt explicatio veteris tabellae anaglyphae Homeri Iliadem atque ex Stesichoro Arctino et Lesche Ilii excidium continentis et emissarii lacus Fucini descriptio*. Rome.
Fantuzzi, M./Tsagalis, C. (eds.) (2015), *The Epic Cycle and its Ancient Reception: A Companion*. Cambridge.
Farina, A. (1968), *Studi Stesicorei. Parte prima: il mito di Elena*. Napoli.
Ferrari, G. (2000), "The Ilioupersis in Athens", *HSCP* 100: 119–150.
Ferrari, W. (1938), "L'Orestea di Stesicoro", *Athenaeum* 16: 1–37.
Ferreira, L.N. (2008a), "Io e Marpessa: uma análise dos ditirambos XIX e XX de Baquílides", *Humanitas* 60: 57–73.
Ferreira, L.N. (2008b), "O canto de Arion de Metimna (fr. adesp. 939 *PMG*)", *Boletim de Estudos Clássicos* 49: 21–25.
Ferreira, L.N. (2013), *Mobilidade Poética na Grécia Antiga. Uma leitura da obra de Simónides*. Coimbra.
Fialho, M.C. (2007), "O Deus de Delfos na *Electra* de Sófocles", *Minerva* 20: 39–52.
Fialho, M.C./Coelho, J. (2012), "Eurípides, *Hécuba*. Introdução, tradução do grego e notas", in AAVV, *Eurípides*, vol. 2. Lisboa, 175–254.
Fialho, M.C./Silva, M.F.S./Rocha Pereira, M.H. (2005), *Génese e Consolidação da Ideia de Europa*. Coimbra.
Finglass, P.J./Kelly, A. (eds.) (2015), *Stesichorus in Context*. Cambridge.
Finglass, P.J. (2006), "The Ending of *Iliad 7*", *Philologus* 150: 187–197.
Finglass, P.J. (2012), "Ethnic Identity in Stesichorus", *ZPE* 182: 39–44.
Finglass, P.J. (2013a), "Stesichorus and the Leaping Lot", *ZPE* 184: 10.
Finglass, P.J. (2013b), "Demophon in Egypt", *ZPE* 184: 37–50.
Finglass, P.J. (2013c), "How Stesichorus Began His *Sack of Troy*", *ZPE* 185: 1–17.
Finglass, P.J. (2013d), "Thucydides and Hesiod", *QUCC* 105: 161–169.
Finglass, P.J. (2014a), "Introduction", in M. Davies and P.J. Finglass, *Stesichorus: The Poems*. Cambridge, 1–91.
Finglass, P.J. (2014b), "Stesichorus and the West", in L. Breglia and A. Moleti (eds.), *Hesperìa. Tradizione, Rotte, Paesaggi*. Paestum, 29–34.
Finglass, P.J. (2014c), "Thebais?", in M. Davies and P.J. Finglass, *Stesichorus: the Poems*. Cambridge, 358–394.
Finglass, P.J. (2014d), "Hermes, father of the Arabs", *Eikasmos* 25: 181–183.

Finglass, P.J. (2015a), "Stesichorus, master of narrative", in P.J. Finglass and A. Kelly (eds.), *Stesichorus in Context*. Cambridge, 83–97.
Finglass, P.J. (2015b), "Simias and Stesichorus", *Eikasmos* 26: 197–202.
Finglass, P.J. (2015c), "Iliou persis", in M. Fantuzzi and C. Tsagalis (eds.), *The Epic Cycle and its Ancient Reception: A Companion*. Cambridge, 344–354.
Finglass, P.J. (2016), "Statius and Stesichorus", *Ariadne* 22: 45–56.
Finglass, P.J. (2017a), "Dancing with Stesichorus", in L. Gianvittorio (ed.), *Choreutika: Performing Dance in Archaic and Classical Greece*. Pisa/Roma, 67–89.
Finglass, P.J. (2017b), "Ibycus or Stesichorus? S166 Page", *ZPE* 202: 19–28.
Finglass, P.J. (2018a), "Gazing at Helen with Stesichorus", in E. Bakola et al. (eds.), *Gaze, Vision, and Visuality in Ancient Greek Literature*. Berlin/Boston, 140–159.
Finglass, P.J. (2018b), "Stesichorus and Greek tragedy", in R. Andújar, T. Coward, and T. Hadjimichael (eds.), *Paths of Song: the Lyric Dimension of Greek Tragedy*. Berlin/Boston, 19–38.
Finglass, P.J. (2020), "Phaedra between Homer and Sophocles: the Stesichorean connexion", in P. Cecconi and C. Tornau (eds.), *Städte und Stadtstaaten zwischen Mythos, Literatur und Propaganda*. Berlin/Boston, 181–190.
Finglass, P.J. (forthcoming), "Editing Stesichorus", in M. Alexandrou, C. Carey, and G. D'Alessio (eds.), *Song Regained: Working with Greek Poetic Fragments*. Berlin/Boston.
Finkelberg, M. (2012), "Oral Formulaic Theory and the Individual Poet", in F. Montanari, A. Rengakos, and C. Tsagalis (eds.), *Homeric Contexts. Neoanalysis and the Interpretation of Oral Poetry*. Berlin/Boston, 73–82.
Fisher, N./Van Wees, H. (eds.), (1998), *Archaic New Approaches and New Evidence*. London/Swansea.
Fletcher, J. (1999), Review of Karydas (1999), *BMCR* 1999.05.19.
Fogelmark, S. (1975), *Chyrsaigis*, IG *XII*, 611. Lund.
Foley, H.P. (1982), "Sacrifice and Marriage in Euripides' *Iphigenia at Aulis*", *Arethusa* 15: 159–180.
Fowler, R.L. (1998), "Genealogical thinking, Hesiod's *Catalogue*, and the creation of the Hellenes", *PCPS* 44: 1–19.
Fraenkel, E. (1963), "Zu den *Phoenissen* des Euripides", *Sitzungsberichte der Philosophisch-philologischen und der Historischen Klasse des Königlich Bayerische Akademie der Wissenschaften* 1.
Franco, C. (2014), *Shameless. The canine and the feminine in Ancient Greece*, Oakland.
Franzen, C. (2009), "Sympathizing with the monster: making sense of colonization in Stesichorus' *Geryoneis*", *QUCC* 92, 55–72.
Frazer, J. (1890), *The Golden Bough*. London.
Frenzel, E. (1999), *Die Motive der Weltliteratur: ein Lexicon dichtungsgeschichtlicher Längsschmitte*. Kröner.
Friedrich, P. (2001), "Lyric Epiphany", *Language in Society* 30: 217–247.
Friedrich, R. (2007), *Formular Economy in Homer. The Poetry of the Breaches*. Stuttgart.
Führer, R. (1971), "Nachträge zu P. Oxy. 2803 (Stesichoros)", *ZPE* 8: 251–254.
Führer, R. (1977), review of *Supplementum Lyricis Graecis*, *GGA*: 1–44.
Furtwängler, A. (1900), *Die Antiken Gemmen*. Leipzig.
Gaertner, J.F. (ed.), (2007), *Writing Exile: The discourse of displacement in Graeco-Roman Antiquity and Beyond*. Leiden.
Gagé, J. (1950), *Huit recherches sur les origines italiques et romaines*. Paris.

Gagné, R. (2013), *Ancestral Fault in Ancient Greece*. Cambridge.
Galinsky, J.K. (1971²), *Aeneas, Sicily, and Rome*. New Jersey.
Gallavotti, C. (1977), "Um poemetto citadorico di Stesicoro nel quadro della cultura Soceliota", *BANL* 25: 1–30.
Gantz, T. (1993), *Early Greek Myth. A Guide to Literary and Artistic Sources*. Baltimore/London.
Garland, R. (2014), *Wandering Greeks. The Ancient Diaspora from the Age of Homer to the Death of Alexander the Great*. Princeton.
Geel, J. (1839), "De Stesichori Palinodia", *RhM* 6: 1–15.
Gentili, B. (1976), Review of D.L. Page, *Poetae Melici Graeci, Lyrica Graeca Selecta*, and *Supplementum Lyricis Graecis*, *Gnomon* 48: 740–751.
Gentili, B. (1988), *Poetry and Its Public in Ancient Greece*. Baltimore/London.
Gerber, D. (1970), *Euterpe: an anthology of early Greek lyric, elegiae, and iambic poetry*. Amsterdam.
Gigante, M.G. (1987), "La civiltà letteraria dell'antica Calabria", in S.S. Settis (ed.), *La Calabria antica*. Roma/Reggio, 527–564.
Giglioli, G.Q. (1941), "Osservazioni e monumenti relativi alla legenda delle origini di Roma", *BMIR* 12: 3–16.
Glynn, R. (1981), "Heracles, Nereus and Triton: a study of iconography in sixth century Athens", *AJA* 85: 121–132.
Gomme, A.W. (1913), "The legend of Cadmus and the Logographoi", *JHS* 33: 223–245.
González de Canales, F./Serrano, L./Llompart, J. (2006), "The Pre-colonial Phoenician *Emporium* in Huelva ca 900–770 BC", *BABesch* 81: 13–29.
González de Canales, F./Serrano, L./Llompart, J. (2008), "The *Emporium* of Huelva and Phoenician chronology: present and future possibilities", in C. Sagona (ed.), *Beyond the Homeland: Makers in Phoenician Chronology*. Leuven, 631–655.
González de Canales, F./Serrano, L./Llompart, J. (2010), "Tarshish and the United Monarchy of Israel", *Ancient Near Eastern Studies* 47: 137–164.
Gostoli, A. (1978), "Some Aspects of the Theban Myth in the Lille Stesichorus", *GRBS* 19: 23–27.
Gostoli, A. (1998), "Stesicoro e la tradizione citarodica", *QUCC* 59: 145–152.
Graham, A.J. (1960), "The authenticity of τῶν οἰκιστηρων of Cyrene", *JHS* 80: 94–111.
Graham, A.J. (1971), "Patterns in Early Colonisation", *JHS* 91: 35–47.
Greco, E. (2006), "Greek Colonisation in Southern Italy: A methodological essay", in G.R. Tsetskhladze (ed.), *Greek Colonisation. An Account of Greek Colonies and Other Settlements Overseas*, Brill, Leiden/Boston, 169–200.
Green, J.R. (2007), "Let's hear it for the Fat Man: Padded Dancers and the pre-history of Drama", in E. Csapo and M.C. Miller (eds.), *The Origins of Theatre in Ancient Greece and Beyond*. Cambridge, 96–107.
Griffith, M. (1983), "Personality in Hesiod", *CA* 2: 37–65.
Grossardt, P. (2012) *Stesichoros zwischen kultischer Praxis, myhtischer Tradition und eigenem Kunstanspruch. Zur Behandlung des Helenamythos im Werk des dichters aus Himera (mit einem Anhang zum Motivkomplex von Beldung und Heilung in der internationalen Erzältradition)*. Tübingen.
Gruen, E.S. (1992), *Culture and National Identity in Republican Rome*. New York.
Gruen, E.S. (2011), *Rethinking the Other in Antiquity*. Princeton.
Gruppe, O. (1906), *Grieschische Mythologie und Reliongsgeschichte*. München.
Gumpert, M. (2001), *Grafting Helen: The Abduction of the Classical Past*. Wisconsin.

Hall, E. (1989), *Inventing the Barbarian. Greek self-definition through Tragedy.* Oxford.
Hall, E. (1996), "When a Myth is not a Myth? Bernal's 'ancient model'", in M.R. Lefkowitz and G. Rogers (eds.), *Black Athena Revisited.* North Carolina, 333–348.
Hall, J. (1997), *Ethnic Identity in Greek Antiquity.* Cambridge.
Hall, J. (2002), *Hellenicity: Between Ethnicity and Culture.* Chicago.
Hall, J. (2012), "Early Greek Settlement in the West: the limits of colonialism", in K. Bosher (ed.), *Theatre Outside Athens. Drama in Greek Sicily and South Italy.* Cambridge, 19–34.
Halliwell, S. (2000), "The subjection of *muthos* to *logos*: Plato's citations of the poets", *CQ* 50: 94–112.
Hamiaux, M. (2001²), *Les sculptures Grecques 1.* Paris.
Hansen, M.H./Nielsen, T.H. (2004), *An Inventory of Archaic and Classical Poleis.* Oxford.
Hansen, M.H. (2006), "Emporion", in Tsetskhladze (ed.), *Greek Colonisation. An account of Greek Colonies and Other Settlements Overseas.* Leuven, 1–40.
Hansen, W. (2002), *Ariadne's Thread: A guide to International Tales Found in Classical Literature.* Ithaca/London.
Harrison, R.P. (1992), *Forests: the shadow of civilization.* Chicago.
Harvey, F.D. (1967), "Oxyrrhynchus Papyrus 2390 and Early Spartan History", *JHS* 87: 62–73.
Haslam, M. (1974), "Stesichorean Metre", *QUCC* 17: 7–57.
Haslam, M. (1978), "The versification of the new Stesichorus (*P. Lille* 76abc)", *GRBS* 19: 29–57.
Haslam, M. (1990), "3876. Stesichorus, various poems?", *The Oxyrhynchus Papyri* 57: 1–45.
Hawes, G. (ed.) (2017), *Myths on the Maps. The storied landscapes of Ancient Greece.* Oxford.
Hedreen, G. (1995), *Silens in Attic Black-figure vase-painting: myth and performance.* Michigan.
Hedreen, G. (1996), "Image, text, and story in the recovery of Helen", *CAnt* 15: 153–184.
Hedreen, G. (2001), *Capturing Troy. The Narrative Functions of Landscape in Archaic and Early Classical Greek Art.* Ann Arbor.
Hellmann, M.-C. (2002), *L'architecture Grecque.* Paris.
Herington, J. (1985), *Poetry into Drama. Early Greek Tragedy and Greek Poetic Tradition.* Berkeley/Los Angeles.
Hermary, A./Jacquemin, A. (1988), "Hephaistos", *LMIC IV*: 627–654.
Higbie, C. (1995), *Heroes' Names, Homeric Identities.* New York/London.
Hölscher, U. (1967), "Die Atridensage in der *Odyssee*", in H. Meller and B. von Wiese (eds.), *Festschrift für Richard Alewyn.* Cologne, 1–16.
Hopman, M.G. (2012), *Scylla. Myth, Metaphor, and Paradox.* Cambridge.
Horden, P./Kinoshita, S. (eds.) (2014), *A Companion to Mediterranean History.* West Sussex.
Horden, P./Purcell, N. (2000), *The Corrupting Sea. A Study of Mediterranean History.* London.
Hornblower, S. (2004), *Thucydides and Pindar. Historical Narrative and the World of Epinikian Poetry.* Oxford.
Hornblower, S. (2011⁴), *The Greek World.* London.
Hornblower, S./Biffis, G. (eds.) (2018), *The Returning Hero: nostoi and Traditions of Mediterranean Settlement.* Oxford.
Horsfall, N.M. (1979), "Stesichorus at Bovillae?", *JHS* 99: 26–48.
Howald, E. (1939), "Die Sieben gegen Theben", *Rektoratsrede.* Zurich.
Howland, R.L. (1955), "Epeius. Carpenter and Athlete", *PCPS* 3: 15–16.
Hunter, R. (2015), "Sweet Stesichorus. Theocritus 18 and the *Helen* revisited", in P.J. Finglass and A. Kelly (eds.), *Stesichorus in Context.* Cambridge, 145–163.
Hunter, R./Rutherford, I. (eds.) (2009), *The Wandering Poets in Ancient Greek Culture. Travel, Locality and Panhellenism.* Cambridge.

Hutchinson, G.O. (2001), *Greek Lyric Poetry. A Commentary on Selected Larger Pieces*. Oxford.
Icard-Gianolio, N. (2009), "Helene", *LIMC* Suppl: 238–240.
Ieranò, G. (1997), *Il ditirambo di Dioniso. Le testimonianze antiche*. Pisa.
Ingoglia, C. (2000), "Il cavalo di Troia su una *kotyle* corinzia da Gela e nell' *Ilioupersis* di Arctino", *QUCC* 65: 7–14.
Irvine, J. (1997), "Keres in Stesichorus' *Geryoneis*: P. Oxy 2617 (a)–(b) = SCG 21 reconsidered", *ZPE* 115: 37–46.
James, P. (2003), "Naukratis revisited", *Hyperboreus* 9: 235–264.
Jebb, R.C. (1894), *The Growth and Influence of Classical Greek Poetry. Lectures delivered in 1892 on the Percy Turnbull Memorial Foundation in the Johns Hopkins University*. Boston/New York.
Jenkins, I. (2001), "Archaic *Kouroi* in Naucratis: The Case for Cypriot Origin", *AJA* 150: 163–179.
Jenner, E.A.B (1986), "Further Speculations on Ibycus and the epinician ode: S 220, S 176, and the 'Bellerophon' ode", *BICS* 33: 59–66.
Jentel, M.O. (1997), "Skylla", *LIMC* VIII/I: 1137–1145.
Jesus, C.A.M. (2009), "Grinaldas de violetas. Epítetos derivados de *ION* e suas valências na poesia grega", *Humanitas* 61: 31–57.
Jesus, C.A.M. (2017), *Poesia e Iconografia. Mito, desporto e imagem nos epinícios de Baquílides*. Porto.
Johnston, S.I. (1999), *Restless Dead. Encounters between the living and the dead in Ancient Greece*. Berkeley/Los Angeles/London.
Johnston, S.I. (2008), *Ancient Greek Divination*. Malden, MA/Oxford/Chichester.
Jourdain-Annequin, C. (1989), "De l'espace de la cité à l'espace symbolique. Héraclès en Occident", *DHA* 15.1, 31–48.
Kahil, L. (1988), "Helene" *LIMC* iv/1: 498–563.
Karydas, H.P. (1999), *Eurycleia and her Successors: Female Figures of Authority in Greek Poetics*. Lanham/New York/Boulder/Oxford.
Kazansky, N.N. (1976), "Načalo poemy Stesichora 'Razrušenie Troi'", *Vestnik Leningradskogo Universiteta*.
Kazansky, N.N. (1997), *Principles of the Reconstruction of a Fragmentary Text (New Stesichorean Papyri)*. St. Petersburg.
Keenan, V.L. (2016), "Artemidorus and the Dream Gates: Myth, Theory, and the restoration of Liminality", *AJP* 137: 189–218.
Keydell, R. (1935), "Die Dichter mit Namen Peisandros", *Hermes* 70: 301–311.
Kelly, A. (2007), "Stesikhoros and Helen", *MH* 64: 1–21.
Kelly, A. (2008), "The Ending of *Iliad* 7: a response", *Philologus* 152: 5–17.
Kelly, A. (2015a), "Stesichorus' Homer", in A. Kelly and P. Finglass (eds.), *Stesichorus in Context*. Cambridge, 21–44.
Kelly, A. (2015b), "*Ilias Parva*", in M. Fantuzzi and C. Tsagalis (eds.), *The Epic Cycle and its Ancient Reception: A Companion*. Cambridge, 318–343.
Kessels, A.H.M. (1978), *Studies on the Dream in Greek Literature*. Utrecht.
Keuls, E.C. (1974), *The Water-Carriers in Hades: A Study of Catharsis through toil in Classical antiquity*. Amsterdam.
Kim, H.J. (2009), *Ethnicity and Foreigners in Ancient Greece and China*. London.
Kinoshita, S. (2014), "Mediterranean Literature", in P. Horden and S. Kinoshita (eds.), *A Companion to Mediterranean History*. West Sussex, 314–344.
Kivilo, M. (2010), *Early Greek Poets' Lives. The Shaping of the Tradition*. Leiden/Boston.

Konstan, D. (2001), *Pity Transformed*. London.
Kossatz-Deissman, A. (1981), "Amyetoi", *LIMC* I/I: 736–738.
Kowalzig, B. (2007), *Singing for the Gods. Performances of Myth and Ritual in Archaic and Classical Greece*. Oxford.
Kowalzig, B. (2013), "Dancing with dolphins in the wine-dark sea. Dithyramb and social change in the archaic Mediterranean", in B. Kowalzig and P. Wilson (eds.), *Dithyramb in Context*, Oxford, 31–58.
Kowalzig, B./Wilson, P. (eds.) (2013), *Dithyramb in Context*. Oxford.
Krauskopf, I. (1988), "Helene", *LIMC* IV: 498–572.
Krauskopf, I./Touchefeu, O. (1988), "Agamemnon", *LMIC* I: 257–277.
Kron, G. (2013), "Fleshing out the Demography of Etruria", in J.M. Turfa (ed.), *The Etruscan World*. New York, 56–75.
Kron, U. (1981), "Aithra I", *LIMC* I/I: 420–431.
Krummen, E. (2010), "Alcman, Stesichorus and Ibycus", in F. Buddleman (ed.), *The Cambridge Companion to Greek Lyric*. Cambridge, 189–203.
Kurke, L. (2000), "The strangeness of 'song-culture': Archaic Greek Poetry", in O. Taplin (ed.), *Literature in the Greek World*. Oxford, 40–69.
Lamari, A.A. (2010), *Narrative, Intertext, and Space in Euripides'* Phoenissae. Berlin/New York.
Lane Fox, R. (2008), *Travelling Heroes. Greeks and their myths in the Epic Age of Homer*. London.
Lattimore, R. (1964), *Story Patterns in Greek Tragedy*. Michigan.
Laurens, A. (1988), "Hekabe", *LIMC* IV/I: 473–481.
Lazzeri, M. (2008), *Studi sulla* Gerioneida *di Stesicoro*. Naples.
Lebeck, A. (1971), *The* Oresteia: *a study in Language and Structure*. Washington DC.
Lefkowitz, M. (1986), *Women in Greek Myth*. London.
Lefkowitz, M. (1991), *First Person Fictions: Pindar's Poetics I*. Oxford.
Lefkowitz, M. (1993), "Seduction and Rape in Greek Culture", in A. Laiou (ed.), *Consent and Coercion to Sex and Marriage in Ancient and Medieval Societies*. Washington, 17–37.
Lefkowitz, M. (2012²), *The Lives of Greek Poets*. Baltimore.
Lehmann-Hartleben, K. (1943), "Cyriacus of Ancona, Aristotle, and Teiresias in Samothrace", *Hesperia* 12: 115–134.
Lerza, P. (1978), "Su un frammento della *Gerioneide* di Stesicoro", *A&R* 23: 83–87.
Lesky, A. (1967), "Die Schuld der Klytaimnestra", *WS* 80: 5–21.
Lesky, A. (1972), *Die tragische Dichtung der Hellenen*. Göttingen.
Ley, G.L. (1993), "Monody, choral song and Athenian festival performance", *Maia* 45: 105–124.
Lloyd-Jones, H. (1958), review of *The Oxyrhynchus Papyri* 23 (1956), *CR* 8: 16–22.
Lloyd-Jones, H. (1980), "Stesicoro", in A. Stazio, M.L. Napolitano, and A. Pelosi (eds.), *L'epos Greco in occidente. Atti del diciannovesimo convegno di studi sulla Magna Grecia, Taranto, 7–11 ottobre 1979*. Taranto, 9–28.
Lloyd-Jones, H. (2002), "Curses and Divine Anger in Early Greek Epic: The Pisander scholion", *CQ* 52: 1–14.
Lomas, K. (ed.) (2004), *Greek Identity in the Western Mediterranean*. Leiden/Boston.
Lobel, E. (1967), "2619. Stesichorus, Ἰλίου πέρcιc?", *The Oxyrhynchus Papyri* 32: 34–55.
Lobel, E. (1968a), "2735 Choral Lyric", *The Oxyrhynchus Papyri* 35: 9–32.
Lobel, E. (1968b), "A commentary on a play of Aristophanes", *The Oxyrhynchus Papyri* 35: 39–45.
Lobel, E. (1971), "2803. Stesichorus?", *The Oxyrhynchus Papyri* 37: 3–11.

López Monteagudo, San Nicolas Pedraz (1991). "La iconografia del rapto de Europa en el Mediterraneo Occidental", *L'Africa Romana* VIII: 1005–1018.
Loraux, N. (1987), *Tragic Ways to Kill a Woman*. Transl. A. Forster. Cambridge, MA/London.
Lourenço, F. (2001), "An interpolated song in Euripides? Helen 229–52", *JHS* 120: 132–139.
Lourenço, F. (2007), "Helena na Epopeia Homérica", in J.V. Bañuls, M.C. Fialho, A. López, F. De Martino, C. Morenilla, A. Pociña Pérez, M.F. Silva (eds.), *O Mito de Helena de Tróia à Actualidade*. vol. 1. Coimbra/Foggia/Granada/Valencia, 47–53.
Lourenço, F. (2009), "Lírica Coral e Monódica: uma problemática revisitada", *Humanitas* 61: 19–29.
Lowe, N. (2006), "Epinikian Eidography", in S. Hornblower and C. Morgan (eds.), *Pindar's Poetry, Patrons, and Festivals. From Archaic Greece to the Roman Empire*. Oxford, 167–176.
Maas, P. (1929), *Stesicoros*. *RE* III A/2: 2458–2462.
Macedo, J.M. (2016), "Two divine epithets in Stesichorus: Poseidon ἱπποκέλευθος and Aphrodite ἠπιόδωρος", *CPh* 111: 1–18.
MacInnes, D. (2007), "Gainsaying the Prophet: Jocasta, Teiresias, and the Lille Stesichorus", *QUCC* 86: 95–108.
Maingon, A.D. (1979), *Stesichorus and the epic tradition*. PhD diss. Vancouver.
Maingon, A.D. (1980), "Epic Convention in Stesichorus' Geryoneis: SLG S15", *Phoenix* 34: 99–107.
Maingon, A.D. (1989), "Form and content in the Lille Stesichorus", *QUCC* 31: 31–56.
Malkin, I. (1994), *Myth and Territory in the Spartan Mediterranean*. Cambridge.
Malkin, I. (1998), *The Returns of Odysseus*. Berkeley/Los Angeles/London.
Malkin, I. (2003), "'Tradition' in Herodotus: The Foundation of Cyrene", in P. Derow and R. Parker (eds.), *Herodotus and his World: Essays from a conference in memory of George Forrest*. Oxford, 153–170.
Malkin, I. (2004), "Postcolonial Concepts in Ancient Greek Colonization", *MLQ* 65: 341–364.
Malkin, I. (2011), *A Small Greek World*. Oxford.
Malkin, I./Constantakopoulou, C./Panagopoulou, K. (eds.) (2009), *Greek and Roman Networks in the Mediterranean*. London/New York.
Maltomini, F. (1985), "Stesicoro, P.Lille 76.220", *ZPE* 58: 9–10.
Mancuso, U. (1911), "La "Tabula Iliaca" del Museo Capitolino", *Atti della Accademia dei Lincei. Memorie: Classe di scienze morali, storiche e filologiche ser.* 5 vol. 14 fasc. 8: 661–731.
Mancuso, U. (1912), *La lirica classica greca in Sicilia e nella Magna Grecia. Contributo alla storia della civiltà ellenica in Occidente*. Pisa.
March, J.P. (1987), *The Creative Poet. Studies on the Treatment of Myths in Greek Poetry*. London.
Marconi, C. (2007), *Temple decoration and Cultural Identity in Archaic Greek World. The Metopes of Selinus*. Cambridge.
Marks, J. (2008), *Zeus in the* Odyssey. Hellenic Studies Series 31. Washington DC. https://chs.harvard.edu/book/marks-j-zeus-in-the-odyssey/ [Last access 22.05.21]
Marques, S.H. (2014), "Sonho e persuasão na épica homérica", *Humanitas* 66: 23–33.
Martin, R.P. (2007), "The Voices of Jocasta", in *XI International Meeting on Ancient Greek Drama. Theban Cycle*. Delphi, 319–328.
Martinéz, J.L. (1974), "Estesícoro de Himera", *Durius* 2: 311–342.
Massimilla, G. (1990a), "L'Elena di Stesicoro quale premessa ad una ritrattazione", *PP* 45: 370–381.

Massimilla, G. (1990b), "Un Sogno di Giocasta in Stesicoro?", *PP* 45: 191–199.
Maurolico, F.M. (1568), *Sicanicarum rerum compendium*. Messina.
McClure, L. (2006), "Maternal Authority and Heroic Disgrace in Aeschylus' *Persae*", *TAPhA* 136: 71–97.
McInerney, J. (ed.) (2014), *A Companion to Ethnicity in the Ancient Mediterranean*. Blackwell.
McLeod, W. (1966), "Studies on Panyassis – An Heroic Poet of the Fifth century", *Phoenix* 20: 95–110.
Meiller, C. (1976), "Callimaque (P.L. 76b, 78abc, 82, 84, 111c). Stésichore (?) (P.L. 76 abc)", *Études sur l'Égypte et le Soudan anciens = Cahiers de recherches de l'Institut de papyrologie et d'égyptologie de Lille* 4: 255–360.
Meiller, C. (1978), "Stésichore, *P.L.* 76 a (+ *P.L.* 73). Quelques conjectures possibles", *SCO* 28: 35–47.
Mele, A. (2014), "A proposito di Hesperia", in L. Breglia and A. Moleti (eds.) *Hesperìa. Tradizione, Rotte, Paesaggi*. Paestum, 35–52.
Mills, S. (1997), *Theseus, Tragedy, and Athenian Empire*. Oxford.
Mitchell, L.G. (2007), *Panhellenism and the Barbarian in Archaic and Classical Greece*. Swansea.
Montiglio, S. (2005), *Wandering in Ancient Culture*. Chicago/London.
Morakis, A. (2011), "Thucydides and the Character of Greek Colonisation in Sicily", *CQ* 61: 460–492.
Morales, H. (2016), "Rape, Violence, Complicity: Colluthus' Abduction of Helen", *Arethusa* 49: 61–92.
Morel, J.P. (2014), "Eldorado. Les Phocéens et Tartessus", *Hesperìa* 16: 107–130.
Morenilla, C./Bañuls, J.V (1991), "La Propuesta de Eurigania (P. Lille Estesícoro)", *Habis* 22: 63–80.
Morgan, K. (2012), "A prolegomenon to the performance in the West", in K. Bosher (ed.), *Theatre outside Athens. Drama in Greek Sicily and South Italy*. Cambridge, 35–55.
Morgan, L. (1988), *The Miniature Wall Paintings of Thera. A Study in Aegean Culture and Iconography*. Cambridge.
Morrison, A.D. (2007), *The Narrator in Archaic Greek and Hellenistic Poetry*. Cambridge.
Morrison, J.V. (1997), "*Kerostasia*, the Dictates of Fate, and the Will of Zeus in the *Iliad*", *Arethusa* 30: 276–296.
Morton, J. (2001), *The role of the Physical Environment in Ancient Greek Seafaring*. Leiden/Boston/Köln.
Mossman, J. (1985), *Wild Justice. A study of Euripides'* Hecuba. Bristol.
Most, G. (1994), "Simonides' Ode to Scopas in Contexts", in I.J.F. De Jong and J.P. Sullivan (eds.), *Modern Critical Theory and Classical Literature*. Leiden, 127–152.
Most, G. (ed.) (1997), *Collecting Fragments = Fragmente Sammeln*. Göttingen.
Mueller-Goldingen, C. (1985), *Untersuchungen Zu den Phönissen des Euripides*. Stuttgart.
Mueller-Goldingen, C. (2000), "Tradition und Innovation. Zu Stesichoros' Umgang mit dem Mythos", *AC* 69: 1–19.
Müller, A. (2010), *Die Carmina Anacreontea und Anakreon: ein literarisches Generationenverhältnis*. Tübingen.
Müller, K.O. (1840), *History of the Literature of ancient Greece*. London.
Nagy, G. (1990), *Greek Mythology and Poetics*. Ithaca/New York/London.

Nagy, H. (2011), "Etruscan votive terracottas and their archaeological contexts" in N.T. de Grummond and I. Edlund-Berry (eds.), *The Archaeology of Sanctuaries and Ritual in Etruria*. Rhode Island, 113–125.

Nakassis, D. (2004), "Gemination at the Horizons: East and Westin the Mythical Geography of Archaic Greek Epic", *TAPhA* 134: 215–233.

Neitzel, H. (1979), "Artemis und Agamemnon in der Parodos des Aischyleischen *Agamemnon*", *Hermes* 107: 10–32.

Neri, C. (2008), "Trattativa contro il fato (Stesich. *PMGF* 222b, 176–231)", *Eikasmos* 19: 11–44.

Neschke, A. (1986), "L' *Orestie* de Stésichore et la tradition littéraire du mythe des Atrides avant Eschyle", *AC* 55: 283–301.

Nesselrath, H.-G. (2005), "'Where the Lord of the Sea Grants Passage to Sailors through the Deep-Blue Mere No More': The Greeks and the Western Seas", *Greece & Rome* 52.2, 153–171.

Niels, J. (1987), "Theseus" [exp. Section VIII by Susan Woodford], *LIMC* VII/I: 922–951.

Nienmeyer, M. (2006), "The Phoenicians in the Mediterranean: between expansion and presence", in G. Tsetskhladze (ed.), *Greek Colonisation. An account of Greeks colonies and other settlements overseas*. Leiden, 143–168.

Noussia-Fantuzzi, M. (2013), "A Scenario for Stesichorus' portrayal of the Monster Geryon in the *Geryoneis*", *TC* 5: 234–259.

Noussia-Fantuzzi, M. (2015), "The Epic Cycle, Stesichorus and Ibycus", in M. Fantuzzi and C. Tsagalis (eds.), *The Epic Cycle and its Ancient Reception: A Companion*. Cambridge, 430–449.

Obbink, D. (2014), "Two New Poems by Sappho", *ZPE* 189: 32–49.

O'Brien, M.J. (1988), "Pelopid History and the plot of *Iphigenia in Tauris*", *CQ* 38: 98–115.

Oliveira, M.L.F. (1967), "Musas e Violetas em Poetas Gregos", *Euphrosyne* 1: 151–157.

Olson, S.D. (1995), *Blood and Iron: Stories and Storytelling in Homer's* Odyssey. Leiden/New York/Köln.

Ornaghi, M. (2014), "Un poeta senza età. Note di cronografia stesicorea (e alcmânico-saffico-simonidea)", *AOFL* 9: 32–96.

Osborne, R. (1998), "Early Greek Colonization? The nature of Greek Settlement in the West", in N. Fisher and Van Wees (eds.), *Archaic New Approaches and New Evidence*, London/Swansea, 255–269.

Osborne, R. (2009a), *Greece in the Making. 1200–479 BC*. London/New York.

Osborne, R. (2009b), "What travelled with Greek Pottery?" in I. Malkin, C. Constantakopolou, and K. Panagopoulou (eds.), *Greek and Roman Networks in the Mediterranean*. London/New York, 83–93.

Owen, S. (1998), Review to N. Fisher and Van Wees (eds.), *Archaic New Approaches and New Evidence*, London/Swansea. *BMCR* 1998.11.27.

Page, D. (1963), "2506. Commentary on lyric poems", *The Oxyrhynchus Papyri* 29: 1–48.

Page, D. (1969), "Stesichorus: P. Oxy. 2735 fr. 1, 2618 fr. 1, 2619 fr. 1", *PCPS* 15: 69–74.

Page, D. (1971), "Ibycus; Stesichorus; Alcman (P. Oxy. 2735, 2618, 2737)", *PCPS* 17: 89–98.

Page, D. (1973), "Stesichorus: *The Sack of Troy* and *The Wooden Horse*", *JHS* 93: 138–154.

Palaima, T.G. (2006), "Wanaks and related power terms", in S. Deger-Jalkotsky and I.S. Lemos (eds.), *Ancient Greece: from the Mycenaean Palaces to the Age of Homer*. Edinburg, 53–71.

Pallotino, M. (1958), Review of Alföldi 1957 *Die trojanische Urahnen der Römer*, *Studi Etruschi* 26: 336–339.

Papadimitropoulos, L. (1980), "On Apollo's Epiphany in Euripides' *Orestes*", *Hermes* 139: 501–506.
Pardini, A.P. (1997), "Osservazioni minime al testo di Stesicoro", *QUCC* 55: 97–101.
Parker, R.B. (1983), *Miasma: Pollution and Purification in Early Greek Religion*. Oxford.
Parker, R.C.T. (1996), *Athenian Religion. A History*. Oxford.
Parry, M. (1987), *The Making of Homeric Verse*. (A. Parry, ed.). Oxford.
Parsons, P.J. (1977), "The Lille 'Stesichorus'", *ZPE* 26: 7–36.
Parsons, P.J. (1978), "Corrigenda", *ZPE* 28: 287.
Pavese, C.O. (1972), *Tradizioni e Generi Poetici della Grecia Arcaica*. Roma.
Pavese, C.O. (1997), "Sulla 'Thebais' di Stesicoro", *Hermes* 125: 259–268.
Pavlou, M. (2010), "Pindar *Olympian* 3: Mapping Acragas on the periphery of the world", *CQ* 60: 313–326.
Pearson, L. (1975), "Myth and 'archeaologia' in Italy and Sicily", *YClS* 24: 171–195.
Pease, A.S. (1907), "Notes on stoning among Greeks and Romans", *TAPhA* 38: 5–18.
Peek, W. (1958), "Die Nostoi des Stesicoros", *Philologus* 102: 169–177.
Perkins, P. (2009), "DNA and Etruscan Identity", in J. Swaddling and P. Perkins (eds.), *Etruscan by definition: The cultural, Regional, and Personal Identity of the Etruscans*. London, 95–111.
Peron, J. (1979), "Une version "sicilienne" du mythe des Labdacids dans les Sept contre Thèbes d'Eschyle", *Grazer Beiträge* 8: 75–99.
Perrin, B. (1909), "Recognition scenes in Greek Literature", *AJPh* 30: 371–404.
Petrain, D. (2014), *Homer in Stone: The* Tabulae Iliacae *in their Roman Context*. Cambridge.
Picard, C. (1935), *Manuel d'archaéologie grecque. La sculpture. I. Période Archaïque*. Paris.
Pickard-Cambridge, A. (1962), *Dithyramb, Tragedy, and Comedy*, Oxford.
Pinney, G.F./Ridgway, B.S. (1981), "Heracles at the ends of the earth", *JHS* 101: 141–144.
Pipili, M. (1997), "Ilioupersis", *LIMC* VIII/I: 650–657.
Plácido, D. (1989), "Realidades arcaicas de los viajes míticos a Occidente", *Gerión* 7, 41–51.
Podlecki, A.J. (1966), "The power of the word in Sophocles' Philoctetes", *GRBS* 7: 231–245.
Podlecki, A.J. (1971), "Stesichoreia", *Athenaeum* 49: 311–327.
Podlecki, A.J. (1984), *Early Greek Poets and their Times*. Vancouver.
Poltera, O. (1997), *Le langage de Simonide: Etude sur la tradition poétique et son renouvellement*. Bern.
Power, T. (2010), *The Culture of Kitharôidia*. Cambridge, MA/London.
Prag, A.J.N.W. (1985), *The* Oresteia. *Iconography and Narrative Tradition*. Warminster.
Prag, A.J.N.W. (1991), "Clytemnestra's Weapon Yet Once More", *CQ* 41: 242–246.
Pratt, L. (1994), "*Odyssey* 19.535–50: on the interpretation of dreams and signs in Homer", *CPh* 89: 147–152.
Prauscello, L. (2010), "The language of pity: *eleos* and *oiktos* in Sophocles' *Philoctetes*", *Cambridge Classical Journal* 56: 199–212.
Prauscello, L. (2012), "Epinician sounds: Pindar and musical innovation", in P. Agócs, C. Carey, and R. Rawles (eds.), *Reading the Victory Ode*. Cambridge, 58–82.
Prontera, F. (1990), "L'estremo Occidente nella concezione geográfica dei Greci" en *La Magna Grecia e il lontano Occidente: Atti del 29 Convegno di studi sulla Magna Grecia*, Tarant, 55–82.
Pulquério, M.O. (1969–70), "O problema do sacrifício de Ifignénia no *Agamémnon* de Ésquilo", *Humanitas* 21–22: 365–377.

Pulquério, M.O. (1974), "O problema das duas Palinódias de Estesícoro", *Humanitas* 25/26: 265–273.
Pucci, L. (2015), "Osservazioni critico-esegetische su alcuni frammenti dell'*Orestea* di Stesicoro (frr. 210, 11, 212 Davies/ 172, 173, 174 Davies–Finglass)", *SemRom* 4: 15–40.
Rabinowitz, N.S. (2011), "Greek Tragedy: A Rape Culture?", *EuGeStA* 1: 1–21.
Ragusa, G. (2010), *Lira, mito e eroticismo: Afrodite na poesia mélica grega arcaica*. Campinas.
Rawles, R. (2012), "Early epinician: Ibycus and Simonides", in P. Agócs, C. Carey, and R. Rawles (eds.), *Receiving the Komos, Ancient and Modern Receptions of Victory Odes*. London, 3–27.
Reed, C.M. (2004), *Maritime Traders in the Ancient Greek World*. Cambridge.
Reiske, J.J. (1755), *Animadversiones ad Plutarchi labellum de tarda numinis ira, in Locos quosdam Polybii a Latinis interpretibus Livio, Casaubono et Valerio perperam translatos proporit atque examinat Car. Christoph. Foersterus Zittav. Lusat. Cum animadversionibus Io. Iac. Reiskii, V. C. ad labellum Plutarchi de tarda numinis ira*. Leipzig.
Rohde, E. (1872), "Isigoni Nicaensis de rebus mirabilibus breviatum ex codice Vaticano", *Acta societatis philologae Lipsiensis* 1: 25–42.
Rhodes, P.J. (2003) "Nothing to do with democracy: Athenian drama and the *polis*", *JHS* 123: 104–119.
Ribeiro-Ferreira, J. (2005), "Hélade. Pan-Helenismo e Identidade Grega", in M.C. Fialho, M.F. Sousa e Silva, and M.H. Rocha Pereira (eds.), *Génese e Consolidação da Ideia de Europa*. Coimbra.
Ridgeway, W. (1888), "Thucydides VI.2", *CR* 2: 180.
Ridgway, D. (1992), *The First Western Greeks*. Cambridge.
Rigsby, K.J. (1987), "The Phocians in Sicily: Thucydides 6.2", *CQ* 37: 332–335.
Rizzo, G.E. (1895), "Questioni Stesicorea (vita e scuola poetica)", *Rivista di storia antica e scienze affini* 1/1: 25–50 and 1/2: 1–35.
Robert, C. (1881), *Bild und Lied. Archäologische Beiträge zur Geschichte der griechischen Heldensage*. Berlin.
Robert, C. (1915), *Oidipus. Geschichte eines poetischen Stoffs im grieschischen Altertum*. Berlin.
Roberts, D. (1984), *Apollo and his Oracle in the* Oresteia. Göttingen.
Robertson, M. (1967), "Conjectures in Polygnotos' Troy", *ABSA* 62: 5–12.
Robertson, M. (1969), "*Geryoneis:* Stesichorus and the vase-painters", *CQ* 19: 207–221.
Robertson, M. (1970), "Ibycus: Polycrates, Troilus, Polyxena", *BICS* 17: 11–15.
Robertson, M. (1986), "Epeios", *LIMC* III/1: 789.
Robertson, M. (1988), "Europe I", *LIMC* IV/1: 76–92.
Robertson, M. (1990), "Troilus and Polyxena. Notes on a changing legend", in J.-P. Descouedres (ed.), *Eumousia. Ceramic and iconographic studies in honour of A. Cambitoglou*. Sydney, 63–70.
Robertson, M. (1992), "Europe and others. Nostalgia in the late fifth century Athenian Vase-painting", in H. Froning (ed.), *Kotinos: Festschrift für Erica Simon*, Mainz, 237–240.
Robertson, N. (1978), "The myth of the First Sacred War", *CQ* 28: 38–73.
Robbins, E. (1997), "Public poetry: Alcman, Stesichorus, Simonides, Pindar, Bacchylides", in D.E. Gerber (ed.), *A Companion to Greek Lyric Poets*. Leiden/New York/Köln, 221–287.
Robson, J.E. (1997), "Bestiality and Bestial Rape in Greek Myth", in S. Deacy and K. Pierce (eds.), *Rape in Antiquity*. Swansea/London, 65–96.
Rocha, R. (2009), "Estesícoro entre Épica e Drama", *Phaos* 9: 65–79.
Rocha-Pereira, M.H. (1955), *Concepções Helénicas de Felicidade no Além*. Coimbra.

Rocha-Pereira, M.H. (1997), "Estatuto social dos artistas gregos", *Revista Crítica de Ciências Sociais* 47: 23–37.
Rocha-Pereira, M.H. (2005), "Europa: Enigmas de um nome", in M.C. Fialho, M.F. Sousa e Silva, and M.H. Rocha Pereira (eds.), *Génese e Consolidação da ideia de Europa*. Coimbra, 7–14.
Rodrigues, N.S. (2004), "Ἄιγυπτος δὲ γῆ. O Egipto na *Helena* de Eurípides", in J.A. Ramos, L.M. Araújo, and A.R. Santos (eds.), *Percursos do Oriente Antigo. Estudos de Homenagem ao Professor Doutor José Nunes Carreira na sua Jubilação Académica*. Lisboa, 481–496.
Rodrigues, N.S. (2009), "Rodópis no país dos faraós: Itinerários de uma hetera grega", *CFC(G)* 19: 115–123.
Rohde, E. (1876), *Der griechische Roman und seine Vorläufer*. Leipzig.
Room, J. (1992), *The Edges of the Earth in Ancient Thought. Geography, Exploration, and Fiction*. New Jersey.
Rosado Fernandes, R.M. (1962), *O Tema das Graças na Poesia Clássica*. Lisboa.
Rose, H.J. (1932a), "De Acteone Stesichoreo", *Mnemosyne* 59: 431–432.
Rose, H.J. (1932b), "Stesichoros and the Rhadine-fragment", *CQ* 26: 88–92.
Rossi, L.E. (1983), "Feste religiose e letteratura: Stesicoro o dell'epica alternativa", *Orpheus* 4: 5–31.
Rowlands, M. (ed.) (1987), *Centre and Periphery in the Ancient World*. Cambridge.
Rozokoki, A. (2008), "Some New Thoughts on Stesichorus' *Geryoneis*", *ZPE* 168: 3–18.
Rozokoki, A. (2009/10), "The evidence in Plato's *Phaedrus* for the Stesichorean *Palinode*", *Dodone(philol)* 38–39: 425–432.
Rozokoki, A. (2013), "Stesichorus' *Helen* fr. 187 *PMGF*: a new interpretation", *RFIC* 141: 257–269.
Rozokoki, A. (2014), review of P. Grossardt (2012) *Stesichoros zwischen kultischer Praxis, myhtischer Tradition und eigenem Kunstanspruch. Zur Behandlung des Helenamythos im Werk des dichters aus Himera (mit einem Anhang zum Motivkomplex von Beldung und Heilung in der internationalen Erzältradition)*. Tübingen, *ExClass* 18: 201–208.
Russo, J. (1999), "Stesichorus, Homer, and the Forms of Early Greek Epic", in J. Kazazis and A. Rengakos (eds.), *Euphrosyne: Studies in Ancient Epic and its legacy in Honor of Dimitris Maronitis*. Stuttgart, 339–348.
Rutherford, I. (2000), "Formulas, Voice, and Death in *Ehoie*-Poetry, the Hesiodic *Gunaikos Katalogos*, and the Odysseian *Nekuia*", in M. Depew and D. Obbink (eds.), *Matrices of Genre. Authors, Canons, and Society*. Cambridge, MA, 81–96.
Rutherford, I. (2001), *Pindar's Paeans. A Reading of the Fragments with a Survey of the Genre*. Oxford.
Rutherford, I. (2015), "Stesichorus the Romantic", in P. Finglass and A. Kelly (eds.), *Stesichorus in Context*. Cambridge, 98–108.
Ryzhkina, Z.A. (1984), "New variation of the Theban Myth: the Thebaid of Stesichorus" [in Russian, English abstract], *Vetnik drevnej istorii* 170: 112–118.
Saïd, S. (2011), *Homer and the Odyssey*. Oxford.
Sadurska, A.S. (1964), *Les Tables Iliaques*. Warszawa.
Sadurska, A.S. (1986), "Equus Troianos", *LIMC* III/I: 813–817.
Scafoglio, G (2005), "Virgilio e Stesicoro: Una ricerca sulla 'Tabula Iliaca Capitolina'" *Rheinisches Museum für Philologie* 148: 113–127.
Scarpanti, E. (2003), "Sorte e sorteggio in Stesicoro : κλαροπαληδόν (fr. 222b, 223 dav.)", *Paideia* 58: 297–305.

Schneidewin, F.W. (1852), "Die Sage vom Ödipus", *Abhandlungen der Königlichen Gesellshcaft der Wissenschaften zu Göttingen*: 1–50.
Schmid, W. (1929), *Geschichte der griechischen Literatur. Erster Teil: Die Klassische Periode der griechischen Literature. Ester Band: Die Griechische Literatur vor der attischen Hegemonie.* München.
Schwarz, G. (2001), "Der Tod und das Madchen: Frihe Polyxena-Bilden", *AM* 116: 35–50.
Schwartz, W.E. (1904), "Zu Bacchylides", *Hermes* 52: 308–313.
Scodel, R.S. (1980), *The Trojan Trilogy of Euripides*. Göttingen.
Scott, M. (2010), *Delphi and Olympia. The Spatial Politics of Panhellenism in the Archaic and Classical Periods*. Cambridge.
Seaford, R. (1987), "The Tragic Wedding", *JHS* 107: 106–130.
Seeberg, A. (1995), "From Padded Dancers to Comedy", *BICS* 40: 1–12.
Segal, C.P. (1963), "Nature and the World of Man in Greek Literature", *Arion* 2: 19–53.
Segal, C.P. (1985), "Archaic choral lyric", in P.E. Easterling and B.W. Knox (eds.), *The Cambridge History of Classical Literature I: Greek Literature*. Cambridge, 222–244.
Sewell-Rutter, N.J. (2007), *Guilt by Descent. Moral inheritance and Decision-Making in Greek Tragedy.* Oxford.
Sgobbi, A.S. (2003), "Stesicoro, Falaride, e la battaglia della Sagra", *Acme* 56: 1–37.
Shapiro, H.A. (2000), "Helen Out of Doors", in G. Tsetskhladze, A. Prag, and A. Snodgrass (eds.), *Periplous. Papers on Classical Art and Archaeology presented to Sir John Boardman*. London, 271–275.
Shaw, B. (2001), "Challenging Braudel: a new vision of the Mediterranean: a review of Horden and Purcell, *The Corrupting Sea*", *JRA* 14: 419–453.
Sider, D. (1989), "The blinding of Stesichorus", *Hermes* 117: 423–431.
Sider, D. (2001), "As is the Generation of Leaves' in Homer, Simonides, Horace, and Stobaeus", in D. Boedeker and D. Sider (eds.), *New Simonides. Contexts of praise and desire.* Oxford, 272–288.
Sider, D. (2010), "Greek verse on a vase by Douris", *Hesperia* 79: 541–554.
Silva, M.F.S. (2005a), "*Philia* e as suas condicionantes na *Hécuba* de Eurípides", *Ensaios sobre Eurípides,* Lisboa, 93–124.
Silva, M.F.S. (2005b), *Ésquilo. O Primeiro Dramaturgo Europeu*. Coimbra.
Sisti, F. (1965), "La due palinodie di Stesicoro", *StudUrb(B)* 39: 301–313.
Sisti, F. (1976), "Sul nuovo Stesicoro", *Accademia Nazionale dei Lincei. Bolletino del Comitato per la preparazione dell'edizione nazionale dei classici greci e latini* NS 24: 50–54.
Skinner, J.E. (2012), *Inventing Greek Ethnography. From Homer to Herodotus*. Oxford.
Slings, S.L. (1990), *The poet's I in archaic Greek Lyric.* Amsterdam.
Slings, S.L. (1994), Review of Campbell's edition, *Mnemosyne* 4[th]ed. 47: 104–109.
Smyth, H.W. (1900), *Greek Melic Poets.* London.
Solmsen, F. (1934), "ONOMA and ΠΡΑΓΜΑ in Euripides' *Helen*", *CR* 48: 119–121.
Solmsen, F. (1949), *Hesiod and Aeschylus.* Ithaca/London.
Solmsen, F. (1967), *Electra and Orestes. Three Recognition Scenes in Greek Tragedy.* Amsterdam.
Sommerstein, A. (1989), "Again Clytaimnestra's weapon", *CQ* 39: 296–301.
Sommerstein, A. (2000), "The prologue of Aeschylus' *Palamedes*", *RhM* 143: 118–127.
Sommerstein, A. (2006), "Rape and Consent in Athenian Tragedy", in D. Cairns et al. (eds.), *Dionysalexandros: Essays on Aeschylus and his fellow tragedians in honour of Alexander F. Garvie.* Swansea, 233–251.

Sommerstein, A. (2010), *The Tangled Ways of Zeus: and Other Studies in and Around Greek Tragedy*. Oxford.
Sommerstein, A. (2013²), *Aeschylean Tragedy*. London/New Delhi/New York/Sydney.
Sommerstein, A. (2015), "Tragedy and the Epic Cycle", in M. Fantuzzi and C. Tsagalis (eds.), *The Greek Epic Cycle and its Reception. A companion*. Cambridge, 461–486.
Sourvinou-Inwood, C. (1987), "A Series of Erotic Pursuits: Images and Meanings", *JHS* 107: 131–153.
Squire, M. (2011), *The Iliad in a Nutshell. Visualizing Epic on the Tabulae Iliacae*. Oxford.
Stansbury O'Donnell, M.D. (1989), "Polygnotos' Iliupersis: A New Reconstruction", *AJA* 93: 203–215.
Steinhart, M. (2007), "From ritual to narrative", in E. Csapo and M.C. Miller (eds.), *The origins of Theatre in Ancient Greece and Beyond*. Cambridge, 196–220.
Stephanopoulos, T.K. (1980), *Umgestaltung des Mythos durch Euripides*. Athens.
Stewart, E. (2017), *Greek Tragedy on the move: the Birth of a Panhellenic Art Form c. 500-300 BC*. Oxford.
Stuart, J./Revett, N. (1717–1788), *The Antiquities of Athens*. London.
Sultan, N. (1999), *Exile and the poetics of loss in Greek Tradition*. New York/Oxford.
Swift, L. (2015), "Stesichorus on Stage", in Finglass and Kelly (eds.), *Stesichorus in Context*. Cambridge, 125–144.
Taplin, O. (1977), *Stagecraft of Aeschylus*. Oxford.
Taylor, C./Vlassopoulos, K. (2014), *Communities and Networks in Ancient Greece*. Oxford.
Texier, R. (1939), "À propos de deux représentations de la fuite d'Énée", *Révue Archéologique* 14: 12–21.
Thalmann, W. (1978), *Dramatic Art in Aeschylus' Seven Against Thebes*. New Haven/London.
Thalmann, W. (1982), "The Lille Stesichorus and the 'Seven Against Thebes'", *Hermes* 110: 385–391.
Thalmann, W. (1998), "Female Slaves in the *Odyssey*", in S.R. Joshel and S. Murnagham (eds.), *Women and Slaves in Greco-Roman Culture*. London/New York, 22–32.
Todisco, L. (2002), *Teatro e spettacolo in Magna Grecia e in Sicilia. Testi, imagini, architettura*. Milano.
Torre, E.S. (2007), "Helena, de la épica a la lírica griega arcaica (Safo, Alceo, Estesícoro)", in J.V. Bañuls, M.C. Fialho, A. López, F. De Martino, C. Morenilla, A. Pociña Pérez, M.F. Silva (eds.), *O Mito de Helena de Tróia à Actualidade*. vol. 1. Coimbra/Foggia/Granada/Valencia, 55–79.
Torres-Guerra, J.B. (2015), "Thebaid", in M. Fantuzzi and C. Tsagalis (eds.) The Greek *Epic Cycle and Its Reception. A Companion*. Cambridge, 226–243.
Tosi, R. (1978), "Note al nuovo Stesicoro", *MCr* 13: 125–143.
Touchefeu, O./Krauskopf, I. (1981), "Agamemnon", *LIMC* I/I : 336–351.
Touchefeu, O. (1984), "Astyanax", *LIMC* I/I : 929–937.
Touchefeu-Meynier, O. (1992), "Kyklops", *LIMC* VI/I: 154–159.
Touchefeu, O. (1994), "Polyxene", *LIMC* VII/I : 431–435.
Tsagalis, C. (2012), *From Listeners to Viewers. Space in the* Iliad. Centre of Hellenic Studies 53. http://nrs.harvard.edu/urn-3:hul.ebook:CHS_TsagalisC.From_Listeners_to_Viewers.2012. [Last access 22.05.21].
Tsetskhladze, G. (ed.) (1999), *Ancient Greeks. West and East*. Leiden/Boston/Cologne.
Tsetskhladze, G. (ed.) (2006), *Greek Colonisation. An account of Greek Colonies and Other Settlements Overseas*. Leiden/Boston.

Tsitsibakou-Vasalos, E. (1986), "Two Homeric Formulae in the P. Lille poem: θεοὶ θέςαν and ἄναξ ἑκάεργος Ἀπόλλων", *Glotta* 64: 165–184.
Tsitsibakou-Vasalos, E. (1987), "The Metre of the Lille Stesichorus", *GRBS* 28: 401–423.
Tsitsibakou-Vasalos, E. (1988), "The textual problems of the *P. Lille* poem, vv. 228–231", *QUCC* 28: 137–148.
Tsitsibakou-Vasalos, E. (1989), "The Homeric ἄφαρ in the Oedipus Myth and the Identity of the Lille Mother", *Glotta* 67: 60–88.
Tsitsibakou-Vasalos, E. (2011), "Stesichorus' Ἰλίου Πέρςις and the Epic Tradition", *Classics@* 6: Efimia D. Karakantza, ed. The Center for Hellenic Studies of Harvard University [available online in http://chs.harvard.edu/CHS/article/display/3529, [Last access 22.05.21]
Ugolini, G. (1990), "L'ethos di Giocasta tra Stesicoro e i Tragici", *Lexis* 5/6: 57–75.
Urquhart, L.M. (2014), "Competing Traditions in the Historiography of Ancient Greek Colonization in Italy", *Journal of the History of Ideas* 75: 23–44.
Ustinova, Y. (2009), *Caves and the Ancient Greek Mind. Descending Underground in the Search of the Ultimate Truth*. Oxford.
Vagnone, G. (1982), "Aspetti formulari in Stesicoro, *Pap. Lille* 76 a b c: il desiderio di morte", *QUCC* 12: 35–42.
Valenzuela Montenegro, N. (2004), *Die Tabulae Iliacae. Mythos und Geschichte im Spiegel einer Gruppe frühkaiserzeitlicher Miniaturreliefs*. Berlin.
Van Eck, J. (1978), *Homeric Hymn to Aphrodite*. Lexmond.
Vanoti, G. (2005), "Qualche considerazione sui frammenti di Lesches di Pirra", in Mele et al., *Eoli ed Eolide tra madrepatri e colonie*. Naples, 123–134.
Vanschoonwinckel, J. (2006), "Mycenaean Expansion", in G.R. Tsetskhladze (ed.), *Greek Colonisation. An account of Greek Colonies and Other Settlements Overseas*. Leiden/Boston, 41–112.
Vermeule, E. (1966), "The Boston Oresteia Krater", *AJA* 70: 1–22.
Vermeule, E. (1971), "Kadmos and the Dragon", in D.G. Mitten, J.G. Pedley, and J.A. Scott (eds.), *Studies Presented to George M. A. Hanfmann*. Mainz, 177–188.
Vernant, J.-P. (1993), *Figuras, Ídolos, Máscaras* (trans. Telma Costa). Lisboa.
Vian, F. (1987), "Poésie et géographie: les Retours des Argonautes" en *Comptes rendus des séances de l' Académie des Inscriptions et Belles-Lettres*, 131.1, 249–262.
Vlassopoulos, K. (2013), *Greeks and Barbarians*. Cambridge.
Von Norwick, T. (1996), *Somewhere I Have Never Travelled. The Hero's Journey*. Oxford.
Waser, O. (1894), *Scylla und Charybdis in der Literatur und Kunst der Griechen und Römer*. Zurich.
Watson, L. (1991), *Arae: the curse poetry in Antiquity*. Leeds.
Webster, T.B.L. (1970), *The Greek Chorus*. London.
Welcker, F.G. (1829), review of O.F. Kleine (1828), *Stesichori Himerensis fragmenta*. Berlin, *Jahrbücher für Philologie und Paedagogik* 9: 131–168, 251–308.
Welcker, F.G. (1844–67), *Kleine Schriften*. 5 vols. Bonn – Elberfeld.
Welcker, F.G. (1865[2]), *Die epische Cyclus*. Bonn.
Wescoat, B.D. (2012), *The Temple of Athena at Assos*. Oxford.
West, M.L. (1965), "Alcmanica", *CQ* 15: 188–202.
West, M.L. (1969), "Stesichorus Redivivus", *ZPE* 4: 135–149.
West, M.L. (1971a), "Stesichorus", *CQ* 21: 302–314.
West, M.L. (1971b), "Further Light on Stesichorus' *Iliou Persis*", *ZPE* 7: 262–264.
West, M.L. (1990), *Studies in Aeschylus*. Stuttgart.

West, M.L. (1997), *The East Face of Helicon*. Oxford.
West, M.L. (1999), "Ancestral Curses", in M. Griffin (ed.), *Sophocles Revisited. Essays Presented to Sir Hugh Lloyd-Jones*. Oxford, 31–45.
West, M.L. (2002), "'Eumelus': A Corinthian Epic Cycle?", *JHS* 122: 109–133.
West, M.L. (2005a), "*Odyssey* and *Argonautica*", *CQ* 55.1, 39–64.
West, M.L. (2005b²), *The Hesiodic Catalogue of Women*. Oxford.
West, M.L. (2007), *Indo-European Poetry and Myth*. Oxford.
West, M.L. (2011a), "The view from Lesbos", in M.L. West, *Hellenica: Selected Papers on Greek Literature and Thought. Volume I: Epic*. Oxford, 392–407.
West, M.L. (2011b), "The Trojan Saga: History and Prehistory" in M.L. West, *Hellenica: Selected Papers on Greek Literature and Thought. Volume I: Epic*. Oxford, 97–112.
West, M.L. (2015), "Epic, lyric, and lyric epic", in P. Finglass and A. Kelly (eds.), *Stesichorus in Context*. Cambridge, 63–80.
West, S. (1982), "Proteus in Stesichorus' Palinode", *ZPE* 47: 6–10.
Westcoat, B.D. (2012), *The temple of Athena at Assos*. Oxford.
Wick, C. (2003), "Le tirage au sort: un *leitmotiv* dans la *Thebaïde de Lille* et les *Sept contre Thebes*", *MH* 60: 167–174.
Wilamowitz-Moellendorff, E.F.W.U. von (1899), "Die griechischen Technopaegnia", *Jahrbuch des Kaiserlich Deutschen Archäologischen Instituts* 14: 51–59.
Wilamowitz-Moellendorff, E.F.W.U. von (1913), *Sappho und Simonides*. Berlin.
Wilamowitz-Moellendorff, E.F.W.U. von (1925), "Lesefrüchte", *Hermes* 60: 280–316.
Wilamowitz-Moellendorff, E.F.W.U. von (1931–32), *Der Glaube der Hellenen*. 2 vols. Berlin.
Willi, A. (2008), *Sikelismos. Sprache, Literatur und Gesellschaft im griechischen Sizilien*. Basel
Willi, A. (2012), "'We speak Peloponnesian': Tradition and linguistic identity in post-classical Sicilian literature", in O. Tribulato (ed.), *Language and Linguistic Contact in Ancient Sicily*. Cambridge, 265–288.
Willink, C.W. (2002), "The Metre of Stesichorus PMG 15/192", *Mnemosyne* 4th 55: 709–711.
Wilson, P. (2007), "Sicilian Choruses", in P. Wilson (ed.), *Greek Tragedy and Festivals*. Oxford, 351–376.
Winnington-Ingram, R.P. (1933), "The role of Apollo in the *Oresteia*", *CR* 47: 97–104.
Wintle, M. (2006), *The image of Europe: Visualizing Europe in Cartography and Iconography throughout the Ages*. Cambridge.
Woodbury, L.E. (1967), "Helen and the Palinode", *Phoenix* 21: 157–176.
Woodford, S./Kraukopf, I. (1992), "Meleager", *LIMC* VI/I: 414–435.
Wrenhaven, K.L. (2012), *Reconstructing the slave: the image of Slaves in Ancient Greece*. London.
Wright, M.E. (2005), *Euripides' Escape Tragedies. A Study of Helen, Andromeda, and Iphigenia among the Taurians*. Oxford.
Xanthou, M.G. (2015), "Maternal Figures in the Stesichorean Blueprint: Althaea, Callirhoe, and the Lille Queen", *QUCC* 111: 29–57.
Yamagata, N. (2012), "Epithets with Echoes: a study on the formula-narrative interaction", in F. Montanari, A. Rengakos, and C. Tsagalis (eds.), *Homeric Contexts. Neoanalysis and the Interpretation of Oral Poetry*. Berlin/Boston, 445–469.
Zachos, G.A. (2013), "Epeios in Greece and Italy. Two different traditions in one person", *Athenaeum* 101: 5–25.
Zardini, F. (2009), *The Myth of Heracles and Kyknos. A Study in Greek Vase-Painting and Literature*. Verona.

Zeitlin, F. (1986), "Configurations of Rape in Greek myth", in S. Tomaselli and R. Porter (eds.), *Rape*. Oxford, 122–151.
Zeitlin, F. (2012), "A Study in Form: Three Recognition Scenes in the Three Recognition plays", *Lexis* 30, 361–378.
Zervoudaki, E. (1988), "Eurytion", *LIMC* IV/I: 112–117.

Index Rerum et Nominum

abduction XXI, XXXIII, 79, 80, 100, 105–117, 116, 126–132, 137 n.109, 138, 143–156, 254, 255
– Europa's XXXIII, 107–115, 116, 131, 150 n.150, 155, 254
– Helen's XXI, XXXIII, 80, 100, 113, 115–117, 126–132, 138, 143–156, 255
– Leucippe's 154
– Persephone's 79, 109, 110, 116
– Theone's 154
Abraham 14 n.57
Acamas XXI, 50 n.12, 98, 141, 152–154, 255
Acastus 191
Achaeans 38, 57–58, 63 n.65, 64, 66, 81, 82 n.127, 83, 92 n.174, 96, 97, 134, 152, 171
Achelous (river) 14 n.59, 16
Achilles 3 n.5, 8, 26, 29–30, 33, 53 n.27, 54, 55, 72, 83, 122, 127, 159, 161, 176, 182 n.87, 186, 190 n.118, 191 n.124, 247 n.293
– tomb of 73–74, 86 n.140
Acteon 113
Adrastus 206, 249 n.305, 249
Aegisthus 125–126, 126 n.79, 158–160, 171, 174, 178, 184–185, 190, 192, 194, 196
Aeneads 90
Aeneas XXXIII, 3 n.5, 44, 47–48, 50, 70, 82, 86, 87–96, 97 n.193, 98, 150, 254
Aeolus 8
Aerope 186
Aethra 48, 50 n.12, 98, 117, 129, 131, 138, 152
Aetolians 38
Agamemnon XXX, 54, 56, 81 n.125, 83, 84, 89, 96 n.188, 98, 99, 117, 122, 124–127, 129, 136, 157–162, 168, 171–172, 174–180, 184–194, 196 n.137, 198, 220
– death of 81 n.125, 99, 117, 124 n.71, 126 n.80, 184–186, 189, 190–192, 194, 198
– tomb of 193–194, 196 n.137

Agave 113
Agenor 107 n.10, 112, 113
Ajax 77 n.120, 96 n.190, 232 n.233
Alaesa 97 n.193
Alcinous XXVII n.92, 103 n.211, 182 n.87
Alcmeon 189, 201–202
Alpheus (river) 16
Althaea 20–21, 188, 256
Amazons see *Antiope*
ambrosia 173
Amphiaraus 134, 201, 204 n.158, 206, 244
Amphitryon 67 n.89
Amyclae 38 n.118, 168
Amyclas 191
Anatolia 91
Anaxander 135, 202
Anaxibia 161, 186
Anchises 90, 92, 93 n.179, 94
Andromache 48, 49, 98, 71, 257
Antenor 66
Anthemides 42 n.139, 53 n.28
Antigone 21 n.86, 207, 224
Antiope XXI, 153
Aphidnae 129–132
Aphrodite XXVII, 70, 76, 77, 80, 81 n.125, 82, 86, 91, 115, 116–127, 132, 138, 146 n.135
Apollo 84–87, 95, 105 n.3, 106, 108 n.15, 122, 150, 157, 165, 166, 168–169, 171, 178, 197–200, 203 n.157, 220, 221, 235–240, 243, 245
– bow of 157, 197–200
Apsyrtos 131
Arcadia XIX, 44, 177 n.72, 203
Ares XXVII, 34–37, 37 n.117, 41, 81 n.125, 201, 243
Argeia 224
Argives 129, 244
Argolid 158
Argos 58, 115, 129, 132, 134, 168, 207, 208 n.171, 249, 251, 255
Aristomache 47, 98–99
Arsinoe 190

https://doi.org/10.1515/9783110715736-007

Artemis XXIX n.103, 33 n.111, 70, 86, 114 n.42, 125, 130, 134, 150, 159–160, 169, 176–178, 202–203, 203 n.155
Ascanius 89
Astyanax 48, 49, 49 n.7, 50, 70–73, 75
Astymedusa 224
Atalanta 38 n.118, 133, 133 n.97, 134
Athena 7, 10 n.42, 12 n.53, 19 n.81, 32–34, 37, 38, 38 n.118, 40, 46 n.150, 49 n.8, 50, 52, 54, 57, 59, 62, 65, 77 n.119, 80, 102, 104, 119, 120, 121, 123, 170, 182 n.87, 238 n.257
Athens XX n.38, XXI, XXII, XXXI, 7, 116, 128–132, 152, 153 n.156, 160, 161, 235, 242, 242 n.272, 252 n.321, 255
Atreus 30 n.103, 122, 126 n.80, 157, 168, 168 n.42, 173–174, 186–187, 188 n.113
Attica 16 n.67, 128 n.85, 160, see also Athens
audience XIX, XXVIII, XXX, XXXIII, 5 n.10, 15, 19, 27, 28, 31, 41–43, 42 n.139, 45, 46, 46 n.150, 52, 53, 63, 66 n.88, 75, 88, 94–95, 123, 147, 152, 168–169, 173–174, 191, 194, 208 n.171, 226, 228, 243, 252, 255–256
Auge 18 n.80
Aulis 158 n.1, 159–162, 174–176, 180

Baetis 13
Beauty 123
Bellerophon 191
boar hunt 1, 38, 38 n.118, 38 n.120, 38 n.121, 44, 134, 255
Boeotia 38 n.119, 113 n.40, 251
Boeotians 38, 134
bowl of the Sun 4–5, 8–11, 18

Cabires 56
Cadiz 1, 15, 114
Cadmus 107 n.10, 110–114
Calchas 96 n.288, 96 n.190, 148, 154–155, 159, 160, 176, 182 n.91, 236 n.247
Callirhoe 2, 7, 23 n.87, 25–26, 27–37, 78, 230, 256, 257
Calydon 1, 38, 38 n.118, 38 n.120, 38 n.121, 134, 255
Campania 92, 92 n.171

Capanaeus 239
Capharaeus 97 n.193
Capua 92, 94 n.185
Capys 63–64, 92
Cartheia 54
Cassandra 48–50, 50 n.9, 63, 70, 76 n.115, 77 n.120, 85, 98, 124 n.71, 174, 158, 184
– death of 124 n.71, 158, 184
Castalia 16 n.69
Catania XV n.13, XXI, XXII
cattle 5–9, 11, 18, 19, 23 n.87, 24–25, 27, 32, 44, 134 n.99, 247
– Geryon's 5–9, 11, 18, 19, 23 n.87, 24–25, 27, 32, 44
Centaurs XVII, 43–44, 46
Cerberus 1, 9
Chalcidians XXI, 92 n.171
Chalcis 92, 129
Charybdis 97, 97 n.193
Chersonese 85
Chiron 44
choral lyric XXV–XXXII, 165 n.23, 167, 167 n.32, 169
chorus XXV–XXXII, 70, 110 n.26, 166–168, 170, 172–173, 185, 200 n.151
Chrysaor 1 n.1, 3, 23 n.87, 25, 28
Chryses 122
Chrysothemis 161
Chryssipus 205 n.161
Cilissa 190–191
Circe 96 n.189
citharode XXIV, XXVI, XXVI n.80, XXVII, XXX n.113, XXXII n. 127, 166 n.30, 167
Cleolla 186
Cleonae 207, 251–252
Clymene 98
Clytemnestra 21 n.86, 81 n.125, 115, 118, 125–126, 127, 129, 131, 158, 159, 162, 168, 175, 178–189, 190, 191–192, 193, 194 n.132, 196, 198, 203, 217 n.176, 255, 257
– death of 158, 196, 198, 203
Cnidian of Lesches 50, 57, 75, 86
comedy 6, 6 n.18, 6 n.19, 30 n.103, 162, 164, 257
Corinth XXIV, XXIV n.65, 114, 251–252

Creon 205, 207, 216, 220, 222, 226, 244,
Crete 108, 109, 110 n.27, 111–112, 114, 195, 242 n.272, 252 n.321, 254
Creusa 86
Crisa XVII n.25
Critolaus 98, 99
curse 80, 116, 125, 172, 173 n.58, 174, 175 n.68, 206–208, 216, 222, 224, 227, 234
– Oedipus' 175 n.68, 206–208, 216, 222, 224, 227, 234
– Tyndareus' 80, 116, 125
Cyclopes 12, 83 n.133
Cycnus XVII, XXXIII, 1, 2, 33–34, 37, 41, 144 n.128
Cynosema 85
Cyprus 154

Daedalus 58
dance XXVII–XXX, 163
Danaans 58
Danaids 55
Death 86
Deimos 34
Deiphobus 126–127
Dejanira 21 n.86
Delphi XXV n.74, 114, 203, 252 n.321
Demeter 79–80
Demodocus XXVII–XXVIII, 63, 165 n.23
Demophon XXI, 95, 98, 131, 138, 141–142, 147–148, 152–154, 155, 255
Deucalion 252 n.321
Dias 186
Diomedes 37 n.116, 96 n.188, 196 n.137, 239
Dionysus 1 n.1, 44, 113 n.40
Dioscuri 32 n.110, 113, 128–129, 131, 132, 134, 136
dithyramb XXIV, XXIX n.105, XXX n.114, XXXII n.127, 107 n.13, 107 n.14, 165 n.22, 167, 167 n.32
divine assembly 32– 35, 40 n.126, 121, 159
dragon 37, 110 n.26
dream 103, 162, 168, 180–189, 182 n.87, 183 n.93, 193, 195, 217, 217 n.176, 257
– Clytemnestra's 162, 168, 180–189, 193, 195, 217 n.176, 257

– Penelope's 103, 181–183
Dropis XX
Dryopes 38, 38 n.119, 134

Earth 59
Egesta XVI n.21, 92 n.174
Egypt XVI n.19, XXI, 86, 96 n.190, 100, 131, 138, 141–143, 145, 147, 148, 148 n.144, 149–156, 178, 254
eidolon 138, 143, 148–152, 148 n.145, 149 n.148, 150, 178, 182 n.87
– Helen's 138, 143, 148–152
– Iphigenia's 150, 178
Einodia 177 n.72
Electra 161, 162, 173, 185, 189, 192–197, 200 n.151, 239 n.262, 257
Elymians XVI n.21, 92 n.174
Entella XVI n.21
Epeius 19 n.81, 33, 48, 49 n.8, 50–59, 67–68 n.89, 89, 119, 120, 123, 170
Epicaste 205, 216, 223, 224, 225 n.208,
Erechtheus 55 n.37
Erinyes 206, 157, 162, 175, 184 n.98, 186, 189, 198–200, 202, 206
Eros 77, 77 n. 119, 77 n.121, 123, 139,
Eriphyle 189, 201–202, 206
Erytheia (island) 1 n.1, 3, 5–8, 11 n.47, 12–15, 25 n.95, 44, 254
Erytheia 18–19
Eryx 92 n.174
escape XXXIII, 44, 47–48, 49, 50, 70, 82, 87–96, 97 n.193, 98, 105–106, 190, 254
– Aeneas' XXXIII, 44, 47–48, 50, 70, 82, 87–96, 97 n.193, 98, 254
Eteocles 31, 204, 205 n.161, 206–209, 215, 216, 218, 222–226, 229, 231–232, 234, 242–247, 242 n.273, 249–253
Etruria 93, 94
Etruscans XVI n.21, 94 n.184, 94 n.185
Euboeans 92, 92 n. 171
Euphemus XV n.15
Euphorbus (*oikiste*) XV n.15
Euphorbus 42 n.139
Europa XXXIII, 105, 106, 107–115, 116, 131, 150 n.150, 155, 254
Eurycleia (nurse) 186, 189 n.117, 191, 191 n.124

Index Rerum et Nominum

Eurycleia 224
Euryganeia 205, 223 n.199, 224 n.202, 225, 228–229, 229 n.224
Eurymedusa 191
Eurytion 7, 14, 17–20, 23 n.87, 25, 31, 42 n.139
Evander XIX, 44
exile XIX, XXII, XXXII, XXXIV, 155 n.168, 157, 158, 160–162, 179 n.79, 186, 188, 190–197, 200, 203, 215, 242 n.273, 245, 252, 254–255
– Oedipus' 215
– Orestes' XIX, XXXIV, 158, 160–161, 179 n.79, 186, 190–192, 196–197, 203
– Polynices' XIX, XXXIV, 242 n.273, 245, 252, 255

feasts 64 n.71, 158, 160, 163, 171–174, 185, 201
festivals XV, n.10, XXIII–XXV, XXV n.74, XXXI, 46 n. 150, 165–169
François Vase XVII, 38 n.118

Gadeira (Gades) 6, 13, 15 see also *Cadiz*
Garden of the Hesperides 9, 10 n.39, 17–18, 25
Geryon XXVIII, 1 n.1, 2–15, 18–33, 35, 37–46, 118 n.60, 218, 238 n.257, 256
Gorgons 1 n.1, 25
Gorgophone 118 n.60
Gorgythion 40 n.126, 42, 102
Greece (mainland) XIII, XV, XX, XXV, 1, 14 n.59, 16 n.67, 45, 46, 104, 132, 169, 253, 254, 255, 258
Greek 'colonisation' XXIV, 15 n.62, 45–46, 92 n.171, 154, 203, 252
Guadalquivir, see *Tartessus (river)*

Hades 19, 79, 242 n.272
Harmonia 113
Hecate 177
Hector 30, 31, 33, 53 n.27, 53 n.28, 71, 73, 81 n.124, 86–87, 87 n.147, 105 n.3, 106, 135 n.102, 237 n.254, 256
Hecuba 30–31, 47, 49, 50, 70, 73, 75, 78, 84–87, 95, 98, 106, 108 n.15, 150, 178, 217 n.176, 239, 256, 257

Helen XXI, XXXIII, 31, 47, 48, 49, 50, 70, 76–84, 86, 88, 94–95, 98, 100–104, 105–107, 110 n.27, 113, 115–156, 162, 168, 178–179, 189, 255, 256, 257
Helenus 58
Hellespont 14 n.58, 91–92
Hephaestus 7, 42 n.139, 81 n.125, 83, 109
Hera 85 n.138, 150, 185
Heracles XVII, XIX, XXI, XXXII, 1–2, 3 n.5, 3 n.6, 4–12, 17–20, 21 n.86, 22, 23 n.87, 24, 25 n.95, 26, 30–46, 95, 149, 153–154, 198 n.143, 254–255, 256
Hermes 14 n.57, 58, 89, 113 n.41, 150
Hermione (city) 79
Hermione 30 n.103, 79–80
Hesperia 90 n.161, 93, 254
Hicetaon 99
Hilo 21 n.86
Himera (river) 36, n. 187
Himera (city) XV–XVI, XVII n.22, XVIII, XIX, XX n.39, XXII, XXII n.50, XXII n.51, XXIV, 14 n.59, 16, 45, 46, 79, 97 n.193
Hippalces 98
Hippodameia 133
Huelva 15
Hydra 41–72
Hyperboreans 171
Hyperion 9
Hippolytus XXI, 125, 153

Identity (Greek) XIII, XXXIII
Io 18 n.79, 112
Iolaus 18
Iope XXI, 153
Iphianassa 161
Iphiclus 134 n.98
Iphigenia 21 n.86, 75, 86, 105 n.3, 115, 127, 129, 131, 132, 150, 158 n.1, 159–161, 162, 169, 174, 175–180, 180, 203, 255
Iphimede 150, 161, 162, 177, 178
Ismene 207, 224
Italy XV n.14, XVI, XVIII, XIX, XXIV, 5, 6, 44, 91–95, 254
Ithaca 91, 99, 104, 219

Jason 241 n.270, 247 n.296
Jocasta 28 n.101, 157, 205–206, 216, 221 n.194, 223–229, 234–235

Keres 39–41
kerostasia 39, 40 n.126

Lacedaemon 115, 132, 168, 175, 191, 255
Laconia 200
Lagaria 67 n.89
Laius 21 n.86, 205, 206, 208 n.172, 224
Lamia 85
Laocoon 48, 63
Laodamia 168, 175 n.69, 189–191
Laodice 86, 162
Laolytus 224
Latins XVI n.19, 93, 93 n.179, 94 n.185
Leonteus 63 n.65, 154 n.162
Leontini XXI
Leto 18 n.79, 122
Leucippe 108, 154
Locrians XVII n.23, 38, 134
Locris (Eziphyrian) XVII, XVIII, XXII, XXIII
Locris (mainland Greece) XVII n.22
lot, see *sortition*
Lycia 50, 85–87, 106, 108 n.15, 114, 150, 152 n.321

Magna Graecia XV, XVI n.19, XXIII–XXV, 166, 255, 257
Malaga 15
Marmor Parium XX
Maronea 91
marriage, see *wedding*
Matauros 169, 203
matricide 30 n.103, 157–159, 184 n.99, 185, 188, 196, 202
Medea 131
Mediterranean XIII–XVI, XXIV, XXXII, 6, 14, 15 n.64, 16, 95, 114, 155 n.168, 254, 256
Medon 252 n.321
Medusa (Gorgon) 1 n.1, 8, 25
Medusa (Priam's daughter) 75, 98
Megara 21 n.86
Megara (city) 114 n.42
Melampus 134

Meleager XXII, XXXII, 1, 38 n.118, 134, 189 n.116
Menelaus 49, 54, 82–84, 76–78, 80–81, 88–89, 91, 94, 96, 100, 102–104, 110 n.27, 115, 118, 124, 126–129, 135–138, 146, 147, 151–154, 160, 161, 175 n.68, 186, 187 n.112, 256
Menoetes 6, 19–24
Mestra 133
Metaurus XV–XVI, XXII
Minos 107 n.14, 108–109, 252 n.321
mobility XIII, XVI, XXIII, XXV n.74, XXXII, 105, 254
Moirai 39, 230, 237, 238 n.257, 241, 243, 246
Molossians 91
monody XXV
Mopsus 154 n.162
Mount Ida 48, 58, 90–91, 109
Mount Parnassus 190
Muses XXIX, 51, 52 n.23, 120, 122, 139, 141–142, 145–146, 148, 163–165, 170, 172
Mycenae 81 n.125, 113 n.40, 158, 160, 168, 255
Mylae XVI n.19

Naples 92
Naucratis 155–156
Nauplius 97, 160 n.9, 195–196, 195 n.135
Nausicaa XXIX, 109, 182 n.87, 135 n.102
Neilus 252 n.321
Neleus 134 n.98
Neoptolemus 21 n.86, 48, 54, 64, 71–73, 75, 91, 96, 98, 160
Nereids 29, 42 n.139
Nereus 10
Nestor 96 n.188, 98, 175 n.68, 186 n.108
Night 238 n.257
Nile 152
nostos, see *return*

oath 67 n.89, 68, 115, 118, 127, 132–133, 135, 137, 138, 146
Ocean 2–4, 6, 8–11, 17, 25
Odysseus XXVII, 8, 12, 31 n.110, 33, 54, 56, 71, 73, 75, 76 n.115, 81 n.125, 84,

89, 91, 92 n.171, 96 n.188, 96 n.190, 98, 99, 100, 102–104, 121, 122, 158, 159, 160, 171, 181–182, 194, 195 n.135, 196 n.137, 219, 212 n.272
Oeax 195 n.135, 196, 196 n.137
Oedipus 21 n.86, 53 n.25, 175 n.68, 204–208, 215, 216, 217, 222–227, 229–235, 241–244, 246
Oeneus 125, 134
Olympia 7
Olympus 23, 33–34, 147 n.141, 149
omen 48, 50, 65–66, 100, 102–104, 184, 203, 217
oracles 126 n.80, 184, 198, 200, 208 n.172, 226, 229, 235, 248, 252 n.321
Orestes XIX, XXXIV, 21 n.86, 30 n.103, 72 n.106, 96, 99, 118, 157–162, 164, 168, 169, 173–175, 178, 179 n.79, 180, 184–203, 196 n.137, 198, 239 n.262, 253, 255–257
Orthos 7, 19–20, 43 n.140

Palamedes 195–196
Pallantium XIX, XXII, 44
Panhellenism XIII, XXV n.74
Panopaeus 67–68 n.89
Paris 74, 77, 80, 86, 100, 110 n.27, 115, 119, 123, 126–127, 131, 138–139, 143–147, 150–151, 179
Parrhasion 203
Parthenon 50, 55
Pasiphae 116
Patroclus 33 n.111, 41, 56, 182 n.87
Pegasus 14 n.57, 25
Peirithoo 128–130, 132
Peisistratus 102
Peleus 172
Pelias 5, 134, 241 n.270, 247 n.296
Pelopia 126, 174 n.64
Peloponnese XV n.10, XX, 130, 132, 143
Pelops 126, 134 n.98, 147 n.141, 173
Peneleus 42
Penelope 96 n.189, 100, 102, 103, 159, 181–183, 193–194, 217 n.176, 256, 257
Peneus (river) 16
performance XXV–XXXII, 165 n.23, 166 n.30, 167, 169, 170 n.50

Perieres 118 n.60
Pero 134
Persephone 12, 79, 110, 116
Perseus 8, 118 n.60
Phaeacians XXVII, 12 n.53, 103 n.211
Phaedra XXI, 125, 153, 192 n.124
Phalaris XIX
Pharos 151
Philoctetes 21 n.86, 65 n.76
Phobos 34
Phocaeans 15
Phocians 92 n.174, 161
Phocis 160, 161
Phoenicia 110, 112 n.34
Phoenicians XVI n.21, 14–15
Phoenix 109 n.118, 191 n.124
Phoenix (son of Agenor) 107 n.10
Pholus XIX, 5, 43–46, 254
Phrastor 224
Phrygians 92 n.174
Phrygian song 164–166, 171
plea 25, 27–31, 78, 221 n.194, 227, 234, 235, 238–239, 245
Pleisthenes 186–188
Plouto 172
poetic culture XXIII–XXV
professionalism XX n.40, XXIII–XXIV, XXXI, 153 n.156, 166
Polydamas 66, 237 n.254
Polydorus 84
Polygnotus 91, 75
Polymestor 84
Polynices XIX, XXXIV, 31, 175, 204, 205 n.161, 206–211, 215, 218, 222–225, 227, 229, 231–232, 234, 242–243, 245–246, 248–253, 255
Polyphemus 33, 121
Polypoites 63 n.65
Polyxena 48, 49, 50, 55, 73–76, 86 n.140, 87, 257
Pontus 3
Poseidon 25, 32–34, 40, 70, 90, 121–122, 147 n.141, 173, 242 n.272
Priam 48, 49, 50, 71, 73, 75, 81 n.124, 82 n.127, 85 n.140, 86, 98, 99, 104, 186 n.108, 196 n.137
– death of 48, 49, 50, 71

Proitos 133
prophecy 76 n.115, 104, 206–208, 216–223, 227, 230–233, 235, 237–238, 240, 244
Proteus 138, 141, 143, 145, 149, 151, 155, 160
Pylades 160–161, 169, 203 n.155

rape 48–50, 77 n.120, 106 n.7, 111–112, 224
– Cassandra's 48–50, 77 n.120
rescue XXI, 21 n.86, 47, 48, 49, 50, 76–77, 84–88, 95, 98, 106, 108 n.15, 115, 127–129, 131–134, 138, 149, 150, 152, 155, 159–160, 177–178, 180, 190–192, 194, 203, 238 n.257, 255
– Aethra's XXI, 48, 50 n.12, 98, 138, 152
– Hecuba's 47, 50, 84–87, 95, 106, 108 n.15, 150, 178
– Helen's 49, 50 n.12, 76–84, 88, 115, 127–129, 131–134, 255
– Iphigenia's 86, 150, 159, 160, 177–178, 180, 203
return XIII n.3, XXIII n.60, XXXIII, 5–8, 11, 21 n.86, 27, 34, 44, 47, 95–97, 99, 100–104, 121, 132, 151–154, 158–159, 160, 162, 171, 174–175, 182, 183, 185, 188, 190, 192–197, 200, 203, 251, 254, 255
– Achaeans' 95–97
– Agamemnon's 99, 158–159, 171, 174–175, 185
– Demophon's 100, 154
– Heracles' 5–8, 11, 34, 44
– Menelaus' 96, 100, 151–154, 160
– Orestes' 96, 158, 162, 188, 192–197, 200, 203, 255
revenge 96, 99, 118, 157–160, 162, 174, 178, 180, 196 n.137, 198, 253, 256
Rhegium XV n.14, XVI n.19, XXXI, 128 n.85, 169, 203 n.155
Rome 91, 93

sacrifice 21 n.86, 33, 48, 49, 50, 55 n.37, 73–76, 86 n.140, 87, 115, 119, 121, 122, 124–125, 134, 150, 158 n.1, 159–160, 161, 169, 174, 175–180, 190, 206
– Polyxena's 48, 49, 50, 73–76, 86 n.140, 87
– Iphigenia's 21 n.86, 150, 158 n.1, 159–160, 161, 169, 174, 175–180
Sagra XVII n.23
Samians 15–16
Samos 1 n.1, 16, 58
Samothrace 56
Sarpedon 24 n.90, 26, 40, 86, 102, 107 n.12, 108, 114, 191, 237 n.257, 252 n.321
Sarpedonia 1 n.1, 25
Satyrs 83 n.133
Scamander 16, 53, 58, 72
Scamandrios 71–72
Scepsis 90
Scythia 6
serpent 37, 48, 63, 66, 158 n.1, 168, 184, 186, 187 n.112, 188
Sicanians 92 n.174
Sicily XIII, XVI, XVIII, XIX n.30, XXI, XXIII–XXIV, XXX n.117, XXXI, 5, 6, 14, 15 n.62, 44–45, 46 n.150, 92–93, 95, 114, 166, 254
Sicyon XXX, 174 n.64
Sidon XXII, 111
Sidonians 104, 108
Simoeis 16, 52–53, 58, 95
Sinon 50, 58, 68
Sleep 86
solar eclipse XVIII
Sparta XX–XXIII, XXXIII, 74, 84, 96, 99–104, 106, 128, 134, 135–138, 143, 145–147, 150, 151, 153, 168–169, 191, 203 n.156, 254, 255
Spartoi 228
Sphinx 205
stasis (strife) XXXIV, 122, 157, 171, 173, 204, 205, 207, 218, 222, 232, 234–235, 252–253, 255
Stoa Poikile 50
Strophius 161, 190, 192
suitors 115, 118, 127, 132–134, 137, 138, 159, 182
Sun 4–6, 8–11, 18
supplication, see *plea*
Sisyphus 55

Tabula Iliaca Capitolina, see Stes. fr. 105 F.
Talthybius 56, 71
Tantalus 126, 172–173, 196 n.137
Tarentum 10, 169
Tartessus 6 n.21, 14–16, 18, 53, 254
Taurians 159
Tauris 176 n.70, 177, 203
Tegea 38 n.118, 130, 203 n.156
Teiresias 21 n.86, 25, 206–208, 216–223, 226, 227, 229, 230–237, 240, 243–245, 247–251
Telegonus 96 n.189
Telemachus XXXIII, 47, 81, 96, 99–104, 158–159, 160, 192 n.124, 195 n.135, 254
Theban Queen XIV, 25, 27–28, 31, 53 n.25, 157, 207–247, 250, 257
Thebes 53 n.25, 107 n.10, 110, 113, 114, 204, 206–207, 216, 219–252, 254–255
Themis 238 n.257
Theoclymenus 154
Theonoe 154–155
Theseus XXI, 10, 106, 109, 113, 115, 116, 117, 126–132, 137, 138, 142–143, 152–153, 235, 255
Thespiadae 154
Thespius 154
Thessaly 1, 34, 43–44, 177 n.72, 254
Thestius 154
Thestor 154–155
Thestorids 154–155
Thetis 29, 30, 42 n.139, 172
Thrace 16 n.67, 76 n.115, 91, 154
Thyestes 126, 173–174
Timandra 124
Trachis 34
Troad 92, 154
Troilus 49 n.6, 55
Trojan captives 91, 96, 98

Trojan/Wooden Horse 19 n.81, 47 n.1, 48–50, 56–70, 74, 80, 119, 120, 146 n.134, 170, 256
Trojans 42, 45, 47, 48, 50, 57, 59, 62–70, 74, 81, 86–87, 90–92, 94, 98–99, 138, 149 n.146, 150, 182 n.87, 236 n.250, 256
Troy XIV, XXI, XXXIII, 16, 27, 30, 33, 44, 48–76, 78, 80, 84–87, 88 n.151, 89–91, 92 n.174, 93–95, 96 n.192, 97–99, 104, 108, 115–117, 119–120, 123, 124, 128, 133, 135, 138–139, 141, 143–145, 146 n.134, 149–154, 158–160, 164, 165, 170, 171, 174, 178–179, 195 n.135, 196 n.136, 254, 255, 256, 257
Tyndareus 21 n.86, 80, 115–127, 131–132, 133, 135, 137, 138, 145, 146, 184
tyrant XIX
Tyre 15, 112
Tyrrhenus 92 n.171

wandering XXIII, XXXII, 19, 92, 203
Wandering Rocks 97 n.193
water-carriers 55
wedding 113, 118, 125, 128, 134, 136–138, 161, 163, 165 n.21, 172, 229
– Helen's 118, 128, 136–138
wooing 115, 118, 132–138, 146, 182, 254
– Helen's 115, 118, 132–138, 254

Xanthus (river) 14 n.59

Zeus 7, 10, 11 n.48, 14 n.57, 33, 40, 52, 59, 64, 66, 67, 69, 104, 106, 107–114, 121, 131, 172, 182 n.87, 217, 218, 227, 234, 236, 237–238 n.257, 242 n.272, 245, 254

Index of Sources

Accius
Phoenissae 227 n.216

Achilles Tatius
1.1.1–2 108

Acusilaus
Fragments
4 96 n.190
29 109 n.21, 111 n.32
39 96 n.190
450 96 n.190

Aeschines
2.31 154

Aeschylus
Agamemnon
48–59 184 n.95
104–159 17
154 178 n.76
185–246 178 n.76
870 6 n.17
877–886 190
1191–1199 174
1219–1222 174
1233 184 n.95
1380–1405 184
1412–1436 178 n.76
1525–1527 178 n.76
1528 185 n.100
1583–1611 174 n.63
Choephori
32–46 183 n.93
168–232 194
205–211 194
219 194
231–232 194
264–265 239 n.262
269–296 198
514–552 184
523–539 217 n.176
523–550 183 n.93
602–612 38 n.118
734–782 190
896 239
896–898 30 n.103
913–915 190
928–929 183 n.93
941 244
994 184 n.95
1010–1011 185 n.100
1026–1034 198
1047 184 n.95
Eumenides
64–66 198
103 184 n.99
245 244
355 237 n.257
657–659 21 n.86
Persae
176–204 217 n.176
176–230 183 n.93
[*Prometheus Bound*]
164 233 n.236
348 94 n.176
645–657 18 n.79
Seven Against Thebes
217–227 70 n.97
375–376 243
377–383 244
423 243
458–459 243
568–591 244
710–711 217
727–733 243 n.277
745–749 221 n.189
782–784 207
816–818 243
906–991 243
926–932 224 n.204
941–946 243
Suppliants
45 18 n.79
313–315 18 n.79
535 18 n.79
1066 18 n.79

Fragments

73a	6 n.18
74	6 n.17
99 (*Europa*)	107, 108 n.15, 111
131–133	55 n.33
143–144 (*Mysians*)	18 n.80
181	195 n.135
199	6 n.18
238–239 (*Telephus*)	18 n.80
Scholia	
Cho. 733 I 35. 11–12	190

Alcaeus
Fragments

42	123 n.70
283	123 n.70
298	49
307(a)	165 n.24
307(d)	XIX n.30
345	8 n.32
365	173 n.59
395	16 n.69

Alcimus
Fragments

560 F 4	49

Alcman
Fragments

1	XXVI
14	170 n.52
21	XXI n.47, 128
22	129 n.86
79	173 n.59

Alexander Aetolus
Fragments

12	87 n.147

Anacreon 9
Fragments

361	15

Anacreontea
Fragments

54	108

Antipater of Sidon

7.75	XXII

Apollodorus
Bibliotheca

1.8.2	39 n.118
2.103–104	19 n.80
2.4.4–8	67 n.89
2.5.4	44 n.142
2.5.10	6, 10, 11 n.46, 11 n.48, 15 n.63
2.5.11	18 n.77
3.1.1	107 n.10
3.4.1	37 n.117
3.10.8–9	132
3.11	131 n.93
3.12.5	75 n.112
Epitome	
1.23	131 n.89
2.3–5	134 n.98
2.6	154 n.162
5.14	58 n.50
5.17	63 n.63, 70 n.95
5.18	63 n.69
5.20–6.15	96
5.25	86 n.143
6.9–10	196 n.136

Apollonius of Rhodes

4.109	18 n.80
4.224–225	131 n.94
Scholia	
A.R. 1.916–18 (pp. 76–8)	56 n.40

Archilochus
Fragments

122	XVIII n.27
91.14IT	173 n.59
13	232 n.233
131	233 n.236

Aristides
Orationes

1.128	149 n.146, 151 n.152
1.131.1	151

2.234	149 n.146	12.42	16 n. 69
33.2–3	145 n.132	*Dithyrambs*	
		17.28–32, 52–54	107 n.14
Aristophanes		17.29–32	109
Aves		20	134 n.98
160	42	*Fragments*	
Fragments		10	108 n.20
564	6 n.18	20a	134 n.98
278–288	44	42	174 n.60
Lysistrata			
155–156	30 n.103	**Callimachus**	
327–334	55 n.33	*Hymn to Zeus*	
Scholia		1.51	14 n.57
Ar. *Av.* 1406	XXX n.116	*Hymn to Delos*	
Ar. *Pax* 775–780 (p. 38 Olson)	163–164	55–196	18 n.79
Ar. *Pax* 796–799 (p. 39 Olson)	163–164	*Fragments*	
Ar. *Pax* 800 (p. 39 Olson)	163–164	197	58 n.51, 68 n.89
Aristophanes of Byzantium		**Cicero**	
Fragments		*Cato*	
124	107 n.13	7.23	XXII n.56
Aristotle		**Cratinus**	
Poetics		*Fragments*	
1449a15–25	XXX n.117	108	6 n.18
1454b19–1455a	193 n.130		
History of the Animals		**Damastes**	
600a10–16	171 n.56	*Fragments*	
		3	49
Athenaeus			
Deipnosophists		**Damocrates**	
7.297b	1 n.1	*Fragments*	
10.456ef	54	3	96 n.190
10.456g	51 n.17		
11.469ef	9, 11	**Demetrius**	
11.781	11 n.46	*On Style*	
12.513a	162	132–133	165 n.21
13.557a–b	128 n.84		
13.610c	see Stes. fr. 102a F.	**Demetrius of Phalerus**	
		Fragments	
		288 F 5	55 n.38
Bacchylides			
Epinicians		**Dictys**	
1.124	107 n.14	2.44	58
5.19–20	103 n.214	5.13	98 n.201
5.93–154	38 n.118	6.2	98 n.201
8.26–27	16 n. 69		

Dio Chrysostom

2.33	88 n. 151

Diodorus Siculus

4.8.4	6 n.19
4.12	44 n.142
4.17.1–25.1	6
4.337–312	19 n.80
4.63	128
5.4.2	45 n.150
5.48–49	56 n.40
5.70	14 n.57
13.62.4	XV n.16

Dionysus of Halicarnassus
Roman Antiquities

1.45.4–47.1–5	89 n.155, 91 n.169
1.45–48	91 n.168
1.47.2	92 n.174
1.48–64	93
1.72.1	91 n.168

Douris
Fragments

938(e)	16 n.69, 53 n.24

Empedocles
Fragments

31 B 17	232 n.233
26	232 n.233
35	232 n.233

Ennius
Annales

20	93

Ephippus
Geryon 6

Epic Cycle
Aethiopis

3	87
	54

Cypria

arg. 5	195 n.135
arg. 8	159, 176 n.71
arg. 12	195 n.135
1.3	59 n.57
12	128
13	XXI n.47

Europeia (Eumelus)

26	110
27	110 n.28
33	110 n.27

Heracleia (Panyassis)

9	5, 44
12	5
13	5

Heracleia (Pisander)

5	4
9	44

Iliou Persis (Arctinus)

arg. 1	48, 90 n.161
arg. 2	48, 76, 68 n.91
arg. 3	48
arg. 4	XXI, 48, 71, 73, 152 n.154
1	48
3	48, 71
6	XXI, 152 n.154
38	31

Little Iliad (Lesches)

arg. 4	48, 57 n.44, 68 n.90
arg. 5	48, 59, 160
17	XXI, 48, 152 n.154
18	48
25	48
28	48, 76
29	48, 71, 98
30	48, 91 n.166, 98

Nostoi

arg. 1	96 n.188
arg. 2	96 n.188, 154 n.162
arg. 3	96 n.188
arg. 4	96 n.188
1	96 n.188
3	163 n.59, 197, n. 725, 160 n.6
5	96 n.188; 184
10	160 n.8
11	160
12	160 n.6, 160 n.8

Index of Sources

Minyas

5	38 n.118

Oedipodeia

1	205
2	205 n.161, 216 n.173

Telegony

6	96 n.189

Thebaid

2	206, 216 n.173, 234
3	206 n.167, 216 n.173, 222
6	206
7	206
9	206
11	34 n.112

Epicharmus
Fragments

66 (*Heracles and Pholus*)	44

Epimenides
Fragments

16	224

Euphorion
Fragments

80	87 n.147

Euripides
Andromache

10	49, 72
627–631	30 n.103, 77
629	30 n.103, 31 n.107
832	30 n.103

Children of Heracles

419–424	6 n.17

Electra

16–18	192 n.127
107–111	55 n.33
160	185
279	185
416	192 n.127
573–579	194
615–612	196 n.139
699–750	173 n.58
1018–1029	178 n.76
1020–1022	176 n.71
1160	185
1206–1207	30 n.103

Hecuba

21	49
40–105	49
68–97	217 n.176
140	49
172	239 n.262
221	49
342–378	74
402–443	74
557–570	75
618–619	49
629–657	123 n.68
919	49
1229–1243	85

Helen

31–55	150 n.150

Heracles

252–253	37 n.117
389–393	34 n.112
490–493	21 n.86
1187–1188	41 n.135

Ion

95	16 n.69
158–159	103 n.214

Iphigenia at Aulis

51–71	132
98–100	176 n.71
358–365	176 n.71
433–434	176 n.71
457–459	176 n.71
609–612	176 n.71
752	16 n.69
884–885	176 n.71
1108	176 n.71
1150–1152	125–126
[1607–1608]	21 n.86

Iphigenia in Tauris

191–202	173 n.58
214–217	176 n.71
372	176 n.71
537–538	176 n.71
798–799	176 n.71

818	176 n.71	1568	28 n.101, 30 n.103, 30 n.105
856–861	176 n.71		
1235–1244	18 n.79	1584	216 n.173
Orestes		1584–1594	215
1–27	173	1760	205 n.161
29–30	199 n.150	*Suppliants*	
53–60	76	14	242 n.273
249	116, 120	*Trojan Women*	
268	197	427–431	85
269–276	199 n.150	481–485	49
285–293	199	622–630	49
346	172	641–650	49
416	199 n.150	709–799	49
432	196	857	70
479–480	184	890–1059	49, 77 n.119
527	30 n.103	895–1032	78
615–621	196 n.139	1037–1040	49
618	217 n.176	1039–1041	76
622–626	21 n.86	1133–1149	49
658	178 n.76	1175–1177	50 n.10
841	30 n.103	1281	70
982–1012	174	*Cressae*	186
1233	162 n.13	*Danae*	18 n.80
1260	93 n.177	*Dictys*	18 n.80
1644–1660	203	*Fragments*	
1665	199	265–281 (*Auge*)	18 n.80
Phoenician Women		390 (*Epeius*)	54 n.32
12–63	227 n.216	472m	85 n.138, 108 n.16
63–65	207		
64	216	525 (*Meleager*)	38 n.118
64–75	216	588	195 n.135
69–70	235 n.245	752g	8–23 108 n.16
69–76	242 n.273, 250	820	108 n.16
84–87	234	696–727 (*Telephus*)	19 n.80
389–407	249	*Scholia*	
[438–440]	21 n.86	*Andr.* 10 (II 249.7–11)	vide Stes. fr. 107 F.
503–506	21 n.86	*Phoen.* 1760 (I. 414)	205 n.161
666–669	37 n.117	*Or.* 249 (I 123. 8–13)	vide Stes. fr. 85 F.
667	244	*Or.* 268 (I 261. 1–2)	vide Stes. fr. 181b F
670	110 n.26		
834	216	*Or.* 1287 (I 214.6–9)	vide Stes. fr. 86 F.
865–929	222 n.196		
898–969	220 n.189	**Eusebius**	
953–959	250 n.316	*Chron.* Ol. 42.2, 55.1 Ta5(b) Ercoles	vide Stesichorus
1282	221 n.194		
1555–1559	21 n.86		

Index of Sources — 303

Eusthatius
Commentary to Homer's Odyssey
1632.23	11 n.46
1698.2	58 n.49

Hecataeus
Fragments (FGrHist)
76–77	5 n.13
1 F 62	49, 92 n.173

Fragments (EGM)
26	5 n.13
110	18 n.80

Hellanicus
Fragments
31	49, 89 n.155, 91 n.169, 92, 96 n.190
51	37 n.117
77	96 n.190
84	49, 91 n.168, 96 n.190
98	242 n.273
110	6 n.15, 18 n.77
111	6 n.15
152a	96 n.190
153	96 n.190
156	96 n.189
168a	128
168b	130

Herodorus
Fragments
11	194 n.132
65	96 n.190

Herodotus
1.1	18 n.79
1.1–5	105 n.4
1.1.2	111 n.33
1.2.1	110 n.26, 112 n.34
1.23–24	XXIV n.65
1.23–27	XXX n.116
1.24.4–7	XXIV n.66
1.28.2	93 n.177
1.163.1–4	15 n.64
1.170	232 n.233
1.173	252 n.321
2.51	56 n.40
2.112–120	151
4.8–10	6
4.152.2–5	15 n.64
4.147.4	110 n.26
5.12–13	55 n.33
5.42	252 n.321
5.67	XXX n.115
9.73	128

Hesiod
Theogony
24–25	170 n.53
26–28	65 n.75
27	93 n.176
66–69	XXIX n.103
211–217	238 n.257
229	65 n.75
231–282	14 n.57
274–275	25
274–280	8
276–281	1 n.1
284–286	25
287–294	2–3
293	7, 14 n.56
340	16 n.69
361	107 n.12
337–370	8 n.31
468–480	14 n.57
784–787	55 n.33
901–906	238 n.257
979–983	3, 25
980–983	3
1008–1016	93 n.179

Works and Days
11–12	148 n.142
179	234 n.240
188	234 n.240
191	234 n.240
197	202
289	232 n.233
487	14 n.58
568–569	171 n.56

[Shield]
15–77	67 n.89

57–74	34	**Hesychius**	
59	34	ε 5957	79 n. 122
206	XXIX n.103		
273–274	137	**Hipponax**	
425–434	34	*Fragments*	
443–450	34	123	232 n.233
450–461	34		
455–457	34, 41 n.129	**Homer**	
458–462	34	*Iliad*	
463–467	34	1.8–11	122
467–469	34	1.56	59 n.57
[*Catalogue of Women*]		1.265	152 n.154
23a	177–178	1.350	14 n.58
23b	177–178	1.414	29
23a13–27	160	1.474	XXIX n.103
23a.15	162	2.79–83	182 n.87
23a17–26	150	2.87–90	42 n.139
23a.28–30	160	2.100–108	174, 188 n.113
23a.29	178	2.236–239	132 n.95
25.2–13	38 n.118	2.284–335	54 n.29
33a.29	198 n.143	2.299–332	158 n.1
37	134	2.339	132
37.5	136 n.107	2.459–468	72
43a	133	2.468	42 n.139
70.21–23	13 n.55	2.517–526	56
130	133	2.569	168 n.40
135	18 n.80	2.621	186 n.108
137c (Most)	186 n.104	2.753	16 n.69
140	108 n.20, 107 n.12, 109	2.763	186 n.108
		2.800	42 n.139
141	109, 107 n.12	3.99–100	123 n.68
144	109	3.114	152 n.154
150	93	3.143–144	98 n.200
165	18 n.80	3.147	99
176	124–125	3.154–160	77
192	216 n.173, 224	3.172–176	81 n.124
194	186	3.180	81 n.124
196–204	133	3.242	128
197.1–5	136 n.107	3.314–325	242 n.272, 247 n.296
204	133		
240	13 n.55	4.266–267	132 n.95
259	133	4.344–356	81 n.124
Fragmenta dubia		4.370–410	204 n.159
360	18 n.77	4.412–418	239
358	142 n.121	4.473–487	53 n.28
		4.475	14 n.57, 17 n.72
		4.485–487	42 n.139

5.449–453	150	14.379	18 n.80
5.478–481	87 n.148	14.444–445	14 n.57, 17 n.72
5.800–813	204 n.159	14.496–500	42
6.146–148	42 n.139	15.236–262	86 n.146
6.196–205	191	15.546–547	99
6.222–223	204 n.159	15.576	99
6.255	82 n.127	16.126	33 n.111
6.456–458	55 n.33	16.182	XXIX n.103
7.161–199	242 n.272	16.281	231 n. 232
7.271–272	86 n.146	16.433	238 n.257
7.357–364	66 n.86	16.431–461	237 n.257
7.446	14 n.58	16.584	33 n.111
8.66–74	40 n.126	16.656–658	40 n.126
8.69	40 n.126	16.666–683	86
8.302–308	42 n.138	16.793–800	41 n.130
9.126	247 n.293	16.839	33 n.111
9.144–147	176 n.71	17.9–109	42 n.139
9.145	158 n.1, 161 n.11, 161 n.12	17.545–596	236 n.250
		18	83–84
9.179	54 n.29	18.54	29
9.223–306	54 n.29	18.56	42 n.139
9.247	161 n.12	18.285–313	66 n.87
9.287	158 n.1	18.394–397	81 n.125
9.286–289	176 n.71	18.437	42 n.139
9.410–416	26	18.478–608	8
9.529–599	38 n.118	18.491–497	137
9.533–539	125 n.74	18.520–522	38 n.120
10.148–282	54	18.572	XXIX n.103
10.184	32 n.110	19.221–224	40 n.126
10.276	104	19.325	81 n.124
11.107–108	236 n.247	20.238	99
11.709	186 n.108	20.293–308	90
12.13–23	72 n.101	21.8	16 n.69
12.17–33	53 n.28	21.130	16 n.69
12.116	82 n.127	21.195–197	8 n.31
12.135	63 n.65	21.257–263	42 n.139
12.153	63 n.65	21.464–466	42 n.139
12.231	66 n.87	21.599–22.20	86 n.146
12.232	237 n.254	22.82–83	30–31
12.322–328	26	22.82–89	239
12.326	40	22.145–156	53 n.27, 53 n.28
13.185	186 n.108	22.166–187	33
13.732–735	233 n. 236, 233 n.238	22.179–181	238 n.257
		22.202–204	86 n.146
14.113–125	204 n.159	22.208–213	40 n.126
14.321–323	107 n.10	23.62–90	182 n.87
14.324	32 n.110	23.188–191	86 n.146

23.514	186 n.108	4.280–289	80
23.669–670	56	4.333	32 n.110
23.678–680	216 n.173	4.351–362	152
23.679	204, 216 n.173	4.512–539	158
23.836–841	56	4.530–537	160
23.861	242 n.272	6.15–36	182 n.87
24.18–54	86 n.146	6.57	135 n.102
24.27–28	123 n.68	6.69	135 n.102
24.49	237 n.257	6.72–73	135 n.102
24.209	237 n.257	6.101	XXIX
24.266	135 n.102	7.19–20	55 n.33
24.292	103 n.214	7.315	103 n.211
24.315–321	103 n.214	8.73–83	XXVII n.86
24.324	135 n.102	8.251–253	XXVII n.92
24.502	135 n.102	8.260–384	165 n.23
24.545	14 n.58	8.261–266	XXVII n.88
24.525	238 n.257	8.266–366	XXVII n.86
24.556	135 n.102	8.317–320	81 n.125
24.576–579	135 n.102	8.492–493	57 n.43
24.590	135 n.102	8.492–520	48 n.3
24.732–738	71	8.499–520	XXVII n.86
24.775	81 n.124	8.500–510	59
Odyssey		8.506–507	62
1.10	170 n.53	8.579	237 n.257
1.17	237 n.257	9.182–183	12
1.19	59 n.57	9.452–461	158
1.45–78	33	10.205–207	242 n.272
1.65–69	121	10.105–106	55 n.33
1.298	159	10.509	12
1.299	178	11.100–137	219
1.429	186 n.108	11.139	237 n.257
2.349–379	192 n.124	11.270–276	225
2.347	186 n.108	11.275–276	225
3.197	178	11.271–280	205, 223
3.208	237 n.257	11.280	205
3.254–275	158	11.280–281	225
3.254–306	159	11.299	32 n.110
3.258	158	11.405–434	158, 159, 184
3.303–310	158	11.409–416	171
3.303–312	194	11.409–434	160
4.17–19	XXIX	11.423–426	82 n.125
4.125–127	151	11.425	184
4.131–132	151	11.523–524	57 n.43
4.141–146	81 n.125	11.523–537	48 n.3
4.220–234	151	11.555	232 n.234
4.266–289	48 n.3	11.582–592	173
4.274–289	70	11.601–604	149

12.159	72	80	110
14.96–97	158	82	80
14.208	242 n.272	114	110
15.1–42	102	*Dionysus*	
15.43–66	102	5–9	113 n.40
15.53	246 n.292	*Hermes*	
15.67–130	102	483	89 n.154
15.115	104	509–511	89 n.154
15.125–129	104	229	14 n.56
15.160–165	102	*Pan*	
15.164–165	103 n.214	21–24	XXIX n.103
15.170–184	102	*h. Hom. 22*	
15.170–185	256	5	33 n.111
15.180	104		
15.440–442	55 n.33	**Hyginus**	
15.526	103 n.214	*Fabulae*	
16.64	237 n.257	63	18 n.80
18.136–137	233 n.236	81	132
19.188	14 n.57	90.6	75 n.112
19.535–550	181 n.85, 217 n.176	98	176 n.71
		117	192
19.536–545	103	128	154 n.164
20.148	186 n.108	173	38 n.118
20.153–154	55 n.33	178.5	37 n.117
20.356–357	XVIII n.27	261	169 n.47, 203 n.155
21.1–4	134		
21.67–79	134		
22.115	54	**Ibycus**	
23.11	232 n.234	*Fragments*	
Scholia		S151	5 n.10, 49 n.6, 123 n.68
Il. 2.339	132 (= Stes. fr. 87 F.)	S166	XX n.35, 128 n.85, 208 n.171
Il. 3.242	128		
Il. 4.376	205 n.162	S176	4, 5 n.11
Il. 12.292	107 n.10	170	128 n.85
Od. 12.85	1 n.1	177	128 n.85
		290	38 n.118
Homeric Hymns		295	87 n.147
Aphrodite		296	76–77, 167 n.34
196–199	90	298	55, n. 243
Apollo		307	49
14–18	18 n.79		
197	XXIX n.103	**Inscriptions**	
Demeter		*CIG* II 2374	XX n.40
3	80, 110	*IG* II² 7873.G	190 n.119
19	80	*IGSD* II §24	XVI n.19, 93 n.179
55	110		

SEG 12

SEG 43.1102

Isocrates
Encomium of Helen
64

39–41

Lycophron
Alexandra
44–49
265
314–318
314–334
417–1089
424–438
932
1296–1311
Scholia
Alex. 265a (p. 54. 3–5)

Malalas
Chronicle
2.34

Menecrates Xanthius
Fragments
3

Mimnermus
Fragments
12

Moschus
Europa
44–71
110

Nicomachus of Alexandria
Fragments
127 F 3 (*Geryon*)

XVI n.19, 155 n.166
XVI n.19, 155 n.166

120–121, 139, 140, 144–145, 148 n.144
132

1 n.1
87 n.147
86 n.143
76 n.115
96
154 n.162
68 n.89
110 n.26, 112 n.37

86 n.145 = Stes. Fr. 108 F.

112 n.35

96 n.190

4 n.7

109
110

6 n.18

Nonnus
Dionysiaca
13
110–112

Ovid
Fasti
4.207
Metamorphoses
8.298–328
8.331
8.360
13.728–14.74

Papyri
Michigan Papyrus 3250
Michigan Papyrus 3498
P. Duk inv. 752
P. Lille
P. London. inv. 2110
P. Oxy. 2503
P. Oxy. 2619

P. Oxy. 2803
P. Oxy. 4097 fr. 2
P. Robinson inv. 10

Pausanias
1.15.2
1.22.6

1.43.1
2.18.2
2.19.6
2.22.6–7
2.29.3
3.20.9
5.25.2–4
7.2.1
7.21.7
8.7.2–3
8.48.7
8.45.6–7
9.5.10
10.9.5
10.17.5
10.25–27

176 n.71
176 n.71

14 n.57

38 n.118
38 n.120
38 n.118
1 n.1

58 n.53
58 n.53
38 n.118
see Stes. 97 F.
174 n.64
see Stes. 90 F.
47, 50–51, 51 n.18
47, 117
38 n.118
38 n.118

50 n.13
160 n.9, 196 n.137
177 n.72
126 n.79, 127
58
129 n.86
161 n.13
132
XXXI n.124
252 n.321
33 n.111
33 n.111
19 n.80
38 n.118
229 n.224
191
18 n.77
50 n.13

Index of Sources — 309

10.26.1	86 n.142	*Pythians*	
10.26.2–3	57	1.60	170 n.52
10.26.9	57	3.88	112 n.40
10.27.1	57, 75 n.112	4.40	93 n.176
10.27.2	85–86	4.45	33 n.111
		4.145–155	241 n.270
Pherecydes		5.83	124 n.71
Fragments		8.47	112 n.40
10	18 n.80	9.123–125	136 n.106
16a	10 n.39	11	168, 179
18a	4 n.8, 5, 10 n.36,	11.10	93 n.176
	15 n.63	11.17–18	190
22a	37 n.117	11.36	190
95	205 n.162, 224	11.51	124 n.71
96	242 n.273, 250	*Nemeans*	
	n.314	3.21	8 n.32
134	175 n.69, 190,	6.28	170 n.52
	191, 192	7.35–50	96
135	203	10.83–88	26 n.97
142	96 n. 190, 154	*Isthmians*	
	n.162	1.29	241 n.269
144	1 n.1, 96 n. 190	1.54	33 n.111
		4.13	8 n.32
Phrynichus		6.74	241 n.269
Fragments		6.76	112 n.40
3 F 6 (*Pleuroniae*)	38 n.118	8.9–10	173 n.59
		8.30–50	246 n.292
Pindar		8.47	93 n.176
Olympians		*Paeans*	
1.24–27	173 n.60	6	96
1.25–50	148 n.143	6.95–98	124
1.25–55	147 n.141	7	18 n.79
1.35–55	173	12	18 n.79
1.56–63	173	*Fragments*	
1.75–81	134 n.98	48	38 n.118
2	208 n.172, 224	52k	XVIII
	n.203	169	5
2.78	112 n.40	169.18–20	37 n.116
3.1	124 n.71	249a	38 n.118
3.44	8 n.32	326	8 n.31
7	203 n.157	520.32–34	170 n.54
8.29	241 n.269		
10	XVII	**Plato**	
10.14	XVII n.24	*Ion*	
10.13–19	34 n.112	533a	58
13. 58–60	124 n.71	*Phaedrus*	
		59e	93 n.176

243a	see Stes. fr. 91a F.	**Quintus Smyrnaeus**	
Protagoras		*Posthomerica*	
325c–d	191 n.124	12.434–489	66 n.84
Republic		12.580–585	70 n.95
620c	58		
9.586c	see Stes. fr. 91b F.	**Sacadas**	
Symposium		*Fragments*	
223d	93 n.176	2	XV n.10
		Sappho	
Plautus		*Fragments*	
Fragments		1	146 n.135
incer. fr. 1	54 n.32	16	123, 123 n.68
		44	137
Pliny		*Brother's Poem*	XIII n.60
Natural History		*Testimonia*	
3.73	203 n.155	251	XIX n. 30, XXIII n.61
Plutarch			
Moralia		**Semonides**	
De Sera Numinis Vindicta		*Fragments*	
554f–559a	see Stes. fr. 180 F.	1.3	233 n.236
De facie in orbe lunae			
931e	see Stes. fr. 300 F.	**Seneca**	
Parallel Lives		*Agamemnon*	
Agis and Cleomenes		918–946	192
60	184 n.94	*Phoenician Women*	
Theseus		407–651	227 n.216
31–34	128		
32–33	129 n.86	**Simias**	
36.1–2	128 n.84	*Axe* 55 n.32	
Porphyry 111, n. 429		**Simonides**	
		Fragments	
Pseudo-Phalaris		271	18 n.80
Epistole 108: 7; 120, n. 474.		273	see Stes. test. Tb37
		307	171 n.56
Pseudo–Plutarch		*Testimonia*	
De Musica		TT 46–50	XXII n.57
3.1132a–b	13, n. 82		
3.1132b–c	XXVI n. 83	**Solon**	
3.1132c	XXVI n.81	*Fragments*	
3.1132f	XXVI n.82	29	65 n.78
3.1134b	XV n.10	30a	XXX n.116
4	XXVI n. 84		
6	XXVI n. 84		
9.1134c	XXIII n.62		
10.1134e	XXIII n.62		

Index of Sources

Sophocles
Ajax
208	233 n.236
254	196 n.137
654–656	65 n.80
678–682	232 n.233
805	93 n.177

Antigone
49–57	226
245–246	21 n.86
908–912	21 n.86
1023–1032	222, 244
1064–1090	222
1060	222 n.196
1085–1090	250 n.316

Electra
10	
11–14	173
132	192 n.126
168–170	185
263	196 n.139
296–297	185
321	192 nn.125, 126
406–425	192 n.126
410–427	184 n.97
459–460	183 n.93
472–575	184 n.97
478–481	174 n.64
516–633	184 n.97
530–533	179 n.76
601	178 n.76
1132–1133	192 n.125
1221–1222	192 nn.125, 126
1348–1352	194 n.134
1498	192 n.126
	173

Oedipus at Colonus
365–375	207
404–409	250 n.314
410–416	249 n.310
431–460	207
612–615	234
788–789	207
893–906	207
988–993	207
1295–1298	242 n.273, 250 n.314
1330	242 n.273, 250 n.314
1370–1379	207
1518–1521	21 n.86

Oedipus King
177	93 n.176
236–240	21 n.86
320–332	222 n.196
344	222 n.196
360	222 n.196
412–415	21 n.86
444	250 n.316
449	21 n.86

Philoctetes
54–55	65 n.76
591–594	21 n.86

Trachinae
61	239 n.262
572–577	41 n.135
714–718	41 n.135
1130	21 n.86

Fragments
Acrisius
68	18 n.80
69	18 n.80

Aleads
74–96	19 n.80

Atreus and Thyestes
140–141	174 n.64
247–269	174 n.64
738	174 n.64

Danae
165	18 n.80

Iberians
4	6 n.18

Laocoon
373.3–5	90

Meleager
	38 n.118

Mysians
375–391	19 n.80

Nauplius sails in 195 n.135
Nauplius, the fire-kindler 195 n.135
Palamedes 195 n.135

Teucer
576	96 n.191
579	96 n.191

Index of Sources

Helenes Apaitesis
180   154 n.162

Statius
Thebaid
1.328–335   252
1.164   242 n.273
7.470   227 n.216

Stephanus of Byzantium
437.3–5   see Stes. Ta15

Stesichorus
Fragments
Funeral Games for Pelias
1   5, 134
2   5, 134
3   5, 134, 254
4   5, 134, 254
Geryoneis
5   39
6   1 n.1, 25
7   10
10–12
9   12–17, 19, 31, 53, 254
10   7, 17–19, 31
12   20
13   20–22
14   19
15   19, 22–27, 32, 40, 105 n.3, 256
16   27–28, 30, 78, 230
17   7 n. 28, 28–32, 78, 230, 256–257
18   7 n. 28, 32–33, 218 n.184, 238 n.257
19   6 n.22, 7, 35–43, 256
20   43
21   XIX, 5 n.14, 43, 44, 254
22   XIX, 5, 43–44
Helen
84   115, 127–128
85   154 n.162
86
87
88
89
Palinode
90
91a
91a–g
91b
91c
91h
91i–j
Eriphyle
92
93
95
Europeia
96
Thebais
97
Sack of Troy
98
99

80, 115, 116–128, 120, 122, 123 n.67, 131, 164
XX n.36, 105 n.3, 107, 115, 117, 128–132, 255
XX n.36, 115, 118–119, 132–135, 138, 254
115, 118, 135–137
115

XXI n.45, XXIX, 51 n.21, 115, 138, 140, 142, 142 n.117 n.118, 143–146, 148 n.144, 149–153, 164 n.19, 254
100, 138–139, 142, 143, 145–147
146
86, 138, 149–151
138, 139, 147
143, 149 n.147, 151
142

218 n.184
XXIX n.111, 134–135, 136 n.107, 189, 201–202, 204 n.158, 218 n.184
202

37, 107 n.10, 110–113, 228

XXIX n.111, XXX, 25, 27–28, 31, 53 n.25, 204, 207–253, 218 n.184, 257

88 n.151
146 n.134

100	16, 33, 48 n.1, 50–59, 89, 117 n.56, 119, 119 n.64, 120, 123, 164 n.19, 165, 215	*Oresteia*	
		172	123, 148 n.142, 162–167, 170, 171, 172, 174, 215
102	48, 50, 58	173	XXIX, XXIX n.107, 162–167, 170, 171–172, 174, 215
103	50, 59–67, 70 n.95, 117 n.56, 256	174	164–167, 171, 174, 215
104	50, 67–68	175a	97 n. 199, 195
105	XXI, 48, 50, 62, 70, 71, 73, 75, 82, 83, 85, 87–95, 115, 132, 152, 152 n.154, 254	175b	195
		176	196 n.137
		177	128 n.85, 168, 255
		178	75, 86, 127, 162, 169, 175–180
106	76–77, 82, 83, 115, 196 n.137	179	168, 175 n.69, 189–192
107	50, 50 n.10, 70–71, 72–73	180	72 n.106, 180–189, 217 n.176, 257
108	84, 86		
109	50, 84–87, 108 n.15, 150, 178	181	162, 176, 179 n.78, 192–201, 256
110	50, 75, 98		
111	98		
113	50, 78–80	*Scylla*	
114	59, 68–70, 87	182	1 n.1, 85
115	76, 80–84, 103 n.215, 115, 257	*Boarhunters*	
		183	XXII n.55, 38, 134
116	59, 70, 72–73	184	XXII n.55, 134
118	59, 73–75, 95	*Incerti*	
119	73, 74	187	33 n.111
121	95	189	XXII n.55, 188–189 n.116
Cerberus			
165	1	191	20–21, 188–189 n.116
Cycnus			
166	33–35	271	XXIX, XXIX n.101
168	XVII n.24, 144 n.128	272	33 n.111
		277a	51 n.21, 164 n.19, 170 n.52
Nostoi			
169	97–99,	278	XXIX, XXIX n.101, 52 n.23, 164
170	XX, 47, 97, 99–104, 115, 128 n.85, 187, 218 n.184, 254, 256	279	164 n.19
		285	113, 113 n.42
		286	105 n.3, 113
		287	105 n.3, 118 n.60
		288	105 n.3
		296	143 n.132

300	XVIII, XVIII n.27	TTb49–52(ii)	XIII n.2
327	52 n.23, 164 n.19, 170 n.52	TTb50–52	XIII n.2
Testimonia		**Strabo**	
Ta4	XV n.10	1.1.2	8 n.30
Ta5(a)	XXII n.52	3.2.11	see Stes. fr. 9 F.
Ta5(a–b)	XV n.10	8.7.1	252 n.321
Ta5(b)	XXII n.56	13.1.53	90 n.160
Ta5(b)i	XV n.11		
Ta5(b)ii	XXII n.53	**Terpander**	
Ta5(d)	XXII n.53	*Testimonia*	
Ta6	XIV n.9	1–2	XXIII n.63
Ta8(a)	XXII n.56	8	XXIII n.63
Ta8(b)	XXII n.56	13	XXIII n.63
Ta9	XXII n.56	17–20	XXIII n.63
Ta10	XIV n.7, XV n.15, XIX, XXII n.51, 44 n.143	18	XXVI n.81
		21	XXVI n.82
Ta10–14(ii)	XV n.12	**Theocritus**	
Ta15	XV, XV n.15	*Idylls*	
Ta16	XV, XV n.15	7. 149–150	44
Ta17	XV nn.12, 15		
Ta18	XVII n.22	**Theognis**	
Ta18–20	XVII	776–779	165 n.24
Ta19(b)	XVII n.22	1232	123 n.68
Ta28	XVII n.23		
Ta30	XVII n.23, 253	**Theopompus**	
Ta30(a)	145 n.132	*Fragments*	
Ta32	XVII n.23	15.1–2	136 n.104
Ta38–42	XXII n.51		
Ta40	XXII n.51	**Thucydides**	
Ta42	XV n.12	6.2	93 n.177
Ta43(iii)	96 n.193	6.2.3	49
Ta43(iv)	XX	6.2.3–4	92
Ta43(xix)	XIX n.31	6.3.3	XXI n.49
TTb3	88	6.5.1	XV n.15
Tb5(a)	166 n.26		
Tb5b(i)	XV n.11	**Timaeus**	
Tb7	129 n.85	*Fragments*	
Tb9	XIII n.2	566 F 59	49
Tb20	XV n.10	566 F 90	6 n.16
TTb20–24	XXVI n.80		
Tb22	XV n.10	**Triphiodorus**	
Tb37	XIII n.2	*Sack of Troy*	
Tb37–52	88	247–249	65
TTb40–47	XIII n.2	316–314	66 n.84
Tb42	XXVI n.83	493–494	80

Tzetzes
Posthomerica
750.2   97 n.194
Ad Lycophron
513   130 n.89

Virgil
Aeneid
2.35   63
2.50–52   63 n.70
2.154–158   68
9.195–233   66
2.199–227   63 n.69
2.246   63 n.63
2.246–250   70 n.95
6.417–425   1 n.2
7.409   18 n.80
7.789–792   18 n.79

Georgics
4.153   14 n.57

Xanthus (poet)
Fragments
699   see Stes. fr. 171 F.
700   162, 192

Xanthus (historian)
Fragments
765 F 21   73

Xenophon
Cynegeticus
10.19   38 n.120
[*Constitution of the Athenians*]
1.13   XXXI n.120

www.ingramcontent.com/pod-product-compliance
Lightning Source LLC
Chambersburg PA
CBHW020220170426
43201CB00007B/268